Admiral of the Fleet Lord Keyes

PUBLICATIONS

OF THE

NAVY RECORDS SOCIETY

VOL. 122

THE KEYES PAPERS

VOL. III: 1939–1945

THE NAVY RECORDS SOCIETY was established in 1893 for the purpose of printing rare or unpublished works of naval interest.

Any person wishing to become a Member of the Society is requested to apply to the Hon. Secretary, Royal Naval College, Greenwich, SE10 9NN. The annual subscription is £5.50, the payment of which entitles the Member to receive one copy of each work issued by the Society for that year, and to purchase back volumes at reduced prices. The subscription for Libraries and Institutions is £7.00.

MEMBERS requiring copies of any volume should apply to the Hon. Secretary.

Subscriptions should be sent to the Hon. Treasurer, c/o Barclays Bank, 54 Lombard St., London, EC3P 3AH.

THE COUNCIL of the NAVY RECORDS SOCIETY wish it to be clearly understood that they are not answerable for any opinions or observations that may appear in the Society's publications. For these the responsibility rests entirely with the Editors of the several works.

THE KEYES PAPERS

*Selections from the Private and Official Correspondence
of Admiral of the Fleet Baron Keyes of Zeebrugge*

Volume III

1939–1945

Edited by
PAUL G. HALPERN, Ph.D.
*Professor of History,
The Florida State University*

PUBLISHED BY GEORGE ALLEN & UNWIN
FOR THE NAVY RECORDS SOCIETY
1981

First published in 1981

This book is copyright under the Berne Convention. All rights are reserved. Apart from any fair dealing for the purpose of private study, research, criticism or review, as permitted under the Copyright Act, 1956, no part of this publication may be reproduced, stored in a retrieval system, or transmitted, in any form or by any means, electronic, electrical, chemical, mechanical, optical, photocopying, recording or otherwise, without the prior permission of the copyright owner. Enquiries should be sent to the publishers at the undermentioned address:

GEORGE ALLEN & UNWIN LTD
40 Museum Street, London WC1A 1LU

© The Navy Records Society, 1981

British Library Cataloguing in Publication Data

Keyes, Roger Keyes, *Baron*
   The Keyes papers. – (Publications/Navy Records Society; vol. 122).
   Vol. III. 1939–1945
   1. Keyes, Roger Keyes, *Baron*
   2. Great Britain. Royal Navy – Biography
   3. Admirals – Great Britain – Biography
   I. Halpern, Paul G.   II. Navy Records Society
   359.3′31′0924   DA89.1.K4   80–41800

ISBN 0–04–942172–7

Typeset in 10 on 12 point Times by Watford Typesetters Ltd
and printed and bound in Great Britain by
William Clowes (Beccles) Limited, Beccles and London

THE COUNCIL
OF THE
NAVY RECORDS SOCIETY
1981

PATRON
H.R.H. THE PRINCE PHILIP, DUKE OF EDINBURGH, K.G., O.M., F.R.S.

PRESIDENT
The Rt Hon. the Lord Carrington, P.C., K.C.M.G., M.C.

VICE PRESIDENTS
Capt. S. W. Roskill, C.B.E., D.S.C., Litt.D., F.B.A., M.A., R.N.
Sir John Lang, G.C.B.
Richard Hough
Prof. C. C. Lloyd, M.A.
Richard Ollard, F.R.S.L., M.A.
R. J. B. Knight, M.A., Ph.D.

COUNCILLORS
Rear-Admiral P. W. Brock, C.B., D.S.O.
Christopher Dowling, M.A., D.Phil.
The Hon. David Erskine, M.A.
Rear-Admiral E. F. Gueritz, C.B., O.B.E., D.S.C.
A. W. H. Pearsall, M.A.
Prof. Peter Nailor, M.A.
Mrs Susan Rose, M.A., Ph.D.
E. K. Timings, F.S.A., M.A.
J. Gooch, M.A., Ph.D.
P. M. Kennedy, B.A., D.Phil., F.R.Hist.S.
H. Tomlinson, M.A., D.Phil.
P. M. H. Bell, B.A., B.Litt.
Prof. J. S. Bromley, M.A., F.R.Hist.S.
D. K. Brown, M.Eng., C.Eng., F.R.I.N.A., R.C.N.C.
J. D. Brown
Admiral Sir James Eberle, K.C.B.
Sub-Lieut. J. A. Goldrick. B.A.. R.A.N.
Prof. D. M. Schurman, M.A., Ph.D.
Geoffrey Till, M.A., Ph.D.
Cdr. A. R. Wells, M.A., M.Sc., Ph.D., R.N.

GENERAL EDITOR
A. N. Ryan, M.A., F.R.Hist.S.

HON. SECRETARY
N. A. M. Rodger, M.A., D.Phil., F.R.Hist.S.

HON. TREASURER
H. U. A. Lambert, M.A.

PREFACE

The vast amount of material collected by Lord Keyes throughout his long career led to the decision to expand publication of *The Keyes Papers* from an originally planned two volumes to three. Keyes's career does fit neatly into the three distinct phases of First World War, interwar period and Second World War. Probably few of the subjects represented in the Navy Records Society publications can reflect as striking a change in the methods of naval warfare as these papers. A comparison of operations in the North Sea and Dardanelles in 1914–1915 with the invasion of Leyte in 1944 would vividly demonstrate how far technology had advanced in a mere thirty years.

This final phase of Keyes's career, particularly his tenure as Director of Combined Operations, is also the most controversial. In the memoirs of some of the leading personalities of the time, Keyes is apt to appear briefly and not always sympathetically. During the war Keyes followed his usual practice of maintaining extensive records and obviously planned to write his own account of events once peace was concluded. Unfortunately he did not live to do so. It is a great pity for, if his *Naval Memoirs* and *Adventures Ashore and Afloat* are an example, the book would have made excellent reading. This collection of documents may, in a sense, give Keyes a chance to put some of his views into the historical record, although obviously it is at best a somewhat fragmentary substitute for the memoirs he would have written himself. One can only regret this, for Keyes's views are certainly not accepted by everyone and one could have anticipated a lively and interesting debate after publication. Moreover, the limitations of space make it impossible to reproduce the lengthy supporting memoranda which Keyes would have used to justify his plans and which, for that matter, the inter-service planning staffs would have used at times to oppose them. This proliferation of paper after 1939 is another feature which sets the Second World War apart from the First and poses special problems in publishing a collection of documents.

More than half of this volume is focused on a period of approximately sixteen months in which Keyes was Director of Combined Operations. The strictly political aspects of Keyes career are not, for the most part, reflected in the documents reproduced. Furthermore, the period when Keyes served as a liaison between the British Government and the King of the Belgians is referred to in relatively few letters rather than an array of documents. Since this is an aspect of Keyes's career of great interest to the historian, a word of explanation may be in order. The Belgian affair is indeed worthy of a special study of its own but, given the mass of material available, it did not seem expedient to devote considerable space to a problem which is basically diplomatic and military. In line with the stated purposes of the Navy Records Society – to publish documents of naval interest – I deliberately decided to keep the focus on naval or combined operations.

There are strong opinions on personalities and events expressed in these documents. Once again I want to emphasize that they are not being published with any idea of creating sensation. There is really no longer any secret about them: practically all of the documents are open to view at various public repositories, and it is up to the student of naval history, who undoubtedly will come in contact with contrasting views, to make his own judgements.

Documents marked [Holograph] are written in the hand of the author. All other documents are typescript or carbons of the original, identified as [Carbon]. Documents marked [Copy] are usually so indicated by Keyes. Handwriting has become even more of a problem as Keyes and his correspondents grew older and illegible or doubtful words are indicated [Illegible] or by a mark in brackets [?]. There are wide variations in the spelling of place names, especially in regard to Norway, but as long as the meaning is clear I have thought it best to leave the original. Occasionally, and only for the purpose of clarity, punctuation has been added where it was non-existent, and for the same reason paragraphs have been given to long tightly-written letters. Some of the official documents which are awkward to reproduce in terms of space have had their headings edited slightly. The salutation and complimentary closing of letters have, with rare exceptions, been omitted to conserve space. Substantial omissions are indicated by a row of asterisks; minor omissions by an ellipsis. Whenever possible, individuals referred to in the text are identified the first time mentioned. A glossary of abbreviations and an appendix listing operational code names have been added to help the reader through one of the characteristic features of wartime documents.

I should like to thank Lord Keyes for permitting his father's papers to be published, thereby making these publications of the Navy Records Society possible. Throughout the project Captain Stephen Roskill has been a constant source of encouragement and assistance. I thank the Master and Fellows of Churchill College for their hospitality, and I am grateful to Mrs Patricia Bradford, Archivist, Miss Angela Raspin, former Archivist, and Mr A. D. Childs, former Deputy Librarian of Churchill College, for helping in innumerable ways.

I should also like to thank the following for their assistance: Miss A. M. Shirley, Custodian of MSS., Mr A. W. H. Pearsall, Historian, and the staff of the National Maritime Museum, Greenwich; Mr E. K. Timings and the staff of the Public Record Office; Commander R. C. Burton, Head, Rear-Admiral Peter N. Buckley, former Head, Miss V. Riley, Mr T. C. Parsons and the staff of the Naval Historical Branch and Naval Historical Library, Ministry of Defence; Dr Christopher Dowling, Mr Roderick Suddaby and the staff of the Imperial War Museum; Professor Arthur J. Marder; Mr Martin Gilbert; Admiral Sir William W. Davis; Commander Ian B. Sutherland, Secretary to the Naval Secretary, Ministry of Defence; and Mr Joseph Evans, Librarian of the Social Science Division, and Miss Marianne Donnell, Assistant Librarian of the Map Division, Strozier Library, The Florida State University.

I am grateful to the Trustees of the National Maritime Museum for permission to use and reproduce material from the papers of Admiral Sir Herbert Richmond and Admiral Sir Walter Cowan; and to the Trustees of the Liddell Hart Centre for Military Archives, King's College, London, for permission to use the papers of Lord Ismay. The late Mr Michael Tomkinson generously made available the papers of his father Vice-Admiral Wilfred Tomkinson.

For permission to print unpublished material I should like to thank the following: Mrs I. M. Agar (Papers of Captain Augustus Agar); The Earl of Avon (his own papers); Field Marshal Sir Claude Auchinleck (his own papers); Commander R. T. Bower (his own papers); Mrs Phyllis Brabner (Papers of Commander Rupert Brabner); C. & T. Publications Ltd. (Papers of Sir Winston S. Churchill); Miss Martha Cowan (Papers of Admiral Sir Walter H. Cowan); Viscountess Cunningham (Papers of Admiral of the Fleet Viscount Cunningham of Hyndhope); Admiral Sir William W. Davis (his own papers); Commander Richard A. Hall (Papers of Rear-Admiral Sir Reginald Hall); Miss Malise Haydon (Papers of Major-General J. C. Haydon); Lady Ismay (Papers of General Baron Ismay); Mrs Helen D. Kinkaid (Papers of Admiral Thomas C. Kinkaid); Admiral of the Fleet Earl Mountbatten of Burma (his own papers); Viscountess Portal (Papers of Marshal of the RAF Viscount Portal); Admiral Sir Reginald H. Portal (his own papers); Captain George Pound (Papers of Admiral of the Fleet Sir A. Dudley P. R. Pound); Lieut.-Colonel Charles A. Ramsay (Papers of Admiral Sir Bertram H. Ramsay); Lady Briget Plowden (Papers of Admiral Sir Herbert Richmond); and Mr William L. Shirer (his own papers).

Documents which are Crown Copyright appear by permission of the Controller, Her Majesty's Stationery Office. I would also like to apologize to those owners of copyright of unpublished material who, despite my best efforts, I have been unable to reach.

The Department of History of The Florida State University has continued to arrange its teaching duties so as to provide free time for research and writing for which I am grateful.

I owe a special debt of gratitude to Anthony N. Ryan, General Editor of the Navy Records Society, for his untiring work in the thousand and one details involved in producing these volumes.

Tallahassee, Florida   Paul G. Halpern
April 1979

The Council of the Society is once again pleased to acknowledge the generous financial support of the British Academy in the production of this volume.

CONTENTS

	PAGE
Preface	vii
List of Maps and Illustrations	xii
Glossary of Abbreviations	xiii
Part I: FROM THE OUTBREAK OF WAR TO THE FALL OF FRANCE (September 1939–July 1940)	1
Part II: DIRECTOR OF COMBINED OPERATIONS (July 1940–October 1941)	75
Part III: THE FINAL PHASE (November 1941–December 1945)	219
Notes to Introduction to Part I	309
Notes to Part I	311
Notes to Introduction to Part II	324
Notes to Part II	325
Notes to Introduction to Part III	344
Notes to Part III	345
Appendix A: List of Operation Code Names	365
Appendix B: Directorate of Combined Operations – Summary of Naval Resources available and planned as of 27 July 1940	366
Appendix C: DCO's Ships – Situation (correct to 1600 hours, 25 August 1941)	367
Appendix D: Landing Craft and Carriers – Weekly Statement – 15 October 1941	370
List of Documents and Sources	375
Index	381

LIST OF MAPS AND ILLUSTRATIONS

Admiral of the Fleet, Lord Keyes .... *Frontispiece*

MAPS:

Trondheim 29
The Belgian Campaign 47
The Central Mediterranean and Pantelleria 121
The Atlantic Islands 168
The South-West Pacific 278

GLOSSARY OF ABBREVIATIONS

Either official or in common use

A/C	Air Craft
ACNS	Assistant Chief of Naval Staff
ACNS (A)	Assistant Chief of Naval Staff (Air)
ADC	Aide-de-Camp
AF or A of F	Admiral of the Fleet
AGRM	Adjutant General Royal Marines
ALC	Assault Landing Craft
AM	Air Ministry
AOC-IN-C	Air Officer, Commander-in-Chief
ARP	Air Raid Precautions
A/S	Anti-Submarine
BEF	British Expeditionary Force
CAS	Chief of Air Staff
CID	Committee of Imperial Defence
CIGS	Chief of Imperial General Staff
C-in-C	Commander-in-Chief
CMF	Central Mediterranean Force (later Allied armies in Italy)
CNS	Chief of Naval Staff
COS or C of S	Chiefs of Staff Committee
CTC	Combined Training Centre
DCO or D of CO	Director of Combined Operations
DCNS	Deputy Chief of Naval Staff
DDCO	Deputy Director of Combined Operations
D/F	Direction Finding (Radio Navigation)
DNAD	Director Naval Air Division
DNI	Director of Naval Intelligence
DNO	Director of Naval Ordnance
DOD	Director of Operations Division
D of P	Director of Plans
EPS	Executive Planning Section (Joint Planning Staff)
FAA	Fleet Air Arm
FOPS	Forward Operational Planning Section (Joint Planning Staff)
GOC	General Officer Commanding
GOC-in-C	General Officer, Commanding-in-Chief
GQG	Grand Quartier Général
GSO	General Staff Officer

ISPS	Inter-Service Planning Staff
ISTDC	Inter-Services Training and Development Centre
JIC	Joint Intelligence Sub-Committee of the Chiefs of Staff
JPC	Joint Planning Sub-Committee of the Chiefs of Staff
JPS	Joint Planning Staff
LCI	Landing Craft, Infantry
LCM	Landing Craft, Mechanised
LSD	Landing Ship, Dock
LSI	Landing Ship, Infantry
LST	Landing Ship, Tank
LVT	Landing Vehicle, Tracked
MAP	Ministry of Aircraft Production
ML	Motor Launch
MLC	Mechanised Landing Craft (later LCM)
MNBDO	Mobile Naval Base Defence Organisation (Royal Marines)
MTB	Motor Torpedo Boat
MT ship	Ship for carrying mechanical transport
NOIC	Naval Officer-in-Charge
PMO	Principal Medical Officer
RA(D)	Rear-Admiral (Destroyers)
RAAF	Royal Australian Air Force
RAF	Royal Air Force
RAN	Royal Australian Navy
RFC	Royal Flying Corps
RM	Royal Marines
RMLI	Royal Marine Light Infantry
RN	Royal Navy
RNAS	Royal Naval Air Service
RNVR	Royal Naval Volunteer Reserve
R/T	Radio-telephony
SEAC	South East Asia Command
SL	Sea Lord
SLC	Support Landing Craft (later LCS)
S/M	Submarine
SNO	Senior Naval Officer
SS	Special Service (Troops)
TLC	Tank Landing Craft (later LCT)
TSDS	Two Speed Destroyer Sweep
USAAF	United States Army Air Force
USN	United States Navy
USNR	United States Naval Reserve
VACTC	Vice-Admiral Combined Training Centre
VCAS	Vice Chief of Air Staff
VCIGS	Vice-Chief of Imperial General Staff
VCNS	Vice-Chief of Naval Staff
W/T	Wireless telegraphy

PART I

FROM THE OUTBREAK OF WAR TO
THE FALL OF FRANCE
(SEPTEMBER 1939–JULY 1940)

With the outbreak of hostilities in September 1939, Keyes found himself in an extremely frustrating position. He had been too young and junior in rank for the highest commands during the First World War, but he was now considered too old and too senior for active employment in the Second.[1] Once again his rapid advancement in earlier years put him at a disadvantage, for he had been away from active service over eight years. On the other hand, his former Deputy and Chief of Staff, Dudley Pound, now First Sea Lord, was only five years younger. Keyes prided himself on his excellent health, and felt that his age – 67 in October 1939 – ought to be no bar to useful employment. His active temperament made it extremely difficult to content himself with parliamentary duties once the war was in progress. Churchill returned to the Admiralty as First Lord on the outbreak of the war and Keyes's hopes were aroused because the day after assuming office, Churchill had promised to find some use for his old friend's abilities [Document 1]. Keyes quickly became dissatisfied with the way the war was being conducted. As his old friend 'Blinker' Hall, Director of Naval Intelligence during the First World War, remarked, it was discouraging to find the 'same old gaffs being committed'. [2]. Keyes listed a number of mistakes he thought the Admiralty had made including the failure to aid Poland with a naval raid in the Baltic before it was mined in, and what he considered the needless loss of the carrier *Courageous* [3, 4, 6]. In October he proposed to Churchill that he be made Chief of Naval Staff with Pound as his Deputy [5].

Keyes's first significant employment during the war resulted from his close relationship with the Belgian royal family. King Leopold III, bound by his Ministers to a policy of strict neutrality, requested in October 1939 that Keyes come to Brussels and serve as an unofficial link with the British Government on the subject of possible Allied assistance in the event of a German attack.[2] Keyes gladly undertook the mission and travelled to Belgium in late Ocober, again in November, and finally in January. The full story of these conversations is complex and beyond the scope of this volume. The King and his advisers may have been pro-British, but they were not necessarily pro-French, and there were misunderstandings. By January the Belgian Government, alarmed that indiscretions might provoke an immediate German attack, retreated into a policy of strict neutrality. Regrettably the affair left a residue of recrimination among the British, French and Belgians.[3]

During this first winter of the war, Keyes, from his vantage point in Parliament, paid particular attention to the question of the Fleet Air Arm. The information which he received from informants in the services about difficulties in co-operation between RAF Coastal Command and the Admiralty confirmed his opinion that a great mistake had been made in not securing control of flying boats when Fleet Air Arm was re-established in 1937 [7, 10]. On some of these points Keyes seems to have been more Royalist than the King for Churchill apparently found his activities, notably an article in the *Daily Telegraph*, something of an embarrassment which hampered his relations with the Air Ministry [8, 9]. Throughout the war Keyes and his correspondents would continue to regard Fleet Air Arm as a Cinderella service.[4]

In March 1940, Keyes, along with other Admirals of the Fleet, was restored to the active list, and when the so-called 'Phoney War' ended with the German attack on Norway and Denmark the following month, his hopes of active employment were high. In fact, the Norwegian campaign brought about Keyes's most famous action during the war – his speech to the House of Commons which preceded the fall of the Chamberlain Government. On April 7th the Germans began 'Weserübung' and in a daring gamble seized a number of Norwegian ports, including Trondheim in central Norway and Narvik in the north. The German garrisons at Narvik and Trondheim were, however, in a precarious position until the bulk of the German forces which had landed in southern Norway could push northwards to reach them. By chance Keyes was visiting Admiral Sir William James, Commander-in-Chief, Portsmouth, when Lady Keyes was taken ill with the measles. Delayed in his return to London, Keyes was allowed into James's War Room where, on the basis of the information available there, he was appalled by what he considered to be a weak Admiralty response to the German challenge [15]. In his view, the most vulnerable German point was at Trondheim where there was an excellent chance to destroy the isolated garrison.[5] Characteristically Keyes sought an interview with Churchill, and when he finally succeeded in seeing the First Lord on the evening of the 16th, offered to lead the attack himself.

Keyes, as he readily admitted, was not privy to the discussions of the Naval Staff and this placed him at a considerable disadvantage. The Cabinet had indeed considered an attack on Trondheim and an expeditionary force under Major-General Sir Adrian Carton de Wiart had landed at Namsos approximately 100 miles to the north on the 14th, and shortly afterwards another force had landed at Andalsnes to the south of Trondheim. However, the Cabinet gave priority to operations against Narvik in the north. A tentative proposal for a direct attack against Trondheim itself by main units of the Home Fleet (Operation 'Hammer') was made to Admiral Sir Charles Forbes, Commander-in-Chief, Home Fleet, but Forbes expressed doubts about its feasibility in the light of German superiority in the air. By the 16th the Admiralty considered Trondheim's capture to be essential and on the 18th Forbes received a copy of the plan for Operation 'Hammer' and a personal letter from Churchill advocating the attack. In the end the Chiefs of Staff cancelled 'Hammer' on the 19th.[6]

It is questionable how much Keyes knew about the Admiralty plans when he finally managed to obtain an interview with Churchill on the evening of the 16th. The session was stormy; Keyes admitted he was 'very offensive' and concluded by offering to lead the attack himself in obsolete ships [11–13]. Keyes returned to the War College Library at Portsmouth in order to study the Norwegian coast defence charts, and then prepared a plan for an assault on Trondheim to be led by two old 'R' class battleships with two battalions of infantry to be carried in the former dreadnought *Centurion*, now a radio-controlled target ship [14]. Keyes had hoped to present his plan to the Chiefs of Staff on the 24th but they were too busy to see him [15]. Churchill managed to arrange for him to meet Pound on the 25th and the First Sea Lord dubbed his plan 'useful' [16–18, 21]. The Chiefs of Staff were considering a modified plan for the capture of Trondheim ('Hammer 2'); but it would have required two Regular Brigades to be drawn from France, and would have involved a delay of at least ten days. On the 26th, 'Hammer 2' was abandoned on the grounds that there were not sufficient anti-aircraft defences to hold the port and the Military Co-ordination Committee decided to evacuate central Norway.[7] Keyes, however, continued to press his case and there was an angry exchange with Pound over the Admiralty's failure to use his services [18, 19].

The German Navy had left two destroyers in Trondheimfjord, thereby enjoying local naval superiority, and these ships apparently played an important role in driving back Carton de Wiart's force at Steinkjer [21, 22]. Carton de Wiart, when he returned to England, discovered how deeply troubled Keyes was over the implication that the Navy had let the Army down.[8] Keyes had particularly harsh words for Churchill's naval advisers and warned: 'If the scuttle is persisted in the Government will have to go and I shall do my damnedest to speed them.' [20]. On the 30th he was still pressing to lead an assault on Trondheim, but by this time the moment had passed. German troops pushing northwards from Oslo had met troops advancing southwards from the port on the 29th and the decision to evacuate the Namsos and Andalsnes forces had already been reached.[9] Keyes was so aroused by the conduct of the war that he sent a copy of his correspondence with Churchill to the Prime Minister and others in the Cabinet [23-25].

There is much about Keyes's Trondheim plan to remind the reader about the Dardanelles – with which Keyes himself frequently drew an analogy. At this time too Churchill was in a leading role and Keyes was desperately attempting to induce the authorities to adopt a daring plan which might have averted the failure of a campaign. In a similar situation, batteries guarding the entrance to a narrow body of water had to be reduced with the prospect of the Navy giving perhaps decisive assistance to the army struggling on land after this occurred. Once again Keyes's plan was turned down. But there was a new factor in 1940 which was not present in 1915 and this is the source of most of the criticism of Keyes. Airpower played only a minor role at the Dardanelles; in Norway it was likely to be decisive and it was the Germans who enjoyed superiority. The Trondheim project has not been treated kindly by commentators who stress the vulnerability of ships to air attack while confined in the narrow waters of the fjord.[10] They point to the example of the cruiser *Suffolk* which was subjected to repeated and damaging attack after bombarding Sola airfield at Stavanger on the 17th. Keyes's criticism of the Naval Staff who had to actually bear the responsibility has also been considered overly harsh, if not irresponsible.[11] On the other hand, a study of Keyes's plan reveals that it was more than a mere mad dash through the fjord. It was a carefully co-ordinated attack with forces landing on the flanks to neutralize the forts. We now know that German forces in Trondheim were not numerous and in a generally precarious position.[12] One authority has also pointed out that to a certain extent the air danger might have been exaggerated for the single engined Ju 87 Stuka dive bombers operating from southern Norway would have been flying beyond their normal radius of action and some support from Fleet Air Arm might have been available.[13] But Trondheim would have been within the range of the twin engined German bombers, the He 111 and potent Ju 88. Obviously much would have depended on timing, and the frequent changes of plan as well as faulty loading of troops and equipment at the start of the campaign do not inspire confidence. This is not the place for a full discussion of the Norwegian campaign although there are fairly universal doubts that Trondheim could have been held for long even if Keyes's plan had succeeded. The fate of the Trondheim project like the fate of a second assault on the Dardanelles must remain a question that will never be answered.

The bitter aftermath of the evacuation of central Norway brought the famous debates in the House of Commons which ended in the fall of the Chamberlain government and the arrival in power of Churchill.

Keyes played an important role in these debates and has earned a mention in most general histories of the time. This is rather ironic for he was a poor speaker and at first glance hardly the man to stir the House. However, he felt so deeply about what he had to say concerning the conduct of the war that he consulted other more facile parliamentarians. Harold Macmillan advised him to prepare his speech carefully beforehand and read it from notes.[14] Keyes donned his uniform as an Admiral of the Fleet, and this, together with his obvious sincerity, had a tremendous effect according to most accounts. His speech was followed by Leo Amery's famous denunciation and the net result was to bring down the Government.[15]

Almost immediately after the Parliamentary debates the German attack in the west began. Churchill promptly despatched Keyes to act as his personal liaison with King Leopold and an eventful few weeks followed in which Keyes experienced first-hand the impact of modern war [26-32, 35, 38]. He managed to escape to England when the Belgians were forced to capitulate.[16] The Belgian campaign is beyond the scope of this volume but Keyes returned with much admiration for King Leopold and reacted strongly against the tendency of some British and French leaders to make the King of the Belgians a scapegoat for the Allied disaster [31-33, 35, 38].[17] He continued to defend the reputation of the King for the remainder of his life, and had he lived would undoubtedly have played an important role in the controversy in Belgium over the question of Leopold's return to the throne after the war.[18]

Keyes saw Churchill briefly on his return to England on May 28th. He was anxious to go to Dunkirk, but this was vetoed by the Prime Minister.[19] To his great regret, he remained unemployed in the crucial weeks following the evacuation. He felt compelled to remind Churchill of his existence on July 4th, asking if the country was 'so flush of people with the experience I possess' that Churchill could continue to ignore him in that critical hour [34]. Within a fortnight Keyes had his answer. On July 17th Churchill appointed him Director of Combined Operations.

1. *Keyes to Admiral Sir William Reginald Hall*[1]

[Carbon]

22 St. Leonard's Terrace,
London, S.W.3.
18/9/39.[2]

Many thanks for your letter. I have been wondering so much what you are doing. Of course you ought to be D.N.I. again.

As you know I have been urging the Government for ages to send

Winston to the Admiralty, and have repeatedly spoken to the Chief Whip on the importance of sending him there before it was too late.³

When we gave immense emergency powers to the Govt., and we could not get Chamberlain to say that he would form a War Cabinet at once, I wrote to the *Daily Telegraph* – the *Times* won't publish letters from me! – giving my war experience of the conduct of the war, until a really vigorous War Cabinet was formed.

If they had sent him when I wrote that letter and I had been at his side, I swear we would have had a skirmish round the Baltic before it was all shut in with mines. There seems to have been no co-ordination in that very gallant raid on Wilhelmshafen and Brunsbüttel.⁴

The day after Winston became First Lord, he volunteered that when he had had time to look round, he would 'find a mission for me worthy of my abilities', but that was a fortnight ago! I tried to get in touch with him one day, as I thought there was just time to organise a combined destroyer and air attack in the Baltic, before mine laying could be completed, but he was too busy to see me and the hour passed.

I can't go and ask him for a job. Of course I *know* I ought to be C.N.S. with Pound⁵ as my deputy. We have worked together since 1917 when he was my Flag Captain for a short spell in the *Colossus*. Later as Assistant Director of Plans. As Director of Operations afterwards he was invaluable to me when I was at Dover. Then I took him as a special Staff Officer to work out tactical problems when I commanded the B.C.S. He worked under me at the Admiralty when I was D.C.N.S. to Beatty⁶ for nearly four years, and then was my Chief of Staff in the Mediterranean.

He is an admirable Staff Officer, but his judgement has not always been good – I could give you two examples, which affected the future of the Service, once disastrously. Perhaps he can accept big responsibility, I hope so, but don't feel sure. Anyway in war time there is too much for the C.N.S. and 1st S.L. to do, and the C.N.S. ought to be free from all Departmental worries.

Chatfield⁷ – as I knew he would be – is all for safety first. Duff Cooper⁸ told me that he could not get him to consider any offensive plan. He swore that there was nothing to be done but protect trade.

When that ass Shakespeare⁹ said in the House last March, that we had the S.M. menace beaten, I could have strangled him.¹⁰ He got it from Chatfield and Co. and Winston himself was much impressed, when Chatfield took him to Portland to see the anti-Submarine service at work. Of course it is excellent, but I warned him and others in the Govt. that it was a foolish boastful statement, we would be bound to have heavy losses, until well screened and protected convoys could be organised. I don't know what the *Courageous* was doing, but an Aircraft Carrier, so dependent on the direction of the wind, is a terrible vulnerable craft to all forms of attack.[11]

All we are going through now is a repetition of the early days of the last war – as described in Vol I of my *Naval Memoirs*! and the peaceful situation at Dover (when I went there) with no aggressive action for fear of reprisals, is akin to the Govt's policy today.

Of the people at the Admiralty, 2 S.L. Little[12] was my Staff Officer for years in the Submarines, and owes much to me.

The Controller – Fraser,[13] a grand fellow all for the offensive, was Gunnery Commander on my staff in the Mediterranean. He ought to be D.C.N.S.

The D.C.N.S.[14] is a good little man, good staff officer, but I should say cautious. He was Commander for Operations on my Staff.

Ramsay,[15] 5.S.L. was on De Robeck's[16] staff with me, and is a friend.

If you can do anything to get me into the Admiralty, for God's sake get on with it, as I can't sit quiet and good much longer, and one of these days I shall explode in the H. of Commons. I have refrained as I do not want to make Winston's task more difficult.

I believe Winston, Pound and I would be a good combination. Everybody in the House of Commons and many in the Country know that I have been working for five years to get an efficient Navy with its own Air Force, and the restoration of our Sea Power.

I am conceited enough to think that my appointment to the Admiralty would have a cheering effect on the country, and might even make the Germans think...

2. *Hall to Keyes*

The Ropeway,
Beaulieu.
September 19th, 1939.

Very many thanks for your letters. I entirely agree that you ought to be at the Admiralty; not only your experience and mind but the name is of enormous value and would make the German understand that there were no velvet gloves in this affair.

It is as you say exactly the same as the beginning of the last war and if Winston is not careful he will have the same end!! This I should greatly regret as he is the right man for the job but he ought to be properly staffed with men who know how to fight and hurt the other fellow.

I don't think they would ever look at me for any job again; officials hate independence in anyone.

Meanwhile my dear Roger, do press for a huge destroyer programme; we want as far as I can calculate another 200 and they must some of them be capable of making the Atlantic crossing or the Indian Ocean. Without these we shall soon run our present ones to death; my son in law in one of the new ones has only been in harbour long enough to refuel since war began and has not slept in his cabin with clothes off at all!! I don't sympathise with him but I do know and so do you that you can't go on at that rate and keep efficient.

I hope to be up in Town next week for a few days and will try to get in touch with you; it is loathsome sitting here knowing that the same old gaffs are being made; we never learn!! ...

3. Keyes to Churchill

Tingewick House,
Buckingham.
1/10/39.

I am sending you an article I wrote for the *Sunday Chronicle* in March *1938*. I am not responsible for the rather absurd way in which it is presented, or its title.

Most of it, particularly paragraphs 2, 3, and 15, are what you have been urging for years,[17] but I know that if 7 had been adopted then,[18] or even three or four months ago, and you had let me help you out of my experience, the war at sea, which you described so vividly in the House of Commons last Tuesday, would have brought still greater honour to the Navy, and been a still braver and more inspiring tale.

It was so unfair that your inclusion in the Cabinet should have been postponed until the morning war broke out, when the Navy was committed to Chatfield's cautious war plan, and it was too late to rectify the lack of foresight and preparation, which was responsible for the loss of several valuable merchant ships.

It was very galling for you, and for your friends, that your warnings and advice should have been ignored, and that step by step the Government were forced to take belatedly the action you had repeatedly urged, too late to avert war, or to be ready to wage war when it was forced upon us.

It is galling too for me, whose one object in life has been to serve the Navy, that now we are at war once again, the fact that I got specially early promotion for my services in two previous wars should be responsible for my being placed on the retired list at an age (62), when Chatfield (who is less than a year younger than I) and others, promoted Admiral of the Fleet normally, were given five to seven more years of active service.

As I have been debarred from any contact with the Admiralty, or even you except in public, and have never been consulted in any way, either before hostilities broke out or during the past month, I am putting my views as to the conduct of the war at sea up to date in the form of a memorandum,[19] which I enclose...

4. *Memorandum by Keyes*

[1 October 1939]

I have been debarred from any contact with the Admiralty and have not been consulted in any way before hostilities broke out, or since, and I know little more than the 'man in the street' what has really happened.

But some proceedings are obviously open to criticism, and in view of my varied experience in the last war, particularly of operations in enemy waters and their vicinity, and of my intimate knowledge of submarine warfare – its possibilities and limitations, I venture to make some comments.

Presumably, before Mr Chamberlain declared that Great Britain and France would immediately go to the assistance of Poland in the event of German aggression, he consulted the Chiefs of the Staff of the Navy, Army and Air Force, as to how this guarantee could be implemented?

It was obvious that it would be a long time before the Army could be ready to take any action; but I wonder what advice was given by the Chiefs of Staff of the Navy and Air Force, or by the Minister for Co-ordination of Defence?

I suppose that owing to the strained relations with Germany, the Government would not allow H.M. ships to pay their customary Autumn visits to the Baltic; but if these could have been arranged and had been limited to vessels of light draught, capable of navigating the Sound, and submarines – Naval action could have been immediate.

I wonder if this was seriously considered, or if the objections were considered insuperable?

However it seems almost incredible, in view of our guarantee, that between March and the end of August no plan was made for a Naval raid into the Baltic of light vessels, at the earliest possible moment after the Germans crossed the Polish frontier.

Such a raid might well have been a surprise and achieved much. It would certainly have heartened the Poles and given them an earnest of our determination to see the matter through. It should have synchronised, if possible, with the very gallant attack on the Naval Bases in the Heligoland Bight carried out by the R.A.F. It is unlikely that the casualties would have amounted to anything like the number lost in the *Courageous* – to which I will refer later.

What must the Poles and the other small Nations, which are looking to us for help, think of the value of Mr Chamberlain's guarantees, and our failure to carry out any offensive action to make good his brave words, and relieve the Poles of some of the German pressure before they were "liquidated".

It cannot have been very encouraging for other Nations to whom we have given guarantees, and they may well doubt our ability or will to honour them, at any rate until we have more robust and resolute leaders.

On the outbreak of the last war, our submarines were immediately sent into the unknown dangers of the Heligoland Bight, and brought back valuable information, which resulted in the action of 28th August, which had far reaching effects on the Naval war for more than a year.[20]

The success of that operation was jeopardised by faulty staff work at the Admiralty.

To my mind, a cardinal principle in the conduct of Naval operations is to ensure that if a ship or squadron meets another, they should be in no doubt that it is a friend – or a foe.

The recent loss of one of our submarines and the narrow escape of another, owing to faulty dispositions, I consider inexcusable.[21]

That scores of inexperienced R.A.F. pilots have it in their power to make similar mistakes alarms me!

The Admiralty must bear the responsibility for their failure to take steps to minimise the risks which British ships would run from submarine attack when war became almost inevitable. I was astonished to learn that the Admiralty could only communicate with them 'en clair'.

It is amazing – in view of the dangerous situation which had existed for a year or more, and the warning we received of German submarine activity in the September crisis – that no arrangements were made to route British ships at sea or advise them to remain in, or run to British or neutral ports when war threatened. A very simple sealed code could have been confided to the skippers, to be opened on the receipt of a warning signal.

It would be interesting to know how many German ships escaped capture and how many British ships were sunk, owing to the delay of 48 hours, after Poland was invaded, before our declaration of war.

Although nominally not at war, it is difficult to find any excuse for allowing a 10,000 ton tanker to leave Trinidad a day or two before war was declared, or indeed for the loss of 60,000 tons of oil through lack of precautions.

I have always felt convinced from my knowledge of submarines, that the Admiralty were putting too high a value on "A.S."[22] It is wonderful, and used by highly trained, skilled operators, submarines can be located and hunted with great accuracy, but it is exceedingly hard to kill a modern submarine, and there are innumerable false contacts in shoal water, particularly with wrecks about.

I think the employment of a great vulnerable target and valuable ship like the *Courageous* with a complement of 1200, trusting blindly to the skill of two or even four destroyers fitted with "A.S." (possibly not highly trained), cruising about looking for one or two submarines was entirely unjustifiable, and akin to the employment – despite my repeated warnings – of the *Aboukir, Cressy,* and *Hogue* in the Narrow Seas in 1914[23]

I cannot conceive that the presence of the *Courageous,* cruising about off the S.W. of Ireland, could achieve any result commensurate with the risks she was running. Results which could have been attained by other and less extravagant means.

The loss of 500 valuable highly trained men, not to mention the value of the ship and her equipment, was deplorable. On the other hand the possible loss of a few destroyers in a brave foray in the Baltic, which would have raised our prestige and given expression to the offensive spirit which was so often damped down in the last war, but which blazed out when given its opportunity, stands in another category.

As you know, I have fought for years for the development of a Naval Air Service, comprising types which would be supreme in a fleet action and invaluable in the protection of trade. In fact *all aircraft which work with and against ships* – and I enlisted your help to this end.

It is difficult to write temperately of the lack of vision of the First Sea Lords of recent years, and their failure to fight for what was so essential for Naval efficiency, and insist on being given freedom to develop, man and train a service, which in war would be needed to carry out functions which the Navy must control and for which they bear all the responsibility.

The lack of fighting spirit in the Admiralty and Baldwin's[24] obstruction held me up for years. In July 1937 Chamberlain wrote to me, saying he hoped I was satisfied with Inskip's[25] settlement of the Navy v. Air controversy.

I replied that the retention of the flying boats by the R.A.F. was illogical and another political compromise. The handling of these craft is a seaman's job. Inskip was able, however, to give me proof that Chatfield had written to him to say *he* was satisfied, although he had told me that he would insist on having operational control of the flying boats.

I understand that the Navy still has no control over them, but I know that those responsible now for the conduct of the war at sea, would give anything for a fleet of highly trained Naval flying boats and shore based reconnaissance aircraft, both for co-operation with the fleet and the protection of trade.

The existing arrangement is unsatisfactory, inefficient according to Naval standards, and can be positively dangerous to our own vessels.

It is gratifying to know that the enterprising and skilful rescue of a crew sunk by a submarine, carried out by a flying boat lately, was due to the skill and seamanship of a Merchant Navy officer who had joined the R.A.F. in response to their advertisements for seamen, for service in the R.A.F.!

How infinitely better off the Navy would be if it had been developing and training a service which many of us knew would be absolutely necessary in war.

The surrender of the Irish ports[26] to appease De Valera[27] was a crime it is difficult to forgive. Did the Naval Staff acquiesce?

Their possession now as bases for patrols and Naval aircraft would be invaluable, and would have avoided any necessity for using aircraft carriers in dangerous waters.

5. *Keyes to Churchill*

Secret
22 St. Leonard's Terrace,
S.W.3.
4/10/39.

As I told you yesterday, during the week end I wrote you a letter and memorandum,[28] making some comments on the conduct of the war at sea.

I must confess that I was feeling a bit sore that I should have been told no more than the man in the street. However, as I was about to send my letter, Pound invited me to lunch, and we had a long and interesting talk.

I put all the points I had made in the memorandum to him, I don't think he accepted any of my criticisms, although that does not necessarily mean that he is right! Anyhow we cleared the air, and as I told you, I was impressed by the way he is bearing his responsibilities.

After my conversation with him, I meant to refrain from sending you these papers, but you told me nevertheless to send them, so I do so.

I know you mean to find me something to do, directly an opportunity offers; but from what you have said, it seems likely to be nothing to do with the Navy, and I do feel that my experience – four years Deputy to Beatty at the Admiralty, and I did much of his work – my varied war experiences, and the war sense I know I possess, should not be divorced from the Navy.

Towards the end of the last war, when the Admiralty were smothered with a wet blanket, and the daily task was its only concern – Wemyss[29] was sent there as Deputy First Sea Lord, probably on account of his Gallipoli effort, to introduce an offensive spirit and think out measures for prosecuting the war.

He at once sent for me to be Director of Plans, and Pound was one of my assistants.

I do not know who was responsible for the idea of duplicating the First Sea Lord, but there is a good deal to be said for it in war time.

Pound is $4\frac{1}{2}$ years younger than I, and succeeded to the rank of Admiral of the Fleet at the age I was retired from it!

He was Flag Captain of the *Colossus* when I hoisted my flag in her and remained with me for a short time.

He was one of my Assistant Directors when I was Director of Plans, and when I went as Vice Admiral commanding Dover Patrol, he became Director of Operations Division and was of great assistance to me.

After the war when I was commanding the Battle Cruiser Squadron, I got him appointed to my Staff, to work out some tactical problems, and later he commanded one of my squadrons.

When I was D.C.N.S., I got him appointed Director of Plans, and later when I went as C.-in-C. Mediterranean, I took him as Chief of Staff.

As I told you, I had formed a very high opinion of him as a *Staff* Officer, although I had good reason on more than one occasion to doubt the wisdom of his judgement on policy.

If circumstances arise which make you feel that the policy adopted in the last war should be repeated – I hope that you will bear me in mind, as Pound and I have worked together in harmony for some years and were a good combination.

I quite appreciate that this might be very difficult for you to arrange, but it is worth thinking about! I know I am not popular with the Government, but after all neither were you!

This letter is of course *for your eye only* and had better be destroyed.

6. Keyes to Churchill

[Carbon]   1/11/39.

I enclose a letter[30] which I think you ought to find time to read and pass on to Pound.

I don't know of course what you are going to say about the loss of the *Royal Oak* and 800 men.[31] Personally I can't think of anything that can possibly be said to save the head of whoever was responsible for the failure to make Scapa defences submarine proof – in view of all our experience in the last war.

The Germans admit that their success was greatly helped by British negligence, and there is no gainsaying this.

You told me to write my experiences in the Great War for the benefit of those who came after, I did but I don't suppose any of those who are responsible for the Naval conduct of this war ever bothered to read my books. It will interest students of Naval History in the future to see how faithfully this generation is repeating mistakes made by the last.

You never give me an opportunity of talking to you, and I daresay you won't even bother to read this! However I hope some day you will remember that my unique experience is not being made use of in any way, to the astonishment of my friends, when I have to confess to them that I know nothing and have no connection with the Admiralty, after two months of war with you as First Lord!

People who don't love you told me you would let me down, but I still have faith in you and my star ...

7. Commander R. T. Bower[32] to Keyes

Private

Officers' Mess,
Royal Air Force,
Eastbury Park,
Northwood, Middx.
3rd Jan. 1940.

I had over an hour with Royle[33] yesterday and put over my views as strongly as possible.

Today I have sent him the enclosed, and also sent a copy to Winston.[34]

You will see that I am advocating a limited objective, and I am sure that this is the right course – otherwise the antagonism of the Air Ministry, which is always near the surface, will be stirred up.

Also, I think both from what Royle said and from other indications, that someone has been getting at Winston and using the argument that now that the Navy have got the Fleet Air Arm, they have done nothing with it, and merely succeeded in immobilising a lot of valuable personnel which the Air Force would have made much better use of!

It is a subtle form of attack, because there is a substratum of truth in the idea. The carrier-borne aircraft have flown hundreds of thousands of miles in the S. Atlantic and Indian Ocean and, as luck will have it, have not done more than pick up an odd German merchant ship. If only they had found the *Graf Spee*!!

I still fear that Winston and others at the Admiralty are not sufficiently conscious of the fact that the Airmen are still much more concerned not to cede anything to the other services than to deal with the situation on its merits. Whenever one comes into contact with them, that same old aggressive attitude based on twenty years of wrong doctrine and inferiority complex comes out!

I do hope you will go on pushing. *Time is so short.* You carry the guns, I don't, but perhaps I can play *Ajax* to your *Exeter*!...[35]

8. *Rear-Admiral Guy C. Royle to Keyes*

Admiralty, S.W.
26th January, 1940.

There is no question in the Admiralty that what you have written is right and almost unanswerable.[36] The only question we are not too sure about is whether this is an opportune moment for re-opening the old battle *in public*.

We are afraid that such action may have the effect of opening up old sores and embittering relations, which under the present First Lord have already become normal and friendly.

I happen to know that the First Lord has some delicate negotiations in mind in connection with the Coastal Command and the Fleet Air Arm, which if they are to succeed must be conducted in an atmosphere of friendliness and trust on both sides. It is, therefore, more than ever necessary at present not to encourage the idea that the Navy is endeavouring to get public opinion on its side at the expense of the R.A.F...

Very many thanks for your good wishes...

[Holograph]
P.S. I quite agree with you that if people like Lord L. [Londonderry][37] make gross misstatements in the Press they must be corrected.

9. Royle to Keyes

Admiralty, S.W.
3rd February, 1940.

I must thank you for an interesting conversation yesterday on the subject of the Fleet Air Arm. I am still not quite sure whether I made myself absolutely clear as to what we think can be done to improve matters vis-à-vis the Coastal Command.

We do not think it possible or desirable, and I am sure you will agree, to make any drastic changes in the operational control of the Coastal Command. The Navy, having had no say in the training or equipment, is not in a position to suddenly take over its operational control in the middle of a war. We should, however, like to see the following changes if they were possible: –

(i) Combined operation room including Coastal Command and Naval Staff.
(ii) A striking force of Bomber squadrons, say 4, placed immediately under the control, both for operation and training, of the Coastal Command.
(iii) A striking force of torpedo carrying aircraft under the immediate control of the Coastal Command.

NOTE. – This is already provided for, but squadrons have not yet been re-armed with suitable aircraft. They still have the obsolete Wildebeeste which has less range than the Swordfish.

(iv) Four squadrons of long range fighters placed under the immediate control of Coastal Command. This also, I believe, is about to be done.

As I told you, the First Lord is playing with the idea of turning over a number of pilots, etc., from the Fleet Air Arm to Coastal Command in order to release a corresponding number of Coastal Command pilots, etc., to augment the First Line squadrons of the Bomber Command at the expense of Carriers.

Under the above conditions a very awkward situation would arise if the Germans decided to send some more warships out into the Atlantic, so that we are naturally not keen on it, nor would, I think, the Air Ministry or Coastal Command be at all pleased to see our Fleet Air Arm personnel taking over their Coastal Command aircraft.

The First Lord, however, appears to think he will have no difficulty in persuading the Air Ministry to accept this change, although it is extremely doubtful if the Board of Admiralty would accept this severe reduction in Carrier strength.

I know you will treat the contents of this letter as confidential...

10. *Keyes to Churchill*

[Copy]
Tingewick House,
Buckingham.
12/2/40.

I get so few opportunities of talking to you now, so must write this, as time passes and the days are lengthening, and I feel impelled to tell you that it is high time the Admiralty took a strong line and insisted on the Navy being given control over all the aircraft it needs to fulfil its responsibilities, including the protection of British and Neutral shipping in the North Sea from enemy aircraft, which now dominate it from the Heligoland Bight to the Shetland Islands.

You told me that my article and letter in the *Daily Telegraph* had made your relations with the Air Ministry difficult, and prevented your getting what you hoped for, but it ought not to be a matter for bargaining with Kingsley Wood,[38] even if he had the guns to compete with Balfour[39] and that self centred Air Ministry – which I doubt.

If the Admiralty insist on having what they had throughout the last War, i.e. the Naval Air Service needed to give security to the Empire communications, (in 1918–2,500 aircraft of all types and 55,000 men), the Government would have to give it to them, because the Admiralty are responsible and cannot share their responsibility with the Air Ministry, and the nature and strength of the Air Force the Navy needs cannot be left any longer to the whim of the Air Ministry.

They have never tried to understand Naval requirements and have impeded the development of Naval Aviation most damnably during the last 20 years, with the result that the Germans can quite fairly claim that they dominate the air over the North Sea.

Public opinion forced your inclusion in the War Cabinet when war broke out, and public opinion will back you up in anything you do to ensure that the Navy possesses an adequate and efficient Air Service, the lack of which has been responsible for the loss of many British and Neutral merchant ships, with the lives of scores of seamen and fishermen, and also for our failure to take advantage of several opportunities of inflicting losses on the enemy.

Many people, including M.P.s on both sides of the House, have told me that the case I made in my article and letter is unanswerable, and I am sure public opinion will now be strongly in favour of the Navy in this matter, because people are deeply concerned at our shipping losses – and would be even more so, if it were generally known that on frequent occasions, the Fighter and Bomber Commands have failed to act when appealed to for assistance by the ill equipped Coastal Command, and have thus missed golden opportunities of showing their capabilities.

How can we possibly get on with the war, while not only is the Navy denied the control of aircraft which carry out purely Naval functions, but while those functions are divided between the aircraft of three entirely separate Air Commands – often in conflict – with all the consequent time lag and delay, whilst action, or inaction, is discussed on the telephone.

It would be difficult to imagine anything more disturbing and discreditable, than the procedure which followed the discovery by the Admiralty of a damaged enemy vessel in the North Sea, within easy striking distance of Bomber Command; or the excuses made by its C.-in-C. for not attacking it – because the position was too near the German Fighter Bases – (about 180 miles).

After all the German bombers attack our ships right in our Estuaries, hundreds of miles from their bases, and within a few miles of our Fighter bases. It is true that our gallant and skilful Fighters have destroyed some of these enterprising aircraft when they came within sight of our coast, but it is disconcerting to hear so often of badly damaged enemy aeroplanes escaping, apparently unpursued.

Aircraft carrying out Naval functions are, or should be, as in the U.S.A., France and Japan, an integral part of the Fleet, just as much as submarines and destroyers.

There has been nothing so humiliating to our Naval pride and prestige as the German aerial domination of the North Sea and the losses their aircraft have inflicted on unprotected vessels off our coasts since the Dutch Navy entered British Estuaries and Harbours, drove our fishing fleet off the sea, and destroyed Spanish ships in the Downs 300 years ago.

I have no doubt that another Blake[40] will be found to correct the atmosphere in the North Sea, but not until the existing system, which has been given a fair trial in war and has been found dangerously ineffective, is terminated and the Coastal Command becomes part of the Navy and is equipped with an Air Force of the nature and strength to carry out the Naval functions required.

On 1st April 1918 – at a most critical moment of the War – the Naval administration of the R.N.A.S. was broken up, and the Army methods and Military titles and uniforms were imposed on the Naval personnel.

The Admiralty need not go so far as this, and if any of the personnel of the Coastal Command wish to remain in the R.A.F., they should be free to do so, as soon as they can be spared, but the Coastal Command itself must be embodied in the R.N.A.S. War experience has proved the folly of depriving the Navy of its Air Service.

The Admiralty ought also to insist on being free to equip the personnel of the Fleet Air Arm with the aircraft best suited to carry out the Naval functions required of it in this war, whether they are carried in ships, or worked from shore bases, but I do hope that the Admiralty won't overdo the paying off of Aircraft Carriers.

You said a good deal to me about the failure of the *Ark Royal* to locate the *Graf Spee,* but she carried out the work of a number of cruisers which would otherwise have been required, but do not exist! and I am confident that the Carriers will justify their existence if more German raiders come out.

The *Bismarck* and the new "Deutschland" will probably cause you much anxiety before this war ends!

As you know I have had a fairly stormy life, fighting for things I considered necessary for the honour of the Navy and the welfare of the Country, but I never fought for anything more vitally important than the restoration of the Naval Air Service, which is of ever increasing importance in a modern Navy.

Before the last War, I thought it was essential to train and develop the Submarine Service for work overseas, and to this end tried to free it from the hampering effects of the Vickers monopoly. I could make no headway until you came to the Admiralty, saw the necessity and took a hand. I think our combined effort was a good one.

You and Freddie Guest[41] were of great help when I was fighting in the House for the restoration of the Naval Air Service, and the memorandum you wrote for Inskip in April 1937, (of which you sent me a copy) concurs in the case I am making now. (Extract attached.)[42]

Chatfield would not realise the urgency of the matter in 1937, (as he believed in the Anglo-German Naval Treaty) and I could not induce him to insist on having at once what he knew would be essential in war because he said he was "an astute campaigner and would get it all in time."

At the Other Club on Thursday I tried to inspire him to take a hand now, but he declared that he had no authority and was no longer Minister for Co-Ordination of Defence except in name. He said it was for the Admiralty to demand what the Navy needs. He admitted that the present situation was very unsatisfactory from the Navy's point of view, and will I am sure back you up in the Cabinet. So ought Hoare[43] – judging by my correspondence with him when he was First Lord.

You initiated the R.N.A.S., which when the last war ended was the finest Naval Air Service in the world; then unfortunately you lost interest in it, but you can make it possible to reorganise it for this war, before it is too late, if only you will take a hand at once, and make the Government put an end for ever to the political compromises and face saving devices from which the Navy has suffered for the last twenty years.

The Air Ministry have had their chance of providing Naval co-operation and have failed lamentably.

Recent events and avoidable losses have provided you with the strongest possible case for relieving the Navy of an intolerable handicap. Are you going to play the hand? Or have I got to go on battling alone for something I know to be essential, and will eventually have to be done, in order to restore confidence in British Sea Power and its ability to give protection to our fishing fleets and merchant shipping, and attack the enemy when he puts to sea?

I don't want to raise the matter in the House of Commons, but I am assured of much support if I do.[44]

I am sending you a copy of my correspondence with the Prime Minister (Chamberlain) on the subject, when the last political compromise was perpetrated in 1937 . . . .

P.S. Personally I believe that after the first shock is over, the Coastal Command would prefer to be under the Navy – with whom it has excellent relations – than with the Fighter and Bomber Commands under the Air Ministry, which has neglected its interests so shockingly.

11. *Keyes to his wife*

[Holograph]   22, St. Leonard's Terrace,
S.W.3.
16.4.40.

I hope you are feeling much better.[45] I travelled up with *Baralong* Herbert[46] and Peter Du Cane[47] who says it is time we went to stay with him. He says the little son is all right *now,* he has had to have an operation because he could not pass his food through his tummy.

I got in touch with Bracken[48] and told him I insisted on seeing Winston. He arranged it about 7 p.m. I had to wait a long time. While I was with Steele [Seal],[49] I let myself go. [Seal] is the senior private secretary.

Before I left the House of Commons I saw the Italian journalist. He said he wanted to correct the German propaganda in Italy. I told him exactly what I thought of the Italians for backing Germany over her Scandinavian exploits, his paper's pro-German attitude, etc. He asked me what Narvik meant. I told him (what I suggested to W.C.)[50] He also asked me what was the value of aircraft against ships. I said Mussolini had banked on his aircraft. He would get a rude awakening.

Peter Du Cane told me how hard we could hit Italy who depended on Narvik for nearly all her iron ore. The journalist said the interview would go straight over to Italy and be given good publicity. The theory that *Scharnhorst* and "Blücher" [class] cruisers intended to do what I have suggest[ed] came to me while I was talking to the Italian.[51] I am pretty certain that was the idea.

I started off by telling W.C. of this. He did the weary Titan again – discredited my theory, told [Seal] later it was out of the question. They would not have dared to go there. They would have been torpedoed up there by our submarines – can you imagine anything so foolish, if he really thinks that is the answer he ought not to be allowed to have anything to say to operations! What he really did not like was that I should have suggested something his tired staff had not thought of – I said it did not matter whether I was right or not it was very good propaganda.

Then I suggested something – that he should get the old "R's"[52] and any other obsolescent ships and prepare to smash up the Norwegian ports. He was very tired he said 2 or 3 times, so I said too tired to listen to me I said all the things I have said I would say and more. Too tired to win the war. He said I had worked myself into a state of excitement, he could quite understand my feeling disgusted at being out of it – but – he had to take the advice of his professional advisers. I said I was not excited, but very angry, and was beginning to wonder what I had been backing in him for nearly a generation. I wondered if he realised what history would have to say about this last week of inaction. This after he told me they were very anxious about Italy. I said no wonder the neutrals were beginning to wonder if we would win – when we sat down and waited a week. Why hadn't we struck at once. He rang the bell ½ way through and said he was sorry he was tired and must rest – [Seal] came in – and I said does this mean you're dismissing me? I have got more to say. [Seal] seeing he was very de trop – hurried out – I had let myself go to him for 20 minutes before I went in – *He* said my idea was of course the right one and had not been suggested by a soul, anyhow it was 1st class propaganda.

Winston gave me a chance of hitting back when he said I was not fit for command, I had been unemployed so long. That is of course what D. Pound Co. must be saying. I said don't think I am jealous of Cork[53] – I commend you for your appt. Of course it isn't a big enough appt. for me – I could be much more use than that if I weren't barred from helping – Cork was 7 or 8 years junior to me and less than a year younger. What did he mean I wasn't fit? I had kept myself young and fit – I then went out, dictated the typewritten paper[54] and wrote the letter to W.C. and left it marked secret and personal – by that time it was 9.30 or later and Winston was coming along the passage (dinner time) as I went out. He said: "Oh my dear" – and was quite affectionate. I said: "I have written some notes for you and have left them" – he thanked me and said he would read them carefully – so I gave his arm a squeeze and said good night. I had a cold dinner at 10 – and so home to bed.

I tried to telephone twice but got no answer. However Culler's door was open – it was 10.30 – and she was very glad to see me – There was a telegram from Katherine[55] to say she was not coming.

I think I touched Winston pretty hard and he evidently does not bear any malice. I really was very offensive!

I have just found this [writing] paper. What infuriated me was his ringing the bell and dismissing me like that – saying he worked so many hours a day, was very tired, I really must go – did I think they had not considered all these things – then I let myself go. Please keep the copy of my letter to Winston. He was very jumpy and thoroughly alarmed about Italy. I said my straight talking to "Ciano's"[56] paper might make them think. He didn't know Italy is dependent on Narvik. Peter Du Cane has the closest relations with Italy as all his MTB engines come from Italy and he goes there often.

I will send your mother's bag and this letter by train as I don't suppose this would reach you tomorrow – It is now midnight. I will try to find out tomorrow where Geoffrey[57] is. I will add a line tomorrow. Good night darling. I had several nice things said to me about my article by M.P.s and the man who looks after my coat! – and [Seal] – Oh I forgot to tell you I told W.C. that I had written the article and had backed the Admiralty but I was not at all sure that their action during this last week merited it. He evidently approved of the article and was grateful for it. I learnt from Bower that some of the Cabinet were for going in at Bergen, they (the people on the spot) were quite ready to go right in with several hundred Marines and 3 or 4 cruisers – but cancelling orders were given at the very last minute. My friend Harcourt[58] prayed the WT would arrive [Random mark] (Sleep!) too late – but alas it didn't – that was why I dwelt on their inaction. Good night darling. Quite like old times!

I told Winston that N.C.'s [Neville Chamberlain] "wait until the next crisis" had killed my liaison with King Leopold[59] – if they had only given me the unqualified guarantee – which both Anthony Eden[60] and he thought quite all right – *at the time,* I could have kept a close liaison – would have acquired merit with the Belgian Govt. for being the King's friend and *their* man – instead of being taboo because they thought I was trying to commit the King.[61] I am afraid each neutral will wait until he is attacked.

Wednesday, 17.4.40.

I hope you are feeling quite well again. Diana[62] and Katherine seem to be coming up for luncheon tomorrow. I will tell her to bring you up a nightie and anything else which came home from the wash last week. I enclose her letter and Diana's.

I think I will come down on Thursday evening if I can – and it looks likely. Particularly if I have to write an article – in which case I will bring the typewriter down – it will have to go off on Friday evening. You see how pleased they are. Diana congratulatory, so I suppose even Elizabeth[63] approves. Algy Boyle[64] "very interested."

I have:
"Made a pile of all my winnings,
and risked them on one turn of pitch and toss,
And lose and start again at your beginnings,
and never breathe a word about your loss."

I certainly risked all connection with W.C. last night by my ruthless attack. I may have to go again but I don't think he will ever ring his bell to dismiss me again. I won that one at any rate, for Seal who is *very* friendly fled!

Well darling there is not much more to tell you – at least I can't think of anything. I am going to take this to Waterloo and then lunch with Cartier[65] at the Belgian Embassy...

[P.S.] The *Sunday Graphic* wants an article and I mean it to be a stinger for Italy and the neutrals. It is running in my head. I will bring it down in the rough on Thursday night or Friday morning and you shall vet and improve it.

[P.P.S.] *Daily Graphic* tells me M. of Information has released – my blast at the Italian which has been published in full in the Italian press!
Viva la guerra.

12. *Keyes to Churchill*[66]

[Holograph] Admiralty, S.W.
[Copy] 16.4.40.

I enclose my suggestion. I am sure it would be very good for neutrals and I believe would make Mussolini pause.

My interview may never be published in Italy – anyhow I think it ought to be followed up by a good blast of propaganda.

It is sad that I should be considered unfit for command because I have been unemployed so long (having commanded the principal Fleet and premier Station while comparatively young). Some of the great sea captains of old, who were left unemployed for many years, emerged while older even than I am, and struck a resounding blow at sea, and so would I if I got a chance. Anyhow I would have *struck* and not "looked at it" for a week.

However, I did not ask for a command – it is so important not to arouse jealousy! – But I do say that if I had been allowed to keep in touch with events and have access to you and the C.N.S., I might have suggested alternatives to a thoroughly tired Staff – and might yet help you to strike the resounding blow, if this could be done without arousing jealousy.

You provoked action by declaring you would break the Narvik iron ore trade, and were not ready for every conceivable counter stroke (however unlikely) which the enemy might make. You have had the good fortune to defeat a very important one,[67] thanks to the fighting spirit of the Navy – *Renown* as well as the destroyers – not to the prevision of the Naval Staff.

Please bear in mind my suggestion to use the *Resolution* and *Royal Sovereign*. I understand the former is in the Clyde and the latter ½ way across the Atlantic. The expedition I have in mind might be prepared at "Invergordon."

I was very offensive – but I am very devoted to you! – and I only want to help but you won't let me . . .

13. Keyes to Churchill[68]

[Holograph]
Secret and Personal. 17.4.40.

I don't believe Mussolini will dare to go to war, with an unwilling Italy behind him. He certainly won't act if we strike a hard blow at once – and it can be done. Let me organise it – Invergordon is in a military area and could be made secure from spying. Thus the secret could be kept. It is very important that it should be kept absolutely secret, even within the Admiralty.[69] Surely one if not two "R's" could be risked without endangering our Naval strength – and there will be no other Naval enemy if we strike hard now. There must be old cruisers and destroyers – mine sweepers and small craft to make smoke, which could be risked. The R.A.F. must be ready for a great effort in co-operation.

I suppose we have lots of chlor-sulphonic acid, or a modern substitute, for making smoke from funnels and exhausts and by other means. I

PART I: 1939-1940   27

wish we had 100 M.T.B.s. I gather very few are ready.

Pity we can't be ready to do it on St George's Day – Why not? Time passes and much too much has passed. I am confident it is a feasible operation – and it is worth any risk at the moment to hearten the Neutrals.

It *can't* and won't fail if you let me do it and be responsible for it – back my good fortune.

I take it T [Trondheim] and B [Bergen] are the vital spots now and that it is too late for O [Oslo].

I appreciated your telegram very much. Thank you. Our stars are linked. Let me do this for you . . .

14.   *Keyes's Plan for Assault on Trondheim*

[Carbon]   [23 April 1940.]

Proposal for direct assault on TRONDHJEM

It is assumed that the enemy have 2 "Maass" class destroyers in Trondhjem Fiord and that the fixed defences are as shown in C.B. 1817 Plan 4. It is unlikely that the Germans will have had time to erect defences powerful enough to cause serious damage to a cruiser.

Forces Required: – 2 Battleships.
                1 a/c carrier.
                2 cruisers & 1 A.A. cruiser.
                2 flotillas of destroyers.
                Centurion carrying 2 battalions of infantry.
                2 "Q" ships each carrying 1 company of infantry.
                1 Small vessel of shallow draft carrying 200 marines.
                1 Small vessel of shallow draft carrying 100 marines.
                R.A.F. aircraft.

Composition of forces:

Force "A"   2 Battleships.
                     1 Flotilla of destroyers.
Force "B"   1 Cruiser.
                     1 Destroyer.
                     1 Small vessel carrying 200 marines.
Force "C"   1 Cruiser.
                     1 Destroyer.
                     1 Small vessel carrying 100 marines.

Force "D"	Centurion. 2 Q Ships. 1 A.A. Cruiser. 6 Destroyers.
General Plan	(Zero hour is dawn)
Z–2 hours.	Aircraft drop parachute flares over Trondhjem Fiord 5 miles south of the Forts. This would: – (a) Attract the attention of the lookouts in the forts. (b) Make it more difficult to see objects on the north side of these forts. (c) Silhouette the land for our ships proceeding to Skjorn Fiord. *Force B* proceeds into Skjorn Fiord keeping on the north shore away from the Forts. R.A.F. carries out heavy bombing of aerodrome (*VAERNES*).
Z zero hour.	*Force A*. Battleships anchor in berths north and north-west of STORFOSEN Island (63°–40′N 9°–25′E) in previously buoyed positions and are protected from submarine attack by the flotilla of destroyers in Force A. Commence bombardment of forts at BRETTINGNES and HYSNES. Ranges 22,000 and 25,000 yards respectively. Aircraft spotting. *Force B*. Cruiser anchors north-west of GALTEN Island (63°–42′N 9°–53′E) and bombards SELVENES Fort. Range 12,000 yards. Aircraft spotting. The small vessel carrying 200 marines runs itself ashore in FEVAAG cove (63°–41′N 9°–52½′E) supported if necessary by the fire of the destroyer. 200 Marines land. 1st objective – BRETTINGSFJELD (922 feet). *Force C*. Small vessel carrying 100 marines runs ashore at RODSTEN (63°–37′N 9°–36′E). 1st objective – capture high ground westward of SELVENES Fort. *Force D*. Assemble south of STORFOSEN Island. *Aircraft carrier*. As requisite for flying aircraft on and off. Objectives of aircraft (F.A.A.): (a) Provide 3 spotters for bombardment. (b) Provide protection from enemy bombers. (c) Prevent reinforcements being sent by water to the forts.

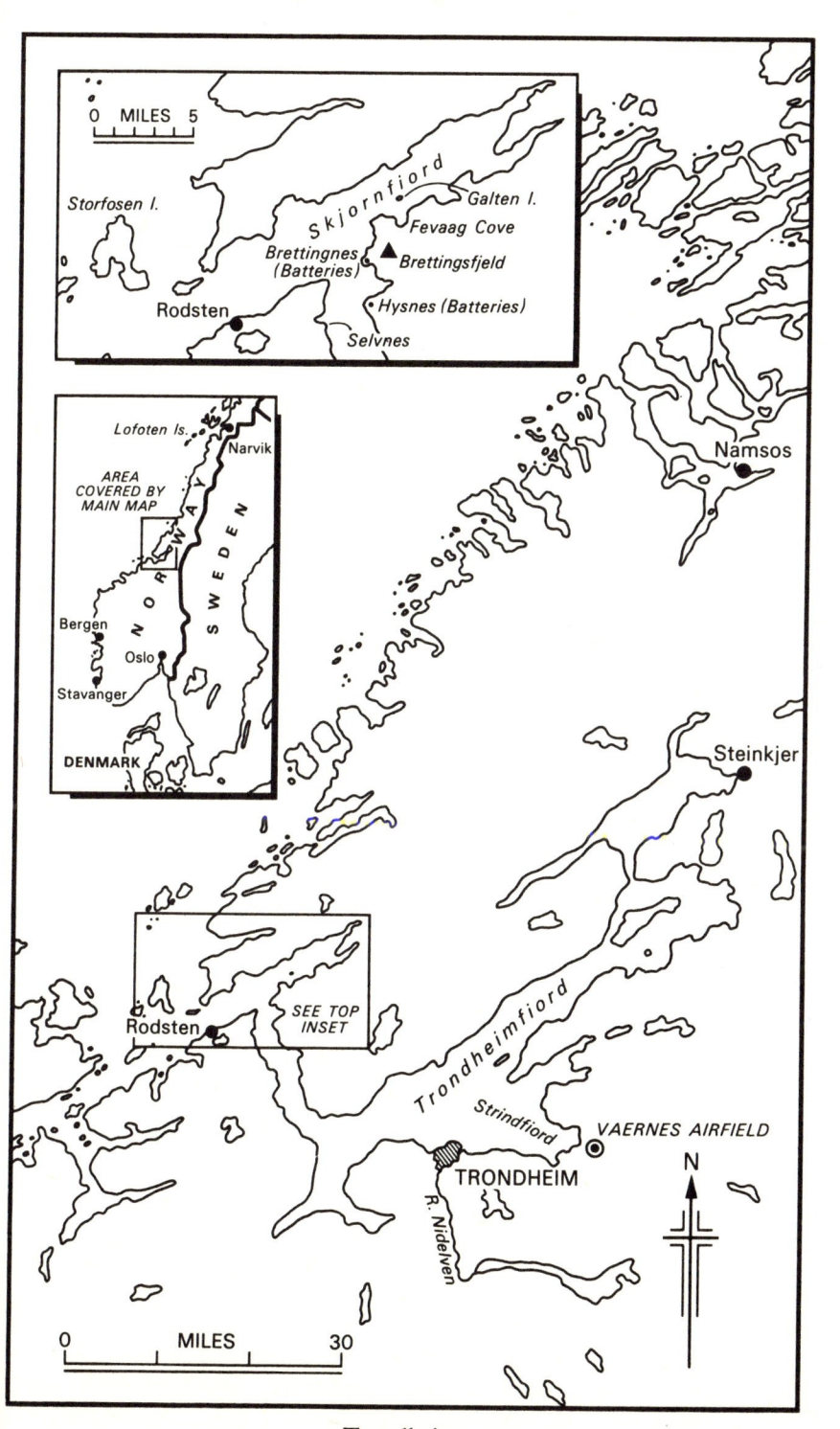

Trondheim

Z + 1
hours.

By this time forts should be damaged – if not destroyed.
Marines of Force A advance to their second objectives – namely to capture BRITTINGSNES and HYSNES Forts.
Marines of Force B advance to their second objective to capture SELVENES Fort.
Force D is joined by the cruiser of Force C and proceeds towards mouth of TRONDHJEM Fiord at full speed. At the mouth of the Fiord Force D is also joined by the cruiser of Force B. Ships then proceed in the following order: –
3 Destroyers sweeping with T.S.D.S.
Cruiser of Force B.
Cruiser of Force C.
A.A. Cruiser.
Centurion.
2 Q Ships.
3 Destroyers.
After passing through the narrows into STRIND Fiord the tasks would be as follows: –
Cruisers: Sink any German warships in the harbour before they can torpedo *Centurion*.
1 Cruiser then to bombard aerodrome.
1 Cruiser – counter artillery work against German military artillery.
A.A. Cruiser provide A.A. protection.
Centurion: anchors as close as possible to ELVE Harbour, and dominates railway swing bridge.
1 Q Ship enters outer basin and secures alongside.
1 Q Ship enters inner basin.
Destroyers act as requisite and ferry men ashore from *Centurion*. Dominate road and railway along South shore of STRIND Fiord to prevent reinforcements reaching the town.
Troops landed from *Centurion* and Q Ships, should with the support of the ships be able to capture the main part of the town enclosed by River NIDELVEN.

Note. Destroyers should be fitted with smoke-making apparatus, in case it is required, and every preparation should be made for using M.T.B.'s. M.T.B.'s to be prepared to make smoke or to proceed through TRONDHJEM Fiord and attack enemy vessels with torpedoes. But the stroke should be made immediately the military expeditions north and south of

TRONDHJEM are ready to co-operate. It should *not* be dependent on weather conditions suitable for M.T.B.'s.

(Signed) Roger Keyes
23.4.40.

15. *Keyes to Churchill*

[Carbon] 24.4.40.

First Lord.

The C.I.G.S.[70] said he would try to arrange for the Chiefs of Staff to see me this morning, but after waiting in the War Office some time, he wrote me a note to say: –

> "We cannot yet take the 'T' scheme. I'll try to let you know today when we can. We have to appear in front of the War Cabinet all this morning and have no time for anything else."

And so time passes!

The following are the notes[71] which I prepared for the Chiefs of Staff meeting which did not take place.

Circumstances kept me in Portsmouth most of last week – and so I took the opportunity of inspecting the Marine M.N.B. H.Q. in Fort Cumberland, which happens to be within the Command of the Division of R.M. of which I am the Colonel Commandant.

As I was staying with the Commander-in-Chief,[72] I had access to his War Room – Coast Defence reports – charts, and such information as the C.-in-C. had from intercepted signals.

It was obvious of course that the seizure of Trondheim Fiord is the key to the situation in Norway at present.

I studied the operation deeply, prepared a plan of action,[73] and I am absolutely convinced – from my experience as C. of S. to the three Admirals who successively commanded the Allied Fleet in the Dardanelles and Gallipoli Campaign – and during the last year of the war as Admiral Commanding all operations on the Belgian Coast – that this operation can be carried out without undue risk, mainly by old vessels, the loss of which cannot appreciably affect our Naval strength.

The essence of success is secrecy, and I do not propose to go into details of my plan, but I hope to have an opportunity of giving the outline to the First Lord and First Sea Lord without further delay.

Before I do so, I would like to know what the C.I.G.S. would require of the Navy, when the Fiord was free of enemy ships and fixed defences?

What the C.A.S.[74] could do in the way of air co-operation, since more would be required than could be given by the Fleet Air Arm. Ample R.A.F. co-operation would therefore be essential and of infinite importance, if it can be generously given.

My knowledge of the military situation is of course limited, and I have been dependent on such as came into the Portsmouth War Room intercepts – by no means all of which could be decyphered.

The question of what ships can be spared, I can go into with the C.N.S. later. But perhaps the C.I.G.S. could say what is essential for the Navy to do, from his point of view. And the C.A.S. what air co-operation he can give. The Aerodrome could be made untenable by gun fire, and before long it should be in our hands, but I do not know its possibilities.

The essence of such an operation is careful staff work. That the leader of each unit should know exactly what is expected of him. That the officer to whom the operation is confided should be given a free hand as to its conduct, and that he should be determined to carry it to a successful issue, and be absolutely confident of his ability to do so.

The most complete secrecy is of course essential.

It will be necessary to have a few modern destroyers to enter the fiord, in company with the old cruisers. I think the French would gladly place two or three of their fine leaders – which I understand are already in Norwegian waters – under my command, if the leadership was given to me. I have found of late that my professional reputation seems to stand higher in France and abroad generally than apparently at home!

16. *Churchill to Keyes*

[Carbon] Admiralty, Whitehall.
[Copy] 24. 4. 40

It astonishes me that you should think that all this has not been examined by people who know exactly what resources are available, and what the dangers would be. I will however ask the First Sea Lord whether he can receive you.

You will, I hope, appreciate the fact that I have to be guided by my responsible Naval advisers, and that it is not open to me to make the kind of appointments you and Eva have in mind on ground of friendship . . .

17. Keyes to Churchill[75]

[Carbon]

22, St. Leonard's Terrace,
S.W.3.
26/4/40.

After my conversation with Pound yesterday, I cannot believe that he does not trust my judgment – or my ability to carry this business through successfully – so don't delay.

I know there is a Brigade of Marines at Aldershot training, whether it is yet ready for such an operation I can't say, but during my inspection of the Royal Marines at Eastney last week, I saw hundreds of highly trained Reservist[s] and Pensioners, and splendid young men – both Volunteers and Militia. No doubt the other two Divisions have similar forces to draw upon.

The Royal Marines – who had not had a sailor Colonel for 130 years – asked for me to be made Colonel Commandant, and would go anywhere in the world for me.

Let the Navy and its Sea Soldiers do the first stroke, which can be followed up at once by all troops available, directly the enemy ships and shore defences inside the fiord are destroyed.

With the command of the sea in the fiord, the Germans in that area could be harassed, destroyed or rounded up. If military action is prompt the delays which have occurred at Narvik would probably be avoided.

The operation I have in mind is a combination of Wolfe[76] and Saunders[77] in the St Lawrence; of what might have been done in the Dardanelles and Gallipoli; and what was done at Zeebrugge and on the Belgian Coast generally in 1918; and in fact of almost every brave tale in our sea history, re-acted by the Navy of today.

It runs through the books you inspired me to write, but can never have had time to read, or you would not have hesitated to listen to me!

Can't you see my vision, it has been my constant companion for days; I have tried so hard to open your overworked tired eyes to see the immense possibilities which lie ahead of us, and which are worth some risk.

Of course it is the duty of a Naval Staff to examine "exactly what resources are available, and what the dangers would be".

Hawke,[78] warned by his pilot of the shoals and dangers ahead, said, "You have done your duty, maintain the present course, crowd on more sail," and the victory of Quiberon Bay saved Quebec and made the conquest of Canada possible.

Beatty, warned by Chatfield of the danger of unknown minefields and submarines, continued on his course at full speed, and saved the situation in the Heligoland Bight on 28th August 1914 – and brought you much credit since you were responsible for bringing it about, after the Naval Staff had turned it down.

The responsibility of course now lies with you and Pound, and I pray that it may be given to you to make a right decision, and employ me to carry it out. I am confident that an operation, on the lines I have outlined to Pound, cannot fail to achieve decisive results – and then there will be no question of hostile Neutrals.

Pound told me you were prepared to take great risks in a similar stroke some days ago, for a large scale landing, but decided against it, in view of the Military situation at that time. It is obvious now, even from official communications, that the Military situation is extremely critical and needs a bold stroke to save it.

18. Keyes to Pound

[Carbon]

22 St. Leonard's Terrace,
S.W.3.
26/4/40.

You told me just now that my plan was most useful, but you had nothing more to say about it to me at present. I can't believe that the First Lord would object to making use of me now, in view of my past services and experience. I hope that you are not preventing it in this hour of peril?

After all I have had more experience in making war and in combined operations of this kind than anyone in the Navy. If you are blocking me now, you are taking a very heavy responsibility on your shoulders.

I would like to remind you of some advice you gave me some years ago, which was very unfortunate.

You persuaded me against my better judgement to urge Beatty to let Madden[79] in as First Sea Lord for his two remaining years on the active list. My first effort failed, but over persuaded by your idea that it would end the Beatty-Jellicoe dissensions in the Navy, I sent a destroyer 800 miles in pursuit of his yacht with a second appeal and an A.F.O. you gave me about tenure of office in the Admiralty (which we found afterwards had no bearing whatever on Beatty's case).[80]

Beatty distrusted Madden, and was determined to hold the fort until I was ready to relieve him at the Admiralty, and in his reply, he expressed grave misgivings, but he acted on the advice you had given, and bitterly regretted it for the rest of his life.

It wasn't good advice, apart from the effect it had on my future, it accentuated the dissensions, and enabled Madden and Field[81] to fill all the key positions with their friends, to the detriment of the Navy. I cannot believe that the Invergordon mutiny would ever have occurred, if I had been First Sea Lord, and I am quite certain there would have been no London Naval Treaty. I am also convinced that the Navy would have been developing its own Naval Air Service without any restrictions for the last ten years.

No-one knows better than you how deplorably the London Naval Treaty arrested Naval construction, and how greatly the Navy and its splendid young airmen are suffering for the lack of the Naval Air Service I would have insisted on having.

So you see what a far-reaching effect the advice you gave 14 years ago is having on the conduct of the sea war, for which you are now responsible.

I think you owe me and the Navy some reparation, and you can do this by giving me the opportunity of running this inshore combined operation, and give the Navy the benefit of my experience and power of leadership.

I ought not to have had to *force* a plan on the Naval Staff's notice or to remind you, of all people, of my fighting qualities.

I should not have ignored you if our positions were reversed! ...

19. *Pound to Keyes*

Admiralty, S.W.
29th April, 1940.

I cannot imagine what caused you to suggest in your letter[82] that I had been, as you put it, "blocking" you and very much resent the suggestion that I should do such a thing either in your case or that of any other Officer.

In making recommendations to the First Lord for appointments, I am guided by one thing and one thing only, and that is that the Officer should be the most suitable for the appointment.

Both the First Lord and I have been fully aware of your burning desire to serve and how much you must feel in not being in the thick of things. You will realise, however, I am sure, that appointments for Admirals of the Fleet are not easy to come by.

I am not aware that you have had to "force" a plan on the Naval Staff's notice because as far as I am aware you had made no approach to the Naval Staff previous to coming to see me, although I had heard that you had approached both the First Lord and the C.I.G.S.

If there is one thing which no one can accuse us of here it is that we are not ready at anytime to listen to any suggestions which anyone has to offer . . .

20. Keyes to Churchill

[Holograph] House of Commons.
28. 4. 40.[83]

I hope you will read this and still act for there is yet time. At any rate read the last paragraphs on page 4 and the last 3 on page 2, 1st on page 3.[84]

If the scuttle is persisted in the Government will have to go and I shall do my damndest to speed them.

21. Keyes to Churchill

[Carbon] 22 St. Leonard's Terrace,
S.W.3.
29/4/40.

I am not very quick with my tongue, and was not nimble enough to stem the flow of words you used to justify the shocking inaction of the Navy at Trondhjem, for which you and your pusillanimous, self-satisfied, short sighted Naval advisers must bear the responsibility.

We have been three weeks at war on the Norwegian Coast, and many mistakes which were made in the conduct of the Gallipoli Campaign by the Admiralty and Government have been, or are about to be, repeated on the Norwegian Coast.

It is indeed a sorry tale. You were scathing, when I referred 11 days ago to the verdict which history would pass on our Naval inaction, and said you were making war not history. Well you won't have to wait for history for the scathing denunciation you have merited.

The Norwegians who appealed to me to try and influence you, (because they thought you were my friend and would listen to me) told me that anyone could have told your Staff that the thrust from Namsos was doomed to disaster, unless we possessed command of the sea in the Trondhjem Fiord.[85] And so it proved a few days later.

The Norwegian Naval Attaché said that he was not consulted as to this, but naturally thought that the Staff Officer who interviewed him must be aware of such an obvious fact from the maps and charts.

He went on to say that your Staff appeared to be obsessed with the fear of mines, which he said could hardly be regarded as very serious in waters of a depth of 200 fathoms.

You, Winston, spoke contemptuously yesterday of my plan, and said it astonished you that I should have imagined: "That all this has not been examined by people who know exactly what resources are available and what the dangers would be."[86] How wrong you have been proved! They never thought of the danger to the Army their inaction would entail.

I had proposed a plan of attack,[87] which would have given us command of the waters of the fiord with a few old ships, and would have dominated the Vaernes Aerodrome until the Army were in a position to capture it. My plan also provided for a striking force of Marines, to be carried mainly in an almost bomb proof ship (the *Centurion*)[88] for amphibious war within the fiord. By using Marines in the initial stage, when the time factor was of vital importance, the Navy would be independent of delays consequent on combined action with a General, who might not work with the Admiral as well as Wolfe did with Saunders off Quebec.

The Namsos thrust might well have succeeded but for the inexplicable ineptitude of your Naval Staff in not realising that command of the sea in the Trondhjem Fiord was the key of the whole situation, and worth some sacrifice to obtain.

I tried to submit this particular point to you for the consideration of the Staff on Sunday evening 21st April, after I had had an opportunity of studying the Coast Defence charts in the War College library at Portsmouth, but you were "too tired" to see me.

I did so because on the 16th April, when I pointed out the dangers of naval inaction, and suggested making use of one or two of the "Royal Sovereign" class to hammer a way into Trondhjem – you replied that those ships were not available, since war with Italy seemed almost inevitable.

You then rang your bell and tried to dismiss me like an importunate beggar. Having been made to feel thoroughly unwelcome in the Admiralty by the Staff and yourself, I only had limited means of knowing what was going on, the strength of our forces and those of the enemy, so my plan using a few old ships was of necessity only an outline, which could, however, be speedily developed by trained staff officers.

I tried again to see you on 23rd April but was passed on to a Staff officer without any qualifications to discuss secret war plans with me.

I then tried to see the Prime Minister, but he said it was a Naval matter, he could not go behind you.

Eventually at midnight on the 23rd, I saw the C.I.G.S. and asked him if command of the sea in the Trondhjem Fiord would be of value to the Army. He said it would be of infinite value. He told me that it had been intended to attack with almost the whole fleet, to force a passage into Trondhjem and deliver a large scale attack, but the project had been dropped.

He promised to try and arrange for me to attend a Chiefs of Staff meeting, and sent a car to fetch me next morning. But after waiting a couple of hours at the War Office, he sent me a message to say that they could not see me that day; and later he told me that the other two Chiefs of Staff had declined to see me!

When I returned from the War Office, I wrote you my memorandum of the 24th,[89] but I don't suppose you ever took the trouble to read it, since I saw it later in Pound's possession, with a very personal and private note to you attached, which mentioned my wife, and which I can't believe you would have passed on, if you had noticed it.

On 25th I received a letter[90] from you which astonished me, and I wrote you the reply it deserved. However, I did not send it, but sent my memorandum of 26th[91] instead, because my only object is to defeat the enemy, and by then Pound had asked me to come and see him, which I did at 7 p.m. on the 25th.

I gave him my plan of action and he was obviously interested, but assured me that a large scale operation had been prepared to land an army inside the fiord, but it had been dropped because the pincer thrusts from North and South of Trondhjem were proceeding successfully, and it was *not considered necessary to go inside the fiord*.

He admitted that now things were going wrong at *Steinkjet*, it would be necessary, *if* it was decided to capture Trondhjem, and he asked me to leave my plan, which I did. I then wrote you my memorandum of 26th.

The next day I telephoned to Pound, to ask him if he had anything to say to me about my plan. He said it had been very useful, but he had nothing further to say about it at present.

The Norwegians having again told me how desperate the situation in Norway was becoming, I made one last effort to see you to try and persuade you to take immediate action before it was too late to secure Trondhjem, the real key of the situation.

* You told me that the Naval Staff had prepared a plan, using large forces, under the Commander-in-Chief himself; and declared that there was no difficulty whatever in taking ships past the forts in the narrows. Of course there isn't, and I offered to do it with a few old ships, as better ones could not be spared because of the Italian menace.

* What in Heaven's name is the use of making plans if you don't put them into execution before a critical situation arises. Are we always to be too late and caught napping, because your Staff are so

immersed in their daily task, and have not the imagination, courage or resolution to make war vigorously.

* It infuriates me to think that the Navy should be so let down by the Admiralty, and be responsible for allowing one German destroyer and torpedo boat (not 3 modern destroyers as I thought) to exercise sea power within the Trondhjem Fiord by giving mobility to a force, which was thus enabled to cut off the advance guard of the Namsos troops and hold up the whole expedition, after three weeks of Naval inaction.

* I have tried hard to help you and your Naval Staff, and have as you know been ready to work in any humble capacity, but have been consistently ignored, and now I give it up, and am going to devote all my energies to defeat all those who stand in the path which leads to victory; and hope to save the Army from being any longer dependent on limited and pusillanimous Naval co-operation, which is all that they can expect from the Navy, as long as the sea war in the Southern area of Norway is conducted by the Naval advisers, on whose advice you say you must rely.

It has been torture to me for the past three weeks, to see one golden opportunity after another pass, while our inaction has given the enemy time to establish themselves so strongly, and thus make the task which our fighting men will have to face infinitely more difficult and costly in the end – like Gallipoli.

You told me that I was living in the past war, and that this one was far more formidable. All the more reason to take warning from the last war, to counter attack at once, and not give the enemy time to accumulate war material, bring up reinforcements, and establish his position with aerodromes.

The Gallipoli Campaign with all its infinite possibilities was lost by hesitations, delay, and fear of responsibility after the first setback. By fear of mines, which could be swept; by fear of concealed torpedo tubes, which did not exist; and by fear of concealed howitzers, which could not be successfully attacked by our flat trajectory guns, but which were about as inaccurate as aerial bombardment.

The Norwegian Campaign will be defeated by similar hesitations and delays, and because the Navy and Army have not had sufficient air support.

If the people responsible for the mess into which we have drifted cannot be induced to steel their hearts and make bolder and more prompt decisions, they will be swept away.

The Norwegians tell me that there can be little doubt that the Allies have abandoned all thought of securing Trondhjem, and they fear that they mean to evacuate Southern Norway, only retaining a hold on Narvik. If that is really the truth – and you gave me no hope to the contrary – it is indeed a shameful and disastrous decision.

At a critical moment, when the whole world is looking to see if we have the guts to see this matter through, and can be counted on to give effective protection to friendly Neutrals – with Italy, Russia and Japan sitting on the fence, waiting to come in on the winning side – you are going to run away from aerial bombing, (which you told me had inflicted comparatively little loss after weeks of intense effort), in case the percentage of hits might go higher!

There is still just time now to make a tremendous effort to turn the tide of retreat by capturing Trondhjem with its good harbour and Aerodrome, and make certain of possessing this essential strategic Base for landing the heavy artillery, tanks and anti-air equipment which the Army needs so badly for the prosecution of the war on more even terms.

If you don't do it now and allow the Germans from Oslo to reach it first, they will have this strategic Base and will soon fortify it and make it practically impregnable, and how will you turn them out of it then? It won't be possible from Narvik, and if we withdraw there, as you suggested might be necessary, it will be a shameful surrender painfully reminiscent of the evacuation and Suvla.

* Give me the small force I asked for – as a Commodore if you like – and the Royal Navy and its Sea Soldiers will show the world that they can stand up to any German air attack, until the Army and Air Force are ready to take advantage of our being able to exercise sea power in the Trondhjem Fiord.
* This plan can't fail, and if it is done immediately, I am absolutely confident of success. We will strike a blow which will help to decide the issue, cheer our friends, and make the hostile Neutrals pause.
* For God's sake put your trust in me and don't waste any more time.
* We will have to do it in the end, and it will be far harder if you let the Germans from Oslo get there before us.

22. *Keyes to Churchill*

[Carbon]
22 St. Leonard's Terrace,
S.W.3.
30/4/40.

I fully understand the Naval situation as you put it to me last night, and all your own difficulties. I do appreciate the very efficient way in which the day to day task of the Naval Staff has been organised and carried out to ensure the protection of trade and the blockade of Germany. But I do feel very strongly that in some other respects the conduct of the Sea War has been deplorably pusillanimous and shortsighted. This opinion is shared with bitter resentment by many Naval Officers with whom I have been thrown in contact lately, and I am told it is pretty prevalent throughout the Fleet.

I know of course that you "must be guided by the advice of your principal Naval Adviser," but this is not generally realised by the Country, nor in the Navy generally – which is very unfair to you, since they attribute to you power you evidently don't possess.

The delay in taking offensive action when Germany first seized several Norwegian ports, before they had time to organise defences, is angrily commented on, and it is pretty generally known that Horton's[92] farseeing disposition of our submarines, to counter the possibility of the German amphibious expedition (which was known to be preparing) being directed against Norway, was frustrated by their withdrawal – ordered by the Naval Staff.[93]

It was obvious that the encircling movement of the troops to capture Trondhjem must be accompanied by the destruction of the ships and fortifications defending Trondhjem Fiord.

You know that I have been urging this for over a fortnight, and when you told me of the anxieties of the Italian situation, and the difficulty of sparing one or two of the older capital ships to carry out the operation, I prepared a plan to do so with oddments, which I knew could be spared without any risk to the strength of the Fleet.

You told me that the Naval Staff had prepared a plan of action, which was about to be put into effect, but it was abandoned, owing to the apparent success of the two "pincer movements", and that there was no difficulty about forcing a way into Trondhjem Fiord.

Why in Heaven's name then was it not done? It is not much use making plans unless they are put into action in time to avert a disaster like the one at Steinkjer, and when it is properly understood how damnably the Admiralty have let the Army down and its share in the failure of the Military expedition to capture Trondhjem, the Navy will not forgive the Admiralty.

Even if it may be found necessary to shorten the line by abandoning our effort to capture Trondhjem, the essential key position in Norway, and leave it in the possession of an enemy more daringly directed; the Navy must be allowed to purge its failure there by wiping out the Trondhjem defences and the feeble German Naval force (2 torpedo craft) which has been making full use of its command of the sea in the fiord to frustrate the British thrust from Namsos.

We ought to have had command of the waters of the fiord a fortnight ago, in which case the Namsos force would have had the support of our Naval guns, and the assistance of a sea-borne striking force to harass the enemy and make his position untenable.

If we had concentrated on this, Trondhjem with its good quays and aerodrome could and should have been in our hands, defended against air attack, before the enemy had had time to develop their air power to the extent they have been able to, owing to our inaction.

With Trondhjem in our possession we could have landed large forces, properly equipped with heavy guns, tanks etc., and established a well defended base, and the enemy would not have been able to drive us out so easily. There would then have been no question of our abandoning the Norwegians, as apparently we are about to do.

It is not fair to blame the War Office for this failure, as the Army was put in an impossible position [at Steinkjer].

I have had unrivalled experience of amphibious warfare and combined operations, and could have given advice which if taken would have averted this catastrophe into which we have drifted through lack of foresight and resolution.

Steinkjer will stink in the nostrils of the Navy until this disgrace is wiped out. When it is friendly Neutrals will trust us, and Italy may yet pause before she dares to challenge the British Navy.

I have been busy all day seeing people, and have collected a great deal of support for my views as to the immediate necessity for a smashing Naval blow at Trondhjem – whatever may happen later.

The French Ambassador gave me an interview this morning, agreed with me, and said that he would pass my views on to Paris at once.

I had a long talk to Simon,[94] who by now will have put the matter to the Prime Minister. The latter was too occupied to see me, but sent a message to say that if I could get your support, the Cabinet would support you.

When am I going to be allowed to take a hand in the conduct of the Naval War? I know I represent the fighting spirit of the Navy, which has proved again – as it did in the last war – that it will carry through any hazardous enterprise, given the opportunity.

If my advice had been followed in 1915 when I fought on, almost singlehanded, to be allowed to force the Dardanelles (which is now accepted as having been a feasible operation) the flower of the Turkish Army would have been cut off and decisively defeated, and we would have been spared the Palestine, Salonika and Mesopotamia campaigns.

Bacon[95] and Jellicoe[96] had to be got rid of by the Lloyd George Govt. before I was allowed to wage war in the Dover Straits and on the Belgian Coast.

Is my Great War experience to be made no use of because the air factor has become more formidable? I am one of the few sailors who has had the opportunity of using it, and am fully alive to its immense value to the Navy, its dangers and its limitations.

I made one great mistake 14 years ago, when commanding the Mediterranean Fleet, by following the advice of my Chief of the Staff – Pound – and urging Beatty (who intended to hold his office until I was ready to succeed him as First Sea Lord) to let Madden in for his last two years of active service, as Pound maintained that this would put an end to the so-called Beatty–Jellicoe controversy in the Navy. However Madden left no stone unturned in order to keep me out, otherwise I would have been in a position to prevent the limitations of the London Naval Treaty, and to insist on our freedom to develop the Naval Air Service, from the lack of which we are suffering so desperately today.

Give me the small force I asked for and the Royal Navy and its Sea Soldiers will show the world that they can stand up to any German air attack, until the Army and Air Force are able to exploit our ability to exercise Sea Power in the Trondhjem Fiord.

If this is now too late we can at least withdraw with our Naval prestige unimpaired.

I understand that it is feared that torpedo tubes may have been mounted in the Narrows, but even if they do exist, this can be overcome.

In any case, the hazards which the force will have to face will be trifling in comparison to those we successfully challenged at Zeebrugge, and the results may be infinitely more important in this critical hour...

23. *Keyes to Churchill*

[Carbon]
22 St. Leonard's Terrace,
S.W.3.

1/5/40.

I am so torn with anxiety that I have felt compelled to write the enclosed letter to the Prime Minister,[97] and have sent him my last letter to you[98] – with the paragraph about Pound's advice to me omitted. I added "at Steinkjer" to the 5th Paragraph on page 2 to make it clearer...

Time is passing so rapidly, and I am convinced that the action I am taking is the best possible way in which I can help our Country's cause, the Navy and incidentally you...

24. Keyes to Neville Chamberlain

[Carbon]

22 St. Leonard's Terrace,
S.W.3.
1/5/40.

I enclose a copy of a letter which I have written to the First Lord,[99] the gist of which I hoped he would convey to you and your War Cabinet today.

I do so, as I fear that in his loyalty to his principal Naval Adviser, he might hesitate to give support to such a severe indictment of the inaction of the Naval Staff.

I need hardly say, that it is distasteful to me to criticise an officer who has served under me on and off for 42 years, and who I selected for important Staff posts in my command on several occasions since 1917.

I hate too doing anything which may annoy Winston for whom I have a great affection and admiration, but I am so absolutely convinced that the critical situation into which we have drifted can still be relieved, and possibly even retrieved, by following the course I have been recommending without success for the last fortnight that I feel compelled to act as I am doing. The fate of the Country in this critical hour is more important than any personal considerations, and action has been already too long delayed.

I am sending a copy of this letter and mine to Winston to Halifax,[100] Simon, Hoare and Stanley,[101] and have told Winston that I have done so... [102]

25. Lord Halifax to Keyes

Foreign Office, S.W.1.
2nd May, 1940.

One line to thank you very much for your letter of yesterday, and for sending me a copy of your letter to the First Lord about Norway.

I am sure that Winston and the rest of the Cabinet are fully seized of all the considerations which you urge...

26. Keyes to his wife[103]

[Copy]

18th May, 1940.

I am afraid it is a long time since I wrote and I have lost all count of time and am feeling a bit weary, but *not* down hearted though these continual retreats are rather dispiriting for the troops. I have not seen much of ours yet, but have asked to be told where R. W. Fus. are and will try to see Jimmy[104] today, if I can manage it. Distances are great and the roads are terribly congested with troops, transport and hundreds of thousands of refugees, old men, women and children, on bicycles, on foot and in farm carts, it is simply heartbreaking. Every now and then the road is bombed and low flying aeroplanes dive down and machine gun the roads. I must say the people are brave and plod along doggedly. For instance one sees a young mother with a baby on the handle bars of her bicycle, an old woman being dragged in a small handcart and 100 other tragic combinations, whole families walking along, including children of 4 to 5. They nearly all carry a little bedding or a blanket, but that is all. This trek has been going on ever since I arrived, I have never watched anything more hateful.

I wish our smug faced school marms with their cries for better education – more pay, etc. – League of Nations Union, Peace at any price people could see all this and realise how fortunate they are that they have – up to the present – been spared war, *because* of the armed forces they have done their best to get rid of as incentives to war. It does seem sheer irony that the principal villain of the London Naval Treaty should be 1st Lord in the war he helped to bring about.

I am sending you copies of my messages to Winston, which were cut short by the flight of the Embassy – I could say a lot more about that but will refrain.

I spent the night of 10th–11th (May), or such as was left of it, at the Embassy. The next 4 nights in that nice house near the Château where the King lived. There were two elderly spinster sisters, an aunt and an invalid mother, so they could not leave. The brother who lived near-by and had several small children left about 15th.

The Château belongs to Vicomte de Benghem [Beughem?], it is quite charming with a lovely garden (Château de Melis, Lippeloo is name of village) – no harm mentioning it now we have left.

My room had a basin but only cold water laid on, but an electric boiler, I could get hot water in a few moments. After the second day I found they had a bath room, hot water had to be made by a little coke burning geyser – all very new and up to date – spotlessly clean very good linen. The household washed my clothes, mended a hole in my socks and really mothered me! They were charming and kind.

I found I was rather helpless without a car and as I have to drive in and out of Brussels 20 miles 2, 3 and once I think 4 times in the day, I came to the conclusion I must have one – so the Military Mission bought me one for £350 – hope I haven't to pay for it?! – a brand new Packard. They hired a first class chauffeur for 600 francs a month – about £6 – and the King said I was to have a gendarme attached to me – a most charming good looking and magnificent young man – armed to the teeth.

The 4th night when it was decided that we must clear out early the next morning – I slept the night in the Château in the room of the Major commanding the Gendarmerie attached to the King. We went off about 8.30, a convoy of 4 cars, Colonel Van Caubergh[105] in mine with me, we drove to Ghent, the G.Q.G. – Grand Quartier Général.

Yesterday morning we went to a Château about 6 miles from Ghent. The Master of the Court arranged to billet me in the Burgomaster's house ½ a mile away. I must say I was very angry as the King said I must always in future stay in the same house, and that he had told the Master of the Household so, Major Van den Heuvel.

It wasn't too pleasant at Lippeloo as one heard a great deal of gunfire and machine-gunfire and bombing of the road 200 yards from my house, but there were lots of troops nearby and what they were bombing was the communications of the French army. But at Château Gavère we were away from anywhere except the Gendarmerie guarding the King and this morning the house was shaken by bombs and gunfire.

Van den Heuvel got a good dressing down from the King when he realised I had to go out after dinner last night. V. den H. looked very crestfallen and came out to see me off and kept out of my way this morning. I don't want to be captured alone by the enterprising Germans. If I am it will have to be in good company after a fight. My chauffeur and I were all alone.

Our last day at Willebroek, the G.Q.G. 20 miles from Brussels, I went in to see if there was any possibility of telephoning from the old Military Mission (Embassy) house, and also to get a good oculist to see Capt. de Pret, a 12th Lancer whose eye looked too awful after a motor smash which knocked out General Needham[106] the head of the Mission. They are both in England by now I expect. Poor Needham is a very heavy man and had not an idea what happened – de Pret had only one thought – tho' he looked too awful – to pass on the information he had got from B.E.F. GHQ before he collapsed.

I found two boys in the Military Attaché's office – they had been civilians a week before in Brussels – they had been put into private's battledress and talking French well were used for telephone work and liaison. They came on duty at 5 a.m. to find everyone had fled except a corporal and 8 men, who turned out the guard for me! Their gallant bearing was balm to my outraged.

I felt too sick and ashamed for words. All day long those boys listened to urgent telephone calls wanting action – and contemptuous scathing comment, when they could only reply that the Embassy had gone, destination unknown – I did not send the telegram 6 – tho' I was

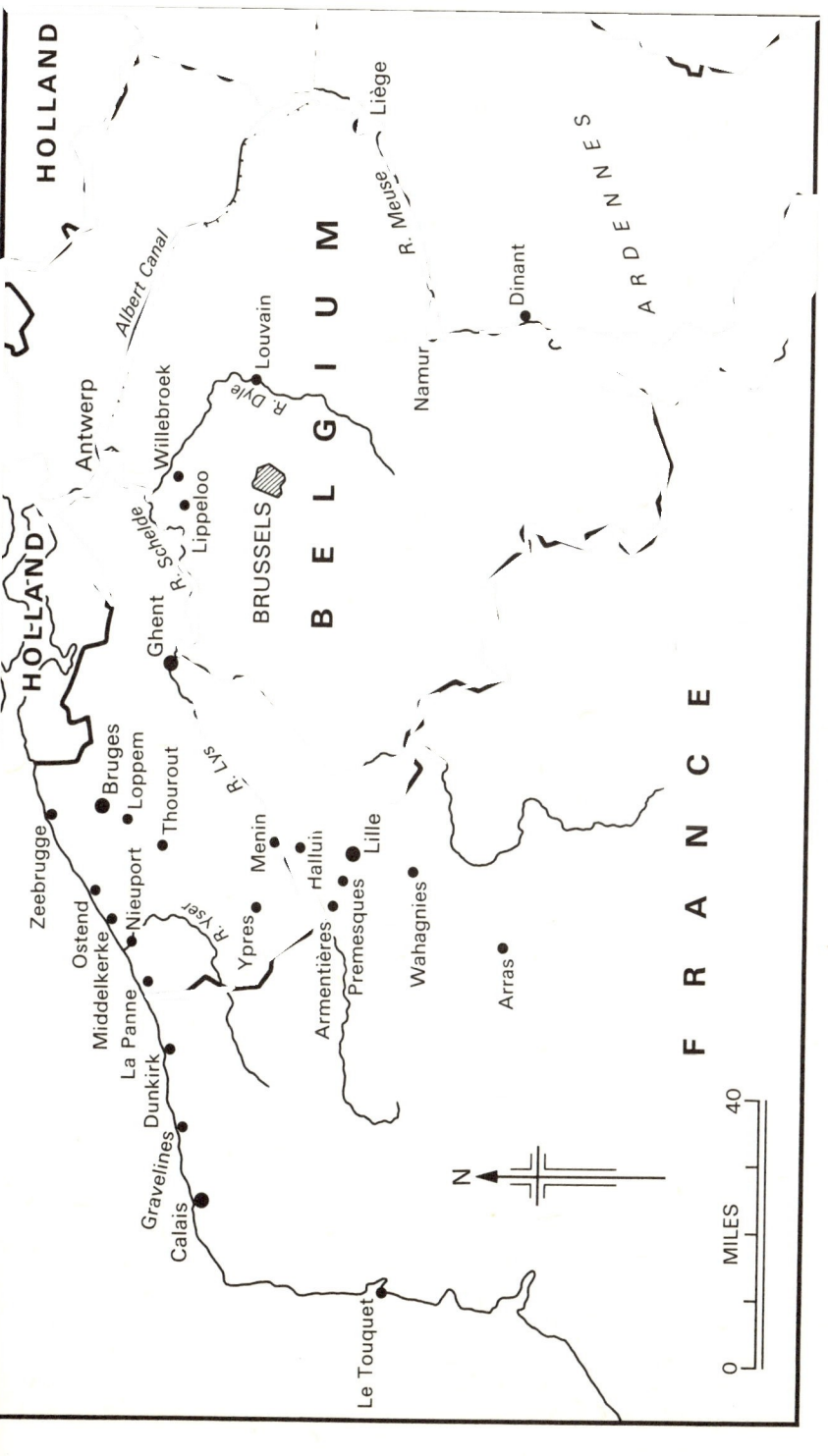

The Belgian Campaign

very tempted to send it but refrained. It was not until 8 hours after they had gone that there was any chance of the Government being allowed to go. I stopped L.O.[107] on 14th and 3 times on 15th. Left him at 8 p.m. The Military Attaché said it was then too late to go – but he was off at 2 a.m. before I could take a hand again. Please treat all this as *very secret,* and don't mention to anyone. They have fled again from the next place, and will be in England or France soon. It embarrasses me very much. The Frenchman went too.

Prince Charles[108] has been in the last two châteaux – I have quite got to like him – His principal man Golfini was the officer who brought the King's £1,000 to Dover[109] – and he lunched with them on board the Q.E. [*Queen Elizabeth*] at Malta.[110] He has only one eye, a black patch over the other. He remembered Geoffrey and Roger in sailor suits – he is a charming fellow.

I don't care for Van den Heuvel – but Van Caubergh, General Van Overstraeten[111] – who I think is splendid now – and a Major Corthouts who commands the Gendarmerie are all good companions, also a Captain of "the Gardes" attached to Prince Charles – I forget his name.

I think the calm courage of the King and Van Overstraeten and the behaviour and morale of the Belgian troops is quite splendid now – I saw a long line of Chasseurs Ardennais who have been fighting since the morning of the 10th (May) in the Ardennes, then two days in Namur – bombed all the way at intervals 250 kilometers – they were fine – they have bicycles (push) and horse transport.

If you see or hear something nice about Belgian morale and these people, it will be "Moi qui parle", lunching with the King today we listened to the 1 o'clock news and heard a great deal about the British and French – nothing about the Belgians.

I have just heard where Jimmy is – miles away – they are doing splendidly. It is cruel luck for the army to be let in once again for a long retreat through no fault of their own, and the Belgians would never have had to retreat like this, if the French had not let the Germans cross the Meuse with 1,000 tanks.

All my love to you all – tell Diana I will see Jimmy as soon as I can. We will be 30 miles from here tonight. I am longing to hear from you . . .

[P.S.] We leave soon – in an hour or two.

Later, 18th May.

I did not forget Geoffrey's birthday and thought of him this morning, I do hope you have good news of him.

A Colonel Davy,[112] 3rd Hussars, has joined Needham's staff to find that he is now in charge. Major Hailey[113] who was 2nd is a splendid fellow – and two or three of the young ones make one feel proud – they go off into the blue and come back with valuable information. They are all awfully nice to me and say I am a Godsend! I do help them a lot. Davy was just leaving for Narvik when he was ordered here, he came like I did and arrived just in time to evacuate the G.Q.G. at Willebroek – Has not been with the Regt.

Sandford the sailor who has been demolishing things at Antwerp and destroying all the oil[114] – was in great difficulties – I took him in to the King and Van Overstraeten who did all he wanted – only to be checked again by some general on the spot – so I drove to Antwerp full speed 50 kilometers – and settled the matter. It made rather a long day – before I got to bed at midnight (last night).

Sandford is a grand fellow, I hoped he would come here today on his way home. He is in N.I.D. Do ask someone in the Admiralty to get him to come and see you, he can tell you a lot I can't write. I meant him to take this – but he apparently went straight on to Calais. He had a party of real tough bluejackets and an R.N.V.R. Midshipman with him. They were to escape in lorries. Antwerp was a city of the dead, not a man, woman, dog or cat moved – but there was a woman and a child and a dog in the Naval Control office! So I dare say there were others hidden away – but it looked a city of desolation.

I forgot to mention in my last trip into Brussels – on 16th – there is a wonderful double one-way traffic road – between Brussels and Antwerp – as I came down it from Willebroek there were quite 200 great busses waiting to take troops away – asking for trouble, our fighters were about which saved them – but when I came back 2 hours later there were 3 *enormous* bomb holes, one in a ploughed field – one evidently fell *on* a bus, there was nothing left that one could not have lifted with one hand and it smashed up one or two others – and a 3rd big hole which was in a space between two busses.

I am waiting for the King to go on to our next G.Q.G. We are going to stay in a château which I went to twice in 1918 – I won't say more until we leave it.[115]

The young airmen were splendid, I have talked to several who have made forced landings (Secret). But I think even the two Airmen in the Mission agree the separate Air Service is, or ought to be dead. There is no such thing as an independent Air Service in war – the time lag is deplorable and dangerous and might have been disastrous but for my direct appeal to Winston.

One young airman, a boy of 22, shot down 3 – his squadron got 28 and only lost two. I think I mentioned him before – if not I shan't forget the story and will put it on record.

Another called Rotheram (?) – so I said do you come from County

Meath, and have your family a pack of Harriers? He said they did! (Ballymacad? Harriers). The King happened to pass when I was talking to him so I presented him – He was thrilled to the core – and said he'd not forget that day.

I have had a peaceful day today and feel rested. Van Caubergh is charming and looks after me well. I share an office with him here opening out of the King's room – we are in a convent.

The M. of F.A. and P.M. have just been here – our Embassy has fled again to where I got my [Ordre de] Leopold and Croix de Guerre in 1918 (La Panne). Next hop England?! The King *ordered* the Govt. to come nearer.

All my love. I don't know when I will be able to send this.

27. *Keyes to his wife*

[Copy] G.H.Q., B.E.F.,
20/5/40.

The King asked me to come here [Wahagnies] to see Lord Gort,[116] so I drove down last night with a Col. Davy in 3rd Hussars who is now head of the Needham Mission. We came through the most awful congestion of refugees, the worst I have seen yet, and as "a v. big man[117] was arriving" from London during the night, I stayed on to see him before going back.

The enclosed are duplicates of some papers for my records, which I sent to you yesterday, No. 1 in duplicate. I hope you have got them by the time you get this – also a very long letter telling you all, or nearly all!, I have been doing since I joined the King. I gave it to a Commander Lewis R.N. who with one civilian called Ratho (Wrathall[118] really) (I think), he certainly deserves his name to be recorded, were running Ostend, shipping off thousands of refugees and doing everything the Consul General and his staff ought to have been doing, but they fled with the Embassy after a few bombs had fallen. They didn't go far – the very edge where King A.[119] used to live [La Panne] – and where Q.E.[120] is now. They have since hopped it over the border to a place Lynes[121] used to live at [Dunkirk], where I hope they were in time for a good bombing it got. I expect they are home by now.

A letter came to the Mission addressed to L.O. [Oliphant] from his wife in Le Touquet. Some funny fellow sent it here to be returned to England *"Not known in Belgium."*

I went to Zeebrugge yesterday meeting streams of Dutch [French?] soldiers trekking into Ostend. Busy day yesterday, lovely bath here last night and slept six hours on end in a lovely room – going back to a place [Bruges] I once rode into.

Curiously enough we are living in a small château belonging to a member of the family who own the big Château which King A. was in before we rode into B [Bruges], which King George stayed in when he did the coast battlefields with me, and which the Kaiser stayed in the night we attacked Z.O. [Zeebrugge-Ostend].

Must stop now. Am sending this to 22 and will get the A.D.C. to find out if you are there or Tingewick. Will try to see Jimmy on my way back...

28. *Keyes to his wife*

[Copy]   23.5.40.

It seems ages since I wrote but I don't suppose it really is, but I have lost all count of time. My messages to W. [Winston], of which I have copies, fill in the gaps and tell the dates. I will try to tell the story since my last letter, which I sent off from a place called Wahagnies. I will look it up on the map later. A lovely modern country house but left far behind now.

When I got back to my friend [King Leopold] I sent another telegram, and when I got a reply, not a very wise one, I sent another.[122] I felt inclined to add – you may have been at Harrow, but "Floreat Etona". In fact I said it to Anthony Eden on the telephone yesterday! He is a grand fellow, my friend.

There is a direct cable from the place I am in now [La Panne] – where my friend's father shyly pressed his highest order into my hand – I was here the day before yesterday, and at the telephone, but not here, yesterday – and today I was here in the morning a bit (it is 35 miles from where I live) and came back in the afternoon and may have to wait until 8.30 p.m. We have been at the place I told you of in my last letter ever since. The Major, Van den H [Heuvel], is *extra civil* since he was spoken to – and gave me a lovely room with hot and cold water in two basins – and my friend has made me honorary member of his bathroom, also I get my underclothes washed!

My chauffeur is a marvel, he valets me too, and my gendarme is a very fine fellow. I spend much time on the roads and some of them *are awful*. I go to O [Ostend] often and once to Z [Zeebrugge], near there I lunched with some French naval officers who were very civil.

One day I went to the place where the Gate is [The Menin Gate at Ypres] and found Geoffrey's[123] name. That was a momentous visit. My friend from Syria[124] – who was at Lausanne – was there and delighted and surprised to see me. My friend [King Leopold] was there and Billotte[125] the co-ordinator of the 3 armies. Gort ought to have been, but the message never reached him, so Van Overstraeten and I went off to what we thought was G.H.Q. – anyhow we got on the telephone – Betty Hodges' husband Kimmins arranged it for me! Then we got Gort and got back to Y. By the time we left it was dark and we had a hideous drive home. Billotte said he was nervous because it seemed possible that the Germans had got through and might be unpleasantly close to the route he had to take. Half an hour later he was mortally injured in a motor smash.

My friend's chauffeur drove far too fast – I went for Van O. [Overstraeten] who was with him and said he really ought not to allow it. It was too dangerous. It was moonlight, but we could not use lights – we were passing farm carts of refugees and every sort of vehicle going our way and the opposite way – guns, lorries, etc., etc. It was of course much worse for my chauffeur – over and over again we were saved by seeing one of the motor cyclist gendarmes – who go behind my friend's car and sometimes in front – swerve over to the right and use his brake, which fortunately showed a fairly bright red light – then we swerved and missed something going the other way by inches. I found myself saying "prenez garde" – which of course is not helpful, as you know! So after watching 2 or 3 narrow escapes I lay back, closed my eyes and soon went to sleep and woke up 1½ hours later at our Château! So that was all right! But we heard before we finished dinner about 10.30 p.m. that Billotte was fatally (probably) injured, he died today. It was cruel luck. The Almighty is chastening us properly – *everything* goes wrong.

My friends [the Belgians] are playing up splendidly and my friend could not be finer – but the others [the French], not so good. It is hard luck on the Belgian and British armies – and ours twice in a generation – to have been led up a wrong path only to retreat. There has been very little fighting, and as far as I can find out Jimmy's people have not been engaged – distances are so great – cross country journeys almost impossible – information hard to come by – I will make every effort to see Jimmy, but I have been so awfully rushed with vitally important missions I have not been able to manage it.

Yesterday I went to G.H.Q. in quite a new place [Premesques] and lunched with Gort – 2 hours from where I work and live – found they were almost on bully beef – so I bought 4 fowls and a lot of vegetables for them and sent the provisions by an officer of the Needham Mission going there. I drove down here with Munster[126] (who was U.S.S. for War but couldn't stand H.B.[127] so joined Gort as principal A.D.C.), as Gort wanted him to telephone to W. [Winston] He was away and we both talked to Anthony Eden, who was frightfully friendly. I think they are grateful to me.

I had a long talk with W. this morning. He asked me to call him up at 7, but they were at a Cabinet, and he asked me to stay on, so I am having dinner with the Lady [Queen Elisabeth], an hour or so ago de Cartier was talking to Willy de G. [Grunne][128] so I took the telephone and gave him the message for you – and within ½ an hour got your answer saying Geoffrey was well and Roger[129] on 3 weeks leave. I suppose his *Wyvern* is out of action.[130] I thought he might be on this coast.

I got a message from you through Seal to say you had sent my things to Bertie Ramsay[131] at Dover, so I may get them in time, but we are awfully cut off.[132] I am afraid Dover got bombed last night – these people thought so and say the German communique says so.

24th May

W. did not call me up, as they promised he would at 8.30, so I called him about 9.45 – and I did not get away until 10 p.m. My journey home was quite frightful, and I do not mean to be caught on the road again at night. I told Winston this morning that if I was more use alive than dead, he better not let me in like that again.

I got home after midnight and found an important letter for me, and I came to the sea again this morning. Did not see the Lady [Queen Elisabeth] as my friend asked her to move to a place inland a bit. Comtesse Carton de Wiart – a cousin of our General[133] – is in attendance. I stayed by the sea for an hour, my lovely motor was going rather badly, dirt in the carburettor the chauffeur thought – now we are ¼ way to O [Ostend] quite broken down – it is a bore – and frightfully important for me to get on.

11 p.m., 24th May

It happened that my breakdown was one of those extraordinary chances that seem to come my way; if I had not been stopped by the roadside I would have gone on to Ostend and back to Bruges, and have missed my friend [King Leopold] who wanted me very much – at quite another place, which I will describe later, anyhow it is a modernised mediaeval castle with a moat, in which my friend, his Mother and van O. are living in.[134]

The K., Q. and I dined in her bedroom – the others in quite a big mess. Before dinner I helped him to write something – after dinner – we listened to the 9 o'clock wireless and were immensely impressed with

King George's inspiring speech, much the best I have ever heard him make.

I must go to bed, I am dead dog weary...

25th May

Had a good night – when I went to G.Q.G. I found Piers Mostyn, so I telephoned at once to W's Secretary to tell you. Winston answered, but as we were inland I put him off until I could get to the seaside.

Yesterday I begged him to send Dill[135] out at once to learn from Gort the situation. They begged me to try to get him sent. They did not want anyone else. W. put me on to him on the telephone – and he has been to G. [Gort] – is about to see my friend [King Leopold] – and go straight back. I will get him to take this.

In haste. All my love.

Piers will stay with us. Colonel Davy was his Company Officer at Sandhurst and made him an Under Officer. All my love.

I am trying my best to get in touch with Jimmy. Best love to Diana. Tell her we are all in great heart.

W. was *v.* nice to me yesterday...

29. *Keyes to his wife*

[Copy] 27/5/40.

I sent you a long letter and some very important papers by General Dill. I hope you got them all right. Since then I have had a pretty hectic time.

I went to Z. [Zeebrugge] to see if the blockships had been well and truly laid. To find that the French Admiral had omitted to tell the French General, who held that sector, that they were expected – on the other hand the General had been told to expect German landing parties – so when he saw them coming he opened fire with guns and machine guns, and the blockship people thinking that the Germans were already there, sank their ships off the Mole!!! Quite useless.

I was inspecting the inner lock gate, with some French and Belgians, when 3 German aeroplanes came and dropped 3 very heavy bombs, one of which came *very* near to us. They circled again, by that time we had got into one of the shelters made by the Germans against our bombing in 1918, and we stayed there until they went away. They dropped a lot of incendiary bombs, which set the grass on fire but did not get a house.

As I passed through O. [Ostend] it was burning furiously in places and some oil tanks and oil trucks on the railway were ablaze. I went on to my seaside place to talk to W. He was very friendly and nice – but did not grasp the gravity of the situation – in spite of my efforts. However, he evidently did later when Dill returned and other information had come in.

I came back to the castle and had dinner again in the Queen's room with the King and Prince Charles, and so to bed where I remained for 7 hours.

Yesterday morning I went to our Mission and then, after a talk with the King, went off with a Major Cockburn, now in the Mission, to see Gort. C. has a black eyeglass in his right eye – he told me he lost his eye in the last war – a fine fellow.

We were told it might be dangerous to go through Y [Ypres] and we had great difficulty in finding a way in, as the bombs had smashed up the road. Eventually we made detour and came through the [Menin] gate with Geoffrey's name on it, and out the other side. I was sad to see the cafe where they so kindly gave Munster and me coffee and would not let us pay – next door to the Hotel de Ville where we had the meeting with W. [Weygand] from Syria – was destroyed, poor Y.

Armentières was frightfully knocked about and a dozen wrecks of our lorries were lying about. I do hope the nice people escaped. I only stayed 20 minutes with Gort, left alone, leaving C. behind to get everything up to date. They strongly advised me not to go through Y again, as it is within gun range and was getting it hot, so I made a detour and came through various places, one where Dickie[136] was in billets when he was killed.

I had an important message for the King – and then at once went to the seaside to talk to W. On the way back 2 low flying Boches were machine gunning the roads, so we got out, which everyone does, and lay under the bank by the roadside. My gendarme tried to get me to wear his tin hat and would not wear it himself since I wouldn't. While we were lying there I found a new laid hen's egg!

When I got back I had dinner in the Queen's room with her – the King joined us later. I went to bed fairly early – but was woken at 5 by Willy de Grunne – when I was very fast asleep after 2 wakeful hours – just got off again at 6, when a message came for the King and I had to go in and wake him. I am just off to the seaside.

I heard last night that Colonel Davy had sent Piers home. I will telephone this for you – one of Winston's secretaries is very good about getting messages for you.

The route to my seaside resort had been badly bombed just before – we passed 7 enormous holes – one each side of the Nieuport bridge.

I talked to W. and Dill – and then went back to the King and wrote a message for him. Had a talk with Winston from here – G.Q.G. – had to be very cryptic, and he put me on to Archie Sinclair[137] – S. of S. for Air.

One thing is absolutely certain – a unified Air Service will not survive this war – if I can help it. I nearly wept last night when I heard all that it had been doing – and knew all it might have done to save the situation here. They are all over us today – it isn't pleasant.

I lunched with the King at... [probably Bruges] just he, Van O. and I. I had an opportunity of asking a favour this morning and begged that Roger might be given an M.T.B., or at any rate a place in one. They may play a great part here.[138] Winston told me he had told you I was doing splendid work.

I had a talk to Tom Phillips and I said I thought it was a shame Winston had brought personalities into his speech – one could not consider them in a struggle like this. He said – of course all that had been forgotten. So I said by me also...

[Notation that the letter was not signed or finished.]

30. Keyes to Churchill

[Copy]

22 St. Leonard's Terrace,
S.W.3.
4/6/40.

I know what a heavy burden you are bearing, and as the future must be our only concern, I have not bothered you. I understand, however, that you are going to make a statement this afternoon, so I would remind you, that I only spoke to you alone for about five minutes, and only for a few minutes to the Cabinet, since when I have not been consulted in any way.

As you know, speaking does not come very easily to me. I came straight from the train after three days of pretty strenuous effort, without any real sleep, and without any preparation or time to collect my thoughts. I may not have been able to present a very clear picture of what occurred during those last crowded hours in Belgium, nor have been able to do justice to the continuous efforts made by King Leopold to facilitate the operations of the B.E.F. after the 20th May, when he learnt that it was to deliver an attack to the South West, in co-operation with the French Northern Army.

He warned us then and several times afterwards (see my telegrams to you) that the Belgian Army would be forced to capitulate, if the Germans succeeded in driving a wedge between it and the British Army, which was likely, if the attack to the Southwards was persisted in.

On the 24th May, with grave misgivings, the Belgian Army withdrew from the line of the Schelde to the Lys, in order to release a number of British Divisions, and conform to the withdrawal of the B.E.F. to the strongly prepared frontier defence system, preparatory to their Southern offensive.

After four days continuous fighting, during which the Belgian Army delivered a number of counter attacks, inflicted heavy losses on the enemy and took some hundreds of prisoners; despite continuous intense aerial bombardment from low flying aeroplanes – which the R.A.F. could do nothing to prevent – the Belgian Army, short of food and ammunition and without any rest, cracked and was routed, and could do nothing further to assist the B.E.F.

Having insured the flooding of the Yser (5 days earlier) and the withdrawal of the two French Divisions from Zeebrugge to Nieuport in Belgian buses and lorries, when he realised that defeat was inevitable, the King asked for an Armistice, in order to spare the remains of his fugitive Army, and the masses of civilian refugees, who thronged every town, village and road in the small part of Belgium left to him, who were being mercilessly and continuously bombed and machine gunned.

It should be remembered that the Belgian Army consisted of Walloons and Flemings, both of whom hate the French, who have always treated them as inferiors, and many of the Flemings are actively pro-German.

This Army was held together thanks to the inspiring leadership of King Leopold, and fought bravely for 17 days, under dispiriting conditions of retirement forced upon them.

Had the King left, as his Ministers ceaselessly urged him to, from the 14th May onwards, the B.E.F. might well have been left in the air on the Dyle, rather than being forced by circumstances *in France* to abandon the Belgian Army on the 27th May.

I had a talk to Gort this morning, and we both felt that "judgement should be suspended until all the facts are known," since communication between the two Armies was well nigh impossible during those last crowded hours.

Personally I hope that you will soon no longer think it necessary to allow the vilification of a brave King to go on unrestrained, "in order to raise the morale of the French", for whose failure on the Meuse both the Belgian and British Armies have had to pay so dearly...

P.S. As the *Daily Mirror* of 30th May has included me in their libellous vilification, I have issued a writ against them.[139]

31. *Keyes to Lord Gort*[140]

[Copy] 12th June 1940.

As you must know, I have done everything I could to help you and the Army since last October, and throughout your brief campaign, and you may be quite certain that it will be my constant endeavour to go on doing so.

I am glad we had that talk last Tuesday morning (4th June) since it cleared the air a bit. I wanted to see you as soon as possible after you arrived because I feared that if you were going to be as unfair and ungenerous to the Belgians as Macfarlane[141] was, when I talked to him on Monday night (3rd), you would lay yourself open to a severe counter attack when all the facts are known. I knew too that the Prime Minister was to make a statement on 4th June, and I thought it would be as well that we should help him to make a fair one.

Since this was impossible, I wrote a letter to the Prime Minister, of which I enclose a copy.[142]

However, he probably did not read it before he made that bitter and very unfair attack on King Leopold,[143] no doubt to please the French, who are seeking a scapegoat to cover their defeat on the Meuse, for which the British and Belgian Armies have had to pay so dearly.

Before I go further, I would like to say that I am sure your gallant spirit and unrivalled fighting record was an inspiration to your splendid army throughout that frightful retreat, from which it emerged bludgeoned but undismayed, and most gloriously unbeaten in spirit. But in fairness to others I cannot leave it at that, and I don't think I could do you a better service than to place certain facts frankly before you now. Having done so, I will leave the matter until the war, or this phase of it is over.

I was behind the scenes at G.H.Q. and G.Q.G., as well as being in close touch with King Leopold, and have been able to place all the evidence on record – some of which is probably unknown to you.

Since I spoke to you, I have heard that you have been attributing most of the blame for your misfortunes to having had *your left flank exposed, without any warning from King Leopold that he was about to capitulate.*

Do you really think that that is a fair statement? in view of the repeated requests made to you on 26th–27th May for help from the

B.E.F. *to prevent the Belgian Army's right flank being turned*, which you were unable to give; and in view of the warning to you and the Government from 20th May onwards that the King would be forced to capitulate if the British and Belgian Armies became separated, which he regarded as inevitable if the British attack to the Southward was persisted in. An opinion shared by the C.I.G.S. and you at the time. (See Enclosure 2).

Although this attack was never delivered, the preparations for it were persisted in for six fateful days, and the withdrawal of the British Divisions to take part in it left the Belgian right flank, and indeed the whole Belgian front line, dangerously weak, as was repeatedly pointed out to you and to Churchill from 20th May onwards, and by King Leopold to Dill on the 25th.

I enclose copies of telegrams and messages bearing on this matter, as I gathered from you that some of your records have been lost.

When I stayed with you at Wahagnies on the night of 19th May it was evident to me that your one object was to withdraw to the seaports as soon as possible, and that even then you did not expect to be able to save much of your equipment. On the morning of the 20th when the C.I.G.S. (Ironside) arrived and gave you the Cabinet's instructions to prepare for an attack you made no secret of your consternation. When the World knows all the facts, which of course will be published someday, the responsibility for all the suffering your Army had to endure and the overwhelming of the Belgian Army will most surely be placed on other shoulders than those of King Leopold.

You may not like the passage I have marked in my letter to Churchill,[144] but there is documentary proof of the fact, apart from the remark you made to me at Ypres on the 21st May: — "Do the Belgians think us awful dirty dogs?" I said "No" and referred you to King Leopold's message to Churchill, of which a copy was sent to you (See Enclosure 3).

I am afraid harsh things will be said by the Belgians later if the responsibility for the B.E.F.'s misfortunes and the exposure of its left flank is attributed to their King. There is of course irrefutable proof that the sacrifice of the B.E.F. and the Belgian Army was primarily caused by the collapse of the French Army on the Meuse and its loss of morale, but other considerations and ill judged decisions contributed to the immensity of the misfortune.

The order given to you on the 20th May by the C.I.G.S. for an offensive to the Southward in co-operation with a thoroughly demoralised French Army, at a moment when your communications were cut and you were running short of food, munitions, and everything needed for further offensive action, was deplorably misjudged.

For this the War Cabinet must bear all the responsibility, although no doubt the plan was urged by the French Government, in the first place, and before Weygand arrived on the scene (19th May). The C.I.G.S. having apparently been unable to dissuade the Cabinet from putting forward such a hopeless plan, you were put in the difficult position of having to carry out an operation, which you knew was doomed to failure, or of declining, and refusing to jeopardise your Army any further by delaying its withdrawal to the Northward.

You may remember what I said at the time: — "Why don't you tell the Government to go to the devil, and insist on being given a free hand?" to extricate your Army from the appalling situation into which it had been placed through no fault of yours. After all you bore all the responsibility for success or failure, and you alone were in a position to judge – in view of the local conditions and the morale of the French with whom you had to co-operate – whether it was possible to carry out the Government's orders or not.

I offered to do anything I could to help, and you assisted me to write a Military appreciation as to what the Government's order meant, but you would not let me say that you had seen it and approved of it, which would have strengthened my hand when I tackled the Prime Minister about it.

Before leaving G.H.Q. I had a telegram cyphered and sent through the War Office to the Prime Minister (See Enclosure 2). On my return to Bruges I only told the King that it was proposed to extend the B.E.F. to the Southward, in a Southerly direction, and it was hoped by our Government, that the Belgian Army would be able to keep contact.

Later that evening the King asked me to let our Government know his views and his anxiety to help our splendid Army to extricate itself from the impossible position into which it had been placed by the French reverse on the Meuse. I then sent a telegram to the Prime Minister (See Enclosure 3).

The King expressed to me his grave misgivings owing to the success of the German thrust and the apparent loss of morale of the French Army. He said he could not understand why we did not realise that the only chance now of extricating the British Army was to swing to the North West at once, strengthen our contact with the Belgian Army, and cover Dunkirk and the Belgian ports by occupying the Lys-Gravelines line.

To my first telegram of the 20th, I received a reply from the Prime Minister (See Enclosure 4) and in reply to the King's message of 20th (See Enclosure 5) which arrived just before the meeting with Weygand at Ypres on 21st May.

It was a misfortune that Weygand's message to you – asking you to meet him at Ypres on the 21st May – did not reach you, and that I could not find you in time to meet him there. You might possibly have been able to dissuade him then, but I doubt it, since Billotte – who was as opposed to this offensive as you were – acquiesced in it.

King Leopold told me that he was very loath at the Ypres meeting with Weygand to throw doubts on the ability of the British and French Northern Armies to close the gap between them and the French Army in the South – 'since the offensive spirit was in the air', although he was tempted to point out that the offensive had been delayed too long and that the only real help now, at this late hour, was to establish a cover to Dunkirk and the Belgian ports in order to withdraw the British and French Armies which were separated from the main Army by the German thrust. He had agreed, however, to do what he could to help by relieving the British and French Divisions, and later he agreed to take over the line of the Lys as far as Halluin in order to release British Divisions to carry out the offensive contemplated by General Weygand, although this necessitated his placing practically the whole Belgian Army in the line of about 100 kilometers, opposite which a considerable number of German Divisions had been identified.

King Leopold pointed out that the well prepared frontier line to be held by the British on his right flank was very strong and was unlikely to be seriously attacked, but that to be held by the Belgian troops was weak and would be comparatively lightly held and would thus invite attack. He feared that if seriously assaulted with strong air support the Germans would break through, sever the connection between the two Armies, and overwhelm the Belgian Army.

The line of the Lys was the last that could be held, there being no natural defences behind it to cover the ports and vital stores and munitions depots, which were all to the East of the Yser. He asked me to telegraph a reply (See Enclosure 6) to the Prime Minister's Message (See Enclosure 5).

On 21st May and during the next few days, I motored hundreds of miles in order to speak to Churchill from La Panne on the end of a cable which was safe as far as Belgium was concerned, and I did my utmost to make him understand the gravity of your position. He would not listen, and even abused me for the statements in the Military appreciation you gave me. If I had only been free to say it was really yours, I might have been more successful.

He would not accept my contention that, if this counter attack to the Southward was insisted on, it was bound to separate the Belgian and British Armies, as it did, for it cannot be denied – as I have already said – that although your attack was never delivered, the preparations for it dangerously weakened the line held by the Belgian

Army, laid it open to an overwhelming attack, and delayed the withdrawal of the B.E.F. for six precious days.

During the night of the 23rd the Belgians relieved the French 68th Division, which was still under the King's orders, and he sent it, in Belgian vehicles, across the Yser to take up the Gravelines Line. On reaching Nieuport, the van heard a rumour of German tanks approaching and turned and fled back in panic, causing great confusion on the road (over which I happened to be returning to Bruges from La Panne at 11 p.m.); eventually the division was pulled up at Thourout and sent to Gravelines in Belgian vehicles on 24th May.

On 24th May, when I saw Weygand's message to you: — 'Fight like a Tiger', I was in despair and begged Churchill to send Dill out at once in the hope that he would be able to stop the offensive before the B.E.F. was committed to it, since I knew that that was what you wanted. I also told him and Eden that someone *must* be appointed to co-ordinate the operations of the 3 armies – as Blanchard[145] was doing nothing to that end – and I suggested you, saying I knew King Leopold would approve, and hoped they would persuade the French to agree.

When Dill returned from G.H.Q. on 25th and told the King and me optimistically that the offensive must go on, despite the length and the weakness of the Belgian line and the numerous German Divisions threatening it, I thought the future looked pretty grim, and I went again to La Panne to warn Churchill – without much effect.

On the morning of the 26th May I went through Ypres to see you and ask what I could do to help; you were much too occupied to tell me what you proposed to do, but said it would be helpful if the Belgian Army could fall back towards the Yser. It was so obvious that you were in a very tight place, that I hurried back to Bruges and gave the King and Van Overstraeten your message.

They said that they would do anything that was possible to help, but the Belgian Army was itself in a very precarious position and had no reserves, and the only possible way to save the situation now and relieve the pressure on the Belgian Army, which was hard pressed and suffering from ceaseless and heavy low bombing attacks, was for the R.A.F. to intervene, and the B.E.F. to strike at the flank of the German Divisions advancing between the Schelde and the Lys, with every prospect of destroying their communications and bridgeheads. I found that this appeal had already been sent to you, and it was passed four or five times by telegram and messenger from 1030 on 26th onwards, with no response.

General Van Overstraeten admitted to me that it might be difficult for you to mount your artillery for such an attack if preparations to deliver the attack to the Southward, ordered by Weygand, were well advanced; he stressed, however, that it was the one possible chance of saving their right flank and their Army from being overwhelmed, and it was an opportunity for the British Army to inflict a severe defeat on the German Infantry of which these Divisions were mainly composed; also that a success here would insure the retention of Ostend and Nieuport for some time, and give two more ports for evacuation.

The King and Van Overstraeten promised to do what they could about withdrawing towards the Yser, so I sent you a telegram (See Enclosure 8) before going to La Panne to speak to the Prime Minister.

I was much relieved to learn from him that the attack to the Southward was off. He was astonished to hear that you had not told me or the G.Q.G. of the instructions you had received. He said that it was only fair that King Leopold should know your instructions as soon as possible. As the telephone line was not absolutely safe I asked him to send a cypher message at once to the British Mission at Bruges.

On my return to Bruges I learnt that the King had gone into the matter of further retirement towards the Yser with his General Staff, and they maintained that it was a physical impossibility to do so. They declared that withdrawal over open roads without adequate fighter support was very costly. One battalion on march N.E. of Ypres was practically wiped out that morning by about 60 low bombing aircraft.

They reiterated that an attempt must be made at once to restore the situation on the Lys by a British counter attack on the *vulnerable flank of the enemy* if a disaster was to be averted, and that the opportunity for this might only last a few more hours. They pointed out that there could be no question of the Belgian Army retiring across the Yser; under the pressure the enemy was exerting it would mean abandoning all their munitions, stores and food. The King had given the order to his Army to hold the line of the Lys to the end; their artillery had been told to stand to their guns until either their ammunition was expended or their guns had been overrun.

There can be no doubt that when it was obvious that the B.E.F. had no intention of coming to the Belgian Army's assistance it lost heart. I went to La Panne again that evening and told the Prime Minister and Secretary of State for Air that unless the R.A.F. could do something to counter the German low bombing attacks and lighten the Belgian Army's burden it was bound to crack, and was unlikely to stand another day of it, having already endured three without respite.

During the night of 26th–27th I received your message for the King – (See Enclosure 9). I need hardly say that I did not show this to him as the only movement of the Belgian Army had been forced upon it by enemy pressure, which the B.E.F. had been unable to ease, despite the help of the 12th Lancers. The Belgians had no reserves. A Belgian Mechanised Cavalry Division which was hurried down from the left flank was practically wiped out in its efforts to support the right flank, and they had brought up the ill equipped 15th Division (Infantry without artillery or machine guns) from the Yser, and thrown them into the battle. These elderly second line troops were much shaken by low bombing attacks, and were probably the Belgians of whom you spoke so contemptuously.

That night (26th) King Leopold gave orders for the French 60th Division, which was still under his direction, to be moved across the Yser to Nieuport in Belgian lorries and buses. At that time it was open to question whether the Yser would be reached first by the Panzer Divisions driving east along the coast, or by the German Divisions attacking the Belgians from the Eastward.

I understand that the big stone bridge across the Yser at Nieuport was not blown up, but you have the French to thank for that. Nieuport was, or should have been, occupied by the French. I was on the bridge at 2 a.m. on 28th and know it was mined and French Naval units crossed it later that morning.

At 1230 on the 27th I sent you a message from the King (See Enclosure 10). At that time he hoped to be able to hold on for another day, but the enemy broke through in several places that afternoon.

The situation had now arisen which the King, and you, foresaw on 20th May. Being unable to be of any further use to the B.E.F., having flooded the Yser (five days earlier), mined its bridges and removed all the French troops across the Yser, he asked for an Armistice in order to avoid the further slaughter of his sorely tried people who crowded every town, village, and road, and were being ruthlessly bombed.

Telephone communication between Bruges and G.H.Q. had been almost impossible for some days, but at about 1700 on 27th, when the King told me his Army had collapsed and he was asking for a cessation of hostilities, a cypher telegram was sent to you and the War Office by wireless. The War Office received it at 1754. I motored at once to La Panne with Davy, and when I telephoned to the Prime Minister he telephoned to A.C.I.G.S. and asked him to repeat the news to you, in case the wireless message did not get through.

The Prime Minister was not at all surprised in view of the repeated warnings, but he told me that I must make every endeavour to persuade the King and Queen to come to England with me, and he dictated a message which he said I should have received that afternoon (See Enclosure 12).

I went back to Bruges, and Davy then went to Middelkerke to arrange for the embarkation of the British Mission. Bruges was crowded with refugees and was being heavily bombed at intervals. I saw the King at G.Q.G. and after some difficulty found the Queen in Bruges, but nothing would induce either of them to leave their country, as they said their people would need them and they could be more use to them there than in France or England.

I left at 10 p.m. on 27th for Nieuport and was fortunate enough to fall in with Colonel Davy and Major Hailey, who after seeing the Mission embarked in the British steamer *Aboukir* at Ostend, and being anxious about my safety, went to Nieuport with a few men to look after me. To this they owe their lives, for nearly the whole Mission and Air Mission – about 70 officers and men – were lost when the *Aboukir* was torpedoed.

I deeply deplore their loss for throughout the campaign I was in close touch with the officers, both Military and R.A.F., and was immensely impressed by their energy and keenness and their anxiety to do everything they could to help the B.E.F., particularly during those last critical days and hours when they made every conceivable effort to make your G.H.Q. realise the perilous position into which the Belgian Army had been placed, and the consequent danger to the B.E.F.'s left flank.

I presume that you told your Belgian Liaison Officers of the instructions you received on the night of 25th–26th after Dill's return, but they were never communicated to G.Q.G.

The Prime Minister's message to the King (See Enclosure 11) did not reach me until I returned to England on the 28th. Had the King been informed of these instructions – as in all fairness he should have been on the 26th – he would have been justified in then taking any steps which he thought fit to avoid the ruthless slaughter of his Army and people.

When I saw the Prime Minister and his Cabinet immediately after I arrived in London there was no question of blaming King Leopold for laying down his arms to avoid further sacrifice of his people when he could do no more to help the B.E.F. and the French. How could there be when the last message from the Prime Minister, which the King ought to have received 36 hours before he took any action, clearly indicated that we were about to leave the Belgians to their fate (See Enclosure 11). At that time they did not know that I had been unable to deliver it! Now of course it is convenient to forget all about it. I found only bitter resentment against King Leopold for ignoring their appeal and declining to come away with me, for reasons which he had previously given in a letter to the King (See Enclosure 13 and also Enclosure 7).

After all, many thousands of men of the French Army laid down their arms within a few days of the outbreak of this campaign under infinitely less trying conditions than those endured by the Belgian Army and people for nearly 3 weeks. Yet no one – very properly at the moment – blames the French, so it seems to be damnably unfair to throw all the blame on the Belgians, and try and make their King a French and British scapegoat.

I hope that you will find time to read this, and that it may be useful to you when you are making out your report on the proceedings of the B.E.F. between the 19th and 28th May 1940 . . .

Enclosure 1 [Reproduced as Document 30.]

Enclosure 2   Telegram   20th May 1940.

To: Prime Minister   *From:* Admiral Keyes

I understand that the orders to B.E.F. brought by C.I.G.S. amount to abandonment of junction with Belgian Army and to fight South Westwards. In this case the Germans will quickly drive wedge through to North of B.E.F. and there is the present threat to South flank by tank attack now proceeding. B.E.F. very tired, congestion on roads with refugees makes movement very difficult and I gather that any reorganisation of British Divisions to South Westward of Lille area can only develop very slowly. Am returning to Bruges and I do not propose to tell the Belgians that B.E.F. intends to desert them yet.

Enclosure 3   Telegram   20th May 1940.

To: Prime Minister   *From:* Admiral Keyes

On my return to Belgian G.Q.G. I told the King of the proposal to extend the B.E.F. Southwards so that part of it could operate in a Southerly direction.

The King pointed out that the Belgian Army existed solely for defence, it had neither tanks nor aircraft and was not trained or equipped for offensive warfare. He also told me that in the small part of Belgium left there was only sufficient food for fourteen days, possibly less, owing to the influx of refugees.

He did not feel that he had any right to expect the British Government to consider jeopardizing perhaps the very existence of our ten Divisions in order to keep contact with the Belgian Army. He wished to make it clear that he does not want to do anything to interfere with any action which may be considered desirable for the B.E.F. to undertake towards the South, if the circumstances make it necessary. He realises, of course, that such action would finally lead to the capitulation of the Belgian Army.

The King asked me to try to ascertain the intentions of the British

Government if the German thrust towards the sea succeeds in separating us from the main French forces in the South.

It must not be thought that he has lost heart or faith, but he feels he owes it to us to make his position perfectly clear.

I have sent a copy of this to Lord Gort.

Enclosure 4   Telegram   20th May 1940.

To: Admiral Keyes   *From:* Prime Minister

Cannot understand what sort of solution you have in mind. B.E.F. will make every effort to sustain and shield the Belgian Army during movements which are indispensable to its life and further action. Please acknowledge.

Enclosure 5   Telegram   21st May 1940.

To: Admiral Keyes   *From:* Prime Minister

Weygand is coming up your way tomorrow to concert action of all forces. Essential to secure our communications Southwards and strike at small bodies intruding upon them.

Use all your influence to persuade your friends to conform to our movements. Belgian Army should keep hold of our left flank.

No question of capitulation for anyone. We greatly admire King's attitude. German thrust towards Lille must not succeed separate us from main French forces.

Have complete confidence in Gort and Weygand who embody offensive spirit vital to success.

Enclosure 6   Telegram   0130   22nd May 1940.

To: Prime Minister   *From:* Admiral Keyes

Reference to your telegram, the King feels that you do not appreciate the difficulty of keeping in touch with the left flank of the B.E.F. if it operates to the South as you suggest.

He would like above all things to continue to co-operate with the B.E.F. if this were possible; but it is a physical impossibility under the existing geographical conditions. Moreover the Belgian Army has now provisions for 13 days only.

His Government are urging him to fly with them to Le Havre before the Army finds it necessary to capitulate. Of course he has no intention of deserting his Army and he considers that he can serve his country better by staying there rather than as a fugitive with a Government which represents no-one while outside the country.

The King asked me to thank you for your message and to say that if the British Government understands his motives, he does not care what others may think.

Enclosure 7   Telegram   1320   25th May 1940.

To: Prime Minister   *From:* Admiral Keyes

The King was told last night by his Ministers that Lord Halifax was telegraphing to me to persuade His Majesty to withdraw with his Government.

I have now received your message 71941 of 24th May.

For the last eleven days the Ministers have been urging the King to fly with them. The four who by his orders have remained here spent some hours last night urging him to go with them at once; thus deserting his Army at a moment when it is fighting a stern battle to cover the left flank of the B.E.F.

Deprived of the King's leadership the capitulation of the Belgian Army would inevitably be hastened and the B.E.F. endangered.

King Leopold has written to the King to explain his motives for remaining with his Army and people if our Armies become encircled and the capitulation of the Belgian Army becomes inevitable.

Dill takes letter and a special Order of the Day by the King to his Army.

I trust that H.M. Government will not be unduly impressed by the arguments of the Belgian Ministers who, apparently, have no thought but the continuation of a political regime whose incapacity and lack of authority have been only too apparent during the last fortnight. Their example has been followed by nearly all the local authorities and the result has been absolute confusion. Moreover they urged the British and French Ambassadors to precede them in order to justify their own flight – a course which did not add to the prestige of the two countries.

Enclosure 8   Telegram   1610   26th May 1940.

To: C.-in-C.   *From:* Admiral Keyes

Have delivered your message.

They will do their best but consider an immediate counter-offensive by B.E.F. on the Lys is only way of averting disaster.

PART I: 1939–1940 69

Enclosure 9 Telegram 2155 26th May 1940.

To: Admiral Keyes *From:* Lord Gort

Following personal to H.M.

His Majesty the King of the Belgians has on two occasions been good enough to assure Lord Gort that the safety of the B.E.F. was a primary consideration in his mind.

Lord Gort is bound to observe that the proposed movement of the Belgian Army which dangerously exposes the left flank of the B.E.F. is a breach of His Majesty's expressed intention.

Enclosure 10 Telegram 1230 27th May 1940.

To: Lord Gort *From:* Admiral Keyes

Reference your message for King.

He wishes you to know that his Army is greatly disheartened. It has been incessantly engaged for four days and subjected to intense air bombardment which the R.A.F. has been unable to prevent.

The knowledge that the Allied Armies in this sector have been encircled and that the Germans have great superiority in the air has led his troops to believe that the position is almost hopeless.

He fears a moment is rapidly approaching when he can no longer rely upon his troops to fight or be of any further use to the B.E.F.

He wishes you to realise that he will be obliged to surrender before a debacle.

The King fully appreciates that the B.E.F. has done everything in its power to help Belgium and he asks you to believe that he has done everything in his power to avert this catastrophe.

Enclosure 11 Telegram[146] 0320 27th May 1940.

To: Admiral Keyes *From:* Prime Minister

Impart the following to your friend. Presume he knows that British and French are fighting their way to coast between Gravelines and Ostend inclusive and that we propose to give fullest support from Navy and Air Force during hazardous embarkation. What can we do for him? Certainly we cannot serve Belgium's cause by being hemmed in and starved out. Only hope is victory and England will never quit the war whatever happens till Hitler is beat or we cease to be a State.

Trust you will make sure he leaves with you by aeroplane before too late. Should our operation prosper and we establish effective bridgehead we would try if desired to carry some Belgian divisions to France by sea. Vitally important Belgium should continue in war and safety King's person essential.

Enclosure 12   Message dictated over telephone.[147]   0730 27th May 1940.

To: Admiral Keyes   *From:* Prime Minister

Belgian Embassy here assumes from King's decision to remain that he regards the war as lost and contemplates separate peace.

It is in order to dissociate itself with this that the Constitutional Belgian Government has reassembled on foreign soil. Even if present Belgian Army has to lay down its arms, there are 200,000 Belgians of military age in France and greater resources than Belgium had in 1914 on which to fight back. By present decision the King is dividing the nation and delivering it into Hitler's protection.

Please convey these considerations to the King, and impress upon him the disastrous consequences to the Allies and to Belgium of his present choice.

Enclosure 13   Commandement de l'Armée Belge
                                                    Grand Quartier Général,
                                                              25th May 1940.

[Extract from letter from King Leopold to the King. Given to General Dill at Bruges on 25th May and delivered on 26th May.]

Belgium has held to the engagement she undertook in 1937, by maintaining her neutrality and by resisting with all the forces at her disposal, the moment her independence was threatened. Her means of resistance are now nearing their end.

After the first reverse of the morning of 10th May, when my Country was treacherously attacked without warning, the Belgian Army succeeded in withdrawing and establishing a good line of defence in co-operation with her Allies.

But retreat from day to day was imposed upon the Allied Armies in Belgium by military events which took place outside the Country. The Belgian Army withdrew in good order until it reached the position it is now holding. It is impossible to retreat further. The development of the battle now in progress is wearing out my Army. The whole cadre of officers and staff being in action, there is no possibility of creating a new military force. Therefore the assistance we can give to the Allies will come to an end if our Armies become encircled.

In spite of all the advice I have received to the contrary, I feel that my duty impels me to share the fate of my Army and to remain with my people. To act otherwise would amount to desertion.

Whatever trials Belgium may have to face in the future, I am convinced that I can help my people better by remaining with them, rather than by attempting to act from outside, especially with regard to the hardships of foreign occupation, the menace of forced labour or deportation, and the difficulties of food supply.

By remaining in my Country, I fully realise that my position will be difficult, but my utmost concern will be to prevent my countrymen from being compelled to associate themselves with any action against the Countries which have attempted to help Belgium in her plight.

If I should fail in that endeavour, and only then, would I give up the task I have set myself.

Leopold.

(Taken by hand by General Dill.)

32. Lord Gort to Keyes[118]

[Copy]

Nobel House,
2 Buckingham Gate,
London, S.W.1.
18th June 1940.

I have to thank you for your letter of the 12th June and I am bound to say it contains certain passages which are at variance with my recollection of events. However, I know you will be in agreement with my view that in these pressing times it is advisable, to quote your own words, that "judgement should be suspended until the facts are known."

There I feel it will be better to leave the matter until hostilities are over...

33. Keyes to Lord Gort[149]

[Copy]

26/6/40.

Thank you for your letter. I was all for leaving the inquest until after the war. But in the meantime, so many officers of the B.E.F. and others are saying what you said – before I sent you documentary evidence to prove how unfair you were in your condemnation of King Leopold, that I think the truth will have to be made public, if these stories persist . . .

34. Keyes to Churchill

[Carbon]   4/7/40.

That was a grand speech – and my best congratulations on the strong line you took over the seizure of the French Fleet. The tremendous reception you received after you told us that the Navy had been used offensively was heartening.[150]

It is now more than five weeks since I returned from Belgium,[151] and I have not bothered you as you apparently have no wish to see me or have anything to do with me. So I was very surprised when someone sent me a copy of your article in the last *Sunday Chronicle*, and it was gratifying to read all the nice things you used to think about the value of my offensive spirit.

It is sad that in this war you have never made any use of it, and that I have only been able to act offensively by word of mouth which is not my strong suit. But you must have noticed that in my somewhat stormy career I have never hesitated to attack those who blocked the road to victory (as Jellicoe and Bacon did in 1917).

When I was trying to persuade you to take action in the Trondhjem Fiord, which would have spared the Navy the stigma of letting down Carton de Wiart's troops, you told me you had responsibility without power – power rested with the three Chiefs of the Staff – so I went into action on your behalf as I have done so often since I fought your battle for the Dardanelles 25 years ago. You brushed aside my indictment, saying that the two small German vessels had been overlooked by the aeroplanes, but all the same the Admiralty knew they were there and they thoroughly deserved my strictures. You deprecated my "casting aspersions on my old Staff Officers" – a remark you might have spared me, since you ought to have known why I did it and how distasteful it was to me.[152]

Nevertheless I am told that my speech was decisive in helping you to get the freedom and power you needed – evidently Chamberlain thinks so as he cuts me dead.

When I returned from Belgium I found over 400 letters commending my action and welcoming the result, including scores from the fighting sailors for whom I spoke – from Admiral of the Fleet to Able Seaman – and since then many have written expressing surprise that those responsible for so many distressing incidents should still have it in their power to let the Navy in for another *Glorious* disaster.¹⁵³ I wonder if their overcaution or Somerville's¹⁵⁴ is responsible for the escape of the *Dunkerque*?¹⁵⁵

During my time in Belgium I strained "every nerve and sinew" to keep you informed of what was happening and of the B.E.F.'s plight, which I could not induce Gort to do for himself. He would not even let me say that the Military appreciation I gave you was really his!

I came back with intimate practical experience of modern war and German methods added to my varied experiences in wars of the past – but you have not spoken to me, except for five minutes immediately I arrived in London on 28th May.

Apart from considerations of a friendship, which has been steadfast from my side, is the Country so flush of people with the experience I possess and the qualities you so handsomely attributed to me in your article that you can afford to continue to ignore me in this critical hour?

P.S. I don't of course know what you are doing about Southern Ireland but here is a suggestion, which I think should be acted upon *immediately*, unless the question of its defence is already satisfactorily settled.

That the Governments of the Dominions should jointly give the Government of Southern Ireland a brief ultimatum to the effect that the security of the sea communications of the British Empire can no longer be jeopardised by their neutrality, and that the Dominion troops will occupy the country to defend it, with or without their permission.

35. *Keyes to Vice-Admiral Wilfred Tomkinson*¹⁵⁶

[Holograph]
Tingewick House,
Buckingham.
6.7.40.

I wish we could have a yarn. I'd like to tell you all about my Belgian campaign. I saw modern bloody war and invasion at its worst and am lucky to be here! Oddly enough I tried to block ZO [Zeebrugge–Ostend] again but it was much harder to do with French cooperation than German opposition and tho' Z was blocked, O Blockship had to be used thanks to the French attacking the Z one thinking they were German invaders.

They insisted on taking charge of the Belgian ports and coasts, only they forgot to tell their French troops we were coming, but did tell them to beware of seaborne German attack.¹⁵⁷ That left nothing to be done but blow up O ship. When I got back to London the French Captain who was charged with pressing the button came to call on me in Katherine's house where Eva[158] and I live – to tell he had been ordered by his senior officer not to do it. J.S. [Somerville] "talked" himself into that job and proved himself a Parker[159] rather than a Nelson *blast him*. He is a pal of Alexander's.[160]

Why didn't they send me or ½ a dozen others who could have done better. I would have had the guts to talk to the French Admiral and the guts to sink their ships – other than by *indirect* fire and mines which misfired. I owe him one for Invergordon and I won't hesitate to criticise – when this story is corroborated. I was told it by DOD – foaming at the mouth, almost, when he told the tale.

I am out to 1000/3 because I told W.C. and his War Cabinet *exactly* what I thought when I got back from Belgium. *I was right* and proved to be – but they don't like plain speaking – and I have not been spoken to since 28th May – and then only for 5 minutes alone with W.C. – 5 minutes with the Cabinet.

Any chance of seeing you? I can't write any more. I found over 400 letters when I got back and haven't read ½ of them since.

I have written the whole of the story of the Belgian Campaign – and placed it on the shelf – to quote W.C. in Parliament, from which the historian will take it when he seeks documents to tell his tale. It *won't* be the lying tale W.C. told in H. of C. – and King Leopold will be proved a worthy son of his father. He sacrificed his army to try to save the BEF before *it deserted* him . . .

PART II

DIRECTOR OF COMBINED OPERATIONS
(JULY 1940–OCTOBER 1941)

Anyone with the slightest knowledge of Keyes's character would realize how much he chafed at his unemployment during the critical situation which followed the fall of France in the early summer of 1940. His letter to Churchill on July 4th [Document 34] was an example of this. But while he fretted Churchill was actually about to discover a position which seemed tailored to Keyes's abilities. Even though the British Army had been driven from the Continent, the Prime Minister hoped that at least the German occupation might be made uncomfortable by means of raids. On June 17th the Chiefs of Staff, without Churchill's approval, had appointed Lieutenant-General A. G. Bourne, Adjutant-General of the Royal Marines, to be Commander of Raiding Operations with operational command of the independent companies raised by the War Office and initially intended for guerilla operations in Norway. Bourne's directive indicated he was to be 'Adviser to the Chiefs of Staff on Combined Operations' and he was given command of the Inter-Services Training and Development Centres for the development and production of special landing craft and equipment [36]. Churchill apparently came to the conclusion that these operations might assume a wider scope and that it would be expedient to have a more senior officer in charge [39]. Keyes, with his experience of combined operations at the Dardenelles, seemed an excellent choice and on July 17th Churchill appointed him Director of Combined Operations. He was to assume Bourne's duties and resources and form contact with the service departments through General Ismay as representing the Minister of Defence.[1] No new directive was issued to Keyes, and Churchill wrote in his memoirs, 'His close personal contact with me and with the Defence Office served to overcome any departmental difficulties arising from this unusual appointment.'[2] Events would demonstrate that this assessment was overly optimistic.

Keyes found comparatively little material to work with [38]. His Directorate only extended over slightly more than 1,250 men, 15 LCA and 4 LCM; but he was overjoyed at finally finding an outlet for his energies which might make use of his past experience, and set to work enthusiastically building, or more correctly creating, an organisation [37]. In August a Combined Training Centre was established at Inveraray in Scotland. Keyes also found it desirable to remove his headquarters from the Admiralty. His idea was to establish a true inter-service organisation and this would have been difficult had he remained where his organisation would always have seemed to be a mere division of the Admiralty. Keyes was successful in establishing his headquarters at Richmond Terrace, with only a naval operations section [Assistant Directorate of Operations Division (Combined Operations)], and later a material section [Director of Naval Equipment (Combined Operations)], remaining at the Admiralty.[3]

The Combined Operations organisation was to a certain extent regarded with misgivings by the established services and, as General Sir Leslie Hollis, former Secretary of the Chiefs of Staff Committee, has written 'came in for a special loathing from the Admiralty' which regarded it as a potential rival and resented Keyes's great seniority. The relationship between Pound, now First Sea Lord, and his former Commander-in-Chief was particularly delicate and 'this juxtaposition of rank and authority suited neither of them.'[4] The Commandos – as the independent companies came to be called – were also in competition for supplies and equipment at a period in the war when comparatively little was available.[5] Keyes knew that his plain speaking during the Norwegian campaign had obviously not endeared him to the Naval Staff, and he came to feel they were blocking him. He also began to resent the various planning staffs and committees composed of relatively junior officers who seemed to do little but cast cold water on his proposals. The somewhat indeterminate position of the DCO led to difficulties, as did his known personal relationship with Churchill. At times Keyes was to feel the Prime Minister bent over backwards to avoid the appearance of favouritism. Keyes found it difficult to get his advice taken and he was not consulted in the preparations for the abortive expedition to Dakar [40–42]. By the end of October Keyes had come to the conclusion that he could be of little use to Churchill in the prosecution of the war as long as he was in any way under the Chiefs of Staff Committee, and proposed that instead the DCO be directly responsible to the Chief of Staff. Keyes went even beyond this, and suggested he become Churchill's Deputy with the Chiefs of Staff under his direction as far as combined operations were concerned [42]. Sir John Colville, Churchill's Assistant Private Secretary in 1940, has written that the Prime Minister was strongly tempted by the suggestion.[6]

The scope of raiding operations was severely hampered by the lack of means to carry them out. This was particularly true in regard to assault craft and vessels specially adapted to carry them. Moreover, from September 1940 until the end of the year the Commandos were placed under the command of the C-in-C Home Forces for use in the event of a German invasion.[7] The situation was further complicated by the uncertain attitude of Spain and the possibility she might enter the war on the side of Germany and render the use of Gibraltar as a base impossible. Spanish belligerency might also be followed by an invasion of Portugal. These possibilities raised the problem of securing the strategically located Spanish and Portuguese possessions in the Atlantic, notably the Azores, Canaries and Cape Verde Islands. All of this meant detailed planning for a contingency which might never arise, but following the spectacular German successes against Norway and France it was not inconceivable the Germans might attempt to secure at least some of the islands by airborne assault, and investigation of German records after the war indicates the idea was considered.[8] We now know that when Hitler met Franco, the Spanish Chief of State, at Hendaye on the French-Spanish border on October 23rd 1940 he was unsuccessful in inducing the Spanish to enter the war. But all of this could not be known in London and the danger of these important islands falling into German hands had to be guarded against. Consequently considerable resources were locked up in preparing for a threat which never materialized.[9] These resources included 4 Commandos which Keyes thought could be put to better use elsewhere [42, 44, 46].

Keyes was aching to undertake some offensive action and, remembering the use of maritime power by Pitt the Elder during the Seven Years' War, he thought the proper place to make use of such amphibious forces as they possessed was in the Mediterranean. Here Keyes chose as his objective the Italian island of Pantelleria located between Sicily and Tunisia some 150 miles to the north west of Malta [43]. Churchill had asked Keyes in September if he had ever considered the possibility of capturing the island. Keyes replied that he had thought of it a good deal and that he considered it quite feasible.[10] This Operation, designated 'Workshop', would occupy the major portion of his attention for the remainder of the year.

Keyes planned to seize Pantelleria with approximately 2,500 Commandos, embarked in ships which would peel off from a Malta bound convoy during the hours of darkness. Naturally he wanted to lead the force in person and would gladly have reverted in rank to Rear- or Vice-Admiral in order to do so [45, 47]. Keyes was never certain the busy Prime Minister would see all of his minutes and on November 19th he appealed for a personal interview [48]. Operation 'Workshop' caught Churchill's imagination and during an air raid on the night of the 19th he sent an armoured car to Keyes's home in Chelsea to bring him to a meeting of the Defence Committee, at which the Prime Minister strongly supported the operation. The meeting ended with an order to Keyes to prepare the necessary plans. Keyes was overjoyed for Churchill told him he would not have anything to do with it 'unless you do it and lead it'. Keyes's diary for the period November 19th to December 9th [49] provides a vivid picture of Keyes's enthusiasm, the hesitancy of the respective staffs, and their interaction with Churchill who clearly emerges as the major force in pushing the operation as far as it went.

The plan for Operation 'Workshop' called for landing in two isolated bays in the south and east of the island with the objective of capturing the island's military headquarters and the main defensive battery while a diversionary bombardment of the town itself was to be carried out by one or two cruisers from the westward [54]. The assault was to commence at 2 a.m. with the aim of completely capturing the island within 12 to 24 hours. Both Keyes's staff and the Joint Planning Staff considered the plan from a purely tactical point of view to have a good chance of success against Italian resistance.[11] But from a strategic point of view the Chiefs of Staff doubted there were sufficient air or naval resources to retain Pantelleria after its capture. Admiral Sir Andrew Cunningham, Mediterranean Commander-in-Chief, was also strongly opposed to 'Workshop', especially as he had other and in his view more important uses for his light craft [55b]. Churchill's signal to Cunningham with its references to the example of Zeebrugge suggests that Keyes had influenced the Prime Minister perhaps more than he realized [55a].

There was a clear division over 'Workshop' between Churchill and Keyes on one side and the Chiefs of Staff on the other. Admiral Sir William W. Davis was then a member of the Joint Planning Staff (Future Operational Planning Section) lent to Keyes for the operation and acting as liaison between the different factions. He remembers: 'To some extent I found myself the "meat in the sandwich" between those powerful forces, but I always maintained that though risky the operation itself – the assault on the island – had a chance of success provided of course the weather did not turn wholly unsuitable.'[12]

But however bright the tactical prospects of 'Workshop' might have been, the strategic aspect was another and more controversial matter. Cunningham remained unshaken in his opposition, largely on the grounds that, while the island might be relatively easy to capture, its retention would be more trouble than it was worth.[13] He was not impressed by Keyes's arguments and even less inspired at the prospect of Keyes coming out to the Mediterranean [53, 77]. Whether or not Churchill would actually have overruled his professional advisers on 'Workshop' must remain an open question for by mid-December the situation had altered sufficiently to give them new and strong arguments for at least postponing the operation. General Wavell's offensive against the Italians in the Western Desert had begun on December 9th and had within a few days achieved great success. But this raised the prospect of a German counter-stroke to bolster their Italian allies and such a move might be directed at the Atlantic Islands. It therefore seemed unwise to lock up amphibious forces, shipping and naval escorts while the situation was so uncertain and 'Workshop' was postponed until the moonless period in January [55c].

Not surprisingly Keyes was appalled when he learned of the decision and one can easily understand his frustration [56 – 62]. He remembered from the Zeebrugge-Ostend operations in 1918 the difficulties in keeping keyed-up troops well motivated during repeated postponements, but he hoped 'Workshop' might still take place the following month. He was destined to be disappointed for 'Workshop' was completely abandoned at the end of January.[14] The arrival in strength of considerable German airpower in the Mediterranean – which Keyes was still inclined to depreciate – had greatly diminished the chances of success [67, 68].

Three of Keyes's Commandos, including the one in which his son Geoffrey was serving, were sent to the Middle East at the beginning of February 1941. Keyes was dismayed for he interpreted this as a futile dispersion of the amphibious striking force he had so painfully assembled. Moreover, signifiant operations would now be excluded until new Commandos were available [64]. Keyes and his commanders feared it would be difficult to keep the enthusiastic volunteers, who had the right to request transfer back to their old units, in the Commandos if these élite troops continued to remain unemployed [64]. At one point Keyes's language against the Naval Staff became so strong that Churchill was moved to rebuke him [65].

Keyes had also seized on an alternative to 'Workshop' called 'Yorker'. This involved a landing on the island of Sardinia at Cagliari, and Keyes tried to use the prospect of 'Yorker' to avoid the dispersion of his Commandos [66, 69]. He was unsuccessful. His continued frustration in efforts to wage offensive war led him to write another long letter to Churchill asking that he be permitted to lead the raid on Sardinia and recounting his frustrations with the Naval Staff since becoming DCO. Keyes ended by proposing Churchill make him either Under-Secretary of Defence or First Sea Lord and Chief of Naval Staff; and should the First Lord, A. V. Alexander, not accept him – for the second time – then Churchill should appoint him as First Lord in place of Alexander [70, 71]. Churchill returned the letter remarking that it was impossible for him to receive one of that character [72].

Keyes was quite ready to resign if, in his eyes, he was not to be 'a real Director of Combined Operations' [73]. On March 14th he received partial satisfaction when a new directive was issued giving the DCO, under the general direction of the Minister of Defence and Chiefs of Staff, the duty of training the special service troops and landing craft personnel, initiating operations for these troops, and the responsibilty for the planning and execution of raiding operations which involved not more than 5,000 men [78]. Keyes was to advise the Chiefs of Staff on technical aspects of opposed landings, and be present at those meetings where that part of the plan was discussed. Moreover he would be responsible for the development of special equipment and craft required for opposed landings and have under his command and direction the Inter-Services Training and Development Centre.[15]

In March 1941 Keyes was able to carry out a successful raid from home waters [80]. This was Operation 'Claymore' – a descent on the Lofoten Islands in northern Norway – which foreshadowed similar raids after Keyes had left office.[16] Keyes himself, thinking in terms of major overseas amphibious operations, tended to downgrade the affair [76]. On the other hand, he would obviously have loved to take personal command of the supporting naval forces and issued strong hints to the C-in-C Home Fleet along this line [74]. They were politely declined [75].

The Atlantic Islands remained a major concern in the spring of 1941 because of the possibility that the recent success of the German Afrika Korps in the Mediterranean theatre might now induce Spain to enter the war. Keyes was deeply involved in the planning for Operation 'Puma', the seizure of Grand Canary Island.[17] He remembered the German initiative in Norway and advocated seizing the islands as a preventative measure [81–84]. Of course Keyes realized this could well provoke Spanish hostility which would make Gibraltar untenable for the fleet, but he considered possession of the islands 'infinitely more important' for the battle of the Atlantic. He tried to enlist the support of Anthony Eden, but the Foreign Secretary remained non-committal towards this proposed violation of Spanish neutrality [85–87].

Keyes also tried to involve the Americans in his plans for the Atlantic Islands. His Secretary, Paymaster-Captain Herbert Woolley, a retired officer married to an American, who had been with Keyes at the Dardanelles, returned to the United States in June to be attached to the British Mission in Washington. Keyes took advantage of his old friendship with the influential American financier Bernard Baruch to arrange for Woolley to have an interview with President Roosevelt [89]. In July Woolley was able to present Keyes's plans for 'Puma' to the President and his adviser Harry Hopkins. The Americans appeared to be far more interested in the Azores and these discussions had no effect on the operations or on Keyes's fortunes. However, as the United States was still neutral, Woolley's detailed report provides an interesting picture of these apparently unofficial conversations concerning the island possessions of other neutral powers, as well as the activities of the British Mission in Washington [90].

Although in retrospect the German attack on Russia on June 22nd removed any possibility that Spain would enter the war on the side of the Axis or that the Germans would devote the resources necessary to seize one or more of the Atlantic Islands, the force for Operation 'Puma' remained in being throughout the summer of 1941. Moreover, the original convoy was expanded into a much larger one and 'Puma' became 'Pilgrim'. This force was destined to be tied up until February 1942.[18] Keyes, constantly anxious for offensive action, thought it wrong to keep their only amphibious force locked up for an operation which was less likely than ever to take place. He felt that with the Germans tied down on the eastern front the moment was ripe for offensive action, and proposed either a major raid under full fighter cover across the Channel or using the 'Pilgrim' force against Sardinia in the Mediterranean [93–96].

On August 10th 'Pilgrim' Force conducted a large scale exercise – 'Leapfrog' – at Scapa Flow which was intended to serve as a dress rehearsal for the actual operation. Exercise 'Leapfrog' set in motion the chain of events which led to Keyes's dismissal as DCO. There were many mistakes committed during the exercise and Keyes was outspoken in his criticism of its conduct [98].[19] The joint commanders, Lieutenant-General H. G. Alexander and Rear-Admiral L. H. K. Hamilton submitted, in turn, a report to the Chiefs of Staff Committee in which they claimed that 'the machinery for the execution of combined operations, including training, is basically at fault' for the difficulties revealed by 'Leapfrog'. They recommended that 'Force Commanders be directed to deal solely with the Service Ministries and not be partially responsible to an outside Directorate, thus avoiding divided control at the outset, which is bound to lead to confusion and chaos.'[20]

The controversy over 'Leapfrog' coincided with Keyes's questioning of the viability of 'Pilgrim'. He proposed as an alternative plan that a major force including carriers, and possibly American warships, be sent to coerce the Spanish into yielding the island for the duration of the war. If they resisted they were to be overwhelmed [100]. He also objected to the Naval Staff's intention to send some of the smaller ships of 'Pilgrim' force to Freetown before the autumn and winter gales made their passage across the Bay of Biscay too hazardous [98, 99, 101–105]. This in his opinion was folly, for it would split their amphibious force and deprive them of the smaller ships necessary for undertaking operations in home waters. Added to the existing friction, Keyes's challenging of 'Pilgrim' was intolerable to the Chiefs of Staff. Their feelings are perhaps best expressed by General Pownall, then Vice Chief of the Imperial General Staff:

'Roger Keyes is a great nuisance. As Director of Combined Operations, a post invented by Winston, he butts in continually on matters concerning the "Pilgrim" Operation – because it is seaborne. Under Alexander and Hamilton who must be responsible for the training of the men for the operation for whose success they are responsible, it is in good hands. But Keyes continually interferes and not only with them but also with the Chiefs of Staff. Keyes continually criticizes the strategical aspect of the whole thing, and that is no business of his whatever. But Winston put him in and it's the devil of a job to get him out. Not that Winston has any real faith in him, I'm sure. But his nominees, good or bad, remain.'[21]

Pownall, former Chief of Staff to Lord Gort in the BEF, had been the object of Keyes's criticism for his role in the closing days of the Belgian campaign the year before and there was little love lost between the two. But his remarks clearly indicate that relations between the Chiefs of Staff and the Director of Combined Operations had reached the crisis stage. In early September the Chiefs of Staff proposed the creation of a new inter-service organisation dealing with combined operations. They pointed out to Keyes, in a conciliatory fashion, that most of his proposals had been incorporated in the area dealing with training and equipment.[22] Not surprisingly Keyes raised a major objection to the greatly reduced role he would have in the planning and execution of operations [97, 98]. According to the Chiefs of Staff the Director of Combined Operations would now become an 'Adviser on Combined Operations' with no powers of initiation, command and execution such as the DCO had possessed. The memoranda involved in this reorganisation are far too voluminous to reproduce. The Chiefs of Staff were willing to meet some of Keyes's objections, but they remained firm on the major point that the DCO would become an adviser [106]. Keyes's protests were noted at the Chiefs of Staff meeting on September 29th, but they endorsed their new memorandum and submitted it to the Prime Minister.[23] Churchill accepted these proposals and warned Keyes that he would find it very hard to resist the advice of all his responsible experts [107]. Keyes's conscience, however, would not permit him to accept and he explained why in a long letter on October 2nd and again on the 4th [108, 109].

Churchill, apparently with great reluctance, came to the conclusion that Keyes must go. He wrote Keyes on the 4th that he had no choice but to arrange for his relief [110]. According to Colonel Hollis, then Secretary of the Chiefs of Staff Committee, the letter caused him considerable grief and he was ready to stop it the next morning if it had not yet been sent.[24] Keyes himself had been prepared to make alternate suggestions to the Chiefs of Staff, but Churchill told him the decision had been reached, it was too late, and he would be relieved on the 19th by Captain Louis Mountbatten [111, 112]. Initially, Mountbatten had the title 'Adviser on Combined Operations'. Keyes was obviously hurt that Churchill did not see him or at least wait until the Chiefs of Staff had examined his new proposals before arranging for his relief [113]. Churchill, however, was anxious to avoid becoming involved in a personal argument and it is easy to imagine how painful such an interview would have been [114]. He also rejected Keyes's proposal that he be permitted to go out to the Middle East as adviser to an organisation to be established there for the study of combined operations [115, 116]. Churchill did try, unsuccessfully as it turned out, to obtain a high office for Keyes in Northern Ireland, but he continued to refuse a personal interview [118, 121].

There is a danger in publishing a collection of documents such as these that the disputes they reflect will present an overly negative picture of Keyes's tenure as DCO. One must point out his very considerable achievement, after starting with little in the way of men and material, in establishing a Combined Operations Headquarters, sheltering it from jealous service ministries, and laying the foundations for an organisation which would grow in size and complexity and play such a major role in the great amphibious operations later in the war. Moreover, Keyes with his fiery spirit no doubt contributed enormously in helping to instill and encourage the particular dash and élan which made the Commandos famous. One can only quote Brigadier Fergusson, author of the authoritative history of combined operations, who wrote: 'It was part of his tragedy that he could only see what he had failed to do out of all that he thought could and should have been done.' Fergusson concluded:

> 'His biggest achievement was the actual setting up of C.O.H.Q. (although former Commandos, full of strange oaths and mindful of the days when they were bearded like the pard, still swear by him, and maintain that it was he who endowed them with much of their legendary spirit). C.O.H.Q. could never have flourished in infancy under the roof of any one of the Service Ministries, nor under an officer of whatever calibre who restricted his allegiance to any one Service. It would have been a tender plant indeed if the Prime Minister's close relationship with Keyes had not acted as a cloche. And technical development, for which Keyes himself had little bent, was able to flourish to some degree under his protection, though it had no great share of his enthusiasm.'[25]

Keyes was indeed unfortunate to have taken office at a period in the war when the resources to implement his great plans were lacking. It is striking to contrast the numbers of men and types of equipment with which Keyes worked with the vast amount of men and material available two or three years later. But this serene perspective was not available to Keyes in October 1941 and he keenly felt his removal from an active role in the war, and regretted even more the opportunities for his Commandos which he felt were being neglected [117].

36. *Directive to General Bourne*[1] *on Raiding Operations*

[Copy]

SECRET
C.O.S. (40) 468
17th JUNE 1940

WAR CABINET
CHIEFS OF STAFF COMMITTEE

RAIDING OPERATIONS: DIRECTIVE TO GENERAL BOURNE

We have approved the attached directive[Ø] to Lieut. General A. G. B. BOURNE, C.B., D.S.O., M.V.O., who has been appointed Commander, Raiding Operations, and adviser to the Chiefs of Staff on combined operations.

(Signed) R. E. C. PEIRSE
V.C.A.S.
T. S. V. PHILLIPS
V.C.N.S.
R. H. HAINING
V.C.I.G.S.

Ø Annex.

ANNEX
DIRECTIVE

To:- LIEUT. GENERAL A. G. B. BOURNE, C.B., D.S.O., M.V.O., Royal Marines.

1. You are appointed Commander of Raiding Operations on coasts in enemy occupation and adviser to the Chiefs of Staff on combined operations.

Raiding Operations

2. The object of raiding operations will be to harass the enemy and cause him to disperse his forces, and to create material damage, particularly on the coastline from Northern Norway to the western limit of German-occupied France.

3. We propose to give you, within the limits of the forces and equipment available, and subject to directions which you receive from time to time from the Chiefs of Staff, complete discretion in the choice of

objectives and the scale of operation undertaken. The Joint Intelligence Sub-Committee have been instructed to help you in the choice of suitable objectives. You are to keep the Chiefs of Staff informed of the operations you propose to carry out.

4. Six independent companies and a School of Training in Irregular Operations have already been raised by the War Office. These and the irregular commandos now being raised will come under your operational command and any administrative suggestions you may wish to make, e.g., for the organisation of units, their location in the United Kingdom, etc., will be met as far as they can be.

In addition the War Office have taken preliminary steps to raise parachutist volunteers, of whom a number will be placed under your command. When raised, they will be trained by the Air Ministry and the War Office according to your requirements and advice.

5. Should you want further independent units, over and above those already raised, you should discuss your requirements with Service Department and advise us accordingly.

6. Certain raids by the independent companies have already been planned by the General Staff in the War Office. You should make yourself acquainted with such projects at once and take over control of any planned raids when you deem it advisable.

7. Irregular actions of various types are undertaken from time to time by the Service Intelligence Departments. There must therefore be close touch between your staff and these departments, in order that your several activities shall not interfere with each other and that, on occasions, co-operation may be possible.

Combined Operations

8. Your second role will be to take over command of the Inter-Services Training & Development Centres and to act as our adviser on the organisation required for opposed landings.

9. Three brigade groups are being detailed for special training in combined operations as soon as they can be equipped. Of these one may be made available at your request for purely raiding operations, in which case it would, of course, be placed under your command. You will, however, be responsible for supervising the technical training of all troops earmarked for combined operations.

In addition we wish you to press on with the development and production of special landing craft and equipment and to advise us, when the occasion arises, as to its allotment.

10. If it is decided to undertake a combined operation, detailed plans will be worked out by the Service Departments (through the medium of the Inter-Service Planning Staff) and the commander designate. Both will require your technical advice and help.

Relations with other Staffs
11. We are directing the Inter-Service Planning Staff to consult you whenever they receive a combined operational project for examination, which implies a landing on a hostile shore.

You should maintain close liaison with this staff and also with the operational and intelligence staffs of the Service Departments and with the Inter-Service Project Board. At the same time, you will have direct access to the Chiefs of Staff Committee, who will also advise you of any combined operations which are envisaged.

Headquarters and Staff
12. Your headquarters will be at the Admiralty. You should let us know as soon as possible what staff you need.
13. An Officer of the Royal Air Force will be attached to your staff, who will also be responsible, under the Air Ministry, for the development, as far as the Air Force are concerned, of parachute troops and other air requirements for raiding and irregular operations.

Secrecy
14. You will appreciate the paramount need for secrecy.

37. *Keyes to Churchill*

[Holograph] Richmond Terrace,
Whitehall, S.W.1.
22.7.40.

My dear Winston,

I must tell you how happy I am – and that I am most grateful to you for giving me this oportunity of proving that I am not as useless as my detractors, whoever they may be, would have you think.

I am your very devoted,

Roger

[P.S.] I am going slow, as you advised me to, and when I have got both feet well in the stirrups and I am ready, my knees well dug in, to take on any obstacle, I will come and tell you.

38. *Keyes to Admiral Sir Walter Cowan*[2]

[Holograph]
Richmond Terrace,
Whitehall, S.W.1.
28.7.40.

I was very glad to hear from you. I wondered what you would do when the war really began. I am glad you had such a wonderful season before it started.

I have been eating my heart out, Churchill tried hard to find a job for me but Pound & Co. told him I had had my chance in the last war – it was not fair to the younger generation if we were employed – I did not want rank – pay or uniform. I only wanted to be in a position to know what was going on and make suggestions.

However I was "taboo" at the Admiralty. I only heard what was going on in Norway by chance. Eva got German measles while we were staying for one night at Admiralty House [Portsmouth] to see my son who was then in a destroyer. So we had to stay about a week until she was allowed to travel, and I was able to go into James' War Room, and I was simply shocked watching the gutless way the naval campaign was being run – and the fate which awaited Carton de Wiart at Trondjhem if we did not go into the Fiord – there was nothing to stop us. I fought for about a fortnight as hard as I have ever fought in my life for anything, to get them to do anything offensive, and when they said they couldn't afford the ships owing to the Italian situation – I said I'd do it with a couple of old obsolete cruisers and 2 or 3 destroyers. I thought there were 2 or 3 German destroyers inside – but as a matter of fact there were only a destroyer and a TBD which smashed up the head of our column and landed troops behind them and took 200 prisoners. There were only 4 old 8" dated 1901 – in shields, and two torpedo tubes on rafts. The guns could be knocked out by a battleship or 8" cruiser outside their range. C. d. W. told me he came down expecting to find British vessels where [?] he found 2 Germans.

During the winter I went 3 times to Brussels at the invitation of the much maligned King Leopold and arranged a wonderful liaison for the B.E.F. – they were given every sort of information to help them take up the [line missing] . . . High Command gave them in the event of Belgium being attacked, and thanks to me the French also got all they wanted.

It was the Belgian Govt. who declined to have any Staff talks. The French were determined to fight in Belgium and hoped of course to keep the war out of France. When the truth is known, and I have put it on record in the War Office and Foreign Office backed by much documentary evidence and cypher telegrams, it will be established that the King did everything in his power to save the BEF and help it to withdraw – even to the extent of sacrificing his own army – before the *BEF* left it to its fate. When history is written it will be recognised that the King and I did our utmost to save the BEF from its fate. It is not a pretty story. I will tell it to you when we meet. I left Bruges at 10 p.m. on 27th [May] with the Germans in the outskirts in a plain cloth suit of the Queen's Secretary – and escaped from Nieuport just before dawn in an MTB having seized a fishing boat as dawn was breaking and we feared the German bombers which roared overhead all night would spot us at daylight. All the Belgian Mission – a splendid lot of soldiers and airmen who I had seen a lot of throughout the campaign (British Mission to Belgian Army) were in a ship which left Ostend at midnight and was torpedoed by an MTB which then machine gunned them in the water – only one Air Force officer survived – and 2 or 3 men out of 70 – a Colonel and a Major having seen the Mission off safely then got 8 men and came to look for me. To that they owe their lives.

I forgot to mention that directly that war started W.C. got the Govt. (he was still 1st Lord) to send me out to Belgium and I flew at once.

It was very interesting – but heart breaking, having to retire every night and fight every day in a weaker position – because the French failed about 100 miles away from us. The French were too awful. The Belgians fought very well.

I wasn't popular when I got home and told the *truth* which was not what W.C. or the Govt. wanted to hear – and for seven weeks after I let myself go at a Cabinet . . . immediately I arrived in London – I did not see W.C., but on 16th July he sent for me and offered me the appointment which I suppose you saw in some confidential list of appts., the 3 Chiefs of Staff gave instructions that it wasn't to be given any publicity. I am having a very interesting time, but there is very little equipment – and all the kind of craft I want were lost in Norway or at Dunkirk.

I am off to Scotland on Wednesday until Sunday, but if you are in London next week I'd like immensely to have a yarn with you.

I am in the same sort of position as I was in 1917 when I was dragged down from the Grand Fleet – only this time for the 3 services – but I don't suppose that I will be told – as I was by Rosie[3] – to do the things I urged myself. I hope I shall see you soon. It is grand of you to serve as a Commander under your brother . . .

[P.S.] The fox hunters and polo players have played up well in this war, as of old.

39. *Keyes to Tomkinson*

[Holograph]

Richmond Terrace,
Whitehall, S.W.1.
29.7.40.

Many thanks for your letter.

W.C. did not speak to me for 7 weeks after I got back from Belgium – and said exactly what I thought! It was not popular then but I proved right.

But a fortnight ago he sent for me and offered me the appt. which had been held by Bourne, – and Bourne elected to stay on as my deputy rather than go back to the AGRM.

It certainly is an interesting job with great possibilities *when* the aircraft and naval craft needed are available. At present we are immobile. I have many interesting things to see – last week I flew to Manchester – or rather an aerodrome near by and on Wednesday I am going to the N.W. of Scotland. I was delighted to find that Geoffrey had volunteered and been selected for one of the corps that come under me...

I had a wonderful day last week with W.C. looking at an armoured Brigade in Northamptonshire – as we lunched and dined in the train and did not get back until 10 p.m. I had a good innings – and got a good deal off my chest. I wish Hitler could have heard us at dinner. W.C. was in boisterous form. I must say he is a great fellow! He said to me à propos of his getting me a job: "You have a great many detractors." I said: "So had you – but you are there now in spite of it." He replied: "There are no competitors for my job now, I didn't get it until they had got into a mess."

Among the Regts. we saw was Peter W. Powlett's,[4] but as bad luck would have it he was away on 48 hours leave with Katherine seeing their babies at his people's in Cornwall. Also Randolph[5] [Churchill] looking like Goering[6] – Winston asked me to get him into one of my Corps and I have arranged for him to go into one commanded by old Joe Laycock's[7] son[8] – who when a subaltern in the Blues went round the Cape in a windjammer before the mast.

W.C. meant the job for me from the outset – but the 3 C. of S. appt.'d Bourne when W.C. wasn't looking! He had not enough guns – and I really believe was glad to get me. Old Godfrey[9] is filling his place temporarily – frankly (not for anyone but you) I would prefer the positions reversed...

40. *Memorandum by Keyes*

SECRET [Richmond Terrace, S.W.1.]
C.O.S. (40) 635 [16th August, 1940.]
[Copy]

WAR CABINET

CHIEFS OF STAFF COMMITTEE

PLANNING FOR COMBINED OPERATIONS

Memorandum by the Director of Combined Operations

Reference C.O.S. (40) 468,[10] paragraph 10, my experience to date of the system outlined leads me to propose the following modifications in procedure in order that fuller use may be made of the combined operations knowledge of this Directorate.

2. I recommend that when an operation has passed the Joint Planning stage, the detailed tactical planning be made by the Combined Operations Directorate instead of by the Inter-Service Planning Staff; the latter staff being called upon for details of shipping, etc. This was done in the case of the KIRKENES project.

3. Also in the next stage, when the Commanders are appointed, that this Directorate should be responsible for making arrangements for providing the Commanders with all the necessary Intelligence, for assisting them with advice as required, and for placing them in touch with the Inter-Service Planning Staff. This Directorate would also be responsible for assisting the Commanders in any arrangements necessary for Combined Operations training, and for ensuring that the arrangements made by the Inter-Service Planning Staff were such as to ensure the carrying out of the Commanders' detailed plans.

4. Finally, I recommend that it be considered to be within my responsibility to represent my views to the Chiefs of Staff on the Commanders' plans, if for any reason I considered it to be in the public interest for me to do so. This does not include matters of detail in the plan which must, of course, be the responsibility of the Commanders.

41. Keyes to Churchill

[Holograph]
[Copy]

Offices of the War Cabinet,
Richmond Terrace,
Whitehall, S.W.1.
24.8.40.

Are you going to risk failure at Dakar?
Do you think for one moment that if you had sent me to Oran I would not have:
1. Gone in myself and used all my personal influence and prestige with the French Navy to persuade the Admiral to accept the honourable terms offered.
2. If unsuccessful, that I would not have insured the destruction of all the French vessels of military value before nightfall.
I could not have laid off like Parker at Copenhagen.
However, I have faith in Almighty God – and you – and Orion is blazing in the southern sky . . .

[P.S.] And I am learning to "wait and not be tired of waiting" – "being lied about" – "of being hated" – patiently [?] confident that I will before long be given the opportunity of proving that the youth of the Navy and Army will act as offensively overseas and face death as contemptuously as the young knights of the air do every day . . .

42. Keyes to Churchill

Secret and Personal
[Carbon]

31.10.40.

Prime Minister
You told me to come to you direct if I wished. I have not troubled you with my difficulties and I have been very patient, but golden opportunities are being missed and I am convinced will continue to be missed unless you give me the power to plan and organise combined operations and be responsible to you – *direct* – for their execution.[11]

The C.I.G.S. has done everything in his power to help me and I have established very good relations both in the War Office and Air Ministry. I have a splendid body of troops – properly equipped thanks to your intervention – and a fighting Brigadier at my disposal, but I am thwarted at every turn by the C.N.S. who seems to dominate the Chiefs of Staff Committee as far as Combined Operations are concerned.

You told me early in last May that the C.O.S. Committee had all the power and might well lose the war – It will certainly postpone the winning of the war as long as it is constituted as it is and retains the power it still apparently possesses.

I represented my difficulties to General Ismay[12] a week ago and he promised to try to get the Committee to reconsider my minute of 16th August[13] but I have heard nothing since.

However in the meantime after watching the delays and miscarriages in connection with the preparation of BRISK,[14] and the failure to make immediate use of the forces available at Home in offensive action in the Mediterranean, I have come to the conclusion that I can be of little use to you for the prosecution of the war as long as I am in any way under the Chiefs of Staff Committee.

I attach a diagram of the organisation which I believe to be essential for the efficient and prompt prosecution of Combined Operations[15] – But better still would be to make me your deputy, with the Chiefs of Staff under my direction, so far as Combined Operations are concerned.

It would be quite impossible to exaggerate the fierce resentment which is felt by young officers including a number of Captains and Commanders in the Admiralty over the repeated miscarriages which have been condoned, the lack of offensive direction and the fact that *we are always too late.*

I have been much in contact lately with officers in the Army who are spoiling to wipe out the humiliating defeats the Army has suffered.

Are the Navy and the Army never to be allowed to strike offensively and prove that they are as valiant as their brothers in the R.A.F.?

43. *Proposal by Keyes for the Capture of Pantelleria*

(a) *Keyes to Churchill*

Most Secret[16]

2nd November 1940.

[Carbon]

You will be glad to hear that at a Chiefs of Staff meeting I attended this morning Phillips,[17] who represented the C.N.S., said that they had discussed my proposition to capture Pantellaria last night, and it attracted them immensely. C.I.G.S. and C.A.S. concurred and instructions were given that the project was to be studied by E.P.S. and my Directorate.

It can't fail if it is properly planned – prepared for – and prosecuted fiercely. After Pantelleria is garrisoned a Commando might stay there for a bit to raid from there – and the remainder go on to Crete.

We could carry 4 Commandos in two "Glen" liners. One is in

service – another, though much delayed, should be ready in all respects by 30th November.

(b) Keyes to Chiefs of Staff

[Carbon]
MOST SECRET
D.C.O. No. P 18.   30th October, 1940.

Chiefs of Staff Committee.
1. I desire to draw attention to the possibilities of a small Combined Operation which I consider to be within the scope of the troops which have been specially organised for offensive operation under my direction.
2. Pantellaria appears to offer great possibilities as a British base

(i)   for staging aircraft to the Middle East.
(ii)   for controlling the Tunis-Sicily Channel.
(iii) for making air attacks on Italy and Sardinia (even Genoa is within 500 miles of Pantelleria).
(iv)   as a threat to Tunis to curb the projects there of the Vichy Government.

3. The main advantage of Pantelleria over Malta is the excellent aerodrome with its underground hangers, repair shops and storage. Since 1935 Italy has spent well over 100 million lira on the construction of these facilities, defences, harbour works, water supply, etc. There are at least 9 underground hangers and it is reported that they can accommodate upwards of 200 bombers and fighters.
   Here exists a ready made air base well protected against air attack where our bombers might safely be based. The importance of such a base would be enhanced if the Italians succeeded in reducing the facilities of Malta as an air base in the staging of aircraft reinforcements to the Middle East.
4. The capture of Pantelleria would not entail a major operation in the sense that land forces required would be very limited and the duration of the operation would be brief. Initial surprise should suffice to effect the landing of sufficient force to overcome the garrison which cannot be large on account of the limitations of the water supply.
   There are a number of possible landing places, though admittedly not sandy beaches, within 2 to 4 miles of the aerodrome and of all the fixed defence positions.

5. Malta is under 140 miles distant so that aircraft could be quickly flown there as soon as the aerodrome falls into our hands.
6. The defences consist of: –

> 6 11" guns
> 26 4.7" guns
> 68 3" A.A. guns.

The position of all these batteries is known but the information about the garrison is scant. It is estimated that it does not exceed one Battalion of Infantry in addition to the personnel manning the fixed defences.

44. *Keyes to Churchill*

[Carbon] 5th November, 1940.

In the attached paper[18] to the Chiefs of Staff I have asked for the return of the four Commandos standing by to carry out "Brisk" as Brigadier Morford,[19] the officer appointed to command the operation, says he does not need them. Moreover, it appears neither he nor the Joint Planning Staff consider "Brisk" a feasible operation in the face of organised German opposition until the summer months – A conclusion which leaves me speechless.

Under the circumstances I do not think the Commandos who are trained for offensive warfare and spoiling to fight should be sidetracked for an operation which only entails the overcoming of Portuguese resistance and may never be undertaken.

I am most strongly of the opinion that the capture of Pantelleria and the arrival of Commandos in Crete should be pressed forward with the greatest despatch. If you will place this operation under my direction, with your backing, I will use every endeavour to ensure that we will not be too late once again.

45. *Memorandum by Keyes*

[Holograph] [7th November 1940.]

Copy of note given to Winston at the "Other Club" on ½ a menu on the night of 7th Nov. 1940.

"Let me take two or three thousand of my 'braves' to Crete to TEASE the Italians in the Aegean, annoying them on the way out.

Degraded to Rear or Vice Admiral if necessary.
After I have organised them for raiding I can fly home."

46. *Keyes to Churchill*

[Carbon]   14th November, 1940.

You asked me more than two months ago if I thought that we could capture *Pantellaria*[20] and I told you that I had thought a great deal about it, and I was sure we could.

I asked for aerial photographs to be taken – as the only ones available were three years old – but after waiting some weeks was told that none could be taken until an operation was approved!

On *7th October* I was told to prepare four Commandos to carry out "Brisk", which I did, but the matter was taken out of my hands as the C.N.S. did not consider that the operation was a raid. Subsequently Brigadier Morford returned to England and was given command of the operation. He told me that he did not require the Commandos and could do the operation as originally arranged without them.

On the 30th October I suggested the operation *P* to the Chiefs of Staff and at a Chiefs of Staff Meeting on 2nd November I was told by V.C.N.S. that he and the C.N.S. were strongly in favour of it and was directed in conjunction with E.P.S. to prepare an outline plan. I asked that the photographs might be taken without any further delay. Air Marshal Portal[21] directed that this should be done at once and they have arrived today.

On the 2nd November I received a Joint Planning Staff paper in which it was stated that neither they nor Brigadier Morford, the Officer appointed to command "Brisk," considered "Brisk" feasible, in the face of German organised opposition, until the summer months!

In the circumstances, on the 5th November I asked for the return of the Commandos in order that they might be trained for the other operation.

At a Meeting of the Chiefs of Staff on 11th November, the C.N.S. told me that there had been some misunderstanding – Brigadier Morford had been directed to prepare a revised plan for "Brisk" to meet the case of the Germans forestalling us – and I was instructed that the Commandos were to remain part of the "Brisk" force.

I submit that: –

(1) Immediate offensive action against the Italians is of paramount importance. That my Commandos should be released from the side-track, into which they have been diverted, to carry out a problematic

operation under a Brigadier who would storm the gates of Hell if ordered to, but who can only think of difficulties directly he has supreme responsibility – like 99 per cent. Naval and Military officers.
(2) That orders be given at once for the 3 "Glens"[22] to be ready by the end of November to embark 6 Commandos for the MEDITERRANEAN. The DUTCH and BELGIAN vessels[23] to follow directly they are ready.
(3) In the meantime other arrangements should be made to assist to accommodate the regular troops under training at INVERARAY. This should present no difficulty and I will make the necessary arrangements.
(4) No Naval Staff bearing responsibility could be induced to force the DARDANELLES.

No Naval Staff would have considered for one moment the storming of ZEEBRUGGE and other operations I undertook on the Belgian coast.

History repeats itself. In September, 1917, I was withdrawn from command of a battle squadron in the Grand Fleet to be Director of (Offensive) Plans at the Admiralty. I was thwarted at every turn. It was not until the opposition of Jellicoe and Bacon was eliminated that I was allowed to wage offensive warfare in the Narrow Seas, which I did from the 1st January, 1918, until the end of the war.

Don't tell a soul yet that you are going to send Rear or Vice Admiral *R.K.* to the MEDITERRANEAN to capture *Pantelleria* and organise 3,000 special troops for the Commanders-in-Chief of the MEDITERRANEAN Fleet and MIDDLE EAST to carry out raids from *Malta, Pantelleria, Crete* and perhaps farther afield *in the Aegean*. I am sure the two Commanders-in-Chief would be delighted to agree, and after this has been done *R.K.* can fly home and resume his rank and appointment.

There could be no more effective or striking way of aiding GREECE in her hour of peril.

[Holograph] I would like to go to Scotland with my Brigadier not later than Monday night to start intensive training of each unit for its respective task and to ensure success – we can't fail. I beg you to approve and back a winner.

47. *Keyes to Churchill*

[Carbon] 15th November, 1940.

The attached paper[24] has been submitted to the Chiefs of Staff by the

Joint Planning Staff. It blows hot and cold and like the recommendations of most councils of war – if acted upon – would result in nothing being done.

Of course it is important to raid and capture Islands in the Dodecanese and raiding troops should have been on their way to Crete long ago.[25] I urged this on 29th October but nothing has been done except to sidetrack the raiding troops and all the vessels ready to carry them for the problematic operation against the Portuguese Islands.

Admittedly the capture of *Pantelleria*[26] would have less effect on Turkey and Greece than an island in the Dodecanese but as a blow to Italy's prestige it would probably have a far greater effect – especially as the Joint Planning Staff do not consider the capture of Rhodes or Leros as feasible operations, *yet at any rate*.

As no doubt the Italians are already expecting an expedition against the Dodecanese, an attack on *Pantelleria* would almost certainly constitute a strategic surprise for Italy, and could be undertaken on the way to Crete without delaying action against the Dodecanese.

It may be noted that the Joint Planning Staff have not made any suggestions for the *immediate* despatch of troops and vessels to Crete to carry out offensive operations or taken any other steps except to refer a number of suggestions, we have made, to the Commanders in Chief of the Mediterranean and Middle East for their consideration.

The Commanders in Chief, however, have not the means – which we possess – to carry out these operations. Of course they would welcome the co-operation and help which could be given by my Directorate, and the specially trained troops and seamen, and vessels and boats which we have been preparing, and I beg you to despatch 6 Commandos to the Mediterranean as I have asked in my minute of the 14th at the earliest possible moment.

I have just been asked to attend a meeting of the Chiefs of Staff tomorrow (Saturday) morning. I will do my best to persuade them to take this action.

48. *Keyes to Churchill*

[Copy]

D.C.O.'s Office,
War Cabinet Office Annexe,
Richmond Terrace, S.W.1.
19.11.40.

If my friendship and my devotion to you for so many years means anything to you, please send for me soon.

I am tormented by the delays and hesitations which I am powerless to overcome, and the golden opportunities which will slip by unless you take a hand now and insist on proper use being made of the Commandos to harry the Italians . . .

49. Diary of 19 November to 9 December relating to Operation 'Workshop'[27]

On 19th Nov. 1940 after seeing the report of the C of S meeting on 16 Nov. I wrote a minute to C of S to point out that I had dissented from the conclusion and wished the views I had given placed on record.[28] I asked General Ismay to come and see me on 18th and told him to see to it that my statements were put on record.[29] I also prepared a statement giving the history of 'Brisk'[30] for the Cabinet (see record). However in the afternoon I felt he might never read them and that I must try and get into personal touch with him. So I wrote him a note.

About 9.30 p.m. on 19th a constable came to the house (telephone broken down) and said Capt. Woolley[31] wished to speak to me – he would take me to Gerald Road P. Station. When I got there I found 6 or 8 sergeants and a young police officer who said a car was being sent to 22 at once. So I asked him to send me back there. After waiting some time I went to 'K' post to telephone – the ARP station at the bottom of Royal Avenue. I got into touch with Woolley who told me a car was on the way to me. Shortly afterwards an armoured car arrived and drove me to Down Street, and through an ordinary street door I was taken to [a] lift which took me down into the depths of the old Down Street tube station which had been transformed into a most comfortable living quarter – shut off at intervals with gas tight doors.

A secretary then showed me into a conference room in which I found the P.M., the 3 Secretaries of State, the 3 Chiefs of Staff and an Air Commodore who was being given a draft telegram regarding the dispatch of fighter planes to the Middle East. After 5 to 10 minutes discussion the Air Commodore left and the P.M. opened the question of 'Workman',[32] the code name for the operation in which I am so deeply interested.

It was evident that he had made a close study of the minutes I had written him and he put my case admirably, drew me out and gave me every opportunity of urging the operation and our ability to carry it out, despite the conflicting claim of 'Brisk', etc. He was scathing when obstacles were raised and once turned to Ismay and said: "General, take a note, the Council is resolved to do nothing." When A.G.[33] said the C.-in-C. Med and Middle E [ast] should be consulted, he said: "Why, to put another committee on to find out all the reasons why it should not be done?" – "Consulted – NO – told we propose to do it – have they any remarks to offer."

He blistered the JPS EPS[34] reason for *not* doing it – the proposed Javelin(?), etc., said he proposed that we should now take the 1st and 2nd readings and any suggestion that transpired could be raised when it was passed in the 3rd reading. Alexander[35] then said he proposed the 1st and 2nd readings be passed – I asked for orders – could I call off the 4 Commandos side-tracked for 'Brisk' – provide whatever troops Brigadier Morford wanted – carry on with the training and take it that I would have 2 "Glens" and 4 destroyers to carry 2500. I was told *yes*.

Winston then saw us all off. 1st Lord, 1 S.L. took the armoured car first. Then Winston took me down to the depths again, asked me if I really wanted to do [it] and do it myself. I said of course I did. He then said, "I tell you frankly that I am not going to have anything to do with it unless you do it and lead it". I might have to take off a stripe or two. I said I would willingly do that. He then took me down deeper still and showed me his bedroom like a sleeping car but about twice the size. He told me he only slept there about once a week; he preferred to be in the middle of things near the War Room. Clemmy,[36] he said, insisted on coming up and she was in the next cabin.

We then said good night. I thanked him for giving me such a wonderful opportunity. He said he might be consigning me to my death – but he knew I would not mind that.

And so to bed – the armoured car took me back and as I got out at 22 I was happy to see Orion ablaze, despite the brilliant moon, standing upright and 4 square.

During our meeting Colville,[37] the secretary, came in and told W. that the air raid was very heavy. It was pretty fierce as I came along in the armoured car (a 12th Lancer one) C. gave the places in London and said Birmingham was having a very heavy raid. 5 planes were already down.

I went to bed feeling very happy and full of hope.

All sorts of difficulties were raised on *20th,* and I was asked to preside over a committee of EPS and Morford to reconsider the requirements of 'Brisk' and 'Workman'. Every kind of difficulty was raised. I flamed a bit and declared that I would not tolerate excuses and delays – Morford must say what he wanted to overcome the Portuguese and perhaps a few Germans.[38] I would take the rest. Later Colonel Jacobs[39] brought me the minutes – I added Morford's name – since *he* required numbers, etc. – I would not admit they were necessary and I added a para. to make it clear that if it were in the interest of the

conduct of the war it could be brought off at any moment and 'Workman' dropped.
There are many snags ahead but I don't mean to be beaten.

27 Nov. Lunched at Dorset Hotel – lunch given by several M.P.'s to P.M. After lunch I told him I wanted to see him and he asked me to come in his car but I could not collect my cap in time and he did not wait, but sent for me at 9 p.m. I saw him for 20 minutes or so and he then told me definitely that I was to have command of the enterprise and that it would not be necessary to degrade me – I would remain an A. of F. and that my direction would make it clear that my command afloat would be limited to the vessels actually taking part in 'Workshop' operation.

28 Nov. To Glasgow by day. Slept at Railway Hotel.

29th Nov. Motored to Inveraray – arrived lunch-time. In afternoon walk to top of look-out hill – dined with Hallett[40] at Naval Centre.

30th Nov. 6.30 motored out to watch 1st Royal Scots landing to carry out a scheme at head of Loch. Bren carrier, 16 ton tank, etc. All N.O.'s [Naval Officers] dined with me.

1st Dec. At Inveraray. Watched 1 R.S. land – v.g. Embarked in *Kingfisher* for Lamlash, lunched with 11 Commando. In *Kingfisher* to Fairlie – drove to Glasgow – dined with Jack Aird – in sleeper to London – arrived Monday morning.

2nd. to find Eva, Geoffrey and Roger at No. 22.

3rd. Asked for 5 officers, 4 d.'s [destroyers] for 2 "Glens", 4 for ops., [and] for floating mines to be carried in "Dido".

4th. Attended C. of S. meeting in forenoon with Haydon[41] – put plan briefly. Pound suggested I should see Harwood.[42] He thought it should be possible to provide 2 more destroyers and a "Dido". Harwood came to see me before lunch – also General Bourne; told the latter to tell Morford not to be too grasping about 'Brisk'. Then turned to Harwood who had grown very fat since I had last seen him – his appearance and his look-out was profoundly disturbing to me. (He used all the arguments with which my staff had been bombarded ever since the operation had been raised by me. I said, "You are going to repeat all the Naval Staff's objections to doing anything offensive".) He started at once that the whole operation was all wrong strategically and ought not to be carried out. The troops ought to be used to attack the Libyan coast and cut the Italian line of communication on which the life of the Italians in Libya depended; even the water had to be carried overseas and along the coast inshore – we ought to attack them near Benghazi and at the same time block the harbour. So I sent for the chart and said: "All right only you will have to give me the *Queen Mary*, the *Queen Elizabeth* and *Aquitania*, and then you won't be certain of blocking the harbour mouth. Do you think for one moment that the C.-in-C. Med. would undertake to cover such an operation – and even if the C.-in-C. Middle East could provide the troops we had no means of disembarking them or indeed carrying them there – was I to take on the Italian mechanized Army with 2500 men – what other operation could he suggest – Dodecanese the P.M. considered politically inexpedient."

The C.-in-C. had pointed out that the whole communications of the Italian Libyan Army went across the narrow part of the Straits past Pantellaria – what better way could there be of attacking the Italian line of communication than at sea in the narrow strait from Pantellaria. Harwood said it was too soon – we could not exploit the capture – we could not afford to garrison Pantellaria, provide anti-air defence, etc., etc., or equip the aerodrome – we had no aircraft to base there, etc. It would be necessary to do it later on, of course, but not now. I said, "And let the Greeks knock the Italians out of the war without any help from us."

I presume what would happen – I would take my 2500 troops to the Med. and do nothing – even the responsibility would no longer be mine and the C.-in-C. would certainly *not* take the responsibility for providing the cover for any operation which could affect the war. At best we might be allowed to capture one or two *un*important Islands in the Dodecanese. We hadn't the means to transport the troops in sufficient numbers to capture Rhodes or Leros. I told him it shocked me to think that Harwood of the River Plate could be so blind to the possibilities of offensive action against Italy. Even if we had no fighters for Pantellaria it was, as I pointed out to C.A.S., who agreed, an invaluable outpost for the Malta fighters to land for fuel and ammunition and, if damaged, to be repaired in the bomb proof hangers. I told him how I needed support from the staff who spent all their time producing arguments against offensive action. If they would address their investigations into other combined operations – "Brisk" for instance, which had been hanging round my neck like an old man of the sea for many weeks – because Morford wanted more men and landing craft to hold the hands of a few Portuguese and possibly a few 5th column Germans than I asked for to capture Pantellaria. I told him to look into this (I wanted one of the "Ulster Monarchs"[43] – there was a 3rd which could be taken for 'Brisk') and said it was distressing to find that he had absorbed all the Naval Staff's determination to do nothing within the 4 days he told me he had been at the Admiralty – I suppose it all emanated from Blake.[44] It was dreadfully reminiscent of Norway and explained why I could not induce W.C. to undertake offensive action against Trondheim, etc., etc. He left me, I hope feeling ashamed of himself, and promised to look into the 'Brisk' force.

Later in the day he said we could have the *Royal Scotsman* and possibly 2 more destroyers. He doubted whether the "Dido" could be spared.

So I went to bed feeling happier.

The P.M. had invited the C of S to dine and after dinner he, they and the Defence Ministers discussed 'Workshop' until after 2 a.m.

5th. We learnt that the C of S had damned it in heaps. They said the plan was incomplete. *I* had evidently not considered using smoke – or carrying any explosives ashore. The P.M. said he thought that the conduct of the operation might be left to the Commander to whom it was confided who was confident of success. If the C of S were opposed to it he had to take note of their advice. *But* he considered himself free to use his own judgment – *So I was told*!! Also that he drafted a telegram to the C.-in-C. Med[45] to ask if he would suggest any use being made of these troops for carrying out raiding operations on the Libyan coast, and told him to consult C.-in-C. Middle East.[46]

It was confirmed in the course of the day that *Royal Scotsman* was available and would be sent to Lamlash and I was asked to attend a C of S meeting.

6th. I was asked to attend C of S meeting at noon and took Hornby[47] as Haydon was at his H.Q. near Reading. Pound told me that they were looking into the matter but he hoped they could give me 10 destroyers, i.e. 3 a side in addition to the 4 protecting the 2 "Glens"; the Scottish "Monarch" and possibly a "Dido" or two for gun support.

We had all been asked to attend a meeting with the P.M. at 9 p.m. but Pound said he would try to put it off until Monday as they would only be flogging over the same ground as on Thursday night, they hadn't got C.-in-C. Med's reply, etc. At the moment I thought it a great mistake – We, Haydon and I ought to be up north, free from the Staff interference, training and preparing operation order, etc. However it turned out for the best.

7th. On Saturday Davis[48] came back as usual depressed – better to seize the two small Dodecanese Islands – it ought to bring Turkey in, they would not want to be left out of a share in the loot, etc. I told him not to bother about the strategic opinion of the J.P.S. and E.P.S., etc., and to get on with the plan for the meeting taking into account the added forces.

In the meantime at about 9 a.m. I was asked to speak to the P.M. on the telephone and he asked me to come down and stay the night and bring my Brigadier. I said I thought he had better see Haydon who would command the troops. He agreed and I said we would be down before dark. He said anytime I liked but he did not get up until dinner time as he worked all day in bed. I meant to start at 4 but found Davis with his new story which I glanced through. I said it looked all right and would do for the meeting. I might decide to do something quite different – and in any case I wanted him to work out a plan for releasing the "Glens" at once, and clearing them so that they could go directly after the first flight left, and to redraft the plan on these lines. He asked me if he could show the plan to the D. of Plans – he had been telephoning for it at short intervals all the afternoon. I said No, I was damned if he could. What the hell had it to do with the D. of Plans. I was far better qualified to judge as to the feasibility of a plan than he was. I did not intend to stand any more interference from the Naval Staff. The responsibility was mine, etc. He was very upset and said it would make it very difficult for him if he did not show it to Daniel.[49] So to ease his anxiety I consented, but made up my mind to put an end to Naval Staff interference. All this delayed our departure and we did not get to Chequers until 7.45.

However the butler told me that the P.M. was still dictating and had not had his bath so I bathed. Mary[50] was doing hostess – Clemmy being in bed for dinner after a long day inspecting a house.

At dinner I sat next to Winston and Diana[51] and he told me in a low voice that the plan I gave to the C of S meeting was ruination. I had not made any provision for making smoke, for destroying wire and gun emplacements, etc. I was furious and started to say exactly what I thought about it. So W. said we'd better wait until after dinner. However it started the tale that no one had any chance of getting on [in the Mediterranean Fleet] unless they played polo and Tommy Thompson[52] who was there told how he hoped to get promotion so sold me a pony I wanted. He did watch carefully while I played it in a trial chukker and told his friends that he was going to put the price up £10 for every goal I got and £5 for an airshot which had a good chance of getting a goal if I had hit it. I got 3 goals and one airshot so the price ought to have been £135 but he wanted his promotion very badly so only charged for the airshot and let me have the pony for £105. I think it was all pure invention though I did give him £105 for Slaney. Anyhow the story went well. I asked him if he knew that I had made the 2nd polo ground [at Malta] by stealing one of the very few men's football grounds. He said, "No." I said I didn't either but that was one of the stories passed round by Field & Co. to prevent me becoming 1st Sea Lord. I quoted a bit of the first verse of "IF" to Winston.

After dinner we started at once. I told him that the plan was of course only an outline. There was no question of its being a detailed plan. We could make that when we could get away to our ships and boats and men; as it was from day to day the number of vessels available was altered each time I was asked to provide a plan – and some wretched little committee, EPS, JPS, started to criticise it. They pestered my staff with hostile criticism of the strategic value of P. [Pantellaria] and never failed to try to discourage Davis, the staff officer. Every night he left me fired by enthusiasm; every morning he came to me after his morning talk with the JPS depressed and despondent. One morning he even depressed the brigadier telling him that the Naval Staff considered that it would be impossible to land the 2nd flight – both the brigadiers considered that the operation must be called off – I asked them what the hell they thought I would be doing – tamely acquiescing in the destruction of the landing craft by the enemy's batteries. I walked about the room cursing them, damned JPS and EPS and said they were determined to sabotage the whole plan. Winston said that he was quite able to make the decision to deliver the attack against their advice if he was satisfied that the plan was a good one and offered a good chance of success. He wanted to know the plan. I said, having made the plan, only this evening Harwood has told me on the telephone that I could only have 4 destroyers altogether for *all* purposes, but could have the *Royal Scotsman* and the *Karaya* [*Karanja*] with 4 ALC's and an SLC. The P.M. had ordained that only 2 destroyers were to leave home waters and if that was adhered to we could only have 4. Eventually we explained the plan. W. was restless because I introduced a cruiser – or two – but I stuck to it. He told me he was favourably impressed with Haydon – and that he told his plan well – before we went to bed about 1.30 W. had promised me six destroyers. He said he could not understand the Admiralty outlook – or rather P.'s [Pound's]. They had enormous commitments in convoys at sea – were losing ships in great numbers – but for an offensive operation they were not prepared to face any loss. He said the opposition to 'Workshop' had hardened considerably since they had learnt that I was to do it! And he growled something pretty bitter about jealous old men.

9th. The C of S asked me to attend their meeting at noon on Monday 9th Dec. The CNS said that it depended on the opinion of the War Cabinet at their meeting tonight but he hoped that it might be possible to let us have 6 destroyers – 3 a side, and 2 "Dido" class cruisers – I said I presumed he had seen the plan I sent the C of S on Saturday evening. It had been prepared in a great hurry as I had been asked to go to Chequers and after I had approved of my Staff Officer's draft I had come to the conclusion that directly after the first flight left the "Glens" the remainder of the troops, etc., could be embarked in destroyers (as I indicated in my covering minute) at once, thus leaving the "Glens" to rejoin the convoy long before daylight. It would be a great relief to me to know they were back with the (Malta) convoy and no doubt to the C.-in-C. Med. and himself.

I said before going any further I was anxious to clear up certain points and to know exactly where I stood. When I was made D. of C. O. I naturally thought I should have something to do with Combined Operations and that I had been selected for the appointment because I had had far more experience than any one living soul in the planning, the execution and finally the responsibility for the conduct of combined operations. But I soon found that my experience was not wanted – no one in the Admiralty at any rate had any use for me. I was too old, I lived in the atmosphere of the last war and much to that effect. As a matter of fact I was responsible for the planning, the preparation and watched the execution of the landing of 10,000 men in two flights of 5,000 simultaneously – of them 9000 landed dryshod within ½ an hour.[53] The fact that 1000 got wet and their second flight of 500 men were delayed was due to the Army insisting on their landing in a place we had been unable to survey.

We had the means to do this in craft which had come out to the E. Med. from England under their own power, assisted by occasional tows on[ly], and arrived by the middle of July 1915, less than a year after the [war's] outbreak. Now after 15 months we had no means of transporting and landing more than about 1000 men simultaneously.

'Alloy'[54] and 'Shrapnel'[55] were or were supposed to be already at short notice to start when I took office. But when they were transferred to 'Menace'[56] my department found that they were utterly unready from a shipping point of view. I made some proposals to ensure that the shipping miscarriage akin to those of Gallipoli, Norway, etc., would not be repeated. They were approved but then my connection with 'Menace' ceased. The plan for capturing Dakar was fantastically foolish – (and was made by ISPS).[57]

The Naval and Military Commanders[58] had the civility to call on me but my offer to help in any way was simply ignored. The Admiral was sweating with apprehension at what was in front of him. And he succeeded in thoroughly alarming the General. The Admiral's only response to my suggestion that I might help was: "Oh, you had 6 months to prepare for Zeebrugge – we have to be ready to sail within a very few weeks."

I believe the 6 months' preparation for Zeebrugge was one of the d—d lies put about to discredit me. I had heard it from other sources. Turning to CNS I said, "It is a lie as you know." Then to the other C of S I said: "As a matter of fact when I was D of P and CNS was one of my deputies *he* proposed the blocking of Zeebrugge and Ostend. I thought it madness, in view of the fact that they were covered by the most powerful system of fortifications in the world – 250 guns of 4-in. to 15-in. calibre. He said he thought it might be done under cover of smoke. That attracted me enormously and I naturally thought the Admiralty, which I had just joined, had provided smoke making apparatus. I then requested him to draw up a staff appreciation of the project and under his direction an appreciation was made which covered every conceivable point – the type of ship – the amount of concrete that could be put in them in view of the draft of water – the possibilities of running the blockships in, the timing for an approach at night, or at dawn – the dates on which it could be carried out having regard to tide and moon, etc. – and under the DNO's (?)[59] direction an admirable appreciation was prepared which would be of great value to the Commander selected. That was the proper way to make use of the Staff – my contribution was to the effect that the plan of action *must* be the responsibility of the Commander – and that the hazard was no greater than that undertaken by the infantry and the tank corps every time an attack was launched on shore – and that the Navy were spoiling to emulate the deeds of their brothers in arms."

I had in mind the awful sacrifice that the Army had made in the Passchendaele offensive in order to deny the Flanders bases to the enemy, a necessity according to Sir John Jellicoe, if we were to be able to continue the war during 1918 – an utterly false premise since the Submarines could have cover from the Heligoland Bight even if the Flanders bases were captured.

I said when I took command of the Dover Patrol on 1st January 1918 and was given a free hand to attack Zeebrugge I had to start from zero. As the CNS knew, the Plan outlined in the Staff appreciation bore little resemblance to the plan I actually carried out. The appreciation was, however, most useful. I had to select the ships, make arrangements for them to be fitted out, select the naval personnel – raise a marine brigade, train the personnel – and since, to my consternation, I found no means for making smoke existed other than throwing sulphur into an iron pot and burning it which made a red hot glow visible 20 miles, I had to set to work to get a smoke making system designed, – thanks to Brock[60] of firework fame this was done, but it was dependent on Chlor Sulphonic acid. At the end of February Brock told me that there was only enough in the country to make smoke for the expedition for 2 hours and I had insisted on 3. This would take a month to provide even if all the Chlor Sulphonic acid in the country were sent to Dover. This was ordered and the production of saccharine was shut down until I was satisfied. The operation could only be carried out during about 5 days in each lunar month and the first possible date in the Staff appreciation was given as 14th March – and that was dependent on the operation being approved at once – say 6th Jan. 1918. I could have been ready by 14th March but for the lack of sufficient Chlor Sulphonic acid to make smoke and unforeseen delays in the fitting out of ships. This postponed the expedition, which was otherwise ready, a lunar month and I actually sailed for the first time on 11th April, 3 months and 11 days after the first action was taken by me on taking up my command. So much for the oft-told lie.

With regard to 'Workshop', the Italians attacked Greece on 28th Oct. On 29th I proposed to send one or two Commandos out to Crete for raiding in the Dodecanese. That was all that was available at that time owing to 'Brisk'. The next day, 30th, I suggested capturing Pantelleria on the way – giving reasons for doing so.

A day or two later the C. of S. informed me that they approved of I. but thought II. was very attractive and should take preference. I have addressed myself to carry out this instruction, to get ships ready, reclaim Commandos from 'Brisk' and generally prepare for the expedition – but find opposition at every turn from the JPS and EPS, the people who, in my opinion, ought to have been helping me to put the C of S decision into practice. Hesitation and delays were exasperating until the 19th November when I was summoned to Down Street and the operation was generally approved. After everyone had left the P.M. asked me if I was prepared to carry out the operation – and if I wanted to. I said of course I wanted to and was quite ready to take off 2 or 3 stripes in order to make is easier for the Flag Officer afloat.

From that time onwards my staff had had nothing but carping criticism from the JPS and EPS who thought the project strategically unsound. The force at my disposal was changed 3 times. Each time I was asked to submit an outline plan only to be criticised by the JPS and EPS. My Staff Officer for operations having been laid low by an appendix, I had borrowed an Admiral's Staff Officer from the FOP's[61] who became fired by enthusiasm by the end of each day but returned the following morning thoroughly depressed after his morning meeting with the JPS. On one occasion I found my stout-hearted brigadier in a most depressed frame of mind – the Naval Staff having informed him that the landing craft could not survive the first landing and he could not hope to get more than 1000 men on shore, even if he had a complete surprise. These individuals who had probably never seen a shot fired laid down the law about risks and dangers.

The whole operation was child's play to those I had conducted on the Belgian coast. I had taken 135 light vessels to within a few hundred yards of the fortifications I had described. "Yes, but you had smoke." "Yes, but the smoke blew back after the first quarter of an hour and my vessels stood up to a most terrific fire for more than an hour and in my destroyer I frequently had to run in making a heavy smoke to cover my small smoke makers. Out of the [blank] odd destroyers I only had one sunk and one badly damaged and they belonged to the small group of 3 which literally were alongside the fortifications; my own escaped. This was due to the change of wind. I only lost 3 M.L.'s . . . though 30 odd were making smoke within a few hundred yards of the fortifications and they were often laid bare. With this experience I maintained the risks run at P. [Pantellaria] would be infinitesimal to those I experienced – but these young men ruled otherwise."

I understood that at the meeting on the night of the . . . . . . my plan was described as immature – no provision for smoke, for taking explosive in – I said I believed I was the first person ever to use smoke offensively, that when I became D of C.O., as I attached the greatest importance to making smoke I sent for the Engnr. R.-A. responsible for its development and was shocked to find that, although all sorts of ingenious methods had been devised to make smoke, that it was still my Brock system – for the MTB's could only produce it for 10 minutes – while I had insisted on 3 hours.

I found that the ALC's would be dependent on smoke floats – trusting to SLC's which were fitted for making smoke and for throwing smoke bombs, but there were only 2 available!

It was not my fault that at this stage of the war smoke making was far behind that at the end of 1918. As for not carrying explosives, the whole training and composition of the Commandos was based on demolition. I did not contradict my brigadier but he had not lived with the Commandos and watched the work as I had.

I would remind the C of S that I had suggested: I. Crete; II. Pantellaria – they had plumped for P. – and since then the JPS and EPS had done nothing but crab it and discourage my people – Pound demurred – and I said whatever his assertions were that was a fact and as recently as Saturday when he told me to see Harwood I naturally thought Harwood was coming to help – and was in favour.

Pound said they were all out to help and to give me as much as they could and said it depended on the meeting that night. I thanked him and said I was sorry I had had to speak so harshly but I had had a *very* trying time during the last 3 weeks.

Final Meeting [9th Dec.] At 9.30 p.m. on Monday I was told to appear in the War Room with all the exhibits. I took Haydon, Hornby, Knox[62] – the model photographs, etc. – in one of the other rooms – in the Council room where I was interviewed after my Belgian visit – P.M., 3 Defence Ministers, 3 C of S, Attlee[63] and Beaverbrook[64] and secretaries. P.M. asked Pound to state his case. He did so quite admirably – giving all the pros and cons – among the former were all the arguments I had put forward in my long fight – absence of other objectives – hardening of defence likely – possible infiltration of Germans – value in lines of communication – another airport, etc. I don't think any fairminded judges could have summed up otherwise than *for* an offensive on 'Workshop'. The sting was in the tail – he ended up by quoting a long telegram the Admiralty had sent that afternoon in which they pointed out all the cons – and made it clear that the responsibility would be *his*. (C.-in-C. Med's.).

There was one *con* of his own to which I took great exception. He stated that the Naval Staff did not consider it possible to land more than 1600 men.

Winston's reaction was remarkable and rather insulting, at least I landed in Africa – I believe at Benghazi – and laid the foundation of an Italian Empire. Another Roger would capture the Workshop which would not have liked to have had such things said to me. He said, "You aren't going to wait for an answer to that telegram. There can only be one answer." The C.-in-C. had already expressed his objection to 'Workshop'. He considered it inexpedient, risky and would have no effect on the war. He, W.C., did not agree with his view. In a few short scathing sentences he gave the C.-in-C.'s probable reply and said, "Well, we had better go on with the business. Your telegram cannot alter the situation with which we are confronted – whether we are to carry out 'Workshop' or not."

There was a brief interlude before the reading of the telegram – Pound, having said not more than 1650 men could get ashore, asked that Haydon might leave the room. The CIGS said he did not want to discourage Haydon but in his opinion it was 3 to 1 against.

In the other room I gave the naval plan, Haydon the military. I said that I felt, tho' I might be wrong, that it might be our good fortune if the wind made it only possible to land on one side, and we were making a plan to that end. I strongly protested against Pound's declaration that only 1650 would get ashore. I was confident of landing the whole force.

Finally W.C. said, "Sir Roger, are you prepared to carry out the operation and what do you consider the odds against it?" I said I was ready to carry it out and I did not think it could fail.

W.C. said, "Now we will adjourn to the other room" and that he had finished with us. I said before we parted company I would like to give them a little ancient history. It would not take 2 minutes.

Roger II of Sicily[65] caputred the Workshop in 1123, and later would play a great part in the destruction of the present Italian Empire. This amused Winston but he said that before we accepted the precedent we ought to examine what happened to Roger II later. He might have come to a disastrous end.

50. *Keyes to Churchill*

[Copy]

D.C.O.'s Office,
War Cabinet Office Annexe,
Richmond Terrace, S.W.1.
20.11.40.

A thousand thanks for your promise last night. I won't let you down.

This is our enterprise which will surely be the forerunner of much offensive action in the Mediterranean and elsewhere, and it would never have got past the Committee stage but for the way you handled the opposition last night.

I have always felt confident that some day I would be given the opportunity of striking a blow which would help you to get on with the war. I know I have sometimes been inconveniently importunate! – forgive – for now I am convinced that the hour has come.

As I got out of the armoured car last night – or rather in the small hours, there was our friend Orion ablaze – despite the brilliant moon light – standing upright and four square in the Southern sky – Surely a harbinger for a feat of arms which will restore the confidence of the Army, from every unit of which my splendid Commandos are drawn, quicken the pulses of our friends and confound our enemies.

I am very grateful for the chance you are giving me...

51. *Keyes to Admiral Sir Herbert Richmond*[66]

D.C.O.'s Office,
War Cabinet Office Annexe,
Richmond Terrace, S.W.1.
21st November, 1940.

Very many thanks for your letter of the 15th, which I only received today. I very much appreciate the nice things you said about my share in recovering control of the Navy's aircraft. It is tormenting to think of what might have been if *Chatfield*[67] had only had any guts. We ought of course to have had complete control of what is known as the

Coastal Command. I had mobilised the support of Winston and Freddie Guest, two of the originators of the unified air service; even Moore-Brabazon[68] in the end, and practically the whole House. *Chatfield* had only to insist.

First he declared to me that he would insist on having operational control of all shore-based aircraft needed by the Navy, and a hand in the manning and training of them, and would go to the point of resignation to that end.

I pointed out that this would only perpetuate dual control. He must go the whole hog; and I asked him to circulate a memo. I sent him on the subject to his Naval colleagues. He said he could not do that as they agreed with him. I then sent a copy of the memo. to Hoare (First Lord) and all the Sea Lords. Hoare was very receptive and vowed he would back the Sea Lords up.

Eventually *Chatfield* demanded all I wanted him to, and said he would insist on being given it.

When Neville Chamberlain announced the decision that the Fleet Air Arm was to be returned to the Navy, but that the Coastal Command was to remain entirely under the Air Ministry, both as to administration and operational control, and wrote to me saying he hoped I was now satisfied, I told him that I was profoundly disappointed and he replied that if the Admiralty was satisfied, why could not I accept it? I heard too from Inskip that *Chatfield* had warmly thanked him for all he had done! When I upbraided C. he wrote, "I am an old campaigner and we will get all we want in the end."[69] The war came first.

Even the transfer of the Fleet Air Arm was sabotaged for more than two years.

Cunningham of Dakar[70] (not Andrew of the Mediterranean) could not compete with the Air Ministry and could not induce *Chatfield* to fight. Ramsay, the Commander-in-Chief East Indies, was called back but could not prevail against the Air Ministry. We started the war in a state of transition and for his failure to organise the Fleet Air Arm, he was broken *by Winston.*

The Coastal Command Commander-in-Chief[71] really did all he could to help and was anxious to come under Admiralty control – as he had been throughout some manoeuvres which took place shortly before the war.

The Air Ministry would not agree and many opportunities were missed owing to the fact that the Coastal Command had no long range torpedo aircraft, no fighters or bombers of their own, and the Commanders-in-Chief of the Fighter and Bomber Commands would not co-operate. This is a sorry story but it is a true one. I have done everything in my power to get the Admiralty to insist on the Coastal

Command being directly under Admiralty control, but although it is far better equipped than it was at the beginning of the war, we suffer frightfully owing to its conflicting allegiances.

Imagine what we could have done if we had been allowed to develop our own air service during the last few years. All the best torpedo-carriers are shore based under the Coastal Command, and they have achieved nothing yet.

[Holograph]
Private

I did not like to dictate the rest of this letter, but I hope you will be able to read it.

As a student of Naval History can you think of anyone who has been given greater opportunities of serving the Navy and the Country than Chatfield – 5 years 1st Sea Lord – then Minister of Defence – and in a small War Cabinet when the greatest war the world has ever seen, broke out – moreover the friend of the last two Prime Ministers and much in their Councils.

Glorious is a shocking story, as you say. Bower is not a pleasant fellow but his story in the H. of C. was the truth,[72] and if he had only stuck to that, instead of going off on his own grievances, it would have had much more effect.[73] It is not generally known that 10,000 men were in transports unescorted – French and British – and it was just chance that they were not caught unconvoyed too. My son was in one of them.

You will wonder what this paper means [the heading D.C.O.] – and what I am doing. During the winter I went 4 times to Brussels, 3 at King Leopold's invitation, to make the liaison between the B.E.F. and his G.Q.G. which his Govt. would not allow. Gort or anyone else could have been driven round in plain clothes wherever he wished from December – until the Belgian campaign started – and I affirm that the B.E.F. and our expeditionary R.A.F. could have had *any* information they wished if the Military Attaché had made proper use of the wonderful facilities I obtained for him – and the B.E.F. had been more enterprising.

When the war broke out on 10th May I was asked to join King Leopold. I flew to the frontier and arrived in the small hours of the day following the German invasion.

When I came home on 28th May I was not very popular for I said exactly what I thought to W.C. and the Cabinet – which was that King Leopold had been a most loyal ally, that he had done every conceivable thing to help the B.E.F. to the extent of sacrificing his own army – before he was deserted by the B.E.F. It was not until then, and he had sent 2 miserable French Divisions across the Yser in Belgian Lorries and Busses, that he asked for an armistice to put a stop to the ruthless slaughter of the hundreds of thousands of refugees who thronged every road, hamlet and town in the small part of Belgium left to him who were being mercilessly bombed. My report which is based on a day to day diary and numerous telegrams and recorded telephone conversations is accepted now. I think it might interest you to read it – it is recorded in the F.O. and W.O. If I had known as much as I do now my letter to Gort[74] (a copy of which is with my report) would not have given him one bouquet. He lost or destroyed every record, but the British Mission's (Military) records came away with me by a happy chance.

After the Norwegian debate, which I took part in just before I went to Belgium, I must confess I was surprised to find the C.-in-C. and the Naval Staff still in office and apparently not at all discredited – all ready to do something glorious. What infuriates me is that they have tried to make D'Oyly Hughes,[75] a splendid fellow, the scapegoat for that frightful miscarriage.

Secret.

On 16th July W.C. sent for me and offered me this appointment. ("Director of Combined Operations" – a misnomer tho' he did not mean it to be.) I believe the Admiralty – or the one most responsible objected very much. However I have no more to do with the Admiralty than the W.O. or Air Ministry. On paper it seemed wonderful. I was to have operational and training command over 5000 troops – all volunteers – selected from almost every unit of the army for amphibious warfare, and command of any raid up to 5000 men – a host of ships and specially designed landing craft – 500 parachutists, etc., etc. I have been here 4 months and have not been able to do anything yet. I am also supposed to give technical advice on all combined operations – and I have an army corps of 2[?] divisions *there.*

This is a very indiscrete outpouring! Please burn it at once and let me know you have received it and done so.

I would like immensely to have a yarn with you and get ideas from you. I wasn't far from you at an aerodrome seeing off the parachutists.

I can't think temperately of the way in which the rescue arrangements we made were cancelled by the Naval Staff after they were promised. I don't think I have ever been so inspired and thrilled as I was by the bearing of these splendid young men. Let me know if you come to London...

52. Richmond to Keyes

The Master's Lodge,
Downing College,
Cambridge.
November 22, 1940.

Very many thanks for your most interesting – if depressing – letter;[76] depressing in that it tells of so many lost opportunities. Alas, the more I read of our past wars the more do I see how we flounder about, though I'm bound to say it was the politicians who made the mess in the past much more than the seamen and soldiers; for they vacillated and lost time, and, through being unable to make up their minds and come to decisions promptly, were so often too late. Now, it seems, it is not they only who cannot decide and act, but our own people. I'm bound also to say that I have never had a great opinion of Chatfield. He has always seemed to me a "lath painted to look like iron"; an excellent gunnery officer, certainly, but not a strategist or a statesman. No man, as you justly say, has ever had greater opportunities than he; he had the confidence of the Prime Ministers, he would have had the country behind him if he had chosen to stand out for the needs of the Navy. Our shortage of destroyers is a scandal.

As to the coastal command aircraft, of course it was plain they should have been transferred to the Navy. I wrote something about it at the time – I forget where – pointing out the absurdity of making a distinction between A/C based on board ships and those based on shore. The true test is the function on which they are employed. All ships and vessels are, after all, based on ports, so why it should have been imagined that there is something different in A/C passes the wit of man.

The real misfortune is that we have had a succession of weak First Sea Lords, beginning with Madden who was nothing short of a calamity and earned the O.M. for being subservient to the Labour Government. Madden, whom I had known ever since he was First Lieut. of the *Vernon*, never had the glimmerings of anything outside technical matters. Poor Tam Field, a delightful person and a sick man when he took the job on, had no courage when it came to standing up to Ministers. He allowed the 50 cruiser agreement to go through,[77] and made no protest when Alexander and one or two other Ministers issued a preposterous Cd paper in which it was said that the number of our destroyers was dependent on the number of enemy submarines! I told him it was sheer and disgraceful cowardice on the part of the Board, and of himself in particular, to let that statement go out to the public without protest from the Sea Lords. Fisher[78] was as bad. I said much the same to him about either that or another surrender and his reply was that if he was to resign someone else would be got who would agree; why should he lose his job?

I see from your letter that the *Glorious* affair was even worse than I had thought. I am aghast that the convoy with 10,000 troops should also have been unescorted. On what grounds such risks were taken will have to be explained some day. What, I wonder were our battleships and cruisers doing while that operation was in progress? If there is one outstanding lesson in our long experience it is that the movements of troops across the sea in large bodies provides the occasion for battle. How carefully our old men always arranged their covering and escort forces! On the Narvik occasion cover was, I imagine, impossible, as it was throughout the convoy movements in the last war; indeed it was for lack of recognising that fact, and trying to cover a convoy, that we suffered one of our losses; an error we did not repeat but escorted the convoys with strong forces afterwards. I fail utterly to understand how we could gamble with the lives of thousands of our men, and of our ships, in the way we did. Were we afraid of risking the battleships as we were at First Narvik? By not sending strong escorts we suffered a double loss; the *Glorious* and two destroyers were sunk and the opportunity of destroying their attackers was lost. It makes one despair when such things are done.

I do trust we are going to make every effort to smash Italy during the winter months. She has played into our hands and we should press her for all we are worth in this Albanian business. I do not of course know what the significance of Kassala and Gallabat[79] is, but unless they are of first rate importance it seems to me we should take our A/C from there and put every possible one that we can into Greece and the Adriatic. That fleet in Taranto must be our principal objective alongside the Italian army in Albania.

It's no less astonishing that we should have thrown away all our landing craft. The same thing happened before the last war. I remember the War Office refusing to vote the money for the upkeep of those we had, saying that there never would be any landings anywhere as all the Army was going to France; and when I tried to get the question of what was to be done about the German naval bases in the colonies it was simply turned down as a ridiculous suggestion.

I hope we are not allowing ourselves to be bluffed about invasion. I don't underrate, I think, the possibility that an attempt may be made but one cannot lose sight of the fact that a threat of invasion is a most useful form of diversion and feint. We were had by precisely such a threat on that occasion in 1756 when we kept all our fleet in Home Waters until it was too late – and so lost Minorca.

I wish you luck in your present job. I prayed for just such a thing in the last war, early in the campaign in the East. Tug Wilson[80] turned it down. I had a lovely scheme for a small combined force to harry the Syrian coast, but he could not see the possibilities that were open to such a body. You may be assured that I am as silent as the grave concerning what you told me.

Yes, I should very much like to see your report on the Belgian campaign if you will spare it for a few days; so pray do send it to me. I am in the unhappy condition of being disabled by a heart attack which laid me out last February and until the damaged part of the heart has mended I can do no more than walk an occasional mile – a hateful condition when there is so much that even at our age can be done, in one way or another...

53. Keyes to Admiral Sir Andrew Browne Cunningham

[Carbon]
Secret and Private.[81]   3rd December, 1940.

Very many congratulations on your success in the Mediterranean – That was a grand performance of the Fleet Air Arm[82] – If we had only been free to develop the latter during the past twenty years, how much further ahead we would be now.

I daresay you do not know much about my appointment here. I have had it for four months but owing to lack of landing craft, vessels to carry them, aeroplanes to drop parachutists and the objections raised by certain brass bound soldiers in the War Office, who hate the very thought of my irregular troops, I found it exceedingly hard to make any progress. Also the withdrawal of these troops for the defence of Great Britain delayed their organisation and training.

Though I am called Director of Combined Operations, it has so far been a mis-nomer as the Directive I inherited confines the responsibilities of my Directive to giving technical advice on Combined Operations, and to the training of regular troops for amphibious warfare at a training establishment at Inveraray and at a number of other establishments where naval crews are trained to man the landing craft. However it does give me definite command of raiding operations carried out by the five thousand irregular troops we have raised and trained.

There are now seven Commandos, that is 3,500 volunteers drawn from almost every Corps and Regiment in the British Army – killers every one of them – spoiling to fight. There are also – 1,500 more, trained on the same lines in the Independent Companies, which are now being organised on the Commando system – Two "Glen" liners ready, each carrying two Commandos, 11 A.L.C.'s, 1 S.L.C. and 2 M.L.C.'s, and one "Glen" liner just completing, similarly equipped (this one is at the moment required for a special service) – Two Dutch ships[83] (25 knots) each carrying a Commando, 2 M.L.C.'s with 14-ton tank on board and 6 A.L.C.'s or Eurekas (fast American shallow draft rum runners which can be run ashore carrying about 20 fully armed men). These ships will be ready in January – Six Belgian cross channel steamers (18 to 20 knots) to carry 300 troops, or 500 for a short trip, and 8 A.L.C.'s or Eurekas. I am afraid only two of these have the endurance to come out to the Mediterranean and they will not be ready until February.

The A.L.C.'s, M.L.C's, T.L.C.'s and rum runners are now coming into service fairly fast, and it is quite time the offensive was launched.

It seems to me that the only raiding operations – on a scale within our present means – to affect seriously the course of the war, must be in the Mediterranean.

For a long time I have been urging that a strong force of my troops should be sent out to you for raiding operations as soon as landing craft and transports to carry them are ready. The delays and hesitations have been exasperating.

You will have heard about what is known as 'Workshop'. I hope you approve. I have been striving to be allowed to do that for ages. Every sort of difficulty was raised until, at last, the Prime Minister took a hand. He told me that he wished me to take command – so I said I would take off two or three stripes in order to do so. However I understand I am to retain my rank but that my directive will not in any way interfere with the naval command afloat and will only include the light craft when they are actually taking part in the attack.

If you and Wavell want them, I would urge that the two Dutchmen and two of the Belgians and another 1,500 men be sent out to you as soon as possible. With such a force, it would be difficult to put a limit to what they might be able to do in the way of harrying the Italians.

We are also training a number of volunteers for raiding operations in the submarine punts.

If you have no objection I would stay for a bit and organise this force – before going home – either from Crete or from Malta or the Workshop...

54. *Brief for Operation 'WORKSHOP'*[84]

[Holograph]   9 December 1940.

WORKSHOP

Dispositions at Outset of Operation

Reference: MOSAIC 1/22,500 dated 23.11.40.

On West Side
  (i) Z.1 with one Battalion on board (850–900 men).
  (ii) Two destroyers ready to close Z.1 and take off men *not* included in first flight (i.e. 405 men to be taken off).
  (iii) One destroyer waiting to escort Z.1 away as soon as she is empty of troops.
  (iv) One destroyer with Commanders and staffs on board and 75 men.
  (v) Z.3 with Reserve on board (up to 550 but unlikely to be so many).

On N.W. Side
  (i) One cruiser waiting to bombard town. No bombardment until it is clear landing is discovered – then intense until limit of safety which will be 0200 hours, or thereabouts.

On East Side
  (i) Z.2 with one Battalion on board (850–900 men).
  (ii) One destroyer ready to close the Z.2 and take off men *not* included in first flight (i.e. 405 men to be taken off).
  (iii) One destroyer waiting to escort Z.2 away as soon as she is empty of troops.
One other cruiser standing by to take on any target that may be ordered.

The Landings.

1st Flights
  (i) At 2315 hours 495 men leave the Z.1 and a similar number leave the Z.2.
  (ii) These 990 men should reach their landing places at *2345 hours.*

Tasks of First Flight on Western Side

Landing Place No. 2 (1900^x in width) – *285 men in first flight.*
A.⎫ *50* men to secure No. 2 Landing Place and block the motor road
B.⎬ (100^x–200^x away) and to cut any communications running along it.
C. *100* men to put out of action the guns at No. 6 Battery (700^x away – steep climb in one place at gradient of 1 in 1¼).
D. *50* men to put out of action the guns at Battery No. 5 (1800^x away).
E. *50* men to move south from Landing Place No.. 2 clearing up local defences and cooperating in attack on Batteries No. 8 and 9 which are 4100^x away, i.e. 2 miles 580 yds.

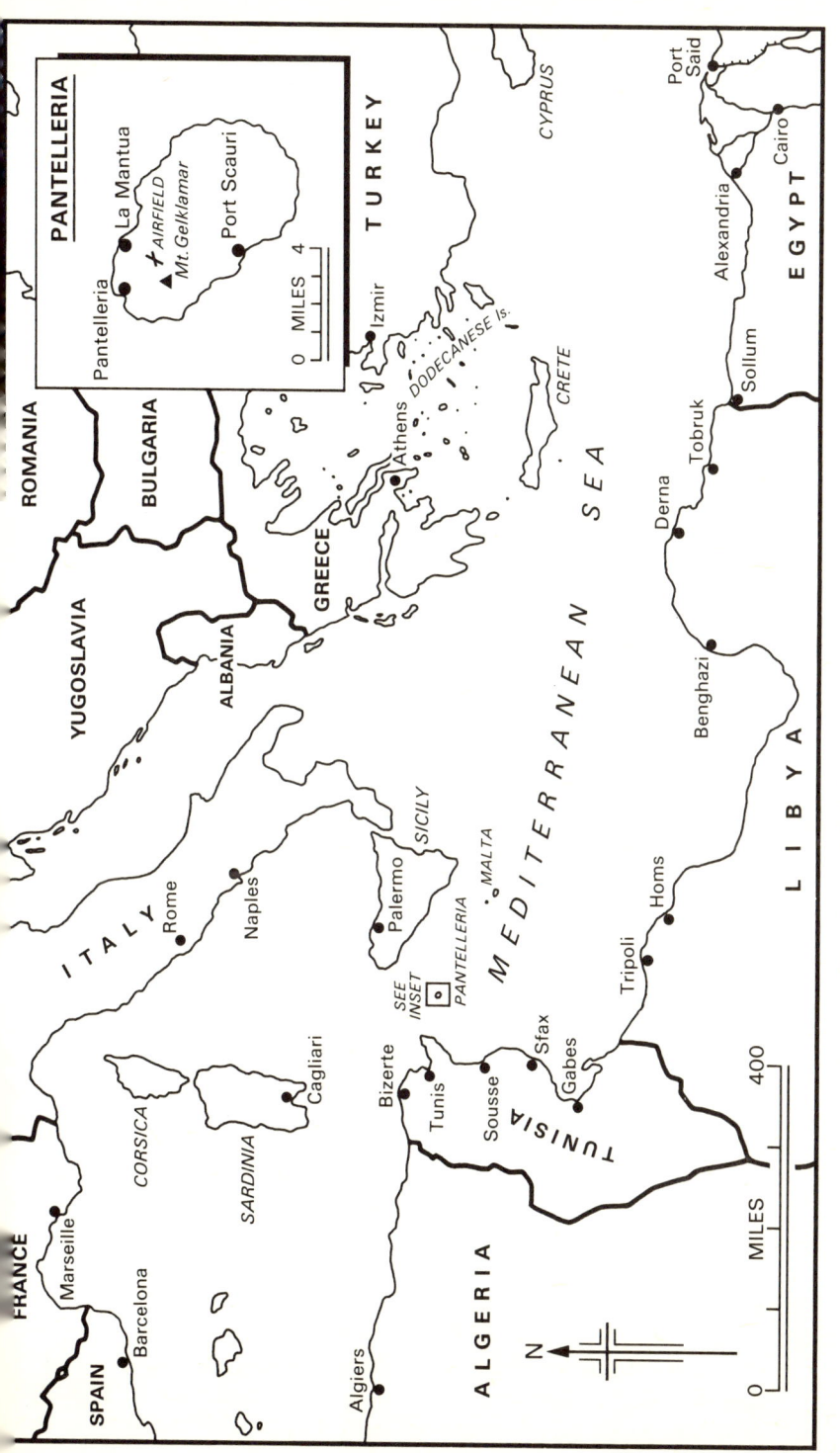

The Central Mediterranean and Pantelleria

In addition 35 of the 400 required for main task of capturing Workshop will be ashore at 2345 hours.

Landing Place No. 4 (1500^X in width)

G.
H. } 25 men to secure the landing place and block the motor road which is 350^X away and a climb of 330 feet at an average gradient of 1 in 3¾.

I. 185 men to put out of action Batteries Nos. 8 and 9 which are 4000^X away, i.e. 2 miles and 480 yds.

Tasks of First Flights on East Side.

Landing Place 1A (1500^X)
 (i) 70 men to secure the landing place, block the motor road, and cut any communications running along it.
 (ii) 175 men to put out of action Batteries No. 16 and 17 which are 2500–2700^X away or an average of 1½ miles and a climb of 180 feet.

In addition there are also 40 men ashore at 2345 hours for the aerodrome task (210 in all required for this).

Landing Place 1B (750^X in width).
 (i) 20 men to block the motor road and to cut any communications running along it. Road is 200^X–300^X away from the landing place.
 (ii) 190 men to capture L.D. Battery immediately south of L in La MANTUA. (650^X away from the landing place with a climb of 80 feet at a gradient of 1 in 4) and to capture Battery No. 18 which is only 200–300^X away from the landing place with a climb of 80 feet at a gradient of 1 in 4.

Notes:–
 (i) The landing places have practically all got an immediate climb in of 20′ or just under. Each Battalion will have 40 twenty-foot scaling ladders to deal with this problem.
 (ii) The photographic interpretations indicate that there may be walls round Battery No. 5, Battery No. 8 & Battery No. 9. These walls are not more than 6′ high and there are gaps in them.
[Paragraph (iii) apparently omitted in oral presentation.]
 (iii) We have 150 Bangalore torpedoes and can get more if we want them. Their principal use is against wire which we must prepare for though no indication of its existence has been discovered in the photographic interpretations. Each Bangalore torpedo is 10 feet long – and 2″ in diameter – and has a fuse which must be lighted. It is about the same weight as an A.T. rifle (36 lbs). It *can* be

carried by one man, but more easily by two. The effect of its explosion is to clear a 10′ gap in a fence.

Movements during the period in which 1st Flights are being landed.

At 2315 hours when the 1st Flights leave Z.1 and Z.2 the destroyers close those ships and take off the remaining personnel (405 from the Z.1 on to two destroyers and 405 from the Z.2 on to one destroyer). Three quarters of an hour is allowed for this transshipment which should therefore be completed by midnight.

After the destroyers having taken personnel on board, the Z.1 and Z.2 will leave the neighbourhood each escorted by a destroyer.

The destroyers with personnel on board will then either remain in the positions previously occupied by the Z.1 and Z.2 or they will, if the conditions are favourable, move closer inshore and thus reduce in length and in time the inward passage of the second flights.

Tasks of the Second Flights.

On the West Side of WORKSHOP.
 (i) At 0025 hours the landing craft having put the first flights on shore reach the two destroyers and are ready to pick up their second load. An allowance is made for 3 A.L.C.'s being damaged in taking the first flight in and thus only eight are being relied on at this stage.
 (ii) The 405 men in the two destroyers will take 30 minutes to get into the landing craft and a further 30 minutes to get ashore. Thus a further *405* should reach Landing Place No. 2 at *0115 hours*.
 (iii) The task of this 2nd Flight of 400 is to capture the town of Workshop and to prevent any craft still in the harbour from leaving. The town is 3 miles 220 yds away by road or 2 miles 580 yards across country.

On the East Side of WORKSHOP.
The timings are the same as for the west side – that is to say the 2nd Flight of 405 men should reach Landing Place No. 1A at 0115 hours.
The tasks to be performed are:
 (i) 210 men move to capture the aerodrome and the wireless station which are 2 miles and 680 yards away, and nearly 600 feet above sea level.
 (ii) 105 men to pass inland of Battery No. 18 and to put out of action Batteries No. 19 and No. 1. No. 19 Battery is $1\frac{3}{4}$ miles away. No. 1 Battery is $3\frac{1}{2}$ miles away.

The above distribution to tasks leaves a reserve of 80–90 men in the hands of the Battalion Commander.

Landing of the General Reserve.

1. The General Reserve which is carried in the Z.3 can number up to 550.

    If taken by the landing craft returning from the 2nd Flight it will mean two trips. If this method is employed then the first trip of 320 men should reach the shore at 0245 hours and the second trip of 230 men should reach the shore at 0415 hours.
2. Alternatively if the situation ashore allows and the conditions are favourable the Z.3 could be run in to Port Scauri and the whole reserve be put ashore from the jetty. Port Scauri is just under 6 miles from the town of Workshop and four miles from the aerodrome. It is unlikely that such an operation would be practicable before about 0230 hours.
3. Whenever the Reserve is landed one of its tasks will be to deal with the guns at M. Gelklamar.

Alternative Arrangements

1. Should the weather conditions be such as to allow landings to take place on the West Coast of Workshop but *NOT* on the East Coast then the whole force would be put ashore at Landing Places Nos. 2 and 4. The detailed timings of this operation have not yet been fully examined.
2. Should the weather conditions be such as to allow landings to take place only on the Eastern side of Workshop then the operation would be cancelled.[85]

55. *Exchange of Signals between the Admiralty and Commander-in-Chief Mediterranean concerning Operation 'Workshop'*

(a) *Admiralty to C.-in-C. Mediterranean*

[11 December 1940]

AIDAC.*   IMMEDIATE.

Following from Prime Minister. Personal and Most Secret.

Your 1319 29th November and various telegrams about WORKSHOP. We have considered whole matter exhaustively. D.C.O. Sir

* Probably signifying 'What follows is only to be decyphered by an officer'.

Roger Keyes will execute it with full control of all forces employed and final plans are now being prepared by him. His appointment will not be Naval but limited to these combined operations. If necessary he will waive his Naval rank. Cannot feel air counter attack will be serious having regard to size of Island, broken character, many mountains and detached fort in which comparatively small attacking force will be intermingled with defenders. Enemy aircraft will not know who hold what till all is over and even then Italian Flag may be displayed on soft spot.

(ii) Capture of WORKSHOP no doubt a hazard. It may be surprisingly easy. It may be a heavy prop. But Zeebrugge would never have got past scrutiny bestowed on this. Besides we are dealing with Italian sedentary troops not Germans. Commandos very highly trained especially trained volunteers for this kind of work. Weather and fixed date of convoy or detection of attackers in approach stages would of course prevent attempt in which case whole outfit will go to Malta or Suda Bay for other enterprises. If position is favourable nothing will be stinted.

(iii) Apprehensions that you have that A.A. guns, etc. will be diverted from Eastern Mediterranean and new commitments created may be mitigated by capture of enemy A.A. which are numerous. Enemy unlikely to attempt recapture even though garrison left will be small. Commandos will come away after handing over to regular troops and be available for further operations. Our reports indicate bulk of civil population has already been evacuated. One hopes for increasing air command of Mediterranean making maintenance easier.

(iv) Comparing WORKSHOP with other operations you mention in future called MANDIBLES[86] (R) MANDIBLES kindly weigh following considerations. MANDIBLES require 10 or 12 thousand men and is far [Corrupt group] affair if 2 bigger ones are to be taken. Little ones you mention would stir up all this area without any important reward unless process continued. Secondly captures in MANDIBLES area would excite keen rivalry of Greek and Turk [Corrupt group] which above all we do not want now. Thirdly our reports show MANDIBLES slowly starving and perhaps we shall get them cheaper later. Apart from above trying WORKSHOP does not rule out MANDIBLES afterwards unless ships and landing craft are lost which they may be. I am quite willing to study MANDIBLES with you and work upon it has already begun here. Also perhaps operations on enemy's land communications along North African shores may present opportunities.

(v) On strategic grounds WORKSHOP gives good air command of most used lines of enemy communications with Libyan army and also increased measure of air protection for our convoys and transports passing so-called Narrows. Undoubtedly blow to Italy at this time create consternation besides [Corrupt group] this we need to show ourselves capable of vehement offensive [Two corrupt groups] action.

(vi) Outfit leaves 18th and zero might be 10 days later. Before then we shall take stock of the whole situation including results obtained from Libyan battle. Whilst I am anxious to have everything ready it may well be better alternatives will present themselves.

T.O.O. 2145/11 Dec. 1940.
T.O.R. 0357/12 Dec. 1940.

(b) C.-in-C. Mediterranean to Admiralty

[12 December 1940]
AIDAC.   IMMEDIATE.

Request following may be passed to Prime Minister.

Your 2145/11. I fully appreciate your view about the advantages to be gained from WORKSHOP and as stated in my 1233/10 every effort will be directed to ensure the success of the operation. I have never questioned the feasibility of WORKSHOP given thorough planning but my concern has always lain in its subsequent maintenance.

2. The hard fact is that my resources are strained beyond their limits already and the extra burden means that something else will have to suffer in consequence. The real point of difference is that in my view the advantages to be gained are outweighed by the disadvantages resulting from having to withdraw ships and light craft from other and more important work. The calls on my forces increase almost daily, for instance today I am arranging for the supply of the Army in the Western Desert and for the removal by sea of some 20,000 prisoners. All these calls by so much reduce the Fleet forces available for offensive action at sea.

3. As regards air counter attack on WORKSHOP I agree that it will not greatly affect the capture but when it comes to landing supplies, disembarkation of casualties and change round of garrisons the work will have to be carried out without any A.A. defence unless we have been able to seize A.A. guns and ammunition.

4. The organisation for command appears likely to lead to awkward and unsatisfactory situations.

5. As regards the MANDIBLES perhaps the strategic implications seem to loom larger to us out here than at home. In Spring, 1941 if not before it seems that we may well be faced with a drive Southeast by Germany and I suggest that the importance is incalculable of ensuring that our line of communications to Greece, Turkey and the

Dardanelles is not menaced by enemy ports and aerodromes on its flank.

6. The MANDIBLES are already alert to the fact that now we are in Crete they may be attacked at any time and in consequence the capture of the outlying islands will not affect that aspect. What such capture will do is to accelerate the starving process, scare the enemy, and give us better jumping off grounds for the eventual attack on the two big objectives.

T.O.O. 1615/12 Dec. 1940.

(c) *Admiralty to C.-in-C. Mediterranean*

[15 December 1940]

IMMEDIATE.   *AIDAC.*

Personal from First Sea Lord.
(a) Since Operations EXCESS[87] and WORKSHOP were contemplated the general situation has changed in following respects: –

(i) Our success in Western Desert must have wide repercussions in both Italy and Germany and latter instead of waiting for spring before embarking on any major move may now consider it necessary to take some action to bolster up Italy or to restore the prestige of Axis.

(ii) There are indications of something being afoot which is connected with French Port in Bay and either Spain or Azores.

(iii) The Spanish action in Tangier of replacing the International Administration by a Spanish may or may not have some connection with German action in Spain.

(iv) Our situation in Middle East is temporarily secure.

(b) Taking above factors into consideration it appears undesirable that we should at present time be committed to operations which will lock up all available shipping suitable for transporting M.T. and personnel apart from considerable Naval escorting forces.

(c) It has been decided therefore that operations EXCESS and WORKSHOP shall be postponed until moonless period in January.

(d) This decision will have the following advantages: –

(i) Med. Fleet will be free to concentrate on any operations which are necessary to assist the army in exploiting magnificent success they have achieved.

(ii) *Malaya* need not be sent to join Force "H" if such an operation would be inconvenient to you.

(iii) It will not be necessary to station *Barham* at Malta.

(iv) You will be relieved for the moment of any commitment in connection with maintenance of WORKSHOP contemplated. Force "H" will be free to deal with any German seaborne expedition.

(e) The following precautions have been taken: –

(i) Force "H" less *Sheffield* left Gibraltar A.M. December 14th for Azores patrol, R.F.A. Oiler *Orangeleaf* will join Force "H" to refuel destroyers.

(ii) Subsequently one cruiser and one submarine will be maintained on this patrol.

(iii) 3 "U" class submarines have been added temporarily to Bay of Biscay patrol.

(iv) Operation TRUCK which is Home Force half only of Operation BRISK and Operation SHRAPNEL are at short notice.

(f) This message has been passed by L/T in F.O.'s cypher to V.A.M.
T.O.O. 0137/15
T.O.R. 0659/15

56. *Keyes to Churchill*

[Carbon]

White House,
Lamlash.
17th December 1940.

It distresses me that you should be so embarrassed by having found me employment for old friendship sake. It is of course all wrong that any such consideration should be added to the burden of your immense preoccupations.

If my withdrawal would relieve you, pray tell me so and I will find some other way of helping you to win the war more speedily than your Chiefs of Staff and those dreadful staff committees will allow you to.

As Maxton[88] said – no doubt it was ordained on the battlefield of Blenheim that you would lead the British Empire to victory in this critical hour. But I am sure it was also ordained in the battles of Gallipoli that I would help you to that end. For when you fell out of your battle to force the Dardanelles, and thus hasten victory, I carried on against overwhelming odds with no help from anyone until Wemyss backed me – too late. That ill fated campaign would still be Churchill's Gallipoli gamble if I had not persisted and proved by carrying a hundred per cent greater hazard to success, that you and I were justified in our opinion that the Dardanelles could have been forced by ships despite the old parrot cry that ships can't fight forts (I read your minute on General Irwin's[89] contention with approval).[90]

You don't make it easy for me to help you when you turn down a request for an interview with such cold disapproval – and, when I persisted, by overwhelming me with reproaches as you did that evening.[91]

I am tongue tied in a battle of words but I hope I persisted long enough to make you see that although I recognised the wisdom of holding your hand until the situation clears,[92] it seemed to me very unwise to leave such a splendid striking force and shining sword to rust and lose its temper in the Highlands when all the alternative objectives such as Workshop, Grind,[93] Brisk, Alloy, Shrapnel, lie East and West of the Straits about seven days to the Southard. During those seven days on passage to the Straits, the situation should clear and you might then be able to take the initiative and strike first instead of leaving it to the Germans to do so. They will not be blind to Workshop's immense strategic importance directly on the line of Italy's communications with Libya nor to the danger of allowing it to fall into our hands – and will certainly not be influenced by the considerations advanced by the C.-in-C., Mediterranean, and other hostile critics.

A few minutes reflection after you left on Saturday [14th] convinced me that your proposal would be turned down by them as impossible and that it would be pure waste of time on my part to stay in London.[94] I felt that I would have failed in my duty to you if I neglected to give you my views, which after all are based on great experience and successful achievements which so far have been denied to your Naval and Military advisers – apart from Wavell who is happily free from cramping influences.

Since you would not see me I tried to see Halifax, whose views seemed to me to be sound, but he was not in London so I saw Alexander and after begging him to make his Naval Staff help rather than impede me, I put to him my view as to the risk of keeping the only amphibian fighting force we possess so far from its potential fields for immediate action. Perhaps he did not take that in, or did not like to convey it to you on an open line – since he does not seem to have prepared you for it as I hoped he would. However, Harwood and I lunched together on Sunday [15th] and I put my view to him and asked him to consider the possibility of escorting my small expedition to Workshop in time for the next dark period which ceases after the 1st January. I suggested that it might be done without calling seriously on the C.-in-C., Mediterranean, since Excess was off and the "Glens" would be released soon after midnight and could get within air cover of Malta before first light.

I think he was impressed with the force of my arguments, and he promised to study the possibility of providing an escort for my small force if it should be decided to strike this month.

Twice I have failed to help you. I did all in my power to do so in the Norwegian campaign, and made an enemy in the process.

Again I failed to persuade you in Belgium. I have not bothered you with the tale but some day I believe you will read it with interest and will appreciate my effort.

Now I offer you a Workshop. "Three times is a lot". It will be necessary to capture it eventually but infinitely more difficult if the Germans are permitted to forestall us.

I strongly advise you to have arrangements made to get my force to Workshop by 1st January unless it is immediately required for Brisk, Alloy, Shrapnel, Grind or some other offensive action.

Any further delay will take the heart out of the troops who volunteered for the Commandos some months ago in the hope of seeing actions since they have already been brought to a high pitch on more than one occasion only to be bitterly disappointed. Brigadier Haydon entirely agrees with this view...

57. *Ismay to Keyes*

MOST SECRET AND PERSONAL

Offices of the War Cabinet,
Richmond Terrace,
Whitehall, S.W.1.
17th December, 1940.

The Prime Minister has just instructed me to give you the following message:–
1. It was definitely decided by the Defence Committee with the Prime Minister in the Chair last night, that Workshop is to be postponed and is not to sail with Convoy W.S.5(a).
2. The Prime Minister is very sorry that you and your fine troops should be disappointed at the eleventh hour but, in the general situation with which we are now confronted, there was no other alternative.
3. The Prime Minister feels sure that advantage will be taken of this postponement to press on with training, particularly in landing operations. Meanwhile, the Commandos should be kept at three days' notice.
4. The Prime Minister hopes that the above will enable Officers and men to be granted short leave for Christmas. He feels sure that all ranks have had impressed upon them the necessity for not talking about the nature of their work and training.
5. The Prime Minister very much hopes that you have been able to get a little rest after your very strenuous weekend and that you are keeping well.

I am trying to telephone the contents of this letter to you at once

(11.30 a.m.) but communications are not always easy. Accordingly, I am sending this by the hand of Lt. Courtney in case I cannot get through.[95]

58. *Keyes to his wife*

[Holograph] 18.12.40

I am very fit. In all my stormy [?] career I have never had more bludgeoning knocks than those of the last 3 weeks – culminating in the last 3 days.[96] However I am confident and determined despite every kind of difficulty and obstacle to strike a blow for the country which will make you proud darling. You and your faith are a wonderful help and inspiration to me – Woolley is simply pure gold.

I had a very friendly message from Winston[97] who evidently regretted his outburst on Sunday. He said he "hoped" very much that you were "able to get a little rest after your very strenuous weekend and that you are keeping well." When we got to Fairlie there was too much sea for the *Freesia*'s boat. I signalled to her ... to go to Ardrossan ...

I then drove to Ardrossan but it was far too rough on the bar for the *Freesia* to come in, however a gallant old Commander[?] commanding a yacht ploughed out with Woolley and me on board and brought us to Brodick[?]. I was on the beach at midnight watching a landing – and so to bed – What 50 year [old] Admiral would go the length I do? Even if he had the heart and nerve and sinew to do it.

Roger was in battle dress looking fine and fancying himself in it. He is doing splendidly and has acquired much merit. He is at Greenock[?] now meeting his beloved MTB. It is all thanks to him that we shall have 2 – no thanks to the Naval Staff. They will be invaluable.

He and Geoffrey enjoyed the Ball the Duchess of Montrose was arranging and they evidently pleased her – I haven't seen her yet. We shall be here on and off until about my Mother's wedding date [12 Jan.]. I think you'll find it in the family bible. But I'll see you before that – I may be coming south. Everything a bit unsettled except as to that date. All my love ...

59. *Keyes to his wife*

[Holograph]
Douglas Hotel,
Brodick, Arran.
19.12.40.

I wish I could hear from you. I hope Robin[98] is well on his way to being fit again and Diana with him.

I wish I could tell you what we are doing. Woolley tells me that his wife and he have a theory – proved a score of times – that things always happen in twos. When he got orders to join me – she said "Of course – and it will go on." I am going through it all again – and this is akin to the torturing delays of the past – and I shall have to fire the troops this evening or tomorrow – as I did the (Zeebrugge) men in the Swin who were looking sideways at me.

I am expecting Roger and Geoffrey back this afternoon – and as I shall be embarking about noon and have 100 things to do – I must stop.[99]

This will be my address until – probably 12.1.41 . . .

[P.S.] I daren't go from here much [?] – only I wish I could be in two places at a time – sometimes. There are so many hostile enemies to fight. I have written to Katherine.

60. *Keyes to Churchill*

[Carbon]

Office of D.C.O.,
Lamlash.
22nd December 1940.

I am grateful to you for your kind message which Ismay conveyed to me on the 18th.[100] Of course it crossed my letter of the 17th[101] I much appreciate your inquiries as to my health. I am very fit, thank you, and thrive on sixteen to eighteen hours a day of strenuous effort when there is an enemy to fight.

After I left you on Sunday evening, I dined with Eva and she came to see me off at Bletchley station and insisted on waiting for nearly two hours – as the train was delayed by air raids. Meanwhile planes roared overhead twice, flying low, but spared the station. Then I had a wonderful night's rest in the train, and arrived here before dark on Monday in time to mount an exercise in a sheltered anchorage, despite a strong gale. I wanted to see how the Guards Commando shaped, as they had had little experience embarking and disembarking out of A.L.C.'s (Assault Landing Craft). I watched them land admirably at midnight and slip away silently and almost invisibly, in their rope-soled boots, and disappear – armed to the teeth – with their scaling ladders, demolition charges, etc.

Your instinct for delay was probably my good fortune – if the Germans don't forestall us in too great strength. There have been so many delays since the Chiefs of Staff approved of the operation, in principle, on 2nd November, and you confirmed it and offered me the command on 19th November, and we really have not had time to do all the preparative work I wanted to do. Bad weather also interfered with the exercises I wanted to carry out, and opportunities were missed while I was away.

I was impatient for the reasons I gave you last Sunday, but putting it off a month (about three weeks really) will enable me to prepare as polished and finished a plan as the one for which I was responsible and acquired merit, on a previous occasion.

I want to stay here because I think it is essential that I should share the trying period of waiting with this magnificent striking force. I dar'nt let them loose all over the country and must keep them happy and enthusiastic on this island. I know you will guard my flanks on the Whitehall front.

I have told the Commandos in each ship that they only exist as Commandos, with the status and all the privileges they prize so highly, because you willed it. That you had faith in them and were determined to give them the opportunity of striking blows and performing feats of arms which would stir the world. You had done me the honour of giving me command of a splendid striking force of soldiers and sailors, the spearhead of all oversea offensive operations. I had promised you that I would keep it burnished and highly tempered, ready to carry out any service you might call upon us to undertake and that I was convinced that you would soon give us the opportunity for which we were so eagerly waiting. We soldiers and sailors must therefore stay in this island and be ready to strike the moment you call upon us.

Their shouts of approval and cheers must have echoed on Goat Fell.

If you have nothing else for us to do, I beg you to give instructions for my force to sail in time to reach Workshop on 22nd January, the first suitable date. That will leave eight days in case we have to pass by, on account of bad weather, and wait at Malta until the weather suits.

If we had sailed on the 18th, it would have only have given us two or, at the most, three days in hand for such a contingency. I believe the next convoy is due to sail about the 11th January, which fits in with this proposal.

I am sending Davis, the admirable staff officer lent to me by my good friends, your F.O.P.S., to clear up a few points and give any information that may be required. He will come back with the F.O.P.S. plans for further operations in the Mediterranean, which should be of great help to the C.-in-C.'s out there.

I know that my age, and suggestions that my health is not good – have often been advanced to discredit me. I wonder if Alexander could find an Admiral of say 45 to 55, apparently his limits of age, with the will to force his heart, nerve and sinew to do what my frail carcase stood up to during those 18 days in Belgium last May and has stood up to for the last month, since you offered me command of this force. Or could sustain the mental strain of trying ceaselessly to persuade others to see the goal ahead and refrain from seeing only potential dangers. Dangers which – my experiences have taught me – are not nearly so formidable as their fears picture.

Or take full responsibility for the conduct of a hazard which might possibly fail.

Or have the moral courage to withdraw if circumstances arose that jeopardised success, or called for sacrifices which the end did not justify.

I wonder.

Anyhow, a thousand thanks to you for giving me this chance of proving once again that I can do all these things and that the passage of years has had no more effect on my judgment and ability to act vigorously than it has had on your ability to stand up to any strain and lead us to victory.

St. Vincent[102] was at his zenith as First Sea Lord when he was older than I am now, and hoisted his Flag again after that.

I am younger than Howe[103] was on his Glorious First of June and I don't suppose either of them possessed such a spare and healthy body.

Winston – back me in this and you will never regret it . . .

61. *Brigadier Hornby to Keyes*

[Holograph]   Offices of the War Cabinet,
Richmond Terrace,
Whitehall, S.W.1.
Sunday 22nd [December 1940].

I have received your letter by hand of Pay/Lt. Davis & send this back by same means. As there are several points to deal with in that letter I will number them.

1. Personal. You must please continue to trust me. I was a little shaken the other evening when you rather suggested that I was not helping & didn't approve your plans, etc. If I don't agree with you I will say so (as I did originally for 'Workshop'). But once my objections have been settled or overruled there is only one boss in this party & that is you. Whatever may appear to be the case please remember that I am in fact your Deputy; things are not easy this end & I have to do a lot of placation & at times what you call blarney to get people to say & do what we want.

2. Maund.[104] He was never "at home" here & his heart was in the Admiralty.[105] Disregarding his personal opinions he has worked most wholeheartedly in the execution of your demands. He is seldom out of his office & has really put in a lot of time squaring things up. It is thanks to his energy & drive that the SLC's & M.T.B.'s were made ready & despatched.

3. Compasses. I agree with you so very much. It has always seemed quite wrong to me to accept a compass-less boat but I have always been assured that it was not possible. Knowing little of these matters I must accept our Naval advice. I have however raised a proper stink about it & attach a note.

4. I am asking C.O.S. to agree to the despatch of 2 "Glens" & 2 S.S. Battalions to Middle East at once. (What happens on the way is nobody's business). Having achieved that we can add *R. Scotsman*, etc. to house the Bde Staffs & oddments. By keeping one "Glen" back we can satisfy the P.M.'s demand to remain "crouched" & not "spread eagled" by maintaining a potential striking force during January, which could be further hotted up by the 'Brisk' ships. If we ask for more than 2 "Glens" there will be the usual argy-bargy & nothing will happen. You are in the strong position of having a compact & prepared force. I will not mention 'Workshop' – as such – since the Admiralty opposition has not flagged. There is *no hope* of the two Dutch ships being fitted out & ready before late January & I would like to send them to Inveraray to finish their own training & to assist in 1st Corps training. Ditto the first two Belgians (There is some doubt as to whether these would do the passage to M.E. in winter – my informant is Commander Fell who has one of them.)

If you will agree to this we can: –
1. Lull Admiralty suspicion.
2. Stop any talk of spread eagling.
3. Continue training & development at home.
4. Let you loose with 2 "Glens" + ??

Therefore early in February we will be able to afford one "Glen" & two Dutchmen which we can cram full of S.S. tps & despatch to wherever you (and/or Haydon) happen to be.

5. Censorship was established within one hour of your demand. Good work on Hollis'[106] part.

6. The P.M. is asking if Commandos are to be given Christmas leave. I presume not in view of the fact that you have padlocked the island. Please confirm this by telephone either to me or to Hollis. It obviously refers to R.C.[107] & I would beg of you not to give him any extraordinary facilities as I am sure that would not go down well in the War Office.

7. I had a long & interesting talk with Gen. Haining.[108] I wanted to

check up how the wind was blowing from that quarter & I found him just the same, heartily on your side & eager to carry out 'Workshop' or anything else.

8. I enclose a signal X. Will let you have the reply.

9. I am sure that we ought to have a regular courier service. I can't spare anyone from here & you have a good many trustworthy officers up there. Will you please consider it. If I had nothing to return I would keep the man until there was a message.

10. In the meanwhile & in order to keep our hand in I am trying to tee up operation "Castle" (Josing fjord). This only requires about 100 S.S. tps + some sappers & I will get the former from No. 1 Bn. Please concur...

62. *Keyes to Churchill*

[Copy]

Office of D.C.O.,
at Lamlash.
24th December, 1940.

I am sending Randolph officially to carry this despatch to you. I know he wants to come back as soon as possible, and when he tells you what we are doing here, that you will release him. He has done grandly, Bob Laycock tells me, and I mean to make proper use of his brain and initiative when he has won his spurs.

Please insist on sending us into the Mediterranean or in that direction with the next convoy.

I did not mean to bother you with the attached history,[109] and I hope you will not consider it necessary to make use of it, as I want to get the Naval Staff on my side as well as the C.N.S., who declares that he is, and V.C.N.S. I know is. It is "with great truth and verity" a statement of fact which cannot be questioned.

I loved your talk to the Italians – the best ever I think.[110] I wish you could give one to the French Navy in North-west Africa and the Mediterranean, after we capture Workshop, and remind them how they and their Fathers served under a British Admiral to whom I was Chief of the Staff, and later under my Flag, in two great offensive strokes during the last war – in the Dardanelles and on the Belgian Coast. Tell them to forget Oran and Dakar and sail with us once again, to purge the seas of the Nazi barbarians, who have fouled them, and to take a hand in destroying for ever the pretentious Italian claim to own the Mediterranean and possess Corsica, Tunisia and Jibuti.

If the Naval Staff cannot find enough destroyers why not let me have one or two Frenchmen? Muselier[111] offered me his sword when De

Gaulle[112] left him behind, and said he would serve as a Capitaine de Frégate, if necessary. It might be better to use a more junior officer as I shall only be a Commodore. It would have a very good effect on the French Navy if one of their vessels took part in our enterprise. I always made a great point of including French craft in my operations on the Belgian Coast. No doubt, that was responsible for the officers of the Navy subscribing to give me a piece of Sèvres when I was C. in C. Mediterranean, and for so many of them coming on board my Flagship to call on *their Admiral*.

There are wonderful things to be done in the Mediterranean. I would give anything to get in touch with Weygand and Ismet Inönü,[113] who sat under my chairmanship at Lausanne for several weeks,[114] both of whom have kept alive the friendship we made then . . .

63. *Memorandum by Chiefs of Staff Committee*

[Copy] [31st December, 1940.]

PRIME MINISTER

Sir Roger Keyes was informed yesterday, 30th December, of the decision (Flag A) about "Workshop".[115]

2. He returned immediately from Scotland where he had been visiting the Special Service Troops under training. He reports that these troops are now trained to the highest pitch and keyed up for action. He considers that, unless they get on the move soon, they will lose heart and apply to return to their units. For this reason he feels that they should not be held in this country till February as at present decided.[116]

3. Sir Roger Keyes proposed that "Workshop" Force should sail with Convoy W.S.5(b) on the 7th January, and after proceeding via the Cape, should carry out "Workshop" Operation from the Eastern Mediterranean.[117]

4. It was suggested that one solution would be for "Workshop" to go through the Western Mediterranean with the delayed "Excess" at the end of January.

5. This was considered an unacceptable alternative, since it would mean detaching destroyers from the Western Approaches during January and keeping a proportion of them permanently in the Central Mediterranean for maintenance duties at an earlier date than now contemplated.

6. A third course considered by the Chiefs of Staff was to send

"Workshop" through with delayed "Excess" without carrying out the Operation en route.

This is not recommended as "Workshop" Force would not reach the Eastern Mediterranean appreciably sooner than if it leaves the United Kingdom on 7th January via the Cape; more destroyers would be needed as part of the escort, and these would have to come from the Western Approaches. The valuable "Glen" ships would be risked without the compensation of doing "Workshop" at a very early date.

7. The Chiefs of Staff recommend that Sir Roger Keyes's proposal in para. 3 above should be approved. It will not interfere with "Truck" (modified "Brisk").

8. If you approve this recommendation, it is requested that a decision may be given today.[118]

64. *Keyes to Churchill*

D.C.O.'s Office,
22.1.41.

As Minister of Defence you appointed me Director of Combined Operations and made a point of my having direct access to you.

On some important occasions when I wished to see you about the prosecution of a combined operation – generally to warn you that the Naval Staff were jeopardising success and risking forestallment by causing avoidable delays – I have been told that you were too busy to see me. So I felt impelled to write: I daresay you could not find time to read my minutes, but they remain on record and there is ample evidence that my warnings have been fully justified. Last night I was given the same answer and now you have given me no choice but to write to you again.[119]

On the advice of your Chiefs of Staff (really Naval Staff) you have now apparently cancelled the deplorably delayed operation you confided to me and, without realising it, you propose to break up the splendid little amphibious force which I have organised, trained and inspired, for that is what it amounts to.[120] Although new landing craft are coming in fairly fast now, with the departure of the "Glens" the only fast transports we possess fitted to carry them are the *Karanja*, two small Dutchmen and two smaller Belgians, giving a first flight of less than 1,000 men and their equipment. The two Belgians have a very limited range of action.

Eight Commandos, which have been trained to a high state of efficiency, volunteered because they wanted to fight, and I am told by the Commanding Officers that the great majority of those who are left behind are certain to apply to return to their units. They have every right to do so under the terms of their enlistment after an action or six months' service, and many did last December until I spoke to them and, on the strength of your promise to me, vowed that I would put them across the enemy. The Brigadier and the Commanding Officers tell me that there is no prospect of recruiting officers or men of the right sort to fill vacancies, at any rate until the Commandos have been allowed to do something to justify their existence and the intensely hard training to which they have been subjected.

As I am not allowed by the Chiefs of Staff to have anything to do with the direction of combined operations, I devoted my energies to training an amphibian force. Since, by your ruling, there are no objectives in home waters, eleven weeks ago I suggested to the Chiefs of Staff sending some Commandos to the Mediterranean to raid enemy territories and capture islands. This was approved a few days later.

In view of our very limited resources for landing troops against opposition, it was obviously impossible to capture territory or large islands, and since you did not approve of stirring up the DODECANESE, I concentrated on an operation which you rightly declared "would be electrifying and would greatly increase our strategic hold on the Central Mediterranean." The J.P.S., E.P.S. and J.I.C. have always considered this operation too hazardous and, because they did not initiate it, have since done everything in their power to delay action. Meanwhile they planned a number of operations for which we have neither the trained troops, the landing craft nor the transports to carry them – enterprises which they must know could not possibly be carried out at this stage of the war or, indeed, for a long time to come. Nevertheless, they have served as red herrings to divert attention from the one valuable operation which can be carried out with our existing amphibian force.

After reading the J.P.S.'s proposals for the capture of YORKER,[121] it is clear that there is no prospect whatever of employing any Special Service troops West of MALTA.

Having risked a valuable convoy through the narrows of the SICILY Channel in broad daylight, after German aircraft were known to be in Italy, the Naval Staff are now so scared by the result of their folly that they have at length succeeded in stopping a feasible *night* operation and depriving the MALTA fighters of a greatly extended field of action which would be invaluable to them, even if we cannot yet afford to station aircraft there.

Their ceaseless efforts to discredit the operation from every point of view apparently only succeeded after producing an absolutely bogus maintenance plan and by playing on the fears of the Chiefs of Staff to take the responsibility of risking ships and troops within range of German dive-bombers.

I have had some modern experience, and every stout-hearted sea-going sailor[122] with whom I have discussed bombing, including several who were in the thick of it in NORWAY and at DUNKIRK, declare that, though alarming at first, one soon gets accustomed to it and that the risk from it is greatly exaggerated, particularly that from dive-bombing against opposition.

Is the arrival of German dive-bombers in SICILY really going to be allowed to prevent the passage of ships through the Mediterranean from West to East? We defeated this type of aircraft at home and no doubt, judging by the figures of those already destroyed, are defeating them at MALTA.

Our convoys pass through the Channel with little loss. The Germans seem to keep up a steady flow of sea-borne transport down the Channel, suffering little or no loss from surface vessels or aircraft, and yet our Naval Staff are allowing the arrival of German aircraft in SICILY to deny the use of a sea to us. It was suggested to me by one of your excellent F.O.P.S. that we should pass our transports along the Algerian coast, and if the Commanders in Chief wanted troops, for instance, to co-operate on the Libyan coast in the attack on BENGHAZI, they could follow the route taken by Italian supply ships until they are out of range of the Sicilian dive-bombers.

Are you really going to send three "Glens" round the Cape when they and our Commandos could play a great part in hastening the defeat of the Italians in the Mediterranean and on the African coast? Have you quite lost faith in me?

I do beg you to be guided by braver counsels. We have the Italians on the run – are we going to run away from the German aircraft after the first knock? From all accounts, we have hit them back very hard.

I most strongly advise you to disregard the faint-hearted advice of the Naval Staff, who have always been obsessed by fear of air attack, and pass four thousand Special Service troops – the three "Glens" and *Karanja* can carry them – direct through the Mediterranean to the Middle East. No one would ever blame you for taking my advice in such a matter, least of all the British public and the sea-going officers and men of every rank, judging by the hundreds of letters I received at the time of the Norwegian fiasco. Everyone is sick to death of the Naval Staff, which has not one successful offensive stroke, but many unhappy miscarriages to its credit, and has never failed to allow the enemy to forestall us.

When it is generally known, as it will most certainly be sooner or later, that they succeeded in delaying the passage of a highly-trained amphibian force through the Mediterranean until we were forestalled by the Germans, and then stopped it altogether through fear of German air atack; thus sabotaging an enterprise which the Chiefs of Staff recommended eleven weeks ago, you were anxious to carry out, I was about to lead, and my Brigadier and Commanding Officers were eager to undertake, it will surely be difficult to justify their continued retention in office after their past record. The ability of a few comparatively junior Staff Officers – who have no practical experience in war and have nothing but their fears to guide them – to stifle offensive efforts so deplorably, is even more inexplicable.

I am ready to take charge of this amphibian force as a Commodore and take it to the Middle East through the Mediterranean. I would suggest that all the Naval Staff need be told is that I am going to do so. If the Commanders in Chief don't want it for early action anywhere else, and wiser counsels about Workshop prevail before we pass there, we could easily take it with part of the force, whose landing craft could be replaced by those which have already arrived in the Mediterranean round the Cape. I am quite prepared to hold Workshop with 2 or 3 Commandos until it is quite convenient to the Commanders in Chief to provide for its defence, equipment and maintenance. With its bomb proof underground shelters for aircraft and its aerodrome, I cannot believe that recognition of its great value as an outpost to Malta for giving fighter cover to ships passing through the Sicily channel will be long delayed.

At any rate I would go quite prepared to carry out this enterprise at the shortest notice, taking full responsibility, if I am given the option of doing it.

Whatever you do, don't break up my amphibian force, and please don't waste time and opportunity sending it round the Cape now. When I asked you to do so before, I was impatient because I feared forestallment and was told definitely by the Chiefs of Staff that I would arrive quite as soon by that route as I could by going direct – owing to the impossibility of providing earlier escort – besides I hoped that you would divert us before it was too late.

I know you meant me well and intended that my unique experience in combined operations should be made use of, and I hoped that as Director of Combined Operations I might be able to give valuable service. However, the Chiefs of Staff Committee decided otherwise and left me nothing to do other than organising the training of amphibian forces over which the Directive I inherited gives me command.

I am very grateful to you for your effort to employ me. I really have been very patient and done my best to work with the Naval Staff. They and their committees made it quite impossible and my position is intolerable. There is no such office as Director of Combined Operations, and your ruling as to raids gives me nothing to do in Home waters even if I could raise the force to do it. I know I could help you win this war but you must give me more authority if I am to be able to do so. I am your very devoted friend and supporter but I cannot bear to see you and the country being let down by craven-hearted advisers. How could Wavell and Cunningham have produced such wonderful results in the Middle East if they had been hampered as you are being whenever any offensive action is suggested.

Please give me an interview today or tomorrow in order that I may know where I stand and how I can best help you and the country . . .

65. *Churchill to Keyes*

Personal and Private 10, Downing Street,
Whitehall.
January 24, 1941.

I do not think you ought to write me letters[123] of this kind on matters which affect those under whom you are serving.

It is not possible for me to argue out with you privately, either by letter or in conversation, every decision of the Defence Committee which affects your Command. My burdens would become intolerable if I were to attempt such a thing.

You and your Commandos will have to obey orders like other people. And that is all there is to be said about it. [Holograph] I am vy sorry if you are not pleased. I do my best . . .

66. *Keyes to Churchill*

[Carbon] Offices of the War Cabinet,
Richmond Terrace,
Whitehall, S.W.1.
25th January, 1941.

Thank you for your letter[124] which I received this morning. I know you are anxious to do your best for me.

I shall always put my duty to the country – and to you as long as I can serve you – before any other consideration, and in this matter I know I have done my duty to both.

When you offered me the appointment of D.C.O. you made it clear that I was under the Minister of Defence and had direct access to you. I do not feel I owe any allegiance to the Naval Staff which denies me the right to criticise their actions when I consider they are contrary to the interests of the country.

Portal is a friend and I have a great respect for him. He has given me his views as to the ability of the German Dive Bombers to interfere with
(i) the approach to Workshop, and its retention after we capture it.
(ii) the passage of vessels through the Sicily Channel.

I have given him my views[125] and have made some suggestions which I hope he will pass on to you. He told me he was going to "Chequers" tomorrow.

I have also seen my friend Davis (one of your F.O.P.S. who was lent to me and has been with me some weeks in Arran). He has given me an outline of a marvellous plan for an attack on Yorker which appeals to me immensely – as much as Workshop – and the latter would naturally follow after it. It is so bold and original, it could never be anticipated and unless the WOPS in that island are very much more determined than those in Libya, it could not fail. I understand it will have to go up to you through the tortuous Naval Staff Channels – I do trust it will reach you rapidly, for immediate action will be necessary since it would require all the landing craft we possess. If it were accepted at once and prepared for vigorously, it could be mounted for the dark night period which ends on the first of March and we might, for once, avoid being forestalled.

I am going to Tingewick for Sunday and to Scotland on Monday night. I do appreciate the magnitude of your burdens and hate to think of adding to them, but I do beg you once again not to break up your one striking force in this critical hour. I only hope the F.O.P.S. Yorker plan will provide the solution . . .

67. *Keyes to Air Chief Marshal Sir Charles Portal*

[Carbon]   25th January, 1941.

I am sorry to have missed you today. I have been thinking so much of what you said yesterday about the dive bombers. I am told that if a fair analysis of all the attacks on ships and convoys were made, it would be recognised that the risk of being knocked out by them is greatly exaggerated. I do appreciate that they are a menace if there is no fighter support but I understand the *Formidable* will shortly be available and, even if some of the dive bombers move to Sardinia, very few hours fighter cover will be required for the convoy before night fall and the ships would be under cover of Malta fighters or out of reach of

Sicily dive bombers to the Southward by daylight if not stopping at Malta. 'Workshop' would be timed to ensure this.

If the convoy goes along the Algerian coast it might well escape notice. After all we cannot make war without any risks and I do think we are overcautious where surface ships are concerned.

Since I saw you I have heard of a new 'Yorker' plan which appeals to me immensely – as much as 'Workshop'. I have had a reply from the Prime Minister – quite a friendly one, but I don't propose to say anything more about the break up of the Commandos at the moment, though it is inevitable unless we can find something for them to do, which seems very doubtful if the "Glens" and their landing craft go off round the Cape.[126]

You might consider my remarks about passing fast ships through the dive bomber area at night – and if you concur pass it on to the P.M. Also the very limited risk from dive bombers in "Workshop" – for instance against stout hearted people like mine, who will sit down and take them on with Bren guns. Surely it would be impossible to exaggerate the value of 'Workshop' aerodrome and bomb proof aircraft shelter for giving fighter cover to ships passing W to E. It seems to me folly to neglect any means to take it promptly and deny it to the enemy...

68. *Portal to Keyes*

SECRET AND PERSONAL

Air Ministry, (Dept. OA)
King Charles Street,
Whitehall, S.W.1.
26th January, 1941.

Thank you for your letter of yesterday.[127] I am sorry that I was unable to see you in the morning.

I am afraid that I do not know about the *Formidable* but if the Germans are in Sardinia and Sicily I do not see how a convoy doing eighteen knots could be within range of one or other of their aerodromes for less than twenty-four hours, which means that they would have to be protected for at least twelve hours of daylight. Adequate protection against the concentrated attack which must be expected would require many times more fighters than we could put up, and if a carrier were used that ship must also be liable to attack. I therefore cannot subscribe to the view that it would not be unduly hazardous under present conditions to pass valuable ships through the Narrows...

69. Keyes to Churchill

[Carbon]

H.M.S. *Glengyle*,
28th January 1941.

I am so glad you saw me yesterday. I do so fully appreciate your burdens and difficulties and I would give anything in the world to be in a position to help you. It is cruel misfortune that you, of all people, should be dependent for technical advice on people who are so obsessed by their responsibilities that they can only see the difficulties and dangers of every offensive operation that is suggested to them.

I do realise that you had no choice but to drop 'Workshop' in view of the opposition which had been marshalled against you by the C.-in-C., Mediterranean, the Governor of Malta and the Naval Staff. If the latter however recommend the F.O.P.S. 'Yorker' plan, I beg you to seize on it and hold them to it by stopping the "Glens."

Such a raid with the means to exploit it, if it proves successful as you and I know it would be, followed by 'Workshop,' would be a wonderful reply to the German invasion of Sicily. A friendly Corsica would enable us to exploit it to the full.

As I have criticised the Naval Staff to you, I thought it would be only straight and proper to let Alexander know that I have done so – particularly after the opening remark of your letter to me of the 24th January.[128] As a matter of fact I had already arranged a meeting with him at 4 p.m. yesterday before I received your letter of 24th.

Alexander told me that he had supported the despatch of the "Glens" round the Cape, but before doing so had actually left your meeting for a few minutes to telephone to the Controller's Department to find out how we would stand with landing craft after the "Glens" had sailed, and had learned that we would shortly have 34 A.L.C.'s apart from those required for training, and that had decided him.

I had some difficulty in making him understand that troopships to carry landing craft are the governing factor and that there was no prospect of increasing the number we possessed – these have been delayed month after month despite the personal efforts of the Controller to help me by speeding them up.

I told Alexander that, on a false premise, he had, in fact, concurred in the breaking of a splendid striking force into two parts, each too weak to take a decisive part in any operation East or West of Malta.

Seven or eight weeks must elapse before the "Glens" and their Commandos and such local forces as the C.-in-C.'s could muster, and train, could be launched against 'Mandible'. Events were moving rapidly in the Middle East and in the interval either the Germans might be able to frustrate us by organising defensive measures which the

C.-in-C's would be reluctant to challenge – or if the Germans were unable to do so 'Mandible' would fall into our hands in due course – (You have often said so yourself).

Meanwhile an excellent plan was being prepared to raid 'Yorker', and exploit it, but the only possible way of carrying it out was by using the whole of our striking force.

His staff of course knew that the influx of A.L.C.'s did not alter the situation as he imagined, but having frustrated 'Workshop' they were delighted to send the "Glens" abroad so that the execution of any action for which they might be held responsible would be impossible – and more to this effect.

I told him that his planners were apparently in favour of the new 'Yorker' plan, probably because they knew that the departure of the "Glens" made it impossible, but if the Defence Committee approved of it, I begged him to use every endeavour in his power to speed up the Naval arrangements for carrying it out.

I do sympathise with you in losing Randolph. That my two sons should be sailing on this wild goose chase, would be more than I could bear if I did not still hope that wiser councils will prevail . . .

70. Keyes to Churchill

[Carbon] 3rd February, 1941.

I saw the last of the three Commandos who sailed in the "Glens" on Friday, the envy of all those who were left behind. I gave your love to Randolph, who is delighted to be one of the lucky ones. So many of our mutual friends have sons in that splendid party. It is the flower of my striking force, made up to the full strength of three Commandos and with specially selected crews for the landing craft.

As a result of seven months' experience and two months of intensive training, I am preparing a memorandum for you on the direction of combined operations.[129] I am afraid it is rather long, but do please find time to read it.

It contains also a proposal for an operation which might be carried out at the same time as 'MANDIBLE', in the other end of the Mediterranean, if I am given authority to make preparations at once . . .

PART II: 1940-1941 147

71. *Keyes to Churchill*

[Carbon]
MOST SECRET & PRIVATE

Offices of the War Cabinet,
Richmond Terrace,
Whitehall, S.W.1.
4th February, 1941.

I have not bothered you with my difficulties more than I could help, since you appointed me D.C.O. and gave me an outline of what you wished me to do, and the men and vessels I would have under my control. I was very grateful to you, for it seemed to me a wonderful opportunity for being of real service, and I had visions of waging the kind of amphibious warfare which has always appealed to me, and of which I have had far more experience than any living soldier or sailor.

You put a ban on pin prick raids generally and small operations which could not really affect the enemy's war effort. I was fully in agreement with this policy, and I hoped before long to help to mount amphibious strokes, akin to those launched by the elder Pitt[130] two hundred years ago, but I have been sadly disillusioned.

I won't weary you with a long tale of my efforts to come to some working arrangement with the Naval Staff – the record is on the shelf ready for the historian, with those of my endeavours to avert the Trondheim fiasco; to get you power as well as responsibility; and also (with the help of the King of the Belgians) to get the B.E.F. away before it was too late, and thus avert Gort's "great victory at Dunkirk".

Three extracts will suffice to show that I cannot possibly be of any use to you in the prosecution of our war effort under the existing regime: –[131]

* * *

You have directed me to make my Commandos up to 5,000, and I have given my views as to the possibility of re-creating a spearhead, as good as that which has just been dissipated, by dividing it into two parts – neither of which is large enough to play a decisive role in an operation of the magnitude you told me to concentrate on.

Brigadier Haydon and I are forwarding a detailed report as to how it is proposed to bring the remaining Commandos at Home to full strength and raise three more. It will be about four months before the latter will be ready for service. So the old Commandos must have priority.

But it really is not fair to me (or the country) to limit my energies, readiness to accept responsibility, initiative and power of leadership to raising and training the personnel for a problematical combined operation, for which the Naval Staff have neglected to provide adequate transport and landing craft, and which will never be launched as long as the present C.N.S. and the Staff Officers who represent his views on the various Joint Service Committees remain in office.

When it was apparent to me that the C.O.S. Committee had no intention of making use of me for the planning and preparation of combined operations, I turned to the one active responsibility within my directive, which would enable my experience to be made use of, i.e. executive command of raiding operations carried out by my Commandos up to 5,000.

After an infinite amount of opposition, both in the War Office and the Admiralty, and thanks only to the knowledge that you were backing me, I have been able to organise and train a splendid striking force of about 4,000 officers and men in Commandos, and the officers and crews of all the landing craft which can be carried in the only existing transports fitted to convey them to a hostile landing place. A wonderful spear-head for an amphibious stroke.

No-one can say that I have not made every possible effort to use it offensively in waters in which it could have played a decisive part in driving Italians out of the Mediterranean and confining them to Italy itself.

In your most optimistic moments you could not possibly have foreseen the amazing success which Wavell and Cunningham have had in North Africa. If my force had been let loose under my leadership in the Mediterranean, which it would well have been several weeks before the Germans arrived there – but for the hostility and timidity of the C.N.S., I do not believe any limit could have been placed on what we might have achieved, by a succession of assaults on islands large and small, which the Italians in their present state of morale would never have withstood.

It is tormenting to reflect on the golden opportunities we have lost by failing to make use of the only sea-borne striking force we possess, or can re-create for some time to come.

The haste with which the three "Glens" were despatched, and the way in which the three Commandos were embarked, so that they were no longer the highly trained amphibious unit I had prepared for immediate action anywhere[132] – drives one to the conclusion that the one object of the Naval Staff was to get this striking force well away before it could do anything for which they might be held responsible – especially as the "Glens" and all the arrangements for their sailing were removed from my control.[133] You may remember their anxiety to send my force away round the Cape before, on the 7th January.

It is hard to believe that it was only sheer incompetence to understand the first principles of war. Anyhow the result is the same and the ships will have to be unloaded and reloaded at Cape Town, if the force is to be ready for use on arrival in the Mediterranean, or if you want it to go into action before it enters it, which seems possible.

If the D.C.O. is to be of any use to the Minister of Defence, he must be his representative on the C.O.S. Committee for all matters concerned with Combined Operations.

There is a way in which this folly of dispersal might be turned to our ultimate advantage and to the utter confusion of the enemy if we only pursue a bold course.

I quite appreciate that a sufficient Naval force must be kept in Home waters for the vitally important duty of safeguarding our sea communications, particularly with America, and containing the German surface fleet. Having insured this, I suggest that everything that can possibly be spared should be used offensively in the Mediterranean.

Give me an absolutely free hand (as I had in 1918) to prepare and lead an expedition to raid 'Yorker' and hold its harbour[134] and aerodrome long enough to allow a small expeditionary force to land and exploit the raid by capturing the whole Island, as proposed by your F.O.P.S.

We will have to do it now without the flower of my troops and more than half the trained Naval personnel. However they should be the spear-head of a similar campaign in the Eastern Mediterranean.

I shall have to start again at my beginnings and build up my force, by making use of all the landing craft we possess in Home waters and improvising means of carrying them – so much for the Naval side of the striking force – It can be done.

I can produce nearly 2,700 Commando troops now, who can be trained with the Naval personnel in two or three weeks. I am a Colonel Commandant of the Marines, and Bourne the A.G. would gladly put his two Brigades under my command – about 2,500 of them are by now well trained. Attached to the Marines is a Battalion of Argyll and Sutherland Highlanders, who have been working with them for several months. I believe they are now pretty good and could be counted as Marines – (as the 2nd Queens were in the *Queen Charlotte* on the glorious 1st of June). I would then have a striking force of about 6,000 which, as a sailor, I could legitimately command. A combined operation of this nature must be conducted by one supreme Commander, and this raid must be a Naval Occasion.

Can you think of one successful hazardous combined operation of any moment since the capture of Quebec, when Wolfe and Saunders worked with such wonderful co-operation? I tried so hard to get their example repeated off Gallipoli, but it seems almost impossible to get soldiers or sailors or their respective Ministries to accept responsibility – each tries to place the burden on the other's shoulders.

A Chiefs of Staff Committee, aided by little people on the various Joint Committees, can be relied upon to do NOTHING.

I assaulted a position with about 1,200 Bluejackets and Marines, which no soldier, other sailor, or Government for that matter, would have accepted responsibility for attacking. But a courageous First Lord[135] and First Sea Lord[136] accepted the responsibility of giving me a free hand and I did not disappoint them. I believe the Government knew nothing about it until it was all over. I do not know why, but soldiers, sailors and politicians always seem to shrink from the responsibility of an amphibious operation – As you know so well to your cost.

I do hope that Cunningham and Wavell, who seem to be working splendidly together, will find a resolute Leader for my striking force in the Eastern Mediterranean and that it will not be wasted.

I trust the news, that we have sent our one striking force to the Mediterranean round the Cape, will reach the enemy, for then we may yet be able to capture 'Yorker' and 'Workshop' before the Germans forestall us there. They must anticipate an attack on 'Mandible' but they cannot possibly think that we would undertake so formidable a task as 'Yorker' without it, particularly after their occupation of Sicily. But we cannot afford to waste time discussing it in Committee. It was suggested a week ago but nothing has been done to make it possible. Give me a free hand to take charge of the planning and preparation at once, or is this enterprise too heavy a burden for you to bear against the strenuous opposition which it is sure to arouse in the C.O.S. Committee? The Joint Committees will work overtime to damn it.

Why not throw them overboard[137] – no-one will blame you if you allow Keyes of Zeebrugge to carry out a raid far less hazardous than Zeebrugge and infinitely less dangerous than the prompt stroke which followed three weeks later at Ostend.

If you cannot do this, why not let me share your burden as Under Secretary for Defence? In such a capacity I could ensure that when a decision for undertaking an operation is made, the preparations for carrying it out are not held up by Committees, but prosecuted vigorously. It is hateful to see you being let down, as you so often have been by your technical advisers.

Or failing this, make me C.N.S. (for which my varied experience and the responsibilities I have borne in peace and war fit me). I would give the ardent spirits who are spoiling to fight a chance, and I would represent the Navy on the C.O.S. Committee with the knowledge and the desire to make full use of its ability to wage amphibious warfare.

If Alexander won't take me as First Sea Lord [Added in holograph: "For the second time! "] – why not make me First Lord. What is the use of having a First Lord in wartime like Alexander? – Who understands *nothing* about war and has not the knowledge to select the right kind of people to form the Naval Staff we so sorely need at the moment.

In my conversation the other day, as I told you, he took credit for having consented to sending the "Glens" round the Cape – not on the advice of his Naval Staff – but only after he had consulted the Controller as to when new landing craft would be delivered. If he had put the real issue, the Controller would not have given such stupid advice, and there could only have been one answer, since Fraser is a fighter and has, I know, had his eye on the Mediterranean for a long time.

Several Admirals have been successful First Lords in time of war – Hawke, Keppel,[138] Howe, St. Vincent and Barham.[139] St. Vincent was at his zenith as First Lord when he was 70, and later hoisted his Flag again when he was 72. Barham was 79 when, as First Lord, he was entirely responsible for the masterly campaign which preceded Trafalgar.

My love for polo is one of the weapons used against me, but the fact that I got into the final of a first class Tournament at Cowdray as a full Admiral aged 57, and won ties playing 1 against star backs like Jack Harrison and the brothers Fanshawe of the Bays, and played the following year as an Admiral of the Fleet, *ought to be counted to my credit*.

The people who lie about me and hate me don't mention that for 4½ years I administered the Submarine Service in every Department – construction, maintenance, personnel – and raised it from the little mobile minefield of Fisher's[140] and Bacon's original conception and trained it into a fighting force, which never hesitated to seek its targets in enemy waters.

They don't mention that I was brought down from command of a Division of Battleships in the Grand Fleet to be the First Director of Plans. Nor that, when Bacon could not be induced to carry out our plans and Jellicoe would not order him to do so and they were dismissed, I was given a free hand to execute the plans I had recommended and was successful both in the Dover Straits and on the Belgian Coast.

They don't mention that, for nearly four years, I was D.C.N.S. to Beatty, in that strenuous period after the war when the Navy had to struggle for its existence, with little help from you – naturally as Chancellor of the Exchequer bent on defending the public purse. Beatty trusted me, left much to me, and was often away for weeks at a time, in America, and when his wife was ill and he took her abroad. I attended every C.I.D. meeting in five different administrations. The Navy has to thank Beatty and me for Singapore, which Alexander did his best to destroy and did shut down. In the fight we put up in the Committee over which Birkenhead[141] presided – for just sufficient cruisers to give some semblance of security[142] – on more than one occasion I conducted our case. One day I fought you for 8″ cruisers to replace our old 7.5″ and was complimented by Birkenhead. I have a letter you wrote me a few months later commending the wisdom of our steady replacement programme, which assured the maintenance of the essential building yards and firms.

You persuaded me to go into Parliament, where I have been for seven years, fighting under your banner for all the things which we knew were necessary, if the Empire was to survive, and to quote your simile "to give the lobster a new shell". Why don't you let me help you now to use its claws?

I can't help not having the glib tongue apparently needed for political advancement, and, as you know, I have never sought it in peace time, but I have much more administrative experience and power of leadership than the majority of politicians, who talk themselves into Cabinet rank.

As First Lord, I could have a Labour Under Secretary. That ought to satisfy the Labour Party and surely something might be found for Alexander more in keeping with his outlook and capabilities.

Ever since I went into the House, I urged, in Press, in Parliament, in public speeches and private conversation, the vital importance of your being persuaded to join the Government of the day to reorganise our defences – many times to Margesson.[143] There was only one reply – no Prime Minister would ever have you, because you would dominate any Government of which you were a member.

No-one could ever dominate you. You can do anything you like in the country – if you would only realise it, and nothing you could do would be more popular with people who matter and the man in the street than to employ me properly. Anyhow, I would only add to your burdens if I stayed where I am, under the existing conditions at the Admiralty, and I must ask you to release me from the appointment of D.C.O. if it is to remain as it is at present.

If you won't do any of the things I have suggested, you had better drop me out of an aeroplane in North Africa, somewhere near Weygand,[144] and I will do my best to bring him and the French Navy in on our side. Anyhow I can't stay in England doing nothing.

I place myself and my sword at your service, but I am not prepared to stop in the dead alley into which I have been forced without any power to do anything of any value to the country.

72. Churchill to Keyes

Private

10, Downing Street,
Whitehall.
February 5, 1941.

It is quite impossible for me to receive a letter[145] of this character, I am sure it would do you a great deal of harm if it fell into unsympathetic hands. I therefore return it to you with its enclosures. If you wish to write on matters affecting the Commandos, pray do so to General Ismay . . .

73. Keyes to Churchill

[Carbon]

Offices of the War Cabinet,
Richmond Terrace,
Whitehall, S.W.1.
6th February, 1941.

I imagine from your letter of 5th February[146] that you have read all the papers I sent you. My minute of 4th February[147] was meant only for your eye – which I thought was sympathetic. It was typed by my Secretary who has been with me on and off for 26 years and he took it himself to your Secretary who assured him that it would only be seen by you.

The attached minute of 30th January to the C.O.S. Committee relates to only one of many miscarriages,[148] which would have been avoided if they had allowed me to be a real Director of Combined Operations.

The concluding paragraph shows how impossible it is for me to continue in that Office and, if you cannot make a satisfactory change, I must ask you to release me.[149] To acquiesce in the existing conditions would be to condone inefficiency which is seriously impeding the prosecution of the war and thus delaying victory.

You ought to know me well enough by now to realise that I never have and never will allow any personal considerations to come between me and what I consider to be my duty to the country . . .

74. Keyes to Admiral J. C. Tovey[150]

[Carbon]

21st February, 1941.

Most Secret and Personal (Copy sent to Brigadier Haydon)
With reference to the P.S. of my letter of 20th February, 1941,[151]

I have taken this question up with the Chiefs of Staff Committee and they have decided that the decision is to rest with you. My directive, as Director of Combined Operations, gives me "Command of Raiding Operations on coasts in enemy occupation." My instructions from the Chiefs of Staff Committee, approved by the Prime Minister, for CLAYMORE,[152] are as follows: – "The Operation . . . . . will be planned, organised and executed under the direction of the Director of Combined Operations in consultation with the Commander-in-Chief, Home Fleet, and Dr. Dalton's[153] organisation."

I hesitated to ask you to let me embark on one of your vessels, as a degraded Commodore for instance, to take command of the Operation, but if you were prepared to do so I would of course take full responsibility for pressing home the attack or calling it off, as I know you would if you were able to be present.

If, in view of the decision of the Chiefs of Staff Committee, you would like me to come up and take command of the inshore vessels, I would of course be delighted to do so.

I don't want to cut any young Captain out of an opportunity of winning his spurs and though the possibility of any real opposition is very remote, I quite appreciate you may prefer to give one of your excellent Captains his chance, and in that case I know you would support him in whatever he might decide to do.

All good wishes . . .

[Added in holograph:] I have told Haydon to tell you of our efforts to put it across the WOPS.

75. *Admiral J. C. Tovey to Keyes*

By hand of Officer only.   H.M.S. *Nelson*,
                                                        23rd February 1941.

Thank you for your letters. With enemy U-boats taking station on our front door step I was afraid it might not be possible to spare destroyers for your operation. I don't think some people realise how very short of destroyers we are in this war; at the moment I have nine serviceable plus three still working up. And although up to date we have not been fortunate in finding trouble, we do go out periodically looking for it. Constant demands occur for screens for capital ships proceeding to and returning from escorting convoys, patrolling the Faroes channel, minelaying operations, escorting ships on passage, capital ships exercising, etc.; we used occasionally to think we were fairly hardworked in destroyers last war but the work did not compare with what is demanded continuously of them nowadays.

I have considered many types of operations off the Norwegian coast, but the shortage of both cruisers and destroyers is such that whether one likes it or not careful consideration must be given to whether the object is worth the possible risk to the forces employed. Occasionally some people appear to get the curious idea that such operations are not undertaken due to the lack of courage or spirit of adventure of the officers and men. You, I know, will realise how ridiculous and offensive such an idea is, the officers and men of today are simply magnificent and are certainly no less gallant than the fine fellows of the last or any previous wars.

'Claymore' in many ways is attractive, as you see it has not been easy to find the destroyers and I have only agreed to doing so on the assumption that the possible complications have been thoroughly examined and considered by you and your staff. Points that I have in mind are the effect on the Norwegians: that they are mostly pro-British I understand, but whether they are to the extent of meekly watching their fishing industry and their source of livelihood being destroyed in front of their eyes I don't know. It seems almost inconceivable that some of them won't resist and if they do, however ineffective their resistance it will certainly entail loss of Norwegian life. Serious resistance, calling for covering fire from destroyers would obviously involve serious loss of life. It is an operation which can not be lightly repeated and how serious the result of complete success would be to the Germans it is difficult to gauge but I cannot visualise it as being very serious; it will be an irritant more than anything else. Of course it may encourage the Norwegians, but our experiences with the French do not encourage that view.

However, I assume that you know the answer to these questions and consider the 'object' well worth while and I will see that the Naval side of the operation is organised and carried out as efficiently as possible. Although the responsibility of the Senior Naval Officer will be considerable I really don't think there is any necessity for you to take command, I have complete confidence in Captain Caslon,[154] S.N.O. and the other destroyer commanding officers.

My principal hope, a very slight one I fear, is that the enemy may send out surface forces to try and intercept and I intend being out myself in *Nelson,* with *King George V* and two cruisers to give them satisfaction if they do.

The most doubtful feature is the weather, always unreliable at this time of year and we have just had a fine spell which is more than our quota.

I dislike strongly the Ministry of Information trying to make a Hollywood show of it, but I presume that for some good reason this has been approved by the highest authority.[155].

I am arranging for a submarine to provide a W/T beacon for the approach in case of low visibility and I regret that this means keeping the transports waiting here longer than I would like. The opportunity will be taken to calibrate the ships' D.F. and to get a very thorough understanding between the two services involved.

I am not too happy about security, as there is a constant flow of civilian workmen backwards and forwards to the mainland, but we are taking what steps we can. Enemy planes make fairly frequent reconnaissance flights over this base, but I hope they will take the transports for warships or minelayers; our initial courses when we sail will, I hope, give the impression of one of our fairly frequent minelaying expeditions.

Good luck to the expedition and your conception . . .

P.S. Since writing the above reports have been received of several more attacks by U-boats on merchant vessels in the North Western Approaches. And I have had no alternative but to urge the Admiralty very strongly that eccentric operations such as 'Claymore' should be postponed until enemy U-boats have been taught that they cannot operate in these waters. In my opinion there is no comparison between the importance of the two objects.

76. Keyes to Tovey

Private
[Carbon]   25th February, 1941.

Thank you very much for your letter.[156] I do most fully appreciate how desperately short you are of destroyers. Frigates and destroyers – it has always been the same story down the ages.

I thoroughly agree with you in all you say about these little sideshows in general, and in this one in particular. It was inspired by Dalton's party and arranged while I was in Scotland training troops and crews for Assault Landing Craft for a *real* Combined Operation, which could not have failed to hit the enemy very hard.

During one of my visits to my office here I saw the Norwegian Naval Attaché and Chief of Staff and put to them the views you have expressed so clearly as to destroying the property and livelihood of Norwegians. However, they declared they were strongly in favour of destroying plant of value to the Germans and capturing Germans and "Quislings", and since they have provided a very keen contingent, I will be sorry on their account if "CLAYMORE" cannot be carried out. I rather thought that the Prime Minister would consider it a waste of effort. However, Dalton urged him to agree to it and he approved – reluctantly, I believe – while I was in Scotland.

When I was appointed D.C.O. and was told by the Prime Minister of the wonderful craft, aircraft and troops I would have at my disposal, I had visions of helping him to carry out amphibious warfare akin to that waged by the first Pitt two hundred years ago. With his approval I set my face against pin-prick raids and made up my mind to prepare something which would really affect the conduct of the war.

Then for some time my troops were handed over to C. in C. Home Forces for anti-invasion defence. By the time I got some of them back in October, I had come to the conclusion that it would be a very long time before we would be able to carry out any oversea operation of any value near[?] Home Waters. On the other hand, there seemed to me an almost unlimited field for sea-borne operations, such as capturing islands and generally harassing the Italian coastwise communications in the Mediterranean and Middle East, and I have been trying since October to get my Commandos and the vessels which can carry assault landing craft into the Mediterranean.

I asked Haydon to tell you of our efforts and how they have been frustrated. It was a bitter disappointment. However, I live in hopes.

It is difficult to make the Inter-Service planners and staffs realise that our ability to wage amphibious warfare in the face of aerial reconnaissance depends on the possession of ships capable of transporting troops and assault landing craft sufficiently fast to approach and launch an attack during dark hours. The landing craft which we are building in great numbers and are accumulating in the Mediterranean will be of no value until we can improvise vessels to carry them rapidly to enemy waters.

I only hope, as you suggest, that the enemy may try to attack "CLAYMORE" with surface craft and thus give you the opportunity you are seeking. Later on we may be able to work together for the overthrow of the enemy in Norway by doing something much more worth while.

I am very glad you have given the command to a destroyer officer. I have always felt that they and submarine officers never got a fair share of peace-time promotion, but in war they have always proved their worth. On that account I was delighted to see your appointment.

[Holograph] I send you with all good wishes Wavell's lectures in pamphlet form.[157] I believe 2 or 3 editions are sold out already . . .

77. *Admiral Andrew Cunningham to Keyes*

[Holograph]
Commander-in-Chief,
Mediterranean Station.
10th March 1941.

I saw Sir Walter[158] yesterday & he gave me the copy of your letter.[159]

Actually I had the original – and answered it, but on examination I think my reply went down with so many other letters in the *Hyperion* when she was mined off Pantellaria.

In it I gave you my reasons for opposing "Workshop." *The chief one being* the difficulty of supply after capture.[160]

I am very glad it did not take place. I think it would have been a disaster, the whole sea that morning was alive with German dive bombers & as you know the *Illustrious* was badly knocked about so I don't suppose the "Glen" ships would have lasted very long.[161] Further we are having enough difficulty at the moment in supplying Malta without having to supply an Island 150 miles beyond.

We had a set back at Castelorizzo. The Commando took the island easily but were bombed out of it.[162] I think these commandos out here, where they are never out of range of aircraft, must have some means of defence landed right behind them.

Walter Cowan told me you were anxious to come out here for the proposed operations.[163] I really do not think it would work. There is a young Rear Admiral & Major General in charge – do you not think that your presence would embarrass them?

Actually due to other moves we have had to put the operation off for I fear nearly two months.[164] Most disappointing. It is the only thing that will put an end to mining the Canal, which is bothering us all so much at the moment.

I am glad to see that the "Glens" have brought me out a couple of M.T.B.'s. I have been asking for them for so long – I want to shake up the Dodecanese. They are just the things for island warfare.

The Lofoten affair judging by the press appears to have been a good show. I suppose some of your experts were in it.

All best wishes & please forgive me for not tumbling to the fact that your answer was sunk sooner...

78. Directive to the Director of Combined Operations

(a) *Note by Major-General Ismay*

SECRET.
C.O.S. (41) 166.
14TH MARCH, 1941.

COPY NO. 34

WAR CABINET.
CHIEFS OF STAFF COMMITTEE.

DIRECTIVE TO THE DIRECTOR OF COMBINED OPERATIONS.

Note by Major-General Ismay.

The Prime Minister has approved the amendments to the Directive to the Director of Combined Operations, which were put forward by Admiral of the Fleet Sir Roger Keyes, and agreed to by the Chiefs of Staff on the 11th March (see Annex to Minutes of C.O.S. (41) 79th Meeting and Minutes of C.O.S. (41) 93rd Meeting, Minute 1). The Prime Minister has also added a new paragraph at the end of the corrections to paragraph 2(e).

A copy of the Directive in its final form is attached.

(Signed) H. L. ISMAY.

Great George Street, S.W.1.,
14th March, 1941.

(b) *Enclosure*

SECRET.

DIRECTIVE TO THE DIRECTOR OF COMBINED OPERATIONS.

The responsibilities of the Director of Combined Operations were laid down in a directive issued to Lt.-General A. G. B. Bourne by the Chiefs of Staff in June 1940.[165] In view of the changes which have taken place since that date, it is desirable that these responsibilities should be re-defined.

At the same time, it is to be recognised that the division of responsibility between the Director of Combined Operations on the one hand and the Joint Planning Staff on the other is not capable of precise definition. There must always be border-line cases which will have to be settled as they arise by mutual consultations.

General Scope of D.C.O.'s Responsibilities.

2. The Director of Combined Operations is responsible, under the general direction of the Minister of Defence and the Chiefs of Staff, for: –

(a) The Command and training in irregular warfare generally, and in landing operations in particular, of the troops specially organised for this purpose, i.e. the Special Service Troops.

(b) The supervision of the technical training in landing operations of such other troops as may from time to time be earmarked for enterprises which call for this particular type of training.

(c) The development, including experiment, research and trial, of all forms of special equipment and craft required for opposed landings.

(d) The initiation, within the general policy prescribed, and the planning and execution of operations by the Special Service Troops, reinforced if necessary by small forces – naval, military and air – which are not normally under his command.

For the purpose of making plans he may have any assistance he requires from the Joint Planning Staff. In this connection, the Prime Minister has laid it down as a guide that the Director of Combined Operations should be responsible for the planning and execution of raiding operations which involve not more than 5,000 men.

(e) The provision of advice to the Chiefs of Staff on the technical aspects of opposed landing operations. When the Chiefs of Staff Committee are considering an operation which involves an opposed landing, the Director of Combined Operations should be present, when that part of the plan is under discussion.

Similarly, when the Joint Planning Staff are directed to prepare or wish to suggest outline plans for an operation which involves an opposed landing, they should first consult the Director of Combined Operations.

Subject to: –

(a) his concurrence that the opposed landing is practicable;

(b) the general nature of the project being approved by the Chiefs of Staff and Defence Committees.

D.C.O.'s staff and the Joint Planning Staff will work in conjunction; the Joint Planning Staff preparing the General Plan and the Director of Combined Operations' staff preparing that part relative to the opposed landing. Subsequently the Commanders designate will consult the Director of Combined Operations and his staff when working out their plans.

The above does not apply to the work of the F.O.P. section, who will receive their instructions both as to what they plan and who they consult, from the Minister of Defence Office.

(f) The provision of advice to the Chiefs of Staff on the tactical use and allocation of carriers and landing craft for Combined Operations. The Director of Combined Operations will be responsible for the training of Naval personnel in so far as opposed landings are concerned, including officers and men of carriers, landing craft and beach parties.

He will have under his command and operational control carriers and landing craft for raiding purposes, which will include such Transports as are from time to time allotted by the Admiralty for this purpose.

Administration.

3. The routine administration of the Special Service Troops including maintenance and movements, will be the responsibility of the War Office. The D.C.O. is, however, responsible for advising the War Office as to how these units can best be organised, armed, equipped and located, to meet his particular needs.

Special Equipment and landing craft.

4. The Director of Combined Operations will have under his command and direction the Inter Services Training and Development Centres.

Authority for Operations.

5. The general policy for raiding operations will be laid down from time to time by the Chiefs of Staff in accordance with the direction of the Prime Minister and Minister of Defence.

79. *Richmond to Keyes*

[Holograph]

The Master's Lodge,
Downing College,
Cambridge.
March 15, 1941.

It was Drake himself who said that about "the advantage of time & place . . . once being lost is irrecoverable." And if you want to add another reminder of the importance of not losing or wasting time, here is another great fighting man's saying – Oliver Cromwell: "Give me leave to tell you that I do not believe that in any war that ever was in former times nor in any engagements that you have had with others, this Nation had more obligations upon them to look to itself – to forbear waste of time, precious time." (1656)

You refer to Chatfield & his share in our unpreparedness. His sins go very far. Unless I am mistaken he was one of the "Naval Experts" who advised Chamberlain that the cession of the Irish bases would expose us to no danger. How any seaman could have said such a thing passes my comprehension; but the Admiralty *did* say it, and they said it in flat contradiction to the Admiralty of 1921, as Churchill reminded the House in his speech of May 8th 1938. Truly, we've been unfortunate in our naval advisers from Madden onwards! To them we are indebted for our 50 cruisers & our 150,000 tons of destroyers. They lacked the courage to oppose those ignorant & misguided Labour politicians; for I will not do them the disgrace of saying they were themselves so utterly ignorant of sea warfare as not to know that the number of both those [?] classes was not a relative matter, but an absolute one; & that under no conceivable circumstances could 50 cruisers give our trade the defence it needs. Alexander, in his last speech, shows that he has at long last learnt the truth (Hansard, 5th March, p. 927) & now knows that "a certain absolute strength" is called for.[166] But why the deuce could not Madden or Field or Fisher tell them that, & insist upon the public's knowing that this was the opinion of the Board of Admiralty? I told Tam Field plainly [?] that he & his colleagues were either cowards or that they were too intent on holding their jobs to do their duty to their country; and I am convinced that I was right.

You might cast your eyes – if you have any leisure, which I daresay you have not – on a small book I've just done on British Strategy – purely a historical sketch, but you can read between the lines. And another will shortly follow on Invasion in which I have shown that our security against invasion has, in the final analysis, always depended upon the superiority of our flotilla & frigate (M.T.B., destroyer of today) forces in the Channel & Narrow Seas, which the French transports & their defending gun boats & gun sloops could not face. It was because of that British flotilla superiority that Napoleon had to devise his great schemes to get his battle fleet into the Channel & support the passage of the barges. Unfortunately, as our naval history has been written, all the attention has been concentrated on Nelson, Cornwallis[167] & Villeneuve[168] – the foundations, unquestionably, of the structure of defence; but the foundation because of the support they afforded the flotillas which opposed the barges & prevented them – the flotillas – from being overwhelmed by superior battleship force. But we, neglecting our flotillas, have today not enough to protect the trade, and I hear it said that naval assistance cannot be expected for over 30 hours! To that position have our Maddens, Fields & Chatfields reduced the Navy & their country! It makes my blood boil. All I got for putting these facts out in my various writings was abuse & condemnation.

But go ahead with your plans. I pray to hear that you have got into those particular islands referred to in your earlier letter. I should not weep my eyes out if I heard we had taken Massawa from the sea & finished up the naval situation in the Red Sea with the destruction of whatever destroyers & submarines there are in those waters & so set free our forces for service elsewhere. Good Heavens! The scope for your [?] efforts, well prepared, & in ample force.

Incidentally, I find that the force regarded generally as the maximum for such operations in the old days seems to have been 10,000.

80. *Tovey to Keyes*

Commander-in-Chief,
Home Fleet.
31st March, 1941.

Thank you so much for your letters. Caslon was excellent and it was a pleasure to see the way the sailors and soldiers worked in together, with only the one idea of making the operation[169] a success.

When the *Queen Emma* and *Princess Beatrix* arrived up here I was rather distressed to find what a short time they had been in commission; fortunately weather conditions were unusually good and Kershaw[170] and Brunton[171] both got well down to it and achieved as high a standard of efficiency as was possible in the time.

In my covering letter to the report I have referred to the need for carrying spare gear for the landing craft. The lack of spare parts did cause us considerable anxiety, and did in fact stop me carrying out a full scale realistic exercise under way and in rather a lop for fear of damaging the davits or the landing craft.

The weather for the landing could not have been kinder; my impression was that any swell or a strong stream might make it difficult to get the landing craft away and would almost certainly have entailed damage to the davits and hoisting gear which would have prevented rehoisting.

When he arrived Haydon did not appear to appreciate the limitation of supporting fire from high velocity naval guns, though I think Hornby did. Haydon also thought that the destroyers would go right in to the various harbours, which of course under the circumstances I could not permit.

Not until about twenty-four hours before the expedition sailed did I see some photographs of the harbours showing what a large number of craft might be found in them; had I known earlier it might have been possible to make arrangements to bring some of them away.

I was disappointed at *Tartar* being in such a hurry to sink the *Hamburg*,[172] but I had been so insistent on the necessity for adhering rigidly to the time laid down for re-embarkation that he probably felt he had no time to spare.

It was disappointing that no enemy ships gave our supporting forces a chance; we were shadowed throughout the next day by enemy aircraft but not even bombers came out to give us a shot.

May I add that it was a great pleasure to all of us to work with your force. The obvious efficiency and the fine spirit of Haydon and all his officers and men filled us with admiration and gave us a feeling of complete confidence . . .

81. *Keyes to Brendan Bracken*

[Carbon] 15th April, 1941.

Your Messrs. Eyre & Spottiswoode want to re-publish the GALLIPOLI part of my Memoirs, which is out of print.

They say "it is a historical document and should remain as a permanent record."

They want me to write a new preface, "as GALLIPOLI is likely to be a war theatre for some time to come. We ought, I think, to do this new edition now if we are to do it at all."

My book emphasizes the tremendous opportunities which are open to those who possess sea power and are prepared to use it boldly in order to wage amphibious warfare. It is, moreover, a vindication of Winston's brilliant strategic effort which only failed because he was jockeyed out of power by jealous enemies – and I was supposed to be too junior to be allowed to carry it through.

The moment would be more propitious still if this publication synchronised with another bold amphibious stroke, inspired by Winston, and this time carried through by him and me.

Nearly three weeks ago the Chiefs of Staff almost enthusiastically approved of my forming an amphibious striking force of three Brigades and the vessels to carry them. I have done everything in my power to speed up its formation – the fitting out of the ships, etc. – but it will be ages before it is ready to strike under the existing system, by which every move has to be vetted and approved by inter-service committees.

It is simply tormenting to think of what is happening in NORTH AFRICA now and the opportunities we missed of making it impossible for the Germans to drive us back into EGYPT.

I had a letter from Cunningham to-day, dated 10th March,[173] in which he says that the operations for which half my assault carriers and three Commandos were sent out to the MEDITERRANEAN had had to be put off for about two months.

"*Time* drinketh up the essence of every great and noble action which ought to be performed and is delayed in the execution."

I do not believe that Winston's highest hour will come until he gives me the power to strike an amphibious blow which – like the forcing of the DARDANELLES – would alter the whole course of the war . . .

P.S. I have told Eyre & Spottiswoode to start the new edition at once. I will ask Winston to vet my preface to this new edition of the DARDANELLES campaign when I have written it.

82. *Keyes to Ismay*

Most Secret   24th April, 1941.
[Carbon]

I have established such good relations with the Chiefs of Staff – thanks to your good offices – and recently with the I.P.S. through my staff. The new D.D.C.O. will, I am sure, get on good terms with the J.P.S. and I am anxious to avoid anything which might upset the harmony!

But a month has passed since my proposal to form a striking force was so warmly approved in principle by the Chiefs of Staff Committee, nevertheless all my efforts have failed to get executive action taken. The inter-Service committees have, no doubt, been considering all the details and are being helpful but time passes and action is essential if we are not to be forestalled once again.

Inter-Service Committees can, of course, give invaluable help, but joint authority and responsibility is bound to reproduce the miscarriages and confusion which have characterised almost all Combined Operations in the past.

If the Chiefs of Staff Committee, with the approval of the Minister of Defence will make me responsible for detailed planning, and the preparation and training of the amphibious force necessary to mop up all the Atlantic Islands, no more time will be lost.

As you will see from my minute I have assumed that they will do so.

"The advantage of time and place in all martial actions is half a victory, which being lost is irrecoverable." Drake's "place" was Cadiz – the most formidable Spanish naval base. Let us also go for the most formidable "place" directly Spain is threatened, and refrain from disturbing the others before it is captured. They will fall into our hands without much effort, once we have secured CHUTNEY.[174]

83. Keyes to Churchill

[Carbon]   9.5.41.

I do fully appreciate the difficulties of the War Cabinet in connection with the seizure of PUMA.[175]

As D.C.O. I have done everything in my power to organise an amphibious force capable of carrying the operation to a successful issue against any opposition the Spaniards and Germans are likely to be able to mount against us for a few weeks to come, and I am going north on Sunday night to supervise exercises and rehearsals which we have arranged, to give the Commanders and their forces experience of the practical side of the business.

It was originally arranged that PUMA force would be ready to sail on the 17th May, but now apparently it will not leave until 22nd – or be able to carry out the operation before the 1st June, – the last day of the next dark period – because this date is governed by the day on which the *Ark Royal* can be made available to take part. If this could be put forward the expedition could with great advantage sail a few days earlier, as originally intended, and thus leave a little time in hand for possible delays. The danger of serious damage being inflicted by air attack on the assembled armada cannot be ignored and the sooner the convoy can get out of home waters the better. Delay of course also adds to the dangers of secrecy being compromised.

So far the matter lies within my Directorate. In view of the vital importance of denying the Atlantic Islands to the enemy and seizing them for our own use, I venture to make some suggestions on the general implications.

If the expedition does not sail in time to deliver the assault on 1st June the prospects of surprise will diminish rapidly in the next three or four days. After that surprise can hardly be hoped for and the hazards of the assault will be greatly increased.

Further, if it is considered imperative to wait indefinitely until either the Germans infringe Spanish neutrality or persuade Spain to join the Axis, the attack cannot be mounted to deliver the assault in less than about 17 days, during which the enemy will have time to forestall us, and the capture of PUMA against the defences and air force which the Germans will have had time to organise will be a very formidable operation needing far larger forces than those which are being assembled and trained – especially if it has to be done in moonlight.

It should be remembered, too, that we have not the means to carry a larger assault force – all the vessels and assault landing craft are already included in the PUMA force, and even they cannot carry all the specially trained troops which could be made available.

You mentioned this morning that the Norwegians complained that we had brought disaster upon them by laying mines in their waters. Surely the Germans had made every preparation for their Norwegian coup, and their advance forces were already hidden in merchant vessels in Norwegian harbours before a mine had been laid by us.

Anyhow, we may be absolutely certain that, unless this time we forestall the Germans, formidable action will be taken by them to prevent our seizing the Islands, after they have involved Spain in the war, long before we are in a position to strike!

It may be said that our action in attacking PUMA will precipitate an attack on Gibraltar which will make it untenable for our Fleet. But for the Battle of the Atlantic the possession of the Islands is infinitely more important than our ability to keep ships at Gibraltar, and in my opinion the temporary abandonment of the harbour can be faced if the Islands are in our hands, since we make so little use of passage through the Mediterranean from West to East, and in any case the enemy could not prevent passage during the dark hours.

The Spanish Foreign Minister has openly discredited us and expressed his opinion as to the certainty of a German victory and the seizure of PUMA would be a fitting reply to his Nazi talk and the seizure of Tangier.[176]

Germany will act whatever we do if it suits her, and she has only refrained so far because it has not been convenient to strike in that direction. Action on our part may well throw her timetable out of gear and that of Spain who is waiting on events.

The Spanish Islands belong to a potential enemy. The Azores to a friendly nation. I never could understand our anxiety to seize the Azores in preference to the Spanish Islands. A propos of your remark yesterday that the question of capturing PUMA was considered eight months ago and was turned down as being beyond our power – I was never consulted, and I certainly would not have agreed that it was not a feasible operation. Eight months ago it would have been far easier than it is now, since German infiltration is becoming increasingly serious, as is evident from the latest intelligence.

I do not think we should infringe Portuguese neutrality if it can be avoided, but with the Spanish Islands in our possession we would be in a position to act with overwhelming force directly Germany threatens Portugal.

If the Germans move into Spanish Morocco I cannot believe that Weygand and a great many French soldiers and sailors would not be ready to resist a German-Spanish attack. Our presence in the Atlantic Islands in force and our readiness to help them would surely strengthen their will to resist.

Let us be prepared to tell Weygand we will help to ensure his hold on Dakar and Casablanca, which after all are the keys to the French African empire and in the hands of an enemy would jeopardise victory in the Battle of the Atlantic.

Let us then tell the French Navy to let bygones be bygones on both sides and remember the wonderful co-operation of the British and French Navies in the last war, when we fought as comrades in the Dardanelles, and in the Dover Straits. Many of those in high positions now served with me in the Dardanelles and under me in the Dover Straits. The Captain[177] of the *Jean Bart* at Casablanca[178] is the son of Admiral Ronarc'h,[179] my most loyal friend and colleague at Dunkirk, when I was in command of the Dover Patrol including several French vessels.

At no time during your period of office has your prestige stood higher in the world than immediately after our attack on the French Fleet at Oran. It is deplorable that your intentions were not thoroughly fulfilled and that any vessels were allowed to escape.

In my opinion nothing could raise British prestige higher at this moment than the seizure of the Spanish Atlantic Islands. By doing so we would show strength and determination, rather than fear of consequences and what others may say of us. The Americans would, I

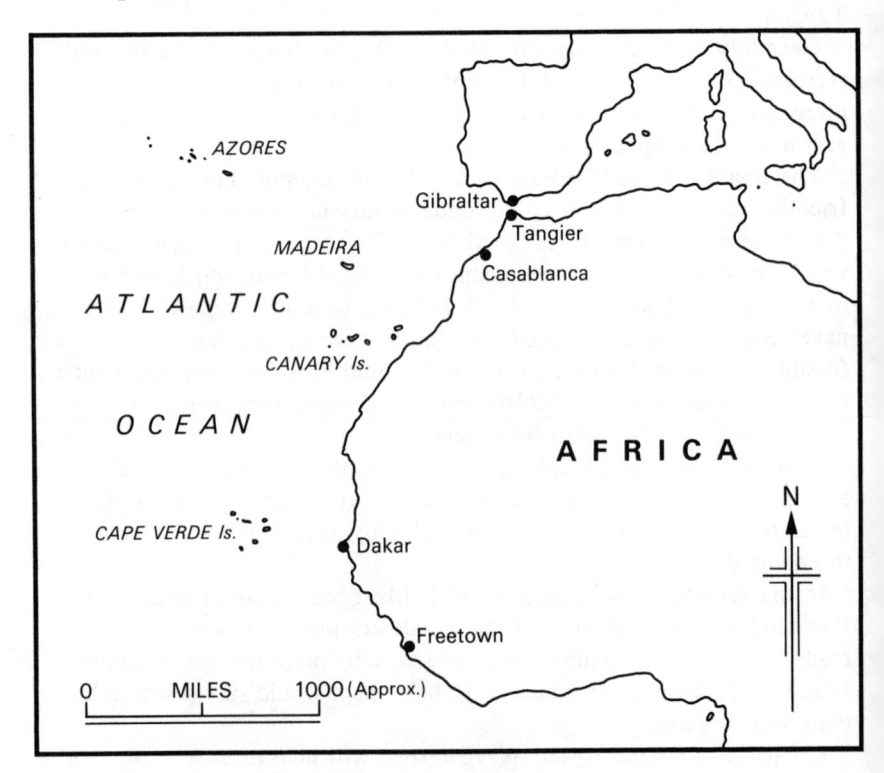

The Atlantic Islands

am sure, be deeply impressed and pleased that at last we were one move ahead of Hitler.

I would offer one more suggestion – Do not consult President Roosevelt but offer him a 'fait accompli' – he will not like to commit himself beforehand but he will follow public opinion.[180]

Let us seize the opportunity while the opportunity lasts. These matters are vitally essential to victory in the Battle of the Atlantic, and we cannot afford to risk failure.

84. *Keyes to Churchill*

[Carbon][181]   10th May, 1941.

Many congratulations on your great personal success on Wednesday.[182] Many of my friends on both sides of the House were very critical before you spoke, but your heartfelt retort to L.G.'s[183] taunt both amused and delighted them and me.[184] It bore out what I had told them and renewed their faith.

What a different position we should be in, in the Mediterranean and Middle East now, if the brakes on your wheels had not arrested your desire to capture YORKER and WORKSHOP while there was yet time and opportunity.

But the fear of air attack has been the keynote of the "NO" men's strategy. Fortunately Hamilton[185] of PUMA, who has come unscathed through a score of attacks during the Norwegian Campaign, shares my view to the full.

Another remark I often heard during the two days debate was "why must we always be forestalled? Why cannot we do the "rough stuff" and forestall the Huns when they are obviously preparing to infringe neutrality?"

It was noticeable during the debate that there was invariably applause for any reference to dropping "kid glove" methods.

You asked me if I had seen the plan. It is my original plan, much strengthened on the Naval side by the Naval staffs readiness to give Hamilton vessels which I never thought would be forthcoming.

Hamilton and Sturges[186] are stout-hearted fellows. I suggested the latter when I persuaded the Chiefs of Staff to let me organise the striking force. Pound could not have nominated a better man than Hamilton, who served with me as a midshipman and commanded a destroyer under me in the Dover Patrol.

[Holograph] I told Anthony[187] on Friday that I would submit an appreciation on 'Puma' to you . . .

85. Keyes to Eden

[Carbon] 12th May, 1941.

I enclose an appreciation of PUMA which I told you I was sending to Winston, and a covering note.[188] Also extracts from letters and minutes to the Chiefs of Staff which record my ceaseless efforts to organise a striking force for immediate use.

Tormenting delays wasted a month, but at length the formation of the force was approved and two good commanders were appointed in joint command. I have placed all my resources at their disposal and, except in an advisory capacity, I am no longer in the picture. The Joint Staffs optimistically decided that the expedition would be able to sail on the 17th May, and I must say the Inter-Service Staffs, since 24th April, have been working with feverish haste. The two commanders too are working on the right lines, but the organisation of an amphibious force is not as easy as all that, and there really was not time to have everything on the top line at such short notice.

I was going to Scotland last night to watch the exercises and rehearsals I had arranged, but I am told that these cannot now take place until the night of Wednesday/Thursday, so I am going north on Tuesday night. The reason of the delay is not quite clear, but I understand it is due to the detailed orders of the Joint Commanders being insufficiently detailed for practical purposes, and revision has been found necessary. However, I hope and think the expedition can be got ready to sail by the 22nd.

You said on Saturday that you had a fortnight in which to decide, but the expedition must sail on the 22nd if the assault on PUMA is to be delivered on the 1st June, the last night in the next dark night period. Failing this they will then have to wait nearly three weeks, when the nights will be shorter, or add to the hazards by making the assault in the light of the moon – to say nothing to jeopardising secrecy and giving time to the Hun visitors (including a late Hun C.G.S.) to help the Spaniards to strengthen the defences and possibly reinforce the air force.

"Procrastination is the thief of time" – "Time is half a victory which, being lost, is irrecoverable."

We might almost lose the Battle of the Atlantic if the Germans establish themselves in the Atlantic Islands, Dakar and Casablanca; at least, victory would be dangerously postponed . . .

86. *Keyes to Eden*

[Carbon] 12th May, 1941.
Most Secret and Personal.

In a separate envelope for Secretary of State only.

Please find time to read the attached letter[189] to you and the "appreciation" at once. The history of my effort can wait.[190]

I know the Almighty has given me an instinct for war and the vision to see what is essential in its prosecution. I could give many proofs. Moreover I have always been lucky. Winston would be wise to make me C.-in-C. and Governor General of the Atlantic Islands and give me the opportunity of trying to bring my one time warm friend Weygand (who nearly embraced me at Ypres on 21st May, 1940) and the French Navy once again into alliance with us for the preservation of their African Empire – which means so much to us.

My relations with the French Navy have been quite unique since 1915. I could give you proof. I was unemployed and had nothing to do with Oran. If I had had, I believe I would personally have blarneyed the Admiral – or, failing that, destroyed all the vessels there. Dakar – if I had been in command as I know you and Winston wished – would have gone differently. Joint or divided counsels can never be satisfactory.

Persuade Winston to back my good fortune in this matter, and you and he will never regret it . . .

87. *Eden to Keyes*

MOST SECRET & Foreign Office,
PERSONAL. S.W.1.
15th May 1941.

Thank you very much for your most secret and personal letter of May 12th.[191]

Of course I fully appreciate the importance of what you say; and the Defence Committee are giving the most careful consideration to your views . . .

88. Keyes to Richmond

[Holograph]

Offices of the War Cabinet,
Richmond Terrace,
Whitehall, S.W.1.
11.6.41.

I am afraid I have been a long time answering your admirable letter. There is indeed no answer to your criticism. I am sending you Hansard of yesterday's debate – it reflects the uneasiness of the country generally. Of course the P.M. got away with it.[192]

I think these ever lasting inter Service conferences of the Chiefs of Staff who deal with every trivial detail hour after hour day after day – and their satellites the Joint Planning Section, JPS, under whom sit the Executive Planning Section, EPS, advised by the J.I.C., Joint Intelligence Committee – are the source of all our troubles, as I think I have told you before.

If one can persuade the P.M. and C.'s of Staff Committee to approve of a policy – or an operation – one can be certain that action will be delayed for days and even weeks by the JPS, EPS and the JIC "exploring every avenue." In the case of an operation – of seeking for every conceivable objection to action being taken – In one or two cases I have in mind – objection to an operation within our powers because they want to carry out a far more formidable one which we have not the means to undertake.

I think when you historians take the records down from the shelves to tell your story you will find a sorry tale of wasted opportunities.

The P.M., to my knowledge, has tried to hold the C.'s of Staff to the decisions they originally made, but has not liked to override them. As L.G. [?][193] put it to me, "the iron of Gallipoli entered his soul" and since J.F. [Fisher] walked out and broke him, he has feared to challenge his professional advisers.

I think these recent events have brought home to him the need for a change. But what form it will take Heaven only knows.

In the meantime I have once again built up an amphibious force of considerable size, well equipped with armoured vehicles, tanks, etc. which our landing craft can carry. It is difficult to write about all this, I wish we could meet.

Do you ever come to London? I spend a good deal of time in Scotland. I spent 10 nights in the train in the last 3 weeks, most of the intervening nights on beaches since we must work by night. As old Dummy Oliver[194] used to say, the Downing Street Front and Whitehall are all important in war, and I daren't leave it for long.

If you come up, let's arrange to meet . . .

[P.S.] As one member said, I too blame the Army, it never could be induced to fight for air power. Gort acquiesced in conditions he should have declined to accept.

89. *Keyes to President Franklin Delano Roosevelt*

[Carbon] 12th June, 1941.

I know you will remember coming to Dover in 1918 when I commanded the Dover Patrol, and will not have forgotten my visit to the White House seven years ago when Barney Baruch[195] brought me to see you at your invitation.[196]

I remember I came away with the vivid impression that you meant to bring our two countries together if trouble threatened. The extent to which you have succeeded in doing so is a miracle and we are profoundly grateful.

I venture to introduce to you Paymaster Captain Woolley who was with me in every sort of tight place during the last War – in the Dardanelles, the Dover Straits, and off the Belgian coast in 1918.

He left the Navy some years ago and met a charming American lady, and is now returning to America as I feel that with his knowledge and contacts there he can best serve our Navy with its mission in Washington.

For the last ten months he has been my Secretary and perhaps you will give him an opportunity of telling you what I am doing in my appointment as Director of Combined Operations – which means waging amphibious warfare – and how I think our two Navies might co-operate if the occasion arises in the "Battle of the Atlantic".

I am, Mr. President,
With great respect,

90. *Captain Herbert Woolley to Keyes*

Most Secret & Private 3001 Dent Place, N.W.,
Washington, D.C.
26th July 1941.

I felt very sad when I said goodbye to you. We had been through such a lot and you had had to fight every inch.

* * *

We de-ammunitioned at Norfolk and passed up the Chesapeake on

Sunday [29 June], getting in late on Sunday night.[197] It was just like coming home to me. There was a squeeze to get us into our berth and lengthy conversations between the pilot and the people on shore as to why we weren't shorter, etc., etc., amused us considerably. Two new cars were ready to take us up to Washington when we finally berthed at about 10.30 p.m. but no customs or immigration officials were there. I made friends with the police and they collected them from their homes to pass us through about midnight. The customs man in plain clothes who took charge was a first class gangster type, with a big cigar – but everything was done in a very kindly fashion. They didn't open anything at all – we only had to fill out forms. We then put all the luggage in one car and travelled in the other. We admired its newness but it was too new and came to a dead stop a few miles out of Washington. We got it going down hill but eventually had to transfer to a taxi – arriving at the Wardman Park Hotel about 2.30 a.m. – found not a word of my wife. But early next morning called the American Express and found her hotel and she came straight over. It was splendid to be together again. Marion had been there since the 26th but was sure I would come all right – she is such a brave girl.

I saw Admiral French[198] who was very friendly. He asked after you and was very interested in what you had been doing. I soon found there wasn't a real job for me in the Repair Mission. We found a nice apartment at $80.00 per month with air conditioning in the living room.

I found Captain G. D. Owen – an old friend in the *Valiant* – on Captain French's staff. We went to tea with them and met Admiral[199] and Mrs Dorling there. I heard from him that poor Admiral Larken[200] had lost his boy in Submarines – he died of some sort of food poisoning I believe. I do hope you have had good news of Geoffrey and Roger by now. I would very much like to hear the story of their adventures.

I sent off your introductory letters – but I first got a message from the White House that Harry Hopkins[201] wished to see me. I told Admiral French and got his permission. At 11:00 on Wednesday 9th I drove in to the White House and felt in good form in one of my new Savile Row suits. Mr Hopkins had not been well and we had our talk in his bedroom suite. He was seated in a big armchair talking on the telephone to the Minister of War but motioned to me to take another by his side.

We had a really long talk – more than an hour and a half. He told me that they had had a telegram from Mr Winant[202] advising them that they should obtain information from me. We covered a very wide field. I gave him the history of Combined Operations as best I could. I told him of the difficulties and trials and your endeavour to build up an assault force to cover any of the small operations. That you now had a fine force, fully trained and ready for 'Puma'. That you attached the greatest importance to 'Puma'. I gave him the arguments as strongly as I could. He listened very attentively and I am sure fully understood them. He replied that America could not assist in taking any of the islands (I had not said you asked for any assistance) but would provide some 80,000 good marines or troops to hold them after we had seized them. He asked about the Azores and I explained that 'Puma' took up all our available carriers, landing craft, etc., and that we had a 'bluff' force standing by for them. He got out a big map and I ran over all the argument about 'Puma' again and told him that you considered that if we were forestalled again it would be a difficult nut to crack. He said he was not sure whether the Americans would include defence of 'Puma' if we did seize it. He said he quite saw the importance of taking 'Puma' but he was afraid we would be bombed out again. He thought that the French would fade out and the Germans would come through North Africa when they wanted to and would establish air bases on the African coast facing 'Puma'. I did not agree with his argument and pointed out again that as 'Puma' was of such great importance in the Battle of the Atlantic we must not be forestalled and must hold it against bombing if necessary (it certainly wouldn't be worse than Malta) and it would take a long time before the Germans could get the air bases ready, to deliver any sort of a serious airborne attack on them after they had been occupied by good troops.

We discussed carriers and craft – first flight – commando troops – the despatch of the "Glens", etc., etc., the importance of seizing an aerodrome and defence of beaches in the early stages, etc., etc. He asked questions about you and how fit you were. I told him quite truthfully how hard I had found it to keep up with you. He took it for granted that you would command any amphibious force we sent out. I did not tell him of the errors made in appointing inexperienced commanders, etc. He said that when he saw you at Chequers you were very cross.[203] I told him I remembered the occasion and that it was not at all surprising as you felt that there was something that ought to be done and that it was of vital importance. He agreed with me that you were a real fighter and would see anything through.

He said our Naval Staff here had given them nothing and appeared to know nothing about combined operations. He said that your experience and knowledge were very important and he felt that I had a good knowledge of your views; and that from our talk he considered it most important that I should see the various American Commanders and run over things with them, see their plans, craft, etc., and he felt I would be most valuable to them.

I explained that my duty had been as Secretary. He said that made no difference and that he wished me to ask Admiral Little[204] to suggest to the American Chiefs of Staff that they could make use of any knowledge I had and call on me at any time. He said I would also learn something from them and that the work should be done on the basis of exchange of information. He said he was anxious that I should see the President as he was very much interested in the subjects we had discussed. I was not anxious to approach Admiral Little and told him so but he pressed the matter. He said he could ask for me or the President could but that would only annoy every one. It had to be done through our Mission and at their suggestion. He said he considered the matter very urgent and that if I were able to start working with them that afternoon it would not be too soon. He said they had plans prepared for all the Islands and that they would let me into their most secret matters.

He ran through the Russian situation and said he had just had a talk with their late minister in Russia who had the theory that the Russians would have about 800,000 fairly good troops come from Siberia to the Urals and that they would have about 1,000,000 left to fall back there on the European side – and they would be able to hold a front there – that they had good steel factories, etc., behind that line. The important thing was for America and England to help them somehow now, or after they had been driven back they might make a deal with Germany – whereby they would get most of their territory back under strong conditions favourable to Germany. He asked my view whether our Navy could do anything. I reminded him of Archangel open in the summer – but we know the Germans are advancing in that direction – and of course the Navy has a great deal on its hands and it is a long way to go. Then again one comes back to 'Puma' which holds all our craft, etc., from operations elsewhere.

He was very keen on pin prick raids and I explained why they had been dropped. I told him how you visualised a strong series of amphibious attacks and wished to build up a force along the lines of the great Pitt. (I had taken care to read up Pitt's naval strategy the night before so knew something about it.)

I got on very well with Mr Hopkins and he told me to report to him any difficulties as he was anxious they should make use of me at once. I got him quite enthusiastic on what England and America could do together with their great command of the sea – but he made no promises about pressing for 'Puma'. Mr Hopkins did not say why he had called for me and did not show me Mr Winant's telegram until I had been there some time.

I saw Admiral French and he passed me on to Admiral Little – regarding their wish to make use of any information I might have. In the meantime I had a call from Captain Beardnell [Beardall],[205] U.S. Naval Attaché to the President to say that the President wished to see me at 12: 45 next day.

PART II: 1940–1941   177

Admiral Little was very friendly and said he thought it might be a good idea to have me attached to his mission, in addition to my work with Admiral French, so as to advise and be available when required regarding combined operations. He said he wished General Wemyss[206] and Air Marshal Harris[207] to see me as it was a matter for all three of them to decide.

The next day I went to the White House – where Beardall met me in the Lobby outside the executive offices. He told me that the President had received your letter[208] and was very anxious to see me. The Russian Ambassador was inside so I had to wait until 1.05 p.m. The new Attorney General was waiting to go in. I met General Watson,[209] U.S. Army Attaché to the President, and enjoyed him. They thought five minutes would be enough for me and Beardall said the President usually did all the talking. He came in with me and sat in the background. The President rose in his chair and seized me warmly by the hand and said, "So we meet again" – and then told me to make myself comfortable in the chair by his desk. He immediately asked after you and I told him you were in very good form. He asked if I remembered when you put him across the Channel in a destroyer and flew his Flag for him. He said they found mines off Dunkirk and anchored for the night within range of the German batteries but nobody bothered. He evidently had talked with Mr Hopkins after our conversation. He launched right away into questions about the Islands. I once more went over the arguments re 'Puma', etc., and I think pleased him by showing him I took it for granted he would know all about the importance of the harbour there, etc. He asked if you thought you could take it. I told him that you were satisfied you could, that you had a fine body of men thoroughly trained, and that your plan had the concurrence of the Chiefs of Staff.

He switched to the A – zores (as he called them). He said, "confidentially and quite frankly, your diplomacy has failed in Portugal about these islands" – I replied that I was not surprised and he laughed – and continued that he was trying to work privately through the American Minister in Lisbon to get them to agree to the Americans occupying the Islands for defensive purposes, and suggesting that it would be a good spot for their Government then to retire to if Portugal were attacked. He said he had hopes something would come of this. He said he had some very good troops with very good commanders whom he would be willing to put into the various islands after we had taken them but emphasized that that did not include 'Puma' but meant all the others including Cape Verde. He said he wished me to see that they had available all the necessary information so that they could occupy them immediately after we had seized them (this seems an important point as it would free you to do the other islands quickly but does not help about 'Puma'). He said it was very important to have all the plans about occupation and defence worked out very well in advance. He said we could do the job of seizing the islands much quicker than they could from America. I impressed on him the importance you attached to 'Puma' and the trouble attaching to delay, and what it would mean if forestalled again.

He switched to the work done by the mission here and asked me a number of questions which I was able to answer quite well as I spent my first few days reading through all the files here.

We discussed landing craft and he said the Americans had a new type for use in landing through breakers which he would like me to see. I explained the difficulty of carrying out a surprise assault during the period when the nights were short – he clearly had not realised that properly before. He asked details of the numbers of troops you had, etc., etc. He said he wished me to see everything they had and said that plans should be exchanged, etc., etc. He then turned to Beardall and said see that Comdr. Woolley sees (he then named all the senior American Naval and Army Commanders). He said he was very grateful to me. That he had very much enjoyed our talk – he was most interested in it and that he must see me again in a few days so that we could continue it.

Both the President and Mr Hopkins clearly took it for granted you would command any amphibious operation we sent and also clearly considered you were the one person for such an undertaking and had full confidence in you.

Before leaving I told the President how Marion and I had sat listening to returns coming in over the radio the first time when he was elected President until the excitement was too much and Marion said, "I think we had better go to the hospital now." Our daughter Diane was born that night. The story pleased him and he laughed and repeated, "You don't say" – "You don't say".

There had been rattles on the door handle but the President had motioned me to stay and when I left I found that my five minutes had been stretched into half an hour. I gathered from Beardall that he thought that the President had really enjoyed the talk. I told Beardall that I thought he had better do nothing about me seeing the various American Commanders and explained how the matter was being handled through Admiral Little. The President told me how much he liked our sailors and that one of them from one of the ships refitting met an American girl who asked him what the "H.M.S." on his ribbon stood for. The sailor replied without any effort at all: "H'I Mustn't Say".

I am very grateful to you for my two interviews as I will always be able to look back on them with interest. I hope I did some good re 'Puma' – I certainly pressed its importance on them.

In the next few days I was sent for to see General Wemyss and Air Marshal Harris. General Wemyss asked me many questions about your forces, craft, first flight, etc., etc. Air Marshal Harris was interested but said really none of them knew much about combined operations and he was going to recommend that they have me attached. I did not hear anything for a day or two more when I saw Admiral Little at a propaganda picture re the Oerlikon gun – very good. He asked me to come and sit next to him and said that they had sent a wire to the C.O.S. Committee in London as they felt it necessary to have their approval before having me attached to their Mission, etc.

* * *

The C.O.S. Committee no doubt passed the message they received from here to you for your concurrence or otherwise. I believe I can be helpful – I naturally learnt a great deal from reading the papers, watching the exercises, etc., and being with you so much and from your arguments to the C.O.S. Committee and with our own staff – based on practical experience on so many different occasions – which drove the numerous points home.

Admiral Little's mission here seem[s] rather apathetic (I am not really qualified to say though, as I am not in touch with their activities). General Wemyss and Air Marshal Harris both seemed to have a poor opinion of the American forces' capabilities if they came into the war. They said that their staff work was neglected. A decision would suddenly be announced and they would then try to put it into effect at the utmost speed without any properly worked out staff plans. They thought the result in war would be a nasty shock to them. Another thing was that the Americans thought they knew everything already. I think this a wrong estimate of them. They have an inferiority complex and don't like to be shown they are wrong but I am sure a great deal can be done with them – if tact is used and care is taken to compliment them on any point where they have progressed as far or further than we have. Especially by telling them we have learnt a lot from that particular point and are adopting it. They are quick in intelligence and will learn and adopt a lot from us if we avoid the attitude of talking down to them. We have much too much the superiority complex – so much so that more often than not we don't realise this ourselves and we are so conservative generally that we don't adopt new things in the eager way they do. As General Wemyss says, they have a bad way of going off full speed on a thing for two or three days and then forgetting all about it just when they were getting really started on it.

If they use me at all – I hope to be allowed to run over with them all you have done and to be able to show them the right way in which their assault forces should be built up. I think we should give them all we know and encourage them to the utmost to prepare properly now. If they come into the war this force will be a most valuable asset and I think the mere fact of having it would make them want to use it. The President is obviously more interested in Naval warfare than any other form of warfare and sees the great possibilities. I think, from what Harry Hopkins said, their Chief's of Staff resent civilian interference and both he and the President have to go a round about way in dealing with them. If you approve, I would like to have a copy of our progress reports, the reports on the Inveraray exercises, the pamphlet on landing craft, the pamphlets on communications and the use of Air forces in combined operations, the various pamphlets prepared at Inveraray on the use of Engineers, the removal of obstacles, etc., and the form giving the details of our various craft and carriers, remarks on the use of smoke. I have a great deal of it in my memory but Americans like exact details and they are sure to ask me the exact weight of an A.L.C., the type of can used to carry petrol for use by the aircraft when the aerodrome is first captured, etc., etc. The documents would increase the weight of any talks I have with them. It would be much better if they ask for me to be detached to them altogether so that I can be with them as much as possible.

I hope you have seen Harry Hopkins while he is in England. I am sure that the President or he will be quite willing to see me again anytime if you have any particular matters I should put before them. Mr Hopkins told me to keep in touch with him and report progress.

* * *

I do feel so very grateful to you for having had me with you and for letting me take a small part in your great struggles to make people see light and get something done. You have been so very kind to me in letting me come here. I do hope I am not too selfish.

Please give my very kindest remembrances to Lady Keyes. I do hope you are both very well and that the great day will come soon but not too soon for me . . .

91. *Keyes to General Auchinleck*[210]

[Copy][211]

Offices of the War Cabinet,
1A Richmond Terrace,
Whitehall,
London, S.W.1.
2nd August, 1941.

I enclose a précis of correspondence which has passed between the Middle East and the War Office and between the Chiefs of Staff and myself.[212] After stopping the arrangements made by the Chiefs of Staff for the return of one "Glen" ship and S.S. troops not required by you for amphibious warfare, the Prime Minister said he wished Commandos in the Middle East to be reconstituted. Perhaps he will ask you about this at Chequers.

Directly the Italians made war on Greece and we occupied Crete last October, I recommended sending the "Glen" ships and S.S. troops to the Mediterranean because I felt there was a tremendous field for amphibious warfare in the Middle East. There were irksome delays, the Germans forestalled us, and I think that a great opportunity was missed. Eventually our three best ships and three fine Commandos (1,600 strong), which had just undergone most intense training night after night for many weeks, left on 1st February to go round the Cape. In the meantime circumstances made it impossible to carry out the amphibious operation for which they were intended to be the spearhead.

Although the ships and landing craft have been mainly engaged in evacuating troops, I think they have proved their worth for amphibious operations. Nevertheless I have no doubt history will record that opportunities were missed of using them and S.S. troops effectively in their proper role.

Combined operations are very difficult to carry out. With dual control, there are so many conflicting influences and responsibilities; but there are tremendous possibilities in the waging of amphibious warfare if opportunities are seized during the lifetime of the opportunity. I am sure striking results can be achieved by intensive training, careful planning and reliable information, – shades of Bardia, where the 7th Commando was launched, under difficult weather conditions, to attack objectives which did not exist! Castelorizzo was captured and lost before our S.S. troops arrived; from all accounts, there were deplorable miscarriages.

As a result of my experience as Chief of the Naval Staff throughout the Dardanelles campaign, and later on the Belgian coast when I had an independent command, I made up my mind that for the capture of a beach or oversea position the assault must be carried out by selected troops of high morale, especially trained in night operations. I consider a daylight assault on a defended beach sheer folly. The development of air power has not only added to the hazards of daylight operations, but has made tactical surprise much more difficult. Hence high speed in the approach is essential.

The size and weight of the assault depends on the number of fast transports we possess and the number of assault landing craft they can carry. These, and their capacity, are very limited, and we can only afford to carry fighting men in the transports and landing craft, which deliver the assault to secure the beaches preparatory to landing the expeditionary force, vehicles, tanks, etc.

A few battalions of Royal Marines, consisting also of volunteers for sea service have been specially trained for the preliminary assault, and for this they and the Commandos are surely best fitted.

Of course, given time, regular units could be similarly trained, but I do not suppose you would get more than about 500 fighting men out of a battalion and they would not all be volunteers for amphibious warfare and hazardous service, as is the case of every officer and man of the Commando's 500.

As you will see from my correspondence with the C.I.G.S., I have had great difficulty in making good the gap in the S.S. Brigade, which I was directed to do after the departure of the S.S. troops for the Middle East.

I do not begrudge them for a moment if they are going to be made use of in the role for which they have been trained.

I do hope you will consider re-forming a small Brigade of Commandos of high quality. If you do, and you give them opportunities such as Wilson[213] gave the 11th Commando in Syria,[214] I am confident they will not disappoint you . . .

92. *Auchinleck to Keyes*

[Holograph]
War Office.
3rd August 1941.

Thank you for your letter of the 2nd August.[215] I know you will believe me when I tell you that I yield to no one in my admiration for the fine qualities of the officers and men who compose the commandos. They are magnificent. I still adhere to my opinion that they are an uneconomical organization and not really suited to our "make up." However, I am not bigoted in my ideas and if I have commandos at my disposal I will make sure that they are used to the best advantage and given every chance to prove their worth. I know you will be glad to hear that last night at Chequers it was decided to reconstitute a commando in the Middle East. I will see that this is done as expeditiously as possible . . .

PART II: 1940-1941

93. *Memorandum by Keyes*

[Carbon]
MOST SECRET

D.C.O.'s Office,
War Cabinet Office Annexe,
1A Richmond Terrace,
Whitehall, S.W.1.
6th August 1941.

MEMORANDUM BY D.C.O.

The plans which are being studied for future offensive operations do not apparently envisage major action before 1942.

Now that the Germans are deeply involved on their Eastern Front, the moment seems ripe for offensive action.

On another paper I have suggested a raid across the Straits within range of fighter cover, with a few units borrowed from 'PILGRIM',[216] but this of necessity can only be a small raid since we have not the means yet to launch and supply an offensive on the Continent.

We have, however, the power to deliver a considerable stroke overseas if the whole of our amphibious striking force could be made available. At the moment it is being held inactive for 'PILGRIM' — an operation which may never take place.

The war in Russia and the policing of the conquered states must greatly strain the German resources. The air raids by the R.A.F. will surely provoke retaliation and attract German aircraft to the Western Front and, with the Russian campaign hanging fire, the German air force must be pretty well stretched. It seems doubtful whether the Germans could provide much assistance for Italy, if we attack her many vulnerable islands.

Plans for the capture of SARDINIA were prepared before the Germans forestalled us in the Mediterranean. The Sardinians have never been amenable to the Fascist regime, which now also seems to be thoroughly discredited in Italy. The capture of SARDINIA might well encourage the Italians to turn to us to help them throw off the German yoke, which must be detestable to them.

'PILGRIM' force, with a few additional units which the Joint Commanders do not wish to make use of, but which are available, could provide an amphibious force capable of capturing and holding the island. Fast transports and raiding craft can carry a striking force sufficient to take CAGLIARI and its aerodrome, and the aerodrome of ALGHERO and the seaplane base at PORTO CONTE during the first flight; followed by the expeditionary force for which vessels have been taken up. It could be augmented, possibly by the Canadian Brigade, if further shipping could be made available.

We have the means now to disembark tanks and guns speedily directly on to beaches by the two "Maracaibos",[217] but directly the controlled minefield guarding CAGLIARI has been put out of action, the port will be available.

Thus we could exercise considerable pressure on the enemy in the Western Mediterranean without drawing on Malta, the Mediterranean Fleet or the Middle East.

Events may move very rapidly now, and I suggest that 'PILGRIM' Force should not be held inactive for only one object, since it is the only amphibious force we possess or can possibly possess for a long time to come.

In the summer of 1918 there was little prospect of bringing the war to a victorious conclusion that year. However, the success of the August offensive was most encouraging and on the 9th September, 1941, I was asked to attend a meeting at MT. CASSEL at which Marshal Foch[218] announced that we were going to finish the war before the winter. He outlined a plan for the recapture of the Belgian Coast in which the forces under my command were to co-operate. Steps were taken at once to get reinforcements from the troops who were being held for the defence of Britain, and for a possible offensive in 1919. Within six weeks the recapture of the Belgian Coast was completed, and the German Army was defeated everywhere within three months.

94. *General Sir H. R. Alexander[219] to Keyes*

SECRET   21st August, 1941.

I am returning the papers you sent me which I have read with much interest.[220]

I do not feel I can give a useful opinion on the projects for the capture of Sardinia and a raid on the French Coast, as I should require more detailed information as to latest enemy strengths, defences, etc. and air photos to study.

As regards the strategic advantages to be gained – this again can only be assessed by those who have full access to all information.

I have sent a copy of this letter to the C.I.G.S. . . .

PART II: 1940-1941 185

95. *Memorandum by Keyes*

MOST SECRET D.C.O.'s Office,
D.C.O. No. B. 1/224 War Cabinet Office Annexe,
[Carbon] 1A Richmond Terrace,
London, S.W.1.
27th August, 1941.

Chiefs of Staff Committee

The plans which have been studied for future offensive operations do not apparently anticipate major action before 1942; and these are on such an ambitious scale that they would require far more shipping and landing craft than we possess, or are likely to be able to acquire from abroad or construct here for a long time to come.

At the moment practically the whole of our means of prosecuting amphibious warfare has been absorbed in the PILGRIM expedition, which may never be necessary.

Four months ago, PUMA Force, carried in fairly fast vessels, had, in my opinion, every prospect of success. However, in the meantime the Germans have had practically a free hand to organise and strengthen the Spanish defences, and undoubtedly the military hazard is very considerably increased.

It is true that PUMA Force has been reinforced, but from the Navy's point of view this has only added to its responsibilities and difficulties. Instead of the original PUMA's small and fairly fast convoy, PILGRIM Force now consists of twenty-nine transports and M.T. ships and about thirty men-of-war, of varying sea-going qualities and speeds – which limit the convoy as a whole to 10 knots – and includes several vessels depending on fuelling at sea and some really not suitable to carry troops on a stormy ocean passage. If this armada of about sixty ships sails in mid-September, it is nearly certain to encounter one or more Autumn gales in the Atlantic during its passage of about 2,000 miles. Apart from enemy action and the certainty that this slow convoy cannot possibly achieve the tactical surprise counted upon four months ago, the Naval hazards cannot be taken lightly now, and they will certainly increase as the winter draws on.

I understand that a decision as to whether PILGRIM expedition will be launched in September will not be given for about a fortnight. Even if this cannot be anticipated, I would strongly urge that detailed plans should be prepared at once for making use of the whole or part of the force on some other enterprise, in order that we may be ready to act in the new dark night period towards the end of September. For instance, a raid on the French coast under full fighter cover, on the lines of 'RANSACK'[221] but on a larger scale; or the capture of the CHERBOURG peninsula, with the object of holding it until the destruction of the Naval port and all its resources is complete. In this case I would recommend the simultaneous capture of the CHANNEL ISLANDS, to give advance air bases for our fighters to re-fuel and ammunition.

I can quite appreciate that the moment may not yet have arrived to embark on a campaign in the Western Mediterranean while there is any prospect of GIBRALTAR being immobilised as a Naval and air base by enemy action, though I think the difficulties of passing ships through the Straits, should GIBRALTAR be besieged, are not insuperable. However, when it is considered opportune to exercise pressure on ITALY, I would recommend the capture of SARDINIA, which could be achieved by the PILGRIM force, augmented, possibly by Canadian troops, without drawing on MALTA, the Mediterranean Fleet or the Middle East Force.

The war in RUSSIA and the policing of the conquered states must greatly strain German resources and limit the aid which she could give ITALY. Now that GERMANY is so deeply involved on the Eastern front, the moment seems ripe for offensive action.

Events may move rapidly on the continent, we have a fine amphibious striking force capable of inflicting a very severe blow across the Channel or overseas, and if we can only get rid of the PILGRIM commitment – which is holding up action – we might make some progress towards waging war against the enemy, for which the whole world is waiting.

96. *Keyes to Churchill*[222]

[Copy]   D.C.O.'s Office,
Whitehall.
2nd Sept. 1941.

I have been longing to see you since you came back from your wonderful expedition,[223] as I have much I wish to say to you. I do beg of you, if you have any regard for me, to send for your D.C.O. and listen to him for a few minutes.

With reference to a remark you made to me in April a year ago, you are now in a position to prevent the Chiefs of Staff losing the war, but they will certainly postpone victory as long as they are guided by the advice of the Inter Service Committees of comparatively junior officers, without practical war experience to justify their dictation as to what can or cannot be done.

Their chief object seems to be to array all the difficulties and dangers of any offensive operation which is within our powers to carry out, generally by proposing as preferable something far more hazardous and formidable, which they know to be impracticable.

The Chiefs of Staff originally were as keen as we were about the capture of PANTELLARIA and could easily have been roused to enthusiasm about the capture of SARDINIA, but it was those marplots, the Inter-Service Committees, who frightened the Chiefs of Staff and arrayed every conceivable argument against an offensive action which could not have failed – before we were forestalled by the Germans.

I was for three years Naval Attaché in ROME, and knew the quality of the Italians. Wavell's five-day raid which turned into a complete rout of the Italian Army in LIBYA would have been anticipated in these two islands, with equal success.

If you had left me as Governor of SARDINIA and its dependency PANTELLARIA, I would not have lost them, through sheer ineptitude, as CRETE was lost.

I have had a great entente with Alan Brooke,[224] and made friends a year ago with Montgomery.[225] They are both spoiling for offensive action, and Brooke's staff and mine are examining various projects I have proposed, since German invasion this year is surely impossible.

If I take the responsibility of guaranteeing to land all the military force Brooke needs to carry out offensive action of value in the prosecution of the war, and Brooke is prepared to carry it out under this guarantee, please seriously consider our advice and over-ride the pusillanimous objections to the Inter Service Committees.

It remains to be seen whether the R.A.F. can be induced to cooperate effectively and if the Military Commander will be ready to undertake the offensive when faced with the responsibility of carrying it out! At ZEEBRUGGE inter-service complications were absent. I had Navy, a Marine assaulting force and R.N.A.S. all under my supreme command, and I had unlimited authority.

Anyhow, if only for old times' sake, please send for me. It is so difficult to write letters, which may never be read by you and which may be seen by others.

I waste all my time writing in order to try to persuade others to do what I would do, if I had the power and responsibility, just as I did as Director of Plans for four months in the last war, when the Admiralty was so obsessed with the daily task that they had neither time for nor interest in offensive action. When the opposition had been eliminated, I was given power and a free hand to wage offensive war in the Narrow Seas, with success.

Even in the China War, as a young Lieutenant, when happily there was no such thing as wireless, I was able to carry out one or two quite decisive strokes without having to seek the permission of superior authority, which resulted in my early promotion.

I am so consistently discredited by your advisers that I have to blow my own trumpet to remind you that I have not yet acquired patience and am tired of having to waste time and energy in trying to overcome the supine objections of our own people, in order to be allowed to make real war on the enemy...

97. Keyes to Hollis

[Carbon]   10th September, 1941.

I enclose a copy of the remarks I made from my notes this morning.[226] It is practically what I said yesterday, but the many interruptions confused the issue.

I do hope the C.N.S. will agree to my recommendations as to the Dutch and Scotsmen,[227] at any rate, and that he will persuade the P.M. likewise before it is too late.

I think a copy of this should go to the P.M. in view of yesterday's meeting, but I don't suppose he will read it...

[Postscript in holograph] You might give one of the attached to each of the C of S to show how faithfully history repeats itself.

98. Memorandum by Keyes

[Carbon]   n.d. [10 September, 1941]

There are a great many papers here and I am afraid you will not have had time to study them, but I hope you will endeavour to do so some day soon, because they do bring out the immense difficulty of waging amphibious warfare generally, and of overcoming the hazards of an opposed landing in particular.

2. The point which I wish to emphasise in my minute of 2nd September[228] is that the Naval Commander must bear the sole responsibility for the naval conduct of the expedition, once he has accepted the command of the Naval force and the Military Commander's plan. He cannot share this responsibility with anyone if he also accepts as sufficient the ships, landing craft, implements, etc., which the Admiralty are prepared to give him, and the air co-operation guaranteed by the Air Ministry.

3. In order to fulfil his responsibilities he must land the force the

Military Commander considers necessary, to seize and cover the beaches, on which it is proposed to disembark the expeditionary force and the armoured units which the Military Commander needs, with sufficient speed and certainty to enable him to overwhelm the local defence before the enemy are able to bring up superior forces.

4. I attach the greatest importance to speed in the approach of the assault force in order to give some prospect of tactical surprise and, in my opinion, the initial attack must be undertaken at night by specially trained troops and naval personnel of high morale carried in fast ships.

5. On 25th March I suggested to the Chiefs of Staff the formation of such a naval and military amphibious force and recommended its assembly at Inveraray to be trained under my direction as laid down in paragraph 2(f) of my directive.[229] This was approved in principle on 28th March. Executive action was taken on 23rd April but on 24th it became part of PUMA force and was placed under the Joint Commanders. I was thus deprived of the opportunity of training the force which I thought necessary in the light of my experience in the last war and during the many weeks I devoted myself to preparing a similar force for WORKSHOP.

6. I would not venture to lay down the law as to how the Military Commander should conduct his campaign, but having watched opposed landings in GALLIPOLI, against greatly inferior defence measures to those which are likely to be encountered against the Germans, – and which were supported by a Naval force far greater than that apparently available for the GANDO landing; and having also motored hundreds of miles between the British and Belgian Armies throughout the campaign in May, 1940, and had opportunities of watching the decisive manner in which the modern German methods so completely defeated ours; I would urge that unless he is prepared to strike fiercely and advance as rapidly as the Germans do, the Navy are likely to be called upon to carry out yet another evacuation.

7. These remarks may appear to be obvious platitudes, but reference to my criticisms on the conduct of LEAPFROG[230] and the remarks on opposed landings by the Force Commanders clearly show that they are not appreciated by them, although the Force had been actually under the command of Joint Commanders[231] for three months.

8. I fully recognise that the Naval and Military Commanders must be absolutely responsible for their plans and for the execution of them when approved by the Chiefs of Staff and the Minister of Defence. It is, however, obvious that they and the E.P.S. need the experience which they make no secret of lacking (in the Force Commanders' paper of 23rd August) and require help and guidance in the preparation of their plans and in the training of the personnel if failure is to be avoided. I have mentioned the E.P.S., but these remarks only apply to

the Naval members of that Committee. The Military members have always been helpful and the R.A.F. members have not been hostile to my Directorate, as far as I know. The Naval members of the E.P.S., however, cannot be dissociated from the recommendations in the Joint Commanders' paper, particularly as I understand it was actually submitted to the Naval Director of Plans.

9. A new "inter-service organisation for dealing with combined operations", which I have been asked to agree to by the Chiefs of Staff Committee, establishes the procedure actually followed in 'PILGRIM' and apparently cuts me out of the planning of combined operations altogether once the Commanders have been selected. This is not in accordance with paragraph 2(e) of my directive. I am quite ready to accept the entire responsibility for the efficient training of the Naval personnel of the amphibious striking force – as laid down in paragraph 2(f) of my directive – provided it is recognised that this is *my* responsibility and I am given executive authority by the Chiefs of Staff and Minister of Defence.

Paragraph 2(f) runs "The Director of Combined Operations will be responsible for the training of the Naval personnel in so far as opposed landings are concerned, including officers and men of carriers, landing craft and beach parties."

10. I called attention to another matter: last December, one or more Staff Officers compiled and circulated in the Admiralty a paper condemning me and my Directorate and suggesting our elimination. This came to my notice as it was also circulated secretly in my office, while I was at Lamlash training the troops and landing craft for 'WORKSHOP'.

I thought it was essential, therefore, to get the directive I inherited from Bourne re-affirmed and strengthened, if my experience was to be made use of . . . . . This was done last March.

In the early stages of 'PUMA', the Directive was observed and I think was of considerable help to Hamilton. The 'THRUSTER' Commanders were housed in my office and were very appreciative of our help. I think Admiral Willis[232] gave excellent advice to the Government – I helped him to do so. My connection with 'THRUSTER' was, I am told, much resented by the E.P.S.

When 'PUMA' was brought forward and turned into 'PILGRIM' early in July, and the whole plan had to be re-cast, I offered similar facilities to the Joint Commanders, but Hamilton rejected them and preferred to work entirely with E.P.S., and from about 8th July onwards I have been absolutely ignored; so has para. 2(e) of the directive you gave me, Hamilton and the E.P.S. being entirely responsible for 'PILGRIM' and the rehearsal ('LEAPFROG') he organised in SCAPA FLOW.

11. My criticisms on 'LEAPFROG' roused the E.P.S. to fresh efforts to eliminate the D.C.O. and this time the paper was forwarded over the names of the Joint Commanders and actually submitted by the Naval Director of Plans. It is, in effect, a repetition of the previous effort and its recommendations absolutely eliminate the D.C.O. from all connection with the preparation, planning and training of a combined operation. The following passage in this paper is of interest: – "After our experience with operation 'PILGRIM' and the results of exercise 'LEAPFROG', it is obvious that the study of opposed landings is still in its early stages and that there is still a great deal to be learnt. It is only from practical experience on a large scale that faults and difficulties will come to light."

'LEAPFROG', however, was intended to be the final rehearsal before the expedition sailed, and in my opinion was a waste of time and effort which could have been avoided if an area such as ARRAN had been selected. Further, 'LEAPFROG' clearly demonstrated that the Naval personnel and beach parties need intensive training before they engage in an enterprise against the enemy.

I recommend therefore that the Transports and Landing Craft and beach parties of the assault striking force be assembled in LOCH FYNE under the command of Commodore Warren[233] and trained by the Combined Training Centre under my command and direction.

It will thus be possible to train the Infantry and Armoured Brigades as desired by the War Office.

12. I called attention also to my difficulties in planning and executing operations, e.g. I did not know till after Lofoten operation had taken place that C.-in-C. Home Fleet had declined to allow the destroyers to act in close support of the landing as I had requested him to do. I had given the Brigadiers an assurance that this close support would be forthcoming.

13. I said that if I had been consulted when the decision was taken to send certain ships of the 'PILGRIM' force – some of which were actually under my command for operational control (under 2(f) of my directive) – I might have been able to induce the Chiefs of Staff to accept my view that the despatch of the Dutchmen and Belfast vessels [to Freetown] on the grounds of unseaworthiness is not justified. Vessels which cross the North Sea and Irish Sea at high speed in any weather could, by careful handling, weather any Atlantic gale. It seemed to me illogical since other craft no more seaworthy and unable to make the passage without refuelling were being left behind.

I recognise the difficulty of the Chiefs of Staff in changing their recommendations at the eleventh hour but I begged the C.N.S. to give further consideration to the despatch of the fast vessels which were so urgently needed for raiding operations in Home Waters, if we are to be in a position to strike across the Channel or North Sea should the course of the war make this desirable. I would not be so insistent if I were not convinced that the ability of the Force Commanders to carry out the 'PILGRIM' expedition as constituted at present would not be jeopardised by these vessels remaining at home.

I said that I did not know how they proposed to mount the expedition efficiently, dispersed as it will be, but it seemed to me an exceedingly difficult and complicated operation.

99. *Keyes to Churchill*

[Carbon]

D.C.O.'s Office,
War Cabinet Office Annexe,
1A Richmond Terrace,
London, S.W.1.
11th September, 1941.

It gave your friends who stood by you in adversity a tremendous thrill to watch you take your place at the head of the nation and give such an inspiring lead in another world crisis, but you are not an easy person to serve. I asked you to help me on Tuesday night [9th], and you only added to my difficulties by interrupting and confusing me – so much so that I felt obliged to ask the Chiefs of Staff to see me the following morning in order to make my points clear, so that there should be no misunderstanding on their part.[234]

I pointed out that 'LEAPFROG' disclosed the inexperience of the Joint Commanders – on their own confession. The ineptitude of the Naval control when things went wrong showed that the Naval part of the assault striking force must be properly trained and organised before 'PILGRIM' force is ready to engage in an enterprise against the enemy. I recommended that the transports, landing craft and beach parties of the assault striking force should be assembled in LOCH FYNE and trained by the C.T.C. under my command and direction, since the success or failure of a combined operation must depend on its efficiency.[235]

I said I was quite ready to take the full responsibility for ensuring the efficiency of the force, provided that it was recognised that this was *my* entire responsibility and I was given executive authority by the Chiefs of Staff and Minister of Defence.

Pound seemed inclined to agree. I urged him to reconsider the despatch of the five small transports for the reasons given in the attached extract from minutes, and he said he would do so – but time passes and they sail on the 16th.²³⁶ Are you really going to allow this to happen against your D.C.O.'s advice?

I called the attention of the Chiefs of Staff to other matters concerning my directorate, and I hope Pound appreciated the impropriety of the attitude of certain Naval Staff Officers towards me, and the fact that my directive had been completely disregarded, to the detriment of efficiency, through the life of the 'PILGRIM' force (2 months). Anyhow he was propitiative and promised to "straighten matters out."²³⁷

On Tuesday you preferred the advice of the Joint Commanders, who were responsible for the failures and miscarriages of 'LEAPFROG', but were apparently satisfied with it since they gained elementary experience from an ill-considered and abortive rehearsal.

I strongly recommend you to read my remarks on this exercise – which I forwarded to the Joint Commanders – before you take any irrecoverable step. I beg you to consider the alternative plan for 'PILGRIM',²³⁸ which you would not let me develop on Tuesday. I attach a brief outline.²³⁹

It would help so much if you would occasionally interview your D.C.O. and listen to what he has to say. Otherwise you might just as well not have one, and leave the conduct of combined operations to inexperienced officers to experiment with. This might spare you the annoyance of my importunity, but it will not help you to win the war. It may involve you in another misadventure – or more likely still, end in your advisers again persuading you to do nothing.

The report of the occupation of SARDINIA by the Germans is a tormenting thought, when one reflects on what you suggested and I was so anxious and ready to do months ago – and now we are forestalled again.

I do my best to serve you and the country, but I find it increasingly difficult. "The credentials of ZEEBRUGGE are now on the Council table", but are persistently ignored . . .

12th September

Since writing this I have heard Roosevelt's speech.²⁴⁰ I am quite ready to fly over tomorrow to explain matters to him. I showed you his letter in which he said, "I am delighted to hear of your work as Director of Combined Operations. I feel very certain, incidentally, that the words 'combined operations' are going to mean a great deal more between our two Naval services."²⁴¹

100. *Memorandum by Keyes*

[Carbon] [11th September, 1941]

AN ALTERNATIVE PLAN FOR THE CAPTURE OF 'PILGRIM'

The inevitable delay in launching 'PUMA' has made an assault on the GANDO beaches – which is still the basis of the 'PILGRIM' plan – much more hazardous. If the latest intelligence reports are accurate, I consider, in the light of my practical experience, that such an attempt would result in a disastrous repulse. The strengthening of the defences would probably also defeat the original plan to rush the harbour at night and land Commandos from small transports on to the quays, since, in my opinion, the approach of the large armada of 'PILGRIM' force, including several slow ships, precludes any prospect of tactical surprise.

If these intelligence reports are greatly exaggerated, as contended by the Joint Commanders, and the defences have not been overhauled, strengthened and organised by the Germans, it is, of course, another matter; but it does not seem to me reasonable to suppose, if the Germans intend to attack GIBRALTAR, that before launching the attack, they will not make the capture by assault of such an invaluable alternative base a very formidable undertaking, if they have not done so already. The Joint Commanders appear to be relying on the negative evidence of aerial photographs, but since we successfully camouflage defences to hide them from aerial observation, the enemy should be given credit for doing likewise.

I have always been fully alive to the importance of capturing 'PILGRIM' and, in fact, on 23rd April I urged that it should be given first consideration in preference to 'THRUSTER', at a moment when the Joint Commanders of 'THRUSTER' were actually working out their plan and that operation was at short notice. At that time 'PUMA' held third place in the Chiefs of Staff priority list for operations against the Atlantic Islands.

As I still consider it of vital importance to capture the island, and do not consider 'PILGRIM', as at present constituted, has a reasonable prospect of doing so, I have given much attention to an alternative plan. I consider that we could obtain possession of the island if an overwhelming powerful Naval force, with carriers in supporting distance, appears off the harbour and an ultimatum is delivered demanding the surrender of the island for the duration of the war, with diplomatic guarantees for its future after the enemy was finally defeated, and its sustenance in the meantime. If the ultimatum is rejected, the civilian population should be given time to withdraw. The town and harbour defences should then be destroyed. In my opinion, the harbour could then be entered by warships and small transports under cover of the guns of the Fleet. A bridgehead would thus be secured for the development of a military campaign against the garrison of the island, should they continue the struggle.

I recognise that while powerful German units are in being, we might be unable to provide a sufficiently powerful fleet to overawe the defence and justify their surrendering to force majeure. I think, however, that a sufficiently powerful British force could probably be made available to ensure the capture of the harbour in the manner I have suggested if the ultimatum is rejected.

If the Americans who, after all, are also deeply concerned could be induced to co-operate in a Naval demonstration on a very large scale, I think there is every prospect of securing the island without alienating Spanish supporters in Spain and South America by killing a large number of Spaniards.[242]

101. *Keyes to Ismay*

[Carbon] 16th September, 1941.

I am sorry to hear you are off as I always look to you to help me to help the P.M.![243]

However I can't do more than I have done to try to make the P.M. see that PILGRIM as it stands is sheer folly.

Despite this we are dispersing a number of valuable ships, which we may urgently need before long in home waters – and are keeping a number of others unemployed – when they are urgently wanted by the Ministry of War Transport . . .

102. *Keyes to Chiefs of Staff Committee*

[Carbon]
MOST SECRET
D.C.O. No. P. 34/3 16th September, 1941.

With reference to J.P. (41) 754 of 13th September, 1941, I have already recorded my opinion that constituted as it is and dispersed as it shortly will be more than 3000 miles apart, 'PILGRIM' Force will not be able to capture the island by assault as planned against the opposition which the Germans are certain to organise before they launch an attack on Gibraltar.

I consider therefore that there are no reasonable grounds for withholding the immense quantity of shipping entailed from service of national importance.

I strongly recommend, however, that such vessels as are required to carry the assault striking force, including a few M.T. vessels, should be assembled in LOCH FYNE and administered and trained by V.A.C.T.C. under my direction. These vessels would also be utilised for carrying out the training programme desired by the War Office.

103. *Ismay to Keyes*

SECRET AND PERSONAL   16th September, 1941.

Many thanks for yours of the 16th September,[244] enclosing a copy of your minute No. P.34/3 of the 16th September to the Chiefs of Staff.[245]

As our Mission to Russia is now engaged in practically all-day talks with the American team and may be leaving for Moscow very soon, I have had to cut myself off – more or less – from my normal work. I have, however, asked Hollis to see that a copy of your minute is submitted to the Prime Minister as soon as it has been considered by the Chiefs of Staff, together with their conclusions thereon.

I feel quite sure, however, that the Prime Minister and the Defence Committee will not be prepared to deprive themselves of all possibility of doing PILGRIM during the winter months, even though this involves an undesirable detachment of force at Freetown, and the retention of shipping that can ill be spared from other services...

104. *Brigadier Charles Haydon to Keyes*

[Holograph]
Secret and Personal   17.9.41.

Thank you very much for your letter. I am delighted to hear about Geoffrey and I am sending a letter which I hope Dexter will be able to forward.

It will be fun to see Roger again. I think I shall almost miss the beard now.

* * *

I wrote a letter to Ely [?] the other day saying that we must *not* allow ourselves to be immobilised because the Dutchmen[246] and so on are being moved away. We should, I am sure, be delivering a series of blows, even though each one may be small.

The cumulative effect on the enemy, not to mention the moral effect on our own people, would be great.

Some of the suggestions recently put up by officers from the Commandos only implicate very few men and I do hope they will be regarded favourably and allowed to go forward. They would be such a stimulus to everyone and would set others thinking of new ways and means. I should like to see a great week planned on every night of which one or more small raids took place not only on the French coast but on the Norwegian coast as well. Material results might not be great but the nervous strain and the doubt as to whether it was not all leading to something bigger would certainly exist and tend to grow.

From the Commando point of view the employment of even a small patrol has results on morale out of all proportion to the size and scope of the operation. They feel they are doing something to earn their keep and their whole outlook lightens.

I hope so much that you will come up and see us.

I am sure it would do you good to get a few days in the country air and it would do us all good to have you here. We gave demonstrations of cliff climbing and overcoming obstacles to General Alexander the other day and have now been asked to repeat them for the Infantry Brigade.

I am very glad as it will do the Commandos good and they will enjoy it I am sure . . .

105. *Keyes to Eden*

[Carbon]
MOST SECRET AND PERSONAL
D.C.O. No. P.34   17th September, 1941.

You may remember I wrote to you last May about the island in which we are so interested, and said I feared that delay would make the enterprise a great hazard.[247] I fully recognise that it would have been, and still is, impossible for the Government to jeopardise the security of Gibraltar by premature action elsewhere.

In the light of my practical experience I am strongly of the opinion that the naval and military hazards of PILGRIM — which is quite a different proposition to the original PUMA — are very considerable.

Winston has accepted the advice of the Joint Commanders and placed on record that I am absolved from all responsibility, but I cannot divest myself of the responsibility of trying to prevent what I consider may well result in another misadventure. I have suggested an alternative which in my opinion would succeed, and if the Americans can be induced to join in sufficient strength we would probably get all we want without killing a lot of Spaniards.[248]

Anyhow I have done my duty in placing my views before the Secretary of State for Foreign Affairs![249]

106. Memorandum by the Chiefs of Staff

SECRET
C.O.S. (41) 59
27th SEPTEMBER, 1941.

WAR CABINET.
CHIEFS OF STAFF COMMITTEE
INTER-SERVICE ORGANISATION FOR COMBINED OPERATIONS

Memorandum by the Chiefs of Staff

We have been considering our Organisation for dealing with Combined Operations in the light of recent events and with an eye to the future.

2. There are, in our view, two outstanding principles which must be recognised as affecting all major operations. These are: –
(a) The responsibility for tendering advice to the Prime Minister, the War Cabinet or Defence Committee on the strategical aspects and general feasibility of any operational plan must rest with the Chiefs of Staff.
(b) Once the Commander or Commanders have been appointed for an operation the detailed planning, the training of the forces allotted and the execution of the operation must be the responsibility of those officers.

3. The above principles must govern Combined Operations which are a specialised form of warfare, and for which special technique and training are needed. But over and above the responsibilities which devolve upon the Chiefs of Staff on the one hand and on the Commanders on the other hand, as set out in paragraph 2 above, we see that there is a definite need for a special Inter-Service Organisation which can give its full time to studying the special requirements of Combined Operations and to assisting in the training of the forces required for them.

4. To win the war it will be necessary, eventually, to undertake a large scale operation across the seas. The time has come when the Army at home has progressed far in the training for its primary role of the defence of this country, and we consider that we should begin now to

train a large part of our Home Forces for amphibious operations. This will be a big task and will require the help of a large and well developed organisation.

5. The actual training of troops is, of course, the responsibility of their Commanders. But skilled advice in training for special operations must be available to the Commanders and to their staffs. Furthermore, schools of instruction on a large scale will be required both for officers and for senior N.C.O.'s. One of the functions therefore of the Inter-Service Organisation, which we have in mind, will be to organise and provide the teaching at these schools and to provide officers skilled in this form of operation at the big training camps which will be necessary. This system would be analogous to that existing in the Royal Artillery which has proved most satisfactory.

6. There is much specialized equipment which is peculiar to Combined Operations and it is essential that research design and development of this equipment should be furthered. This then would be a second function of our Combined Operations organisation.

7. A third function would be the study and development of the tactics and technique to be used in all forms of combined operation, varying from raiding patrols up to the full scale invasion of the Continent. Close liaison should be maintained with the organisation for the development of air borne forces.

8. The Planning for large scale operations will be carried out in accordance with the procedure described in the diagram at Annex I.[250]

9. To carry out the functions which we have outlined above, we propose that an inter-service organisation should be set up under an "Adviser on Combined Operations". The Adviser would preside over an Inter-Service Committee consisting of the Directors of training of the three Services, which would deal with questions of training and technical policy. Questions of detail in connection with training, equipment and the administration of the training arrangements, would be dealt with by an Inter-Service Sub-Committee of which the Deputy Adviser on Combined Operations would be the Chairman. (A diagram showing the proposed machinery for dealing with training and equipment is attached at Annex II).[251]

10. We have discussed very thoroughly the position of the Commander-in-Chief, Home Forces in our Combined Operations organisation.

If large-scale land operations on the Continent are undertaken the Army forces employed will be those now under the command of Commander-in-Chief, Home Forces, and it is logical for the detailed planning and execution of such operations and the training of the troops to be employed to be carried out by Commander-in-Chief, Home Forces, in conjuction with the appropriate Naval and Air Commanders-in-Chief.

11. Similarly, so far as the Army is concerned, there are, particularly after so much purely defensive work, considerable advantages in delegating the planning and execution of large scale raids on the Continent, in accordance with outline plans approved by the Chiefs of Staff, to Commander-in-Chief, Home Forces. In each case, the Commander-in-Chief, Home Forces, should obtain the advice of the Adviser on Combined Operations in the planning and preparation for the operations.

Raids

12. The Planning and execution of small cross channel raids, in so far as the Army is concerned, will also be the responsibility of the Commander-in-Chief, Home Forces. The Commander-in-Chief will decentralise this responsibility to Commands as he thinks fit.

The Commander-in-Chief, Home Forces or the Commander-in-Chief of the Command concerned:
(a) should obtain the advice of the Adviser on Combined Operations, and
(b) should ensure that the planning of any operation is concerted with the Royal Navy and the Royal Air Force from its inception.

Combined Training Centres

13. We propose that the Combined Training Centre at Inveraray and such other Combined Training Centres as may be established, should be the focus of all training for landing operations. These Centres will receive general directions on training and equipment policy from the Inter-Services Committee and Sub-Committee visualised in paragraph 9.

Special Service Troops

14. The Special Service troops will be allotted to the Combined Training Centres and will be under the Command of the Commandants of the Centres until such time as they are allotted to any particular operation, when they will automatically be placed at the disposal of the Commander of that operation.

                         (Signed) DUDLEY POUND
                                  " J. G. DILL
                                  " C. PORTAL.

107. Churchill to Keyes[252]

[Copy]

PRIVATE AND CONFIDENTIAL

10 Downing Street,
Whitehall.
30 September, 1941.

My dear Roger,

I hope you will find yourself able to come to an agreement with the Chiefs of Staff upon the modification of your original directive. Your title of "Director" does not correspond to the facts. Special operations once decided upon in principle must lie in the hands of the commanders chosen, who have to back them with their reputations and their lives. I am convinced that excursions from this country to the continent, unless entrusted to specially chosen commanders, must have behind them the authority and resources of G.H.Q. Home Forces. In both cases the responsibility for advising the Defence Committee and the War Cabinet can only lie with the Chiefs of the Staff. These are facts which must be accepted.

It seems to me that very large spheres of important and interesting work will be open to you as Adviser under the new arrangement, and that some of the causes of friction in the past will be removed. I should find it very hard to resist the advice of all my responsible experts. I trust therefore that you will fall in with the plans which have now taken shape.

Yours very sincerely,
(Signed) Winston S. Churchill

108. Keyes to Churchill

[Carbon]

D.C.O.'s Office,
War Cabinet Office Annexe,
1A Richmond Terrace,
London, S.W.1.
2nd October, 1941.

Thank you for your letter,[253] from which I gather that, on the advice of the Chiefs of Staff Committee, you are terminating my appointment as D.C.O.

You made it quite clear at the meeting you presided over on 9th September that you were not in any way influenced by my advice. I fully appreciate your difficulties and I do not wish to add to them by bringing you into a controversy, since it is evident that you are still labouring under restrictions and difficulties which do not appear to have been lightened since those unhappy days of the Norwegian campaign, eighteen months ago.

I have tried to make it clear to the Chiefs of Staff that I cannot accept such a sweeping reduction of status and an absurd title which means nothing, as a substitute for the appointment you gave me in July, 1940, strengthened by a directive which they gave me, with your approval, as recently as the 14th March.[254] I pointed out that nothing had occurred in the meantime to justify such a drastic change of policy, and that the title of "Adviser" is not one that has ever been used in the Services, in which there are many Directors.

The only excuse the Chiefs of Staff could offer for changing my title was that the Joint Commanders might object to it! They might just as well have objected to the presence of the *Director* of Military Training and the *Director* of Military Operations, who attended the PUMA exercises with me, and who did not hesitate to criticise the General of Marines – somewhat unfairly, I thought. But they were determined that a soldier should have command of the expedition, and seemed to resent any troops being under a Marine.

Writing and talking do not come as easily to me as they do to you, and I find this ceaseless wordy warfare very trying; but I am preparing a paper which I intend to hand to the Chiefs of Staff shortly. I hope they will accept my advice and recommendations.

With reference to your remarks about the responsibility of Joint Commanders, you say that "the conduct of operations once decided upon must be in the hands of the Commanders, who have to back them with their reputations and their lives." I have always maintained that the Commanders of expeditions must be given a free hand; but for amphibious operations the force employed must be thoroughly trained if success is to be achieved. It is not sufficient, on the day of battle, to have a highly trained staff which appears to be the War Office's main concern, – very important, but the knowledge and quality of the leader or leaders is of *vital* importance, particularly if events do not go according to plan. To employ untried and inexperienced leaders, however brave and ready they may be "to throw their caps over the fence" (your remark), is to court disaster.

If they are worth their salt, they should be ready to take – from an experienced senior officer – expert advice, and train with their force to fit themselves for the great responsibilities they will have to bear; otherwise not only they but many of their men may have to pay with *their* lives unnecessarily for the inexperience of their leaders.

I have never questioned the authority of the Chiefs of Staff and I have established excellent relations with the C. in C. Home Forces; I am certain I can work well with him, and I can't believe that he would be so petty as to object to my title.

With reference to your last paragraph, I merely become "Adviser" and Chairman of another inter-service committee. I cannot agree that there is any "large sphere of important and interesting work open to me", although Pound spent half an hour trying to persuade me to believe this, on the grounds of the enormous expansion contemplated.

It is difficult to make even a Chief of Staff appreciate the limitations of beach landings, and the physical impossibility of landing large mechanised forces and getting them clear of beaches quickly enough, if the enemy possesses even widely dispersed mechanised forces within reach, and the absolute necessity for seizing ports and sheltered harbours before the disembarkation of a large modern mechanised army can be undertaken.

The Chiefs of Staff had not apparently realised, when they talked of vast expansion, that we would not have had the naval craft available nor the means of getting them in sufficient numbers to train more than about three divisions during the next six months, even if they had not "irrigated" away a number of valuable vessels and landing craft,[255] on the advice of the Joint Commanders, and tied up many more in PILGRIM force, 33% of which the Joint Commanders insist on retaining, inactive.

It is almost impossible to make a soldier, and even some sailors, realise that a combined operation is entirely a naval responsibility until the Navy has made it possible to seize a beach and cover it, preparatory to landing the expeditionary force, and to reinforce it sufficiently rapidly to enable the military commander to overwhelm the local defences, before the enemy can bring up a superior force. Once ashore, the military commander's task is no different to any other military operation, except that he may get gun and air support from seaward. The naval commander's task, however, continues to be one of tremendous responsibility, for he has to ensure the Army's communications, in the face of enemy action from the air, sea and submarine.

You, of course, understand all this and probably consider these remarks platitudes, but I have not yet succeeded in making the Chiefs of Staff really understand what amphibious warfare involves, and I assure you that it was a closed book to Hamilton and Alexander in Scapa Flow on 10th Aug. As Hamilton is R.A. (D) at Scapa and has many other preoccupations, and Alexander is C. in C. at Salisbury, I don't suppose they will be able to devote much time to the study of amphibious warfare. It is frightfully galling to see the transports and landing craft of our one and only amphibious striking force lying fallow in the Clyde and at Sierra Leone, 3,000 miles apart, still under Hamilton's command, when they ought to be undergoing intensive training, under my direction, to fit them to land the spearhead of any amphibious operation which may be required at short notice in enemy-occupied territories.

My experience in the last war and in the training for WORKSHOP last winter has taught me the vital importance of an amphibious striking force of highly trained seamen and troops to deliver the initial night assault, on the success or failure of which the whole fate of an amphibious expedition will most surely depend. I tried to raise and train such a force in March, after the one I had personally trained day and night for several weeks, sailed for the Middle East on 1st Feb. I asked for the two Brigades of Marines and the S.S. Brigade, and all the fast ships available, to be assembled and trained by the C.T.C. under my direction, because my experience in this war has brought home to me the painful fact that the Army, led and staffed and taught as it is at present, cannot yet be relied upon to carry out the hazards of an opposed night landing.

Although the Chiefs of Staff approved, nothing was done until the end of April, when the force I recommended was formed, and at the same time placed under inexperienced Joint Commanders. The naval part of this force, *which has not yet been trained,* failed deplorably on the 10th Aug. The Joint Commanders of PILGRIM, in recommending my elimination, actually attributed the naval failure to faulty training; but the naval force had been out of my hands under Hamilton's command for four months – in fact, ever since it was formed. It never will be trained until it can be released from PILGRIM force and goes to the C.T.C. to be trained and inspired in its desperate venture, under my direction.

I suppose you realise that, deprived of my support and leadership, the Commandos will disappear. Since General Haining left the War Office and was succeeded by Pownall,[256] there have been persistent efforts to discredit their value.

I pointed all this out to the Chiefs of Staff, and suggested that as they had many responsibilities and concerns, my experience and such qualities as I possess would be of great value to them and the country if they trusted me as their D.C.O. "Combined operations are a highly specialised form of warfare" which I have deeply studied, and in which I happen to have more practical experience than anyone else. Surely the Joint Commanders need not be ashamed of taking advice from an experienced senior officer like me.

I have never made a confidential report about an officer without showing it to him, and in consequence have lost some friends and made some enemies. I listened to a sentence in your speech on Tuesday in this connection, which I found encouraging, but my plain speaking about the failures of the Naval Staff and Joint Commanders, and Gort's Chief of Staff, have brought this storm down upon me, with yet a third attempt to eliminate my directive. I don't intend to bow to it, but you, of course, are all-powerful and could easily terminate the appointment you gave me, although I have not failed you in any way, and I am very little older.

On the 17th July, 1940, the Chiefs of Staff Committee agreed:—
(a) That it was desirable that Sir Roger Keyes should assume the title of "Director of Combined Operations."
(b) That it was undesirable that any publicity should be given to the appointment.

Consequently I have been anonymous for more than a year. But it is known to a great many, since those who have passed through my hands and are under my control and guidance have made no secret of the debt they owe to my leadership and inspiration, and the fact that I *am* their Chief. They know too what battles I have had to fight for their very existence.

You see, I have a name and a reputation that is pretty widely recognised in other countries. Presumably on that account the Chiefs of Staff Committee considered it desirable not to advertise the fact that I was once again concerned with amphibious operations.

Now they wish to make use of my name and reputation in the role of an "adviser", who can be made a scapegoat when things go wrong – as was done by the Joint Commanders in that outrageous paper presented by the Director of Naval Plans over their signatures – or be ignored when his advice is inconvenient. You cannot expect me to lend my name and reputation to the new organisation the Chiefs of Staff propose for the conduct of Combined Operations, which I *know* will break down if it is ever put to the test in an amphibious enterprise. If I am to be in any way connected with Combined Operations, responsibility must be delegated to me by the Chiefs of Staff to prevent the recurrence of a long series of miscarriages, which I have not been able to avert even under my present directive, and which have impeded progress and efficiency and our ability to wage war overseas.

However, I won't bore you with more details, but I will make my recommendations and give my advice to the Chiefs of Staff, and I hope that they will be wise enough to accept them.

There are such wonderful things to be done now, if you could only induce your Chiefs of Staff to allow you to do them. I think Alan Brooke might play, and I have always found Dill and Portal easy to work with, but I am afraid Pound and his Joint Planning Staff and Executive Planning Staff are rocks on which any bold plans will founder...

[P.S.] Since seeing you last night I have looked up in Hansard the passage in your speech on Tuesday which appealed to me so deeply – [cutting from Hansard attached]²⁵⁷.

If to-day I am very kindly treated by so many Members in all parts of the House, it is certainly not because I have followed public opinion in recent years.

I know I am right to urge you not to risk losing the confidence of our great people in these days of trouble.

You asked for a plan to capture Trondheim. Ask Dill to tell you the plan that your E.P.S. and J.P.S. have put forward. It would be laughable, if it were not so tragic, that not only those people whose miscarriages were a by-word in the Service during the Norwegian campaign, and who were responsible for letting down Carton de Wiart so deplorably in his efforts *to carry out the same plan*;²⁵⁸ but also those who were responsible for the most disgraceful debacle in the history of the British Army – which was only saved from becoming an overwhelming disaster by your inspiring call to the seafarers of Great Britain and their wonderful response – should still be in office and holding key positions in the combined operations organisation, which the Chiefs of Staff wish you to establish, and in other vital services.

If you had shot, or at least disgraced, ——— and ———, instead of showering honours upon them and giving them important appointments, you would probably have been spared the failure of the thrust in Libya for which you risked so much – the flight from Greece – the dreadful fiasco in Crete, etc.

Read Roger Keyes's War Diary of the Belgian Campaign and his correspondence with Gort. Then read *The General*, by Forester²⁵⁹ (the author of Hornblower), and you will understand why the Generals of to-day shrink from running any risk of repeating the slaughter for which the Generals of 1914–18 were responsible, and why they cannot now be induced to fight.

Read Roger Keyes's criticism of the conduct, by the Joint Commanders and the E.P.S., of LEAPFROG, and you will realise why I am so anxious to spare the country further amphibious miscarriages by being given the authority by the Chiefs of Staff to be a real DIRECTOR of Combined Operations.

How shocked our great people would be if they only knew how badly you, their leader, were being served.

109. Keyes to Churchill

[Carbon]

D.C.O.'s Office,
War Cabinet Office Annexe,
1A Richmond Terrace, S.W.1.
4th October, 1941.

You said you would like to see the foreword of my *Fight for Gallipoli*. The proof has just come; I hope there is nothing in it you object to! or would like altered? The publishers suggested that you might write a brief foreword but I pointed out that as the whole book was a vindication of your policy it would hardly be decent.

I had a long talk with Dill yesterday and I think made him understand that although it would be much easier and pleasanter for me to fall in with your wishes, it would be rotten of me to do so because I knew that under the organisation which Pound and the Naval Staff have been intriguing to force on me since last August (1940) we should drift on as we have been doing, inviting disaster if an amphibious expedition is ever launched.

Dill asked me why I did not explain all this to you. I said I had tried to on paper but it was obvious that you could not find time to read my memoranda – I had proof of this. You never gave me an opportunity of speaking to you, presumably because you did not want the Chiefs of Staff Committee to think I had any influence with you. He had seen how badly you treated me on the 9th September no doubt because you wished to impress this upon them and the Joint Commanders. I said I had the impression that you nearly made a right decision that day but obviously found it difficult to do so against their advice, and now our ability to wage amphibious warfare anywhere had been dissipated – just as that splendid striking force which I had trained has been dissipated in the Mediterranean.

Why do you so continually dwell on my age? St. Vincent was at the zenith of his power at 70 and hoisted his flag in an anxious hour when he was 71. Howe was 68 on the glorious First of June. They must both have been years older than I am in body. I have not yet found it necessary to "*force* my heart and nerve and sinew" – nor found "the longest day too long" (A.L.G.). I have not yet found time to acquire the obviously valuable habit of resting for 3 or 4 hours in the afternoon.

I remember almost twenty years ago when you were living in temporary retirement in Sussex Square you said to me, "You know, Roger, we have only about 10 years of active life left". Ten years later I played in the final of the Cowdray Tournament in first-class company. Ten years later still, you had won for yourself a position which no Englishman has ever previously attained. At the moment I am being thwarted at every turn by stumbling blocks, but in the end they will be stepping stones to my goal, namely, the proper use of amphibious power – Britain's greatest weapon in the past, misused in the Dardanelles, through no fault of yours – still unemployed in this war owing to the pusillanimous folly of your principal naval adviser. I think you and I still have about ten years left in us, bar accidents, because the sacred fire within will never be quenched while we have life.

I know I am destined to play a decisive part in helping you to win this war. Why postpone the day? . . .

110. *Churchill to Keyes*[260]

[Holograph]

10 Downing Street,
Whitehall.
4. X. 41.

My dear Roger,

I am sorry that you do not feel able to fall in with proposal wh the Chiefs of the Staff have made to you. I have really done my best to meet yr wishes. I have to consider first my duty to the State wh ranks above personal friendship. In all the circumstances I have no choice but to arrange for yr relief.

Yours vy sincerely,
Winston S. Churchill

111. *Keyes to Ismay*

Secret and Personal.

D.C.O.'s Office,
War Cabinet Office Annexe,
1A Richmond Terrace, S.W.1.
11th October 1941.

I am delighted that you are safely back. I have missed you very much this last fortnight. Hollis has been very good and has done all he could to help, but has not had the "guns" or the inside knowledge you have to put the matter to the Prime Minister, who could have squared things up in a ten minutes' interview, if you had been here to help – as he could now, if the matter is put squarely before him.

You will remember that I wrote to the Prime Minister in February asking him to release me from the appointment of D.C.O. unless I was recognised as such, and given the authority to be a real Director of Combined Operations. He then deputed you to go into the matter with me, and in the course of our discussions, on the 6th March, I said that the Prime Minister should find some new name for me, as I could not be called "D.C.O." under the first revised directive you suggested. It implied responsibility for the planning and preparation of combined operations, whereas I had none.

You then suggested some amendments and the Directive of 14th March, which was given to me by the Chiefs of Staff and approved by the Prime Minister, was the result.

This Directive held good until early in July, when it was completely ignored by the Admiralty Staff and Joint Commanders and the new proposals put forward by the Chiefs of Staff on the 16th September were, no doubt, designed to regularise what had in fact been the procedure for two months. In the meantime, in order to get rid of the friction which existed, I had suggested a Committee should be set up over which I should preside, consisting of senior officers representing the three Services. The War Office and Air Ministry had agreed to their Directors of Training sitting on this Committee, and I made a great point of the Naval member being an A.C.N.S., thus ensuring that my relations with the three Services should be through senior and responsible officers. I only suggested that this Committee should deal with training and equipment; however, I had it in mind that these officers had better be the medium of my relations with the three Services in all matters.

This suggestion was adopted by the Chiefs of Staff and embodied in their memorandum of 16th September, which proposed that, in addition to being Chairman of the inter-service committee on training and equipment, I should be employed very widely in an advisory capacity and called "Adviser on Combined Operations". Otherwise their proposals virtually terminated my appointment of D.C.O.

On 22nd September I forwarded some comments on this paper but, while accepting most of the proposals, I pointed out how completely the responsibilities, which had been confided to me as lately as 14th March, had been removed. As a result of these comments, Hollis told me, the Chiefs of Staff had incorporated some of my suggestions in a revised memorandum of 27th September,[261] but did not find themselves able to change their views on the main issues.

I had a frank talk with the Chiefs of Staff on the new memorandum on 27th September, but pointed out that the alternative appointment they were offering me was no substitute for the appointment which I had been given; for instance, I was deprived of the command of the Combined Training Centres, which, after all, owed something to me; and there were important matters which the memorandum left unsettled. I handed in some proposals for a revision of my directive, which they said they would consider.

A few hours later Hollis wrote to say the Chiefs of Staff intended me to retain command of the Combined Training Centres, and on 2nd October Hollis asked me to meet the Chiefs of Staff on the 3rd, to discuss the matter further with them.

In the meantime I had received a letter from the Prime Minister dated 30th September,[262] in which he said he hoped I would find myself able to come to an agreement with the Chiefs of Staff upon the modification of my original directive.

I therefore asked Hollis to postpone the meeting, as I was preparing a paper making further suggestions to meet the Chiefs of Staff's wishes. I told the Prime Minister I was doing so, and hoped that they would accept my proposals.

I re-examined the whole matter during the week-end, and on Monday morning, 6th October, I forwarded my proposals to Hollis.[263] That day I received a letter from the Prime Minister written on 4th October,[264] before the meeting which Hollis said he would arrange with the Chiefs of Staff had taken place. In this the Prime Minister said he must put his duty to the State above personal friendship, and he had no choice but to arrange for my relief. If it is really in the interests of the State to deprive it of my services and experience, and he wishes to dismiss me, there is nothing more to be said.

In the proposals I sent to Hollis for the Chiefs of Staff's consideration, I suggested that as I was to preside over the Directors of Training of the three Services, I should be called "Director of Combined Training". I suggested that the inter-service committee over which I was to preside should be widened to cover all matters concerned with combined operations.

In addition to the command of the combined training centres, which the Chiefs of Staff wished me to have, I asked for the command of the landing craft, carriers, transports, etc., and the training of their personnel (as in my original directive) until such time as any of them was specifically allocated for an operation, when it would pass under the control of the Commander appointed for the operation. Thus I would be in a position to ensure that the training was properly carried out, both in ships and training centres, and would be able to hand over an efficiently trained force to the Commander appointed.

I do not think "Adviser on Combined Operations" is a good title, and in view of what has happened I certainly don't want to force my advice on anybody who doesn't want it.

It is clear that the Chiefs of Staff do not wish me to have anything to do with the execution of combined operations. It is only fair to say that, although the Prime Minister wished me to have command of raiding operations, and I have had powers under my original directive, I have never exercised them because I realised the difficulties involved.

The Prime Minister told me he wished me to undertake command of the WORKSHOP expedition, but, alas, that never came off!

Having planned the Lofoten expedition and trained the force I asked the C. in C. Home Fleet to give a stout-hearted Captain an opportunity of winning his spurs.

In the case of the recent reconnaissance raids in the Channel, I have made the plans and placed the forces at the disposal of the Admiral at Dover and C. in C. Portsmouth to carry out the operations.

Taking everything into consideration, if the Prime Minister wishes me to remain, the Chiefs of Staff had much better limit my responsibilities to the direction of combined training, and call me "D.C.T." ...

[Holograph]
Prime Minister

You wished to see the attached letter from Sir Roger Keyes again, and possibly to discuss it with the First Sea Lord.

H.L. Ismay
13. X. 41.

[Holograph]
P.M. has seen.
    J.H.P. [Peck][265]
    13. X.

112. *Churchill to Keyes*

[Copy]

10 Downing Street,
Whitehall.
14th October 1941.

My dear Roger,

On September 30 I wrote you a serious letter about the need for you to accept the proposals of the Chiefs of Staff in regard to the scope of your appointment.[266] On October 2 you replied that you could not accept 'such a sweeping reduction of status'.[267] On October 4 I told you by letter[268] that "in all the circumstances I have no choice but to arrange for your relief". On October 6 you wrote further emphasizing this position. You have since on October 11 written to General Ismay indicating other alternatives which would be agreeable to you[269] In the meanwhile action has proceeded in accordance with my letter to you of October 4, and it has been arranged that you should be relieved on

October 19 by Louis Mountbatten[270] who will be given the rank of Commodore First Class and the title of Commodore C. There can be no question of going back on any of these arrangements.

I need not waste words on the pain and labour which this matter has caused me. In war time especially everyone has to do what he thinks is his duty without undue regard for personal or political associations. This, I am sure, will be your view.

Yours very sincerely,
(Signed)   Winston S. Churchill

113. Keyes to Churchill

[Carbon]   D.C.O.'s Office,
15th October, 1941.

The last two sentences of your letter of 14th October[271] admirably express my view.

One of your qualities that I have always appreciated most in our long friendship is that you never have an "arrière pensée". You may be quite certain that I shall have none either. Please don't feel pain on my account, I have none; I only grieve to have let down my splendid Commandos. I have so often had to break disappointments to them and have always told them to have faith in me since you had vowed to give me opportunities of putting them across the enemy. The War Office appear to be determined to break up the S.S. Brigade and disperse the Commandos and I beg you to see me about this before any irrevocable step is taken.

I do think, however, that before dismissing me, you might have found time to see me, or at least waited to appoint my relief until after the C.O.S. had examined the proposals, which I told you I was making in my letter of 2nd October.

These proposals were actually the "other alternatives" mentioned in my letter to Ismay,[272] which were not ready in time for the C.O.S. meeting to which I was invited on 3rd, so it was postponed by arrangement with Hollis to early the next week, and they were in his hands on the morning of the 6th October, when I received your letter of 4th saying you were arranging for my relief. Hollis then told me that the C.O.S. meeting was off as the matter was out of their hands.

I don't think the Chiefs of Staff could have rejected these alternatives – which I made to meet your wishes – for they went a very long way towards meeting theirs! There is ample evidence of this.

Dickie Mountbatten is a splendid fellow and a live wire with lots of drive. He always makes a study of anything he undertakes and will no doubt do everything in his power to overcome the difficulties of executing amphibious operations. I will do all I can to give him a good start...

114. *Churchill to Keyes*

10, Downing Street,
Whitehall.
October 16, 1941.

Thank you very much for your letter.[273] I was sure you would do your best to give Mountbatten a good start. I did not think it would be a good thing for us to get involved in a long, personal argument about official matters.

I am following up the suggestion which Brendan [Bracken] made to you and I hope, though I cannot promise, that something will come of it... [274]

115. *Keyes to Churchill*

[Copy]

22 St. Leonard's Terrace,
S.W.3.
16th October, 1941.

Thank you for your letter[275] and for the kind suggestion which Brendan made on your behalf. I understand from him that this cannot in any case mature for some months.

Since seeing Brendan, a telegram has come in from Cairo asking approval for the establishment of an organisation for the study and planning of combined operations and opposed landings.

I shall be very grateful if you will allow me to go out for a suitable period, to act as adviser in this matter out there.

This would be in keeping with the recent proposal of the Chiefs of Staff that I should become adviser on combined operations, and ensure that the experience I have gained as D.C.O. would be utilized, with a probable saving of time in many directions. I hope very much that this proposal will commend itself to you, as I am most anxious to be of immediate service, whatever the future may hold for me.

I have no wish to involve you in any personal argument on official matters, or the past, but I beg you to see me before any decision is taken as to my future...

116. Churchill to Keyes

[Copy]

10 Downing Street,
Whitehall.
17 October 1941.

I am sure it would not be a good thing for you to go out to the Middle East at this juncture, or on so vaguely defined a mission. I am actively pursuing the other matter, and the Home Secretary has already written to Mr Andrews.[276] I shall hear in a few days, and then I shall be very glad to have a talk with you . . .

117. Keyes to Churchill

[Copy]
Most Secret

22 St. Leonard's Terrace,
London, S.W.1.
21st Oct. 1941.

Prime Minister

My appointment as D.C.O. having been terminated, I feel free to submit to you, for the consideration of the War Cabinet, the following observations and suggestions, which are based on much practical experience in war, and my fruitless efforts to get combined operations launched during the fifteen months I have held this appointment.

In my opinion, 'Pilgrim' has not been a feasible operation since August last. If we want the islands they could be secured in the way I have suggested, provided Roosevelt will co-operate.[277] There is therefore no longer any justification for keeping a large force of urgently needed transports and M.T. vessels locked up indefinitely and dispersed for this operation.

If the ships which were sent to Sierra Leone – despite my urgent protests – had remained in England, the S.S. troops and Marines could have carried out the large-scale raids which I have suggested, such as beating up Merlimont and Le Touquet Aerodrome, or the Fokker Wolff Aerodrome and the seaside resorts which harbour the German personnel on the peninsula South of Brest.

They could even have secured and covered the landing places on the Cherbourg Peninsula and the aerodromes in the Channel Islands, to enable extended fighter cover to be given.

Personally I think this would have been worth while, if the Army could be induced to capture the peninsula and hold it until every German and military objective had been captured or destroyed.

Raiding operations in Norway since the nights have lengthened

119. Keyes to Churchill

[Copy]

22 St. Leonard's Terrace,
S.W.1.
28. 10. 41.

Now that you have the answer from Mr. Andrews, I hope you will give me the interview you promised me.

I think you might have spared me the rest of your letter...

120. Keyes to Ismay

Tingewick House,
Buckingham.
30/10/41.

Thank you for your visit last night. You have always been helpful during the past 15 months of disappointments and frustration, and I am sure you wish me well in my efforts to defeat the enemy.

Please read carefully the marked passages in the accompanying papers.[281] I am absolutely convinced that it would be very much in the interests of the State, and indeed Winston's too, if my advice was followed.

One more request, please read the attached note[282] to him. It is what I asked you to say last night, as a reply to his message to me, and I would be glad if you would leave it with him...

121. Keyes to Ismay

Tingewick House,
Buckingham.
30/10/41.

I am still very attached to Winston – I can't think why, for he has given me a very raw deal and has now added insults to injury, for I hear he has given to Mountbatten all that he agreed to allow the Chiefs of Staff to take away from me.

I know he wished me well when he gave me the appointment of D.C.O. 15 months ago. He was fully alive to the difficulties I should encounter, of which he warned me himself, but I would have repaid him 100 fold in service to the State, if he had only had the resolution to continue to sustain me in my difficult task.

If he will reflect, he will find that I have never failed him nor given him bad advice in this war or the last, and I do beg him to carefully consider the recommendations I have made in my minutes of 11th Sept.[283] and 21st October.[284]

Time passes and there are such golden opportunities for amphibious strokes in the Mediterranean now, if our splendid striking force is properly directed and courageously used.

At present the Royal Marines and S.S. troops are being messed about in Pilgrim Force, the existence of which and the dispersal of its ships, long after the opportunity of using the force had passed, has stifled all offensive action.

Please urge Winston to get them away from hidebound Army control, which is taking the heart out of them, and send them out to the Mediterranean, where under a Marine General and Naval control, they could be of enormous value to the Army in offensive warfare; as proved by General Wilson's use of the Scottish Commando in the Syrian Campaign.

Neither this striking force, nor the one which went to the Mediterranean and was disintegrated, would have existed but for me, and I really think Winston owes it to me to seriously consider my advice in this matter.

Tell him I have no intention of writing to him again, or having anything more to say to him, until he squares yards with me in the interview I have asked for so often, and which he promised me in his letter of 17th October.[285]

PART III
THE FINAL PHASE
(NOVEMBER 1941–DECEMBER 1945)

Once again in the autumn of 1941 Keyes found himself unemployed in the midst of a war in which victory was at best still a long way off. It was a frustrating situation for he did not feel that his 69 years were a handicap to active employment. Now that he was removed from the scene, he also feared that an unsympathetic staff would repeat their past mistakes and fail to seize the opportunities to use his beloved Commandos properly [Documents 123-5, 130]. There is a certain note of bitterness which creeps into Keyes's correspondence at this unhappy stage in his life for he had heard of ugly rumours about his alleged influence over Churchill. Keyes, with considerable justification, thought the Prime Minister had actually bent over backwards to avoid charges of this nature, and he could not escape the suspicion that his removal from office had been the result of intrigue [126, 127, 129].

The year closed on a tragic note for Keyes when his eldest son Geoffrey, now serving in the Commandos, was killed in November leading the famous raid on Rommel's headquarters in North Africa.[1] The daring nature of the raid far behind enemy lines meant that reliable information was slow in filtering out and at first Keyes hoped his son might have been wounded and was a prisoner of war [131]. Unfortunately near the end of 1941 his death was confirmed [132]. Geoffrey Keyes was awarded a posthumous Victoria Cross which his father received personally from the King the following June [140].

Keyes busied himself in Parliament and in the winter of 1942 began an active campaign of speeches on behalf of National Savings at Navy Weeks throughout the country. His outspoken criticism of inefficiency and slackness in the dockyards aroused the ire of Union leaders, not to mention certain officials in the Government, and once again Keyes was in the midst of controversy [136].[2] He also retained his close interest in the Fleet Air Arm [133, 135]. This was a particularly black period in the war for the Allies, and Keyes and his frequent correspondent Admiral Sir Herbert Richmond, now Master of Downing College, found much to criticise in the conduct of the war where the spectacular Japanese successes in the Far East seemed to confirm the validity of their past warnings [134, 138, 139].

Keyes's dissatisfaction with the conduct of the war led him into a somewhat dubious political adventure when he seconded the motion of censure introduced in the House of Commons by Sir John Wardlaw Milne [138, 139]. He had wanted an opportunity to address the House but had always seemed unable to secure the attention of the Speaker. The debate would give him an opportunity.[3] However, while Wardlaw Milne's attack was directed at Churchill, Keyes's attack was directed at the Prime Minister's advisers [140]. The motion went down to overwhelming defeat and Keyes found himself with strange and unwelcome companions in the division lobby. Churchill seemed to realise that Keyes's role in the affair had not been directed against him personally, and later in the year when the two met at the Other Club in October he offered Keyes a peerage [141, 142]. Churchill would, however, throw the motion of censure back at Keyes the following summer when Keyes complained about remaining unemployed [151, 152].

Keyes accepted the peerage which was announced in the New Year's Honours list for 1943. He chose as his title Baron Keyes of Zeebrugge and of Dover, and his arms included as supporters a sailor of the Royal Navy in blue working rig, and a Royal Marine in field service dress, armed and equipped for trench raiding. Keyes had accepted the peerage largely because Churchill had hinted through his emissary, Brendan Bracken, Minister of Information, that it might be easier to employ him if he were in the House of Lords. Keyes also realised that the most outspoken opponent of the Navy on the question of naval aviation – his wife's brother-in-law Hugh Trenchard – was now a peer and it would be advantageous to have a forum in which to answer him [143, 144]. The sparks began to fly quickly.

On January 27th Keyes was introduced in the House of Lords with Admiral of the Fleet the Earl of Cork and Orrery and Lieutenant-Colonel Lord Lovat (then serving in the Commandos) as his sponsors. The debate that day concerned Fleet Air Arm and in a provocative speech, Trenchard blamed the Navy for its relative backwardness in aircraft and suggested that 'the best way of making certain that the Fleet Air Arm was properly equipped was for it to be taken over by the Royal Air Force, who have the knowledge to re-establish this branch on a sound footing.'

This was too much for Keyes who had been privy to much of the long controversy with Trenchard and the Air Ministry over the question in the interwar period. He departed from custom by intervening in the debate on his very first day in the House of Lords to recall some of the history of the problem. Keyes declared: 'My noble friend Lord Trenchard says it is all the Admiralty's fault. Well, it may be. I hold no brief for the Admiralty; but if the Navy had been allowed to develop its aviation and had not been deprived of it in 1918, we should have been in a very different position today. Now let us wipe out what is past and start afresh.' He concluded by appealing to Lord Sherwood, the Air Ministry representative in the House of Lords, to assist him in his quest to see that the Navy was properly equipped with all the aircraft it needed to fulfil its responsibility. His rebuke of Trenchard led Lord Cherwell, the Paymaster-General, to congratulate him on his intervention and remark: 'We are pleased to see that he [Keyes] is faithful to his habit. He starts by closing with the enemy and lets off his broadside as soon as he has an opportunity.'[4]

Later in the spring of 1943 Keyes became interested in the case of Admiral Sir Dudley North who had been relieved from his command as Flag Officer commanding North Atlantic Station in October 1940 after having allowed Vichy French reinforcements to pass through the Straits of Gibraltar. They ultimately reached Dakar and Churchill thought their arrival was one of the major reasons for the failure of the British-Free French expedition (Operation 'Menace') against the strategically located port.[5] The Admiralty denied North's request for an inquiry or court martial and Keyes joined the number of high naval officers (including Somerville, Andrew Cunningham and Bertram Ramsay) who thought North was being made a scapegoat for the set back at Dakar. As Keyes put it, he was yet another victim of 'that dreadful administration' at the Admiralty [147–150]. North chose to avoid public controversy during the war and did not begin his efforts towards vindication until after Keyes had passed from the scene. Had Keyes lived he would probably have played a substantial role among those who later assisted North in the long effort to clear his name.[6]

At the end of February 1944 Keyes suffered a detached retina in his right eye. Although the first operation for its repair was successful, a near miss during an air raid while Keyes was still in the hospital apparently caused the retina to become detached again. After hopes that it would heal proved futile, Keyes was forced to undergo a second operation. It was not successful and Keyes suffered a permanent loss of vision in his right eye [154, 155]. By now the war was moving towards a victorious conclusion and the work of the Combined Operations organisation was an important factor in the successful invasion of Normandy on the 6th of June. Keyes sent letters of congratulation to Admiral Sir Andrew Cunningham, now First Sea Lord, and Admiral Sir Bertram Ramsay, naval commander of the operation. He received gracious replies [156, 157] and in early July was given the opportunity to spend two days in Normandy touring the beaches and artificial harbours in both the British and American zones.[7]

The trip to Normandy had been a prelude to a longer voyage, for Bracken in his capacity as Minister of Information had suggested, and Churchill had approved, that Keyes undertake a goodwill mission to Australia and New Zealand. Lady Keyes would accompany him as his secretary. The couple left England at the end of July travelling by way of the United States and Canada. In Washington Keyes had an interview with President Roosevelt and Fleet Admiral Ernest King, C-in-C of the US Navy and Chief of Naval Operations. Keyes's charm must have been as powerful as ever and his prestige among the Americans evidently high, for King, who was not noted for his excessive love of the British, made extremely generous arrangements for Keyes's tour. He even arranged for a naval transport plane to fly to Vancouver to pick up Keyes and his wife and bring them to San Diego where Keyes received a grand tour of the training establishments in Southern California [163]. Lord and Lady Keyes flew to Honolulu in a naval transport and here Keyes met Admiral Chester Nimitz, C-in-C of the US Pacific Fleet. Nimitz took Keyes with him for a day at sea aboard a carrier and Keyes spent another day in the command ship of Vice-Admiral Richard L. Conolly observing the training of troops destined for the campaigns in the Pacific Islands.

Anyone who has followed Keyes's career this far would hardly be surprised to learn that he was extremely anxious to witness one of the American operations, and no doubt had been using his considerable ingenuity towards securing such an invitation ever since he arrived in Washington. He was successful, for after he reached Australia he received word that General Douglas MacArthur had invited him to visit his advanced headquarters at Hollandia on the island of New Guinea [160]. And again we can almost anticipate Keyes's next step. On October 7th he wrote his wife from Hollandia: 'I am going to stay with Conolly darling. I hope you won't mind very much but I know you want me to see things and there is so much to see.'[8] Admiral Thomas Kinkaid, C-in-C of the Seventh Fleet had arranged for Keyes to embark in Admiral Conolly's flagship *Appalachian* to observe the impending invasion of Leyte in the Philippines. Keyes had therefore succeeded in extending his goodwill tour into participation in one of the major combined operations of the war. Lady Keyes must certainly have anticipated her husband would do something along this line. Keyes wrote her a few days later: 'I do miss you very much darling – and look forward very much to my flight back to you, but I would not miss this – and I know you would not wish me to. It will be invaluable in the postwar battle to come for sea power properly equipped with air components.'[9]

Keyes's diary for this period is reproduced [161]. It is of great interest for one can sense Keyes's wonder at the vast naval and air operations which characterised this Pacific campaign. In many respects it represented the fulfilment of his wildest dreams concerning combined operations. There is also a considerable note of satisfaction at the crucial role played by carrier-borne aircraft, for the American success justified what Keyes had been fighting for since the end of

World War I. As he watched the LCI's, LCM's and 'Alligator' landing craft, and perhaps thought back to the whalers towed by steam pinnaces at Cape Helles and Anzac, it must have been hard to believe that less than thirty years had elapsed. Keyes was, however, looking forward to the post-war period and the future development of British forces. With perhaps a twinge of conscience that he might seem to be enjoying himself too much, he asked Bracken to emphasise to the Prime Minister that this first-hand knowledge would be useful and that this was the real reason he had arranged to accompany the American forces [167].

Keyes took a lively interest in everything about him. His papers contain slips of paper on which he jotted down the characteristics of ships and equipment he saw, the types of aircraft flown in, the flying time and distance flown, and similar details. He also retained his critical eye, and after the Leyte invasion suggested to MacArthur's Chief of Staff that the Americans might be wise to make use of night landings [164]. Keyes's experience at the Dardanelles had given him a deep and lasting aversion to daylight landings on a hostile shore.

On the evening of the day of the invasion Keyes suffered an accident. Japanese aircraft attacked the invasion flotilla and smoke was put up. A new type of smoke float proved to be poisonous and Keyes along with a number of others on the bridge of the *Appalachian* were gassed [165]. The accident prevented him from embarking in the battleship *Tennessee* as he had been scheduled to do, and so he missed the night action of Surigao Straits in which the American fleet performed the classic manoeuvre of 'crossing the T.' in what may well be the last encounter between capital ships [165].

Keyes recovered from the gassing and returned to a strenuous tour of Australia and New Zealand. But he was 72 and the accident undoubtedly took its toll. Keyes was warned not to fly at altitudes above 10,000 feet without oxygen, but on the flight from Australia to New Zealand his pilot climbed to 13,000 feet and there was no oxygen aboard the plane. Although tiring easily, he continued the New Zealand tour and returned to Australia in the new year. After reaching Adelaide he was finally ordered to bed by a doctor for a complete rest [166]. When he was well enough to travel, Keyes returned to England by way of Ceylon, where he met with Mountbatten, now Southeast Asia Theatre Commander [169], and the Middle East, where he visited his son's grave in Libya.

The naval operations in Leyte Gulf were destined to be Keyes's last experience of active service – ironically with a foreign Navy. The gassing aboard the *Appalachian* and the high altitude flights without oxygen had permanently damaged his heart [170, 171]. His health was now poor but his spirit remained undaunted, as for example, when he did his best to defend King Leopold who was encountering strong opposition against his return to the Belgian throne.[10] Keyes's intentions to participate more actively in the King's defence as well as future debates over naval air power, and also to continue his memoirs, remained unfulfilled. He died quietly in his sleep on the morning of 26th December 1945. The funeral service was held at Westminster Abbey. In the procession led by a band of the Royal Marines with muffled drums from the Horse Guards Parade to the Abbey, six Admirals of the Fleet (Tyrwhitt, Chatfield, Cork and Orrery, Forbes, A. B. Cunningham, and Somerville) marched as pall bearers along with Field Marshal Alexander and General Laycock. Keyes's coffin was placed on a gun carriage, drawn by bluejackets. Burial took place in the cemetery at Dover next to the graves of 66 men who had died in the Zeebrugge action. There was a proposal that Keyes be buried in Nelson's crypt at St Paul's Cathedral but the Admiralty declined on the grounds that he had never commanded one of Great Britain's major fleets in action.[11] A plaque was, however, placed there in memory of both Keyes and his son Geoffrey. Churchill spoke at the unveiling of the tablet on 27th April 1950 and pointed out that from China down to the last period of his life Keyes 'sought glory in the face of danger, and his intense impulse for action was always armed with the highest degree of naval skill and technical efficiency' while his 'exploits afloat and ashore will always excite the enthusiasm of the youth of Britain and are also full of guidance for the leaders of the Royal Navy.' Churchill added: 'There radiated from him the Commando spirit to which we owe so many glorious episodes', and concluded that 'in many ways his spirit and example seemed to revive in our stern and tragic age the vivid personality and unconquerable and dauntless soul of Nelson himself.'[12]

122. *Ismay to Keyes*

SECRET AND PERSONAL.　　　　　　Offices of the War Cabinet,
　　　　　　　　　　　　　　　　　　　Great George Street, S.W.1.
　　　　　　　　　　　　　　　　　　　　　　3rd November, 1941.

Thank you so much for seeing me last Wednesday (29th October) and for your letter of the 30th.[1]

I took the first opportunity of telling the Prime Minister of our talk, and he read through the note which you wrote for his eyes as a reply to his message.[2]

I myself have read through the two other papers[3] enclosed with your letter most carefully, and I will again put them to the Chiefs of Staff Committee at the first opportunity.

Meanwhile, there is an important point which I feel that I ought to raise with you at once. In the course of our talk last Wednesday, you were good enough to show me a number of papers, some personal, some demi-official, and some official, but nearly all dealing with highly secret matters. I am very anxious about these papers on security grounds, and I have looked up the Official Secrets Acts on the subject. The relevant extract is enclosed.

It would obviously be a disaster of the first magnitude if these papers were to fall into wrong hands while the war is in progress; and it is clearly very difficult, if not impossible, for a private individual to ensure their safe custody at all times. Might I therefore suggest that I should arrange for the custody of these documents in our secret archives. They would be listed and sealed in a special box; to which arrangements could be made for you to have access. If you agree, may I send an officer to take them over as soon as possible . . .

123. *Keyes to Tomkinson*

[Holograph]

Tingewick House,
Buckingham.
4. 11. 41.

It is a long tale and I won't weary you with it. But my appointment of DCO has been abolished; it has always been a difficult one, because D.P. [Pound] and the Naval Staff have never forgiven me for my speech about the Norwegian fiasco. It was all right as long as Winston, who gave me the appt. – and warned me of the hostility in the Admiralty – supported me – but my ceaseless battle to try to put the splendid amphibious force I had raised across the enemy became irritating to him and on the spur of the moment he told me he wished me to accept a very considerable modification in my office (which the C. of S. wished to introduce). My "Commandos", their ships, etc. were to be taken from me. I was in fact to be Chairman of yet another Interservice committee and to be called "Adviser on Combined Operations" – as they always ignored my advice – and took all my executive authority away – I told Winston that I could only suppose he wished to terminate the appt. of DCO – I was not prepared to accept the new one as a substitute. So he telegraphed, I believe without saying a word to the Admiralty, to Mountbatten in Honolulu to fly home at once and be Commodore 1st Class (C) and adviser "On Combined Operations"!

L.MB [Mountbatten] told me that he protested to W.C. – he owed much to me, etc. – but W.C. said, "Don't worry about Roger, I am giving him a great promotion," a peerage and an appt. which would be pleasant in peace time and carries 8000 a year – but quite outside of the war effort. Anyhow it isn't coming off for reasons I won't go into.

I hate leaving my splendid people but the whole position was becoming intolerable. It is an unpleasant tale of intrigue and jealousy. There is one bright thing in the story – Geoffrey's gallant action, and the feat of arms which the Commando put up when it was given the opportunity. No other Commando has been given a fair deal and the other 2 in the M.E. have been disbanded – The Army is determined to get the 8 at home completely under their control, if they succeed that will be their end. Although W.C. allowed the C. of S. to take them from me, I believe they are being left under MB!

However I have faith and I am convinced I shall get an opportunity yet of helping to put it across the Hun – Somehow – only it doesn't look very hopeful yet – since no one seems to want to fight when the interservice committees (Councils of War never want to fight) have done with tabulating all the dangers and difficulties.

Winston *wants* to fight and has backed me twice *almost* to the starting day but he funks overriding the C. of S. who are ruled by the J.P.S., E.P.S. – J.I.C.'s. Since all combined operations are primarily a naval responsibility all the difficulties emanate from the Admiralty – and the Army are terrified of another evacuation – and can only think of late 1942 or 1943 – But what is wrong with late 1941 and early 1942 say I! It is curious how history repeats itself, I always seem to be fighting our own side to get on with the war. I am not beaten yet! ...

124. *Keyes to Ismay*

Secret and personal. Tingewick House,
Buckingham,
6/11/41.

Many thanks for your letter of 3rd Nov.,[4] which I received last night, and for passing on my answer to the Prime Minister's message.

I do hope that action is being taken on the two papers I sent you. Of that fine force of three Commandos (1500 men) – which I spent several weeks training personally before they went to the Middle East – five officers and 110 other ranks are all that remained on 14th October.

Even the Scottish Commando, which had just performed an

amphibious feat of arms of which the Army might well be proud, were told almost immediately afterwards that they were going to be disbanded, and were kept hanging about guarding an aerodrome in Cyprus in a state of uncertainty as to when this would take place for three months. By the time they were told of their reprieve, most of the officers and men – who had only volunteered in the first instance for six months – had gone back to their units, as no one seemed to take any further interest in them.

As my informant remarked: – "They don't know troop psychology at all and in an assorted show like this, it is ten times as hard to keep up enthusiasm, after the hammer blows they have dealt us." This will surely also happen at home, if they are messed about by the Army.

I have been repeatedly told by Generals, since I first started to raise the Commandos, that any battalion with a little training could produce equally good shock troops – well let them, but in the meantime let the Navy in the Mediterranean have the Royal Marines and these already trained S.S. troops, who have been disappointed of any action up to now. They know that their only hope in the future is linked with the Navy. The War Office and the Army Commanders have never had any use for them, nor for the Royal Marines for that matter. Vide J.P.(41) 100 "Future Combined Operations" which expresses the views of the War Office representative on the J.P.S., 6/2/41.

Ask the Prime Minister to consult General Bourne about this, he has always been anxious to see the Marines properly used, and he knew that the S.S. troops would be highly trained Marines before long under my direction, and so they are.

The outlook of the Commandos is clear in a number of letters I have received, and I enclose some quotations from them.

I am sure that they will never be given a proper chance in Home Waters, now that all overseas operations are to be the responsibility of C.-in-C. Home Forces; but there are wonderful things to be done in the Mediterranean, if these splendid amphibious troops are only boldly and skilfully used. That they should be properly used is surely of infinitely greater importance to the State than the personal feelings of individuals, who have had their opportunities and failed to make proper use of them.

About the other matter you mentioned. When I received the Prime Minister's letter of 14th October,[5] in which he told me that Mountbatten would relieve me on 19th, it did not leave me any time to go through my papers and settle things in my office, as I wanted to say goodbye to the two training centres in Hampshire, the C.T.C. at Inveraray, and the seven Commandos who are scattered about in different places on the West Coast of Scotland.

I did not get back to London until the 20th, so I had my papers sent to my house and was going through them when you came to see me. While there, they never left my personal care and I even took them to bed with me! And you may be quite certain that anything I have retained will be kept in safe custody. I am, however, grateful for your kind offer to give me a lock up in your secret archives, and I will avail myself of your offer when I come up for the Parliamentary Session next week.

I really am not the irresponsible person the Prime Minister suggested in the closing paragraph of his last letter[6] – which I think he might have spared me – I meant to have referred to this when you came to see me. Please assure him that he may be absolutely certain that I will scrupulously respect secrets regarding the various Operations which are impending, and will not run the slightest risk of jeopardising success or causing loss of life by any indiscretion on my part . . .

125. *Ismay to Keyes*

SECRET AND PERSONAL
Offices of the War Cabinet,
Great George Street, S.W.1.
11th November, 1941.

Many thanks for yours of the 6th November.[7] I will send an officer to collect the papers whenever you say the word.

I gave your message to the Prime Minister last night, but I am certain that your assurance was redundant. My only fear in raising the question of the papers was the possibility of secret agents, or rather unauthorised persons, laying hands on them.

The other points in your letter are at this very moment being given the most earnest consideration, but the pros and cons are very evenly balanced. In any event, I am sure that you need have no fear of the Commandos getting into wrong or unsympathetic hands . . .

126. *Keyes to Ismay*

Most Secret
22 St. Leonard's Terrace,
S.W.3.
14th Nov. 1941.

Thank you for your letter of 11th Nov.[8] received last night. Some of the papers I intended to ask you to deposit in your secret archives are at the moment in the possession of Mountbatten, when he returns them, I will ask you to send for them.

In the Prime Minister's last letter[9] to me, he says: – "I am quite sure you have not been the victim of intrigue," and goes on to say: – "Your very high rank and personal association with me also cause embarrassment and friction."

I have been wondering what this meant, for as You know, I have had no personal association with the Prime Minister for many months, and he has repeatedly refused to even see me in regard to my office and has never failed to reject my advice, when it conflicted with that of the Chiefs of Staff.

By a lucky chance today, I have at last learnt why the Prime Minister has been shunning me as if I had the plague, instead of helping me in my difficult task; and I suppose it is also the reason why he terminated my appointment at the request of the Chiefs of Staff so ruthlessly, without hearing my side of the question; and despite the vows and promises he made to me, each time I had to break disappointments to my ardent people.

I had heard some time ago that Wing Commander James[10] had remarked to certain M.P.s, that he hoped that I "was not going to be given a high Naval command, as it would cause tremendous feeling in the Navy." As I was already D.C.O. and there was no question of my being given a high Naval command, I did not bother about it at the time, as before I had an opportunity of asking him what it was all about, I heard that he had returned to Spain.[11]

However, I asked him today why he had said this, and he told me that his duties in Spain often took him to Gibraltar, where he frequently visited the ships there, including the *Ark Royal,* and he heard there was bitter resentment at the Prime Minister's interference in Naval matters, which was all attributed to *my alleged influence over him*! For instance: – The unfair way in which Dudley North[12] was made a scapegoat for his alleged failure to stop the French cruisers going through the Straits. James told me that this was also particularly resented in the Embassy at Madrid, as they knew who was really responsible and were shocked when North was superseded.[13]

Another incident for which my influence was held responsible was the Court of Enquiry held by Lord Cork on Admiral Somerville's alleged reluctance to engage the enemy in the Western Mediterranean.[14]

I knew nothing of either of these incidents until long after they had occurred!

In fact my evil influence over the Prime Minister was said to be responsible for this odious head hunting and almost every miscarriage and failure of the Naval Staff which has occurred for the last year – except perhaps the loss of the *Glorious,* when her splendid Captain – who was killed – was made the scapegoat by the Naval Staff, to the disgust of his many friends.

I asked James why he had not told me of all this, and given me the chance of refuting these lies, but he told me he felt he had done the right thing by bringing it to the notice of the Prime Minister through YOU. Don't you think that you might have warned me of this damned intrigue, instead of passing on – what You must have known were lies – and thus making my difficult position infinitely more difficult by making the Prime Minister not un-naturally reluctant ever to see me.

As I told you before, all this intrigue was started by Captain Maund (now Captain of the *Ark Royal*), who had been Asst. Naval Director to General Bourne and resented my advent, as up to then *he* had been the Naval authority on combined operations. At his request therefore I agreed to his exchanging appointments with my representative at the Admiralty, where he set to work to undermine my position and was responsible for circulating in the Admiralty and (during my absence in Scotland) secretly in my office, a paper suggesting that my Directorate was redundant and should be abolished, and recommending that he should be the authority on combined operations at the Admiralty! all the executive work being undertaken by the Inter Service E.P.S.

However last January this paper came to my notice, and on my return from Lamlash I sent for him and told him exactly what I thought of his disloyalty, which I reported to the V.C.N.S. Having been found out, he applied to go to sea, and although Pound told me later he had been well scrubbed, he was actually rewarded by being given the command of the *Ark Royal,* where he has been carrying on his good work busily bringing my name into odium by putting about these lies in the Fleet at Gibraltar; and incidentally of course, he was responsible for Wing Commander James' mischief *making through you to the Prime Minister.*

Meanwhile the seeds of intrigue he had sown against me in the Naval Staff were bearing fruit. They had never forgiven me for my exposure of the Norwegian fiasco, and considered the office the Prime Minister had given me – with the object of prosecuting combined operations more effectively and offensively – was a reflection on them. With the result that the Naval Director of Plans actually persuaded the Joint Commanders to sign that mischievous document, making similar recommendations, which he forwarded with his covering remarks to the Chiefs of Staff, behind my back, on 23rd August.

You told me that you had scotched this second effort to get rid of me, but the Naval Staff soon returned to the charge, and this time persuaded the Chiefs of Staff to make recommendations to the Prime Minister which resulted in terminating my appointment – obviously because these rumours had "caused him embarrassment and friction." Yet I am told that there is no intrigue against me!

I have also been told by senior officers who have come back from the Eastern Mediterranean, that they had been told that I was responsible for holding up the attack on the Dodecanese, by persuading the Prime Minister to concentrate on 'Workshop'. You know the facts.

I do not believe for one moment that all this engineered hostile and slanderous criticism of me really represents the feeling of the *fighting* Navy, judging by the many scores of letters that I received after my speech about the way the Navy let the Army down at Trondheim and lately from sailors and soldiers, who have been in contact with [my] work during the past 15 months. They all look to me to give a lead in the waging of amphibious warfare, and having seen me on the beaches day and night in the worst Winter weather, do not consider me too old and useless!

It is of course most annoying for the Prime Minister that anyone should be under the erroneous impression that I influence his actions in any way, and I sincerely sympathise with him; but it is damnably infuriating for me, that not only have I failed to persuade the Prime Minister to do anything I have recommended throughout this war, but that I have been blamed for many unpleasant things that neither I (nor he for that matter) have had anything whatever to do with, on account of my so-called but non-existing personal association with him; but which has helped to bring about my ignominious dismissal, at a moment when I should be in a position to do great service to the State, if he would only have been induced to accept my expert advice, and reject that of his "expert Advisers", who have succeeded in frustrating all offensive action that both he and I have tried to undertake.

Quite apart from any question of friendship, which has been loyal and steadfast on my part, I think the Prime Minister owes me very considerable amends for my humiliating downfall and all the slanders I have suffered on his account.

I think too, that you owe it to me, to see that he reads this letter as he has never accorded me the interview he promised me. Perhaps it may help him to put the true interests of the State before the personal feelings of people, who have had their opportunities and failed to take them and a few jealous unscrupulous Naval Staff officers, who only succeeded in eliminating my Directorate when backed by the V.C.I.G.S.[15] (who owes me a grudge too, because I exposed his efforts to make a scapegoat for his own shortcomings).[16] However, I gather from Mountbatten that now I have been got rid of, he will be allowed to retain the Commandos – the Army's demand for which was made the final excuse for breaking up my Directorate . . .

15th November.

P.S. Since this was written, I see Nemesis has overtaken Maund!¹⁷ I hope if he is ever employed again, it will be somewhere where he cannot make further mischief.

I know although he was Cork and Orrery's Chief of Staff throughout the Narvik Campaign he worked against him, and when he came back libelled him right left and centre (he tried to do so to me), and no doubt his lies then had a good deal to do with that Admiral of the Fleet's undoing. I asked Cork what he thought of him, and he told me that he had never come across anyone so utterly disloyal. An opinion in which I heartily concur. I am of course bringing these facts to the notice of the First Lord.

127. *Ismay to Keyes*

MOST SECRET AND PERSONAL Offices of the War Cabinet,
Great George Street, S.W.1.
17th November, 1941.

Thank you for your letter of the 14th November.¹⁸ I will send an officer for the papers as soon as you let me know that you are ready to hand them over.

I am reluctant to dwell on the past, but I must dispel the illusion that anything which James said to me had the remotest effect on the events of last month.

So far as I remember the interview, James said that there was a lot of criticism at Gibraltar against your influence on the Prime Minister in naval matters, and against the influence of a certain other member of the Prime Minister's Staff (who may be nameless) in political matters. I explained to him (a) that the story was ridiculous since your share of responsibility was strictly confined to Combined Operations, while the "other man's" responsibilities were even more circumscribed, and (b) that, in any event, I did not pass on this kind of tittle-tattle to the Prime Minister.

It is, as you know, inevitable that anyone who is near the Prime Minister should become the subject of criticism; and if I were to pay any attention to this kind of thing and, still more, if I were to make a habit of passing on this uninformed gossip to the Prime Minister, I should only be doing him and the Country a grave disservice.

You therefore have my categorical assurance that I did *not* pass on James' story and that, so far as I know, no breath of it ever reached the Prime Minister's ears. Further I am certain, even if it had, that he would have taken no notice of it. As you know far better than I, he is the last man in the world to be influenced by popular clamour, or petty intrigue.

As you particularly requested it, and as I happened to get a fleeting opportunity last night, I mentioned the gist of your letter to him . . .

128. *Keyes to Richmond*

[Holograph]
Private   18.11.41.

I have not heard from you for ages. I suppose you gave up all hope of ever spurring me into action!! As a matter of fact my ceaseless efforts to *make* war overseas has caused so much friction with the Chiefs of Staff Committee and their satellite interservice committees, who manage to stifle action, that the P.M. decided on their recommendation to abolish the office of D.C.O. They recommended that I should be called "Adviser on Combined Operations," deprived of all executive responsibility and command, and be Chairman of yet another Interservice Committee, on the Training and Equipment for Combined Operations. So I told the PM he had terminated my appt. – and as they had *never* listened to my advice & I did not wish to be Chairman of a Committee I could not accept the appt. W.C. actually thought that promotion to "another place" and a high office in no way connected with the war would appeal to me – but it does *not* while we are in the middle of a bloody war, and something must be done to speed up action by getting rid of all that impedes it.

Some months ago Eyre & Spottiswoode who bought my bankrupt publisher's business asked me if my Gallipoli story could be republished as it was sold out and still in demand. So I wrote a foreword in the hope that it would encourage the PM to override the stonewall opposition from which I have been suffering from for the last year or more. It should have come out 2 or 3 months ago but by a curious chance it actually appeared yesterday when the papers were full of my downfall which had hitherto escaped notice tho' it occurred a month ago, with the result that I had a rotten weekend pestered by reporters . . .

129. Keyes to Ismay

Most Secret
22 St. Leonard's Terrace,
S.W.3
19/11/41.

Thank you for your letter of 17th Nov.[19] I am glad to hear that you were not the person who passed on the information James gave you, although I still think that you might have warned me of these slanders.

I am under "no illusion that anything James said to you" had the remotest effect on *the events of last month*; however the suggestion that the Fleet resented *my alleged influence* with the Prime Minister and regarded me as responsible for many unpleasant actions (taken by the Naval Staff) which were attributed to him, undoubtedly reached him. Otherwise what possible excuse can he have for shunning me as he has for many months, and affording me no opportunity of giving him advice on combined operations as Minister of Defence, which he had told me he expected me to do.

He obviously does not read my letters, and your giving him "the gist" of them leaves me in no doubt as to what he really knows about it.

After all I am considered the expert on amphibious warfare and combined operations, and that was obviously the reason he gave me the appointment of D.C.O. – although he warned me of Pound's hostility at an early date.

It was clear to me from the first that Pound and his satellites on the Naval Staff deeply resented my appointment, and considered it a reflection on their ability to conduct combined operations – which of course it was, after the Norwegian fiasco.

There is abundant evidence of this on record.

I enclose a copy of Maund's memorandum,[20] which I forgot to send with my last letter.

The two subsequent efforts – the 2nd, signed by the Joint Commanders and forwarded by the Naval Director of Plans, and the 3rd, forwarded to the Prime Minister by the Chiefs of Staff – are in the War Cabinet records already.

I maintain that these three documents and the story of my alleged evil influence over the Prime Minister – spread in the Fleet by the author of the first – after he was found out, and sent to *Ark Royal* – constitutes a very unpleasant intrigue, which has been successful in eliminating me, and completely disorganising the splendid amphibious striking force I have built up; and it has prevented it being used – as it most certainly would have been, if the Prime Minister had followed my advice.

After I received my new Directive in March 1941, the Prime Minister told me to communicate with him through you, and on the 24th April I wrote you two letters,[21] one of which I asked you to show to the Prime Minister with my Minute of 24th April to the C.O.S. Committee (a copy of which I enclosed), during a tour you were about to undertake with him.

I happened to meet him just before he started – and he said he had something important for me to do. I told him I had given you these papers, which I particularly wished him to read, and he promised to do so in the train.

On your return you said you had not had an opportunity of showing them to him!

If he had then read the letter I sent you, and acted on it, we should have had a highly trained amphibious force ready to carry out any action – including 'Puma' – and would have avoided tying up for the past six months a large force and shipping – urgently needed – for 'Pilgrim' operation, long after it was a feasible operation; thus depriving us of the means of striking amphibious blows elsewhere.

In fact the determination of the Naval Staff to prevent me having any hand in the direction or execution of any combined operation has, as you know, wasted a great deal of their time and mine, and it has certainly impeded the war effort.

I wrote to you because the Prime Minister sent you to see me, instead of according me the interview which he had promised me; but as you don't show him my letters, it is hardly a substitute for an interview.

However, now that I am no longer in uniform in a subordinate position, the whole thing is on a different plane, and perhaps it is not fair to expect you to do anything further . . .[22]

P.S. I am glad to hear that Pownall is leaving the War Office, but after what I saw of him in Belgium, it alarms me to think of his having any position of responsibility.

130. *Keyes to Richmond*

[Holograph]

Tingewick
Dec. 3, 1941.

Many thanks for your letter of 26th. I can't of course write of what I wanted to do and was ready to do a year ago. My speech was not a "personal statement" in the Parliamentary sense.[23] Had I wished to make one it would have been simply devastating and very embarrassing to W.C. D.P. and his passive defence satellites deeply resented my office as a reflection on their ability to wage amphibious war – as it was, shades of Norway & Dakar! They never forgave me for my strictures on the Trondheim fiasco. W.C.'s retort that I was only out to do another Zeebrugge was, as he knew, damnably unfair. I never suggested taking a hand until after *14* days during which I tried to persuade the Admiralty to go into the Fiord because C. de Wiart's Namsos thrust was doomed to failure unless we occupied its waters – and all I said came true. This is all on record. When I was told that they had a plan but it entailed using the whole Home Fleet and we could not afford to risk it or take it from its strategic base owing to the threat of war with Italy, I said nothing would impress Italy more than a smashing success against the German Fleet which was taking such liberties. I then suggested a simple plan which W.C. admitted in the House was better than theirs – and offered to make myself responsible for it, in the vain hope of goading them into action. However W.C. skated over the exposure I made – concentrated on my self seeking – and rebuked me for casting aspersions on my old friends and chosen staff officers, etc., D.P. – T.P.[24]

As my post of DCO was subordinate to the committees on which they sat – C of S and VCOS – it is not surprising that they did not rest until they got rid of me. W.C. felt that he could best put an end to the friction by promoting me to the other House and giving me an appt. of "great dignity", without any reference to me. He did not realise that nothing outside the ring in which I can fight the King's enemies – overseas or within our gates – would appeal to me. I warned him that I was determined to speed up the war machine and gave him notice I was going to attack on Tuesday. My one object was to try to force them into action before it is too late.[25] I knew they would know what I meant – they have been hesitating and proscrastinating for many weeks. It is too late to take full advantage of it.

Winterton's[26] silly intervention turned some people's thoughts in the direction I want – action – and have been urging action for many months – starting the day Italy crossed the Greek frontier.[27] They were strokes akin to Pitt's – the phrase I used "electrifying the world", etc. – were W.C.'s own[28] for he supported me – but he will never override the C. of S. Committee – they were all for it to start with but the sub committees marshalled all the difficulties and dangers – exaggerated difficulties of supply, etc. – and the COS shrank from the risks – put it off – put it off – and then the Huns came. The Commanders and the Army hardly came into the big thing I have been fighting for – amphibious striking force under naval responsibility, 2 Brigades of R.M. and my S.S. Brigade – under a Marine General – a splendid fellow and a young Admiral chosen by me – such a force *has* been available since April, light tanks, A.A. guns, artillery, etc., in fast ships with the means to land them. First the Army insisted on a General superseding my Marine – because tanks, etc., and another Brigade had been added. They have been held idle since August for something I've told them they *can't* do now that we have been forestalled there.

When the story is told after the war it will be recognized as a major tragedy – *I mean 6000 highly trained amphibious troops* where *you* would put them now. D.P. & Co. really ought to be impeached. It is simply tormenting.

As for Trondheim – read the young American girl who was "Looking for trouble." – She was in Rome and said nothing encouraged the Italians more to come into the war than our naval failure in Norway. And Shirer's[29] *Berlin Diary* declares that the Germans were fearfully anxious about Trondheim – "If the British had forced a passage into the fiord the Norwegian gamble would have failed!" I wish we meet sometime . . .

131. *Keyes to Tomkinson*

[Holograph]

Tingewick House,
Buckingham.
24.12.41.

That was a splendid card you and Joan sent us. You always find the best.

I have promised that nice fellow George Hall[30] who was Civil Lord in the 2nd Labour Govt. to come down for Aberdare's Warship Week opening on 22nd Feb. They have offered to put me up – but if you can give me a bed I'd love to come, there are 101 things I'd like to talk to you about. We have been very anxious about Geoffrey.[31] We heard about 1st Decr. that he had been missing since 24th Nov. He went on rather a desperate business about 200 miles behind the enemy's lines – and evidently did not expect to get back – I don't know if it is any connection but it looks like it – *Glenroy* was torpedoed and put into Malta[32] – and evidently posted this letter – same day (as the letter) Baillie-Grohman[33] telegraphed that he was reported P of W. He hoped to confirm later. We live in hopes and faith.

It is tormenting to think that instead of 5000 to 6000 S.S. troops & 2 Marine Brigades – light tanks, etc., which I have been trying to get into the Mediterranean for months – we only had Geoffrey's 4 officers, 110 men – left – when they decided to restart the S.S. troops and form a DCO office out there – after disbanding the Commandos. Just think of what they might have done –and might be doing now. I'll tell you all about it when we meet. It all gets back to D.P.'s damned jealousy. I think the War Cabinet and Naval Staff will come very badly out of it when all the facts are known – and it is realised that we have had a splendid amphibious force lying idle.

The Japs have taught us how to make use of amphibious power to threaten the Empire which was built up with it.

It alarms me to think of what D.P. and W.C. are up to in the U.S.A.!!

I wrote that article, the gist of a speech which was short circuited by the Govt. making it a secret session instead of the debate we demanded. The *D.T.* [*Daily Telegraph*] would not publish it. Camrose[34] is in Trenchard's[35] pocket – and said it was a very weak case for a Naval Air Service – It was all Phillips' fault, he could have had all the fighter cover he wanted, etc.[36] So I gave it to the *News Chronicle* which had been backing the plea for a Naval Air Service.

Algy [Boyle] is very annoyed with me I gather! About *News Chronicle* – and my speech which was not a personal statement in the Parliamentary sense, I could have made a devastating one if I had wanted to. It was an effort to spur the war machine into sending the amphibious force to the Med – as W.C. and Co. knew.

He wanted to, but he is absolutely *ruled* by D.P. It is strange – I have not seen him to speak to for 5 months. The friction was all over the failure to use sea power – and W.C. really thought a peerage, etc., would please me and make up for all his broken vows and my disappointments!

Anyhow I am free to fight on – and in the Secret Session had the whole House with me (except the Treasury Bench). I expect that Algy will be sicker still with me before I finish and do help to win this war, which we deserve to lose. After all Algy would not have gone to Dover if I had not fought Bacon, J.R.J. [Jellicoe] & Co. and beaten them. We are just where we were in the winter of 1917 – passive defence as far as the war effort in London is concerned – the people in the M.E. [Middle East] have guts and enterprise but they ought to have made use of amphibious power.

I hope all goes well with all yours & trust Peter flourishes. Every good wish from us all for you all . . .

132. *Keyes to Richmond*

[Holograph]

Tingewick House,
Buckingham.
4.1.42.

My wife and I were deeply touched by your kind letter. Letters such as yours are a real help and consolation.

We have not given up hope that our son may be alive. Although his death was officially confirmed in Cairo, we find that it is solely based on the Sergeant's report who followed my son into the H.Q. and escaped to join Col. Laycock who was waiting at the R.V. 20 miles away. The only other man taken into the house was a Captain Campbell and he and the Sergeant carried Geoffrey out, it was dark and fighting was going on. They may well have been mistaken in thinking that he was dead. So many men have been left for dead and survived. Campbell was wounded later in the leg and is missing – presumably a wounded prisoner of war – and we have faith and hope that they may be together in an Italian hospital.

From his last two letters it was clear that he was preparing for an enterprise and on 8th Decr. we received a letter which he said would only be posted if he did not get back – also a telegram from an Admiral in the Mediterranean saying that he was reported to be a prisoner of war, but there is no confirmation of this. The casualty people at the W.O. are making enquiries on the lines I have suggested – and do not accept Cairo's official confirmation. The cruel thing was that the Cairo message was broadcasted at 8 a.m. on 31st and my 3 daughters in different parts of the country and my son in a cruiser on the way back from the Norwegian raid[37] heard it for the first time like that. The War Office censor rang up after midnight to warn me that he could not stop it being published.

You asked about the LITANI river, here is an extract from a lecture given to the Commandos at home by Laycock when he came back after the C.'s-in-C. had disbanded the Commandos out there, which was stopped, but too late to save any except the handful who collected round my son.

Please keep the *News Chronicle* article. One published in the *Daily Telegraph* on Friday – an obvious reply to it, shows why Camrose who had published my naval air propaganda since 1935 refused to take my last effort. Trenchard had taken a lot of trouble to "get" him. In 1918 the RFC broke up the RNAS in a fortnight as far as my fine command was concerned – and naval officers were *forced* to wear military uniform and adopt military ranks at once. I spoke 4 times in the House to show how the Air Ministry was sabotaging the Govt. decision of 1937.

An Admiral Cunningham[38], *not Andrew,* in charge of Naval Air was defeated [?] and got rid of. Alec Ramsay, C.-in-C. East Indies, was bought home to take it over – and also failed – when Winston found what hopeless chaos there was Ramsay was made the scape goat and has been unemployed ever since the winter of '39 – a cruel injustice. The complacent and self satisfied attitude of the *D.T.* man is difficult to tolerate!

My wife and I are so very grateful to you and Lady Richmond and will always prize your letter which expresses so beautifully what many others have tried to convey . . .

133. *Rear-Admiral Alexander H. Ramsay to Keyes*

[Holograph]   Bagshot Park,
Surrey.

This is for your own ears only.

26 Jan. '42.

I do not blame Winston, at the time he was just about to become P.M. He could not stand a row with Kingsley Wood, who was at that time more or less the star of the Cabinet as far as the people were concerned. Clever as a monkey, full of advertisement and totally against any cooperation. Few people will realise what I went through, with 3 First Lords & 3 First Sea Lords during the crisis taking over the F.A.A., against the wishes of the Cabinet & Air Force & I am sorry to say the Admiralty. My predecessor Cunningham did nothing for 2 years, met me when I came home with tears in his eyes on the edge of a nervous breakdown, in fact he left just before he was found out. Instead of saying he could not take it on like I would have in his place, he said he would take 5 years to take over in peace time. I took over in 2. When I started we were 60 pilots short, no reserves, 80 observers & 175 back gunners short, we were just about to launch 2 new carriers & after I left Pound's boast was that he had given 100 pilots to the air force (to make friends), 6 months later I found out that they were exactly 100 pilots short.

I had to make the first Estimates for 34,000,000 for aerodromes, personnel, etc.

It took me 6 months after taking over to get the Ad^l Personnel dept. to take over the personnel, & the same with guns, bombs, etc.

At the same time I had [to?] find & fight for new aerodrome rights, all this single handed.

To show you what it meant, I was 2 sergt. & 10 corpl. fitters short & the Air Min^{try} delayed me 3 months making a Cabinet matter out of it. They knew full well that Stanhope[39] or any 1st Lord would not rise up to it with the political pull they had.

Every paper I wrote on aerodromes & personnel was submitted by the Treasury to Air Ministry before they would approve, & you can imagine how the Air M. loved this method of delaying.

The large personnel pamphlet I issued re the maintenance organisation, etc. & sent to A.M. for remarks, they took 6 months to answer, but I had to go on building, not knowing whether they would pull all the wires [?] out or not.

It was just perfect hell, then Winston came & said he was not sure of the use of the Fleet Air Arm and all the expenditure of money, I had to begin explaining all A.B.C. which my nerves would no longer stand.

Then I wrote a really rude minute to the Board saying Cabinet decision was wanted & that it was no use waiting for Air Ministry about an armament camp, which they had promised me on paper, but on asking them to turn it over, they explained that they had never given the date, hardly the way to behave between officers.

Winston met K.W. on it & Seal the private secretary gave him my pamphlet which was only meant for the Board & I believe Winston actually read it through, he never told me, but obviously this was the last straw.

It was only later that I found Phillips had been working hard against me, where all the trouble of the F.A.A. was really due to him, where he had been 5 years there in Plans, putting forward 14 cruisers without [?] any provision. Phillips like a lot of Admirals never believed in the air & now poor devil he knows.

Winston said that being protected by cloud he was quite right to carry out the operation, when on manoeuvres in peacetime I have prayed for those very conditions.

I am afraid as regards Chatfield I offended him because I wrote from East Indies to congratulate him on obtaining the principle for the Fleet to have its own air arm but regretting that no details of any sort had been agreed on because it meant we had nothing & the A.M. would make anything a Cabinet decision, which they did.

I know my methods were dictatorial, but they had to be as I knew I only had 2 years & I did it within a month, though the A.M. suggested continually that during the crisis it ought to be postponed.

Thank God I trained them in night flying, etc., & kept them busy. In fact in Abyssinian crisis two carriers 100 miles apart kept in touch with each other all night & attacked all night.

I don't believe they would have had a Taranto[40] without this training & with *Bismarck*[41] & sinkings in the Med^n the F.A.A. has certainly justified itself.

There was an awfully good article in the *Evening Standard* of 25th against the dead hand of Lord Trenchard, who at the beginning of the war asked how I was getting on & said he thought it was a good thing we had to fight for it.

How can the Army get on without their artillery, the old horse [?] artillery they can not move up at the rate of mechanised troops, it is not only bases [?] in rear [?] they must bomb [?], but they must be at the army's instant command for artillery support. However having been at sea all my life and refused an Ad¹ billet 3 times, they offered me Greenwich Hospital & surprised & offended I didn't jump at it.

Enough said, I have tried to keep quiet, but the [illegible] & all the F.A.A. know what I have done & they always greet me. Lyster[42] himself said to me how grateful he was & said that none of my organisation had been altered, not bad.

Enough said. Thanks for your sympathy . . .

134. *Richmond to Keyes*

Master's Lodge,
Downing College,
Cambridge.
Feb. 16, 1942.

Singapore is as good as gone I fear.[43] We build a great base for the fleet and then do not provide ourselves with the fleet for whose use it was built. Jellicoe recommended a "Two Ocean Navy" and his proposals were scorned. We preferred to trust to luck and refused to consider the possibility that when we were engaged either in Europe or the Far East the gangsters in the other hemisphere would fail to take the opportunity of our difficulty. Dimly, perhaps, some allowed themselves to hope that if Japan attacked us in the East, the U.S.A. would fly to our help. They forgot the old doctrine of the first Lord Stanhope:[44] "Our Navy pride themselves on doing their own service without any obligation to foreign help." So, with a navy so reduced by the Macdonalds,[45] Arthur Hendersons,[46] Alexanders, Wedgwood Benn[47] and the other contrivers of the criminal London Treaty (some of whom now are apotheosized or occupy the seat of the First Lord or in the House of Lords) with the cowardly assent of Madden, Field and Chatfield (whose defence of the Admiralty in the matter of the Irish bases was a disgrace) we can now barely hold our own against Germany and Italy but can do nothing to stop Japan's career of conquest in the East. And Parliament has blandly assented to it all.

Here, however, is a matter which, if not promptly attended to will add to our misfortunes; and not ours only but also those of Russia and China. If you were a German with Japan as your ally what would you urge her to do as soon as possible? When she has secured her hold on Singapore would you not wish her to get possession of Trincomali? There lies the best port in the Indian Ocean at the very centre of it. With a naval force there the Burma Road is as effectively cut as it would be at Rangoon, the route of the armies' supplies to Egypt, Persia and Russia is within reach of effective attack by the Japanese navy – battleships, "pocket-battleships," cruisers and submarines; there is a huge oil installation there; there is a great maidan close to the harbour admirably suited for an aerodrome. There are no defences other than those light guns, up to a 9.2 for defence against cruiser attack; for the basis of the defence was command of the sea. I venture to think that if Japan were to send 4000 men or even less tomorrow they would land without the smallest difficulty on the open beach – for the N.E. Monsoon is now practically over – and take the place in their slippers.

I wrote to Winston to point this out last week and his Secretary replies that he will have the matter looked into. There is no time for this customary "looking into" – indeed it is disturbing that he should make such a reply and not be able to say at once that proper measures have already been put in train. What measures are needed? Plainly, fighting ships, aircraft and a strong military garrison. Troops alone are not enough, for an enemy has a wide choice of where to land along the whole of the east coast. If some of those long ranged bombers with which the R.A.F. bombs Mannheim and other German centres with so little effect in stopping German armies were sent to Ceylon, they might perform some useful service in assisting to hold the line of communications on which the security of Egypt, of China and of Russia – in so far as the last depends on the war material we and the Americans send her is concerned. I see fears being expressed [that] Japan is wheedling Vichy to give her the use of Madagascar. It may be true. Diego Suarez is a fine anchorage – I always planned that it should be the first object of my attack in a war with France. But it may equally be a blind to divert our attention from Ceylon; or, for that matter, she may, in her wide sweeping ambition nourished by her successes and confident in her power, want both the great islands.

Can we spare battleships from home or the Mediterranean. If not, how are we going to protect the Route up the East Coast of Africa against heavy ship attack by Japan? Is it possible that we can now ignore the danger of the Italian battleships taking part in any operations in the Levant, because of the risks they would run from submarines and air? Only someone more acquainted with the conditions out there than I am can answer that, but it need[s] immediate answer. As I think I have said to you before, the neglect of the Admiralty to follow up Taranto and Matapan with attacks on the damaged ships, the dockyard at Taranto and the town of Taranto itself which we ought to have blotted out with its workmen was extraordinary to me and I begged Alexander more than once to see to it.

We must have heavy ships in the Indian Ocean quickly, and we must forestall the Japanese in Ceylon. Is it possible to persuade those who direct our strategy that we shall help ourselves and our allies far more effectively if we ensure the safety of the sea routes which supply the army in Egypt, the army in Persia, the Russian army and the army in India, to say nothing of maintaining the communications in the Indian ocean and South Pacific, than by bombing Cologne and the marshalling yards of this or that line of railroads in Germany? Have not all the forecasts of the R.A.F. been falsified in regard to the effects of their attacks on German production? I venture the belief that 50 torpedo planes or even 50 bombers in Celyon next week, with a complement of fighters if they can be got there, would be worth double the number over Germany or occupied France. Command of the sea is what matters, and that is a thing the Air staff have never understood. They have always wanted to fight their own war, independently of the other services and with a separate object. That they have done well in keeping the *S.* and *G.*[48] in Brest for all these months since March last is true. But the damages they have thought they had inflicted on them do not now appear to have been great. The ineffectiveness of the bomber against the ships both in harbour and at sea has been demonstrated. All, I gather, that the Navy could do was to send half a dozen Swordfish planes whose torpedoes are apparently not particularly powerful. The contrast between the efficiency of the Japanese with their naval air arm and ourselves with our divided organisation is patent and plain.

Do, if you can, rub in to Winston the facts which the map disclose; that a navy holding ports on the west coast of Malaya – Penang, Moulmein, Port Swettenham – can slip a force into the Andamans as a stepping stone and then a stronger one into Ceylon; and, from Trincomali and the Malay ports, will effectively close the approaches to Madras, Calcutta and Rangoon, isolate China, and cut into the Cape route, seizing Madagascar if it chooses so to do, Vichy or no Vichy. Get him to insist that the Air force shall regard as its first duty the prevention of those dire events as far as it lies in their power by the despatch of air forces to Ceylon, and the Admiralty to find a means of sparing heavy ships without whose protection the armies will lose their supplies. Forgive a letter with rather a lot of repetition in it . . .

135. *Lieut.-Commander Rupert Brabner*[49] *to Keyes*

[Holograph]
R.A.F. Tain,
Ross-shire.
14.3.42.

I hear from the Mayor of Folkestone that you are to open the Warship Week there on March 20th. I wish I could be there to help welcome you but I am afraid we are being well and truly worked up here.

I am sure your presence will do much to invigorate the town. While it has escaped severe war damage the degree of misery there is high as many have left or have been evacuated and the remainder are very badly off. I think you will agree that to suffer in silence without the relief of occasional action which we have is a good quality of courage and there have been comparatively few complaints from the constituency.

I tried like blazes to get down for the debate on the War Situation and Naval Estimates but was prevented by Hunnish activity up here. I was so glad to see that a really determined effort is being made to do something about our aircraft. I know that you have been trying for years to get some interest taken.

Quite honestly, Sir, the real trouble is that the Board of Admiralty do not care two hoots about the F.A.A. and are incapable of holding their own against the Air Ministry. The Fifth Sea Lord[50] is a damn good fighter but he is only one among many more senior officers. The best man we have for getting things done is Captain Caspar John[51] who is at M.A.P. He ordered Spitfires for us off his own bat and got a fearful trouncing for it but we are getting them at last.

I have tackled Alexander again and again and he has to do him justice, listened, but it is all Greek to him and he, in my opinion, is easily satisfied with official excuses.

One continually hears still at the Admiralty "Oh this is good enough for the Fleet Air Arm" and so on. Alexander admitted to me that the Albacore was a mistake and the new T.B.R. has been continually sniped at and held up both by the Air Ministry and M.A.P.

It is only when we are caught short in Norway without a decent Fighter – in Crete without any Fighters and so on, and now in the Channel, that the inadequacy of our equipment is shown up. The storm, however, always dies down and nothing seems to come of it. Alexander is the man who ought to keep up the pressure but doesn't.

As for Esmonde[52] and his chaps – you will perhaps know that their Fighter escort failed to materialise, and while he was shot down by ship's fire, most of the others were wounded or destroyed by these F.W. 190's.

This is not just an idle moan and it has been boiling up for months. I cannot however get up in the House and say these things without presumably resigning my commission. I suppose if one were really courageous that ought to be done.

I am afraid this is rather long and has little to do with Warship Weeks but I do wish you the greatest success in starting this week and I apologise for not being there to welcome you...

136. *Keyes to Tomkinson*

[Holograph]

Tingewick House,
Buckingham.
8.4.42.

Many thanks for your letter. I have had such hundreds of letters encouraging me to go on in my efforts to speed up the war machine[53] – so many from workers themselves who hate the T.U. interference and its inability to control the bad elements and to stop strikes. W.C. is completely under the thumb of Bevin[54] & Co., the T.U. Bosses, Morrison,[55] the "Conshie"[56] of last war, now a little despot. A.V.A. [Alexander], who deprived us of a Navy and the means to rebuild it rapidly when we shook off the blasted London Naval Treaty, licks Winston's boots and is a great pal of *"Dudley's"* and so we drift on.

I heard from Algy [Boyle] today, he had written to ask for Roger's address and I forgot to answer – "incidentally R. had sent him a ship card for Christmas." He says he suppose[d] I was "too busy with your *politics!*" I have no politics – but a burning desire to speed up the war and serve my country. I love Algy but find him rather trying nowadays – he is typical of the arm chair blokes in the U.S. [United Service] Club who thought Geoffrey's gallant effort "not quite cricket", who think because I try to stir up the Admiralty to action I am serving my own ends. They (D.P. & Co.) and they only are responsible for our failure to make use of amphibious power in the Libyan Campaign. Auchinleck – too late – would have given anything for 5000 Geoffreys – with all the means to land them in fast ships of no military value. Only Wavell's C. of S. had disbanded the 1500 I sent out. Geoffrey had only 1 officer and 17 men with him and he trekked 2 days up 1600 ft. 250′ behind the battle front – having almost swum on shore. ⅔ of his force could not land owing to rubber boats capsizing, etc. Lyttleton[57] admitted to me that the force D.P. broke up against my advice – and hot protests – would have put Rommel[58] in the bag.

Algy and his friends – what the hell did they do for their country while I have been striving for *ten* years to wake the country up. 7 years ago W.C. told me "Why [do] you have a 2 power standard". The Air is the only thing we want. That was when Italy was still a friend and Germany had no Navy. I said yes but what about Japan – he replied with a shrug you have lost the Far East – we can't build up for that or words to that effect. It explains so much now.

Would we have stopped the S.M.'s going through the Straits in which Algy and you played so great [a] part? Or stirred up the hornet's nest on the Belgian coast if I had not fought Bacon & Co. and L-G [Lloyd-George] hadn't got rid of him – and Jellicoe – since he would not get rid of Bacon. I hate your being unemployed and displaced for that old dead head B. D.P. is a nasty brute. Willie [?] James says he has always been vindictive – but until we get rid of him and A.V.A. I don't see how we can get on. I hope you can read this. Love from us both to you both . . .

137. *Captain Augustus Agar*[59] *to Keyes*

[Holograph]

The Cottage,
Compton, Nr. Winchester.
6.6.42.

This is just a note to let you know that I am safely back in England once again, and after a short leave in my home hope to be given another ship or action job.

A letter of mine to you, when I heard Geoffrey was missing was on the way but I doubt if you received it. We had no details other than those published in the Press which were all unanimous of his courage and leadership.

You can well imagine how I feel over the loss of my ship – and also *Cornwall*[60] – but on the credit side we did manage to survive two thirds of the crew, entirely due to the fine discipline and unselfishness of the men themselves. We were in the water for 30 hours (two days and one night) with only two leaky whalers to support our community, a large number of whom were badly burned and wounded. The men were just magnificent, & those who could swim just set about collecting wreckage and helping the others, until we had enough to pack everybody into a compact party on improvised rafts with wounded in the two boats (altogether 500 men). This on the Equator with hot Tropical Sun overhead. I won't dwell on details. The whole thing was over so quickly. From start to finish not more than 10 minutes before the ship disappeared under the sea.

I can only say that the attack was well timed, well delivered, and most courageously executed by our enemies. That is all and we must do the same ourselves and learn our lessons.

I hope there will be a chance of seeing you in London in the course of the next week or two when I have to go to the Admiralty to square up things. One has been out of touch during the last six months but I heard young Roger was in *Arethusa*, where I hope he is happy, and am sure he is doing well. Had there been time before we left England last year, I would have taken him with me in *Dorsetshire* and am glad now for his sake that this was not to be. Please give my love to your wife and I hope your family are all very well . . .

138. *Richmond to Keyes*

Master's Lodge,
Downing College,
Cambridge.
June 29, 1942.

I don't suppose I can say anything that you don't know as well as I do. If time admits before you speak[61] you might have a look at the July *Fortnightly* in which I have tried to drive into the dull heads of the people that there is no difference between "sea power" and "air power" any more than there [is] between sea power and destroyer power, or submarine power, or torpedo boat power. The aircraft is simply one of the many types of flotilla craft, without which a modern navy is lacking in one of its constituent units. If you can rub that in – it simply can't be said too often – do. The other thing is the cry of that ass Trenchard that it is better to destroy the submarine in the place it is produced than to "hunt" it on the trade routes. Some of my correspondents say the same. They forget: (a) that the German Submarines are not the only enemy craft we have to tackle. There are the German aircraft, surface men of war from *Tirpitz* to E boat, raiders and mines; there are the Italian and Japanese navies with their aircraft. All the bombing in the world will not affect those other vessels and instruments, and it has not reduced the submarines sufficiently to justify a policy which has lost us the command of the Mediterranean, our possessions in the East, our naval base at Singapore, which has resulted in Australia being threatened with invasion, and in Suez, the Red Sea, and our East African colonies being now in imminent danger of being lost, and their recovery most difficult and costly. How any sane man can justify such an abuse of strategy passes my understanding. It is a strategy which ignores the vital, and as I had imagined the hitherto accepted principle of the "liaison of arms." It pretends that the principles of war, as we have always interpreted them, do not apply to air forces. As a matter of fact, Trenchard said so to me on one occasion at the C.O.S. Committee, when I said that those principles ought to be defined in identical terms in the text books of the three services.

I wish too you would find it possible to explain to these inconceivably stupid people what the meaning of the words "Sea Power" is. Most of them seem to suppose that it means strength in fighting ships and no more in spite of all that Mahan[62] (whom they now consider out of date) said about it sixty years ago. Ships are one of the elements of which sea power consists. Sea power is the power of using the sea for one's own purposes and depriving the enemy of its use – a totally different thing. Its elements are all those types of vessels and craft capable of taking an effective part in the direct operations at sea of which the aim is the control of the sea, the bases without which those craft cannot operate, and a merchant navy and shipbuilding industry sufficient to carry our trade and troops across all the seas and to repair and replace losses. The blindness and ignorance of our politicians, and the apathy or cowardice of the successive Boards of Admiralty, during the last 25 years have allowed all these three elements to be emasculated. Our cruiser and destroyer strength was reduced, in direct opposition to every principle (See my remarks on that damned fellow Alexander in the *National* which I sent you), the Irish bases were thrown away without a protest from Chatfield and his colleagues, the merchant navy was allowed to be driven out of business by the state aided merchant fleets of the foreigners, who (Japan in particular) subsidised speed and produced those fast transports which they now possess, while we were giving a miserable two millions to the tramp service and building 9 knot ships which make $6\frac{1}{2}$ in convoy, and at the same time shutting down our shipyards whose skilled men were emigrating to the United States. It is Parliament which bears the responsibility for these measures which have crippled our sea power, Parliament which should be the watch dog upon our ministers and Admiralty and see that they are not guilty of dereliction of their duty.

There may yet be time, if Auchinleck can hold Egypt, to recover. It can only be done if the strategy is altered and the old principles acted upon – singleness of object, concentration of effort of all the services upon that object. What that object should be is as plain as can be, namely the recovery of the command of the sea. Bombing German shipbuilding yards won't do it. It may – I daresay it does – reduce output; but it does not reduce German output enough to preserve our shipping – or stop the Japanese in the Pacific and restore us the 90 per cent of the rubber and 60 per cent of the tin we have lost, or open the road for supplying China, or enable us to revictual Malta and stop Rommel's supplies, or clear the way for the Murmansk convoys. It will not prevent the loss of Egypt if the present battle goes against us.

And it will not, as the advocates of it claim, depress the determination of the German people so long as Hitler can continue to show them victories.

So drive all this, or as much of it as you can, home. It is only ignorance that stands in the way. Bombing provides headlines and advertisement but it does not win wars. Good luck to your efforts, though I hope you will not drive Churchill out of office. There is a very short supply of talent in the country and who would replace him from the C3 ranks of our politicians.

One final word, and a personal one. I grieve for you in your loss that has been at last confirmed. I need not say more for you will well know how much my heart is with you and Lady Keyes in your deep sorrow...

139. *Richmond to Keyes*

Master's Lodge,
Downing College,
Cambridge.
July 4, 1942.

Many thanks for your letter. I confess I was very sorry to see you going into the lobby with some of that unsavoury mob. I thought Bevan's[63] speech a disgrace to Parliament and the innuendoes of others equally vile. But on the question of the conduct of the war, apart from that of production, I am heart and soul with those who say it has been misdirected, and in my belief that misdirection is due to Trenchard and the school of thought that he and his friends have created, not forgetting that most poisonous person Brigadier General Groves[64] who, in his *Behind the Smoke Screen* did all in his power to damage the relations between the Navy and Air force.

As I think I have said to you before, I found, when I was at the Imp. Def. College that the Airmen were fixed in the delusion that the Air should fight a war of its own independently and without the least connection with the other services. Unhappily, it seems, Winston has been got at by these people. Hence the starvation of the Navy and Army. The defence of the bombing policy *now* (it is a new defence) that it is the same as that of the attacks we used to make in our old combined operations against the naval bases of the enemy – Drake at Lagos, Nelson at Copenhagen, and dozens of others. Of course the circumstances are entirely different today. On those occasions what we attacked was the concentrated strength of the enemy in the shape of a large body of big fighting ships. The whole Danish Navy was taken at the second Copenhagen attack in 1807 by Gambier.⁶⁵ There is no comparison whatever between these raids on the shipyards and those expeditions. I don't deny that they injure his production though no figures have been given to show precisely what has been effected. But I see that the last – yesterdays – attack on Bremen was the 97*th*; and how many there have been on Hamburg I forget. Yet in spite of it all the German submarines have multiplied sufficiently to sink over 300 American ships and plenty of ours, and the bombing does nothing whatever to the Italians and the Japanese. The fact is that it is an attempt to close the stable door after the horse has been stolen, and it closes (if indeed it *does* close, which I doubt) one door only, the German. It is the enemy in the field that has to be destroyed, that mass of submarines, small craft, aircraft and other surface ships which have succeeded in driving us into the narrow corner of the Levant and enabled Rommel to be reinforced, prevented us from reinforcing Auchinleck, and thereby, if we have to leave Alexandria, leaving the command of the Medn. in the enemy's hands. The aircraft that might have stemmed this advance by action in the Med. against the naval and air forces in the Italian harbours have been bombing Cologne and so forth and earning great headlines for the R.A.F. while we lose our possessions, our trade and our troops.

The *Times* cut down both my letters and has not inserted a reply I sent to that extremely stupid and misrepresenting letter of Longmore's.⁶⁶ I think it is somewhat improper that he should be allowed to accuse me of opposing the sending of reinforcements to Egypt or troops to other points when if anything *was* clear it was that I had said the army and air force should be employed to assist the navy to obtain command of the sea; and how in the world could they do that without crossing the sea? Of course the man is a fool, and unless I am greatly mistaken it is he who is primarily responsible for the loss of Crete, where the navy was as badly let down as it has ever been in the whole of history.

The bother is what can we do against this conspiracy of the Press, and the whips who shut you out of the debates?

The *Times* will print Trenchard at length and also the fool cries of the Wedgwoods, Browns and Longmores, the *D.T.* is in Trenchard's pocket. The *Manchester Guardian* is free and I shall see whether I can get a word in in that quarter. There's a debate at Chatham House on July 7. Colvin⁶⁷ is reading a paper. If I can I shall go. I believe Colvin is sound. Drax⁶⁸ tells me he means to speak. Could you be there?

The sooner they shed that mountebank Alexander and the ineffable Pound the better. I don't know Horton but he has a fine record. How right to refuse the command of the Grand Fleet unless he was properly supplied. I wish a few more admirals had courage in this matter and would make their opinions known.

My Hansard has not yet come. When I shall have read it I think I shall make the debate the subject of my next *Fortnightly* article. I hope you, and others in the House, saw and digested my "Sea Power and Air Power" in the July number.

To think of those utterly contemptible Italians being on top in the Med!!!! Who can't fight either on land, at sea, or in the air, though they could sneak into Alex and sink the *Q.E.* and *Valiant*.[69] That is about the measure of their powers...

140. Keyes to Tomkinson

[Holograph]   Tingewick House,
Buckingham.
12.7.42.

Thank you very much for your letter about Geoffrey's V.C. which touched Eva and me very much. You had known him as a little boy and I know recognised his qualities. We have had such wonderful letters from his school masters and a tutor we did not know at Eton. He always stood up for the under dog, and two told us that little boys in trouble always turned to him. It has been wonderful too to hear from his Regiment and two old Colonels of another age who commanded the Scots Greys, their pride in him, their first V.C. I will send you a copy of Laycock's report on which Sir Alan Cunningham[70] recommended him for the V.C.

I can't bear your being relieved like that. I know how it was done – and how some like that fat ass Maxwell[71] at Newcastle stay on – why Davies, V.C.[72] was moved – and Maund was given the *Ark Royal* and Portal[73] an old "R" battleship.

I would like to have a yarn with you. Alexander and D.P. [Pound] *must* be got rid of. I have said all I said in the debate on 1st in secret session without avail and much more. I had of course to leave much out but W.C. and his War Cabinet could read between the lines. It was D.P. and no other who prevented any use being made of about 4000 Commandos in the M.E. in Nov. '40 – Feb. '41 – when Wavell with 30,000 rounded up 250,000 Italians. In Sept. '41 we had a tremendous amphibious force which would have turned the scale in that Libyan battle: 4 Brigades, a large tank force, Field Guns, AA guns, etc. – in fast vessels of no military value – D.P. alone stopped it being made use of – divorced its ships from the men by 3000 miles. It is an awful tale. I wrote 4 stinkers to the War Cabinet, and it was because they would not listen to me I refused to accept the new appt. offered me – "Adviser on C.O." and Chairman of a Committee on Combined Training.

The appt. given to M.batten but since then they have given him all they took from me and much more. They could not have found a more able organiser and staff officer – but what is wanted is someone with the guts to make big decisions – and W.C. won't do that unless his C. of S. Committee will take *all* the responsibility. He is not the W.C. of 1914. He has never forgotten how Jackie F. [Fisher] broke him.

The original motion saying that we were not satisfied with the Central Direction of the war was backed by a number of Conservatives but they all ratted nearly. Having said I would support Wardlaw-Milne[74] on the understanding he was not making a personal attack on W.C., I could not run out. It was awful going into the same lobby as A. Bevan, Silverman,[75] etc., etc. I just looked through them as if they did not exist when they welcomed me – and walked by them.

The Govt. were really – at least W.C.'s party – very grateful to me for almost sinking the censure with a heavy near miss if not a torpedo direct hit. Who can honestly say that they are satisfied with the central direction of the war with Bevin and Morrison afraid to rule – unable to deal with strikes except by bribery – and W.C. going from one naval misfortune to the next guided by D.P.

Willie James told me D.P. sent for all the C.'s -in-C. and told them there was much too much talk going on criticising the Admiralty, particularly on the loss of the *Prince of Wales* and *Repulse* – and he proceeded to try to justify sending them out. He said he hoped they would put a stop to this kind of talk – 2 of them said, "but you have not told us anything that justifies our contradicting what the whole Service is feeling," or words to that effect. Nevertheless D.P. goes on. The squadron despatched under James Somerville to the Far E. of which I cannot speak – and what it was expected to do simply amazes me.[76]

Let me know if you come to London – I do hope you have good news of your Peter. Young Roger is in the Mediterranean in the saucy A—— [*Arethusa*]. Very much involved in the convoy battle when [?] a [illegible] ship was sunk.

With love to you all from [words missing] Thank[s] for your letter which we do value . . .

P.S. Katherine's Peter was last heard of in Java.

141. *Keyes to Field Marshal Smuts*[77]

[Copy]

Tingewick House,
Buckingham.
24/10/42.

I can't tell you what a pleasure it was to meet you again and hear your vigorous confident words – both in the Royal Gallery and more so even in the privacy of the Other Club.

As you know I am devoted to Winston and we were warm friends and allies, when we were both fighting to try and make the country realise that we must re-arm or perish.

As you saw, he has no 'arrière pensée' over the fact that I seconded the motion on the Central Direction of the War.

Personally I feel that in doing so I rendered him a great service, by calling attention to the real culprits responsible for our failure to make use in the Mediterranean of Britain's time honoured and most valuable weapon – amphibious power – in the critical days when its bold and proper use would have turned the scale to complete victory.

I send you a copy of my speech, because it happens to mention you – and you probably have only seen extracts, if you have seen it at all. It indicates what Winston and I wanted to do, and I out of my experience knew could be done, and which would have been done, if Winston had felt free to follow his instincts & my advice.

It is all so reminiscent of those black days in 1917, when Jellicoe could only see salvation through the Army battering its way over the Passchendaele Ridge to capture the Belgian Naval Bases, and could not be induced to order Admiral Bacon to act offensively with the Dover Patrol.

Then your War Cabinet took a hand and acted ruthlessly, without any consideration for the personal feelings of Jellicoe and his friends – and a new atmosphere was created and the tide turned. I had all this in mind when I spoke on 1st July and hoped Winston would do the same and shake himself free of those who have impeded his offensive war efforts.

I tried to call and say goodbye before I left London – as I am unemployed now except when Parliament is sitting – but they told me you were away for the day – I learnt afterwards – inspecting my old hunting ground – Dover – where your War Cabinet gave me a free hand to hunt and harry the enemy across the Narrow Seas in 1918.

In case you leave before I return, goodbye and good luck; it was like a breath of fresh air to see and hear you again, as for me, this war has been one of complete and tormenting frustration of all my efforts to carry out worth while Combined Operations; coupled with a deep personal sorrow for a sacrifice, which I feel might have been spared, had we struck amphibiously on a grand scale, as I tried so hard to do in both 1940 and 1941 . . .

142. *Keyes to Churchill*

[Carbon]
Tingewick House,
Buckingham.
26th Oct. 1942.

I was much moved by your saying the other night that you "would much rather have Geoffrey alive than Rommel dead," as I had been missing a word of sympathy from you about it, although amongst the many hundreds of letters we received, there was none that touched us more than Clemmy's – while you were in America.[78]

In Geoffrey's last letter – only to be posted if he did not return – he told us he had "a wonderful opportunity of serving the cause" and he was evidently prepared to sacrifice his life for it, as he told us not to worry if he did not get back.

Thank you very much for your offer of promotion to the peerage. Of course I should be proud to accept a peerage as a reward for good service, but I would like to talk to you about it before you take action.

I know you had every intention of doing me well and making use of my services, and a year ago (17th Oct.) you said you would be very glad to have a talk with me, when the matter you had in mind was settled; it fell through, but we have not had our talk yet! and I vowed I would not write to you again, until you sent for me.

However, you broke the ice at the Other Club last Thursday, and somehow I always feel that we are destined to work together for the country and that you will need my luck in war, for which I know I have a flair.

You, who were left in the wilderness so long, when your great gifts would have been of such value to the country, must surely realise what I have been through during the last year – completely out of the war, my only value, apparently, being to induce people to invest in War Savings!

It was kind of you to arrange for me to sit next to Smuts the other night, it was a memorably bright spot in a very black year for me . . .

143. Keyes to Richmond

[Holograph] 1.1.43.

Many thanks for your letter. My lectures are on 17th–24th Feb. and 3rd March.[79] It is very good of you and Lady Richmond to offer to have me to stay. The Master of Trinity had invited me to stay and I had a letter (when the dates were fixed) from him about it at the same time as yours. I said we were old friends and had a lot to talk about, but I never saw you nowadays. So would go to you one night. I hope that is all right? Would you say which night would suit you best? Perhaps you would mention it to Trevelyan.[80]

The Admiralty are always afraid to say anything which might annoy the Air Ministry and I expect that they would get out of answering a question in the House of Commons by saying it was not in the public interest – and a question to the S.S. for Air would certainly be evaded. I very much doubt aircraft getting many SM's. Tho' I believe they do get them occasionally now they have been induced to use depth charges. I really don't think Trenchard has done himself or his cause any good by his foolish article and absurd letter "summing up" the controversy.

Private. I hope you weren't very shocked at my New Year Honour! When Pound & Pownall – Gort's C. of S., who I fell foul of over the Belgian Campaign – succeeded in getting all my executive authority taken away from me – and I declined to accept the new appt. of adviser and Chairman of an Inter Service Committee, Winston was very anxious to make it up to me and without any reference to me arranged for me to be a Governor General and a peer – the former fell through and I declined the latter. But when Smuts was over here – we had made friends when he was in the Cabinet which gave me such a free hand in the last war – he and Winston and I had a great entente one night and Winston renewed the offer.[81] I did not accept it then – but later it was conveyed to me that he would find it easier to employ me if I went to the "Other Place". As I went into the House of Commons to fight for the restoration of our sea power and freedom for the Navy to develop its own vitally important air service – and the chief enemy[82] and obstacle has a seat in the House of Lords, I hope to be able to take him on there. I have cut out the article and all the letters and I think they will be of great help in clarifying the question. I think Cork, Sempill[83] and I could stage a debate in which his fallacies could be well exposed. Winston is a clever politician and might be useful. I look forward very much to coming to Cambridge as I told Trevelyan, but with some trepidation mainly at the thought of lecturing to you!! Tho' I did not add this! All good wishes for 1943 and many thanks to you and Lady Richmond for saying you will put me up...

144. Keyes to Richmond

[Holograph]
Tingewick,
5.1.43.

Thank you very much for your kind letter and for all you say which I value and appreciate.

I refused a peerage 15 months ago and the alternative appointment of "Adviser" without any executive authority which was offered to me, and said I would go on ½ pay and fight for all I considered for the prosecution of the war. I was promptly sent a copy of the Official Secrets Act![84] I know W.C. has felt very badly about the way he let me down and he has avoided seeing me alone since Sept. 1941. When Smuts was here we had a great entente at W.C.'s "Other Club" and we 3 had a great "buck". Smuts has been a friend since the last war when he was in the Cabinet which gave me such a free hand in 1918. At the end of the evening W.C. renewed his offer of a peerage.

I thought it well over and eventually accepted about a month ago. If I had taken it in 1941 I would not have felt free to attack the direction of the war and the gutless failure of the Admiralty to undertake amphibious operations. They don't mind risking losing aircraft, submarines and soldiers but to risk a surface ship is something they won't face – even if they are of "no military value" as my landing craft carriers were. Heaven knows we lose enough in the daily task, as in the Dardanelles – but for an offensive hazard they will risk nothing. Why didn't we launch 5000 to 6000, as we could have, in fast "carriers" to short circuit the Axis in Tunisia and Bizerta. My General[85] who was with Eisenhower[86] and planned all the *night* landings in N. Africa, with as much darkness in hand as possible, my way, told me it was purely a naval consideration. The risk of a few thousand highly trained night fighters might well have spared the 1st Army many more thousands and weeks of time.[87] Well I have said it all in Secret and to a great extent in Public Session. I have told Bevin, Morrison and Alexander exactly what I think of them. I have got the whole House of Commons practically on our side about Navy's right to develop its own aviation in order to exercise sea power unfettered by the A.M. Now the principal enemy of the Navy is in the House of Lords and I intend to lay myself alongside him. It is a bore that he is connected by marriage and has just written me a nice letter welcoming me into the House of Lords! But one can't let private considerations interfere with one's duty in a vital matter!!! I wish I could speak like Chatfield and Cork but at any rate Bill Boyle and I will work together in absolute accord.

I won't say it was the decisive factor but Trenchard's article and letter helped me to make up my mind! Neither my wife nor I were very keen – in fact it left us cold – but a wonderful lot of telegrams and letters warmed us up immensely – and none I appreciated more than yours my dear Richmond . . .

[P.S.] I have such a lot to tell you (particularly Dieppe)[88] and talk about and look forward to seeing you at Cambridge. I have unburdened myself in a quite illegible letter which I hope you will manage to decypher.
I keep my name of course.

145. *A. Ramsay to Keyes*

[Holograph]

Brechin Castle,
Brechin, Scotland.
n.d. [February, 1943].

Many thanks for your kind letter, I thought your extempore speech quite excellent and not too bitter.[89]

After watching the passive decay of the F.A.A. for 3 years, I almost came round to the Trenchard point of view that the Navy didn't want it at heart & never understood it.

I think that both you & Lord Cork have stirred it up sufficiently to make them buy the best Yank aircraft, which is really the best we can do now for this war, as it takes such a hell of a time to develop a good machine, and anyhow the aircraft nowadays is built round the engine. You will never get the Air Min^{ty} to allocate the best or even best but one.

A great fault was made when Beaverbrook got the Admiralty to put back their priority for 3 months, the latter now know that this virtually meant 16 months.

I am afraid you will never get Pound to wage war on the behalf of the F.A.A. as it is an unpopular war and Air Min^{ty} has such immense political prestige.

You will see 9 years ago a plea was put in for dive bombers to do away with the beautiful accurate? high pattern-precision bombing, this was refused, you will also note that all ships sunk by Yanks have been with dive bombers, also Japanese successes.

Trenchard states that it is no use without air superiority, well it is no use to the Germans according to him (viz Tunis) but as we are to have air superiority surely this mobile artillery will be invaluable to our army especially in a landing when accuracy is required to silence batteries, Trenchard will tell you that with determined gunners, the latter will always get them [?], maybe, but if you have a lot of them they will silence the gunners & I don't believe the old Germans or fortifications would stand it. Also you can afford to lose them, they should be cheap to build in man hours & the pilot need only be trained for the one thing. All you lose is one rapidly trained pilot per[?] machine. When I think of the number of times we could have used them it makes my heart sick.

The Italian Fleet was out five hours, bombed by Yanks & our machines[?] with high precision, result one hit & one ship sunk by our submarines.

I agree with you it is no good trying to convert Trenchard. He has a one track brain & has had it since 1916, "to have one Air Force", even to the point of prolonging the war 2 years, thank God he can't lose it.

I am afraid I am of little use as I can not enter the political arena placed as I am.

But I honestly think that with this last debate you will have stirred up enough & to go too far will only injure the F.A.A.

However, I think a whack at the treatment of the personnel in promotions might do good. Portal[90] ought to have been made an R.A. last Xmas.

Air Min[ty] will make it I fear as difficult as possible, as regards myself they actually carried out sabotage, removing[?] workmen from F.A.A. factory.

Every Naval Officer should have to go to a carrier or air base some time in his career.

Sorry, but I do feel useless. I also feel P.M. is not a believer in F.A.A. really, but thinks along the lines of Seversky.[91]

Best of luck to you & hope to see you when I come south.

Should love a copy of Chatfield's attack in Hansard...

[P.S.] I hope you will excuse my inadequate address but I have not found out what your proper title is.

146. *Captain Reginald H. Portal to Keyes*

(a) *Letter.*
Personal

A.C.N.S.(A.)'s Office,
ADMIRALTY, S.W.1.
2nd February, 1943.

Thank you very much indeed for your kind letter of congratulations – I am indeed proud to be in my present position and if I can do any good for the Fleet Air Arm – that is all I want.

2. I think our noble friend's outburst in the House of Lords,[92] and his previous recent letters in the newspapers, are lamentable. When the Heads of the Services are trying to kill controversy and bury the hatchet for the duration, in order that we may win the war, why should he come forward with all this vitriolic and antiquated stuff to disturb a show which is really running very well considering the conditions under which we are working.

3. May I suggest that when you reply to him you trounce him first for his most unsporting attack on your "pigeon" at the time you were due for your maiden speech, secondly for his most unpatriotic attempts to disturb the present harmonious working between the services under the existing charter (which cannot in any case be changed fundamentally for the duration) and thirdly for the gross inaccuracies of his statements in your House on 27th January.

4. I think the line to take is that he is an arrant mischief maker and that the stuff he is trying to put across now is really nothing but Fifth Column work as far as the war effort is concerned; and I believe that the better side of the Air Ministry would agree. Boyd[93] and I have pledged ourselves to try our damnedest to get on with the other side to win the war – that is the only object and I believe they are ready to help.

5. Really the only major bone of contention between us now (apart from the principles of control of shore based aircraft – a decision on which cannot be forced at the present juncture) is over the question of priorities for material, in a very limited field, and that is a question on which only the War Cabinet can decide – their decisions ought to be clear cut and definite and then there would be no more trouble.

6. I feel that with the prejudice that he must have raised against himself on Wednesday you would score heavily by denouncing his doings as subversive to the War Effort and that the Navy's shares would rise by such a broad-minded representation of the case (as you could give). At the same time you could re-affirm your views on the broader questions of principle and say that it is obvious that in the most critical phase of a major war they must remain for consideration as principles only.

7. I attach some remarks on some of the major untruths in Wednesday's diatribe which you may find useful.

8. Good luck in your attack. Please give my kind regards to Lady Keyes...

P.S. The M.A.P. is definitely doing his best for us and I feel it is vitally important to say nothing that might make trouble between him and A.V.A. [Alexander]. Once the Government have given priorities I am sure Stafford Cripps[94] and his people will do their level best to give us all they can – but I expect you know this as well as I do.

(b) *Annexe – Remarks on Statements by Lord Trenchard*

A. *"Failure to provide the right type of aircraft is the direct responsibility of the Admiralty."*
This is not so. The *designs* of the new types are good enough; the failure to get them is due to past Ministers of Aircraft production (and the bad management of certain firms).

B. *"Aircraft produced to Admiralty requirements have failed to stand the test of war."*
Considering the devastating work that has been done by naval aircraft (Taranto, *Bismarck*, Rommel's supply lines, etc.) this is a far fetched statement – The Swordfish[95] is still the best of its class for certain naval requirements and I believe that something with the same characteristics will always be a requirement.

Also our fighters dominated the Mediterranean air against shore based aircraft in the early days of the war.

The reason we have not up-to-date Fleet Air Arm types now is given at A above.

C. (i) *"The Admiralty selected their own manufacturers"*
   (ii) *"The designing of F.A.A. aircraft became entirely an Admiralty affair"*
   (i) Is totally untrue – we have always had to take the factories we were given, (in the early days by the Air Ministry, and later by the M.A.P.).
   (ii) The Admiralty have no charter to design aircraft. They only state requirements and the firms design, under the Air Ministry (in the old days) and now under the Ministry of Aircraft Production.

Our basic trouble in the past has always been the small number of firms allotted to us and their limited capacity. If you want a new type of aircraft you ought to build to *at least 3 designs* and then one will probably come out right. If you have to bank on *one*, as we have had to in the past, (and there is no second or third string to your bow) then if anything goes wrong you get just the delays from which we have been suffering.

D. *"The Admiralty scoffed at the Torpedo machines but the R.A.F. realized their value and kept them going . . . down to 1937 . . ."*
(The reference to the Swordfish in this connection – Col. 815 of Hansard – is obscure and ludicrous! It was designed by Fairey's for

the *Admiralty* as a private venture at the instigation of the then D.N.A.D.!).

The Admiralty has always tried to develop offence and defence together. Actually the results obtained by Torpedo aircraft and bombers of all kinds against properly equipped ships approximate very closely to Admiralty estimates made before the war.

The aircraft torpedo was developed by Naval Officers seconded to the R.A.F. (because we had no flying experimental establishment of our own) – from 1921–1929 (I was one of them) and the principles of attack were developed in the *F.A.A.*, including the first real massed attacks under the first R.A.A. (Sir R. Henderson,[96] whose Staff Officer I was at the time).

The Admiralty never under-rated the potency of the weapon but they were quite right in their later view that its proper use demanded cover in some form (either from the elements or from a simultaneous attack with other weapons). Plain straightforward attack in broad daylight against a properly equipped enemy is sheer murder.

E. *The Admiralty say "How shall we restore the Capital ship to its supremacy by the use of the Air?".*

What a fantastic statement – The whole trend of modern practice is to regard the Capital ship as the heavy support for the Aircraft Carrier, (which is rapidly coming to be regarded as the core of the Fleet as is witnessed by our large Naval Air Expansion programme) and as the means for delivering the coup de grace to a crippled enemy.

147. *Keyes to Admiral Sir Dudley North*

[Holograph]

Tingewick House,
Buckingham.
17. 5. 43.

Thank you very much for your letter. I feel much honoured by the action of the Committee of the Naval in making me an Honorary Member of the Royal Naval Club for life.

It does not seem 50 years since I joined it!

I have often wanted to tell you what a damned outrage I thought it your being made a scapegoat for the "War Machine's" irresolution and inaction when the French went through the Straits before the attack on Dakar.[97]

With many thanks to you and the Committee . . .

148. *Keyes to North*

[Holograph]

Tingewick House,
Buckingham.
27. 5. 43.

I am delighted to hear that you have an appointment and an interesting one near the battle front.⁹⁸ But I do hope it is not going to incline you to pull your punches when you – as surely[?] you are going to – tell the truth about that dreadful administration which was responsible for *Courageous, Royal Oak*, Norway miscarriages – *Glorious* and a determination not to allow any amphibious operations to be launched – concluding with our failure to land near Tunis and Bizerta.

If I live I am going to tell the tale and anyhow it is all in minutes and letters from me to the P.M., the War Cabinet, the Admiralty, etc., including some mention of their *"head hunting"* to find scapegoats for their pusillanimous ineptitude including your supersession – which I will add to if you will give me the details.

All good wishes. I expect they were trying to mollify you – or put you in the fore front of the battle like Uriah...

149. *Keyes to North*

[Holograph]

10. 7. 43.

I am returning your papers. It really is difficult to write temperately about the matter. It is a shocking story – much worse than I thought, and I knew it was pretty bad. I would much like to help you to vindicate your professional reputation when you decide to act.

It is thoroughly in keeping with the treatment accorded to other flag officers in the past in the Western Mediterranean by Govts. to cover their own discreditable shortcomings. In keeping too with the Admiralty's conduct throughout the war. They have never had a court martial or enquiry about any miscarriage of the many for which they were entirely responsible – *Courageous, Royal Oak, Glorious* – there they tried to put the blame on to D'Oyly Hughes. I always think one of the worst was their refusal to allow the *Renown* and a strong force of destroyers to go into Narvik⁹⁹ and then put the responsibility on to Warburton Lee¹⁰⁰ for going in with a small one to attack a greatly superior one – to say nothing of Trondjhem – Bergen[?] – the escape from Brest of *Scharnhorst* and *Gneisenau* – and our failure to carry out an amphibious operation in the Mediterranean-M.E. campaign while we had command of the sea and air.

I never knew that you had been sent to Oran and had given such wise advice.[101] I expect your outspoken telegram irked them[102] and Pound was anxious to have that poor creature, his friend C., who would be docile he knew.

You must let me have a copy of your papers when you want to act. I expect your present appointment was to keep you quiet! But you must not let anything stop you clearing the matter up after the war.

I will get you a copy of Hansard with the P.M.'s speech. I must confess he has been a great disappointment to me. He does not mean to risk anything on his own. Even the ringing of the church bells had to have the approval of those 3 Chiefs of Staff!!! And if anything goes wrong in the Mediterranean campaign it will be Eisenhower's fault!

That was a good letter of Somerville's. Many thanks for letting me see these papers. I think D.P. and A.V.A. will have a very unenviable place in history and the P.M.'s actions then and his denunciation of King Leopold will not be to his credit in history...

150. *Keyes to North*

[Holograph]

Tingewick House,
Buckingham.
29. 7. 43.

Here is Hansard of 8th Oct. 1940 with the P.M.'s dreadful speech.[103] It is as outrageous as that one he made on 4th June 1940 trying to put all the blame for the British Army's flight to the sea onto King Leopold *as Gort did*. Of course Reynaud[104] told him they had proof of his treachery, and I suppose A.D.P. and A.V.A. did not tell the War Cabinet that they had all the evidence in your possession as soon as you? Perhaps – but he is a politician and he was out to defend the Govt. which was badly shaken by the Dakar fiasco.

We know now that the Governor was packing up and that there would have been no opposition if Cunningham and de Gaulle had had the guts to see the matter through. So a French officer who was there and is now in London says[105] – you and Somerville knew nothing about Dakar?

When you have got all your papers in order do let me see them all again please.

Since I wrote to you Cork has told of his readiness to enquire into your conduct of the proceedings only the Admiralty would not allow it.

I asked Winster[106] who was A.V.A.'s Parliamentary Secretary at the time what he remembered of it. He said he has a note in his diary which he will look up – date, etc. and let me know – It was to the effect that A.D.P. sent a minute to A.V.A.: "This officer (you) should be ordered to haul down his flag forthwith."

He is very anxious to see your papers. It seems that he has a diary in which he noted everything! Incidentally he detests them both. I would not trust him *absolutely* but he is pretty clever and rather vindictive!

As you say you were more fortunate than Byng[107] but the Admiralty and War Cabinet were out for a scapegoat in your case as surely as they were in the days of Byng and Mathews.[108]

All good wishes...

151. *Churchill to Keyes*

Private.
10 Downing Street,
Whitehall.
August 14, 1943.

I am very sorry to receive your letter, and I certainly understand how you feel about not having an active part to play.[109] I can only say that I acted in what I conceived was the public interest and that I do not think it likely that any fighting post will be open to an officer now over seventy. The position of a Prime Minister, which you cite, like that of a Pope or a Judge is quite different.[110]

I cannot feel that you are right in thinking that your services have not been recognized and marked. In a particularly dark hour you seconded a vote of censure on the Government which had it been successful would have relieved me once and for all from my many cares. Most people I think would have considered such an act as a final severance of all public relations. On the contrary, although I knew I should incur criticism both in naval and political circles, I submitted your name to the King for the very high honour of a Peerage because I thought your services to the State made such an award appropriate, and I would not allow any opposition which you had shown to me personally to affect my judgment in this matter...

152. Keyes to Churchill

[Carbon]

Tingewick House,
Buckingham.
22/8/43.

First I want to send you my warm congratulations on the capture of Sicily and my sincere hope that it may only be the prelude to a great and speedy victory. I know how much we owe it to you personally.

I am sorry my letter displeased you, I don't like your reply[111] and cannot allow some of the statements in it to go unchallenged. Letters certainly are a very unsatisfactory means of communication but you have left me no other way, as you have persistently refused to give me an interview since the 5th Sept. 1941, in spite of your promise and many requests – in fact you still seem not to realise how abominably you treated me then, although I have never failed you in any way.

You always harp on my age. St Vincent was urgently recalled at the age of 71 to take command of the Channel Fleet and was engaged in a rigid blockade of the French Fleet for many months. Howe was 63 when he fought his battle on the "glorious 1st June" and he too did not haul his flag down until he was 73. It is recognised that men are far younger physically in our generation than they were in those days. $2\frac{1}{2}$ years ago you evidently did not consider me too old for "a fighting post". Have you forgotten that you said you would not look at the project to capture Pantelleria, unless I was ready to take command of it – it was not my fault that we were stopped on the eve of sailing. You also wanted to send me to Dakar. Don't you now think that it was a misfortune that you were not allowed to do either? I have not deteriorated or lost any of the vigour I had then, but I appreciate that the opportunity of proving that you were right when you gave me command of a "fighting force" has passed, but I don't agree for a moment that age alone should be a handicap, at any rate in the Council chamber, or should only be tolerated in a Prime Minister, a Pope or a Judge; particularly if a soldier or sailor has given proof of good judgment and readiness to accept responsibility and has shown his quality as a leader in war; all the more so if he has great practical experience and achievement to back his advice, on a form of warfare in which responsibilities are great and real practical experience very limited. Many wonderful opportunities have been neglected or missed in this war.

I don't suppose you ever read letters I wrote to the First Lord and Attlee – while you were in America in the winter of 1941–42 and which Attlee said he would pass on to you. You have published so many minutes and speeches to show how right you have always been, so I hope you will find time to look at the enclosed copies of the letters, now, which I think will also find a place in history, and recognition that if my advice had been followed the Country might have been spared much loss and tribulation.

The three American "Commando" landings behind the enemy's lines in Sicily were brilliantly successful and achieved decisive results, while our belated effort with the very small Commando force made available to Montgomery, at least just prevented the Americans having a complete run away race to Messina.[112]

All this provides additional evidence of what could have been done by amphibious strokes earlier in the Sicilian Campaign, when our troops were held up at Catania – and also in the Mediterranean since Dec. 1940, if you had continued to trust your own good judgement, accepted full responsibility and not withdrawn your support from me at the critical moment – for no military reason or failure on my part.

I have just had a letter from a former teacher in the Senior Officers War College in America, telling me that General Patton[113] was one of a much interested audience who listened to a lecture – on Gallipoli and the immense possibilities of Combined Operations generally – which I gave them at their invitation in 1934. American soldiers seem much more amphibious minded and willing to learn than ours.

The original landings in N. Africa and Sicily were masterpieces of skilful organisation, and great credit is due to the Combined Operations organisation, but your "Advisers" missed opportunities in both campaigns of making the best use of our amphibious forces to exploit them and speed up the march to final victory. They still apparently do not understand the vital maxim that in war TIME is everything, and they left most of our specially trained amphibious troops idle at home, during "the greatest amphibious operations in the history of war"!

I hate bothering you with letters, but I feel that I would be failing in my duty to my Country and our cause, if I refrained from continuing to press my views of what I *know ought* to be done, however unpopular it apparently makes me.

You tell me that my services in this war have been recognised and marked. Yes they have been. A peerage is a great honour when given for war services, but as you know I had no wish to be given one as a sop for my dismissal; however your remark about Geoffrey at the Other Club, the night Smuts dined,[114] and the renewal of your offer softened my resentment at the way you had treated me, and later Brendan – your emissary in the first instance – persuaded me to accept it, saying you wanted me to take it and it would make it easier to employ me. So I said that I would be proud to take it, if it was made clear that it was for my war services. My remark, that I had not been given credit or a word of appreciation for the part I played in Combined Operations, does not justify your suggestion that I am not sensible of the high honour the King has done me on your recommendation, or that I am ungrateful.

It is a fact, however, that it was only by accident that my connection with Combined Operations came to light at all – a month after I had left – you had an opportunity of saying a word of appreciation 6 months later, when you announced that Mountbatten had succeeded me and become Chief of Combined Operations, your refraining to do so left it to be inferred by the Press and House of Commons, that I had been superseded for incapacity through my advanced age and that now that they had a vigorous young Chief all would go ahead. Although it was not my fault that we had not gained much glory for the Country, and "altered the whole situation in the Mediterranean" and then neither "the dark hour" nor the vote of censure need ever have occurred.

When you asked for a vote of confidence in Jan. 1942, I particularly wanted to speak and was promised an opportunity by the Speaker, but no doubt at a hint from the Whips, he avoided calling me – as he did at the time of Munich – although I rose every time anyone sat down on both occasions. I thought it vitally important in the interests of the State, and in your interest – since in my opinion they are inseparable – that the blame for the misfortunes and miscarriages from which we had suffered, should go where it belonged, particularly as it was very generally believed and put about that they were due to your over-riding your professional advisers. Therefore when Wardlaw Milne asked me to second the Vote of Censure on the "Central Direction of the War", assuring me that he would make no attack on you personally, I agreed to do so – as it insured my being able to speak and say what I wanted to in your presence. I had nothing to do with any of the other supporters of the motion some of whom were very annoyed with me. You know perfectly well that I did *not* "show any opposition to you personally", in fact most people in the H. of C. including Government Whips and your P.P.S., thought that I had done you a great service by torpedoing the attack on you and making it quite clear where the real trouble lay. In doing so, I hoped to free you from the apron strings of the C.O.S. Committee, whose advice you seem always constitutionally bound to accept, however much it may conflict with what you know ought to be done.

The remarks in your letter about my connection with the vote of censure are as unfair and ungenerous, as those you made about me in the House of Commons on the 8th May 1940.

To refresh your memory, I enclose a copy of my speech in which

I repeated for the nth time my faith and devotion to you. You have certainly tried it very hard these last two years, Winston, and I don't think I deserve it at your hands...

153. *Mountbatten to Keyes*

Combined Operations Headquarters,
1A, Richmond Terrace,
Whitehall, S.W.1.
30th August, 1943.

Thank you very much for your letter of the 26th[115]

There is no one from whom I appreciate congratulations more than you.

Considering the invidious position in which I found myself on being given the great honour of relieving you, I should like to say how deeply I appreciate your kindness and all the support that you have given me.[116]

I am sure you will be pleased to know that I am arranging for Lovat[117] to take three Commandos out to South East Asia for a very special mission I have in mind and that the Royal Marines are starting to raise some more Commandos, so that the party will not only be kept up to strength, but will increase.

Please give my love to Lady Keyes...

154. *Cork and Orrery to Keyes*

[Holograph]

Old Quarry,
Seale,
Farnham, Surrey.
April 10th, '44.

I am so sorry to hear of this set back for you, and had been looking forward to seeing you again after the recess.[118] It must indeed be trying for you having to go through another period of forced inaction.

I should be very much interested to see the "Norseman" you speak of. Thank you for telling the Editor to send me a copy. I wish to God now I had not submitted my Narvik chapter to the Admy.[119] It was quite harmless and only slightly controversial. My original report was, I heard later, suppressed in the Admy & not circulated, presumably by Alexander – although he had no responsibility for any shortcomings.

If after the 24th you are laid up in London I shall hope to come & have a talk with you on these subjects. I hear nothing out of the Admiralty now but cannot say I think much of the propaganda. Too much fuss made about successes. Why should H.M. have been made to telegraph to the *Duke of York*: "I am proud of you." Whoever expected any other result if that battleship once got the battle cruiser *Scharnhorst* under her guns, helped as she was by cruisers & destroyers! [120]

I do not wish to belittle in anyway the dispositions that caught the *Scharnhorst* – but once in the net the rest might almost have been taken for granted? The Norwegian Destroyer was good! [121] The Midget S/M exploit really warmed one's heart,[122] & I am glad the F.A.A. got their chance.[123]

Anyday now I suppose we may hear great news – I wish it were a few years back so that you might have played the part all your career has marked you out for . . .

155. Cowan to Keyes

[Holograph]

H^{d}Q^{rt} 2nd S.S. B^{de}, C.M.F., 30-4-44.

I'm *so* sorry about you – it's such misery lying all these weeks in the dark with little but your thoughts and you'll have got so unfit and out of condition. It would have been so splendid if you could have come & toured all the Commando positions & H^d Q^{rs} & a great uplift for us all but perhaps yet you will. I got your letter on the 26th – 11 days only and the day following your 2nd operation & I'm so hoping that will have been completed successfully & all the trouble behind you. Both these Churchills[124] greatly concerned but v. pleased with your messages. We've given them in the last few days another resounding thump – all the honours with the Partisans who at the end staged a sort of Roman Triumph to show there was no deception – their morale & fighting fire up very high & they care nothing for losses, men or women & quite a few of them in the ranks and amongst the casualties.

May 1st. They've made a great day of it here being of course all Communists but you can't help loving them – a big review, every sort of makeshift uniform including much they took from the enemy in this last battle and more still of their arms & equipment & a complete 4 gun battery – mules loaded with every kind of machine gun & mortar ammunition in biscuit or bully beef boxes & decorated & camouflaged with wild flowers – red poppies in their rifle barrels. I c^d write pages. Whatever they were dressed in it didn't matter – a splendid soldier like lot, real warrior faces & the light of battle in every eye. I've never been so moved & near to crying by any other Soldier Pageant I've ever seen. The General in Command with 32 holes in him known to them all as the bravest living Yugoslav.

On the sea it's just as good, they bundle into any sort of primitive craft & just a few days ago in 2 row boats from another island went over & cut out a v. heavily armed schooner, killed & wounded more than half – the schooner a real good one & the remnants of the crew just fetched in here – about 3 times the number of their captors. Our own lot pulled off a fair good stroke last night & got somewhat "shot up" at about 50 yds range, *v.* few casualties & the enemy annihilated & sunk.

There's really something every day, so many different enterprises & targets to pick from & our Forces with these 2 Churchills just like a pack of the keenest of Foxhounds. In so many ways, land & sea, it's the warfare of 150 yrs back & individual manhood counting all the time & thank God no newspaper correspondents to rot them with indiscriminate and platitudinous vulgar praise. Such a good lot of Yanks too we've got.

It's the Dalmatian Islands we are thrashing about in – as announced by the Germans and our own wireless. Goodbye & affection to your E, & my thanks to her for writing the letter for you . . .

156. *Admiral Sir Andrew B. Cunningham to Keyes*

[Holograph]

Admiralty, S.W.1.
14th June [1944].

It was very good of you to write & congratulate us on the naval success in the invasion. We are all terribly pleased about it & the greatest credit is due to Ramsay[125] & his staff. Myself I feel that the performance of the little minesweepers is outstanding. They have swept up nearly 200 mines of all sorts & the sweeping across the Channel of the invasion forces in weather that must have been pretty nasty for them was a splendid job.

The bombarding forces have also done excellent work. I think the accuracy is still a bit overestimated but there is no doubt that 15" projectiles hurtling over the heads of the soldiers puts great heart into them, and a corresponding lowering of the enemy morale.

The spotting planes were naval Seafires & these young men have done excellently. Unfortunately they have had over 25% casualties. I am still a bit doubtful about accurate spotting by a single seater plane travelling at about 280 miles per hour.

I hope you are quite recovered from your operation & that it was successful. In any count I know you will see as much with one eye as most people do with two.

All best wishes to you & my kind regards to Lady Keyes...

157. Admiral Sir Bertram Ramsay to Keyes

[Holograph]   19. 6. 44.

I was so glad to get your kind letter which gave me great pleasure & satisfaction.

Everything went with a swing which I think surprised everybody, including the Germans, but knowing how well trained my forces were I was fully expecting that 95% of the troops would be brought to the beaches. What did surprise me was the manner in which the troops penetrated the beach defences and the weak opposition of the Coast Defence Batteries. Both of these had been well taken care of by air & sea bombardment but the surprise was the success of the bombing of the Batteries. Most of the guns were put out before the naval bombardment started and as far as I know only one ship was sunk by their gun fire. The beach defences were sighted to enfilade the beaches near H.W. so that as we landed about half tide most of the men were able to get out of the craft unfired at.

The beach obstacles were a nuisance afterwards when, the tide having risen, the craft fouled them and set off the Tellermines attached to them. It took longer than expected to clear them out of the way & our craft casualties, due to this, have been high. I am lost in admiration of the manner in which the navies have tackled this operation. Everyone has done splendidly & really I can think of no weak links.

Communications have exceeded my expectations & I've not heard of a single complaint.

The Americans were slower than the British in getting their beach & far shore organisations going but now, after 14 days, I'm of the opinion that the American organisations are the more advanced. The weather has been our most consistent opponent throughout & was responsible for a large number of craft casualties on D. Day & this in turn affected the immediate build up. We have hardly caught up yet, but still we are by now very firmly established & there is no fear of anything going wrong. I believe that we may witness very surprising results shortly! The troops have their tails right up whereas the Germans are not the formidable fighters that they formerly were. The prisoners are a very mixed lot & certainly disappointing to look at. Their morale has fallen considerably. I have a feeling that we are approaching a situation similar to that of August 1918. I hope that you are well and that the results of your operations are satisfactory. My best respects to Lady Keyes & as always to yourself...

158. *Cowan to Keyes*

[Holograph] At sea, 8-7-44.

Just to tell you I'm homeward bound. I saw young Roger twice for a very few days in that island of Viz in one of those fast small M.V.'s which he had had altered a bit to his own design – full of ideas & hope & enterprise & in process of growing another beard. Then when he came again (he'd been away on the mainland with engine trouble) I went down to have a look at him and found him in the middle of shaving it off again. Now he has gone off on another job in another set of boats & by what he said with rather a free hand to do things which he sh^d be the very man for. Amongst the rather piratical though *most* gallant lot over there for the short time he was – his ship was most noticeably a Man of War – men properly dressed & fallen in for coming into harbour, a very rare thing which both the Churchills commented on to me and I hastened to tell them that this was your son.

You'll have heard we lost Jack C. to my lasting and deep grief.[126] I'd been on every raid & enterprise with him in the 4 months I was there with the two of them, and as you know in any sort of a fight he was just a ball of fire and the soul of an instinctive fighting leader. We had – in order to take the pressure off Tito[127] – to undertake a raid in conjunction with the Partisans at very short notice and without that incomparable 2 Commando of his – had they been with us we'd never have lost him and, furthermore, would have dealt the Germans a far heavier punch than in fact we did, perhaps with fewer losses. We had fought them here & there & off & on for nearly 3 days & nights & he spent all the last day reconnoitering the 2 hills we wanted to knock them off – by himself – and came back more full of confidence than I've ever seen him. But just one unit failed to effectively cooperate. He, playing his bagpipes, and the other Colonel led the other lot up the hill in the dark and won the top and fired off the green lights to say so, but almost at once the Germans counter attacked with great vigour and regained it, both Jack and Manners,[128] the other Colonel, being knocked over & a good many others as well and the pipes stopped. The first time in these 6 months I've been with the 2 of them that I hadn't gone right up & on with Jack & his adjutant, but that night he meant being alone & hadn't even his batman with him – the B^{de} Major & I just had to sit back at the bottom listening & watching & hoping a few hundred yds away & by seeing the green lights go up thinking that all was well until they began to trickle back. His adjutant he left behind at Viz with 2 Commando as they'd hardly any officers left and that was the first time those two had been parted since the Sicily landing. Jack just said he was going to *watch* the fight but as that other lot went wrong I reckon he thought he *must* lead the rest and those bagpipes were his fighting soul. Someday there's a lot more to tell you about them. I'm rather proud to remember that I helped to pack him into them that night and to bang him on the back & God speed him when I'd done it [?].

Dear Roger I do *hope* they may by now have made a proper job of your eyes, those 2 brothers so often asked me for news of you. Sh^d say if I get home [illegible] they'll pitch me on shore round about 14 days from the date of this letter which I hope will start away by air from Gib. All my affection to your Eva...

159. *William L. Shirer to Keyes*

Columbia Broadcasting System, Inc.,
485 Madison Avenue, New York 22, N.Y.
August 25, 1944.

Thank you very much for your interesting letter from Port Washington.

I have always believed that if the Admiralty had allowed you to go into Trondjheim the whole campaign in Norway would have turned out differently. The German High Command was scared to death that the British would take Trondjheim, and they certainly breathed a sigh of relief when they saw that this was not to be done.

I was very sorry to have missed you when you were in New York, but I plan to be down in Washington on Friday, September 1st, and shall try to get in touch with you at the Shoreham...

160. *Royle to Keyes*

[Holograph]
Navy Office,
Melbourne.
3 Oct. [1944].

I had hoped very much to greet you & Lady Keyes at Canberra last Thursday when I was up there attending a War Council meeting.

It appeared, however, that you were lunching out so my endeavours to come to Govt. House were thwarted.

I am sending you a Flag Lieut.[129] whom you may find useful on your journey.

I hope & trust you are receiving all the facilities from the R.A.N. which you require & I hope very much that you may have an opportunity of visiting some of our ships in the operational area.

You will find Ad¹ Kinkaid[130] an exceptionally nice type of officer & one who has seen a lot of active service in this war, chiefly in carriers.

MacArthur[131] is a dual personality, theatrical & inclined to exaggerate in the presence of Aust[ralian] politicians! But full of sound ideas & charm when you get him in his natural state as I hope you will very soon. I thought your broadcast was most interesting & informative last Sunday. We shall look forward to seeing you & Lady Keyes in Melbourne towards the end of the month.

I know you will let me know if there is anything I can do to assist your visit but you appear to be very much in the hands of the High Commissioner at present who jealously guards your person from interlopers like myself! I fear this Govt. requires a lot of Naval Education. They are at present obsessed with air power to the almost complete exclusion of anything else.

We are busy preparing for the arrival of a large British Naval Force which Winston has wished on to Nimitz,[132] I am glad to say, rather against their will. It will be some months before anything really big can arrive but I shouldn't be surprised to see the *Howe* – a few cruisers & some of our best carriers & destroyers arrive fairly soon. They will require a fleet train with them for keeping them supplied in the forward areas.

The U.S. forces up to date have had no really opposed landings except Tarawa – Saipan & perhaps a very little opposition in Pelelieu (Palau).[133] MacArthur's party have had none. They certainly are great believers in using a sledge hammer to smash a nut & to reduce casualties to a minimum wh. is very sound. Philippines may be their toughest job so far. Good luck to you. I hope you have a very successful trip. Kindest remembrances to you & Lady Keyes from my wife & self...

161. *Keyes's Pacific Diary*[134] *4-28 October, 1944*

Oct. 4th. My birthday. Went to Sydney Air Station with Eva and Mr. Martin[135] and took off about 9 a.m. in a commercial Lockheed Lodestar for Brisbane, where we arrived about 12 o'clock – about 450

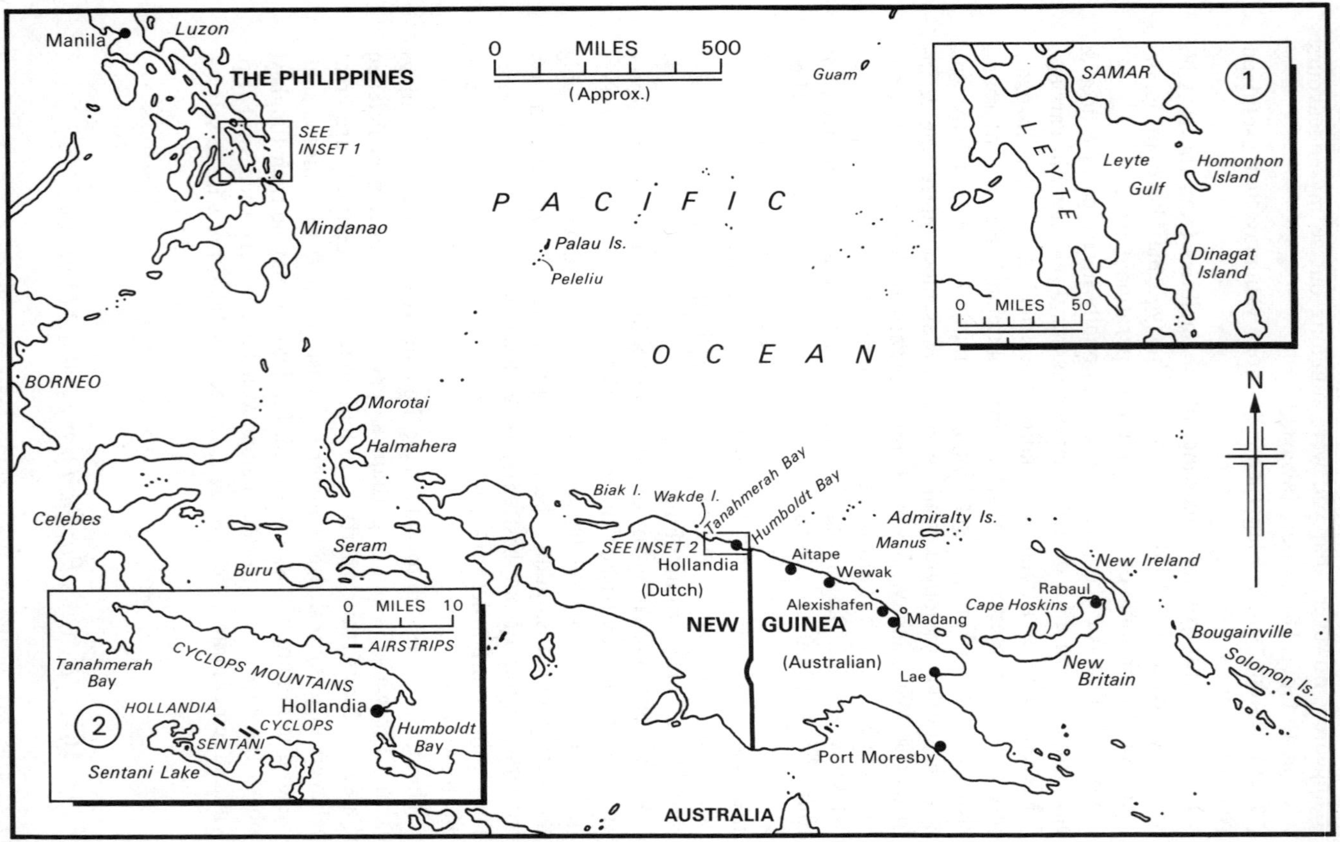

The South West Pacific

miles. Met by Capt. Thomas, R.N.,[136] and lunched at Queensland Club; went to Services Club about 5.30 and addressed about 100 officers – some serving – many Naval – several old ones, most of whom were in Gallipoli. Then to Govt. House to stay with the Leslie Wilson's.[137]

5th. Called at 4.15 a.m., breakfast and left for U.S.N. airfield at 5 a.m. with Lieutenant Tapp, R.A.N., attached to me as Flag Lieut. Took off at 6 a.m. in a "Liberator Express", flying across New Guinea at 15,000 ft. (with oxygen) and arrived at Manus airfield at 3 p.m. (2 p.m. local), a flight of 1690 nautical miles. Met by Commodore Boak,[138] U.S.N. who drove me along the beach captured on 15th March by U.S. troops, covered by U.S. and Australian ships and U.S.N. carrier-borne aircraft. There seems to have been practically no opposition. The Japs were taken completely by surprise and took to the hills, where they have been starved out and eliminated.

The U.S. had already gained an air strip, Momote Aerodrome in the Admiralties on 29th Feb. and Lorengau Aerodrome in [the] Admiralties on 16th March.

The harbour was full of ships, 300 odd, including Admirals Conolly[139] and Royal's[140] Task Forces.

We embarked in Admiral Kinkaid's barge at a quay about 4 miles from the Aerodrome and steamed across the Bay for an hour, passing the new floating dock (with the 35,000 ton battleship *Pennsylvania* in it).

The dock was towed out in ten sections, each a complete ship, they were placed alongside one another; the sides of the dock, folded down for the voyage, were jacked up and the whole bolted together; a wonderful improvement on the Singapore Floating Dock, which was towed out whole with much difficulty, through the Mediterranean and Suez Canal.

Commodore Boak told me it would take the biggest ship in the world, but as it is only 700 feet long, I think the *Queen Elizabeth* might overshoot it too much; however, as there is a staging at one end for longer ships, I daresay it could take her if necessary, anyhow it has the beam and the lifting power.[141]

We landed at his base and I stayed the night with him in a Quonset hut, very comfortable, excellent shower.

6th. We got up at 6 a.m., breakfast at 7 and then to the aerodrome by speedboat and jeep, took off at 9.5, and after flying over Humboldt Bay with about 350 vessels in it, arrived a few minutes later in Hollandia at the air strip 22 miles inland, after a flight of 430 nautical miles from Manus, in Admiral Kinkaid's own Douglas, which he sent over specially to fetch me so I felt much honoured. It is beautifully fitted out with very comfortable chairs, a dining table and a bunk. Admiral Kinkaid and General Sutherland[142] – General MacArthur's

Chief of Staff – met me, and I am to dine with the Admiral tonight, but am staying in the General's H.Q. He is away, so I am to sleep in his bed! His mess is run by a W.A.C. officer, Captain Clarke, whose husband is in the Grenadier Guards, and her father is Sir Norman Brooke[s][143] a late lawn tennis world champion – an Australian – and she was staying with him at Melbourne when she joined up in the W.A.C.'s.

The U.S.A. captured Hollandia Harbour and Airfield between April 22nd and 24th 1944, when Allied troops entered Madang, on 25th they captured Aitape village and on 26th April they entered Alexishafen, Hollandia, and captured Cyclops and Sentani airdromes – 435 Jap planes were destroyed. U.S. casualties were only about 200 killed and wounded, whilst 12,000 Japs were killed, including many who took to the hills and jungle who either were starved to death or killed since. Wewak was by-passed.

On 7th May Cape Hoskins airdrome was captured and on 17th May a landing at Arara (opposite Wakde Island) was made. On the 18th May Wakde Airdrome was seized and the next day troops landed on Liki and Niroemoari Islands (29 miles N.W. of Wakde). When troops landed on Biak Island on 27th May it marked the practical end of the New Guinea Campaign.

The work done by the U.S.A. and U.S.N. Constructional Corps and Engineers is nothing short of a miracle, an enormous gathering housed with good communications.

A great lake lies below the General's H.Q. which is an enormous lath and plaster built house on stilts and most comfortable. I have the General's bedroom, bathroom, etc. There is a big ante-room, well furnished, and a dining room which can seat 25–30, generally about 18. The Mess consists of Lt. General Sutherland, Chief of Staff; General Chamberlin[144] – Chief of Operational Planning; Brigadier General Willoughby[145] – Director of Intelligence – assigned to look after me; an Australian, Lt. Gen. Berryman;[146] and several other Generals, including the Chief Engineer who is responsible for all the wonderful lay out, roads, camps, etc.

All the Generals who escaped with General MacArthur from Corregidor are here, except two who have been killed since in an air crash.

I was surprised to find Admiral Van Hook[147] from Brisbane dining with Admiral Kinkaid, having arrived that morning. I had asked for him at Brisbane and been told he was away for the day, no-one there knew that he had moved his office over here. He left only a few hours after me but came direct instead of going to Manus first, as I did.

Admiral Wilkinson,[148] who is Chief of the big Amphibious Forces now assembled at Manus, one commanded by R.Adm Conolly and the other by R.Adm Royal, had all three flown over to a conference from

Manus where their ships lie. They then told me I am to embark for the operation in Admiral Conolly's Amphibious Command flagship the *Appalachian*; which is a sister ship of the one Eva and I inspected at Honolulu when Admiral C. kindly said he would like to take me. This *was* good news! These two Task Forces are the ones I flew over that last day but one at Honolulu.

Sat. 7th. Admirals Wilkinson, Conolly and Royal flew back to Manus this morning, and at 9.30 a.m. I attended the Naval Staff "Readings" which are held every morning by Admiral Kinkaid; Van Hook was there and 30 or 40 officers. Admiral Kinkaid asked me to say a few words to the officers, which I did. My Flag Lt., Lieut. Tapp, R.A.N., told me that they said nice things about my talk later.

I told them how I started the preparations for amphibious warfare in England in July 1940, etc., and how intensely interested I had been in all I saw at San Diego and Honolulu, on every airfield, Manus and here. How all my dreams about amphibious operations were coming true.

At breakfast time – 7 a.m. – the President of the Philippines[149] and a Philippines General[150] and two or three other Filipinos arrived, they had left Washington on Tuesday 3rd Oct., having picked up a day – they arrived Friday – all flown in a land plane like my flight to Manus – but theirs was a Douglas four engined plane.

Since the President's arrival, he sits on the right of General Sutherland and I on his left. General Blamey[151] also arrived from Australia and I called on him. Wrote letters most of the afternoon.

At dinner in the Mess, Sutherland and I talked about the Belgian Campaign and missed opportunities, he said very nice things about Geoffrey, and later I found *Retreat to Victory* by Alan [*sic*] Michie,[152] which they had read.

Oct. 8th. 9.30 a.m. attended Admiral Kinkaid's Staff meeting and at 10.30 drove to Humboldt Bay down a very good but very dusty road, carved out of and round the hills – 22 miles. Lunched with Admiral Barbey,[153] the Amphibious Commander of 7th Fleet under Kinkaid, onboard his *Blue Ridge* amphibious command ship. He commanded the Navy's assault forces in several operations, including the capture of this place (Hollandia), very interesting and he gave me several photographs of the landings. His Chief of Staff Commodore Noble,[154] U.S.N. and Flag Lieut. Maylard [Mailliard[155]] (married to an English girl, daughter of Glen the portrait painter, but for some reason her surname was Quinney) dined in the Mess. Went to bed at 10 p.m.

9th Up at 6 a.m. Attended Admiral Kinkaid's Staff talk, was then shown two films to illustrate the campaign out here, very good. Rather on the lines of "Desert Victory" – with arrows to show movements, etc. Generals MacArthur, Chamberlin, Sutherland, and Willoughby, and Admirals Nimitz and Kinkaid came prominently into the film. One has been shown in U.S.A. and is said to have had a great success. I hope they do a good one of the next big operation. Wrote letters in the afternoon.

At 5 p.m. we embarked in a fast army motor-boat to cross the lake with General C., Willoughby, Lt. Tapp, Lieut Graham, U.S.N., General Irving[156] – (whose division did the attack on Hollandia from Tanahmerah) – commanding 24th Division, which is to take part in the coming operation.

We were met by our host General Eichelberger[157] – commanding 8th Army U.S.A. with General Swift[158] – commanding 1st Corps, 8th Army; General Byers,[159] General Eichelberger's Chief of Staff. Latter two cavalry officers, we bucked about polo, horses, and it was a most interesting evening. About 8.30 we embarked and went back across the lake, escorted by the three Generals. I wished General Irving goodbye and good luck, he is a fine fellow, looks young and hard, did the landing at Tanahmerah, which Tapp's R.A.N. destroyer supported. Found everyone had turned in when I got back, packed up and so to bed.

Oct. 10th. Up at 6, breakfast at 7, and at 7.30 drove to aerodrome, after farewells to General Sutherland, Captain Clarke (W.A.C.), President Osmeña, General Romolo [Romulo] and other Filipinos and Generals Berryman and Morshead[160] of the Australian Army.

Admiral Kinkaid and his Aide, Lieut. Freeman, came over with us in his plane "Susie Q." Douglas 0. 98 –

Admiral Kinkaid talked to me about the inaccuracies in *The Navy's War* by Fletcher Pratt,[161] very annoying for the author criticises him on pages 227 and 230 for action carried out by Admiral Fletcher[162] not Kinkaid.[163]

(*Note.* Going across the lake passed island with native villages, mat houses set on stilts – on one was a superior mat house, which I was told was probably a Dutch church. The Dutch missionaries have converted most of them to Christianity, but many inland are cannibals! Eichelberger's camp was a Geographical Society's camp. A party came to study the Aborigines, look for metals, etc., found some gold but not in sufficient quantity to pay.)

As we got near the Admiralties the co-pilot came along and told us to put our belts on. Soon after we got some nasty bumps and the engine eased down. We ran out of it in 10 minutes and saw the Islands below us. The harbour was crowded with ships – 560 I was told, of all sorts including several battleships, cruisers and aircraft carriers, transports, L.S.T.s, etc.

When we landed we were met by Commodore Boak, Admiral Wilkinson – commanding our part of the expedition – Admiral Conolly, my host and others. We drove to the harbour along a very dusty road in a glorified very big Jeep with Admirals Kinkaid, Wilkinson, Conolly; and Conolly and I embarked in the *Appalachian*'s boat. I found Wilkinson was in the *Mount Olympus*, the ship Eva and I were shown over in Pearl Harbour Dockyard. The *Appalachian* is the first of her class and has a big 1 on her bows. The *Mount Olympus* is the latest I think.

Admiral Conolly gave me his cabin with shower bath, etc. and big very comfortable bed. I felt badly about it, until I saw his "Emergency Sea Cabin", which though smaller is cooler and has a shower, etc., complete. One of the officers who met us was Commodore Collins,[164] R.A.N. who relieved Victor Crutchley.[165] He did very well in the Mediterranean and sank an Italian cruiser in the *Sydney*. He met two and sank one, the other fled. Lately he has been Captain of the *Shropshire*, given by R.N. to R.A.N. He brought her out, but now he is a Commodore 1st Class in the *Australia*. I said I would like to visit his ship and he asked me to speak to the men. I went onboard at 4 p.m., he had all his senior officers present, Captain Nichols, R.N. of *Shropshire*, whom I met dining with Commodore Boak last week; the C.O.s of the two destroyers and several Staff officers, including a very friendly American liaison officer.

I spoke to the officers and men, said how important these amphibious operations were and how glad I was that Australia was represented. The operation ahead of us would prove the value of sea power and the vital importance of sea-borne aircraft, which alone could take part. Then I told them about Normandy, the mobile harbours, etc. I think they were interested and pleased.

Admiral Conolly, General Arnold[166] – who commanded the troops – his Chief of Staff – Brigadier (?),[167] and I dined onboard the *Mount Olympus* with Admiral Wilkinson. Admiral Kinkaid was staying onboard for the night and going back to Hollandia in the morning.

All the Admirals (21) and all the Generals (5) were there. We selected our dinner at a side table and then scattered to eat it in three big cabins, Kinkaid, Wilkinson and I, General Hodge[168] – commanding the Corps, berthed in the *Mount Olympus*, our two Generals, etc. After dinner we watched a most exciting film of the early Californian days, when the Spaniards were there, about 120 years ago. It was very good, the heroine, a star, very pretty, the hero ? [Tyrone] Power, very dark, quite a Spaniard, just as agile as Fairbanks, a great swordsman and horseman – if he was actually riding and not a "Stand in". There was not a dull moment in the film, watched by all the Admirals, Generals and 100 officers. A much more decorous audience than the bluejackets at Espiritu Santo. We dined early so it was still quite early when Admiral Conolly, his two Generals and I went to the Officers Club, near Commodore Boak's place, an enormous room where officers can get a meal and drink.¹⁶⁹ The ships are *absolutely* dry.

It was a cheery evening, there were hundreds of what Admiral Conolly called "College boys", the new Navy, like our R.N.V.R., they are called U.S.N.R. and wear the same uniform as U.S.N. They sang lustily and it reminded me of the night before we left Tientsin, when Pell¹⁷⁰ and I and several of General Gaselee's¹⁷¹ Staff went to a Sing Song given by the 10th and 11th Regts, which came from the Philippines. I told Conolly and his Generals of this and the refrain or chorus of a song the young Americans sang: "And if anyone says the CHINS can't fight, why tell them to guess again."

This crowd was very cheerful and confident, on the eve of a *very* big show – the biggest to date. I *am* lucky to be in it.

In the Tientsin party we were going into the unknown, and some of our hosts were *not* confident.¹⁷²

We got back about 10.30 p.m. and so to bed, and a good long night as we don't breakfast until 8 o'clock.

Oct. 11th. I stayed onboard, read all the orders and studied plans and photos.

12th. Wrote to Eva everything not confidential, did not give names of the destroyer *Erben* – after an Admiral¹⁷³ of Spanish-American War days – commanded by a Lt. Commander Slayton, whose father had commanded two destroyers in the last war, with whom we lunched, onboard his 2100 ton destroyer. The Commodore of the Flotilla lived onboard and was a polo playing Capt. Marshall.¹⁷⁴ They flew a British Admiral's flag for me while I was onboard.

I dined with General Arnold, who commands the 7th Division, we were photographed together and also with his Staff. He gave me a U.S. dollar note for money to be used in the Philippines when they landed, to add to my "Short Snorter", one side is now covered with the Naval and Military Staffs of our landing. I will get MacArthur and Kinkaid, the Naval and Military Chiefs to sign it, if I get a chance. Kinkaid is in the *Wasatch*.

13th. I stayed onboard and General Arnold took me through his plans and orders, they have wonderful photographs of the beaches. This evening he asked if he might introduce the 3 Colonels commanding his 3 Regiments. A regiment has 3 Battalions and is like our Brigade. One Colonel – Logie¹⁷⁵ – a man of 52, a soldier of fortune, says he was in Gallipoli in our Black Watch, but attached to the Connaught Rangers in 10th Division – and was in 29th Division (?), I can't fit it all in. Says he was at Salonika and Mesopotamia, before he went back in U.S. Army and joined the 9th Foot. Since then he has served with Poles and Yugoslavs and various odd places, including Alaska. He is a very fine big strong man, a real "tough guy".

Colonel O'Sullivan¹⁷⁶ was educated, until he was 16, at Westminster

School wearing a top hat and tails! He asked how Dean's Yard had fared, asked much about that part of London, said he still gets the School Magazine.

Colonel Thagler, [Pachler][177] only 34, was a West Pointer. All three have done the Marshall Islands fight and are confident gallant spirited fellows.

Oct. 14th. Up at 6.15 a.m. and we sailed about 7 a.m. with 9 destroyers (2100 tons), 27 transports and cargo ships carrying the 7th Division.

Admiral Wilkinson, commanding the Assault Group, senior to Conolly, but sails in Conolly's group. Admiral Royal following in U.S.S. *Rocky Mount*, with about 30 ships carrying the 96th Division. There is a Ranger Regiment No. 98, which is going to seize the islands, on either flank of the channel by which the Force enters Leyte Gulf, Homonhon and Dinagat, on "A" minus 3 day; assisted by a regiment of the 24th Division, commanded by General Irving – who I met when I dined with General Eichelberger.

Admiral Barbey has the rest of the Force, 9th Division and [1st] Cavalry Div.

The whole Force is about 60,000 men and there are over 500 vessels engaged, not counting Admiral Halsey's[178] immense 3rd Fleet, with a very large Aircraft Carrier Force under Admiral Mitscher[179]

We hear reports of the great successes the Naval aircraft are having bombing the Pescadores Islands and Formosa, including destruction of 396 aircraft and 27 ships sunk, besides many damaged and 14 probably sunk. 45 American planes were lost in the two days attack.

They are working down the Coast to support our Expedition, by providing fighter cover and destroying enemy aircraft on every airfield within reach, before our "A" Day.[180]

Most of the day I sat in one of the two very comfortable chairs, on the Admiral's bridge, which had been salved from wrecked aircraft in Pearl Harbour. The whole Force got out Paravanes for exercise (very slow!) and fired at "sleeve" targets, towed by Manus based aircraft.

It was very hot in the cabins, nevertheless we had all become Movie fans and we watched one in the Wardroom – "The birth of a Thoroughbred" which turned out to be a 1st class trotter. Then quite a good Fox Century film – "A Real Snob".

It was frightfully hot last night and a long time before I could sleep.

Oct. 15th. It is much cooler today. I had a distinct twinge of gout yesterday, very painful, so told the Admiral's P.M.O., a very nice fellow, who messes with us – Commander Kenny. We were alone at the end of breakfast. He then vetted me very thoroughly, heart, blood pressure, gout, etc. Said I was "pretty good' but there were signs of gout, due he thought to too much meat! I said he might have noticed I always eat very little of the enormous helpings given to me, and last night at dinner, I shied off altogether. He said it was undoubtedly too good living after a low diet. "Pretty good" meant for my age. He vetted me very thoroughly and was evidently pleased with me. I told him about my eye. He said every Task Force carried a first class Oculist and ours was onboard, and might he bring him to see me. He examined my eyes very carefully – said left eye was very good, he noticed the little "floater" but it was nothing to worry about. My right eye was finished – but it would not affect the other eye. He was pleased when I mentioned Williamson Noble,[181] he said he had a great reputation in U.S.A. as one of the best Oculists living. The doctor is giving me some tablets for gout, to be taken with lots of water and bicarbonate of soda, just like Dr Brydone's.

16th. Foot much better, soaked it 3 times in Epsom salted water.

17th. Distinctly better after same treatment.

18th. Much better. Signals coming in show that Halsey's 3rd Fleet has been heavily attacked by Jap aircraft, some damage,[182] a great many Jap planes destroyed. According to the "Radio News Press" 870 to 885 Jap planes were destroyed in seven days offensive and defensive forays. In addition 63 of their ships have been sunk or damaged. Japanese claims of course absurdly exaggerated, they claim between 40 and 52 American warships, including 17 carriers have been destroyed or damaged.

Admiral Kinkaid joined the Force under Admiral Conolly this morning in U.S.S. *Wasatch* with two destroyers. In the afternoon, U.S.S. *Nashville* and two destroyers joined us, with General Mac-Arthur onboard.

On 17th, "A" Day minus 3, U.S.S. *Hughes* – Admiral Struble[183] – carrying 98th Rangers, captured Homonhon Island, to allow minesweepers to sweep. Dinagat Island also captured by Rangers, covered by Squadron of 5 battleships, cruisers and destroyers, under Admiral Oldendorf[184] in U.S.S. *Tennessee*, which later entered Leyte Gulf and softened the defences by intense gunfire. The Japanese will thus have three days notice of our impending attack.

Oct. 19th. Submarines report two large vessels, probably battleships, to S.W. of us steaming to N.E. at 23 knots. Battle orders were issued in the event of their locating our Task Force, which consists solely of transports, destroyer escorts and one cruiser, the *Nashville*.

Although Kinkaid, commanding the 7th Fleet, and Wilkinson – commanding the two Task Forces, were in the convoy, Conolly led it and gave all the orders throughout the passage. When the information about the approach of the Japanese Force was received, he was directed by Wilkinson to make dispositions for the conduct of the convoy and its escorts.

He remarked to me that the fact of MacArthur's presence onboard the *Nashville* would not deter him from making use of her, and he ordered her to be ready to join the destroyers and cover the convoy, which was to withdraw at full speed under cover of smoke, if the Japanese attacked us. I was amused to note that Conolly's own command ship the *Appalachian*, which was only armed with anti-aircraft guns (dual purpose 4" or 5" ?), was to remain with the fighting ships and take command of them.

When he reported his dispositions to Wilkinson, he was promptly ordered to remain with the convoy, so he directed the Captain of the *Nashville* to take command of the covering vessels. However we had no further news of this Japanese Squadron. (But this was in fact the Squadron which attempted to break into Leyte from the South on 23rd Oct.)

Oct. 20th. "A" Day. During the early hours of the morning we steamed through the swept channel, preceded by Admiral Barbey's Force (Which was to assault Leyte ten miles to the Northward of us).

The channel, which was very heavily mined, had not been completely cleared and the American sweepers suffered some loss, however by keeping well to the Eastward the whole Force got into the Gulf without suffering any loss, although the *Shropshire* and one of our transports picked up a mine in their paravanes, which they succeeded in getting rid of without damage. The Australian ships were covering Admiral Barbey's landing further North and I could see nothing of them owing to the smoke of the battle, but they are reported to have done very well and to have given most efficient gunnery support.

At daylight on the 20th the scene was amazing, hundreds of transports, cargo ships, L.S.T.'s (Landing Ship Transports), and L.S.D.'s (Landing Ship Docks), were in the Gulf. The L.S.D.'s are a development initiated by us of the train ferry ships which used to cross the English channel. We fitted out two, each to carry thirteen L.C.M.'s (Landing Craft Motor) each capable of landing a 20 ton tank, or 100 men, to be launched down a ramp, which formed the stern of the train ferry ship, and was lowered down for the purpose. The new L.S.D. was like a floating dock, the stern opened and the vessels she carried were floated out under their own power. (We had been shown one of these at Honolulu, which they said had been built for the British Navy, but taken over by the U.S.A.)

One happened to stop within a cable of the *Appalachian* and I was amused to see an L.C.T. followed by about a dozen L.C.M.'s come out of her ready to land with their cargoes complete.

"A" hour was not until 10 a.m. and in the two preceding hours the

Assault Force was embarked in the Landing Craft carried by the Transports and formed up in several lines abreast, so that wave after wave could approach the beach in rapid succession.

The *Appalachian* moved in very close to watch the assault, and I could follow the movements of the 7th Division very clearly, but could not see much to the Northward of it.

As our Task Force was originally equipped for the capture of Yap, a coral atoll, the assault troops were carried in Alligators,[185] ready to crawl over outlying coral reefs. The first wave were armed with guns, the following waves carried troops, only about 20 in each, and even then they had very little freeboard and it was fortunate that the sea was perfectly calm. On the flanks and at intervals were L.C.I.'s (Landing Craft Infantry), small sea-going vessels designed for carrying about 100 men, who landed from ramps on either bow when the L.C.I. had run her stem ashore. On this occasion they were stripped of everything for carrying troops, and instead were fitted with hundreds of rockets.

Just before 10 a.m. the fire of the battleships, cruisers and destroyers ceased, they had been softening the defences since dawn, as had Naval dive bombers, in a succession of heavy attacks.

As in all previous amphibious operations which the Americans had carried out, the assault troops had immediately followed the lifting of the barrage, and the Japanese, who were in deep trenches and foxholes (which could be clearly seen in the excellent aerial photographs) came up with their machine guns and mortars, expecting to take heavy toll of the assaulting troops, as they had done on almost every other occasion. However, this time a surprise awaited them. The L.C.I.'s darted out ahead of the first wave and ran in close to the shore and turning parallel to it, blasted the foreshore and some hundred yards inland with a tremendous concentration of rocket fire, which wiped out the Japanese, and the troops following close after this new barrage landed apparently without opposition, personally I did not see a single man fall.

It was not until the L.C.I.'s came back to discharge their own dead and wounded that one realised what serious loss would have been inflicted on the assault troops but for this new manoeuver and the gallantry of the young sailors who manned the L.C.I.'s.

When the assault troops had landed they were closely followed by a number of L.S.T.'s, which landed tanks, guns, bulldozers and the heavy transport vehicles direct on to the beach. They were shelled at intervals from the Southern flank by Japanese mortars and mobile artillery, but these were promptly silenced by the fire of the ships, although they generally opened again from another position. However the landing was never impeded and went on well throughout the day.

There were many actions in the air when Japanese shore-based aircraft came snooping round the hills, thus escaping radar detection, and the anti-aircraft fire from the ships was pretty incessant, but the Naval fighters gave us most efficient cover and there was never any heavy concentrated air attack, such as might have been expected with the Jap's air bases within such easy reach. For this, no doubt, we had to thank the splendid force of carrier borne aircraft in Halsey's 3rd Fleet which had been attacking Japanese air bases in Luzon for the last few days.

The only serious casualty among the ships in our vicinity was a 10,000 ton cruiser (*Honolulu*) which was torpedoed well forward and took a heavy list and was well down by the bows. She was flying the flag of Admiral Ainsworth[186] who, at first, thought it would be necessary to beach her, but eventually she was got on an even keel and reached Manus under her own steam some days later, escorted as far as Palau, where she stopped for more temporary repairs, by the *Australia*, which had suffered severe casualties and heavy damage to her bridge, fire control and radar installations and had to be withdrawn for repairs.

21st. This occurred at dawn the following day when a single seater Japanese fighter bomber made a suicide crash landing on her bridge, which was enveloped in flame.

It had been the intention to get the transports and store ships under way during the night of the 20th, but things were going so well and it was desirable to completely clear them and get them away from the danger of attack as soon as possible, so it was decided to carry on landing through the night of 20th, with every prospect of finishing by the afternoon of 21st.

During an air attack on the evening of the 20th a heavy smoke screen was laid to protect the transports, which was very successful, but apparently a few smoke floats of a new type were laid in addition to the ordinary smoke, and many of the officers and men in the ships nearest them were affected including 25 people on the upper deck of the *Appalachian*. Admiral Conolly's Operations officer, an Australian officer onboard and the Surgeon Commander and I suffered most. The bad cases were taken down below to the air conditioned spaces and we were all treated with oxygen. I remained in the Admiral's upper deck cabin with an oxygen mask handy. However, we were all quite badly poisoned by it and I felt very ill for three days and was unable to eat anything.

As Admiral Conolly's Task Force had finished its mission by the evening of the 21st and was to withdraw to Humboldt Bay and Manus in convoy, he had promised to arrange for me to transfer to the battleship *Tennessee* whose Captain Heffernan[187] I had met and who was a great friend of his. However, Surgeon Commander Kenny – who was superintending the embarkation of the wounded on shore when our gassing took place, strongly urged that I ought not to be subjected to any further risk of smoke poisoning, and on the evening of the 21st he took me onboard the *J. Franklin Bell*, a large fast transport, which the Admiral thought would arrive at Humboldt Bay much earlier than his slow moving convoy. However, my ship was diverted to Manus with a slow convoy and only arrived there the same day as the *Appalachian* reached Humboldt Bay, on the 27th Oct.

27th. However, I was glad to go to Manus, because the *Australia* arrived there the same day and I was able to go onboard her and see the damage she had suffered and say a few words of sympathy to her company in the loss of so many of their shipmates, which included the Captain, Dechaineux,[188] and the Navigator killed, and Commodore Collins dangerously wounded. Commander Wright was in command and he told me that the airman came up on the port quarter, killed two men and wounded another manning an A.A. gun aft, and then turned in an[d] crashed against the tripod and his plane fell on the bridge before bouncing overboard, the pilot's smashed body fell onboard. The petrol from the plane and possibly a bomb exploded, and the whole bridge being enveloped in flame, everybody in its vicinity was killed or badly injured. I found the Ship's Company very disappointed that they were not to go back to Sydney or Brisbane for their repairs, as the estimate of time for doing these was about 60 days, instead of about 28 at the American base at Espiritu Santo; and Admiral Kinkaid urgently wanted the *Australia* as soon as possible for further operations in the Philippines.

22nd to 24th. I was kept in bed the first three days onboard the *J. Franklin Bell* still feeling pretty bad and unable to eat, but was well looked after by her Surgeon Commander and the young Pharmacist Mates (Sick Berth Stewards). There were also a good many wounded onboard and amongst the sick was the Surgeon Captain of one of the U.S. hospital ships who was very ill from the same smoke poisoning, and they said had nearly died from it. There were a lot of eye wounds and fortunately the ship carried a famous Boston Oculist, Virgil G. Casten, M.D., and he told me that he thought he had been able to save the eyes of nearly all of them through prompt treatment, in one case he had extracted some metal from behind a man's eye with a of our voyage, which was uneventful.

25th. After three days in bed I was feeling much better and had my meals with the Captain, Oliver Ritchie, who had retired from the U.S.N. before the war and settled in Boston. He was a charming fellow and I made great friends with him during the next three days of our voyage, which was uneventful.

We arrived at 8 a.m. on the 27th at Manus, Commodore Boak had asked me to stay when I returned there, but he was in bed with fever, so I remained onboard.

28th. Next day Admiral Van Hook, who had remained at Hollandia, sent a Lockheed Lodestar plane to fetch me, Admiral Kinkaid's Douglas being under refit. On arrival at Hollandia I was met by Van Hook and General Chamberlin, General MacArthur's Deputy Chief of Staff, who took me to G.H.Q. where I stayed in General MacArthur's room again. The General promised to send me on to Brisbane the next day. That evening General Sutherland arrived with General Kenney,[189] who commands MacArthur's Army Air Force, he had just flown down from Leyte, but I did not see him until next morning, and in the meantime I had a long talk with Generals Willoughby and Chamberlin.[190]

162. *Admiral Thomas C. Kinkaid to Keyes*[191]

[Holograph] United States Fleet,
Commander Seventh Fleet.
Wednesday, 8 November [1944].

Thank you for your kind note regarding the Leyte operations.

Those operations were truly amazing and I am sorry not to be able to tell you personally the story as we saw it in the Flagship.

In the amphibious phase the weatherman was good to us; the preliminary operations of minesweeping, beach-clearance and bombardment offered no great obstacles; the assault troops were landed as scheduled under cover of excellent gun-fire support and direct air support. I could ask for no better execution of a plan. Also, Jap air opposition was very mild considering that they had three days of advance notice due to our preliminary operations.

In the Surigao Straits show, I had plenty of advance information, plenty of time to make adequate dispositions, early information of the enemy advance through the Mindanao Sea from our PT boats, and, to top it off, the Japs advanced on northerly courses through the Surigao Straits in two columns, one four miles astern of the other, directly into the middle of our battle line which formed a perfect T. Can you beat that? Destroyer attacks from both sides followed by simultaneous opening fire by cruisers and battleships, in some cases landing their first salvoes on the target, made short work of the Jap force.

In the battle to eastward of Samar Island our CVE's in an action unique in the history of naval warfare drove off a strong enemy force of battleships, cruisers and destroyers which approached within easy gun range.[192] It is almost unbelievable.

I would like you to know that I greatly enjoyed your visit to 7th Fleet Headquarters at Hollandia as did others who had the pleasure of meeting you. Admiral Conolly particularly mentioned his pleasure at having you on board.

With best regards...

163. *Keyes to Churchill*[193]

[Carbon]
Government House,
Sydney.
8th November, 1944.

When Brendan suggested with your approval that I might go to Australia on a kind of good will mission to talk to the Australian people – I must confess I had in mind the possibility of seeing one or two of the amphibious operations which the Americans are carrying out with such enterprise in the Pacific.

When I was in Washington waiting to see the President, I saw something of Admiral King.[194] I learned from him and his Naval Aviation people that the Seversky School, backed by a strong political element, and the U.S. Army Air Force will make every endeavour to get the Naval Air Service merged in the U.S.A.A.F. on the lines of the R.A.F. – dominated of course, by the military element.

They told me that all the speeches and articles I have written on the need for development of Naval Aviation, and the speeches you made when you supported me in 1937, will be used in the battle which will surely be waged after the war, if the Naval Air Service is to be kept free from outside interference.

I told King that I would, of course, do anything I could to help them, as we would have most surely been "sunk" in the Pacific war if they had not possessed an all-powerful and efficient Naval Air Service. I said I hoped he would give me an opportunity of seeing it at work in some future operation in the Pacific, which of necessity would have to be carried out far beyond the support of shore based aircraft.

He then suggested that I should go down to San Diego and inspect the amphibious bases and training centres on the Californian Coast. Then I could fly to Honolulu to see Nimitz, and the future must rest with him but he would ask him to show me all he could.

King then attached a young Naval Air Service Captain, who picked us up at Vancouver and flew us to San Francisco and then to San Diego in a Naval plane. As my Official Secretary, Eva was allowed to fly in Naval planes as an honorary "WAVE".[195] I was immensely impressed flying down the coast to see the great rows of ships in line abreast in various stages of construction, and on the air-fields many hundreds of naval aircraft, lying with folded wings, waiting to be carried to the Pacific in escort carriers.

The Admiral in Charge of the Training Centres and Depots of landing craft, which extended for miles down the Californian coast, devoted three or four days to show me everything. He was good enough to tell a large company of Officers, including Roosevelt's fine young Marine Son,[196] when he proposed my health, that they owed much to my early efforts and inspiration.

I was taken to the Marine Training Camp on a great ranch 100 miles square which included every kind of territory, jungle, marsh and rough rocky country. They had a great display for my benefit. An attack carried out by the Marines under fire just over their heads and through mine fields and every kind of obstacle. The General remarked that this all started as the result of a visit or two of his boys to one of my Commando Training Camps. Rather more generous than some of our Generals who introduced our training into the battle training of the Army and then did all they could to do away with the Commandos.

After this we flew to San Francisco, and across to Pearl Harbour in a Clipper run by the Navy. There Admiral Nimitz was at great pains to show me everything. I spent one day at sea with him in one of the great carriers of which they now have more than twenty in the Pacific, and inspected one of the little escort carriers of which they have at least fifty ready for action.

I watched the jungle training, and went out in one of their amazing alligators which waddled down a rough beach, swam out to sea, climbed over a coral reef, cruised round the lagoon, then clambered back up the beach. He showed me two great Task Forces equipped with a number of these alligators, some mounting guns, others to carry troops. They were about to embark for the capture of Yap which is surrounded by coral reefs.

I spent a day studying the operation in a Command Ship with Admiral Conolly who had conducted the U.S. landing in Sicily, and had landed our 46th and 56th divisions at Salerno in U.S. landing craft. Since then he has conducted two of the amphibious operations for the capture of Pacific Islands. These two Task Forces sailed in company before I left Honolulu, and Nimitz flew me out to look down from the air at the organization of this enormous armada at sea.

Before I left, Nimitz told me that they might now well by-pass Yap, as Admiral Halsey had experienced very little opposition in the neighbourhood of the Philippines and he had offered to hand over the two Task Forces to MacArthur, if he wished to speed up his advance towards Luzon, and would cover the operation with Halsey's 3rd Fleet.

Nimitz told me that he would ask General MacArthur and Admiral Kinkaid to allow me to watch any operations they might carry out.

Eva and I then flew in a Naval Transport plane heavily laden with packing cases to Brisbane – but they made us quite comfortable.

After a couple of weeks in Australia, and a brief meeting with MacArthur at Canberra, I flew to General MacArthur's headquarters at Hollandia where I stayed for four days, and then thanks to Kinkaid's good offices I flew to Manus in the Admiralties, where I embarked in Admiral Conolly's Flag Ship, which also carried General Arnold commanding the Seventh Division, who had taken part in two of the Island attacks. They were charming hosts and companions.

There was an enormous armada of ships, large and small, and scores of L.S.T.'s and other big landing craft – about a thousand vessels, divided between the Hollandia and Manus anchorages, which are about 400 miles apart.

It is a long story and I will write an account of it, but I want this to go in your Commando transport plane which, I believe, is returning to England to-morrow.

To cut it short I was embarked for eighteen days in ships of the U.S.N. and shared with them the hazards – and there were some! – of an extraordinarily bold and well conducted amphibious stroke. Fifteen hundred miles from the U.S. Naval and Air Bases, right into the heart of enemy occupied territory with powerful Japanese Naval and Air Forces at large.

Nimitz's island captures in the Pacific – of which I believe MacArthur did not approve – covered his right flank, and made it possible for him to capture and hold the Admiralties with its magnificent harbour at Manus, and make his daring amphibious jumps towards the Philippines. The most westerly of Nimitz's Islands in the Palau group covered Yap and was only five hundred miles from our objective in the Philippines.

General MacArthur as C.-in-C. of the South West Pacific bore all the responsibility for this daring and successful enterprise, but one can also have nothing but admiration for Admiral Kinkaid and the ships and aircraft of the 7th Fleet under his Command which made it possible. The U.S. Navy may well be proud that they enabled the Army to get to grips with the Japanese at a spot many hundreds of miles beyond the effective radius of shore based fighter aircraft and within easy reach of powerful Japanese squadrons and land based aircraft.

Of course the final issue will be decided by the U.S. Army, but it was the U.S. Navy with its hundreds of carrier borne aircraft which made it possible for MacArthur to capture territory on which to establish air bases for his U.S.A.A.F. – *seven days* after the original landing, and with all the equipment they needed, carried by the Navy.

Some days prior to the operation, Admiral Halsey's 3rd Fleet and his very powerful force of carriers struck far and wide at the Japanese Naval and Air Bases and took heavy toll of their shipping and aircraft During the operation he was in the offing and his aircraft gave valuable help on one or two critical occasions. I am afraid, however, that he will be criticised for going too far north when he destroyed the Japanese carriers, which came down heavily escorted from Japan, having apparently brought down aircraft reinforcements for the Philippines. A powerful force of four Japanese battleships including one of their latest, and several large and small cruisers and destroyers, said to have come from Singapore – were sighted west of Luzon, and were reported by Halsey's aircraft, which attacked them, to be heavily damaged and "milling around." Airmen, even Naval ones, seem prone to overcall! During the night, the Japanese broke through the channel north of Samar Island and got within fourteen thousand yards of our gallant little escort carriers – we had eighteen with us. The Japanese ships were most gallantly engaged by some destroyers and by scores of young Naval airmen, catapulted and flown from our little table tops at great sacrifice. Planes from Halsey's carriers came tearing down from the North to join in the action, and the Japanese were sent reeling back, but Halsey's fast battleships which he brought down at full speed were three hours too late to cut off and destroy that force.

The old battleships (some of which had been brought up from the bottom of Pearl Harbor and modernized) of Kinkaid's 7th Fleet, cruisers and destroyers which had been covering the landing, engaged and destroyed two Japanese battleships and several cruisers and destroyers which had come up from Borneo and attempted to break into Leyte from the south during the night. The few cripples that escaped were destroyed by Naval aircraft after daylight.

I have an unbounded admiration for the young Naval Airmen who bore all the heat and burden of the day for a week, and gave us cover during many Japanese air attacks from shore based aircraft, they dive bombed the defences and attacked Japanese vessels with torpedoes and bombs with indomitable spirit.

This bold jump towards the Philippines which I had the good fortune to watch must surely discredit the mischievous and pretentious claims of Seversky and his like who have ceaselessly declared that victory can be won by air power alone, and security against aggression in the future can be economically maintained by means of a great International Air Force.

What a lengthy, costly and prolonged proceeding MacArthur's

progress towards the Philippines would have been if his jumps had been limited to the radius of action of the fighters of the U.S.A.A.F. – which they would have been, but for the co-operation of a powerful and daring Naval Air Service, carried under the protection of the U.S. Navy.

But for the bomb which undid Williamson Noble's operation on my eye, I would probably have started a month or two earlier and possibly taken part in the capture of Guam instead of watching this wonderful enterprise. I saw quite a lot with one eye, and don't grudge the other a bit "for the good of the cause", which I believe my experience will help.

[Holograph] Love from Eva and myself to Clemmy . . .

164. *Keyes to Lieut.-General R. K. Sutherland*

[Carbon]

Government House,
Sydney.
18th November, 1944.

I am sending you a copy of some lectures on Amphibious Warfare which I gave at Cambridge early in 1943, before we knew anything about your Amphibious Operations in the Pacific, and before the Sicilian Campaign, though I refer to the latter in some notes at the end.

I was immensely interested in General MacArthur's bold strategic thrust to the Philippines, and am full of admiration for the skill and efficiency of the landing operations which went off so successfully, and without much loss to your troops.

After their experience in the landing at Leyte, in which the L.C.I. rocket craft played such a valuable part, it seems likely that in future, the Japanese will remain in their deep trenches and fox holes until the rocket blast is over, and then jump up with their mortars and machine guns to take toll of your troops, who were spared losses (in the operation I watched) thanks to the L.C.I.'s rocket attack.

I quite understand your objection to landing inexperienced troops in amphibious operations at night. Now, however, you have some splendid battle-worthy troops in your Cavalry Division, Marines, Rangers and in Divisions such as the 7th, which have had valuable experience. I am sure you could get a magnificent body of volunteers for hazardous enterprises, and train them in a few weeks intensively in night fighting. They would, of course, be far superior to the Japanese.

After the softening process by ships and aircraft, to which the Japanese are now accustomed – if a few thousand such troops were landed quietly during the night before the morning on which they expect your attack to be launched, I am convinced you would spring a tremendous surprise on the enemy and achieve a great success.

I will always have a most happy recollection of my stay at your G.H.Q., and the kindness I received from you and Generals Chamberlin and Willoughby and other members of your most hospitable Mess...

165. *Keyes to Churchill*

[Carbon]

Government House,
Sydney.
20th November, 1944.

I wrote in a great hurry in order to send my last letter by your "Commando" plane.[197] I would like, however, to tell you something about the tactical side of the operations I witnessed.

Admiral Conolly and General Arnold, with whom I sailed, had, as I mentioned, taken part in several amphibious operations, and I studied their reports and those of others carried out by the U.S. Marines, Army and Navy.

The landings are always carried out in daylight, after two or three days of softening by gunfire and bombing of the ships and aircraft of the U.S. Navy, and when the barrage was lifted the Japanese knew to a few moments when the assault would be launched. Consequently, they stayed down in their foxholes and deep trenches until the last minute, then came up with their mortars and machine guns, and almost invariably took heavy toll of the assaulting troops.

In the operation I watched they introduced a new factor. At the moment the Japanese had every reason to think the assault would be delivered, and wave after wave of troops were approaching in landing craft in line abreast – a score of L.C.I.'s, fitted to carry hundreds of rockets, dashed in ahead of the landing and running parallel to the coast turned the whole fore-shore and approaches to the beaches some hundreds of yards inland into a blaze of bursting rockets. Then I watched the troops go in and advance some way inland, apparently without much loss.

The Japanese with their machine guns and mortars had been wiped out by the rocket fire. It was not until the L.C.I.'s came back to discharge a number of dead and wounded that one realised that the Japanese fire which was intended for the troops had inflicted serious losses on the gallant young crews of the L.C.I.'s.

I have always been obsessed with the value of night fighting, and have had a horror of day assaults since I watched the landings on "V" beach at Gallipoli being wiped out by a few machine guns in positions on either flank, which could not be destroyed by gun fire, and could not have been attacked from the air by bombs under modern conditions – such as those at Dieppe (I used to preach this to our people and to the Americans who attended my Headquarters in London and the Training Centre at Inveraray when I was D.C.O.).

After I got back to Manus I flew over to MacArthur's Headquarters at Hollandia and put my views to his Chief of Staff, who had just flown back from Leyte, and to his chief planner there – with whom I had made friends during my previous visit. They told me that they had never been able to carry out night operations because their troops were untried and inexperienced, and the Japs were much better at the game. They had been much harassed by Jap troops infiltrating at night. However, they were interested, and I see that a recent capture of one of the outlying islands was carried out by a night attack. Possibly a trial before the attack on Luzon, which they know will be a very tough proposition.

To put my suggestion on record I wrote as follows to General Sutherland, MacArthur's Chief of Staff: –[198]

* * *

I also put it to Admiral Kinkaid after I had discussed it with Conolly who has had lots of experience and he fully concurred it was about time they introduced new methods.

Admiral Talbot,[199] the amphibious Admiral here[200] who was in the Normandy landing, fully appreciates the value of night operations.

To my everlasting regret and by an extraordinarily unfortunate chance, I was prevented from doing much I had intended to do.

We were being rather heavily attacked by Japanese torpedo planes and dive bombers which came snooping round the hills and diving into our anchorage, undetected by the radar, which was otherwise wonderfully effective. The U.S. cruiser *Honolulu* was torpedoed within a few cables of our ship. My Admiral then put up a tremendous smoke screen to cover the transports and store ships, which were discharging their cargoes and building up an immense reserve as rapidly as possible. Much of the smoke was harmless and as effective as I used at Zeebrugge. But unfortunately they had some new float in which there was a poisonous chemical ingredient which affected a great many people, including me and the Admiral's Chief of Operations, who were on the bridge at the time. I found it absolutely suffocating and the Fleet Surgeon advised us to wear gas masks and put one on me, but as my lungs were full of the smoke, it only made matters worse. Luckily for me he put one on himself and then almost passed out, and like many others had to be removed to an air conditioned space below. Then a young doctor removed the gas masks and treated us with oxygen, which cleared my pipes, but I was very sick for three days, whooping up beastliness from my lungs and tummy and unable to eat anything. This prevented me from going ashore to the H.Q. which MacArthur and the President of the Philippines had set up near Tacloban; and worse still from embarking in the U.S. battleship *Tennessee* from which I was to have watched some other special operations. So I missed the night action in which she and her consorts fought and destroyed a Japanese squadron, which came up from Borneo. The Japanese were in two columns and the Americans in line ahead crossed their T and fired salvos by radar as they approached, finding their targets almost at once.

It was very disappointing missing this, but one never knows one's luck, and going to and fro to MacArthur's H.Q. was also not exactly healthy; perhaps a kind Providence was looking after me, thinking my experience may yet be of use to our cause, although I am neither a Pope, Judge or Prime Minister, but an old sailor who has had the opportunity of seeing quite a lot of war, ancient and modern! [201]

In spite of being gassed, I soon recovered and was able to fly back later over New Guinea at 15,000 feet without any discomfort, and have been leading a very strenuous life ever since.

There is one other point I want to make, the Seversky School claims that practically everything can be carried by air. I have flown many thousands of miles in the largest transport planes. Their service is wonderful, but for an amphibious operation in the Pacific, for every ton they can carry, several hundreds of tons have to be carried in ships, including, not only heavy tanks, but the great machines which make the airfields they require, and the petrol they need to enable them to operate.

I have been much amused by Ian Hamilton's[202] *Waiting for the Drums*,[203] and his reference to your getting into every war. (I can sympathize – there were many obstacles to be overcome between London and Leyte). I remember your remarks about this in *The River War*. It is only fitting that in the end you should have had the running of the greatest war of all time to a victorious issue . . .

166. *Keyes to Bracken*

[Carbon]

Government House,
Adelaide, South Australia.
17/2/45.

Since I wrote to you on the 4th Dec. we have travelled many thousands of miles, mostly by plane, but we also did some hundreds of miles in Tasmania by car, and 2500 by car in New Zealand last month.

Our welcome in these last two places was, if possible, even warmer and more enthusiastic than in Australia, where it has been quite wonderful too.

In New Zealand we were the guests of the Government and were sent round in Service planes and Minister's cars, and treated royally everywhere, and laden with gifts and flowers wherever we went, including the Maoris at Rotorua, who gave us a national welcome, the three principal chiefs making long speeches and bringing into them praise of my "warrior son" Geoffrey in the Rommel raid, which they knew all about, as New Zealand troops had been in camp near his Commando, and they had a tremendous admiration for him. One New Zealand retd. soldier brought us a photograph of his grave at Sidi Rafa, which he had gone there to take.

I expect you saw my second letter to Winston[204] in which I mentioned that I had been rather badly gassed at Leyte by a poisonous smoke screen, but had recovered well from it and had actually flown back over New Guinea at 15,000^{ft}, with oxygen of course. The doctors had told me that I might not be able to fly for awhile, but if I did, I must always have oxygen if we went over 10,000 feet.

After this we carried out our very strenuous Australian and Tasmanian tour which involved very heavy programmes everywhere we went and often making three or four speeches a day. I felt none the worse until we flew to New Zealand when a blasted young pilot took us up to 13,000 feet for some time to get a tail wind and make a fast passage. I began to feel pretty bad and asked for oxygen, but they had none onboard! I have not felt really well since and often got tired during our strenuous tour in New Zealand, so when we got here after four consecutive days flying – New Zealand to Sydney 10 hrs, Sydney to Canberra, Canberra back to Sydney, and Sydney to Adelaide – with engagements at all places; Eva insisted on having a Doctor to vet me before going on with the heavy programmes arranged for us here and at Perth.

He and a Consultant he called in both agreed that the high flight without oxygen had strained my heart, and that I must go to bed at once and have a complete rest for a month if I was to avoid really serious permanent damage. He said I ought to have been put to bed a month ago instead of "forcing my heart and nerve and sinew" so long.

Our kind hosts – General Sir Willoughby[205] and Lady Norrie – would not hear of my going to hospital, so Eva and a nurse are looking after me here where we are extremely comfortable.

After a week in bed I felt ever so much better and am now allowed to sit up on the balcony for some hours during the day, but am not allowed to walk about yet; although the doctor says he is "astounded at the rapid progress I have made and my recuperative powers", so no doubt I will be on the war path again before long. Although I may have to give up the idea of having a look at Dickie Mountbatten's war in Burmah on my way home, as I had hoped.

The chief difficulty is to get home. We got seats in the plane leaving Perth for Colombo on the 23rd Feb. but of course the doctor won't hear of that, and he doesn't want me to fly, as it would be awkward if I was taken ill with no doctor onboard; and he thinks it would be better for me to go by sea if possible, however my improvement has been so rapid that he is reconsidering this, and we may fly after all.

This is all being gone into, but not many ships come to Adelaide and I don't want to have to go back to Sydney – two days journey by train and then have to come back through the Panama Canal; as I particularly wanted to return via the Mediterranean. However, no doubt things will turn out for the best in the end.

I shall always be most grateful to you for sending us on this "Good Will Mission" which has been most interesting for us, and I really think it has been a great success judging by the many letters I have received, and I hope you may have had some good reports of it.

You will be interested to hear that during my farewell visit to Canberra Mr Forde[206] – the deputy Prime Minister, came up to me in the High Commissioner's house and said he wanted to tell me: "How much they all admired the way I had taken on the Trade Union Leaders in Sydney."[207] Another Labour Minister told me that one of the T.U. leaders had said that he was "all for me, after my straight talk to them."

You might pass this on to Kemsley,[208] for the information of his malicious Naval Correspondent – Russell Grenfell,[209] with the enclosed two cuttings.[210]

Winston seems to have done wonderful work in the Crimea and at Athens, where he has confounded his enemies and won great credit.

It is rather amusing that the 3000 Dockyard mateys at a mass meeting in the dinner hour of the Sydney Govt. Dockyard, who condemned me for insulting Australian labour – about H.M.S. *Australia*'s repairs – passed a similar resolution condemning Winston for employing British troops to suppress the working class of Greece. They could be easily led but are weak and there is a very nasty Communist element, who are doing infinite harm and strikes are incessant . . .

167. Keyes to Bracken

[Copy]
Government House,
Adelaide, South Australia.
27/2/45.

I meant to tell you in my letter yesterday[211] how immensely valuable my trip to the Philippines with the Americans has been throughout my subsequent tour in Australia, New Zealand and Tasmania.

My audiences were naturally very interested to hear a first hand account of, what is recognized out here, as a very bold and hazardous undertaking which deserved the great success it achieved.

The lessons to be learnt from it are most valuable and important for the Government and people of these outposts of our Ocean Empire, whose vital communications pass through areas of thousands of miles, far out of reach of any shore-based aircraft support; which underlines the necessity of the maintenance of British Sea Power, properly equipped with sufficient Sea-borne Air Power as an integral part of it, on the same lines as that so successfully developed by the United States Navy.

The Naval Boards in Australia and New Zealand are very grateful to me for bringing all this to the fore, as they are very keen to develop their Naval Aviation, and are always up against the Air Force propaganda that Air Power is all that these Dominions need maintain for security, and that they cannot afford to maintain Sea Power as well, which of course is always attractive to any Government which puts Social Services before expenditure on defence.

I found this view prevalent in Canberra, before I went to the Philippines even Menzies[212] rather supported Curtin[213] in an argument we had about it; however, I think they are converted now by recent events, and I was agreeably surprised after a lecture I gave to the Officers of the RAAF Staff College – at their invitation – to hear the Chief of the Air Staff, who was an ardent "Boomer", declare that this war had abundantly proved that bombing had not achieved all that had been expected of it, and had stressed the importance of seaborne aircraft and the necessity for Air co-operation with the Army in the fields – in thanking me for my lecture.

This was after some remarks of mine about the ineffectiveness of mass bombing of Cassino, Caen, Bologna, Aachen, etc., which seemed to have made the task of the P.B.I.[214] only more difficult and costly.

I made great friends with Fraser[215] (P.M. New Zealand) and some of the members of his Govt over all this, and actually won the support of Newall[216] (Gov. Gen.), who was very kind and hospitable, and with whom I made friends despite the battles we fought, when he was Chief of Air Staff.

I thought you might be interested to hear all this, in case Winston thought my expedition to the Philippines was only "bush thwacking" for my own amusement! ...

168. *Keyes to Churchill*

[Carbon]

Tingewick House,
Buckingham.
17/4/45.

What a frightful shock for you and Bernie,[217] when you got back from the Other Club on Thursday night. I do sympathise with you, for I know how much Roosevelt's death means to you and how much you will miss him in the battles to come, before a real peace can be won.[218] It really is a national disaster losing him now.

You told me to write you a note,[219] on my observations at Kandy, and I now enclose it . . .

169. *Keyes to Churchill*

[Carbon]
SECRET & PERSONAL
Prime Minister

17/4/45.

When I was staying with Mountbatten at Kandy, I studied his campaign, present and future, and was much impressed with the good spirit and confidence that prevails there. I was able to tell him and his principal sailor – Douglas Pennant[220] – about my experiences, when staying at MacArthur's H.Q. and with the U.S. fleet, and of the gigantic equipment they have for their daring by-passing strokes by sea and air.

When Mountbatten has more air transport and landing equipment for far reaching amphibious strokes, I am confident that our Pacific war will also go apace, for now that we have command of the sea, and the areas occupied by the Japanese in SEAC's sphere are cut off from reinforcements and replenishments of supplies by sea, it is simply a question of isolating areas and killing the Japanese in them.

When I was there they only had enough landing craft to lift about a brigade and I was told that only about enough for a division was on the way. I talked to Cunningham about this and he told me of the difficulty of reinforcing SEAC, owing to the unexpected delays in the European Campaign, the loss of landing craft on passage in bad weather, and the delay ahead owing to the monsoon; but he assured me that reinforcements would be sent out with all despatch, as soon as it is practicable, so I have really nothing new to say, except that anything you can do to speed up the provision of amphibiously trained troops and the vessels they need, as well as airborne troops, would pay you a big dividend, possibly even Singapore in the near future.

No-one knows better than you the delays which can occur when things proceed down "Service channels", and the value of a dynamic spirit which will overcome difficulties and get a move on, and I am sure you will do all you can to help and support Mountbatten and his splendid command, who have achieved so much under great difficulties.

So far the Americans have had all the limelight, and it would be a great help to our prestige in the Far East if we could retake our own possessions out there speedily, without American help. I know the Australian troops are spoiling to take a hand with us, and are feeling very bitter at being kept out of the Philippines after they had played such a predominant part in the recovery of New Guinea, the base from which that campaign was launched.

170. *Bracken to Keyes*

Admiralty, Whitehall.
1st August, 1945.

Winston was very touched by your message. He is in the best of spirits and is, I think, rather looking forward to serving as Leader of the Opposition.

The comrades have made great promises. We shall now see the effects of their attempts to fufil them.

But politicians are of smaller importance than your health. What do the doctors say about you now? Please send me a postcard . . .

171. *Keyes to Tomkinson*[221]

[Holograph]

Tingewick House,
Buckingham.
3.11.45.

I see you were at Tam Field's Memorial Service. I expect you saw the obituary in the *Daily Telegraph* in which it mentioned his letter to you commending you.²²² Also Dreyer's²²³ article in *The Times*! He was D.C.N.S. wasn't he? And also commended you to Joan.

I have so many pleasant recollections of Tam Field starting 1885 when he was a third term captain – the most powerfully built and developed boy in the *Britannia* – his basin next to mine, a miserable little specimen 4 ft 10″ and a "New". He was awfully good to us and we loved him. Next in China when he did so well – and took it so well my going over his head – Then when I was I.C.S. or Commodore S and he commander in the *Vernon* – Then in the Grand Fleet – and at the Admiralty when I was DCNS and he Controller – we were always good friends or I thought we were. When we met at Marseilles he apparently knew tho' I didn't that he was going to be 1 S.L.²²⁴ I don't think I ever saw him again to speak to except about your case and that was the end.

You are bigger minded than I am – and I don't think even if I had been fit enough to come up I would have gone to his Memorial Service – because most unpleasant tales came back to me from the Mediterranean of the way he used to run me down – not only from my sailor friends – but from friends in a yacht – and I hated the way he allowed you to be made a scapegoat. How typical of Dreyer his apologia in *The Times*.

I am being rather petty and I ought to be ashamed of myself. Well may he rest in peace – he was a charming fellow as I remember him best.

I spent 10 days in London early in the month (Oct.) but I found it rather exhausting and the Dr.'s said if I want to get completely over the heart strain I had better stay quietly down here for a bit [?] longer. However I hope to sponsor Andrew Cunningham on 21st Nov. when he is "enrolled" in the House of Lords.²²⁵ I hope you have good news of Peter and the girls.

With love from us both to you and Joan . . .

NOTES

NOTES TO INTRODUCTION TO PART I

1. Keyes to his daughter Elizabeth, 5 Sept. 1939, cited in Cecil Aspinall-Oglander, *Roger Keyes* (London, 1951), p. 339.
2. *Ibid.*, pp. 343-4. See also Brian Bond (ed.), *Chief of Staff: The Diaries of Lieutenant-General Sir Henry Pownall* Vol. I *1933-1940* (Hampden, Conn., 1973), p. 256; Roderick Macleod and Denis Kelly (eds.), *Time Unguarded: The Ironside Diaries, 1937-1940* (New York, 1962), pp. 115-16, 132-3; Brian Bond, *France and Belgium, 1939-1940* (London, 1975), pp. 49-50. The most detailed account of Keyes's relationship with King Leopold will undoubtedly be the study, *'Outrageous Fortune': King Leopold III of the Belgians*, now in preparation by the 2nd Lord Keyes (Keyes's son).
3. Bond, *France and Belgium, 1939-1940*, pp. 56-9, 67-73; *Ironside Diaries*, pp. 205-8. The Permanent Under Secretary of State for Foreign Affairs was highly critical of Keyes and other unofficial emissaries. See David Dilks (ed.), *The Diaries of Sir Alexander Cadogan, 1938-1945* (London, 1971), pp. 246, 249. Lord Keyes intends to refute the statements of Pownall and Cadogan in his forthcoming study of King Leopold.
4. An extremely hostile account of Keyes's activities is in Sir John Slessor, *The Central Blue* (London, 1956), pp. 481-2.
5. Many years afterwards (in 1968) James claimed that Keyes's Trondheim plan was originated by Lady Keyes who had asked for the Norwegian charts to be brought to her while sick in bed. Cited by Arthur J. Marder, *From the Dardanelles to Oran: Studies of the Royal Navy in War and Peace, 1915-1940* (London, 1974), p. 160, n. 107. There is no evidence in the Keyes MSS. to support this and Document 15 would seem to disprove it. Lady Keyes was indeed ill at Portsmouth at the time, but Keyes had access to James's War Room where he determined 'it was obvious of course that the seizure of Trondheim Fiord is the key to the situation'. In preparing his plan Keyes did study the Norwegian coast defence charts in the War College Library at Portsmouth and this might be the origin of the story.
6. Stephen W. Roskill, *The War at Sea* Vol. I *The Defensive* (London, 1954), pp. 185-7; T. K. Derry, *The Campaign in Norway* (London, 1952), pp. 71-2, 76-7. A full account of the Trondheim plans is given by Winston S. Churchill, *The Gathering Storm* (Boston, 1948), ch. xiv.
7. Derry, *Campaign in Norway*, pp. 80-1; James R. M. Butler, *Grand Strategy* Vol II *September 1939-June 1941* (London, 1957), p. 139. After the war Churchill is reported to have said Dudley Pound hated Keyes and 'if as First Lord he had given Keyes the command there might have been resignations; and the price was too high for this particular risk'. Lord Moran, *Churchill: The Struggle for Survival, 1940-1965* (Boston, 1966), p. 346.
8. Sir Adrian Carton de Wiart, *Happy Odyssey* (London, 1950), p. 176; on Steinkjer see Derry, *Campaign in Norway*, pp. 91-3; J. L. Moulton, *The Norwegian Campaign of 1940: A Study of Warfare in Three Dimensions* (London, 1966), p. 172.
9. *Ibid.*, pp. 200-1.
10. Roskill, *The War at Sea*, I, p. 188; Slessor, *Central Blue*, pp. 278-80.
11. Baron Ismay, *The Memoirs of General Lord Ismay* (New York, 1960), pp. 122-3.
12. Derry, *Campaign in Norway*, pp. 76-7.
13. Moulton, *Norwegian Campaign*, pp. 160-1.

14 Harold Macmillan, *The Blast of War, 1939–1945* (New York, 1967), p. 54.
15 *Ibid.*, p. 56; Duff Cooper, *Old Men Forget* (New York, 1954), pp. 277–8; Major-General Sir Edward Spears, *Assignment to Catastrophe* Vol. I *Prelude to Dunkirk* (New York, 1954), pp. 118–19; Hugh Dalton, *The Fateful Years: Memoirs 1931–1945* (2 vols., London, 1957), Vol. II, p. 306.
16 For details see Aspinall-Oglander, *Roger Keyes*, ch. xxxix; Bond, *France and Belgium, 1939–1940*, chapters iii–iv; and the forthcoming book by Lord Keyes.
17 See for example Keyes's Preface to Emile Cammaerts, *The Prisoner at Laeken* (London, 1941), pp. vii–xviii. A substantial portion of this appeared as 'King Leopold's Loyal Co-operation with Allies in Flanders', *Daily Telegraph*, 20 June 1941.
18 Aspinall-Oglander, *Roger Keyes*, pp. 374–9, 453–7; Bond, *France and Belgium, 1939–1940*, pp. 147–51.
19 A. V. Alexander to Keyes, 28 and 30 May 1940, Keyes MSS. 140/2/3.

NOTES TO PART I

1 Admiral Sir William Reginald Hall (1870–1943). Nicknamed 'Blinker Hall'. Commanded battle cruiser *Queen Mary*, 1913–14; best remembered for his brilliant record as Director of Naval Intelligence, 1914–18; retired list, 1919; MP (U) West Derby div., Liverpool, 1919–23; Eastbourne, 1925–29.
2 The copy in the Keyes MSS. is misdated August.
3 On the day war was declared Churchill became First Lord of the Admiralty – the same post he had been forced out of as a result of the Dardanelles fiasco in 1915 – and the Admiralty sent the now famous signal to the fleet: 'Winston is back.'
4 On 4 Sept., 14 Wellingtons attacked the battle cruisers *Scharnhorst* and *Gneisenau* at Brunsbüttel without scoring any hits. A 2nd wave of 15 Blenheims were directed against German warships in Schillig Roads off Wilhelmshaven. 5 Blenheims returned without finding their targets. The remainder pressed their attack at low level and 1 crashed into the side of the cruiser *Emden* after it was shot down. 3 hits were also scored on the pocket battleship *Scheer* but the bombs failed to explode. Neither ship was out of action for long. 5 Blenheims were shot down by anti-aircraft fire and 2 Wellingtons by fighters.
5 Admiral of the Fleet Sir A. Dudley P. R. Pound (1877–1943). Commanded dreadnought *Colossus* at Jutland, 1916; Director of Plans Div., Admiralty, 1922–5; Chief of Staff to Keyes in the Mediterranean Fleet, 1925–7; Assistant Chief of Naval Staff, 1927–9; commanded Battle Cruiser Squadron, 1929–31; Admiralty representative on League of Nations Advisory Commission, 1932; Second Sea Lord and Chief of Naval Personnel, 1932–5; temporary Chief of Staff, Mediterranean Fleet, 1935–6; C-in-C Mediterranean Station, 1936–9; First Sea Lord and Chief of Naval Staff, June 1939–Oct. 1943.
6 Admiral of the Fleet David Beatty (1871–1936). Created Earl, 1919. Naval Secretary to First Lord, 1912; commanded Battle Cruiser Squadron (later Force), 1912–16; Grand Fleet, 1916–19; First Sea Lord, 1919–27.
7 Admiral of the Fleet Alfred Ernle Montacute Chatfield (1873–1967). Created Baron, 1937. Served as Flag Captain to Beatty in *Lion* at Heligoland and Dogger Bank actions and battle of Jutland, 1914–16; Flag Captain and Fleet Gunnery Officer to C-in-C Grand Fleet (Beatty), 1917–19; Fourth Sea Lord, 1919–20; naval representative at Washington Naval Conference, 1921; Assistant Chief of Naval Staff, 1920–22; commanded 3rd Light Cruiser Squadron, 1923–25; Third Sea Lord and Controller of the Navy, 1925–28; C-in-C Atlantic Fleet, 1929–30; C-in-C Mediterranean Station, 1930–32; First Sea Lord and Chief of Naval Staff, 1933–38; Minister for Co-ordination of Defence, 1939–40.
8 Alfred Duff Cooper (1890–1954). Created 1st Viscount Norwich, 1952. MP (U) Oldham, 1924–29; MP (C) St George's div. of Westminster, 1931–45; Financial Secretary, War Office, 1928–29, 1931–34; Financial Secretary to the Treasury, 1934–35; Secretary of State for War, 1935–37; First Lord of the Admiralty, 1937–38; Minister of Information, 1940–41; Chancellor of the Duchy of Lancaster, 1941–43; representative of H.M. Government with French Committee of National Liberation, 1943–44; Ambassador to France, 1944–47.
9 Rt Hon Sir Geoffrey H. Shakespeare (1893–). Created Baronet, 1942. MP (Nat. Lib.) Wellingborough div. of Northamptonshire, 1922–23; MP (L)

Norwich, 1929–31; (Liberal National), 1931–45; Lord Commissioner of the Treasury and Chief Whip, Liberal Nationals, Nov. 1931–Oct. 1932; Parliamentary Secretary, Ministry of Health, 1932–36; Parliamentary Secretary to Board of Education, 1936–37; Parliamentary and Financial Secretary to the Admiralty, 1937–40; Parliamentary Secretary to Dept. of Overseas Trade, Apr.–May 1940; Parliamentary Under-Secretary of State, Dominions Office, 1940–42.

10   Shakespeare claims that his description in guarded terms of ASDIC (anti-submarine detecting device) did include the caveat the Admiralty did not claim that under all conditions the method was infallible. See Sir Geoffrey Shakespeare, Bt., *Let Candles Be Brought In* (London, 1949), pp. 213–14.

11   On 17 Sept. *Courageous* was torpedoed and sunk by *U.29* while part of a group hunting submarines in the southwestern approaches. The submarine was presented with a favourable opportunity when *Courageous* turned into the wind to recover aircraft. Her loss led to the withdrawal of fleet aircraft carriers from submarine hunting duties.

12   Admiral Sir Charles James Colebrooke Little (1882–1973). Joined Submarine Service, 1903; commanded Grand Fleet Submarine Flotilla, 1916–18; commanded *Cleopatra* in Baltic, 1919; Director of Trade Div., Naval Staff, 1920–22; Captain of the Fleet, Mediterranean Station, 1922–24; commanded *Iron Duke*, 1926–27; Director, RN Staff College, 1927–30; Rear-Admiral in 2nd Battle Squadron, 1930–31; Rear-Admiral Submarines, 1931–32; Deputy Chief of Naval Staff, 1932–35; C-in-C China Station, 1936–38; Second Sea Lord and Chief of Naval Personnel, 1938–41; Head of British Joint Staff Mission in Washington, 1941–42; C-in-C Portsmouth, 1942–45.

13   Later Admiral of the Fleet Lord Fraser of North Cape [Bruce Austin Fraser] (1888–). Created Baron, 1946. Third Sea Lord and Controller, 1939–42; 2nd-in-command, Home Fleet, 1942; C-in-C Home Fleet, 1943–44; C-in-C Eastern Fleet, 1944; C-in-C British Pacific Fleet, 1945–46; C-in-C Portsmouth, 1947–48; First Sea Lord and Chief of Naval Staff, 1948–51.

14   Vice-Admiral [later Admiral Sir] Tom Spencer Vaughan Phillips (1888–1941). Assistant Director of Plans, 1930–32; Chief of Staff and Flag Captain to C-in-C East Indies, 1932–35; Director of Plans, 1935–38; Commodore commanding Home Fleet Destroyer Flotillas, 1938–39; Deputy Chief [after Apr. 1940 Vice Chief] of Naval Staff, 1939–41; C-in-C Eastern Fleet, 1941; lost with his flagship *Prince of Wales*, 10 Dec. 1941.

15   Admiral Hon Sir Alexander Robert Maule Ramsay (1881–1972). 3rd son of 13th Earl of Dalhousie. Gunnery Officer on Carden's and De Robeck's staff at the Dardanelles, 1915; married Princess Victoria Patricia Helena Elizabeth (daughter of Duke of Connaught), 1919; naval attaché, Paris, 1919–22; Rear-Admiral Aircraft Carriers, 1933–36; C-in-C East Indies, 1936–38; Fifth Sea Lord and Chief of Naval Air Services, 1938–39.

16   Admiral of the Fleet Sir John M. De Robeck (1862–1928). 2nd son of 4th Baron De Robeck. Created Baronet, 1919. Admiral of Patrols, 1912–14; commanded Eastern Mediterranean Squadron (including Dardanelles campaign), 1915–16; C-in-C, Mediterranean, 1919–22; High Commissioner for Constantinople, 1919–20; C-in-C Atlantic Fleet, 1922–24.

17   The proposals are: Great Britain should enlist the co-operation of all nations anxious to maintain peace and build up some form of collective action while completing her own rearmament; seek Russian co-operation for the protection of Czechoslovakia and preservation of peace in Eastern Europe; and reorganise industry on a national service basis to avoid profiteering during the period of intense national preparation. Admiral Sir Roger Keyes, 'This Plan Would Stop Hitler', *Sunday Chronicle*, 20 Mar. 1938.

18   Keyes urged delegating the reconstruction of the Navy and its air service to Winston Churchill.

19   Document 4.

20   See *The Keyes Papers* Vol. I, Documents 2–9.

21 The Anson's used by RAF Coastal Command at the beginning of the war lacked sufficient range to cover the patrol line from Montrose to Obrestadt (Norway). Submarines were therefore employed, but it was difficult for them to maintain their correct positions on a diving patrol and on 10 Sept. *Triton* torpedoed and sank *Oxley*. On 14 Sept. *Sturgeon* fired at *Swordfish*, but fortunately missed. The distance between submarines was increased from 12 to 16 miles and on 20 Sept. they were withdrawn as longer range Hudson aircraft had entered service. Roskill, *The War at Sea* Vol. I, p. 66.
22 The ASDIC anti-submarine detecting device.
23 See *The Keyes Papers* Vol. I, Document 17.
24 Stanley Baldwin (1867–1947). Created Earl, 1937. MP (U) Bewdley div. of Worcestershire, 1908–37; Chancellor of the Exchequer, 1922–23; Prime Minister and First Lord of the Treasury, 1923–24, 1924–29, 1835–37; Lord Privy Seal, 1932–34; Lord President of the Council, 1931–35. On the question of restoring naval control over Fleet Air Arm. Baldwin had advised Keyes in 1936 to 'Let sleeping dogs lie.' See *The Keyes Papers* Vol. II, Document 296.
25 Thomas Walker Hobart Inskip (1876–1947). Created 1st Viscount Caldecote, 1939. MP (C) Central div., Bristol, 1918–29; Fareham div. of Hampshire, 1931–39; Solicitor-General, 1922–Jan. 1924, Nov. 1924–1928, 1931–32; Attorney General, 1928–29, 1932–36; Minister for Co-ordination of Defence, 1936–39; Secretary of State for Dominion Affairs, Jan.–Sept. 1939; Lord High Chancellor of Great Britain, 1939–40; Lord Chief Justice, 1940–46; Secretary of State for Dominion Affairs and Leader of the House of Lords, May–Oct. 1940.
26 As part of an agreement concluded in Apr. 1938 by the Chamberlain Government with the Government of Eire, the British agreed to abandon the treaty ports (Queenstown, Berehaven, Lough Swilly) whose use they had retained when the Irish Free State was created in 1921. At the time Churchill had denounced this act of appeasement and warned that in time of war a neutral Ireland might deny Great Britain the use of the bases and render defence of the Western Approaches difficult. This is exactly what happened in 1939.
27 Eamon De Valera (1882–1975). Joined Irish Volunteers, 1913; Commandant in Easter Rebellion, 1916; President, Irish Volunteers, 1917–22; President, Sinn Fein, 1917–26; President of Executive Council, Irish Free State, and Minister for External Affairs, 1932–37; Head of Government of Eire and Minister for External Affairs, 1937–48; Minister for Education, 1939–40; Leader of the Opposition, 1948–51, 1954–57; Head of the Government, 1951–54, 1957–59; President of Ireland, 1959–73.
28 Documents 3, 4.
29 Admiral of the Fleet Rosslyn Erskine Wemyss (1864–1933). Created 1st Baron Wester Wemyss, 1919. Commanded 12th Cruiser Squadron, 1914; Senior Naval Officer, Mudros, 1915; C-in-C East Indies and Egypt, 1916–17; Deputy First Sea Lord, Sept.–Dec. 1917; First Sea Lord, Jan. 1918–Nov. 1919.
30 Not reproduced.
31 Early on the morning of 14 Oct. the battleship *Royal Oak* was torpedoed and sunk with heavy loss of life by *U.47*, which had managed to penetrate the uncompleted defences of Scapa Flow.
32 Commander Robert Tatton Bower (1894–1975). Joined Royal Navy, 1907; in destroyer *Inconstant* at Jutland, 1916; in Submarine Service, 1916–18; Flag Lieutenant to C-in-C Portsmouth, 1918–19; attached RAF Staff College, 1928; retired list, 1931; MP (U) Cleveland div., Yorkshire, 1931–45; returned to active service on outbreak of war and attached to RAF Coastal Command as naval liaison officer.
33 Later Admiral Sir Guy Charles Royle (1885–1954). Naval attaché, British Embassy, Tokyo, 1824–27; commanded *Canterbury*, 1927–29; gunnery school *Excellent*, 1930–32; *Glorious*, 1933–34; Naval Secretary to First Lord; 1934–37; Vice-Admiral Aircraft Carriers, 1937–39; Fifth Sea Lord and Chief of

Naval Air Services, Nov. 1939–Apr. 1941; First Naval Member, Commonwealth Naval Board (Australia), 1941–45; retired list, 1946.

34 Bower advocated providing Coastal Command, which had hitherto been restricted to reconnaissance, convoy and anti-submarine work, with a striking force directly under the command of the C-in-C Coastal Command. At the moment the striking force was merely seconded or placed at his disposal by Bomber Command. Co-operation would also be improved if Coastal Command HQ were at the Admiralty, and Bower termed the provision of the striking force as well as adequate equipment matters of extreme urgency which should be settled within the next few days. Bower to Royle, 3 Jan. 1940, copy in Keyes MSS. 8/16.

35 A reference to the action of 13 Dec. off the estuary of the River Plate in which the 8-inch gun cruiser *Exeter* and the 6-inch gun cruisers *Ajax* and *Achilles* forced the German pocket battleship *Graf Spee* to seek shelter in Montevideo. After expiration of the time limit imposed by the neutral Uruguayan Government, the *Graf Spee* was scuttled.

36 This presumably refers to an article by Keyes expressing the naval point of view about Coastal Command which was published in the *Daily Telegraph*, 11 Jan. 1940. Lord Londonderry then wrote defending the existing system and Keyes replied to it in a lengthy letter. His basic theme was that the Navy must have operational control of aircraft, even flying boats, which performed purely naval functions. Keyes to editor, *Daily Telegraph*, 23 Jan. 1940. Copy in Keyes MSS. 8/16.

37 7th Marquess of Londonderry [Charles Stewart Henry Vane-Tempest-Stewart] (1878–1949). Succeeded father 1915. MP (C) Maidstone, 1906–15; Under-Secretary for Air, 1920–21; First Commissioner of Works, 1928–29, Aug.–Oct. 1931; Secretary of State for Air, 1931–35; Lord Privy Seal and Leader of the House of Lords, 1935; Lord Lieutenant of County Durham, 1928–49.

38 Sir Kingsley Wood (1881–1943). Knighted 1918. MP (U) Woolwich West, 1918–43; Parliamentary Private Secretary to Minister of Health, 1919–22; Parliamentary Secretary, Ministry of Health, Nov. 1924–June 1929; Parliamentary Secretary Board of Education, 1931; Postmaster-General, 1931–35; Minister of Health, 1935–38; Secretary of State for Air, 1938–40; Lord Privy Seal, Apr.–May 1940; Chancellor of the Exchequer, May 1940–Sept. 1943.

39 Captain Harold Harington Balfour (1897–). Created Baron, 1945. Joined 60th Rifles, 1914; attached to RFC, 1915; to RAF, 1918–23; MP (C) Isle of Thanet, 1929–45; Parliamentary Under-Secretary of State for Air, 1938–44; Minister Resident in West Africa, 1944–45.

40 Admiral and General at Sea Robert Blake (1599–1657). MP for Bridgwater, 1640 and 1645; fought in Parliamentary Army, 1644–45; appointed Admiral and General at Sea, 1649; member of Council of State, 1651–52; one of the commanders of the English Fleet in War against the Dutch, 1652–54; destroyed Turkish pirate fleet at Porto Farina, 1655; destroyed Spanish West Indian Fleet at Santa Cruz, 1657; died of fever while returning to England.

41 Captain Rt Hon Frederick Edward Guest (1875–1937). 3rd son of 1st Baron Wimbourne and cousin of Winston Churchill. ADC to Field Marshal Sir John French, 1914–16; MP (L) Stroud div. of Gloucester, 1923–24; Bristol North, 1924–29; joined Conservative Party, 1930; MP (U) Drake div. of Plymouth, 1931–37; Secretary of State for Air, 1921–22.

42 Not reproduced.

43 Samuel John Gurney Hoare (1880–1959). Created 1st Viscount Templewood, 1944. MP (C) Chelsea, 1910–44; Secretary of State for Air, 1922–24, Nov. 1924–June 1929; Secretary of State for India, 1931–35; Secretary of State for Foreign Affairs, 1935; First Lord of the Admiralty, 1936–37; Secretary of State for Home Affairs, 1937–39; Lord Privy Seal; 1939–40; Secretary of State for Air, 1940; Ambassador to Spain, 1940–44.

44 Keyes later noted on his copy: 'As I could not get any satisfactory answer

I raised the matter in the Navy Estimates 27.2.40. As I was told that negotiations were in progress I raised it again in the Air Estimates 7/3/40 by appealing to S. of S. for Air – NOTHING Done – in about April 1941 the Admiralty were given *nominally* at any rate operational control of the Coastal Command.'

45 Letter endorsed by Lady Keyes: 'E.K. having German measles at Portsmouth.'
46 Captain Godfrey Herbert (1884–1961). Commanded Q-ship *Baralong* which sank *U.27* in August 1915; considered a war criminal by the Germans for his failure to take the submarine crew prisoner. Operations Officer on staff of Admiral Bayly, Queenstown Command, 1917–18; retired from Navy after the war to become managing director, Daimler Car div., Birmingham Small Arms Co.; recalled to service and commanded armed merchant cruiser *Cilicia*, 1939–43.
47 Commander Peter Du Cane (1901–). Designer and builder of high speed craft (including record breaking *Bluebird II*, 1939) and MTBs; managing director, Vosper Ltd, 1931–63; Deputy Chairman, 1963– ; pilot, FAA, 1940–41.
48 Brendan Bracken (1901–1958). Created Viscount, 1952. MP (U) North Paddington, 1929–45; MP (C) Bournemouth, Nov. 1945–Feb. 1950; East Bournemouth and Christchurch, 1950–51; Parliamentary Private Secretary to the Prime Minister, 1940–41; Minister of Information, 1941–45; First Lord of the Admiralty, May–Aug. 1945.
49 Keyes obviously meant Sir Eric Seal (1898–1972). Principal Private Secretary to First Lord, 1938–40; Principal Private Secretary to Churchill as Prime Minister, 1940–41; Deputy Secretary of the Admiralty (North America), 1941–43; member of British Supply Council, Washington, 1943; Under-Secretary of Admiralty (London), 1943–45; Chief, Trade and Industry Div. Control Commission, Germany, 1946–47; Director-General Building Materials, Ministry of Works, 1947–48; Deputy Under-Secretary of State, Foreign Office (German Section), 1948–51; Deputy Secretary, Ministry of Works, 1951–59.
50 Keyes told the London correspondent of the *Gazetta del Popolo* and *Telegraffo* that the main German objective was to seize Narvik and deny the export of iron ore to Great Britain, and incidentally Italy, since the Italians could not possibly get any out of the Baltic now. The Germans had used 2 of their most powerful ships and about half their modern destroyer force to seize and hold Narvik and might have taken up positions so as to concentrate all their armaments against any ships attempting to turn them out. They failed because the battle cruiser *Scharnhorst* and 'Blücher' class heavy cruiser 'had not the guts to fight the *Renown*'. Keyes gave their relative armaments and pointed out that if the German ships had been handled like the British ships in the battle off the River Plate the *Renown* would have been at a great disadvantage. Instead, the Germans had fled and left their destroyer consorts to their fate at Narvik, where they were eventually destroyed. Memorandum by Keyes, Keyes MSS. 13/12.
51 Actually, on 9 Apr. the *Renown* was engaged with 2 battle cruisers, the *Scharnhorst* and *Gneisenau* (mistakenly identified as a heavy cruiser). In the brief engagement before the Germans outran *Renown*, *Gneisenau* suffered 3 hits. However, Keyes was mistaken about the role of the German heavy ships. They were never to enter Narvik, but rather to cover the operation and create a diversion away from the Norwegian coast.
52 The old battleships *Royal Sovereign*, *Ramilles*, *Revenge* and *Resolution*.
53 Admiral of the Fleet the Earl of Cork and Orrery [William Henry Dudley Boyle] (1873–1967). Succeeded cousin as 12th Earl, 1934. Naval attaché, Rome, 1913–15; Senior Officer in Red Sea Patrol during the First World War; commanded 1st Cruiser Squadron (in Mediterranean Fleet under Keyes) 1926–28; President, RN College, Greenwich, 1929–32; C-in-C Home Fleet,

1933–35; C-in-C Portsmouth, 1937–39; commanded combined expedition to Narvik, 1940.
54 Document 13.
55 Katherine Elizabeth Keyes (1911–). 2nd daughter of Keyes. Married Major Peter de Barton Vernon Wallop William-Powlett, 1935. Keyes was staying at the William-Powlett house in St Leonard's Terrace.
56 Count Galeazzo Ciano (1903–1944). Married Mussolini's daughter, 1930; Foreign Minister, 1936–43; Ambassador to the Vatican, Feb.–July 1943; one of those who voted for Mussolini's resignation, July 1943; later fled to Germany and, after Mussolini's liberation by the Germans, attempted reconciliation with his father-in-law; arrested by Fascists, tried for treason and executed, Jan. 1944.
57 Geoffrey Charles Tasker Keyes, VC (1917–1941). Eldest son of Keyes. Served in Palestine with Royal Scots Greys, 1938–39; joined Commandos, 1940; killed leading raid on Rommel's headquarters in Libya, 18 Nov. 1941; awarded posthumous Victoria Cross.
58 Captain [later Admiral Sir] Cecil Halliday Harcourt (1892–1959). Lent to Royal Australian Navy and commanded Australian Flotilla, 1935–37; Deputy Director of Operations Div., 1938–39; Director of Operations Div., 1939–41; commanded *Duke of York*, 1941–42; commanded successively 10th, 12th and 15th Cruiser Squadrons (including North African, Sicilian and Salerno landings), 1942–44; Naval Secretary to First Lord, 1944–45; commanded 11th Aircraft Carrier Squadron, 1945; C-in-C and head of Military Administration, Hong Kong, 1945–46; Flag Office (Air) and 2nd-in-Command, Mediterranean Fleet, 1947–48; Second Sea Lord, 1948–50; C-in-C The Nore, 1950–52; retired list, 1953.
59 Leopold III, King of the Belgians (1901–). Succeeded his father, 1934. His decision to surrender to the Germans in May 1940 and remain in Belgium instead of following the Government into exile caused much controversy. Equally controversial was his visit to Hitler at Berchtesgaden in Nov. 1940 in an attempt to obtain additional food supplies for his country and the total release of Belgian prisoners of war. Removed from his palace at Laeken by the Germans following the Normandy invasions, he was liberated in Austria by US troops in May 1945. At this time his return was opposed by the Belgian Government and he remained in Switzerland until 1950 when a plebescite indicated a slight majority of Belgians favoured his return. Leopold returned to Belgium in July 1950 but the Belgian people were bitterly divided by the royal issue and there was widespread disorder. At the beginning of Aug. Leopold transferred full powers to his son Baudoin and formally abdicated in July 1951.
60 Robert Anthony Eden (1897–1977). Created 1st Earl of Avon, 1961. MP (C) Warwick and Leamington, 1923–57; Parliamentary Private Secretary to Secretary of State for Foreign Affairs (Austen Chamberlain), 1926–29; Parliamentary Under-Secretary, Foreign Office, 1931–33; Lord Privy Seal, 1934–35; Minister without portfolio for League of Nations Affairs, 1935; Secretary of State for Foreign Affairs, 1935–38, 1940–45; Secretary of State for Dominion Affairs, 1939–40; Secretary of State for War, 1940; Leader of the House of Commons, 1942–45; Secretary of State for Foreign Affairs and Deputy Prime Minister, 1951–55; Prime Minister and First Lord of the Treasury, Apr. 1955–Jan. 1957.
61 For details see Bond, *France and Belgium, 1939–40*, pp. 66–73.
62 Diana Margaret Keyes (1910–). Keyes's eldest daughter. Married Captain [later Colonel] James Robert Johnson, 1936.
63 Elizabeth Mary Keyes (1915–). Youngest daughter of Keyes.
64 Admiral Hon Sir Algernon D. E. H. Boyle (1871–1949). 6th son of 5th Earl of Shannon. Commanded guard of honour at Windsor during Queen Victoria's funeral, 1901; commanded cruiser *Bacchante* at Dardanelles, 1915; dreadnought *Malaya* at Jutland, 1916; Chief of Staff to Keyes at Dover,

1918; Fourth Sea Lord, 1920-24; retired list, 1924; member, Port of London Authority, 1924-29.
65 Baron de Cartier de Marchienne (1871-1946). Entered Belgian diplomatic service 1892; Minister to China, 1910; Minister to the US, 1917; Ambassador to the US, 1920; Ambassador to UK, 1927-46.
66 Partially reproduced by Aspinall-Oglander, *Roger Keyes*, p. 346.
67 There were 2 engagements in Ofotfjord – 10 Apr. (destroyers) and 13 Apr. (destroyers supported by *Warspite*) – in which the 10 German destroyers of the Narvik force were sunk or scuttled by their crews.
68 Partially reproduced in Aspinall-Oglander, *Roger Keyes*, p. 346
69 Added in margin: 'Don't tell the Cabinet except I suppose N.C. [Chamberlain] would have to be told?'
70 Field Marshal William Edmund Ironside (1880-1959). Created Baron, 1941. C-in-C Allied troops, North Russia, Oct. 1918-Oct. 1919; commanded Ismid force, 1920, North Persia force, 1921; Commandant, Staff College, Camberley, 1922-26; commanded Meerut District, India, 1928-31; Quartermaster-General in India, 1933-36; GOC Eastern Command, 1936-38; Governor and C-in-C Gibraltar, 1938-39; Inspector-General of Overseas forces, 1939; CIGS, 1939-40; C-in-C Home forces, 1940; Colonel Commandant Royal Artillery, 1932-46.
71 Not reproduced.
72 Admiral Sir William Milbourne James (1881-1973). Deputy Director, RN Staff College, Greenwich, 1923-25; Director, 1925-26; Naval Assistant to First Sea Lord, 1928; COS, Atlantic Fleet, 1929-30; COS Mediterranean Fleet, 1930; commanded Battle Cruiser Squadron, 1932-34; Deputy Chief of Naval Staff, 1935-38; C-in-C Portsmouth, 1939-42; Chief of Naval Information, 1943-44; MP (U) North Portsmouth, 1943-45.
73 Document 14.
74 Marshal of the RAF Sir Cyril Louis Norton Newall (1886-1963). Created Baron, 1946. Director of Operations and Intelligence and Deputy Chief of the Air Staff, 1926-31; Air Officer commanding RAF Middle East, 1931-34; member of Air Council for Supply and Organisation, 1935-37; Chief of Air Staff, 1937-40; Governor-General and C-in-C of New Zealand, 1941-46.
75 Partially reproduced in Aspinall-Oglander, *Roger Keyes*, p. 348.
76 Major-General James Wolfe (1727-1759). Quartermaster General of Rochefort expedition, 1758; Brigadier during siege of Louisburg, 1758; commanded expeditionary force sent up the St Lawrence River against fortress of Quebec, 1759; mortally wounded at Battle of the Plains of Abraham, 13 Sept.
77 Admiral Sir Charles Saunders (1713?-1775). MP Plymouth, 1750; MP for Heydon, 1754-75; Commodore and C-in-C Newfoundland Station, 1752; Comptroller of the Navy, 1755; C-in-C of naval forces in the St Lawrence, 1759; C-in-C Mediterranean, 1760; First Lord of the Admiralty, 1766.
78 Admiral of the Fleet Edward Hawke (1705-1781). Created Baron, 1776. Defeated French squadron protecting La Rochelle convoy, 1747; MP for Portsmouth, 1747; commanded Home Fleet, 1748-52; Western Fleet, 1755-56; Mediterranean Fleet, 1756; victor in Battle of Quiberon Bay, 20 Nov. 1759; First Lord of the Admiralty, 1766-71.
79 Admiral of the Fleet Sir Charles E. Madden (1862-1935). Created Baronet, 1919. Fourth Sea Lord, 1910-11; Chief of Staff to C-in-C Grand Fleet (Jellicoe), 1914-16; 2nd-in-command Grand Fleet, 1917-19; C-in-C Atlantic Fleet, 1919-22; First Lord of the Admiralty and Chief of Naval Staff, 1927-30; retired list, 1930.
80 See *The Keyes Papers* Vol. II *1919-1938*, Documents 153, 154.
81 Admiral of the Fleet Sir Frederick Laurence Field (1871-1945). Commanded dreadnought *King George V* at Jutland, 1916; Chief of Staff to Madden, 1916-18; Director of Torpedoes and Mining, Admiralty, 1918-20; Third Sea Lord and Controller of the Navy, 1920-23; commanded Battle Cruiser

Squadron, 1923; commanded Special Service Squadron (including *Hood* and *Repulse*) during World Cruise, 1923–24; Deputy Chief of Naval Staff, 1925–28; C-in-C Mediterranean Fleet, 1928–30; First Sea Lord and Chief of Naval Staff, 1930–33.
82 Document 18.
83 Noted by Keyes: 'Sent this in to Winston on evening of 29th. He saw me later and handed it back to me – and made it clear that he did not intend to do anything.'
84 Those paragraphs marked with an asterisk in Document 21.
85 Keyes's diary notes contain the following: '24th ... Went to H. of C. Met Noel Baker who said Norwegian – late Staff Officer – very anxious to see me – incog. – he turned out to be Councillor at Legation – who told me of their anxieties – asked him to put me in touch with NA [naval attaché]. *25th.* Saw Councillor and NA. Showed the latter my plan – he confirmed my opinion, having local knowledge.' Keyes MSS. 13/12.
86 Document 16.
87 Document 14.
88 The old dreadnought *Centurion* (which Keyes had commanded in 1916) was then employed as a radio-controlled target ship for guns up to 8-inch calibre.
89 Document 15.
90 Document 16.
91 Document 17.
92 Admiral Sir Max Kennedy Horton (1883–1951). Outstanding record as submarine commander in North Sea and Baltic, 1914–18; commanded 2nd Cruiser Squadron, 1935–36; Reserve Fleet, 1937–39; Northern Patrol, Sept. 1939–Jan. 1940; Flag Officer Submarines, 1940–42; C-in-C Western Approaches, 1942–45; retired list, 1945.
93 On 8 Apr. the Admiralty ordered Horton, who had deployed 19 submarines around the Danish peninsula and off the south coast of Norway, to alter some of his inshore dispositions, notably to withdraw *Triad* from Norwegian territorial waters at the entrance to Oslo Fiord. A few hours later German Group 5 including *Lützow, Blücher* and the transport carrying the Army C-in-C and his staff passed the position *Triad* had vacated. Furthermore, it was not until 9 Apr. that the Cabinet decided to permit submarines to sink without warning German merchant shipping in the Skagerrak and Kattegat. In one of the lost opportunities of the Norwegian campaign the British submarines had been forced for 48 hours to refrain from attacking the German merchant ships they watched steaming through the Kattegat. See Rear-Admiral G. W. G. Simpson, *Periscope View: A Professional Autobiography* (London, 1972), pp. 86–9.
94 John Allsebrook Simon (1873–1954). Created Viscount, 1940. MP (Lib.) Walthamstow div., Essex, 1906–18; Spen Valley div., Yorkshire, 1922–31; (Liberal National), 1931–40; Solicitor-General, 1910–13; Attorney-General, 1913–15; Secretary of State for Home Affairs, 1915–16; Secretary of State for Foreign Affairs, 1931–35; Secretary of State for Home Affairs and Deputy Leader of the House of Commons, 1935–37; Chancellor of the Exchequer, 1937–40; Lord Chancellor, 1940–45.
95 Admiral Sir Reginald H. S. Bacon (1863–1947). Naval assistant to First Sea Lord, 1905; commanded *Dreadnought,* 1906; Director of Naval Ordnance and Torpedoes, 1907–09; retired to become managing director, Coventry Ordnance Works, 1910–15; recalled to service and commanded Dover Patrols, 1915–18. For the account of his supersession by Keyes see *The Keyes Papers* Vol. I *1914–1918,* part IV.
96 Admiral of the Fleet Sir John R. Jellicoe (1859–1935). Created Viscount, 1918; Earl, 1925. Commanded Atlantic Fleet, 1910–11; 2nd div., Home Fleet, 1911–12; Second Sea Lord, 1912–14; C-in-C Grand Fleet, Aug. 1914–Nov. 1916; First Sea Lord, Dec. 1916–Dec. 1917; Governor-General and C-in-C of the Dominion of New Zealand, 1920–24; retired, 1924.

NOTES: PART I 319

97 Document 24.
98 Document 22. There are other slight variations.
99 Document 22.
100 Viscount Halifax [Edward Frederick Lindley Wood] (1881–1959). Succeeded father as 3rd Viscount, 1934. Created Earl, 1944. MP (U) Ripon div., West Riding, Yorkshire, 1910–25; President, Board of Education, 1922–24, 1932–35; Minister of Agriculture, 1924–25; Viceroy of India, 1926–31; Secretary of State for War, 1935; Lord Privy Seal, 1935–37; Leader of the House of Lords, 1935–38; Lord President of the Council, 1937–38; Secretary of State for Foreign Affairs, 1938–40; British Ambassador at Washington, 1941–46.
101 Hon Oliver F. G. Stanley (1896–1950). Son of 17th Earl of Derby. MP (U) 1924–50; Minister of Transport, 1933–34; Minister of Labour, 1934–35; President, Board of Education, 1935–37; President, Board of Trade, 1937–40; Secretary of State for War, 1940; Secretary of State for the Colonies, 1942–45.
102 Keyes noted in his diary: 'May 1st . . . The Prime Minister, Simon and Hoare all said that the matter rested with Winston and they would support any action he recommended.'
103 Partially reproduced in Aspinall-Oglander, *Roger Keyes*, pp. 355–6.
104 Captain [later Brigadier] James Robert Johnson (1910-). Husband of Keyes's eldest daughter Diana. Served with 1st bn., Royal Welch Fusiliers, France, 1939–40; wounded and taken prisoner, May 1940; escaped Oct. 1940; subsequently served in Tunisia and Italy; commanded 1st bn., Royal Welch Fusiliers, 1951–54; military attaché, Athens, 1957; retired, 1961.
105 Colonel [later Lieut-General Baron] Alfred Van Caubergh (1891-). An artillery officer and former professor at the Ecole de Guerre. ADC to King Leopold.
106 Major-General Henry Needham (1876–1965). Military attaché, Brussels, Berne and Luxemburg, 1922; military attaché, Paris, 1927–31; Commander, Bombay District, 1931–35; retired, 1935; recalled to service on outbreak of war and subsequently head of War Office Mission to Belgian GQG, May 1940; injured in motor accident 17 May.
107 Sir Launcelot Oliphant (1881–1965). Assistant Under-Secretary of State for Foreign Affairs, 1927–36; Deputy Under-Secretary of State for Foreign Affairs, 1936–39; Ambassador to Belgium and Minister to Luxemburg, 1939–40; captured by the Germans while attempting to join the Belgian Government at Le Havre and interned in Germany, June 1940–Sept. 1941; resumed duties with Belgian and Luxemburg governments-in-exile, London, Oct. 1941–Sept. 1944; retired, Nov. 1944.
108 Charles, Prince of Belgium, Count of Flanders (1903-). Younger brother of King Leopold III. Prince Regent of Belgium, Sept. 1944–July 1950.
109 In 1919 King Albert had contributed £1,000 to the fund for a memorial to the Dover Patrol to be erected on the cliffs of Dover.
110 When Keyes was C-in-C Mediterranean in 1925, King Albert and Queen Elisabeth had stopped at Malta on their way back from a visit to India. Keyes, still recovering from the effects of an aeroplane crash [See *The Keyes Papers* Vol. II. Documents 129, 131, 132], was allowed out of hospital for the day and gave the royal couple lunch aboard his flagship.
111 Major-General Raoul F. C. Van Overstraeten (1885–1977). An artillery officer and former Commandant, Ecole de Guerre; ADC to King Albert and King Leopold; principal military adviser of King Leopold. Van Overstraeten's influence over the King and his role, which may have overshadowed the Belgian General Staff, make him an extremely controversial figure. For a critical view by the Belgian Foreign Minister at the time see Paul-Henri Spaak, *Combats Inachevés* Vol. I *De l'Indépendance à l'Alliance* (Paris, 1969), pp. 62–3. General Brooke's experience with him during an interview with Leopold is recorded in Arthur Bryant, *The Turn of the Tide: A History of the War Years Based on the Diaries of Field Marshal Lord Alanbrooke*

(New York, 1957), pp. 72–3. His own memoirs are: *Albert Ier-Léopold III. Vingt ans de politique militaire belge, 1920–1940*. (Bruges, 1949).

112 Lieut.-Colonel [later Brigadier] George Mark Oswald Davy (1898–). Succeeded General Needham as head of Military Mission to Belgian GQG; commanded 3rd and 7th Armoured Brigades in Western Desert, 1941; Director of Military Operations, GHQ, Middle East, 1942–44; Deputy Assistant Chief of Staff (Operations), Allied forces HQ, Algiers, 1944; commanded land forces, Adriatic, 1944–45; War Office representative with Polish forces, 1945–47; retired 1948; recalled to service, 1956–59.

113 Major [later Brigadier] John Malcolm Hailey (1905–). 2nd-in-command British Military Mission to Belgian GQG, 1940; commanded Field Regiment, Royal Artillery, France, 1944–45; Brigadier Royal Artillery, Far East land forces, 1955; retired, 1957.

114 In the period from the evening of 10 May to the afternoon of 17 May the demolition party for Antwerp is credited with having got away 26 Allied ships, 50 tugs, and some 600 barges, dredgers and floating cranes, while rendering unusable some 150,000 tons of oil. Although some entrances to docks and basins were blocked, 'much that was desirable had to be left undone'. See Roskill, *The War at Sea* Vol. I, p. 210.

115 Le Château Blanc at Loppem.

116 General [later Field Marshal] Viscount Gort [John Standish Surtees Prendergast Vereker] (1886–1946). Succeeded father as 6th Viscount, 1902. During First World War served in Grenadier Guards and awarded Victoria Cross, 1918; Chief of Imperial General Staff, 1937–39; C-in-C of British Field Force, 1939–40; Inspector-General to the Forces for training, 1940–41; Inspector-General Home Guard, 1941; Governor and C-in-C of Gibraltar, 1941–42; Governor and C-in-C of Malta, 1942–44; High Commissioner and C-in-C for Palestine and High Commissioner for Transjordan, 1944–45.

117 General Ironside.

118 Major W. P. Wrathall, a resident of Brussels and veteran of the First World War, had formerly been President of the British Chamber of Commerce in Belgium.

119 Albert I (1875–1934). King of the Belgians, 1909–34.

120 Elisabeth, Queen of the Belgians (1876–1965). Married Albert, 1900; mother of King Leopold and Prince Charles.

121 Commodore [later Rear-Admiral] Hubert Lynes (1874–1942). Commodore, Dunkirk, in command of Allied naval and marine forces, Flanders, June 1917–June 1918.

122 Document 31, Enclosures 3, 5 and 6.

123 Captain Geoffrey Bowlby (1883–1915). Royal Horse Guards. Younger brother of Keyes's wife. Killed near Ypres, May 1915.

124 General Maxime Weygand (1867–1965). Chief of Staff to Marshal Foch, 1914–23; head of French Military Mission to Poland, 1920; High Commissioner in Syria, 1923–24; Chief of the General Staff and C-in-C of the French Army, 1931–35, May–June 1940; C-in-C French Forces in the Levant, 1940; Minister of National Defence, June–Sept. 1940; Governor-General of Algeria and Delegate-General of Vichy Government in French Africa, 1940–41; prisoner of the Germans, 1942–45; prisoner in France, 1945–46.

125 General Gaston-Henri-Gustav Billotte (1875–1940). Commissioned into the Colonial Infantry and served in Tonkin, Shanghai and Morocco before the First World War; Chef of 3e Bureau, Etat-Major Général de l'armée, 1917–18; with Military Mission to Poland, 1920; served in Syria, 1921–24; Morocco, 1925–26; commanded troops in Indo-China, 1930–32; Inspector-General of Colonial troops, 1936; commanded 1st Army Group in north, 1939–40; Co-ordinator of Allied armies in Northeastern France and Belgium, May 1940; died as a result of injuries received in an automobile accident, 23 May.

126 Captain the Earl of Munster [Geoffrey William Hugh FitzClarence] (1906–1975). Succeeded uncle as 5th Earl, 1928. Paymaster-General, 1938–39;

Parliamentary Under-Secretary of State for War, Feb.–Sept., 1938; ADC and military assistant to Lord Gort, 1939–41; Parliamentary Under-Secretary of State for India and for Burma, 1943–44; Parliamentary Under-Secretary of State, Home Office, 1944–45; Parliamentary Under-Secretary of State, Colonial Office, 1951–54; Minister without portfolio, 1954–57.

127 Leslie Hore-Belisha (1893–1957). Created Baron, 1954. MP (Liberal National), Devonport, 1923–42; (Ind.), 1942–45; Minister of Transport, 1934–37; Secretary of State for War, 1937–40; Minister of National Insurance, 1945.

128 Comte Guillaume de Grunne, Grand Master of the Household of Queen Elisabeth.

129 Roger George Bowlby Keyes (1919–). Younger son of Keyes. Succeeded his father as 2nd Baron, 1945. Attended RN College, Dartmouth and served in Royal Navy (North Atlantic, Mediterranean and Adriatic), 1939–45; retired, 1949.

130 The destroyer *Wyvern* had been badly damaged off the coast of Holland by German aircraft.

131 Admiral Sir Bertram Home Ramsay (1883–1945). Commanded *M.25* and *Broke* in Dover Patrol, 1915–19; commanded *Weymouth*, 1924–25; *Danae*, 1925–27; on staff of RN College, Greenwich, 1927–29; commanded *Kent* and Chief of Staff, China Station, 1929–31; on staff of Imperial Defence College, 1931–33; commanded *Royal Sovereign*, 1933–36; Rear-Admiral and Chief of Staff, Home Fleet, 1935; retired list, 1938; Flag Officer Commanding Dover (including Operation 'Dynamo' – the evacuation of the BEF from Dunkirk), 1939–42; Naval Commander, Eastern Task Force (invasion of Sicily), Mediterranean, 1943; Allied Naval Commander-in-Chief, Expeditionary Force (including Normandy landings), 1944–45; lost in air crash 2 Jan. 1945.

132 Keyes had to leave for Belgium at short notice and, as the trip had been by air, travelled light. Lady Keyes subsequently sent a helmet, some field service uniform, and underclothes in a suitcase to be forwarded by the Admiral at Dover. The suitcase eventually arrived at Dunkirk but never reached Keyes in Belgium, and was apparently left behind in the evacuation. Ramsay to Keyes, 21 June and Statement by Keyes, 26 June 1940, Keyes MSS. 12/16.

133 Lieut.-General Sir Adrian Carton de Wiart, VC (1880–1963). Awarded Victoria Cross, 1916; commanded British Military Mission to Poland, 1918–24; retired 1924; recalled after outbreak of Second World War and served with British Military Mission to the Polish Army, 1939; commanded Central Norwegian (Namsos) expeditionary force, 1940; served in Middle East, prisoner of war, 1941; liberated, 1943; special military representative with General Chiang Kai-shek in China, 1943–46; retired, 1947.

134 Wynendaele, 2 miles from Thourout.

135 General [later Field Marshal] Sir John Greer Dill (1881–1944). Commandant, Staff College, Camberley, 1931–34; Director of Military Operations and Intelligence, War Office, 1934–36; Commander, British forces in Palestine, 1936–37; GOC Aldershot Command, 1937–39; commanded 1st Army Corps, BEF, 1939–40; Vice-Chief of Imperial General Staff, 1940; Chief of Imperial General Staff, 27 May 1940–Dec. 1941; head of British Joint Staff Mission to the US, 1941–44.

136 Lionel Bowlby (1892–1916). Captain, Scots Greys. Youngest brother of Keyes's wife. Killed in France, June, 1916.

137 Sir Archibald Henry Macdonald Sinclair [later 1st Viscount Thurso] (1890–1970). Created Viscount, 1952. MP (Liberal) Caithness and Sutherland, 1922–45; Chief Liberal Whip, 1930–31; Secretary of State for Scotland, 1931–32; leader of the Liberal Party, 1935–45; Secretary of State for Air, 1940–45.

138 Keyes had requested the Admiralty to send MTBs to Nieuport.

139 In June 1941 the *Daily Mirror* settled out of court, admitting that there was no foundation for its criticism and that Keyes in asking for suspension of judgement on King Leopold until all facts were known, had acted in accord-

ance with the highest traditions of honour and justice. The newspaper apologised to both Keyes and King Leopold. See Aspinall-Oglander, *Roger Keyes*, p. 379. The statements are printed in: The Belgian Ministry for Foreign Affairs, *Belgium: The Official Account of What Happened, 1939–1940* (London, n.d. [1941]), Appendix 22, pp. 106–10.

140 Reproduced in Joseph P. Kennedy and James M. Landis, *The Surrender of King Leopold* (New York, 1950), pp. 40ff.

141 Major-General [later Lieut.-General Sir] Frank Noel Mason MacFarlane (1889–1953). Military attaché, Budapest, Vienna and Berne, 1931–34; Berlin and Copenhagen, 1937–39; Director of Military Intelligence with BEF, 1939–40; head of British Military Mission to Moscow, 1941–42; Governor and C-in-C Gibraltar, 1942–44; Chief Commissioner, Allied Control Commission for Italy, 1944; Colonel Commandant, Royal Artillery, 1944; retired, 1945; MP (Labour) North Paddington, 1945–46; Chiltern Hundreds, 1946.

142 Document 30.

143 Including the statement 'Suddenly, without prior consultation, with the least possible notice, without the advice of his Ministers and upon his own personal act, he sent a plenipotentiary to the German Command, surrendered his army, and exposed our whole flank and means of retreat.' Quoted in Winston S. Churchill, *Their Finest Hour* (Boston, 1949), p. 96.

144 'Had the King left, as his Ministers ceaselessly urged him to, from the 14th May onwards, the B.E.F. might well have been left in the air on the Dyle, rather than being forced by circumstances *in France* to abandon the Belgian Army on the 27th May.'

145 General Jean-Maurice-Georges Blanchard. Commanded 1st (French) Army and succeeded Billotte as Co-ordinator of Allied Armies, 24 May. The famous historian Marc Bloch gave a description of Blanchard at the Château of Attiches: 'On that occasion I spent more than an hour in the same room as the general. During all that time he sat in tragic immobility, saying nothing, doing nothing, but just gazing at the map spread on the table between us, as though hoping to find on it the decision which he was incapable of taking.' Marc Bloch, *Strange Defeat* (New York: W. W. Norton, paperback edition, 1968), p. 28.

146 Reproduced in Churchill, *Their Finest Hour*, p. 90.

147 Reproduced in Churchill, *ibid.*, p. 91.

148 Reproduced in Kennedy and Landis, *The Surrender of King Leopold*, p. 51.

149 Reproduced *ibid.*, p. 52.

150 On 4 July Churchill reported to the House of Commons on Operation 'Catapult', the simultaneous seizure of all French ships within British ports and the neutralisation of those within reach of British seapower. This effort to ensure major portions of the powerful French fleet would never come under German control had led to considerable bloodshed at Mers-el-Kébir near Oran when Admiral Somerville's Force H opened fire after negotiations broke down. The Conservative Party, which until then had treated Churchill with a certain amount of reserve, joined in the general and sustained cheering at the end of the speech, for the ruthless action was correctly interpreted as a sign that the War Cabinet 'feared nothing and would stop at nothing' despite the seemingly desperate situation created by the fall of France. Churchill, *Their Finest Hour*, pp. 237–8.

151 Keyes had wanted to return to Dunkirk before the evacuation, but both the First Lord, A. V. Alexander, and the Prime Minister insisted he must 'have a thorough rest.' A. V. Alexander to Keyes, 28 and 30 May 1940. Keyes MSS. 140/2/3.

152 On 8 May, in his speech concerning the Norwegian campaign, Churchill said: 'I must say a word about my hon. and gallant Friend the Admiral, to whom we listened with so much pleasure yesterday, when he made the best speech I have heard him make. I sympathize intensely with his desire to lead a

valiant attack and to repeat in Scandinavian waters the immortal glories of the Zeebrugge Mole, but I am sorry that this natural impulse should have led him to cast aspersions upon his old shipmates and his old staff officers, Sir Dudley Pound and Vice-Admiral Phillips, and to speak in disparaging terms of them.' *Parliamentary Debates, Commons,* 5th series, vol. 360, cols. 1358–9.

153 On 8 June, while the evacuation of the last Allied forces from Narvik was ending, the aircraft carrier *Glorious* ran into the *Scharnhorst* and *Gneisenau* which were engaged in a sortie against Allied bases. The *Glorious* had just embarked shorebased RAF Gladiators and Hurricanes and had been ordered to proceed home independently, escorted only by the destroyers *Ardent* and *Acasta*, because she was short of fuel. The carrier was caught virtually defenceless and with her escorts sunk by gunfire with tragic loss of life in the ship's complement, FAA and RAF personnel. The *Acasta* managed to damage the *Scharnhorst* with a torpedo before she was destroyed, possibly saving the other evacuation convoys. Roskill, *The War at Sea* Vol. I, pp. 195–8.

154 Later Admiral of the Fleet Sir James Fownes Somerville (1882–1949). Director of Signal Dept., Admiralty, 1925–27; commanded *Norfolk*, 1931–32; Commodore RN Barracks, Portsmouth, 1932–34; Director of Personnel Services, Admiralty, 1934–36; commanded Destroyer Flotillas, Mediterranean Fleet, 1936–38; C-in-C East Indies, 1938–39; retired list, 1939; Officer commanding Force H, June 1940–Jan. 1942; C-in-C Eastern Fleet, 1942–44; head of British Admiralty delegation, Washington, 1944–45; Admiral of the Fleet, 1945.

155 Actually it was the battle cruiser *Strasbourg* which, along with 5 destroyers, had managed to escape from Mers-el-Kébir to Toulon. The *Dunkerque* was badly damaged by gunfire on the 3rd, and damaged again by air attack on the 6th.

156 Vice-Admiral Wilfred Tomkinson (1877–1971). 1st Lieutenant of Keyes's destroyer *Fame* in China, 1899–1900; commanded *Lurcher* in Heligoland action, 1914; Flag Captain to Keyes in *Colossus*, 1917; Captain of Dover Destroyers, 1918; Chief of Staff to Keyes in the Mediterranean, 1927; Assistant Chief of Naval Staff, 1929–31; commanded Battle Cruiser Squadron, 1931–32; prematurely relieved of his command and made one of the major scapegoats of the Invergordon affair (See *The Keyes Papers* Vol. II, part iii); retired list, 1935; Flag Officer-in-Charge, Bristol Channel, 1940–42.

157 According to one French account Keyes 'made it a special point to congratulate these French soldiers for their faithfulness in carrying out their orders'. Rear-Admiral Paul Auphan and Jacques Mordal, *The French Navy in World War II* (English tr., Annapolis, Maryland, 1959), p. 58.

158 Eva Mary Salvin Bowlby (1882–1973). Married Roger Keyes, 1906.

159 Admiral Sir Hyde Parker (1739–1807). Knighted for services in North America during the war for American Independence, 1779; C-in-C at Jamaica, 1796–1800; commanded fleet sent to Baltic (with Nelson as his 2nd-in-command) as a result of the hostile attitude of the Northern Confederacy, but subsequently recalled for his irresolution, 1801. It was at the Battle of Copenhagen that the celebrated incident occurred in which Nelson disregarded Parker's signal to 'Leave off action' by putting his telescope to his blind eye.

160 Albert Victor Alexander (1885–1965). Created Viscount, 1950; Earl, 1963. MP (Lab.) Hillsborough div. of Sheffield, 1922–31, 1935–50; Parliamentary Secretary to the Board of Trade, 1924; First Lord of the Admiralty (at the time Keyes was passed over for First Sea Lord), 1929–31, 1940–45, 1945–46; Minister of Defence, 1947–50; Chancellor of the Duchy of Lancaster, 1950–51; Leader of Labour Peers in House of Lords, 1955–65.

NOTES TO INTRODUCTION TO PART II

1 Amphibious Warfare Headquarters, *History of the Combined Operations Organisation, 1940–1945* (London, 1956), pp. 12–13; Bernard Fergusson, *The Watery Maze: The Story of Combined Operations* (London, 1961), pp. 50–1.
2 Churchill, *Their Finest Hour*, p. 249.
3 *Combined Operations Organisation*, p. 13; Fergusson, *The Watery Maze*, pp. 54–5; James Leasor, *War at the Top: based on the experiences of General Sir Leslie Hollis* (London, 1949), p. 120.
4 Leasor, *War at the Top*, p. 119.
5 Hilary St George Saunders, *The Green Beret: The Story of the Commandos, 1940–1945* (London, 1949), p. 34.
6 Lord Normanbrook, John Colville, John Martin et al., *Action this Day: Working with Churchill* (New York, 1969), pp. 62–3.
7 *Combined Operations Organisation*, p. 14.
8 For example, on 6 and 26 Sept. and 14 Oct. 1940. See 'Fuehrer Conferences on Naval Affairs' in Rear-Admiral H. G. Thursfield (ed.), *Brassey's Naval Annual 1948* (London, 1948), pp. 135, 141, 143, 145; Walter Ansel, *Hitler and the Middle Sea* (Durham, N. C., 1972), pp. 21, 24–5, 37.
9 Roskill, *The War at Sea* I, pp. 272–3, 380–1; Butler, *Grand Strategy* II, pp. 239, 431–2.
10 Keyes, 'History of Workshop', Keyes MSS. 13/5.
11 Note on Operation 'Workshop' and 'Yorker'. Admiral Sir William W. Davis to the editor, 3 June 1976.
12 *Ibid.*
13 Admiral of the Fleet Viscount Cunningham of Hyndhope, *A Sailor's Odyssey* (New York, 1951), pp. 290–1; Gerald W. Pawle, *The War and Colonel Warden: Based on the Recollections of Commander C. R. Thompson* (New York, 1963), p. 83.
14 Roskill, *The War at Sea* I, pp. 304–5; Churchill, *Their Finest Hour*, pp. 694–5; id., *The Grand Alliance* (Boston, 1950), pp. 57–9. According to Sir John Colville, then Churchill's Assistant Private Secretary, the Prime Minister, when informed on 12 Jan. that the cruiser *Southampton* had been sunk by German dive bombers in the Mediterranean, bitterly regretted having been dissuaded from allowing Operation 'Workshop' to go through. Churchill remarked, 'I flinched, and now I have cause to regret it.' Excerpt from Colville's diary reproduced in Ronald Tree, *When the Moon was High: Memoirs of Peace and War, 1897–1942* (London, 1975), p. 143.
15 *Combined Operations Organisation*, pp. 15, 155.
16 Saunders, *The Green Beret*, pp. 50–1; Roskill, *The War at Sea* I, pp. 341–2.
17 Butler, *Grand Strategy* II, pp. 432–3; J. M. A. Gwyer and J. R. M. Butler, *Grand Strategy* Vol. III *June 1941–August 1942* (London, 1964), pp. 6–8.
18 *Ibid.*, p. 515.
19 Fergusson, *The Watery Maze*, pp. 81–3.
20 'Remarks on Opposed Landings by Force Commanders Operation 'Pilgrim' 23 Aug. 1941, Keyes MSS. 13/1.
21 Brian Bond (ed.), *Chief of Staff: The Diaries of Lieutenant-General Sir Henry Pownall* Vol. II *1940–1944* (Hamden, Conn., 1974), pp. 43–4.
22 Hollis to Keyes, 2 Sept. 1941, Keyes MSS. 13/1.
23 Minutes, COS (41) 336th meeting, 29 Sept. 1941, Keyes MSS. 13/1.
24 Leasor, *War at the Top*, pp. 122–5; Churchill's terse account is in *The Grand Alliance*, p. 542.
25 Fergusson, *The Watery Maze*, pp. 84–5.

NOTES TO PART II

1 Lieut.-General [later General Sir] Alan George Bourne (1882–1967). Assistant Adjutant-General, Royal Marines, 1932–35; Colonel Commandant, Portsmouth div., Royal Marines, 1935–38; Adjutant-General, Royal Marines, 1939–43; Commander of Raiding Operations, June–July 1940; retired list, 1943.
2 Admiral Sir Walter Henry Cowan (1871–1956). Created Baronet, 1921. Commanded *Princess Royal*, 1915–17; 1st Light Cruiser Squadron, Grand Fleet, 1917–20; Baltic Force, 1919; Battle Cruiser Squadron, Atlantic Fleet, 1921–22; Commanding Officer, coast of Scotland, 1925–26; C-in-C North America and West Indies Station, 1926–28; retired list, 1931; during Second World War volunteered for service with Commando Forces (captured and exchanged), winning bar to his DSO.
3 Admiral Sir Rosslyn Wemyss. It was Wemyss who gave Keyes his great opportunity at the end of 1917 by appointing him to command of the Dover Patrol. See *The Keyes Papers* Vol. I, Part iv.
4 Major Peter de Barton Vernon Wallop William-Powlett (1903–). Married Keyes's daughter Katherine, 1935. Major, 3rd King's Own Hussars; served in Libya, 1940–41; Tobruk, 1941; Java, 1942; prisoner of war, 1942–45.
5 Randolph Frederick Edward Spenser Churchill (1911–1968). Son of Winston Churchill. MP (C) Preston, 1940–45; served with Commandos in North Africa, Italy and Yugoslavia; journalist and author (work includes 1st two volumes of a biography of his father).
6 Hermann Goering (1893–1946). Air ace during First World War; commanded Richtofen Squadron, 1918; one of early members of Nazi Party and wounded in Munich Putsch, 1923; speaker of the Reichstag, 1932; Air Minister, 1933, although also Minister-President and Minister of the Interior of Prussia, he was most closely identified with the creation and development of the Luftwaffe; tried as war criminal at Nuremberg but committed suicide shortly before his scheduled execution, 1946.
7 Brigadier-General Sir Joseph Laycock.
8 Lieut.-Colonel [later Major-General Sir] Robert Laycock (1907–1968). Joined Royal Horse Guards, 1927; commanded Commandos in Middle East, 1941–43; Chief of Combined Operations, 1943–47; retired pay, 1947; Governor and C-in-C Malta, 1954–59; Colonel Commandant Special Air Service Regiment and Sherwood Rangers, Yeomanry, 1960–68; Lord Lieutenant of Nottinghamshire, 1962–68.
9 Presumably General Sir William Wellington Godfrey (1880–1952). War Staff Officer on Carden's and De Robeck's staff at the Dardanelles, 1915–16, where he was a strong supporter of Keyes's plans (See *The Keyes Papers* Vol. I, Part ii); Colonel Commandant, Portsmouth Div., Royal Marines, 1933–35; Adjutant-General, Royal Marines, 1936–39.
10 Document 36.
11 Throughout this letter there are marginal notes referring to 6 papers Keyes sent with it.
12 Major-General [later General Sir] Hastings Lionel Ismay (1887–1965). Created Baron, 1947. Assistant Secretary, CID, 1926–30; Military Secretary to Lord Willingdon, Viceroy of India, 1931–33; Deputy Secretary, CID, 1936–38; Secretary, CID, 1938; Chief of Staff to Minister of Defence (Churchill), 1940–45; Deputy Secretary (Military) to War Cabinet, 1940–45; Chief of Staff to Viceroy of India (Earl Mountbatten), Mar.–Nov. 1947; Secretary of State for Commonwealth Relations, 1951–52; Secretary-General of North Atlantic

Treaty Organisation, 1952–57; Vice-Chairman of North Atlantic Council, 1952–56; Chairman of North Atlantic Council, 1956–57.
13 Document 40.
14 The occupation of the Azores in the event of a German invasion of Portugal.
15 According to the diagram, the Director of Combined Operations would be directly under the Minister of Defence, rather than the Chiefs of Staff.
16 Added by Keyes in holograph: 'P.M. had ordered me to consider the capture of P[antellaria].'
17 Rear-Admiral T. S. V. Phillips, Deputy Chief of Naval Staff.
18 Not reproduced.
19 Brigadier [later Major-General] Albert C. St Clair-Morford (1893–1945). Commanded Royal Marine Brigade, 1940–41; lent to Government of India, 1942–43; retired list, 1943.
20 Italicised words added in holograph.
21 Air Chief Marshal [later Marshal of the RAF] Charles Frederick Algernon Portal (1893–1971). Created Baron, 1945; Viscount, 1946. Joined RFC, 1915; commanded British forces, Aden, 1934–35; Director of Organisation, Air Ministry, 1937–38; Air Member for Personnel on the Air Council, 1939–40; AOC in C Bomber Command, Mar.–Oct. 1940; Chief of the Air Staff, 1940–45; Controller, Atomic Energy, Ministry of Supply, 1946–51.
22 The 18-knot 10,000-ton cargo-liners *Glenearn, Glengyle* and *Glenroy* were specially equipped to carry 12 ALC or SLC, 2 MLC and 850 soldiers.
23 Former cross-Channel ferries.
24 Not reproduced.
25 The Joint Planning Staff argued that raids on the mainland of Italy and on the Dodecanese should take preference over the Pantellaria operation because of their effect on Greece and Turkey.
26 Italicised words added in holograph.
27 Typescript marked by Lady Keyes: 'Copy of R.K.'s notes about Pantellaria Plans, C. of S. Meeting, 1940.'
28 At the Chiefs of Staff meeting, the points were made that the island (Pantellaria) if captured would require a considerable garrison to hold and would require a large number of anti-aircraft guns to protect the harbour and aerodrome. While the advantages conferred by the use of this aerodrome would be considerable, the shortage of anti-aircraft guns in Malta, Crete, and the Middle East made it unsound to undertake a commitment requiring further dispersion of anti-aircraft defences. Keyes was asked to prepare a statement showing when the available landing craft carriers would be ready to leave Great Britain, what Special Service troops and landing craft it was proposed to dispatch in them, and an outline of possible raiding operations against the mainland of Italy for which these troops would be suitable. Keyes wrote on his copy of the COS conclusions: 'A very satisfactory *"Do Nothing"* Meeting' Extract from COS (40) 26th meeting (O), 16 Nov. 1940, Keyes MSS. 140/3.
29 Among his points, Keyes emphasised the immense value of Pantelleria – 150 miles N.W. of Malta – as an outpost for aircraft to cover ships passing through or operating in the northern portion of the Malta Channel. He also questioned the large garrison the EPS considered necessary for the island since he doubted that the Italians would undertake an amphibious operation for its recapture unless they had complete command of the sea. Keyes to COS, 18 Nov. 1940, Keyes MSS. 140/3.
30 Not reproduced.
31 Paymaster Captain Hubert Woolley, acting as Keyes's secretary.
32 The capture of Pantelleria, code name later altered to 'Workshop'.
33 Possibly Arthur Greenwood, Minister without portfolio in the War Cabinet. However, this is probably a typographical error and Keyes meant A.S. – Sir Archibald Sinclair, Secretary of State for Air.
34 Joint Planning Staff, Executive Planning Section.

35 A. V. Alexander, First Lord of the Admiralty.
36 Clementine Hozier Churchill (1885–1977). Wife of Winston Churchill.
37 John Rupert Colville (1915–). 3rd Secretary, Diplomatic Service, 1937; Assistant Private Secretary to: Chamberlain, 1939–40; Churchill, 1940–41, 1943–45; Attlee, 1945; served as pilot in RAF, 1941–43; Private Secretary to Princess Elizabeth, 1947–49; First Secretary, British Embassy, Lisbon, 1949–51; Joint Principal Private Secretary to the Prime Minister (Churchill), 1951–55.
38 Brigadier Morford and the EPS proposed for Operation 'Brisk' a plan involving the employment of all 4 Commandos in addition to Force 101, a total of approximately 4,000 troops. Keyes considered this excessive to overcome the resistance of neutrals, possibly supported by a few Germans. He, of course, wanted the Commandos for Operation 'Workshop'. 'A History of Workshop', Keyes MSS. 13/5.
39 Lieut.-Colonel [later Lieut.-General Sir] Ian Jacob (1899–). Military Assistant Secretary, Committee of Imperial Defence, 1938; Military Assistant Secretary to the War Cabinet, 1939–46; retired pay, 1946; Chief Staff Officer to Minister of Defence and Deputy Secretary (Military) of the Cabinet, 1952; Director-General of the BBC, 1952–60.
40 Vice-Admiral Theodore John Hallet (1878–1957). Naval Assistant to Second Sea Lord, 1922–24; Commanding Officer Coast of Scotland, 1929–31; retired list, 1933; returned to service after outbreak of Second World War as Convoy Commodore; in charge of Bray sector of Dunkirk evacuation; with destroyer *Vanquisher* assisted uncompleted French battleship *Jean Bart* to escape from St Nazaire, June 1940; assumed command of Combined Training Centre (H.M.S. *Quebec*) at Inveraray, Sept. 1940.
41 Brigadier [later Major-General] Joseph Charles Haydon (1899–1970). Military Assistant to Secretary of State for War, 1938; Lieut.-Col. commanding 2nd bn., Irish Guards, 1939–40; commanded Special Service Brigade (Commandos), 1940–42; Vice-Chief of Combined Operations Staff, 1942; commanded 1st Guards Brigade (Italy), 1944; British Joint Services Mission, Washington, 1944–45; British Army representative, Joint Chiefs of Staff, Australia, 1946–47; Chief Intelligence Div., Control Commission, Germany, 1948–50; retired pay. 1951.
42 Rear-Admiral [later Admiral] Sir Henry Harwood (1888–1950). Commanded *Warwick* and 9th Destroyer Div., 1929; *London*, 1932–34; Commodore commanding South America division, 1936–39; commanded British forces in action against *Graf Spee* off the River Plate (promoted to Rear-Admiral and awarded KCB), Dec. 1939; a Lord Commissioner of the Admiralty and Assistant Chief of Naval Staff (Foreign), 1940–42; C-in-C Mediterranean, 1942; C-in-C Levant, 1943; Flag Officer commanding Orkneys and Shetlands, 1944–45; retired list. 1945.
43 The *Ulster Monarch* (3,791 tons), *Royal Scotsman* (3.288 tons) and *Royal Ulsterman* (3,244 tons), formerly engaged in passenger service across the Irish Sea, were converted to carry troops and landing craft. The *Ulster Queen*, a sister ship of the *Ulster Monarch*, was converted to an auxiliary anti-aircraft ship and later altered to a fighter direction ship. A 3rd ship, *Ulster Prince*, was used as a store carrier and lost in the Aegean, Apr. 1941.
44 Vice-Admiral Sir Geoffrey Blake (1882–1968). Gunnery Commander in *Iron Duke* at Jutland, 1916; naval attaché to the US. 1919–21; commanded *Queen Elizabeth*, 1921–23; Deputy Director, RN Staff College, 1925–26; Director, RN Staff College, 1926–27; Chief of Staff in Atlantic Fleet, 1927–29; Commodore in Command of New Zealand Station and First Naval Member, New Zealand Naval Board, 1929–32; Fourth Sea Lord, 1932–35; Vice-Admiral commanding Battle Cruiser Squadron and 2nd-in-Command Mediterranean Fleet, 1936–38; placed on retired list as a result of an accident, 1938; a Lord Commissioner of the Admiralty and Assistant Chief

of Naval Staff (Foreign), Apr.–Dec. 1940; Flag Officer Liaison US Navy in Europe, 1942–45; Gentleman Usher of the Black Rod, 1945–49.

45 Admiral [later Admiral of the Fleet] Sir Andrew Browne Cunningham (1883–1963). Created Baron, 1945; Viscount, 1946. Rear-Admiral commanding Destroyer Flotillas, Mediterranean Fleet, 1934–36; commanded Battle Cruiser Squadron and 2nd-in-Command, Mediterranean Fleet, 1937–38; Deputy Chief of Naval Staff, 1938–39; C-in-C Mediterranean, 1939–42; head of British Admiralty delegation in Washington, 1942; Naval C-in-C Expeditionary force, North Africa, 1942; C-in-C Mediterranean, 1943; First Sea Lord and Chief of Naval Staff, 1943–46.

46 General [later Field Marshal] Sir Archibald Percival Wavell (1883–1950). Created Earl, 1947. Commanded British forces in Palestine and Transjordan, 1937–38; GOC in C. Southern Command, 1938–39; C-in-C Middle East, 1939–41; C-in-C India, 1941–43; Supreme Commander, S.W. Pacific, Jan.–Mar. 1942; Viceroy and Governor General of India, 1943–47.

47 Later Major-General Alan Hugh Hornby (1894–1958). Served in France and Belgium, 1914–18; Iraq operations, 1919–20; Middle East, Sicily and Italy, 1939–45; retired pay, 1948; Colonel Commandant Royal Artillery, 1953–58.

48 Captain [later Admiral Sir] William W. Davis (1901–). Deputy Director of Plans, 1940–42; commanded *Mauritius*, 1943–44; Director of Under Water Weapons, Admiralty, 1945–46; Imperial Defence College, 1947; COS to C-in-C Home Fleet, 1948–49; Naval Secretary, Admiralty, 1950–52; 2nd-in-Command Mediterranean, 1952–54; Vice-Chief of the Naval Staff, 1954–57; C-in-C Home Fleet and NATO C-in-C Eastern Atlantic Area, 1958–60.

49 Captain [later Admiral Sir] Charles Saumarez Daniel (1894–). Commanded *Glorious*, 1933–35; Captain D, 8th Destroyer Flotilla, 1938–40; Director of Plans, Admiralty, 1940–41; commanded *Renown*, 1941–43; Flag Officer, Combined Operations and Naval Chief of Staff, 1943; commanded 1st Battle Squadron, British Pacific Fleet, 1944–45; Third Sea Lord and Controller of the Navy, 1945–49; Commandant Imperial Defence College, 1949–51; retired list, 1952.

50 Mary Churchill (1922–). Youngest daughter of Winston Churchill.
51 Diana Churchill (1909–1963). Eldest daughter of the Prime Minister.
52 Commander Charles Ralfe Thompson (1894–1966). Served primarily in submarines in China and in Mediterranean, 1915–31; Flag Lieutenant to Admirals Waistell and Kelly (C's-in-C, Portsmouth), 1931–36; Flag Lieutenant and Flag Commander to the Board of Admiralty, 1936–40; retired list, 1939; Personal Assistant to Churchill, 1940–45.
53 The landings at Suvla Bay during the Dardanelles Campaign, August 1915. See *The Keyes Papers* Vol. I, Part ii.
54 Plan to capture the Azores in the event of Vichy France declaring war.
55 The occupation of the Cape Verde Islands.
56 The British and Free French expedition to Dakar.
57 Inter-Service Planning Staff.
58 Vice-Admiral John H. D. Cunningham and Major-General N. M. S. Irwin.
59 The reference in the typescript is questioned. From the context Keyes probably meant the present CNS, i.e. Pound.
60 Wing Commander Frank A. Brock, RNAS. Son of the founder of Brock's Fireworks. Killed in Zeebrugge raid, 23 Apr. 1918.
61 Forward Operational Planning Section.
62 Captain John Knox, head of the Combined Operations Intelligence Section.
63 Clement Richard Attlee (1883–1967). Created 1st Earl, 1955. MP (Lab.) Limehouse div. of Stepney, 1922–50; West Walthamstow, 1950–55; Deputy Leader of Labour Party in House of Commons, 1931–35; Leader of the Opposition, 1935–40; Lord Privy Seal, 1940–42; Secretary of State for Dominion Affairs, 1942–43; Lord President of the Council, 1943–45; Deputy Prime Minister, 1942–45; Prime Minister and First Lord of the Treasury, 1945–51; Minister of Defence, 1945–46; Leader of the Opposition, 1951–55.

64 Lord Beaverbrook [William Max Aitken] (1879-1964). Created Baron, 1917. MP (U) Ashton-under-Lyne, 1910-16; Chancellor of the Duchy of Lancaster and Minister of Information, 1918; Minister for Aircraft Production, 1940-41; Minister of State, 1941; Minister of Supply, 1941-42; Lord Privy Seal, Sept. 1943-July 1945. Owner of the *Daily Express, Sunday Express* and *Evening Standard*.

65 Roger II (1101-1154). Norman Count of Sicily, crowned King of Sicily, Apulia and Capua, 1130. Roger established considerable North African holdings for what he hoped would be a Mediterranean Empire. The Normans, faced with a cosmopolitan kingdom, proved extremely flexible and tolerant and the court at Palermo was one of the most brilliant of its age.

66 Admiral Sir Herbert W. Richmond (1871-1946). Assistant Director of Operations, 1913-15; liaison officer with Italian Fleet, 1915; commanded *Commonwealth, Conqueror* and *Erin*, 1915-18; Director of Staff Duties and Training, 1918; President of RN College, 1920-23; C-in-C East Indies Squadron, 1924-25; Commandant of Imperial Defence College, 1927-28; retired list, 1931; Master of Downing College, 1936-46. Richmond was a prolific writer on naval subjects and was also noted for his sometimes pungent criticism of contemporaries.

67 Italicised names added later in holograph.

68 John Theodore Cuthbert Moore-Brabazon (1884-1964). Created 1st Baron Brabazon of Tara, 1942. A pioneer aviator and holder of Certificate No. 1 granted by Royal Aero Club for pilots; served in RFC, 1914-18; MP (U) Chatham div. of Rochester, 1918-29; Wallasey, 1931-42; Parliamentary Secretary to Minister of Transport, 1923-24, Nov. 1924-27; Minister of Transport, 1940-41; Minister of Aircraft Production, 1941-42. A member of numerous committees and societies connected with aviation.

69 For the Keyes-Chatfield correspondence see *The Keyes Papers* Vol. II, Documents 298-300, 302-7.

70 Vice-Admiral [later Admiral of the Fleet Sir] John Henry Dacres Cunningham (1885-1962). Director of Plans Div., Admiralty, 1930-32; commanded *Resolution*, 1933; Assistant Chief of Naval Staff, 1936-37; Assistant Chief of Naval Staff (Air), 1937-38; Chief of Naval Air Services, 1938; commanded 1st Cruiser Squadron, 1938-41; naval commander of Operation 'Menace', the unsuccessful attempt to secure Dakar for the Free French, Sept. 1940; Fourth Sea Lord and Chief of Supplies and Transport, 1941-43; C-in-C Levant, 1943; C-in-C Mediterranean and Allied Naval Commander Mediterranean, 1943-46; First Sea Lord and Chief of Naval Staff, 1946-48.

71 Air Chief Marshal Sir Frederick William Bowhill (1880-1960). Officer in Merchant Service, 1896-1912; in RFC (Naval Wing), RNAS and RAF, 1913-18; Director of Organisation and Staff Duties, Air Ministry, 1929-31; Air Member for Personnel on Air Council, 1933-37; Air Officer Commanding-in-Chief, Coastal Command, 1934-41; commanded Ferry Command, 1941-43; Air Officer commanding Transport Command, 1943-45; retired, 1945; Chief Aeronautical Adviser to Ministry of Civil Aviation, 1946-57.

72 The question of the loss of the carrier *Glorious* – sunk by the battlecruisers *Scharnhorst* and *Gneisenau* while escorted by only 2 destroyers at the time of the evacuation of Narvik the preceding June – was raised in the House of Commons on 7 Nov. Commander Bower charged that the evacuation of Narvik was considered of such a secret nature that none but the higher officers were informed it was to take place, and, consequently, the expected co-operation between the staffs of the Admiralty, Royal Air Force Coastal Command, and Vice-Admiral commanding Submarines did not take place. Bower had been on duty as naval liaison officer at Coastal Command at the time and reported they knew nothing of it nor, he charged, did such a highly-placed officer as the Director of Operations at the Admiralty. On 20 Nov. Bower withdrew part of his statement after the Director of Operations had written him stating he was fully informed, but confirming Bower's

account that for reasons of secrecy Coastal Command was not informed. *Parliamentary Debates, Commons,* 5th series, vol. 365, cols. 1540–2, 1986–7. See Roskill, *The War at Sea* Vol. I, pp. 197–8.

73 Bower's charge that after writing the First Lord about these matters he was victimised by being given an inferior command resulted in an acrimonious exchange between himself and A. V. Alexander.

74 Probably Document 31.

75 Captain Guy D'Oyly-Hughes (1891–1940). 1st Lieutenant of submarine *E.11* at the Dardanelles (and described by Keyes in regard to *E.11*'s exploits in the Marmora as: 'A proper man, worthy to be second in command to Nasmith.', *Naval Memoirs* I, p. 428); Captain (S), 1st Submarine Flotilla, 1934–36; Chief of Staff to C-in-C Plymouth, 1936–38; commanded carrier *Glorious*, 1939–40; lost with his ship 8 June 1940.

76 Document 51.

77 At the London naval conference in 1930 the minimum British demand with regard to cruisers was reduced from 70 to 50.

78 Admiral Sir William W. Fisher (1875–1937). Commanded dreadnought *St Vincent* at Jutland, 1916; Director of Anti-Submarine Div., Admiralty, 1917–18; Chief of Staff in Mediterranean Fleet, 1919–22; in Atlantic Fleet, 1922–24; Rear-Admiral in 1st Battle Squadron, 1924–25; Fourth Sea Lord, 1927–28; Deputy Chief of Naval Staff 1928–30; C-in-C Mediterranean, 1932–36; C-in-C Portsmouth, 1936–37.

79 Kassala and Gallabat are on the frontier between Ethiopia and the Sudan. In early July they had been captured by Italian forces who also overran British Somaliland in Aug. The few RAF aircraft squadrons in the Red Sea area kept up a spirited harassment of the Italians. Wavell had as his objective, after securing Egypt in the west, the liquidation of Italian forces in East Africa. Butler, *Grand Strategy* Vol. II, p. 379.

80 Admiral of the Fleet Sir Arthur Knyvet Wilson, VC (1842–1921). Awarded Victoria Cross for heroism at El Teb, 1884. Third Sea Lord, 1897–1901; commanded Channel Squadron, 1901–03; C-in-C Home and Channel Fleets, 1903–07; First Sea Lord, 1910–11; loosely attached in unofficial and unpaid capacity to War Staff, 1914–16.

81 Endorsed by Keyes: 'Duplicate of letter sent to C in C Mediterranean by air – another copy sent by Sir Walter Cowan., 30.1.41.'

82 The successful attack on the Italian Fleet in Taranto harbour by carrier-borne Swordfish aircraft on the night of 11–12 Nov.

83 The former 4,100-ton cross-Channel steamers *Princess Beatrix* and *Koningin Emma*.

84 Note added by General Haydon: 'Following is Brief from which Operation "Workshop" was explained to the Cabinet War Committee in Cabinet War Room under Foreign Office on Monday, 9th December. Present at meeting were: Prime Minister, Eden, Alexander, [Archibald] Sinclair, Beaverbrook, Attlee, Dill, Pound, Portal, with Sir Roger Keyes and self. News of first advance in Egypt came during meeting.'

85 It is interesting to compare this modest 1940 plan with the actual capture of Pantelleria (Operation 'Corkscrew') in June 1943 when the island was virtually blasted into submission by intense air and naval bombardment. Pantelleria had been subjected to heavy Allied air attack in May, and in the period from 6 to 11 June bombing was almost continuous with 5,324 tons of bombs dropped from 3,712 bomber and fighter-bomber sorties, with additional bombardments by cruisers and destroyers. The Italian garrison of approximately 12,000 surrendered on the 11th as an assault force from the 1st (British) Infantry Div. was landing. See Brigadier C. J. C. Molony, *The Mediterranean and Middle East* Vol. V *The Campaign in Sicily, 1943 and the Campaign in Italy, 3 Sept. 1943 to 31 March 1944* (London, 1973), pp. 49–50; Cunningham, *A Sailor's Odyssey*, pp. 542–3.

86 The occupation of the Dodecanese.

NOTES: PART II

87 A fast convoy composed of 3 ships bound for Piraeus carrying stores for the Greek Army, and 1 ship for Malta.
88 James Maxton (1885–1946). MP (Lab.) Bridgeton div. of Glasgow, 1922–46; Chairman of Independent Labour Party, 1926–31, 1934–39. The statement was made 13 May during the debate on the formation of Churchill's Cabinet.
89 Major-General [later Lieut.-General] Noel Mackintosh Stuart Irwin (1892–1972). Commanded 6th Infantry Brigade, 1939; designated military commander for expedition against Dakar, 1940; commanded 2nd Infantry Div.; 38th Div.; XI Corps; IV Indian Corps; Eastern Army, India; GOC West Africa Command, 1946–48; retired, 1948.
90 In a minute on General Irwin's report on Operation 'Menace' Churchill wrote: 'He [Irwin] would make a mistake, however, if he assumed . . . that ships can in no circumstances engage forts with success. This might well be true in the fog conditions which so unexpectedly and unnaturally descended upon Dakar; but it would not necessarily be true of the case where the ships' guns could engage the forts at ranges to which the forts could not reply, or where the gunners in the forts were frightened, inefficient, or friendly to the attacking force.' Churchill to CIGS and Sir James Grigg, 21 Oct. 1940, reproduced in Churchill, *Their Finest Hour*, pp. 681–2.
91 This probably refers to an incident not mentioned by Keyes in his history of 'Workshop'. On weekends when a full moon made Chequers particularly vulnerable to attack from the air Churchill stayed at Ditchley, the Oxfordshire home of Mr Ronald Tree. According to the diary of Sir John Colville, then assistant private secretary to the Prime Minister, after dinner on the 14th: 'Roger Keyes who has been scheming to come to Ditchley for the last two days, rang up and asked point blank. Winston, who is at long last becoming bored with his importunity, refused to speak to him and sent a snubbing answer through me.' However, on Sunday afternoon (15th): 'Sir Roger Keyes, in spite of all injunctions, arrived. He was greeted with indignation by Winston when he returned from Blenheim, but he agreed to talk to him. His whole aim is to undo the decisions reached at yesterday's conferences, namely that Operations "Workshop" and "Excess" should be postponed in view of the threat of developments in Spain and elsewhere. We were all thunderstruck by his audacity: he carries the Zeebrugge spirit too far with private life.' Reproduced in Tree, *When the Moon was High*, pp. 136–7.
92 Keyes was informed at Chequers on the 14th that 'Workshop' would be postponed until the following month. In the meantime the force would be held at 3 days' notice in case it was required elsewhere, notably for the Azores or Cape Verde Islands.
93 Operation for the seizure of Tangier.
94 This reference is not clear, but there is a note [Holograph]: ' "We will end doing *Nothing*." Written by R. K. and passed to General Haining, VCIGS after listening to the P.M. and Chiefs of Staff at Chequers on 14 Dec., 1940', Keyes MSS. 140/3/1.
95 Endorsed by Keyes 'Received 18th.'
96 '*10th December*. I was informed of this decision [Approval for Keyes's striking force, now named 103] to assemble at Lamlash and sail with the convoy on 18 December and left for Arran at once and arrived the following day to find that the ships and troops, which had been much delayed by fog, had only arrived at Lamlash the previous afternoon. Although only 8 days remained for training every effort was made to get the expedition ready to sail on 18th, so as to be able to carry out the operation before 1st January when the dark period ended.

14th December. At the invitation of the Prime Minister, I went to Chequers and was told that owing to the information received, the operation 'Workshop' would be postponed until the following month. In the meantime, Force 103 was to be held at three days' notice as it might be required to operate elsewhere [The Azores or Atlantic Islands].

I stressed the danger of being forestalled by the Germans and suggested that as all the potential objectives were East or West of the latitudes of the Straits of Gibraltar, 7 days distant from 103's base, it might be advisable to sail the Force as originally intended. During the 7 days' interval, the situation was likely to clear, and we might then be in a position to take the initiative and strike first instead of leaving it to the enemy to do so.

However this was not approved and the sailing of Force 103 on the 18th December was definitely cancelled. Extract from Keyes's Paper, 'History of Workshop', Keyes MSS. 13/5.

97 Document 57.
98 Robin E. R. Johnson (1937–). Son of Keyes's daughter Diana.
99 '*17th December.* The three [*Glengyle, Glenroy, Royal Scotsman*] ships, as previously arranged, proceeded to Greenock complete with stores, fuel and water, and embarked landing craft and MTBs. They were much impeded by bad weather, and did not return until the evening of the 19th December.

20th December. In the early morning between 0100 and 0530, a full dress rehearsal was carried out which provided correct timing and valuable experience to enable the operation plans to be perfected.

Brigadier Haydon and I were then able to report that Force 103 was ready to carry out "Workshop" or any other offensive operation required of it.' Extract from Keyes's 'History of Workshop', Keyes MSS. 13/5.
100 Document 57.
101 Document 56.
102 Admiral of the Fleet John Jervis, Earl of St Vincent (1735–1823). C-in-C Mediterranean, 1795–99; defeated Spanish fleet off Cape St Vincent, 14 Feb. 1797; created Earl, 1797; commanded Channel Fleet, 1800–01; 1806–07; First Lord of the Admiralty, 1801–4.
103 Admiral of the Fleet Richard, 1st Earl Howe (1726–1799). Treasurer of the Navy, 1765–70; C-in-C North America, 1776–78; First Lord of the Admiralty, 1783–88; created Earl, 1788; commanded Channel Fleet in victory over French Fleet, 1 June 1794.
104 Captain [later Rear-Admiral] Loben E. H. Maund (1892–1957). Commandant Combined Operations Development Centre, 1938; Naval Chief of Staff for Narvik Operations, 1940; Deputy Director of Training and Staff Duties (Combined Operations), 1940; commanded *Ark Royal,* 1941; Director of Combined Operations, Middle East, 1942–43; India, 1943; Rear-Admiral Landing Ships and Craft, 1944–45.
105 Maund had written a paper in which he argued in favour of the DCO's duties being assumed by a Landing Operations Staff in the Admiralty and the respective Home and Foreign Commanders-in-Chief. According to Keyes's marginal notes, the paper was circulated in the Admiralty and secretly in the DCO's Office in Jan. 1941. Memorandum by Maund, 'DCO Organisation', 11 Dec. 1940. Copy in Keyes MSS. 13/16.
106 Colonel [later Lieut.-General Sir] Leslie Chasemore Hollis (1897–1963). Joined Royal Marine Light Infantry, 1914; Assistant Secretary, Committee of Imperial Defence, 1936; Senior Assistant Secretary in office of War Cabinet, 1939–46; Chief Staff Officer to Minister of Defence and Deputy Secretary (Military) of the Cabinet, 1947–49; Commandant General, Royal Marines, 1949–52; retired, 1952.
107 Randolph Churchill.
108 General Sir Robert Hadden Haining (1882–1959). Deputy Director of Military Operations and Intelligence, War Office, 1933–34; Commandant, Imperial Defence College, 1935–36; Director of Military Operations and Intelligence, 1936–38; commanded British forces in Palestine and Transjordan, 1938–39; GOC-in-C Western Command, 1940; Vice-Chief of Imperial General Staff, 1940–41; Intendant-General, Middle East, 1941–42; retired pay, 1942.
109 A history of 'Workshop'.

110 A radio broadcast to the people of Italy (23 Dec. 1940) in which Churchill concluded: 'Where is it that the Duce has led his trusting people after eighteen years of dictatorial power? What hard choice is open to him now? It is to stand up to the battery of the whole British Empire on sea, in the air, and in Africa, and the vigorous counter-attack of the Greek nation; or, on the other hand, to call in Attila over the Brenner Pass with his hordes of ravenous soldiery and his gangs of Gestapo policemen to occupy, hold down and protect the Italian people, for whom he and his Nazi followers cherish the most bitter and outspoken contempt that is on record between races.' Text in Robert Rhodes James (ed.) *Winston S. Churchill: His Complete Speeches 1897–1963* Vol. VI *1935–1942* (New York, 1974), p. 6325.

111 Vice-Amiral d'Escadre Emile-Henry Muselier (1882–1965). Commanded 2nd Cruiser Div., Mediterranean, 1938; Admiral commanding port of Marseilles, 1939; joined General de Gaulle, July 1940; C-in-C Free French naval forces, 1940–42; C-in-C Free French Air Force, 1940–41; quarrelled with de Gaulle (arrested in Jan. 1941 by Scotland Yard and released after 10 days with a letter of apology from Eden); resigned as Commissioner of Marine in French National Committee and subsequently relieved of his command as C-in-C Free French Navy, Feb.–Mar. 1942; Assistant to General Giraud in Algiers, 1943.

112 General Charles André Joseph Marie de Gaulle (1890–1970). Commanded 4th Armoured Div., 1940; Under-Secretary of National Defence, June 1940; Chief of Free French forces and President of French National Committee, 1940–42; President of French Committee of National Liberation, 1943; President of Provisional Government of French Republic, 1944–46; Premier (with full powers to draft a new Constitution), June 1958–Jan. 1959; President of Fifth French Republic, 1959–69.

113 General Ismet Inönü (1884–1973). Under-Secretary for War, 1918; joined Mustafa Kemal, 1920; Deputy for Edirne in National Assembly; Chief of General Staff, 1920; commanded Western Front and defeated Greek army at Inönü (which he subsequently adopted as his surname), 1921; Minister of Foreign Affairs, 1922; head of Turkish delegation at Lausanne, 1922–23; Prime Minister of Turkish Republic, 1923–24, 1925–35, 1961–65; Leader of the Republican People's Party, 1938–72; President of the Turkish Republic, 1938–50.

114 See *The Keyes Papers* Vol. II, Documents 67–76.

115 'It was decided to let EXCESS go through without WORKSHOP in order to keep the Commandos free for contingencies arising out of the Spanish situation, and also for further training.' Minute by Churchill, 28 Dec. 1940, Keyes MSS. 13/5. The concluding paragraph of this minute, referring to the high value of 'Workshop', is reproduced in Churchill, *The Second World War* Vol. III *The Grand Alliance* (Boston, 1950), p. 58.

116 Brigadier Haydon's letter to Keyes (30 Dec. 1940) concerning the harmful effects on troop morale of the postponement is substantially reproduced in Aspinall-Oglander, *Roger Keyes*, pp. 397–8.

117 '*31st December* . . . I was told that as no destroyers were available to carry out "Workshop" it had been decided to delay its departure until 17th February. The C.O.S. suggested that "Workshop" might go with "Excess" which was delayed at Gibraltar ("Workshop" was originally to have sailed with "Excess" on 18th January). The C.N.S., however, said that "Excess" would not sail until the end of January and would not arrive appreciably earlier than a convoy leaving England for the Mediterranean around the Cape on 7th January, and asked me if I would like my force to sail with it. I said I preferred this to keeping the troops, who were already trained to high pitch, waiting in Arran. I hoped, of course, that wiser counsels would prevail and circumstances would make it possible to send the forces through the Mediterranean before it was too late.

In any case, in view of the opposition which the various Inter-Staff Committees had managed to marshal, I felt it would be far better to get the forces away into the Mediterranean, where there was an immense field for harrying the enemy with sea-borne troops, and the Commander-in-Chief was apparently free from such interference as I was encountering.' Extract from Keyes's 'History of Workshop', Keyes MSS. 13/5.

118 The Chiefs of Staff met the night of the 31st under the Chairmanship of the Prime Minister and decided that Operation 'Workshop' should not go via the Cape with Convoy W.S.5(b) on 7 Jan., but should sail about 17 Feb. as previously decided. Hollis to DCO, 1 Jan. 1941, Keyes MSS. 13/5. Keyes noted '. . . the Prime Minister did not approve for reasons he gave me verbally', 'A History of Workshop', *ibid.* Hornby reported he had recommended to the Chiefs of Staff on 30 Dec. that the Commandos go round the Cape and mount 'Workshop' from Egypt, but was told 'the Prime Minister had already vetoed that, probably, I suggest, because he suspected a plot on the part of the Chiefs of Staff to put WORKSHOP off the map.' Précis enclosed with Hornby to Keyes, 31 Dec. 1940, *ibid.*

119 Keyes learned from the Chiefs of Staff that Churchill had accepted their advice to abandon 'Workshop' and did not wish to discuss the matter. However, he begged Churchill to see him. Keyes to Churchill, 21 Jan. 1941, Keyes MSS. 140/3/1.

120 Three of the Commandos were ordered to the Middle East, to be carried in the 3 'Glen' liners.

121 Sardinia.

122 Added by Keyes in margin: 'Dickie Mountbatten.'

123 Document 64.

124 Document 65.

125 Document 67.

126 On the night of 20 Jan. Churchill and the Chiefs of Staff reached the decision: 'Three "Glen" ships with full complement of landing craft and with the Commandos assigned to these ships on board, less one Commando (which General Wavell already has) should sail at earliest round the Cape to Suez.' The DCO was to stay in England to reorganise and rebuild the remaining Commandos up to their full strength of 5,000. Minute by Churchill, 21 Jan. 1941. Copy in Keyes MSS. 13/5.

127 Document 67.

128 Document 65.

129 Document 71.

130 William Pitt (1708–1778). Created Earl of Chatham, 1767. As Secretary of State in coalition government with the Duke of Newcastle, Pitt was the real leader of war effort against France, 1757–61; Prime Minister, 1766–67.

131 Not reproduced. They included Keyes's minute to the COS's Committee 'after listening to the complaints of the two Commanders of "Menace" as to the futility of the plan given to them and the lack of supply of information. The shipping miscarriages would have been disastrous, if they had not been discovered and remedied by an officer on my Staff, whom I lent to the Commanders. This was the only part I was allowed to play in the preparation of "Menace".'

132 Keyes had visited Inveraray on the arrival of the *Glenearn* to ensure that her captain would train the crews of her landing craft in the same manner laid down for those of the *Glengyle* and *Glenroy*. When the 3 Commandos were ordered around the Cape he embarked the 11th Commando in the *Glenearn*, hoping that 'in the course of the long voyage, the officers and men of the two Services would become the amphibious unit so essential for the kind of operation they may be called upon to undertake.' However, when it was too late to make any change, he found that the 11th Commando had been divided between the *Glenroy* and *Glengyle*, 'separated from the personnel of landing craft which had been trained on precisely similar lines to those on which they had been operating.' Furthermore, owing to overcrowding, 18

officers from the 3 Commandos had to be separated from their troops and embarked in *Glenearn*. Keyes to Chiefs of Staff Committee, 30 Jan. 1941, Keyes MSS. 13/3.

133 The Admiralty had signalled the 3 'Glens' in a widely distributed message that all communications in connection with personnel, material and movements were to be made to the authority concerned and not to the DCO. Copy, *ibid.*

134 Cagliari.

135 Sir Eric C. Geddes (1875–1937). Knighted, 1916. Director-General of Transportation on staff of C-in-C British armies in France, 1916–17; Controller and member of the Board of Admiralty with rank of temporary honorary Vice-Admiral, 1917; First Lord of the Admiralty, July 1917–Dec. 1918; MP (U) Cambridge, 1917–22; Minister of Transport, 1919–21.

136 Wemyss.

137 Marginal note: 'The rest is rather private, R.K.'

138 Admiral Augustus Keppel (1725–1786). Created Viscount, 1782. Commodore commanding North American station, 1754; a Lord Commissioner of the Admiralty, 1766; C-in-C of Grand Fleet, 1778; First Lord of the Admiralty, 1782.

139 Admiral Charles Middleton (1726–1813). Created Baronet, 1781; Baron Barham, 1805. MP for Rochester, 1784; Comptroller of the Navy, 1778–90; a Lord Commissioner of the Admiralty, 1794; First Lord of the Admiralty, 1805.

140 Admiral of the Fleet Sir John Arbuthnot Fisher (1841–1920). Created 1st Baron Fisher of Kilverstone, 1909. C-in-C Mediterranean, 1899–1902; Second Sea Lord, 1902–03; C-in-C Portsmouth, 1903–04; First Sea Lord, 1904–10; Oct. 1914–May 1915.

141 1st Earl of Birkenhead [Frederick Edwin Smith] (1872–1930). Created Baron, 1919; Earl, 1922. MP (U) Walton div., Liverpool, 1906–19; Solicitor-General, 1915; Attorney-General, 1915–19; Lord High Chancellor, 1919–22; Secretary of State for India, 1924–28.

142 On the controversy see *The Keyes Papers* Vol. II, Documents 108–13.

143 Captain Henry David Reginald Margesson (1890–1965). Created Viscount, 1942. Served in 11th Hussars, 1914–18; MP (U) Upton div. of West Ham, 1922–23; Rugby, 1924–42; Junior Lord of the Treasury, 1926–29, 1931; Parliamentary Secretary to the Treasury, and Chief Government Whip, 1931–40; Secretary of State for War, 1940–42.

144 Governor-General of Algeria and Delegate-General of the Vichy Government in French Africa.

145 Document 71.

146 Document 72.

147 Document 71.

148 The division of the 11th Commando between the *Glenroy* and *Glengyle* upon embarkation for the Middle East. Minute of 30 Jan. 1941 not reproduced.

149 There had been no substantial result to Keyes's repeated requests to meet with the Chiefs of Staff in order to elaborate his views on the planning and preparation of combined operations.

150 Vice-Admiral [later Admiral of the Fleet Sir] John Cronyn Tovey (1885–1971). Created Baron, 1946. Naval assistant to Second Sea Lord, 1930–32; commanded *Rodney*, 1932–34; Commodore RN Barracks, Chatham, 1935–37; Rear-Admiral Destroyers, Mediterranean Fleet, 1938–40; 2nd-in-Command Mediterranean Fleet, 1940; C-in-C Home Fleet, Dec. 1940–Nov. 1943; C-in-C the Nore, 1943–46.

151 At the conclusion of his letter discussing points connected with the forthcoming raid on the Lofoten Islands, Keyes wrote: 'I am asking the Chiefs of Staff to decide as to whether these landings are to be pressed home, in the event of opposition, under the cover of supporting fire from destroyers.'

Keyes to Tovey, 20 Feb. 1941, copy in Keyes MSS. 13/6.
152   The raid on the Lofoten Islands.
153   Rt Hon Hugh Dalton (1887–1962). Created Baron (Life Peer), 1960. MP (Lab.) Peckham div., Camberwell, 1924–29; Bishop Auckland div., 1929–31, 1935–59; Parliamentary Under-Secretary, Foreign Office, 1929–31; Chairman National Executive of Labour Party, 1936–37; Minister of Economic Warfare, 1940–42; President of Board of Trade, 1942–45; Chancellor of the Exchequer, 1945–47; Chancellor of the Duchy of Lancaster, 1948–50; Minister of Town and Country Planning, 1950–51; Minister of Local Government and Planning, 1951.
154   Captain [later Vice-Admiral] Clifford Caslon (1896–). Fleet Signal Officer, Mediterranean Fleet, 1929–30; commanded 4th, 18th and 6th Destroyer Flotillas, 1938–42; Chief of Staff, Plymouth, 1943–44; commanded *Nelson*, 1945–46; Flag Officer Malaya, 1947–50; retired list, 1950.
155   The Ministry of Information was most anxious to have a record of the operation and arranged for a Commander from the Admiralty Press Dept. and two officer photographers from the War Office to be embarked for this purpose. Keyes to Tovey, 20 Feb. 1941, Keyes MSS. 13/6.
156   Document 75.
157   In 1939 Wavell had delivered the 3 Lees-Knowles lectures at Trinity College, Cambridge. In 1943 Keyes himself would have this honour [See Document 143]. The lectures were later published by *The Times*; again by Penguin Books; and also form the first 3 essays in Wavell's *Soldiers and Soldiering* (London, 1953). Rommel supposedly had a well-annotated German translation with him during the Desert campaign. John Connell, *Wavell: Soldier and Scholar* (New York. 1964), pp. 203–4.
158   Cowan.
159   Document 53.
160   Keyes underlined the italicised words and added: 'Grossly exaggerated by EPS.'
161   The ships for Operation 'Workshop' were supposed to peel off from the 'Excess' convoy at the appropriate moment. However, during Jan. Fliegerkorps X of the Luftwaffe arrived in Sicily and on the 10th the aircraft carrier *Illustrious*, part of the force covering Operation 'Excess', was subjected to intensive dive-bombing attack and suffered 6 hits from heavy bombs and 3 near-misses. The cruiser *Southampton* was sunk on the 11th.
162   The attack on the small island of Castelorizzo by No. 50 Middle East Commando took place 25–27 Feb. The Italians did react strongly and, in addition to heavy bombing, reinforcements from Rhodes were landed by destroyer. As the Commando's wireless set had failed, Cunningham had no information as to what was going on. The remainder of the Commando was evacuated by destroyer the following night. Cunningham, *A Sailor's Odyssey*, p. 316.
163   An attack on the Dodecanese, particularly Rhodes, for which the 3 'Glens' had been sent to the Mediterranean. *Ibid.*, pp. 306–7.
164   Operation 'Lustre', the transport of British reinforcements to Greece, which began on 5 Mar.
165   Document 36.
166   In presenting the Naval Estimates to the House on 5 Mar., Alexander stated: 'Never in the long history of the growth of our sea power have we had such need of numbers of ships and of men. For a war against an adversary of consequence, the volume of our trade which has to be protected, and the length of our lines of movement and supply, necessitate a certain absolute naval strength in the various classes of ships which is essential for the full exercise of our sea power.' *Parliamentary Debates, Commons*, 5th series, vol. 369, col. 927.
167   Admiral Sir William Cornwallis (1744–1819). Commanded Channel Fleet at time of Trafalgar campaign.

168 Vice-Amiral Pierre-Charles Villeneuve (1763–1806). Commander of the French Fleet at the Battle of Trafalgar.
169 Operation 'Claymore', the raid on the Lofoten Islands.
170 Captain Cecil A. Kershaw, commanding the *Queen Emma*.
171 Commander Thomas B. Brunton, commanding the *Princess Beatrix*.
172 A German-controlled fish factory ship (9,780 tons).
173 Document 77.
174 Grand Canary Island.
175 The Canary Islands.
176 On 15 June 1940 the Spanish occupied the neutral zone of Tangier; on 4 Nov. they assumed administrative control of the international zone; and on 1 Dec. incorporated Tangier in the Spanish zone of Morocco and dismissed British officials. Butler, *Grand Strategy* Vol. II, pp. 238, 430–1.
177 Capitaine de vaisseau [later Vice-amiral d'escadre] Pierre-Jean Ronarc'h (1892–1960). Commanded battery of heavy railway artillery, 1917–19; torpilleur *Tramontane*, 1927; Dunkirk Coastal Artillery, 1932; destroyer *Kersaint*, 1934; cruiser *Montcalm*, 1938–40; *Jean Bart*, 1940; Rear-Admiral commanding Casablanca defence sector, 1941; commanded French naval forces in Morocco, 1942–43; commanded French naval forces in Mediterranean, 1944–47; C-in-C French naval forces in Mediterranean, 1951; retired, 1954.
178 Ronarc'h had managed with great skill the difficult task of getting the uncompleted battleship *Jean Bart* away from Saint-Nazaire just before the arrival of the German army. See Auphan and Mordal, *The French Navy in World War II*, pp. 91–2.
179 Vice-amiral Pierre Ronarc'h (1865–1940). Commanded torpedo-boat and submarine flotillas of Ire Armée navale (Mediterranean), 1908; commanded Brigade of Fusiliers Marins, 1914–15; commanded French naval forces in zone of the Armies of the North, 1916–19; Chief of Naval Staff, 1919–20; retired, 1920.
180 Added by Keyes: 'Note:– (Not in original). This is pressed by my Naval Secretary who is normally a resident of U.S.A. and lived there from 1928–39. His opinion and information are that the Americans are irked by Roosevelt's slowness in yielding to the pressure of public opinion, instead of leading it at a time when speed is such a vital factor.'
181 Carbon endorsed by Keyes: 'Anthony [Eden], Please detach and destroy after you have read it, R.K.'
182 Following Churchill's speech on the war situation on 7 May, a vote of confidence in the Government was carried 447–3.
183 David Lloyd George (1863–1945). Created Earl, 1945. MP (L) Carnarvon, 1890–1931; (Ind.L.), 1931–45; President of the Board of Trade, 1905–08; Chancellor of the Exchequer, 1908–15; Minister of Munitions, 1915–16; Secretary of State for War, 1916; Prime Minister and First Lord of the Treasury, 1916–22.
184 In his criticism of the Government during the debates, Lloyd George had charged Churchill with being surrounded by 'yes-men'. Churchill replied: 'My right hon. Friend spoke of the great importance of my being surrounded by people who would stand up to me and say, "No, No, No." Why, good gracious, has he no idea how strong the negative principle is in the constitution and working of the British war-making machine? The difficulty is not, I assure him, to have more brakes put on the wheels; the difficulty is to get more impetus and speed behind it. At one moment we are asked to emulate the Germans in their audacity and vigour, and the next moment the Prime Minister is to be assisted by being surrounded by a number of "No-men" to resist me at every point and prevent me from making anything in the nature of a speedy, rapid and, above all, positive constructive decision.' *Parliamentary Debates, Commons*, 5th series, vol. 371, col. 937.
185 Rear-Admiral [later Admiral Sir] Louis Henry Keppel Hamilton (1890–1957).

Known as 'Turtle' in the Service. Designated Naval Commander for Operation 'Puma'; Flag Officer-in-Charge, Malta, 1943–45; First Naval Member and Chief of Naval Staff of Commonwealth Naval Board (Australia), 1945–48; retired list, 1948.

186 Major-General [later Lieut.-General Sir] Robert Grice Sturges (1891–1970). Entered Royal Navy, 1908; transferred to Royal Marine Light Infantry, 1912; commanded troops in first occupation of Iceland, 1940; military commander occupation of Madagascar, 1942; commanded Special Service Group, 1943–44; retired list, 1946.

187 Anthony Eden, Secretary of State for Foreign Affairs.

188 Probably Document 84.

189 Document 85.

190 Added in holograph: 'but read the last minute on the last page. Time is being wasted.'

191 Document 86.

192 In the debates of 10 June there was scathing criticism of the Government's conduct of the war, particularly the recent loss of Crete. Churchill concluded his review of the war situation with the words: 'I give no guarantee, I make no promise or prediction for the future. But if the next six months, during which we must expect even harder fighting and many disappointments, should find us in no worse position than that in which we stand today; if, after having fought so long alone, single-handed against the might of Germany, and against Italy, and against the intrigues and treachery of Vichy, we should still be found the faithful and unbeaten guardians of the Nile Valley and of the regions that lie about it, then I say that a famous chapter will have been written in the martial history of the British Empire and Commonwealth of Nations. *Parliamentary Debates, Commons*, 5th series, vol. 372, cols. 162–3.

193 Although the handwriting is not clear, it is probably 'L.G.' for Lloyd George.

194 Admiral of the Fleet Sir Henry Francis Oliver (1865–1965). Director of Intelligence, Admiralty War Staff, 1913–14; Chief of Admiralty War Staff, 1914–17; Deputy Chief of Naval War Staff, 1917–18; commanded 1st Battle Cruiser Squadron, 1918; Reserve Fleet, 1919–20; Second Sea Lord, 1920–24; C-in-C Atlantic Fleet, 1924–27; retired list, 1933.

195 Bernard Mannes Baruch (1870–1965). Noted American financier and presidential adviser. During First World War, Chairman: Commission on raw materials, minerals and metals; Commission in charge of raw materials for War Industries Board; Allied Purchasing Commission; Chairman of War Industries Board, Mar. 1918–Jan. 1919; member of Supreme Economic Council and Chairman of raw materials div., American delegation on economic and reparations clauses, Paris Peace Conference, 1919; Chairman fact-finding committee on synthetic rubber, 1942; adviser to James F. Byrnes, War Mobilization div., 1943; US representative on United Nations Atomic Energy Commission, 1946.

196 See *The Keyes Papers* Vol. II, Documents 260, 285.

197 Woolley had sailed from Greenock in the *California* on 14 June, and transferred at Halifax for onward passage to Baltimore in the *Bulolo*.

198 Admiral Sir Wilfred Frankland French (1880–1958). Rear-Admiral, 2nd Battle Squadron, 1931–32; Vice-Admiral in Charge, Malta, 1934–37; member of Executive Council of Malta, 1936–37; retired list, 1938; British administrative and maintenance representative, Washington, 1941–44.

199 Vice-Admiral James Wilfred Sussex Dorling (1889–1966). Deputy Controller, Admiralty, 1939–41; British Admiralty supply representative, Washington, 1941–44; Flag Officer, Liverpool, 1944–46.

200 Admiral Sir Frank Larken (1875–1953). Naval Secretary to First Lord, 1925–27; commanded 2nd Cruiser Squadron, Atlantic Fleet, 1927–29; commanded Reserve Fleet, 1930–32; retired list, 1933.

201 Harry L. Hopkins (1890–1946). Executive Director and subsequently Chair-

NOTES: PART II 339

man of New York State Temporary Emergency Relief Administration, 1931–32; Federal Administrator of Emergency Relief, 1933; Works Progress Administrator, 1935–38; Secretary of Commerce, 1938–40; appointed head of Lend-lease Programme, 1941; special adviser and assistant to the President of the US, 1941–45. Described by Churchill as 'that extraordinary man, who played, and was to play, a sometimes decisive part in the whole movement of the war.' Churchill, *The Grand Alliance*, p. 23.

202 John Gilbert Winant (1889–1947). Governor of New Hampshire, 1925–27, 1931–35; Chairman of Social Security Board, 1935–37; Assistant Director of International Labour Office, 1935, 1937–38; Director, 1938–41; Ambassador to the Court of St James, 1941–46.

203 Hopkins was in England in Jan. 1941 as personal representative of Roosevelt to Churchill. This was the moment when Keyes was still arguing in favour of Operation 'Workshop'.

204 Admiral Sir Charles Little, Head of the British Joint Staff Mission in Washington, 1941–42.

205 Captain [later Rear-Admiral] John Reginald Beardall (1887–1967). Aide to Secretary of the Navy, 1936–39; commanded *Vincennes*, 1939–41; Aide to President Roosevelt, May 1941–Jan. 1942; Superintendent, US Naval Academy, 1942–45; Commandant 15th Naval District and Commander, S.E. Pacific, 1945–46; retired, 1946.

206 Lieut.-General [later General Sir] Colville Wemyss (1891–1959). Director of Mobilisation, War Office, 1939; Adjutant-General to the Forces, 1940–41; Head of British Army Staff in Washington, 1941–42; Military Secretary to the Secretary of State for War, 1942–46; retired, 1946.

207 Air Marshal [later Marshal of the Royal Air Force Sir] Arthur Travers Harris (1892–). Created Baronet, 1953. Commanded RAF, Palestine and Transjordan, 1938–39; 5th Bomber Group, 1939–41; Deputy Chief of Air Staff, 1940–41; head of RAF delegation to the US, 1941; C-in-C Bomber Command, 1942–45.

208 Document 89.

209 Major-General Edwin Martin Watson (1883–1945). Military Aide to President Wilson, 1915–17, 1918–20; served with AEF in France, 1918; military attaché in Brussels, 1927–31; Military Aide to President Roosevelt, 1933–41; Secretary to the President, 1939–45.

210 General [later Field Marshal Sir] Claude John Eyre Auchinleck (1884–). Commanded Peshawar Brigade, India, 1933–36; Deputy Chief of General Staff, India, 1936–38; commanded Meerut District, India, 1938; GOC-in-C Northern Norway, 1940; GOC-in-C Southern Command, 1940; C-in-C in India, 1941, 1943–47; C-in-C Middle East, 1941–42; Field Marshal, 1946; Supreme Commander in India and Pakistan, 1947.

211 The copy bears the notation: 'Copy of letter sent to General Auchinleck during his brief stay in England.'

212 Not reproduced.

213 General [later Field Marshal] Henry Maitland Wilson (1881–1964). Created Baron, 1946. Commanded 2nd Div., Aldershot, 1937–39; General Officer C-in-C in Egypt, 1939; Military Governor and GOC-in-C, Cyrenaica, 1941; GOC-in-C British troops in Greece, 1941; GOC-in-C British forces in Palestine and Transjordan, 1941; C-in-C Allied forces in Syria, 1941; C-in-C Persia–Iraq Command, 1942–43; C-in-C Middle East, 1943; Supreme Allied Commander Mediterranean theatre, 1944; Field Marshal, 1944; head of British Joint Staff Mission in Washington, 1945–47.

214 The Commando had landed in the opening phase of the Syrian campaign of June 1941 to help secure the passage of the Litani River. Keyes's son Geoffrey, 2nd-in-command, distinguished himself in the action in which, however, a quarter of the Commando were lost. A brief account is in Christopher Buckley, *Five Ventures* (London, 1954), pp. 63–6.

215 Document 91.

216 In July 1941 the 3 operations planned against the Atlantic Islands ('Puma', the largest, against the Canaries; 'Thruster' against the Azores; and 'Springboard' against Madeira) were consolidated into a single enlarged force – 'Pilgrim'. J. M. A. Gwyer and J. R. M. Butler, *Grand Strategy* Vol. III *June 1941–August 1942* (London, 1964), p. 8.

217 The *Bachaquero, Misoa,* and *Tasajera* were shallow draught tankers built to pass over the bars of Lake Maracaibo. Because of their shallow draught they were fitted with bow ramps and converted to land tanks directly on a beach, and therefore became the 1st of the LSTs.

218 Marshal Ferdinand Foch (1851–1929). Commanded 9th Army, 1914; Army group on the Somme, 1916; Chief of Staff to C-in-C French Army (Pétain), 1917; Generalissimo of Allied Armies on the Western Front, Apr. 1918.

219 Lieut.-General [later Field Marshal] Harold Rupert Leofric George Alexander (1891–1969). Created Viscount, 1946; Earl, 1952. 3rd son of 4th Earl of Caledon. Commanded 1st Div., 1938–40; 1st Corps, 1940; GOC-in-C Southern Command, 1940–42; GOC Burma, 1942; C-in-C Middle East, 1942–43; C-in-C 18th Army Group, North Africa, 1943; C-in-C Allied armies in Italy, 1943–44; Field Marshal, 1944; Supreme Allied Commander, Mediterranean theatre, 1944–45; Governor-General of Canada, 1946–52; Minister of Defence, 1952–54.

220 Including Document 93.

221 Raid on the aerodrome at Berck-sur-mer.

222 Partially reproduced in Aspinall-Oglander, *Roger Keyes,* pp. 406–7.

223 Churchill had sailed in the *Prince of Wales* to join President Roosevelt in the *Augusta* at Placentia Bay, Newfoundland. The historic meeting (9–12 Aug.) resulted in the Atlantic Charter, an Anglo-American declaration of joint principles to guide their actions.

224 General [later Field Marshal] Sir Alan Francis Brooke (1883–1963). Created Baron, 1945; Viscount Alanbrooke, 1946. Commandant School of Artillery, 1929–32; Inspector of Royal Artillery, 1935–36; Director of Military Training, War Office, 1936–37; commanded Mobile Div., 1937–38; Commander, Anti-Aircraft Corps, 1938–39; GOC-in-C Anti-Aircraft Command, 1939; GOC-in-C Southern Command, 1939, 1940; commanded II Army Corps, BEF, 1939–40; C-in-C Home forces, 1940–41; Chief of Imperial General Staff, 1941–46; Field Marshal, 1944.

225 Major-General [later Field Marshal Sir] Bernard Law Montgomery (1887–1976). Created Viscount, 1946. Commanded 8th Div., 1938–39; 3rd Div., 1939–40; V Corps, 1940; XII Corps, 1941; Southeastern Command, 1942; 8th Army, 1942–44; 21st Army Group, 1944–45; British Army on the Rhine, 1945–46; Chief of Imperial General Staff, 1946–48; Chairman, Western Europe Commanders in Chief Committee, 1948–51; Deputy Supreme Allied Commander, Europe, 1951–58.

226 Document 98.

227 The cross-Channel and Irish Sea ferries fitted as LSIs.

228 Not reproduced.

229 Document 78.

230 The landing exercise held at Scapa Flow, Aug. 1941.

231 Lieut.-General H. R. Alexander and Rear-Admiral Louis Hamilton.

232 Vice-Admiral [later Admiral of the Fleet Sir] Algernon Usborne Willis (1889–1976). Commanded *Warwick,* 1927–29; Flag Captain, *Kent,* China Fleet, 1933–34; Flag Captain, *Nelson,* Home Fleet, 1934–35; Captain, *Vernon* (Torpedo School, Portsmouth), 1935–38; commanded *Barham,* 1938–39; Chief of Staff, Mediterranean Fleet, 1939–41; C-in-C South Atlantic Station, 1941–42; 2nd-in-Command Eastern Fleet, 1942–43; Flag Officer commanding Force H (Mediterranean), 1943; C-in-C Levant Station, 1943; Second Sea Lord, 1944–46; C-in-C Mediterranean Fleet, 1946–48; C-in-C Portsmouth, 1948–50.

233 Commodore [later Rear-Admiral] Guy Warren (1888–1961). Designated

Senior Naval Officer Landings for 'Puma' and 'Pilgrim' Operations, 1941; Senior Officer Assault Ships and Craft in Combined Operations, 1941–45. ('. . . when [Admiral Sir B. H.] Ramsay was touring the shipping assembled in the Solent just before D-Day, he was accompanied by Warren. . . . Familiar ship after familiar ship came into view; and Warren suddenly realised that there was scarcely one which had not passed through his hands in preparation for battle at some time or another.' Fergusson, *The Watery Maze*, pp. 350–1).

234 Keyes had argued that Operation 'Pilgrim' as presently envisaged had no reasonable chance of success. Intelligence reports indicated the defences of Grand Canary had been strengthened and an assault launched on the beaches at Gando without any prospect of tactical surprise would be repulsed. Minutes, Chiefs of Staff Committee, [9 Sept. 1941] and DCO's Amendments, Keyes MSS. 13/9.

235 The typescript of another copy of this letter has the notation: 'Note. They had been taken away from me, when the Joint Commanders were appointed, and put under them.' Keyes MSS. 13/3.

236 The Prime Minister and Chiefs of Staff had decided to send the slower and less seaworthy ships of 'Pilgrim' force to Freetown in Sierra Leone for the winter months. This would permit the operation to be carried out at a time when bad weather in the Bay of Biscay would make the use of the small vessels hazardous if they had sailed from the British Isles. Keyes disagreed with locking up these valuable craft at Freetown for the whole winter and favoured alternative employment for the 'Pilgrim' force. Keyes to Minister of Defence, 2 Sept. 1941, Keyes MSS. 13/9.

237 Added at a later date in holograph: 'He did so by recommending the abolition of my Directive & suggesting my appt. instead as "Adviser" & Chairman of another Inter-Service committee, R.K.'

238 Document 100.

239 Footnote by Keyes: 'I sent a copy of this to S.S. of F.A. (Eden) & gave a copy to Lord Halifax, R.K.'

240 On 4 Sept. the American destroyer *Greer* had been unsuccessfully attacked by a U-boat off Iceland. President Roosevelt in a radio broadcast on 11 Sept. condemned the attack and declared: 'From now on, if German or Italian vessels of war enter the water the protection of which is necessary for American defence, they do so at their own risk.' According to the historian of US naval operations: 'From the date of the *Greer* incident . . . the United States was engaged in a *de facto* naval war with Germany on the Atlantic Ocean.' Samuel Eliot Morison, *History of United States Naval Operations in World War II* Vol. I *The Battle of the Atlantic* (Boston, 1947), p. 80.

241 The typescript of another copy of this minute has the notation: 'This was only one of many minutes and letters I wrote to Winston and the Chiefs of Staff from the 6th August onwards, pointing out that we had this fine amphibious striking force lying idle, but "capable of inflicting very severe blows overseas." On 6 Aug. I wrote: – "Events may move very rapidly now and I suggest that 'PILGRIM' Force should not be held inactive for only one object, since it is the only amphibious force we possess." [Document 93.] On 27 Aug. I wrote:–"Events may move rapidly on the continent, we have a fine amphibious striking force capable of inflicting a very severe blow across the Channel or overseas, and if we can only get rid of the 'PILGRIM' commitment—which is holding up action, we might make some progress towards waging war against the enemy." [Document 95] R.K., 4/12/41', Keyes MSS. 13/3.

242 Keyes gave a copy of this to Lord Halifax, Ambassador to the US, when he was in England. Marginal note [c. 30 Oct. 1941] on copy in Ismay MSS. IV/Key/8/3.

243 Ismay was a member of the Anglo-American Mission to Russia which departed on the 22nd. His account of the trip is in *The Memoirs of General*

	Lord Ismay (New York, 1960), pp. 230–5.
244	Document 101.
245	Document 102.
246	The *Queen Emma* and *Princess Beatrix*.
247	Document 86.
248	Document 100.
249	In his brief acknowledgement, Eden remarked that happily the Spanish position seemed to be improving. Eden to Keyes, 18 Sept. 1941, Keyes MSS. 13/15.
250	Not reproduced.
251	Not reproduced.
252	Reproduced in Aspinall-Oglander, *Roger Keyes*, p. 408.
253	Document 107.
254	Document 78.
255	This is probably a reference to Operation 'Irrigate'. The Naval Historical Branch has no record of any operation by this name, but from various documents in the Keyes MSS, it appears to have been the deployment to Freetown around mid-September of the smaller ships earmarked for Operation 'Pilgrim' so as to avoid the risk of passage through the Bay of Biscay during the autumn and winter gales should the operation take place later in the year. Keyes MSS. 13/9.
256	Lieut.-General Sir Henry Royds Pownall (1887–1961). Director of Military Operations and Intelligence, War Office, 1938–39; Chief of General Staff, BEF, 1939–40; Inspector-General of Home Guard, 1940; commanded British troops in Northern Ireland, 1940–41; Vice Chief of Imperial General Staff, 1941; C-in-C Far East, Dec. 1941–Jan. 1942; Chief of Staff, 'ABDA' Command, Far East, Jan.–Feb. 1942; GOC Ceylon, Mar. 1942–Mar. 1943; C-in-C Persia–Iraq, 1943; Chief of Staff to Supreme Allied Commander, South East Asia, 1943–44; retired, 1945.
257	'There is only one duty and only one safe course, and that is to try to be right and not to fear to do or say what you believe to be right. And that is the only way to deserve and win the confidence of our great people in these days of trouble.' Churchill, in his speech on the war situation (30 Sept.), was arguing against taking the easy and popular course, and being guided in defence matters by the 'shifting winds of well-meaning public opinion.' *Parliamentary Debates, Commons*, 5th series, vol. 374, col. 517.
258	Added in holograph: '(This time without any prospect of commanding the waters of Trondheim Fiord.)'
259	Cecil Scott Forester (1899–1966). Author whose most famous works were the novels set during the Napoleonic wars and dealing with the career of Horatio Hornblower (the fictional naval officer). *The General*, however, was about the 1914–18 war.
260	Reproduced in Aspinall-Oglander, *Roger Keyes*, pp. 408–9.
261	Document 106.
262	Document 107.
263	Marginal note: '[Illegible] his letter [illegible] he definitely refuses.' The writing, partially obliterated by perforations, does not appear to be Ismay's.
264	Document 110.
265	John H. [later Sir John] Peck (1913–). Assistant Private Secretary to First Lord of the Admiralty, 1937–39; to Minister for Co-ordination of Defence, 1939–40; to the Prime Minister, 1940–46; transferred to Foreign Service, 1946; Ambassador to Senegal, 1962–66; to Mauretania, 1962–65; Assistant Under-Secretary of State, Foreign Office, 1966–70; Ambassador to Republic of Ireland, 1970–73.
266	Document 107.
267	Document 108.
268	Document 110.
269	Document 111.

NOTES: PART II 343

270 Captain [later Admiral of the Fleet] Louis Mountbatten (1900–1979). Created Viscount, 1946, Earl, 1947. Younger son of Prince Louis of Battenberg (after 1917 Marquess of Milford Haven). Fleet Wireless Officer, Mediterranean Fleet, 1931–33; commanded *Daring*, 1934; *Wishart*, 1935; *Kelly* and 5th Destroyer Flotilla, 1939–41; *Illustrious*, 1941; Commodore Combined Operations, 1941–42; Chief of Combined Operations, 1942–43; Supreme Allied Commander, South East Asia, 1943–46; Viceroy of India, Mar.–Aug. 1947; Governor-General of India, Aug. 1947–June 1948; commanded 1st Cruiser Squadron, Mediterranean Fleet, 1948–49; Fourth Sea Lord, 1950–52; C-in-C Mediterranean, 1952–54; C-in-C Allied forces Mediterranean, 1953–54; First Sea Lord, 1955–59; Chief of UK Defence Staff and Chairman of Chiefs of Staff Committee, 1959–65. Killed by IRA bomb, 1979.
271 Document 112.
272 Document 111.
273 Document 113.
274 From the context of other letters the suggestion probably concerned the post of Governor of Northern Ireland.
275 Document 114.
276 Rt Hon John Miller Andrews (1871–1956). MP (Unionist) Co. Down, Parliament of Northern Ireland, 1921–29; Mid-Down and Down, 1929–53; Minister of Labour in Cabinet of Northern Ireland, 1921–37; Minister of Finance, Northern Ireland, 1937–40; Prime Minister of Northern Ireland, 1940–43.
277 Document 100.
278 Keyes sent copies of this memorandum to Eden and Beaverbrook. Keyes MSS. 13/15.
279 Not reproduced.
280 Document 117.
281 'An Alternative Plan for the Capture of "Pilgrim".' [Document 100], and a paper arguing against the despatch of the small landing ships to Sierra Leone.
282 Document 121.
283 Document 100.
284 Document 117.
285 Document 116.

NOTES TO INTRODUCTION TO PART III

1 Saunders, *The Green Beret*, pp. 74–9.
2 Aspinall-Oglander, *Roger Keyes*, pp. 417–22.
3 *Ibid.*, pp. 423–4; George Malcolm Thomson, *Vote of Censure* (New York, 1968), pp. 195–8.
4 *Parliamentary Debates, Lords,* 5th series, vol. CXXV, cols. 815–20.
5 Roskill, *The War at Sea* Vol. I, pp. 309–14; Auphan and Mordal, *The French Navy in World War II,* pp. 184–92.
6 The subject is exhaustively covered in Arthur J. Marder, *Operation 'Menace': The Dakar Expedition and the Dudley North Affair* (London, 1976), chaps. x–xii. The North affair is a complex question, and it is only fair to point out that had Keyes known the full details he might not necessarily have approved all of North's actions. He would, undoubtedly, have agreed with the five Admirals of the Fleet who requested a confidential inquiry in 1953 on the grounds that North's fault was at most an error of judgement or misinterpretation of Admiralty orders rather than a neglect of duty, *ibid.*, p. 235.
7 Aspinall-Oglander, *Roger Keyes*, p. 433.
8 Keyes to his wife, 7 Oct. 1944, Keyes MSS 14/4.
9 Keyes to his wife, 12 Oct. 1944, Keyes MSS 2/31.
10 Aspinall-Oglander, *Roger Keyes*, pp. 453–7.
11 *Ibid.*, p. 461.
12 James. *Churchill, Complete Speeches* Vol. VIII. pp. 7997–8.

NOTES TO PART III

1. Document 120.
2. Document 121.
3. Document 100 and a paper arguing against the despatch to Sierra Leone of the small landing ships destined for Operation 'Pilgrim'.
4. Document 122.
5. Document 112.
6. Document 118.
7. Document 124.
8. Document 125.
9. Document 118.
10. Wing-Commander Archibald W. H. James (1893–). Knighted, 1945. Served in 3rd Hussars, RFC and RAF, 1914–26; MP (U) Wellingborough div. of Northamptonshire, 1931–45; Parliamentary Private Secretary to R. A. Butler at India Office and Ministry of Labour, 1936–38; at Board of Education, 1942.
11. James was Hon First Secretary, British Embassy, Madrid, 1940–41.
12. Admiral Sir Dudley Burton Napier North (1881–1961). Commanded *Caledon*, *Revenge* and *Tiger;* Director of Operations Div., Naval Staff, 1930–32; Chief of Staff, Home Fleet, 1932–33; commanded HM Yachts, 1934–39; Admiral commanding North Atlantic Station, 1939–40; retired, 1942; Flag Officer-in-Charge, Great Yarmouth, 1942–45.
13. On 9 Sept. 1940 Force Y (3 cruisers and 3 large destroyers) sailed from Toulon for Dakar. They had been ordered by the Vichy Government to counter 'Dissidence' or Free French activity in the Gulf of Guinea, notably at Libreville. Admiral North, Flag Officer commanding North Atlantic Station, had ambiguous orders and did not believe they required him to stop a French squadron as long as it was not sailing to an enemy occupied port. Moreover his relationship and control over Somerville's Force H was hazy, and he probably lacked the force to stop the French who had only been permitted to sail by the German-Italian Armistice Commission on the condition that they resisted any British attack. The result was Force Y passed through the Straits unmolested and no British move was made until it was too late to stop them. The French Squadron reached Dakar on the 12th and shortly afterwards played a role in opposing Operation 'Menace', the unsuccessful Anglo-Free French expedition to Dakar. On 15 Oct. the Admiralty informed North he would be relieved and they consistently denied his request for an opportunity to vindicate himself before some sort of enquiry. It was not until 1957 that Prime Minister Harold Macmillan substantially exonerated North in the House of Commons. Roskill, *The War at Sea* Vol. I, pp. 309–14; Auphan and Mordal, *The French Navy in World War II*, pp. 184–7.
14. On 25 Nov. 1940 Somerville, commanding Force H, had engaged a superior Italian force off Cape Spartivento, the southern tip of Sardinia. The action was indecisive, but the Italians turned away. Somerville, primarily concerned with the safety of the convoy he was covering, abandoned the pursuit as he approached the enemy coast. He was criticised by the Admiralty for this and Lord Cork and Orrery was sent to conduct an Enquiry. Cunningham thought this 'a most iniquitous action' since the members of the Board of Enquiry were flown out to Gibraltar before Somerville had submitted his report or even returned to harbour. The Enquiry itself upheld Somerville's actions. The official historian has also termed the handling of the whole

matter 'unfortunate', Cunningham, *A Sailor's Odyssey*, pp. 291–4; Roskill, *The War at Sea* Vol. I, pp. 302–4.

15 Lieut.-General Sir Henry Royds Pownall.
16 Presumably a reference to Keyes's defence of King Leopold's conduct in May 1940.
17 While returning to Gibraltar after successfully launching aircraft reinforcements to Malta, *Ark Royal* was torpedoed by *U.81*. After a prolonged but unsuccessful effort to save her, the carrier was abandoned and sank the morning of 14 Nov.
18 Document 126.
19 Document 127.
20 Not reproduced.
21 One of which is reproduced as Document 82.
22 The letter is endorsed: 'No reply to be sent, M.H.K., 22/11.' The initials are those of Morris H. Knott, Ismay's Secretary.
23 On 25 Nov. Keyes spoke in Parliament of the termination of his appointment as DCO. The tenor and contents of his speech are substantially reproduced in this letter and consisted of an attack on the Inter-service committees and sub-committees which, he charged, had become almost the dictators of military policy instead of the servants they should be of those who bore all the responsibility. Keyes, while praising Churchill's will to victory, argued that until the staff system was overhauled they would always be too late in anything they undertook, and urged the House to help the Prime Minister remove some of the brakes in the war machine of Whitehall. He also mentioned, in declining to comment on recent operations in Libya, that he had recently received a copy of the Official Secrets Act [Document 122], and it is interesting to note that the Keyes File among Ismay's papers has the extract from Hansard containing his speech with this reference carefully underlined. Ismay MSS. IV/Key/17. For the full text see *Parliamentary Debates, Commons*, 5th series, vol. 376, cols. 661–5.
24 Admiral Sir Dudley Pound and Vice-Admiral Tom Phillips.
25 On the effects of the speech see Aspinall-Oglander, *Roger Keyes*, pp. 414–16.
26 Earl Winterton [Edward Turnour] (1883–1962). Succeeded father as 6th Earl (Irish Peerage), 1907; MP (U) Horsham div., 1904–18; Horsham and Worthing, 1918–40; Horsham, 1940–51; Under-Secretary of State for India, 1922–24, Nov. 1924–29; Chancellor of Duchy of Lancaster, 1937–39; Deputy to Secretary of State for Air and Vice-President of Air Council, Mar.–May, 1938; Paymaster-General, Jan.–Nov. 1939.
27 Winterton asked if Keyes had applied his considerations to those going on in Libya.
28 'The effect of "Workshop", if successful, would be electrifying, and would greatly increase our strategic hold upon the Central Mediterranean.' Churchill to Ismay for COS Committee, 28 Dec. 1940. Extract reproduced in Churchill, *The Grand Alliance*, p. 58.
29 William L. Shirer (1904–). European correspondent for the *Chicago Tribune*, 1925–32; Chief of Berlin Bureau of Universal Service and news commentator for Columbia Broadcasting System, 1934–41. His journal was the basis of the widely-read *Berlin Diary* (New York, 1941).
30 George Henry Hall (1881–1965). Created Viscount, 1946. MP (Labour) Aberdare div. of Merthyr Tydfil, 1922–46; Civil Lord of the Admiralty, 1929–31; Parliamentary Under-Secretary of State, Colonial Office, 1940–42; Financial Secretary to the Admiralty, 1942–43; Parliamentary Under-Secretary of State for Foreign Affairs, 1943–45; Secretary of State for the Colonies, 1945–46; First Lord of the Admiralty, 1946–51; Deputy Leader of House of Lords, 1947–51.
31 Lieut.-Colonel Geoffrey Keyes was killed the night of 17–18 Nov. 1941 in one of the most famous and daring raids of the war. This was the attack on Rommel's HQ at Breda Littoria, some 250 miles behind enemy lines. How-

ever, neither Rommel nor his personal staff were in the house assumed to be his HQ at the time. Keyes was awarded the Victoria Cross posthumously. A very full account is in Elizabeth Keyes, *Geoffrey Keyes, V.C.* (London, 1956). See also Fergusson, *The Watery Maze,* pp. 102–5; Saunders, *The Green Beret,* pp. 74–81.

32 *Glenroy* had nothing to do with the operation. The Commando landed from the submarines *Torbay* and *Talisman.*

33 Rear-Admiral [later Vice-Admiral] Harold Tom Baillie-Grohman (1888–). Head of British Naval Mission to China, 1931–33; commanded 1st Destroyer Flotilla, Mediterranean Fleet, 1934–36; commanded *St Vincent* and in charge Boys' Training Establishment, 1936–38; commanded *Ramilles,* 1939–40; attached to staff of GOC Middle East, 1941; Rear-Admiral Combined Operations, 1942; Flag Officer-in-Charge, Harwich, 1944; Kiel and Schleswig-Holstein, 1945–46.

34 William Ewert Berry, 1st Viscount Camrose (1879–1954). Created Baron, 1929; Viscount, 1941. Founded *Advertising World,* 1901; Editor-in-Chief, *Sunday Times,* 1915–36; Editor-in-Chief, *Daily Telegraph,* 1928–54.

35 Marshal of the RAF Hugh Montague Trenchard (1873–1956). Created Baron, 1930; Viscount, 1936. Married the sister of Keyes's wife, 1920; Assistant Commandant, Central Flying School, 1913–14; GOC RFC in the Field, 1915–17; Chief of Air Staff, 1918–29; Commissioner of Metropolitan Police, 1931–35.

36 Presumably a reference to Admiral Tom Phillips and the recent loss of the *Prince of Wales* and *Repulse* to Japanese air attack off the coast of Malaya.

37 Sub-Lieutenant Roger Keyes was then in the *Arethusa* which had supported a 2nd raid on the Lofoten Islands.

38 Admiral J. H. D. Cunningham.

39 7th Earl Stanhope [James Richard Stanhope] (1880–1967). Succeeded father, 1905. Civil Lord of the Admiralty, 1924–29; Parliamentary and Financial Secretary to the Admiralty, Sept.–Nov. 1931; Under-Secretary of State for War, 1931–34; Parliamentary Under-Secretary of State for Foreign Affairs, 1934–36; First Commissioner of Works, 1936–37; President Board of Education, 1937–38; First Lord of the Admiralty, Oct. 1938–Sept. 1939; Lord President of the Council, 1939–40; Leader of House of Lords, 1938–40.

40 On the night of 11 Nov. 1940 Swordfish aircraft from the carrier *Illustrious* attacked the Italian Fleet in its base at Taranto and sank the battleships *Littorio, Duilio* and *Cavour* at their moorings. Although the ships were eventually refloated, the *Cavour* never re-entered service.

41 A torpedo attack on the evening of 26 May 1941 by Swordfish aircraft from *Ark Royal* sealed the fate of the *Bismarck* by scoring a hit which wrecked the battleship's steering gear and jammed her rudders.

42 Rear-Admiral [later Admiral Sir] A. Lamley St G. Lyster (1888–1957). Commanded *Danae,* 1932; 5th Destroyer Flotilla, 1933–35; RN Gunnery School, Chatham, 1935–36; Director of Training and Staff Duties, Admiralty, 1936–37; commanded *Glorious,* 1938–39; Rear-Admiral Aircraft Carriers, Mediterranean Fleet (including attack on Taranto), 1940–41; Fifth Sea Lord and Chief of Naval Air Services, 1941–42; commanded Aircraft Carriers, Home Fleet, 1942–43; Flag Officer Carrier Training, 1943–45; retired list, 1945.

43 Singapore surrendered to the Japanese on 15 Feb. 1942.

44 James Stanhope (1673–1721). Created Viscount, 1717; Earl, 1718. Commander of British forces in Spain, 1708–10; played prominent role in arranging the Hanoverian succession and principal minister of George I; particularly active in conduct of foreign affairs, 1714–21.

45 James Ramsay MacDonald (1866–1937). Treasurer of Labour Party, 1912–24; Prime Minister and Foreign Secretary, Jan.–Nov. 1924; Prime Minister, 1929–31; Prime Minister of National Government, 1931–35; Lord President of the Council, 1935–37.

46 Arthur Henderson (1863–1935). MP (Labour) Barnard Castle div., Durham,

1903–18; Widnes, 1919–22; Newcastle, 1923; Burnley, 1924–31; Clay Cross, 1933–35; Chairman of Parliamentary Labour Party, 1908–10, 1914–17; President Board of Education, 1915–16; Paymaster-General and Labour adviser to Government, 1916; Minister without portfolio in War Cabinet, 1917; Home Secretary, 1924; Secretary of State for Foreign Affairs, 1929–31; President World Disarmament Conference, 1932–33.

47 William Wedgwood Benn (1877–1960). Created 1st Viscount Stansgate, 1941. MP (L) St George's div., Tower Hamlets, 1906–18; Leith, 1918–27; joined Labour Party, 1927; MP (Labour) North Aberdeen, 1928–31; Gorton div. of Manchester, 1937–41; Secretary of State for India, 1929–31; Vice-President Allied Control Commission for Italy, 1943–44; Secretary of State for Air, 1945–46; President Interparliamentary Union, 1947–57.

48 The battle cruisers *Scharnhorst* and *Gneisenau* which had escaped from Brest in a daring dash through the Channel on 12–13 Feb.

49 Commander Rupert Arnold Brabner (1911–1945). MP (U) Hythe, 1939–45. Commissioned in RNVR, FAA and served in *Illustrious, Eagle, Victorious* and *Indomitable;* Crete and North Africa; commanded fighter squadron in *Eagle,* 1942; on Staff of Vice-Admiral Aircraft Carriers at time of landings in North Africa, 1942; Technical Assistant to Fifth Sea Lord, 1943; Joint Parliamentary Under-Secretary of State for Air, 1944–45; lost at sea in air crash, 29 Mar. 1945.

50 Rear-Admiral A. L. St G. Lyster.

51 Captain [later Admiral of the Fleet Sir] Caspar John (1903–). Flag Officer commanding 3rd Aircraft Carrier Squadron and Heavy Squadron, 1951–52; Deputy Controller Aircraft, 1953–54; Flag Officer Air, 1955–57; Vice Chief of Naval Staff, 1957–60; First Sea Lord and Chief of Naval Staff, 1960–63.

52 Lieut.-Commander E. Esmonde. Commanded the Swordfish from *Victorious* which had attacked the *Bismarck,* May 1941. On 12 Feb. 1942 led the 6 Swordfish of No. 825 Squadron in a gallant but hopeless attack on the *Scharnhorst, Gneisenau* and *Prinz Eugen* during their dash through the Channel. All 6 of the obsolete and slow Swordfish were lost. Esmonde was awarded a posthumous Victoria Cross.

53 At the beginning of 1942 Keyes began an extensive programme of speaking in favour of National Savings at various 'Warship Weeks' in different localities. However, Keyes went beyond merely asking his audiences to lend their money and frequently included sharp criticism of mismanagement at the top in the dockyards and idleness and absenteeism among the workers. These remarks, predictably, caused considerable controversy and Keyes was the subject of a critical leader in *The Times* on 19 Mar. For a fuller account see Aspinall-Oglander, *Roger Keyes,* pp. 417–22.

54 Ernest Bevin (1881–1951). General Secretary of Transport and General Workers' Union, 1921–40; Member of General Council Trades Union Congress, 1925–40; MP (Labour) Central Wandsworth, 1940–50; East Woolwich, 1950–51; Minister of Labour and National Service, 1940–45; Secretary of State for Foreign Affairs, 1945–51; Lord Privy Seal, 1951.

55 Herbert Stanley Morrison (1888–1965). Created Baron, 1959. MP (Labour) South Hackney, 1923–24, 1929–31, 1935–45; East Lewisham, 1945–51; South Lewisham, 1951–59; Minister of Transport, 1929–31; Minister of Supply, 1940; Home Secretary and Minister of Home Security, 1940–45; Member of War Cabinet, 1942–45; Deputy Prime Minister, 1945–51; Lord President of the Council and Leader of the House of Commons, 1945–51; Secretary of State for Foreign Affairs, Mar.–Oct. 1951; Deputy Leader of the Opposition, 1951–55.

56 Conscientious objectors to military service.

57 Oliver Lyttleton (1893–1972). Created 1st Viscount Chandos, 1954. Served in Grenadier Guards, 1914–18; MP (U) Aldershot div. of Hampshire, 1940–54; President of Board of Trade, 1940–41; Minister of State representing War Cabinet in Middle East, June 1941–Feb. 1942; Minister of Production and

member of the War Cabinet, 1942–45; President of Board of Trade, May–July 1945; Secretary of State for the Colonies, 1951–54.
58 Field Marshal Erwin Rommel (1891–1944). German officer noted for his brilliant conduct of armoured warfare. Commanded Afrika Korps, 1941–43; implicated in plot against Hitler and forced to commit suicide, July 1944.
59 Captain Augustus Wellington Shelton Agar (1890–1968). Awarded Victoria Cross for exploits against Bolshevik fleet in the Baltic while in command of a CMB, 1919; commanded *Dorsetshire*, 1941–42; Commodore-President, RN College, Greenwich, 1943–46.
60 On 5 Apr. the cruisers *Dorsetshire* and *Cornwall* had been sunk in the Indian Ocean by carrier-borne Japanese aircraft.
61 Keyes had seconded the motion of censure of the Government introduced by Sir John Wardlaw Milne and was scheduled to speak on 1 July.
62 Captain Alfred Thayer Mahan (1840–1914). Officer in the US Navy, 1859–96. President of Naval War College, Newport, Rhode Island, 1886–88, 1892–93; special lecturer at Naval War College, 1910–12; possibly the most influential writer on naval history of his time and author of the classic *The Influence of Sea Power upon History, 1660–1783* (London, 1890) and *The Influence of Sea Power upon the French Revolution and Empire* (2 vols., London, 1892).
63 Aneurin Bevan (1897–1960). MP (Labour) Ebbw Vale div. of Monmouthshire, 1929–60; Minister of Health, 1945–51; Minister of Labour and National Service, 1951; resigned, 1951; Treasurer, Labour Party, 1956–60.
64 Brigadier-General Percy Robert Clifford Groves (?–1959). Joined Army, 1899; joined RFC 1914; Director of Flying Operations, Air Ministry, Apr. 1918; British air representative, Paris Peace Conference, 1919; retired, 1922; Hon Secretary-General Air League of British Empire and editor of *Air*, 1927–29; Deputy Director Intelligence, Air Ministry, 1939–40; seconded to Foreign Office, 1940–45.
65 Admiral of the Fleet Sir James Gambier (1756–1833). Created Baron, 1807. C-in-C of the Fleet in the Baltic, 1807; C-in-C Channel Fleet, 1808–11.
66 Air Chief Marshal Sir Arthur Murray Longmore (1885–1970). Commandant, RAF College, Cranwell, 1929–33; Air Officer commanding Inland Area, 1933–34; Coastal Area (subsequently, Coastal Command), 1934–36; Commandant, Imperial Defence College, 1936–38; AOC in C Training Command, 1939; AOC in C RAF Middle East, 1940–41; Inspector-General of RAF, 1941; retired list, 1942.
67 Admiral Sir Ragnar Musgrave Colvin (1882–1954). Naval attaché in Tokyo, 1922–24; Director Naval Tactical School, 1927–29; Chief of Staff in Home Fleet, 1930–32; Rear-Admiral 2nd Battle Squadron, 1932–33; President of RN College, Greenwich, 1934–37; First Naval Member for Commonwealth Naval Board, 1937–41; retired list, 1942; naval adviser to High Commissioner for Australia, 1942–44.
68 Admiral Hon Sir Reginald A. R. Plunkett-Ernle-Erle-Drax (1880–1967). 2nd son of 17th Baron Dunsany. Commanded *Blanche*, 1918; Director of RN Staff College, Greenwich; 1919–22; President of Naval Allied Control Commission (Berlin), 1923, 1924; Rear-Admiral 1st Battle Squadron, 1929–30; Director of Manning Dept., Admiralty, 1930–32; C-in-C America and West Indies Station, 1932–34; C-in-C Plymouth, 1935–38; C-in-C The Nore, 1939–41; Home Guard, 1941–43; Commodore of Ocean Convoys, 1943–45.
69 On 19 Dec. 1941 the *Queen Elizabeth* and *Valiant* were severely damaged in Alexandria harbour by delayed action mines fixed to their hulls by Italian 'human torpedoes'. Although both ships suffered extensive flooding they were, fortunately, kept on an even keel and enemy Intelligence may have failed to realise the extent of their success. However, both ships were incapacitated for many months and, as the *Barham* had been sunk in late Nov., the Mediterranean Fleet was deprived of its battle squadron. The Japanese attack in the Far East precluded significant reinforcements and

British sea power in the Mediterranean was therefore reduced to its most precarious position since the evacuation of 1796. Roskill, *The War at Sea* Vol. I, pp. 538–9; Cunningham, *A Sailor's Odyssey*, pp. 433–7.

70 Lieut.-General [later General] Sir Alan Gordon Cunningham (1887–). Commanded 5th A.A. Div., Territorial Army, 1938; commanded 66th, 9th and 51st Divs., 1940; GOC East Africa forces, 1940–41; GOC-in-C 8th Army, 1941; Commandant, Staff College, Camberley, 1942; GOC Northern Ireland, 1943–44; GOC-in-C Eastern Command, 1944–45; High Commissioner and C-in-C for Palestine, 1945–48.

71 Rear-Admiral Sir Wellwood George Courtenay Maxwell (1882–1965). Commanded Gunnery School, Chatham, 1923–25; *Ceres*, 1925–27; *St Vincent*, 1928–30; *Valiant*, 1932–33; retired list, 1934; recalled as Flag Officer, Tyne Area, 1939–46.

72 Vice-Admiral Richard Bell Davies (1887–1966). Awarded Victoria Cross for services at the Dardanelles, 1916. In charge of the air section of the Naval Staff, 1920–24; 1926–28; commanded *Royal Sovereign*, 1924–26; liaison officer for FAA at Air Ministry, 1931–33; commanded *Cornwall*, 1933–35; RN Barracks, Devonport, 1936–38; Rear-Admiral, Naval Air Stations, 1939–40; retired list, 1941.

73 Captain [later Admiral Sir] Reginald Henry Portal (1894–). Commanded *York*, 1939–41; *Royal Sovereign*, 1941–42; Assistant Chief of Naval Staff (Air), 1943–44; Flag Officer Naval Air Stations (Australia), 1945; naval representative on Joint Chiefs of Staff Committee (Australia), 1946–47; Flag Officer, Air (Home), 1947–51; retired list, 1951.

74 Sir John S. Wardlaw-Milne (?–1967). Member, Bombay Municipal Corporation, 1907–17; MP (U) Kidderminster div. of Worcestershire, 1922–45; member of Imperial Economic Committee, 1926–29; Chairman, Conservative Foreign Affairs Committee, 1939–45; sponsor of resolution in House of Commons expressing lack of confidence in central direction of the war, 1942.

75 S. Sydney Silverman (1895–1968). MP (Labour) Nelson and Colne, 1935–68; member National Executive Committee, Labour Party, 1956–68.

76 Somerville had assumed command of the hastily assembled Eastern Fleet at the end of Mar. 1942. His force consisted of the large carriers *Formidable* and *Indomitable* and the small carrier *Hermes;* the battleships *Warspite*, *Resolution*, *Ramilles*, *Royal Sovereign* and *Revenge*, 2 heavy and 5 light cruisers, 16 destroyers and 7 submarines. Although the 3 carriers represented a substantial portion of those available at the time, their air complement was much too small to deal with the major Japanese carrier forces which might enter the Indian Ocean. Furthermore, many of Somerville's ships (especially the 'R Class' battleships) were old, slow, unmodernised and ill-protected. His major bases were inadequate and the potential support from shorebased aircraft for reconnaissance or strikes was equally insufficient. By the first half of Apr., the *Hermes*, 2 heavy cruisers, a destroyer and a corvette had been sunk by Japanese carrier-borne aircraft. Roskill, *The War at Sea* Vol. II, pp. 22–3.

77 Field Marshal Jan Christian Smuts (1870–1950). Boer Commando leader and given supreme command of Republican Forces in Cape Colony, 1901; Minister of the Interior and Minister of Mines, Union of South Africa, 1910–12; Minister of Defence, 1910–20; Minister of Finance, 1912–13; commanded troops in British East Africa, 1916–17; South African representative in Imperial War Cabinet, 1917, 1918; Plenipotentiary (with General Botha) for South Africa at Paris Peace Conference, 1919; Prime Minister and Minister of Native Affairs, 1919–24; Minister of Justice, 1933–39; Prime Minister and Minister of External Affairs and Defence, 1939–48; GOC Union Defence forces in the Field, 1940–49; Field Marshal, 1941.

78 Churchill had actually sent a telegram of condolence (2 Jan. 1942) from the US, but it failed to reach Keyes. He immediately had his secretary send a copy. J. Peck to Keyes, 4 Nov. 1942, Keyes MSS 140/3/3.

NOTES: PART III

79 Keyes had been invited to Cambridge to deliver the Lees Knowles Lectures for 1943.
80 George Macaulay Trevelyan (1876–1962). Commanded 1st British Ambulance Unit for Italy, 1915–18; Regius Professor of Modern History, Cambridge University, 1927–40; Master of Trinity College, Cambridge, 1940–51; Chancellor of Durham University, 1949–57.
81 Document 142.
82 Trenchard.
83 Baron Sempill [Commander William Francis Forbes-Sempill] (1893–1965). Succeeded father as 19th Baron, 1934. Served in RFC, Aug. 1914–Jan. 1916; RNAS Jan. 1916–Apr. 1918; RAF, Apr. 1918–July 1919; competed in King's Cup Air Race around Britain, 1924–30; Chairman, Royal Aeronautical Society, 1926–27; President, 1927–30; President British Gliding Association, 1933–42; served in FAA, 1939–41.
84 Document 122.
85 Probably Major-General J. C. Haydon, then Vice-Chief of Combined Operations. Eisenhower wrote Mountbatten on 11 Aug. 1942: "I want you to know I appreciate your handing me the constructive criticism of TORCH [landing in North Africa] by General Haydon.' Alfred D. Chandler *et al.*, *The Papers of Dwight David Eisenhower: The War Years* (5 vols., Baltimore, 1970) Vol. I, no. 421, p. 459.
86 Lieut.-General [later General of the Army] Dwight David Eisenhower (1890–1969). Chief of Staff to General MacArthur in the Philippines, 1935–40; commanded US forces in the UK, July–Nov. 1942; C-in-C Allied forces in North Africa, Nov. 1942–Dec. 1943; Supreme Commander Allied expeditionary force in Western Europe, 1944–45; Chief of Staff, US Army, 1945–48; President of Columbia University, 1948–50; Supreme Commander of North Atlantic Treaty forces in Europe, 1950–52; 34th President of the US, 1953–61.
87 Eisenhower himself believed that Tunis was a great enough prize for the Allies to initially land as far east as Bône. The US Chiefs of Staffs were, however, opposed to omitting Casablanca from their plans and relying entirely on the Straits of Gibraltar for communications. Eisenhower wrote: 'As far as I can recall, this was the only instance in the war when any part of one of our proposed operational plans was changed by intervention of higher authority.' Dwight D. Eisenhower, *Crusade in Europe* (Garden City, N.Y., 1948), pp. 79–80.
88 Operation 'Jubilee', the unsuccessful raid on Dieppe, 19 Aug. 1942. In his lecture Keyes said: 'This generation was taught afresh at Dieppe the lessons which were indelibly impressed on the memories of all who witnessed at Gallipoli, on 25th April 1915, the heroic but unsuccessful and costly efforts to capture in *daylight* a much less heavily defended beach than that of Dieppe.' *Amphibious Warfare and Combined Operations* (Cambridge, 1943), p. 99.
89 Keyes had been introduced in the House of Lords on 27 Jan. with Admiral of the Fleet Lord Cork and Orrery and Lieut.-Colonel Lord Lovat as his sponsors. Shortly afterwards, Lord Trenchard delivered an attack on the Navy blaming them and their ignorance of aerial matters for the poor equipment of the Fleet Air Arm and recommending the return of the FAA to the RAF as the best means of ensuring it would be properly equipped. Keyes could hardly have been expected to sit still for this and, departing from precedent, he intervened in the debate on his very 1st day in the House of Lords. Aspinall-Oglander, *Roger Keyes*, pp. 428–9.
90 Captain Reginald H. Portal, now Assistant Chief of Naval Staff (Air).
91 Major Alexander P. de Seversky (1894–1974). Russian-born pioneer aviator; flew with Imperial Russian Navy, 1915; successful aircraft designer whose P-35 was one of the first all metal planes to exceed 300 miles per hour and whose basic design would in a few years be elaborated upon and developed into the famous P-47 Thunderbolt. In 1942 Seversky published his

widely-read *Victory Through Air Power,* a prophetic work in which he advocated the development of long range aircraft which would operate from home grounds instead of advanced bases turning everything in between into a no man's land and rendering the naval aircraft carrier unnecessary. For a synopsis of his work see Edward Warner, 'Douhet, Mitchell, Seversky: Theories of Air Warfare,' in Edward Mead Earle (ed.), *Makers of Modern Strategy* (Princeton, 1960), pp. 501–3.

92 Lord Trenchard on 27 Jan.
93 Rear-Admiral [later Admiral Sir] Denis W. Boyd (1891–1965). Commanded carrier *Illustrious,* 1940; Rear-Admiral commanding Mediterranean Aircraft Carriers, 1941; commanded Eastern Force Aircraft Carriers (including Madagascar operation), 1942; Fifth Sea Lord and Chief of Naval Air Equipment, 1943–45; Admiral (Air), 1945–46; C-in-C Far East Station, 1948–49; retired list, 1949.
94 Rt Hon Sir R. Stafford Cripps (1889–1952). Younger son of 1st Baron Parmoor. Knighted, 1930. MP (Lab) East Bristol, 1931–50; Solicitor-General, 1930–31; Ambassador to Russia, 1940–42; Lord Privy Seal and Leader of House of Commons, 1942; Minister of Aircraft Production, 1942–45; President of Board of Trade, 1945; Minister for Economic Affairs, 1947; Chancellor of the Exchequer, 1947–50.
95 The Fairey Swordfish, a relatively slow biplane which entered service in 1936, became known affectionately as the 'Stringbag'. Although considered obsolescent by 1939, the Swordfish thanks to its magnificent handling qualities remained in 1st line service throughout the war in Europe and actually outlasted the aircraft (the Albacore) which was supposed to replace it. For details see Owen Thetford, *British Naval Aircraft since 1912* (rev. edn. London, 1971), pp. 132–45.
96 Admiral Sir Reginald Guy Henderson (1881–1939). Flag Captain of *Hawkins* and Chief Staff Officer to C-in-C China, 1919–21; on staff of RN College, Greenwich, 1923–25; commanded aircraft carrier *Furious,* 1926–28; with Naval Mission to Rumania, 1929; Rear-Admiral commanding Aircraft Carriers, 1931–33; Third Sea Lord and Controller of the Navy, 1934–39.
97 See Document 126.
98 Flag Officer-in-Charge, Great Yarmouth.
99 For a discussion of this point see Roskill, *The War at Sea* Vol. I, pp. 173–4.
100 Captain Bernard Armitage Warburton Warburton-Lee (1887–1940). Commanded 2nd Destroyer Flotilla in 1st Battle of Narvik, 10 Apr. 1940; killed in the battle and awarded posthumous Victoria Cross.
101 On 24 July 1940 the Admiralty sent North, then Flag Officer Commanding North Atlantic from Gibraltar to Oran to ascertain the likelihood of the French Navy continuing co-operation with the British. North reported that the French would not surrender to a British force. He later repeated these warnings to Admiral Somerville, Commander of Force H, in the days preceding Operation 'Catapult', the action against the French Fleet at Mers-el-Kébir. See Marder, *From the Dardanelles to Oran,* pp. 204–6, 230–1.
102 On 4 July, the day after 'Catapult', North had placed his objections to the use of force on record in a long signal to the Admiralty which earned him a sharp rebuke. *Ibid.,* pp. 269–70.
103 In speaking of the fiasco at Dakar, Churchill remarked: 'The whole situation at Dakar was transformed in a most unfavourable manner by the arrival there of three French cruisers and three destroyers which carried with them a number of Vichy partisans, evidently of a most bitter type. . . . By a series of accidents, and some errors which have been made the subject of disciplinary action or are now subject to formal inquiry, neither the First Sea Lord nor the Cabinet was informed of the approach of these ships to the Straits of Gibraltar until it was too late to stop them passing through.' Churchill concluded: 'The House may therefore rest assured—indeed it is the only point I am seeking to make to-day—that the mischievous arrival

of these ships, and the men they carried, at Dakar arose in no way from any infirmity of purpose on the part of the Government; it was one of those mischances which often arise in war and especially in war at sea.' *Parliamentary Debates, Commons,* 5th series, vol. 365, cols. 298–9.

104 Paul Reynaud (1878–1966). Unsuccessfully supported in French legislature De Gaulle's proposals for creation of special armoured force, 1936; Minister of Finance, Nov. 1938–Mar. 1940; Premier, Mar.–June 1940; extremely bitter against King Leopold for his surrender, Reynaud hoped to continue the war from North Africa but was unable to overcome the defeatism of Pétain (Vice-Premier) and Weygand (C-in-C); resigned 16 June and was replaced by Pétain who immediately asked the Germans for an Armistice.

105 Keyes's informant was mistaken on this point. Governor-General Pierre Boisson was apparently determined to defend Dakar to the end. See Auphan and Mordal, *The French Navy in World War II,* pp. 188–91. There were, however, persistent rumours that Boisson had been about to surrender. See Marder, *Operation 'Menace',* p. 149, n. 9.

106 1st Baron Winster [Commander Reginald Thomas Herbert Fletcher] (1885–1961). Created Baron, 1942. MP (Lab) Nuneaton div. of Warwickshire, 1935–41; Parliamentary Private Secretary to First Lord of the Admiralty, 1940–41; Minister of Civil Aviation, 1945–46; Governor and C-in-C of Cyprus, 1946–49.

107 Admiral John Byng (1704–1757). Sent to relieve Minorca in 1756; fought inconclusive engagement with French Fleet (20 May) after which in accordance with decision of his council of war he retired to Gibraltar, resulting in the loss of Minorca; tried by court martial on his return to England and convicted of failing to do his utmost to defeat the French Fleet; executed by firing squad 27 Jan. 1757. Although generally acknowledged to have exercised poor judgement, Byng was undoubtedly used as a scapegoat by the Government.

108 Admiral Thomas Mathews (1676–1751). C-in-C in Mediterranean, 1742; fought inconclusive action with French and Spanish Fleet off Toulon, Feb. 1744; after a lengthy series of courts martial concerning the mismanaged affair, convicted of neglect of duty and dismissed from the service, 1747.

109 Keyes expanded a letter concerning possible American interest in Commander C. Varley's project for a 'sea tank' (actually a small submarine) into a long complaint about his treatment during the war; the failure to use in the Mediterranean the amphibious striking force he had created; and what he considered missed opportunities for the majority of Commandos 'left lying idle at home'. He concluded with the statement: 'I have stood up to many hard knocks from enemies, but I certainly never expected such a knock-out blow from you. How much longer are you going to leave me to eat my heart out in idleness?' Keyes to Churchill, 8 Aug. 1943, Keyes MSS. 13/14.

110 Keyes claimed the excuse for getting rid of him on his 69th birthday had been his age and asked: 'You are now 69, do you feel that you ought to be deprived of your great and strenuous job because of your age? Are you going to hand it over to young Anthony [Eden]?', *ibid.*

111 Document 151

112 No. 3 Commando was landed behind enemy lines in the Bay of Agnone in order to prevent the destruction of the Ponte dei Malati, an important bridge on the road to Catania and Messina. Losses were heavy, largely because strong German forces (the 1st Parachute div. and portions of the Herman Goering div.) defended the area. The Commando, in the face of superior forces, could not hold on to the bridge, but were able to create enough confusion to prevent its destruction when the Germans retreated. For details see Saunders, *The Green Beret,* ch. xi.

113 Lieut.-General [later General] George S. Patton (1885–1945). US expert on mechanised warfare. Commanded tank brigade, 1940; 2nd Armoured Div., 1941; organised desert training centre, Indio, California, 1942; commanded

western task force during operations in North Africa, 1942-43; commanded US 7th Army, 1943-44; US 3rd Army, 1944-45; US 15th Army, 1945.
114 Document 142.
115 Not reproduced. Presumably congratulating Mountbatten on his appointment as Supreme Allied Commander, South East Asia.
116 Mountbatten later wrote: 'It was embarrassing for me – a mere captain – to have to take over from this famous Admiral of the Fleet, who had served under my father, and who had been kind to me when he was Commander-in-Chief of the Mediterranean Fleet, and I was a two-striper on his Staff in the 1920s.' Reproduced in John Terraine, *The Life and Times of Lord Mountbatten* (London, 1968), p. 84.
117 Simon Christopher Joseph Fraser, 17th Baron Lovat (1911–). 24th Chief of Clan Fraser. Succeeded father, 1933. Served in Scots Guards, 1934-37; Captain, Lovat Scouts, 1939; joined Commandos and subsequently commanded No. 4 Commando at Dieppe; Lieut.-Colonel, 1942; Brigadier, 1944; commanded No. 1 Special Service Brigade at Normandy landings, 1944; Joint Parliamentary Under-Secretary of State for Foreign Affairs, May-July, 1945.
118 In early Mar. Keyes had undergone an operation in St Mary's Hospital, Paddington, to repair a detached retina in his right eye. Following the operation he was forced to lie absolutely still with both eyes bandaged for 3 weeks. The operation was successful, but unfortunately the concussion from a near miss during an air raid the night of 21 Mar. apparently caused a portion of the retina to become detached again. Keyes returned to Tingewick in the hope the eye would heal, but had to return for a 2nd operation the latter part of April. This was not successful and Keyes lost the sight of his right eye.. Aspinall-Oglander, *Roger Keyes*, pp. 430-3.
119 Cork and Orrery's *My Naval Life* was published by Hutchinson in 1942.
120 *Scharnhorst* had attempted to attack the Arctic convoys but was trapped and sunk on 26 Dec. 1943 by the escorts and covering force commanded by Admiral Sir Bruce Fraser in the *Duke of York*. For details see Roskill, *The War at Sea* Vol. III (pt. 1), pp. 81-9.
121 Presumably the Norwegian destroyer *Stord* which along with *Scorpion*, *Savage* and *Saumarez* delivered the torpedo attack that crippled the *Scharnhorst* and ensured her doom.
122 Operation 'Source', the attack by X-craft (midget submarines) on German heavy units in Altenfiord. On 22 Sept. 1943, *X.6* and *X.7* managed to penetrate the heavily-defended anchorage of the *Tirpitz* in Kaa fiord and cause damage which put the battleship out of action for over 6 months.
123 Operation 'Tungsten' of 3 Apr. 1944 consisted of a raid by carrier-borne aircraft of FAA on the *Tirpitz* just as repairs to damage caused by the midget submarines were completed. Several hits were obtained and the *Tirpitz* was out of action for a further 3 months.
124 Brigadier Thomas B. L. Churchill, commanding 2nd Commando Brigade, and his brother Lieut.-Colonel J. M. T. F. ('Mad Jack') Churchill, commanding No. 2 (Army) Commando.
125 Admiral Sir Bertram Home Ramsay (1883-1945). Commanded *M.25* and *Broke* in Dover Patrol, 1915-19; commanded *Weymouth*, 1924-25; *Danae*, 1925-27; on staff of RN College, Greenwich, 1927-29; commanded *Kent* and Chief of Staff, China Station, 1929-31; on staff of Imperial Defence College, 1931-33; commanded *Royal Sovereign*, 1933-36; Rear-Admiral and Chief of Staff, Home Fleet, 1935; retired list, 1938; Flag Officer Commanding Dover (including Operation 'Dynamo' – the evacuation of the BEF from Dunkirk), 1939-42; Naval Commander, Eastern Task force, Mediterranean, 1943; Allied Naval Commander-in-Chief, Expeditionary force (including Normandy landings), 1944-45; lost in air crash, Jan. 1945.
126 Churchill was captured on Brac Island, but survived the war.
127 Josip Broz Tito (1892-1980). Served in Austro-Hungarian Army, 1913-15; prisoner of war in Russia, 1915-17; fought with Red Army, 1917-20; labour

leader in Croatia, imprisoned for conspiracy, 1928; led Partisan uprising after German occupation of Yugoslavia, and despite Communist affiliation subsequently received Allied backing; Marshal, 1943; Prime Minister of Yugoslavia, 1945–80; President of the Republic, 1953–80.
128 Lieut.-Colonel J. C. Manners commanding No. 40 (Royal Marine) Commando was killed in the action on Brac.
129 Lieutenant Tapp, RAN.
130 Vice-Admiral [later Admiral] Thomas Cassin Kinkaid (1888–1972). Secretary of the General Board, Navy Dept, 1930; Technical Adviser to American delegation at Geneva Conference, 1932; commanded *Indianapolis*, 1937–38; US naval attaché, Rome, Nov. 1938–Mar. 1941, and Belgrade, Mar. 1939–Mar. 1941; commanded Destroyer Squadron 8, June–Nov. 1941; Cruiser Div. 6, Pacific Fleet, and *Enterprise* carrier group (including Coral Sea, Midway, Eastern Solomons, Santa Cruz Islands and Guadalcanal), 1942; commanded North Pacific Fleet (Aleutians Campaign), Jan.–Oct. 1943; commanded US 7th Fleet and Allied naval forces, S.W. Pacific Area, Nov. 1943–Sept. 1945; commanded Eastern Sea Frontier, Jan.–June, 1946; 16th Fleet (subsequently Atlantic Reserve Fleet), 1946–50; retired, 1950.
131 General of the Army Douglas MacArthur (1880–1964). Commanded 42nd div., AEF, 1918; Superintendent, US Military Academy, West Point, 1919–22; Military Adviser to Commonwealth Government of the Philippines, 1935; Field Marshal of Philippine Army, 1936–37; commanded US and Philippine forces during Japanese invasion, 1941–42; commanded US Armed forces in Far East, 1941–51; Supreme Commander Allied forces in S.W. Pacific, 1942–45; commanded Occupation forces in Japan, 1945–51; C-in-C UN forces in Korea, 1950–51; Chairman of the Board, Remington Rand, Inc., 1951–55; Sperry Rand, 1955–64.
132 Admiral [later Fleet Admiral] Chester William Nimitz (1885–1966). Commanded *Augusta*, 1933–35; Assistant Director, Bureau of Navigation, Navy Dept, 1935–38; commanded Battleship Div. 1, Battle Force, 1938–39; Chief, Bureau of Navigation, June 1939–Dec. 1941; C-in-C Pacific Fleet, Dec. 1941–Nov. 1945; Fleet Admiral, Dec. 1944; Chief of Naval Operations, 1945–47.
133 Royle was mistaken as 'overcoming the intricate defenses of Peleliu cost the attackers the highest combat casualty rate (nearly 40 per cent) of any amphibious assault in American history.' E. B. Potter and Chester W. Nimitz (eds.), *The Great Sea War* (New York, 1960), p. 365. The official US Army historian considered the Palaus operation so costly 'that one wonders if the results were worth the effort', Robert Ross Smith, *The Approach to the Philippines* ('The United States Army in World War II: The War in the Pacific Vol. III', Washington, D.C., 1953), p. 573.
134 Typescript copy with pencilled corrections titled 'R.K.'s Expedition to the Philippines'. The diary closely follows the letters Keyes sent his wife while he was with the American forces, but is more complete as Keyes deleted many details from the private correspondence for security reasons.
135 Probably Thomas B. Martin, Press Relations adviser to the High Commissioner of the UK, Canberra.
136 Captain Edward Penry Thomas (1890–). Naval Officer-in-Charge, Darwin, 1939–42, Brisbane, 1943–48; retired list, 1948.
137 Sir Leslie Orme Wilson (1876–1955). Commissioned in RMLI and served in South Africa, 1899–1901; MP (U) Reading, 1913–22; MP (C) South Portsmouth, 1922–23; commanded Hawke bn., Royal Naval Div. at Gallipoli and in France (severely wounded), 1915–16; Parliamentary Assistant Secretary to the War Cabinet, 1918; Parliamentary Secretary to the Ministry of Shipping, 1919; Parliamentary Secretary to the Treasury and Chief Unionist Whip, 1921–23; Governor of Bombay, 1923–28; Governor of Queensland, 1932–46.
138 Commodore James Earl Boak (1891–1956). Commanded advance naval base in New Hebrides, 1943; Manus Island, 1944–45.
139 Rear-Admiral [later Admiral] Richard L. Conolly (1892–1962). Commanded

Destroyer Div. 7, May 1939–Jan. 1941; commanded Destroyer Squadron 6, Jan. 1941–Apr. 1942; Commander Landing Craft and Bases, N.W. African Waters, Feb. 1943–Oct. 1943; commanded TF 53 Southern Attack force (capture of Guam), July–Aug. 1944; commanded TG 79.1 Attack Group 'Able' (part of Vice-Admiral Wilkinson's TF 79 Southern Attack Force, invasion of Leyte), Oct. 1944; commanded Amphibious Group 3 (Lingayen Gulf), Jan. 1945; commanded landing of occupation troops in northern Honshu and Hokkaido, Oct. 1945; Deputy Chief of Naval Operations, Washington, 1945–46; US Naval Adviser to Council of Foreign Ministers, Paris, Aug. 1946; commanded US naval forces, Eastern Atlantic and Mediterranean, Sept. 1946–Aug. 1950; President of Naval War College, Aug. 1950–Nov. 1953; President of Long Island University, 1953–1962; killed in plane crash, Mar. 1962.

140 Rear-Admiral Forrest B. Royal (1892–1945). Chief of US Naval Mission to Brazil, 1939–41; commanded *Milwaukee,* 1941–42; served on Joint Chiefs of Staff, 1942–44; commanded TG 79.2 Attack Group 'Baker' (part of Admiral Wilkinson's TF 79 Southern Attack Force) invasion of Leyte, Oct. 1944; Lingayen Attack Force, Jan. 1945; commanded TG 78.1 Amphibious Group 6 at Zamboanga (Mindanao), Mar. 1945; Tarakan (Borneo), May 1945; and Brunei Bay (Borneo), June 1945; died of a heart attack in his flagship, 18 June 1945.

141 This paragraph is marked 'Omit' and may not be found in other copies of the diary which were apparently circulated.

142 Lieut.-General Richard K. Sutherland (1893–1966). Commissioned 2nd Lieutenant, Infantry, 1916 and served with 2nd Div., American Expeditionary Force, France, 1918; Chief of Staff to General MacArthur, 1939–45.

143 Sir Norman Everard Brookes (1877–1968). Winner at Wimbledon, 1907; played in Davis Cup Finals, 1905–20; President of Lawn Tennis Association of Australia, 1926–55.

144 Lieut.-General Stephen J. Chamberlin (1889–1971). G-4 (Logistics) and Chief of Staff, US Army forces, Australia 1942; G-3 (Operations) S.W. Pacific Area, US Army forces, Pacific, 1942–45; Deputy Chief of Staff and Acting Chief of Staff, US Army forces Pacific and for Supreme Commander for Allied forces, 1945–46; Director, Intelligence, Dept. of the Army, 1946–48; Commanding General, 5th Army, 1948–51; retired, 1951.

145 Brigadier-General Charles A. Willoughby (1892–1972). G-2 (Chief of Intelligence) on MacArthur's Staff, 1941–46. Biographer and ardent defender of MacArthur in later years.

146 Lieut-General [later Sir] Frank Horton Berryman (1894–). GSO (1) 6th Australian Div. at capture of Bardia and Tobruk, 1941; CRA 7th Australian Div. and Commander Berryforce, Syrian campaign, 1941; Deputy Chief of General Staff, New Guinea force, Dec. 1942–Oct. 1943; administrative commander, 2nd Australian Corps, Nov. 1943; commanded 1st Australian Corps, Apr. 1944; Chief of Staff, Advanced Land force HQ, S.W. Pacific area, July 1944–Sept. 1945; commanded Eastern Command, Australia, 1946–50, 1952–53; retired list, 1954.

147 Rear-Admiral Clifford E. Van Hook (1886–1975). Member of US Naval Mission to Brazil, 1927–30; commanded *Portland,* Pacific Fleet, 1940–42; commanded Panama Sea Frontier and Commandant 15th Naval District (Canal Zone), 1942–43; Deputy Commander S.W. Pacific Force, 1943; Deputy Commander 7th Fleet, 1944.

148 Vice-Admiral Theodore Stark Wilkinson (1888–1946). Secretary of the General Board, Dec. 1931–Sept. 1934; with US delegation at Arms Limitation conferences at Geneva, 1933, and London, 1934; commanded *Mississippi,* Jan.–Sept. 1941; Director of Naval Intelligence, Oct. 1941–Aug. 1942; commanded Battleship Div. 2, Pacific Fleet, Aug. 1942–Jan. 1943; commanded 3rd Amphibious Force, Pacific Fleet, July 1943–Sept. 1945; additional duty as Commander of TF 79 (Southern Attack Force, invasion of Leyte, Oct. 1944.

and Lingayen Attack Force, Jan. 1945).
149 Sergio Osmeña (1878–1961). Speaker of Philippine Assembly, 1907–16; House of Representatives, 1916–22; Senator for Cebu, 1922, 1928, 1935; Vice-President of the Commonwealth of the Philippines, 1935–44; President, Aug. 1944–Apr. 1946.
150 Brigadier-General Carlos P. Romulo (1901–). Resident Commissioner of the Philippines in the US, 1944–46; Secretary of Information and Public Relations in War Cabinet, 1943–44; Acting Secretary of Public Instruction, 1944–45; Secretary of Foreign Affairs, 1950–52, 1969– ; Ambassador to the US, 1954–62; head of Philippine delegation to UN Conference, San Francisco, 1945 and at UN General Assembly, 1946–53; President, UN General Assembly, 1949.
151 General [later Field Marshal] Sir Thomas Albert Blamey (1884–1951). Commanded 6th Australian Div., 1939–40; 1st Australian Corps, 1940–41; Australian Imperial Force in Middle East, 1941; Deputy C-in-C Middle East, 1941; C-in-C Allied land forces, S.W. Pacific Area, 1942–45; Field Marshal, 1950.
152 Allan A. Michie (1915–1973). Noted war correspondent. Joined *Time* magazine, 1936; on outbreak of war joined London bureau of *Time* and *Life;* author or co-author of a number of popular wartime books; wrote for *Reader's Digest*, 1947–52; with Radio Free Europe (Munich), 1952–56.
153 Vice-Admiral Daniel Edward Barbey (1889–1969). Chief of Staff to Commander Service Force and Amphibious Force, Atlantic Fleet, 1942; established and in charge of Amphibious Warfare Section, Staff of C-in-C Washington; commanded VII Amphibious Force and conducted all amphibious operations in S.W. Pacific area (including New Guinea, Bismarck Archipelago and Philippines), 1943–45; commanded Caribbean Sea Frontier and 13th Naval District, 1950; retired, 1951.
154 Rear-Admiral Albert Gallatin Noble (1895–). Commanded cruiser *Phoenix*, 1943–44; Chief of Staff to Commander VII Amphibious Force (Barbey), Mar.–Dec. 1944; commanded Eastern Attack Group at Aitape landing and assault on Wakde and Biak (Hollandia Task Organisation), Apr.–May, 1944; commanded Task Group 78.2 at Mindanao landing, Apr. 1945; tactical command of landing at Balikpapan (Borneo), July 1945.
155 Lieutenant William Somers Mailliard, USNR (1917–). Assistant naval attaché, London 1939–40; served with 7th Amphibious Force, 1943–46; Secretary to Governor of California, 1949–51; member (Republican) House of Representatives, 4th District California, 1953–63; 6th District, California, 1963–1974; Ambassador and permanent representative of the US to the Organisation of American States, 1974– ; Rear-Admiral, USNR.
156 Major-General Frederick Augustus Irving (1894–). Instructor, US Military Academy, West Point, 1938–41; Commandant of Cadets, 1941–42; commanded 24th Div., 1943–44 (including Tanahmerah Bay and Leyte); commanded 8th Army Area Command, 1945.
157 Lieut.-General Robert Lawrence Eichelberger (1886–1961). Superintendent, US Military Academy, West Point, 1940–42; commanded 77th Infantry Div., 1942; I Corps (including operations in New Guinea, New Britain, and Philippines), 1942–44; commanded 8th Army, 1944–48; commanded Allied and US ground forces, Japan, 1946–48; retired 1948.
158 Major-General Innis Palmer Swift (1882–1953). Commanded 8th Cavalry, 1936–39; 2nd Cavalry Brigade, 1939–41; 1st Cavalry Div. (including recapture of Admiralty Islands), 1941–44; commanded I Corps (including operations in Dutch New Guinea, Luzon and occupation of Japan), 1944–45.
159 Major-General Clovis E. Byers (1899–1973). Chief of Staff, 77th Infantry Div., 1942; Chief of Staff, I Corps, 1942–43; Chief of Staff, 8th Army, 1944–45.
160 Lieut.-General Sir Leslie James Morshead (1889–1959). Commanded 18th Australian Infantry Brigade, 1939–41; Commandant, Tobruk garrison, 1941; commanded 9th Australian Div. at El Alamein, 1942; commanded Australian

Imperial Force in Middle East, 1942–43; returned to Australia to command II Australian Corps, 1943–44; General officer commanding New Guinea Force, 1944; commanded 2nd Australian Army, 1944; Task Force Commander for Borneo operations, 1945.

161 Fletcher Pratt (1897–1956). Free-lance magazine writer and prolific author including the well-known study of the American Civil War, *Ordeal by Fire* (1935), and one of the first accounts of naval operations in the early stages of the Pacific War, *The Navy's War* (1944).

162 Vice-Admiral Frank Jack Fletcher (1885–1973). Commanded Cruiser Div. 6, 1940–41; Cruisers, Pacific Fleet, 1942; Task Force 61 (Solomons), 1942; Commandant, 13th Naval District, Seattle, Washington, Nov. 1942–Oct. 1943; Commander Northwestern (later Alaskan) Sea Frontier, 1942–45; commanded North Pacific Force and North Pacific area, 1944–45; member of General Board, Navy Dept, 1945–46; Chairman, May 1946–May 1947; retired, 1947.

163 Pratt's criticism referred to the Battle of the Eastern Solomons (24–25 Aug. 1942) in which a Japanese attempt to recapture Guadalcanal was turned back. Admiral Fletcher commanded the carrier task force (Task Force 61) of which Kinkaid's *Enterprise* group was a part.

164 Commodore [later Vice-Admiral Sir] John A. Collins (1899–). Commanded *Sydney*, 1939–41; Assistant Chief of Staff to C-in-C China, 1941; Commodore commanding China Force, 1942; commanded *Shropshire*, 1943–44; Commodore commanding Australian Squadron, June–Oct., 1944; 1945–46; Rear–Admiral 1947; First Naval Member and Chief of Naval Staff, Commonwealth Naval Board, 1948–55; Australian High Commissioner to New Zealand, 1956–62.

165 Rear-Admiral [later Admiral Sir] Victor Alexander Charles Crutchley, VC (1893–). Awarded Victoria Cross for role in attempts to block Ostend, Apr. and May, 1918; commanded *Warspite*, 1937–40; Commodore RN Barracks, Devonport, 1940–42; commanded Australian Naval Squadron, 1942–44; Flag Officer Gibraltar, 1945–47; retired list, 1947.

166 Major-General Archibald V. Arnold, commanded 7th Infantry Div., Feb. 1944–Sept. 1945.

167 Colonel Burton K. Lucas.

168 Lieut.-General John R. Hodge (1893–1963). Commanded XXIV Corps, Apr. 1944–Aug. 1948; commanded US Army forces in Korea, 1945–48; 3rd Army, 1950–52; Chief of Army field forces, 1952–53.

169 According to the historian of US naval operations in the Second World War, Commodore Boak modelled this after the Espiritu Santo Officers' Club, which held the record for the 'longest bar in the Pacific'. Samuel Eliot Morison, *History of United States Naval Operations in World War II* Vol. XII *Leyte* (Boston, 1963), p. 115, n. 6.

170 Captain [later Lieut.-Colonel] Beauchamp Tyndall Pell (1866–1914). Queen's Royal West Surrey Regiment. Served N.W. Frontier, India, 1897–98; South Africa, 1901–02; ADC to General Gaselee in China, 1900; mortally wounded at Ypres, 31 Oct. 1914.

171 Brigadier [later General] Sir Alfred Gaselee (1844–1918). Commanded 2nd Brigade in Tirah campaign, 1897–98; commanded British forces in North China, 1900; commanded Northern Army, India, 1907–08; retired list, 1911.

172 Keyes does not mention the party with the American forces in his *Adventures Ashore and Afloat*.

173 Rear-Admiral Henry Erben (1832–1909). Distinguished service during the American Civil War with gunboats and ironclads on the Mississippi River, naval howitzer battery with McClellan's army during the Antietam campaign, and blockade operations along the Atlantic and Gulf coasts, 1861–65; Commandant of Brooklyn Navy Yard, 1891–93; C-in-C European Station, 1893–94; retired 1894; recalled to service during Spanish American War and placed in command of naval defence system of Atlantic and Gulf coasts as well as the Naval Militia manning the auxiliary fleet, 1898. Erben's Flag Captain

while C-in-C European Station was the celebrated naval historian Captain Alfred Thayer Mahan, but the two were 'hopelessly incompatible' and Erben submitted an unfavourable fitness report on Mahan. See Captain W. D. Puleston, *Mahan* (London, 1939), especially ch. xxii.

174   Captain [later Vice-Admiral] William J. Marshall (1903-). Commanded Destroyer Squadron 48 (Destroyer Screen for Admiral Conolly's TG 79.1), Leyte, 1944; naval attaché, Rome, 1951-53; Executive Assistant and Senior Aide to Chief, Naval Operations, 1953-54; commanded Destroyer Flotilla One, Western Pacific, 1954-56; Director Material, Navy Dept, 1956-59; retired 1959; President, Bourbon Institute, 1959-.

175   Colonel Marc J. Logie, commanding 32nd Infantry Regiment.

176   Colonel [later Major-General] Curtis D. O'Sullivan (1894-1967). Assistant Chief of Staff and G-2, 40th Div. (California National Guard), 1929-39; Chief of Staff, 40th Div., 1939-40; commanded 184th Infantry Regiment, 1941-45; Adjutant of California, 1946-51; commanded 49th Infantry Div., 1950.

177   Keyes probably meant Lieut.-Colonel [later Major-General] Francis T. Pachler (1909-). Commanded 17th Infantry Regiment, 1944-45; Commanding General US Berlin Command, 1954-55; Director of Operations, HQ, Dept of the Army, Washington, 1957-60; commanded 7th Infantry Div. (Korea), 1960-61; Deputy Commandant, National War College, 1961-63; with HQ, US Army Europe, 1963-67; retired, 1967; Commandant of Cadets, Virginia Polytechnique Institute, 1967-72.

178   Admiral [later Fleet Admiral] William Frederick Halsey (1882-1959). Entered flight training, 1934 and designated Naval Aviator at the age of 52, May 1935; commanded *Saratoga*, July 1935-June 1937; Naval Air Station, Pensacola, June 1937-June 1938; Carrier Div. 2, June 1938-May 1939; Carrier Div. 1, May 1939-June 1940; Commander Task Force 16 and Commander Carriers, Pacific Fleet, Apr. 1942-Oct. 1942; Commander South Pacific Force and South Pacific Area, Oct. 1942-June 1944; commanded 3rd Fleet and Western Pacific Task Force, June 1944-Nov. 1945; retired list, 1947.

179   Vice-Admiral Marc Andrew Mitscher (1887-1947). Designated Naval Aviator No. 33, June 1916; pilot in NC 1 which accompanied NC 4 as far as the Azores in first trans-Atlantic flight, 1919; Assistant Chief, Bureau of Aeronautics, Navy Dept, 1939-41; commanded *Hornet*, Oct. 1941-July 1942; Patrol Wing 2, July-Dec. 1942; Commander Fleet Air, Noumea, Dec. 1942-Apr. 1943; Commander Air, Solomon Islands, Apr.-July 1943; commanded Task Force 58, Pacific Fleet (Marshalls, Truk, Tinian-Saipan, Philippine Sea) and Task Force 38 (Central Philippines and Leyte), 1944; Deputy Chief of Naval Operations for Air, 1945-46; C-in-C US Atlantic Fleet, 1946-47.

180   According to Morison, the 3-day (12-14 Oct.) air offensive over Formosa resulted in over 500 Japanese planes destroyed, 2 score freighters, and small craft sunk and many others damaged at a cost of 71 US aircraft. Morison, *US Naval Operations in World War II* Vol. XII, pp. 92-5.

181   Frederick Arnold Williamson-Noble (1889-1969). Consulting Ophthalmic Surgeon, St Mary's Hospital, Paddington and National Hospital for Diseases of the Nervous System, Queen's Square.

182   The heavy cruiser *Canberra* and light cruiser *Houston* were badly damaged, but both were saved.

183   Rear-Admiral [later Admiral] Arthur D. Struble (1894-). Chief of Staff to Rear-Admiral Kirk, commanding Western (American) Task Force at Normandy invasion, 1944; commanded TG 78.4 Dinagat Attack Group (Leyte invasion), 1944; TG 74.3 Amphibious Group 9 (Panay and W. Negros, Philippines), 1945; commanded Minecraft, Pacific Fleet, Sept. 1945; Deputy Chief of Naval Operations, 1948; commanded 7th Fleet (including Inchon and Wonsan landings), 1950; commanded 1st Fleet, 1951-52; retired, 1956.

184   Rear-Admiral Jesse B. Oldendorf (1887-1974). Commanded *Houston*,

1939–41; commanded Aruba Curaçao Area and Trinidad naval base, 1942–43; commanded Fire Support Unit at Pelelieu, Sept. 1944; and Leyte, Oct. 1944; commanded US forces at Battle of Surigao Strait, 24 Oct. 1944; commanded Fire Support Unit Lingayen Gulf and Okinawa operations, 1945; retired, 1948.

185 The LVT, or landing vehicle tracked.

186 Rear-Admiral Walden L. Ainsworth (1886–1960). Known as 'Pug'. Commanded cruiser-destroyer task forces in Central Solomons (including Battle of Kolombangara), 1943; commanded Crudiv 9 (Leyte), 1944; retired 1948.

187 Captain [later Rear-Admiral] John Baptist Heffernan (1894–). Commanded Destroyer Div., Atlantic, 1940–41; Destroyer Squadron, Atlantic, 1942; battleship *Tennessee* at battle for Leyte Gulf, 1944, and at Iwo Jima and Okinawa, 1945; Chief of Staff, 7th Naval District, 1946; Director Naval History, 1946–56.

188 Captain E. F. V. Dechaineux (1902–1944). Commanded *Vivacious, Eglinton,* 1940–41; *Warramunga,* 1942–44; *Australia,* 1944. Died of wounds, 21 Oct. 1944.

189 Lieut.-General [later General] George Churchill Kenney (1889–1977). Commanded 4th Air Force, 1942; Allied Air Force, S.W. Pacific, 1942–45; Pacific, 1945; Commanding General, Strategic Air Command, 1946–48; Air University, 1948–51; retired, 1951.

190 The typescript is endorsed: 'Examined and found correct., R. L. Conolly, Admiral, U.S. Navy, January 18, 1947.'

191 Partially reproduced in Aspinall-Oglander, *Roger Keyes,* p. 446.

192 On 25 Apr., the American escort carriers off Samar Island had been surprised by the powerful Japanese centre force which had passed through the unguarded San Bernardino Strait. Admiral Halsey had mistakenly believed this force, which had been mauled by air attacks, to be in retreat and had turned north with his 3rd Fleet to strike at the northern Japanese force. In the melee which followed 1 escort carrier was sunk along with 3 of the screening destroyers who had attacked the Japanese. 3 Japanese cruisers were sunk by aircraft and the Japanese turned away without pressing their advantage. For the complex manoeuvres making up the Battle of Leyte Gulf see Morison, *US Naval Operations in World War II* Vol. XII, chs. ix–xiv.

193 Partially reproduced in Aspinall-Oglander, *Roger Keyes,* pp. 435–7.

194 Admiral [later Fleet Admiral] Ernest J. King (1878–1956). Assistant Chief, Bureau of Aeronautics, 1928–29; Chief, 1933–36; Vice-Admiral commanding Aircraft, Battle Force, US Fleet, 1938–39; member, General Board, Navy Dept, 1939–40; commanded Patrol Force (Atlantic), Dec. 1940–Feb. 1941; C-in-C Atlantic Fleet, Feb.–Dec. 1941; C-in-C US Fleet Dec. 1941–Dec. 1945; Chief of Naval Operations, Mar. 1942–Dec. 1945; Fleet Admiral, Dec. 1944.

195 The Women's Corps of the US Navy. The name WAVES was derived from the earlier title W[omen] A[ccepted for] V[oluntary] E[mergency] S[ervice].

196 James Roosevelt (1907–). Eldest son of President Franklin Delano Roosevelt. Served (Captain to Colonel) in US Marine Corps Reserve and awarded Navy Cross and Silver Star, 1940–45; represented 26th California District in Congress, 1955–65; US representative, UN Economic and Social Council, 1965–67.

197 Document 163.

198 Keyes quoted Document 164 here.

199 Rear-Admiral [later Vice-Admiral] Arthur George Talbot (1892–1960). Commanded 3rd Destroyer Flotilla, 1937–39; Director of Anti-Submarine Warfare Div., Admiralty, 1940; commanded *Furious,* 1941; *Illustrious,* 1942; *Formidable,* 1943; Naval Commander of Eastern Assault Force ('Sword' Beach), Normandy invasion, 1944; Flag Officer, Force X (Brisbane), 1944–45; head of British Naval Mission to Greece, 1946–48; retired list, 1948.

200 In command of Force X, a landing ship force which was originally to serve with Rear-Admiral Barbey's Seventh Amphibious Force. However, Force X

did not participate directly and instead was used for training a large proportion of the American troops employed in the Leyte landings. G. Hermon Gill, *Royal Australian Navy, 1942-45* (Canberra, 1968), p. 495.
201 A dig at Churchill for his remark the year before that the position of Prime Minister, like that of a Pope or Judge, was quite different, and that it would be difficult to find any fighting post open to an officer over 70. See Document 151.
202 General Sir Ian Hamilton (1853–1947). Chief of Staff to Kitchener and commanded mobile columns in western Transvaal, 1900–02; military representative of Government of India with the Japanese Army in Manchuria, 1904–05; Adjutant-General to the Forces, 1909–10; C-in-C Mediterranean and Inspector-General Overseas Forces, 1910–14; C-in-C Mediterranean Expeditionary Force (Dardanelles campaign), Mar.–Oct. 1915; Lord Rector of Edinburgh University, 1932–35.
203 *Listening for the Drums* (London, 1944).
204 Document 165.
205 Major-General Sir Charles Willoughby Moke Norrie (1893–). Created Baron, 1957. Commanded 10th Royal Hussars, 1931–35; 1st Cavalry Brigade, 1936–38; 1st Armoured Brigade, 1938–40; Inspector, Royal Armoured Corps, 1940; commanded 1st Armoured Div., 1940–41; XXX Corps (Middle East), 1941–42; Royal Armoured Corps, 1943; Governor of the State of South Australia, 1944–52; Governor-General and C-in-C of New Zealand, 1952–57.
206 Rt Hon Francis Michael Forde (1890–). Member of the Legislative Assembly for Rockhampton, Queensland, 1917–22; Flinders, Queensland, 1955–57; member of the House of Representatives for Capricornia, Queensland, 1922–46; Deputy Leader, Parliamentary Labour Party, 1932–46; Minister for the Army, 1941–46; Minister for Defence, Aug.–Oct. 1946; Deputy Prime Minister, 1941–45, 1945–46; Prime Minister, 6–12 July 1945; Australian High Commissioner to Canada, 1946–53.
207 The Australian press had picked up certain remarks Keyes made on his return from the Leyte operation concerning the decision to repair the damaged cruiser *Australia* at an American base because of the notoriously slow Australian yards. Australian union leaders resented what they considered criticism of slack work habits and frequent stoppages, and a considerable controversy resulted. Keyes met with 40–50 trade union leaders at Trades Hall in Sydney and gave them a statement of his views that more could be done on the Home Front. Transcript of the meeting in Keyes MSS. 14/7. See also the account in Aspinall-Oglander, *Roger Keyes*, pp. 446–51.
208 Viscount Kemsley [John Gomer Berry] (1883–1968). Created Baronet, 1928; Baron, 1936; Viscount, 1945. Chairman. Kemsley Newspapers Ltd, 1937–59; Editor-in-Chief, *Sunday Times*, 1937–59.
209 Captain Russell Grenfell (1892–1954). Senior Commander on staff of RN Staff College, Greenwich at time of his retirement, 1937; author of numerous books and articles on naval affairs and history.
210 Grenfell wrote that under challenge from the trade unions Keyes had to admit that he had made an unfortunate mistake and 'had spoken from inaccurate information, and would now doubtless wish to make corresponding amends towards the dockyard workers in Britain whom he had also criticized in the past'. *The Sunday Times*, 12 Nov. 1944.
211 Keyes wrote to Bracken: 'I have made such rapid progress that the doctors have decided that I shall be able to fly to Colombo about the middle of March, as long as there is sufficient oxygen in the plane to keep me supplied if we go up above 6,000 ft. to 8,000 ft.' Keyes to Bracken, 26 Feb. 1945, Keyes MSS. 14/2.
212 Rt Hon Sir Robert G. Menzies (1894–1978). Minister for Railways and Deputy Premier of Victoria, 1932–34; member House of Representatives for

Kooyong, 1934–66; Attorney-General, Commonwealth of Australia, 1934–39; Treasurer, 1939–40; Minister for Co-ordination of Defence, 1939–42; Prime Minister of Australia, 1939–41, 1949–66; Leader of Opposition, 1943–49.

213 Rt Hon John J. Curtin (1885–1945). Member (Labour) of the House of Representatives for Fremantle, 1928–31, 1934–45; Leader of the Opposition, Commonwealth Parliament, 1935–41; Prime Minister of Australia, Oct. 1941–July 1945; Minister of Defence Co-ordination, 1941–42; Minister of Defence, 1942–45.

214 Slang expression in both World Wars meaning 'poor bloody infantry'.

215 Rt Hon Peter Fraser (1884–1950). Leader of New Zealand Parliamentary Labour Party. Minister of Education, Health, Marine and Police, 1935–40; Prime Minister of New Zealand, 1940–49; Minister of External Affairs and Minister of Island Territories, 1943–49; Minister of Maori Affairs, 1946–49.

216 Marshal of the Royal Air Force Sir Cyril Newall, Governor-General and C-in-C of New Zealand, 1941–46.

217 Baruch.

218 President Roosevelt died suddenly on 12 Apr.

219 Document 169.

220 Rear-Admiral [later Admiral Sir] Cyril Eustace Douglas-Pennant (1894–1961). Eldest son of 5th Baron Penrhyn. Commodore commanding British assault force 'Gold' Beach, Normandy invasion, 1944; Chief Naval Staff Officer and Deputy Chief of Staff to Supreme Allied Commander, South East Asia, 1945–46; Commandant Joint Services Staff College, 1947–49; Flag Officer (Air) and 2nd-in-command, Mediterranean Station, 1948–50; Admiral British Joint Services Mission in Washington, 1950–52; C-in-C the Nore, 1952–53; retired list, 1953.

221 Partially reproduced in Aspinall-Oglander, *Roger Keyes*, p. 458.

222 Tomkinson had initially been praised by both the First Lord and First Sea Lord for his conduct after the Invergordon Mutiny in 1931. See *The Keyes Papers* Vol. II, part iii.

223 Admiral Sir Frederic Charles Dreyer (1878–1956). Flag Captain to Jellicoe in *Iron Duke* (including Jutland), 1915–16; Commodore and Chief of Staff to Jellicoe in *New Zealand* on mission to India and the Dominions, 1919–20; commanded *Repulse*, 1922–23; Assistant Chief of Naval Staff, 1924–27; commanded Battle Cruiser Squadron, 1927–29; Deputy Chief of Naval Staff, 1930–33; C-in-C China Station, 1933–36; retired list, 1939; Commodore of Convoys, 1939–40; Inspector of Merchant Navy Gunnery, 1941–42; Chief of Naval Air Services, 1942–43.

224 Field had succeeded Keyes as C-in-C Mediterranean in 1928. Keyes expected to be chosen First Sea Lord when the incumbent, Admiral Sir Charles Madden, retired. However, the First Lord (A. V. Alexander) and Madden chose Field, Madden's former Chief of Staff. See *The Keyes Papers* Vol. II, Documents 200–24.

225 Unfortunately Keyes was too ill to attend and Admirals of the Fleet Lord Chatfield and the Earl of Cork and Orrery served as Cunningham's supporters.

APPENDIXES

APPENDIX A

LIST OF OPERATION CODE NAMES

ALLOY	Capture of the Azores if Vichy France declared war (Summer 1940)
BRISK	Occupation of the Azores (Dec. 1940)
CASTLE	Raid on Jossing Fjord
CHUTNEY	Capture of Grand Canary Island (later PUMA)
CLAYMORE	Raid on the Lofoten Islands
EXCESS	Convoy of fast merchant ships for Piraeus, Malta and Alexandria
GARROTTER	Occupation of Cagliari, Sardinia
GRIND	Seizure of Tangier
HAMMER	Proposed attack on Trondheim
LANDFALL	Passage of convoy of personnel ships through the Mediterranean to the Middle East (sub-plan of EXCESS)
LEAPFROG	Amphibious exercise at Scapa Flow (Rehearsal for PILGRIM)
LUSTRE	Expedition to Greece (Spring 1941)
MANDIBLE	Occupation of the Dodecanese
MENACE	Expedition to Dakar by British and Free French forces
PILGRIM	Capture of Grand Canary Island (elaboration of PUMA)
PUMA	Capture of Grand Canary Island
RANSACK	Raid on the aerodrome at Berck-sur-mer
SHRAPNEL	Occupation of Cape Verde Islands (Dec. 1940–Feb. 1941)
SPRINGBOARD	Occupation of Madeira by invitation
THRUSTER	Capture of the Azores against Portuguese opposition
TRUCK	Home force half only of BRISK
WORKSHOP	Capture of Pantelleria
YORKER	Capture of Sardinia

APPENDIX B

DIRECTORATE OF COMBINED OPERATIONS

Summary of Naval Resources available and planned as of 27 July 1940

(a) *Ships for Personnel*   Tonnage varying from 10,000–3,000

    Available: None
    Earmarked: (Work on 3 ships now being carried out. One will be ready about 15th August.)   5   { 3 'Glen' ships, 10,000 tons, 18 knots; 2 Dutch ships, 3,000 tons, 22 knots }
    Projected (in addition).   6   Isle of Man and Ostend (5) type ships, 20 knots. (1–16-1800 tons, 5–2500 tons).

(b) *Ships for carrying tanks*
    Available: None
    Now being prepared: 2 train ferries, 14 tanks, 12 knots. 4 Turkish horse ferries, 12 tanks, 9 knots.

(c) *Landing craft suitable for putting tanks on to a beach or jetty*

    Available: 4*
    Now being constructed: 26   } M.L.C. speed 7½ knots, 14-ton tank
    Projected, a total of: 105
    Designed: 40-ton tank carrier, speed 10 knots, 3 tanks.

* (Two of these are embarked ready to sail on a projected operation.)

(d) *Landing craft for personnel*

	Available	Now being constructed or bought from America	Projected
Assault landing craft	15*	27	49
Support landing craft	1	7	6
Motor boats	6	81	50
Punts (for use from submarines)	4	24	–
Horse boats	13	–	–

* (These 15 craft are embarked ready to sail on a projected operation.)

Source: Keyes MSS. 13/3.

APPENDIX C

D.C.O.'S SHIPS — SITUATION (CORRECT to 1600 HOURS, 25 AUGUST, 1941)

Ship	L/C's Carried	L/C's Embarked	Troops Carried	Speed Endurance	Position and date	Future Movements	Remarks
Prince Leopold	8 Eurekas or A.L.C. (normally Eurekas)	4 A.L.C. 4 Eurekas	Offrs. – 20 O.R. – 250	22 kts–1,210 18 kts–1,584	Falmouth 22/8 (In hand for A. & As.)		(1)
Prince Charles	–or– 7 A.L.C. +1 S.L.C.	4 Eurekas	–do–	–do–	Govan 23/8 Refitting at Babcock & Wilcox	To Inveraray on completion about 15/9	(2)
Princess Astrid	–do–	8 Eurekas	–do–	–do–	Gourock 16/8	To be refitted at first opportunity	(3)
Princess J. Charlotte	–do–	–do–	–do–	–do–	Being refitted at Cardiff by Mountstuart Dry Dock Co.	Unlikely to be ready for sea until 22/10	(4)
Prince Albert	–do–	none	Nil	22 kts–1,048 16 kts–1,300 12 kts–1,200 (max)	Penarth	Completes 15th Sept.	(5)
Daffodil	13 M.L.C. loaded with 16-ton tanks	Nil	Offrs. – 13 O.R. – 123	–do–	Aultbea 4/8	Returns Inveraray 1/9	(6)
Iris	–do–	6 M.L.C. 9 A.L.C. 2 M.L.C. 1 S.L.C.	–do–	16 kts–9,600 14 kts–12,400	Inveraray 20/8		
*Hydra	9 A.L.C. 2 M.L.C. 1 S.L.C.		Offrs – 180 O.R. – 1515		Greenock 2/8 for repairs	Completes 17/8	(7)

APPENDIX C — Continued

Ship	L/C's Carried	L/C's Embarked	Troops Carried	Speed Endurance	Position and date	Future Movements	Remarks
*Karanja	–do–	–do– +12 11-man punts	Offrs. & N.C.O.s – 283 O.R. – 1487	17 kts–7,600 13½ kts–12,000	Gourock 17/8	To Inveraray	(8)
*Ennerdale Derwentdale *Dewdale	14 M.L.C. each loaded with 10/11½ tons	12 M.L.C. 8 M.L.C. 11 M.L.C.	Reduced M.L.C. crews Offrs. – 5 P.O.s – 15 Ratings – 60	12½ kts–13,000 11 kts –15,000	Inveraray 17/8 Belfast 26/8 Greenock 24/8	To Inveraray	(9)
*Bachaquero	24 16- or 25-ton tanks +1 A.L.C., M.L.C., S.L.C., or Eurekas	None	Offrs. – 8 O.R. – 150	11 kts–5,000	Gourock 16/8	To Inveraray Ready end of October	
*Misoa Tasajera					Gourock 17/8 Greenwell's Yard, Sunderland Taken in hand 23/8 by Barclay Curle, Govan for repairs to propellers	Completion date 31/8 approx.	(10)
*Princess Beatrix	5 A.L.C. 2 M.L.C. 1 S.L.C.	5 A.L.C. 2 M.L.C. 1 S.L.C.	Offrs. – 19 O.R. – 385	22 kts–2,300 20 kts–3,500			
*Queen Emma	–do–	–do–	–do–	15 kts–5,000 12 kts–9,000	Inveraray 18/8	To be docked for bottom cleaning when *P. Beatrix* undocks on or about 31/8	
*Royal Ulsterman	none	fitted with brows	750 all ranks	17 kts–3,000 14 kts–3,500	Greenock 8/8		

APPENDIX C — Continued

Ship	L/C's Carried	L/C's Embarked	Troops Carried	Speed Endurance	Position and date	Future Movements	Remarks
*Royal Scotsman	none	fitted with brows	Offrs. – 50 O.R. – 700	17 kts–3,000 14 kts–3,500	repairs to galley. Completion about 21/8 Troon 19/8	Leaves Clyde in D.S. 10	(11)
*Ulster Monarch	none	fitted with brows	Offrs. – 70 O.R. – 700	17 kts–3,000 14 kts–3,500	Gourock 17/8		

Ships marked * designated for Operation 'Pilgrim'.

REMARKS

(1) Belgians cannot hoist E. coast cobles or more than 2 craft at a time. Fitted with T/W gear.
(2) 35 defects. Requires refit. Tubes burst in centre forward boiler. Tubes distorted in centre after boiler.
(3) Only one turbo-generator. Other gone to *Prince Leopold*. Defects to electrical installation. Defects & leak from for'd F.W. tank.
(4) Defects to main steam pipe, boilers and turbines.
(5) Fitted with T/W gear.
(6) Kite-balloon ship at Aultbea.
(7) F.W. Tanks & filters being cleaned out. Completion date 17/8 approx. W/T not good. Defects to be removed. Boiler cleaning also in hand.
(8) W/T equipment not satisfactory. Defects to be remedied. Will require 14 days. Work cannot be undertaken on Clyde. (V.A.C.T.C.s 1011/21).
(9) Max. hoisting load 30 tons.
(10) *Misoa* to be taken in hand for repairs to galley after 18/8.
(11) Derricks can only lift 5 tons. 48 hrs. notice for steam. To carry out fuelling trials.

Source: Keyes MSS. 13/21.

APPENDIX D

LANDING CRAFT AND CARRIERS — WEEKLY STATEMENT — 15 OCTOBER 1941

Landing Craft		Available at or in transit to Bases (Figures in brackets show numbers arrived)	On Board or in transit to		Total completed (excluding those lost)	Nos. still to be delivered	Forecast Deliveries
1. *A.L.C.*	*Northney*	8	*Glengyle*	11	109	79	15 Nov.
	Inveraray	26[a]	*Glenroy*	11			15 Dec.
	Mid East	9 (9)	*Glenearn*	12			49 later[b]
	Freetown	4 (4)	*Queen Emma*	5			+8 per month afterwards
			P. Beatrix	5			(18 ordered)
			Karanja	9			
			Keren	9			
2. *M.L.C.*	*Northney*	8	*Glengyle*	2	119	20	20 starting December
	M.N.B.D.O.	1	*Glenroy*	2			+5 per month afterwards
	Inveraray	23[c]	*Glenearn*	2			
	Scapa	2	*Queen Emma*	2			
	Freetown	2 (2)[d]	*P. Beatrix*	2			
	Iceland	2 (2)	*Iris*	6			
	Mid East	19 (19)	*Daffodil*	0			
			Karanja	2			
			Keren	2			
			Dewdale	14			
			Ennerdale	14			
			Derwentdale	14			

APPENDIX D — Continued

Landing Craft	Available at or in transit to Bases (Figures in brackets show numbers arrived)		On Board or in transit to		Total completed (excluding those lost)	Nos. still to be delivered	Forecast Deliveries
3. *S.L.C.*	*Northney*	2	*Glengyle*	1	23	9	3 Nov.[f]
	Inveraray	4[e]	*Glenroy*	2			3 Dec.
	Mid East	9 (3)	*Glenearn*	1			3 Jan.
			Queen Emma	1			
			P. Beatrix	1			
			Karanja	1			
			Keren	1			
(b) *H.S.C.* (Heavy Support Craft)						5	Starting December
4. (a) *Mk. 1 T.L.C.* (10 knot)	Mid East	9 (9)			19	nil	6 Oct.
	Detached Service	10					8 Nov.
(b) *Mk. 2 T.L.C.* (13 knot triple)	Doing trials	3			31	38	8 Dec.
	Oban	7[g]					8 Jan.
	Being unbolted	2					8 Feb.
	Awaiting shipment	4					
(c) *Mk. 3 T.L.C.* (elongated twin)	Mid East	15 (3)[h]				120	1 Nov.
							3 Dec.
(d) *B.P.V.* (Beach Protection Vessels)						2	116 later
							2 Nov.
(e) *Indian T.L.C.s* (Mk 2)						10	due end 1942[i]

APPENDIX D — Continued

Landing Craft	Available at or in transit to Bases (Figures in brackets show numbers arrived)	On Board or in transit to	Total completed (excluding those lost)	Nos. still to be delivered	Forecast Deliveries
5. *Z Craft*		(All to Mid East)		44	15 Dec., 15 Feb., 14 May[j]
6. *Raiding Craft* (Higgins Eurekas)			148	100	10 Oct.
Warsash	25				15 Nov.[k]
Inveraray-spares	10				15 Dec.
21st Flotilla	8	*Keren* 2			60 later
22nd Flotilla	8	*Karanja* 2			
23rd Flotilla	8	*Batory* 2			
24th Flotilla	8				
25th Flotilla	8				
Dorlin House	6				
Northney	2				
Dartmouth	18				
Brightlingsea	10				
D.N.I. Liverpool	1				
Mid East	21				
Freetown	9 (0)				
7. *Special Shipping* (Infantry Assault Ships)	*Glengyle*				
	Glenroy				
	Glenearn				
	Queen Emma				
	Princess Beatrix				
	Keren				
	Karanja				

APPENDIX D — Continued

Landing Craft	Available at or in transit to Bases (Figures in brackets show numbers arrived)	On Board or in transit to	Total completed (excluding those lost)	Nos. still to be delivered	Forecast Deliveries
8. Commissioned Transports	Ulster Monarch Royal Scotsman Royal Ulsterman				
9. Raiding Craft Carriers	Prince Leopold Prince Charles Princess Astrid Princess J. Charlotte Prince Albert				
10. M.L.C. Carriers	Iris Daffodil R.F.A. Dewdale R.F.A. Ennerdale R.F.A. Derwentdale				
11. Tank Assault Ships	Bachaquero Misoa				
Tasajera Winettes (3)					January[l] June 1942[m] August 1942
American Winettes (7)					Sept. 1942 Early 1943[n]

APPENDIX D — Continued

Craft which will be available when the construction programme has been completed:—
(Figures in brackets show the numbers lost by enemy action or other causes in 1941)

M.L.C.	139 (11)	Motor Boats based at Warsash	13
A.L.C.	206 (20)	Salmon Cobles	53
S.L.C.	37 (1)	Tank Assault Ships	13
T.L.C.	210 (13)	Infantry Assault Ships	7
Indian T.LC.	10	Raiding Craft Carriers	5 (1)
Z Craft	44	M.L.C. Carriers	5
Eurekas	248 (14)	Commissioned Transports	3
Water Taxis	18		
			1,011 (62)

REMARKS

a Of which 24 are earmarked for operations.
b Completion dates put back due to delay in delivery of engines from America.
c Of which 14 are earmarked for operations.
d To be transferred to Gibraltar.
e Of which 2 are earmarked for operations.
f Subject to arrival of engines and bullet proof plating.
g To await unbolting—one doing Boom Defence Trials at Rosyth.
h Two ships carrying T.L.C.s have been sunk on passage.
i Approved but India state they cannot build them.
j Building in India.
k 10 of these are being shipped to Malaya.
l Being converted at Sunderland.
m These carry 20 tanks.
n The last 4 of these may be altered.

Source: Keyes MSS. 13/7.

LIST OF DOCUMENTS AND SOURCES

PART I

				PAGE
1. Keyes to Admiral Sir William R. Hall	18 Sept. 1939	Keyes MSS. 16/24	7
2. Hall to Keyes	19 Sept. 1939	Keyes MSS. 16/24	9
3. Keyes to Churchill	1 Oct. 1939	P.R.O., ADM. I/9774	10
4. Memorandum by Keyes	1 Oct. 1939	P.R.O., ADM. I/9774	11
5. Keyes to Churchill	4 Oct. 1939	P.R.O., ADM. I/9774	14
6. Keyes to Churchill	1 Nov. 1939	Keyes MSS. 13/12	16
7. Commander R. T. Bower to Keyes	3 Jan. 1940	Keyes MSS. 8/16	16
8. Rear-Admiral Guy C. Royle to Keyes	26 Jan. 1940	Keyes MSS. 8/16	17
9. Royle to Keyes	3 Feb. 1940	Keyes MSS. 8/16	18
10. Keyes to Churchill	12 Feb. 1940	Keyes MSS. 8/16	19
11. Keyes to his wife	16 Apr. 1940	Keyes MSS. 2/30	22
12. Keyes to Churchill	16 Apr. 1940	Keyes MSS. 13/12	25
13. Keyes to Churchill	17 Apr. 1940	Keyes MSS. 13/12	26
14. Keyes's Plan for Assault on Trondheim	23 Apr. 1940	Keyes MSS. 13/12	27
15. Keyes to Churchill	24 Apr. 1940	Keyes MSS. 13/12	31
16. Churchill to Keyes	25 Apr. 1940	Keyes MSS. 13/12	32
17. Keyes to Churchill	26 Apr. 1940	Keyes MSS. 13/12	33
18. Keyes to Pound	26 Apr. 1940	Keyes MSS. 13/12	34
19. Pound to Keyes	29 Apr. 1940	Keyes MSS. 13/12	35
20. Keyes to Churchill	28 Apr. 1940	Keyes MSS. 13/12	36
21. Keyes to Churchill	29 Apr. 1940	Keyes MSS. 13/12	36
22. Keyes to Churchill	30 Apr. 1940	Keyes MSS. 13/12	40
23. Keyes to Churchill	1 May 1940	Keyes MSS. 13/12	43
24. Keyes to Neville Chamberlain	1 May 1940	Keyes MSS. 13/12	44
25. Lord Halifax to Keyes	2 May 1940	Keyes MSS. 13/12	44
26. Keyes to his wife	18 May 1940	Keyes MSS. (Lord Keyes)	44
27. Keyes to his wife	20 May 1940	Keyes MSS. (Lord Keyes)	50
28. Keyes to his wife	23 May 1940	Keyes MSS. (Lord Keyes)	51
29. Keyes to his wife	27 May 1940	Keyes MSS. (Lord Keyes)	54
30. Keyes to Churchill	4 June 1940	Keyes MSS. (Lord Keyes)	56
31. Keyes to Lord Gort	12 June 1940	Keyes MSS. (Lord Keyes)	58
Enclosures:			
2. Keyes to P.M.	20 May 1940		66
3. Keyes to P.M.	20 May 1940		66
4. P.M. to Keyes	20 May 1940		67
5. P.M. to Keyes	21 May 1940		67
6. Keyes to P.M.	22 May 1940		67
7. Keyes to P.M.	25 May 1940		68
8. Keyes to Gort	26 May 1940		68

				PAGE
9. Gort to Keyes	26 May 1940			69
10. Keyes to Gort	27 May 1940			69
11. P.M. to Keyes	27 May 1940			69
12. P.M. to Keyes	27 May 1940			70
13. Extract from King Leopold to King George	25 May 1940			70
32. Gort to Keyes	18 June 1940	Keyes MSS. (Lord Keyes)		71
33. Keyes to Gort	26 June 1940	Keyes MSS. (Lord Keyes)		71
34. Keyes to Churchill	4 July 1940	Keyes MSS. 13/13		72
35. Keyes to Vice-Admiral Wilfred Tomkinson	6 July 1940	Tomkinson MSS.		73

PART II

36. Directive to General Bourne on Raiding Operations	17 June 1940	Keyes MSS. 13/1	86
37. Keyes to Churchill	22 July 1940	Keyes MSS. 140/3/1	88
38. Keyes to Admiral Sir Walter Cowan	28 July 1940	Cowan MSS.	89
39. Keyes to Tomkinson	29 July 1940	Tomkinson MSS.	91
40. Memorandum by Keyes	16 Aug. 1940	Keyes MSS. 13/1	92
41. Keyes to Churchill	24 Aug. 1940	Keyes MSS. 140/3	93
42. Keyes to Churchill	31 Oct. 1940	Keyes MSS. 140/3/1	93
43. Proposal by Keyes for the Capture of Pantelleria			
(a) Keyes to Churchill	2 Nov. 1940	Keyes MSS. 140/3	94
(b) Keyes to Chiefs of Staff Committee	30 Oct. 1940	Keyes MSS. 140/3	95
44. Keyes to Churchill	5 Nov. 1940	Keyes MSS. 140/3	96
45. Memorandum by Keyes	7 Nov. 1940	Keyes MSS. 140/3/1	96
46. Keyes to Churchill	14 Nov. 1940	Keyes MSS. 140/3	97
47. Keyes to Churchill	15 Nov. 1940	Keyes MSS. 140/3	98
48. Keyes to Churchill	19 Nov. 1940	Keyes MSS. 140/3/1	99
49. Diary relating to Operation 'Workshop'	19 Nov. – 9 Dec. 1940	Keyes MSS. 13/5	100
50. Keyes to Churchill	20 Nov. 1940	Keyes MSS. 140/3/1	112
51. Keyes to Admiral Sir Herbert Richmond	21 Nov. 1940	Richmond MSS.	112
52. Richmond to Keyes	22 Nov. 1940	Keyes MSS. 13/25	116
53. Keyes to Admiral Sir Andrew Browne Cunningham	3 Dec. 1940	Keyes MSS. 13/20	118
54. Brief for Operation 'Workshop'	9 Dec. 1940	Haydon MSS., Box 2	119
55. Exchange of Signals between the Admiralty and C-in-C Mediterranean concerning Operation 'Workshop'			
(a) Admiralty to C-in-C Mediterranean	11 Dec. 1940	Cunningham MSS. (ADD. MSS. 52567)	124
(b) C-in-C Mediterranean to Admiralty	12 Dec. 1940	Cunningham MSS. (ADD. MSS. 52567)	126
(c) Admiralty to C-in-C Mediterranean	15 Dec. 1940	Cunningham MSS. (ADD. MSS. 52567)	127
56. Keyes to Churchill	17 Dec. 1940	Keyes MSS. 140/3	128
57. Ismay to Keyes	17 Dec. 1940	Keyes MSS. 140/3/1	130
58. Keyes to his wife	18 Dec. 1940	Keyes MSS. 2/30	131
59. Keyes to his wife	19 Dec. 1940	Keyes MSS. 2/30	131

LIST OF DOCUMENTS AND SOURCES 377

				PAGE
60.	Keyes to Churchill	22 Dec. 1940	Keyes MSS. 140/3	132
61.	Brigadier Hornby to Keyes	22 Dec. 1940	Keyes MSS. 13/25	134
62.	Keyes to Churchill	24 Dec. 1940	Keyes MSS. 140/3/1	136
63.	Memorandum by Chiefs of Staff Committee	31 Dec. 1940	Keyes MSS. 13/5	137
64.	Keyes to Churchill	22 Jan. 1941	Keyes MSS. 140/3/1	138
65.	Churchill to Keyes	24 Jan. 1941	Keyes MSS. 140/3/1	142
66.	Keyes to Churchill	25 Jan. 1941	Keyes MSS. 140/3/1	142
67.	Keyes to Air Chief Marshal Sir Charles Portal	25 Jan. 1941	Keyes MSS. 13/5	143
68.	Portal to Keyes	26 Jan. 1941	Keyes MSS. 13/5	144
69.	Keyes to Churchill	28 Jan. 1941	Keyes MSS. 140/3/1	145
70.	Keyes to Churchill	3 Feb. 1941	Keyes MSS. 13/3	146
71.	Keyes to Churchill	4 Feb. 1941	Keyes MSS. 13/3	147
72.	Churchill to Keyes	5 Feb. 1941	Keyes MSS. 140/3/2	153
73.	Keyes to Churchill	6 Feb. 1941	Keyes MSS. 140/3/2	153
74.	Keyes to Admiral J. C. Tovey	21 Feb. 1941	Keyes MSS. 13/6	153
75.	Tovey to Keyes	23 Feb. 1941	Keyes MSS. 13/6	154
76.	Keyes to Tovey	25 Feb. 1941	Keyes MSS. 13/6	156
77.	Cunningham to Keyes	10 Mar. 1941	Keyes MSS. 13/20	158
78.	Directive to the Director of Combined Operations			
	(a) Note by Ismay	14 Mar. 1941	Keyes MSS. 13/1	159
	(b) Directive to DCO	14 Mar. 1941	Keyes MSS. 13/1	159
79.	Richmond to Keyes	15 Mar. 1941	Keyes MSS. 15/21	161
80.	Tovey to Keyes	31 Mar. 1941	Keyes MSS. 13/6	163
81.	Keyes to Brendan Bracken	15 Apr. 1941	Keyes MSS. 140/3/2	164
82.	Keyes to Ismay	24 Apr. 1941	Keyes MSS. 140/3	165
83.	Keyes to Churchill	9 May 1941	Keyes MSS. 13/13	166
84.	Keyes to Churchill	10 May 1941	Keyes MSS. 13/13	169
85.	Keyes to Eden	12 May 1941	Keyes MSS. 13/15	170
86.	Keyes to Eden	12 May 1941	Keyes MSS. 13/15	171
87.	Eden to Keyes	15 May 1941	Keyes MSS. 13/15	171
88.	Keyes to Richmond	11 June 1941	Richmond MSS.	172
89.	Keyes to Franklin Delano Roosevelt	12 June 1941	Keyes MSS. 15/67	173
90.	Captain Herbert Woolley to Keyes	26 July 1941	Keyes MSS. 15/25	173
91.	Keyes to General Auchinleck	2 Aug. 1941	Keyes MSS. 13/3	180
92.	Auchinleck to Keyes	3 Aug. 1941	Keyes MSS. 13/20	182
93.	Memorandum by Keyes	6 Aug. 1941	Keyes MSS. 13/9	183
94.	General Sir H. R. Alexander to Keyes	21 Aug. 1941	Keyes MSS. 13/9	184
95.	Memorandum by Keyes	27 Aug. 1941	Keyes MSS. 140/3/2	185
96.	Keyes to Churchill	2 Sept. 1941	Keyes MSS. 13/3	186
97.	Keyes to Hollis	10 Sept. 1941	Keyes MSS. 13/3	188
98.	Memorandum by Keyes	10 Sept. 1941	Keyes MSS. 13/3	188
99.	Keyes to Churchill	11 Sept. 1941	Keyes MSS. 13/15	192
100.	Memorandum by Keyes	11 Sept. 1941	Keyes MSS. 13/9	194
101.	Keyes to Ismay	16 Sept. 1941	Keyes MSS. 13/9	195
102.	Keyes to Chiefs of Staff Committee	16 Sept. 1941	Keyes MSS. 13/9	195
103.	Ismay to Keyes	16 Sept. 1941	Keyes MSS. 13/9	196
104.	Brigadier Charles Haydon			
105.	Keyes to Eden	17 Sept. 1941	Keyes MSS. 15/67	196
	to Keyes	17 Sept. 1941	Keyes MSS. 13/15	197

				PAGE
106.	Memorandum by the Chiefs of Staff	27 Sept. 1941	Keyes MSS.13/1	198
107.	Churchill to Keyes	30 Sept. 1941	Keyes MSS. 13/3	201
108.	Keyes to Churchill	2 Oct. 1941	Keyes MSS. 140/3/2	201
109.	Keyes to Churchill	4 Oct. 1941	Keyes MSS. 140/3/2	207
110.	Churchill to Keyes	4 Oct. 1941	Keyes MSS. 140/3/2	208
111.	Keyes to Ismay	11 Oct. 1941	Ismay MSS. IV/KEY/2/2	208
112.	Churchill to Keyes	14 Oct. 1941	Keyes MSS. 13/3	211
113.	Keyes to Churchill	15 Oct. 1941	Keyes MSS. 140/3/2	212
114.	Churchill to Keyes	16 Oct. 1941	Keyes MSS. 140/3/2	213
115.	Keyes to Churchill	16 Oct. 1941	Keyes MSS. 13/13	213
116.	Churchill to Keyes	17 Oct. 1941	Keyes MSS. 13/13	214
117.	Keyes to Churchill	21 Oct. 1941	Keyes MSS. 13/15	214
118.	Churchill to Keyes	26 Oct. 1941	Keyes MSS. 13/13	216
119.	Keyes to Churchill	28 Oct. 1941	Keyes MSS. 13/13	217
120.	Keyes to Ismay	30 Oct. 1941	Ismay MSS. IV/KEY/8/1	217
121.	Keyes to Ismay	30 Oct. 1941	Ismay MSS. IV/KEY/8/2	217

PART III

122.	Ismay to Keyes	3 Nov. 1941	Keyes MSS. 13/17	226
123.	Keyes to Tomkinson	4 Nov. 1941	Tomkinson MSS.	227
124.	Keyes to Ismay	6 Nov. 1941	Ismay MSS. IV/KEY/11	228
125.	Ismay to Keyes	11 Nov. 1941	Keyes MSS. 13/17	230
126.	Keyes to Ismay	14 Nov. 1941	Ismay MSS. IV/KEY/14	230
127.	Ismay to Keyes	17 Nov. 1941	Keyes MSS. 13/17	234
128.	Keyes to Richmond	18 Nov. 1941	Richmond MSS.	235
129.	Keyes to Ismay	19 Nov. 1941	Ismay MSS. IV/KEY/16/1	236
130.	Keyes to Richmond	3 Dec. 1941	Richmond MSS.	237
131.	Keyes to Tomkinson	24 Dec. 1941	Tomkinson MSS.	239
132.	Keyes to Richmond	4 Jan. 1942	Richmond MSS. RIC/7/4	241
133.	Rear-Admiral Alexander H. Ramsay to Keyes	26 Jan. 1942	Keyes MSS. 8/17	242
134.	Richmond to Keyes	16 Feb. 1942	Keyes MSS. 15/21	244
135.	Lieut.-Commander Rupert Brabner to Keyes	14 Mar. 1942	Keyes MSS. 8/17	247
136.	Keyes to Tomkinson	8 Apr. 1942	Tomkinson MSS.	248
137.	Captain Augustus Agar to Keyes	6 June 1942	Keyes MSS. 15/67	249
138.	Richmond to Keyes	29 June 1942	Keyes MSS. 15/21	250
139.	Richmond to Keyes	4 July 1942	Keyes MSS. 15/21	252
140.	Keyes to Tomkinson	12 July 1942	Tomkinson MSS.	254
141.	Keyes to Field Marshal Smuts	24 Oct. 1942	Keyes MSS. 13/16	256
142.	Keyes to Churchill	26 Oct. 1942	Keyes MSS. 13/14	257
143.	Keyes to Richmond	1 Jan. 1943	Richmond MSS.	258
144.	Keyes to Richmond	5 Jan. 1943	Richmond MSS.	259
145.	Ramsay to Keyes	Feb. 1943	Keyes MSS. 8/17	260
146.	Captain Reginald H. Portal to Keyes			
	(a) Portal to Keyes	2 Feb. 1943	Keyes MSS. 8/17	261
	(b) Annexe – Remarks by Portal	2 Feb. 1943	Keyes MSS. 8/17	263
147.	Keyes to Admiral Sir Dudley North	17 May 1943	North MSS.	264

148.	Keyes to North	27 May 1943	North MSS.	265
149.	Keyes to North	10 July 1943	North MSS.	265
150.	Keyes to North	29 July 1943	North MSS.	266
151.	Churchill to Keyes	14 Aug. 1943	Keyes MSS. 140/3/3	267
152.	Keyes to Churchill	22 Aug. 1943	Keyes MSS. 13/14	268
153.	Mountbatten to Keyes	30 Aug. 1943	Keyes MSS. 15/69	271
154.	Cork and Orrery to Keyes	10 Apr. 1944	Keyes MSS. 15/70	271
155.	Cowan to Keyes	30 Apr. 1944	Keyes MSS. 15/7	272
156.	Cunningham to Keyes	14 June 1944	Keyes MSS. 15/70	273
157.	Admiral Sir Bertram Ramsay to Keyes	19 June 1944	Keyes MSS. 15/70	274
158.	Cowan to Keyes	8 July 1944	Keyes MSS. 15/71	275
159.	William L. Shirer to Keyes	25 Aug. 1944	Keyes MSS. 15/70	276
160.	Royle to Keyes	3 Oct. 1944	Keyes MSS. 14/4	276
161.	Keyes's Pacific Diary	4–28 Oct. 1944	Keyes MSS. 14/3	277
162.	Admiral Thomas C. Kinkaid to Keyes	8 Nov. 1944	Keyes MSS. 14/4	291
163.	Keyes to Churchill	8 Nov. 1944	Keyes MSS. 14/4	292
164.	Keyes to Lieut.-General R. K. Sutherland	18 Nov. 1944	Keyes MSS. 14/2	296
165.	Keyes to Churchill	20 Nov. 1944	Keyes MSS. 14/4	297
166.	Keyes to Bracken	17 Feb. 1945	Keyes MSS. 14/2	299
167.	Keyes to Bracken	27 Feb. 1945	Keyes MSS. 14/2	302
168.	Keyes to Churchill	17 Apr. 1945	Keyes MSS. 14/4	303
169.	Keyes to Churchill	17 Apr. 1945	Keyes MSS. 14/4	303
170.	Bracken to Keyes	1 Aug. 1945	Keyes MSS. 15/71	304
171.	Keyes to Tomkinson	3 Nov. 1945	Tomkinson MSS.	304

INDEX

Abyssinian Crisis 243
Admiralty: and failure to aid Poland 3; and Coastal Command 4, 18; and Norwegian campaign 4, 5, 39, 318; and submarine war 12, 13; suspicious of Combined Operations organisation 78, 148; and Operation 'Workshop' 111, 135; and evacuation of Narvik 329–30; and Keyes's appointment as DCO 115, 227; criticized by Richmond over Irish ports 162; and Fleet Air Arm 222, 247–8, 263–4; and Dudley North affair 223, 265–7, 345; decline proposal Keyes be buried in St Paul's 226; criticized by Keyes for failure to take offensive action 228, 259; and Lord Cork and Orrery 271–2; and Somerville's conduct at Cape Spartivento 345–6; *see also* Naval Staff, Pound, Alexander
Admiralty Islands 279, 282, 294. See *also* Manus
Adriatic 117, 272–3
Aegean 98; *see also* 'Mandible', Dodecanese
Afrika Korps 82
Agar, Captain Augustus Wellington Shelton 249–50, 349
Ainsworth, Rear-Admiral Walden L. (USN) 289, 360
Air Ministry: and Churchill 4; and Fleet Air Arm 16, 18, 241, 242–3, 260–1; cricized by Keyes over failure to understand naval requirements 19, 21, 22; and Combined Operations 87–8, 93; and Coastal Command 113; mentioned 262; *see also* Coastal Command, Royal Air Force, Bomber Command, Fighter Command
Aird, Jack 102
Albania 117
Albert I, King of the Belgians 48, 50, 51, 319, 320

Alexander, Rt Hon Albert Victor (later 1st Earl Alexander of Hillsborough): career 323; and Keyes 81, 132; and Operation 'Workshop' 101, 129; criticized by Richmond 116, 244, 246, 251, 253; and despatch of 'Glen' liners around the Cape 145; criticized by Keyes 150–1, 152, 248, 249, 254, 259; and Singapore base 151; calls for a certain absolute strength 162, 336–7; and Fleet Air Arm 247; and Dudley North affair 266, 267; and Lord Cork and Orrery's report 271; mentioned 74, 262, 322, 330
Alexander, Lieut-General (later Field Marshal, 1st Earl of Tunis) Harold Rupert Leofric George: career 340; on Keyes's plans for Sardinia 184; and Operation 'Leapfrog' 83, 189, 191, 192, 193, 203; and Operation 'Pilgrim' 194; mentioned 197, 215
'Alloy' Operation 107, 129
Amery, Rt Hon Leopold Stennett 7
Andalsnes 4, 5
Andrews, Rt Hon John Miller: career, 343; and proposal Keyes be made Governor General of Northern Ireland 214, 216, 217
Antwerp 49, 320
Anzac (Beach) 225
Arnold, Major-General Archibald V. (USA) 283, 284, 294, 297, 358
Atlantic, Battle of the 167, 168, 169, 170, 173, 175
Atlantic Islands: German threat to 80, 82 170; plans for mopping up 165, 166, 168, 194; and the United States 176, 177, 178; mentioned 167, 171; *see also* Azores, Canary Islands, Cape Verde Islands
Attlee, Rt Hon Clement Richard (later 1st Earl): career 328–9; mentioned 111, 268

Auchinleck, General (later Field Marshal Sir) Claude John Eyre: career 339; views on Commandos 182; mentioned 215, 248, 251, 253
Australia: visited by Keyes 223–5, 277, 300–1, 302; threatened by invasion 250; government requires education on naval affairs 277; delays in dockyards 301, 361; development of naval aviation 302; troops anxious to participate in reconquest of British possessions 304
Australia (Navy): supports operations in Admiralty Islands 279; and Tanahmerah landings 282; and invasion of Leyte 287, 289, 290
Azores: and the United States 82, 175, 177; mentioned 79, 127, 167, 340; *see also* 'Brisk', 'Thruster'

Bacon, Admiral Sir Reginald H. S.: career 318; at Dover 42, 98, 256; and Submarine Service 151; mentioned 72, 240, 249
Baillie-Grohman, Rear-Admiral (later Vice-Admiral) Harold Tom 239, 347
Baldwin, Rt Hon Stanley (later 1st Earl of Bewdley) 13, 313
Balfour, Captain Harold Harington (later 1st Baron) 19, 314
Baltic 3, 8, 11, 13
Barbey, Vice-Admiral Daniel Edward (USN): career 357; in Leyte invasion force 285, 287; mentioned 281, 360
Bardia, 181
Barham, Admiral, 1st Baron (Charles Middleton) 151, 335
Baruch, Bernard Mannes: career 338; and Keyes 82, 173; mentioned 303
Beardall, Captain (later Rear-Admiral) John Reginald (USN): career 339; and Commander Woolley 176, 177, 178
Beatty, Admiral of the Fleet, 1st Earl, David: career 311; and Keyes 15, 151; and Heligoland action 33; and Madden 34, 43; mentioned 8
Beaverbrook, 1st Baron (William Maxwell Aitken) 111, 260, 329
Belgium: Keyes's mission to 3–4, 24, 89, 130, 134; campaign in 7, 44–6, 48–56, 66–71, 73–4; operations off coast during World War I 31, 33, 42, 184; *see also* Leopold III, Zeebrugge, Ostend
Belgium (Army): praised by Keyes 48, 52, 90; and Belgian campaign 60–1, 62, 63–6; forced to request armistice 57, 58, 59, 66–71; mentioned 48, 64
Benghazi 103, 140
Benn, Rt Hon William Wedgwood (later 1st Viscount Stansgate) 244, 253, 348
Bergen 24, 27, 265
Berryman, Lieut-General (later Sir) Frank Horton 280, 282, 356
Bevan, Rt Hon Aneurin 252, 255, 349
Bevin, Rt Hon Ernest 248, 255, 259, 348
Billotte, General Gaston-Henri-Gustav 52, 61, 320
Birkenhead, 1st Earl of (Frank Edwin Smith) 151–2, 335
Bizerte 259, 265
Blake, Vice-Admiral Sir Geoffrey 104, 327–8
Blake, Admiral and General at Sea Robert 20, 314
Blamey, General (later Field Marshal) Sir Thomas Albert 281, 357
Blanchard, General Jean-Maurice-Georges 62, 322
Blenheim, Battle of 128
Boak, Commodore James Earl (USN): career 355; at Manus 279, 282, 283, 291, 358
Boisson, Pierre François 353
Bomber Command (RAF): fails to support Coastal Command 19–20, 22, 113; mentioned 18, 314; *see also* Royal Air Force
Bourne, Lieut-General (later General Sir) Alan George: career 325; appointed chief of raiding operations 77, 86–8, 159; and Keyes 91, 102, 149; mentioned 190, 229, 232
Bower, Commander Robert Tatton: career 313; proposals on Coastal Command 314; on Fleet Air Arm 16, 17; on Bergen 24; charges concerning the evacuation of Narvik 114, 329–30
Bownhill, Air Chief Marshal Sir Frederick William 113, 329
Bowlby, Captain Geoffrey 51, 55, 320
Bowlby, Captain Lionel 55, 321
Boyd, Rear-Admiral (later Admiral Sir) Denis W. 262, 352
Boyle, Admiral Hon Sir Algernon D. E. H.: career 316–17; and Keyes 25, 240. 248–9
Brabner, Lieut-Commander (later Commander) Rupert Arnold 274–8, 348
Bracken, Rt Hon Brendan (later 1st Viscount): career 315; serves as

INDEX

intermediary between Churchill and Keyes 22, 213, 222, 269; advised by Keyes of new edition of memoirs 164–5; suggests Keyes be sent on goodwill mission to Australia and New Zealand 223, 225, 292; receives report of Keyes's mission 225, 301, 302–3; anxious about Keyes's health 304

'Brisk', Operation: delays in preparation of 94, 97; and Joint Planning Staff 96; conflicting claims on 'Workshop' 100, 109; proposed force for 103, 104, 327; mentioned 128, 129, 130, 135, 138

British Expeditionary Force: and Belgian campaign 52, 56–7, 59–71, 74, 89–90, 114–15, 322; mentioned 77; *see also* Gort

British Joint Staff Mission (Washington) 82, 175, 176, 179

Brock, Wing Commander Frank A. 108, 110, 328

Brooke, General Sir Alan Francis (later Field Marshal, 1st Viscount Alanbrooke) 187, 205, 215, 340

Brookes, Sir Norman Everard 280, 356

Brunsbüttel 8, 311

Brunton, Commander Thomas B. 163, 337

Byers, Major-General Clovis E. (USA) 282, 357

Byng, Admiral John 267, 353

Cabinet: and Norwegian campaign 4–5, 6, 42, 318; and Belgian campaign 56, 60; and Operation 'Workshop' 106; and Operation 'Puma' 166; and Dudley North affair 265; mentioned 240, 262

Cadiz 165

Cagliari 81, 183, 184; *see also* 'Yorker'

Campbell, Captain Robin 241

Camrose, 1st Viscount (William Ewert Berry) 240, 241, 337

Canada 33, 224

Canada (Army) 183, 186

Canary Islands: necessity to secure 79, 82; mentioned 340, 341; *see also* Spain, 'Puma', 'Pilgrim', Gando

Cape Helles 225

Cape Spartivento 345

Cape Verde Islands 79, 177; *see also* 'Shrapnel'

Cartier de Marchienne, Baron de 25, 53, 317

Carton de Wiart, Lieut-General Sir Adrian: career 321; and expedition to Namsos 4, 5, 72, 89, 206, 238; mentioned 53

Carton de Wiart, Comtesse 53

Casablanca 168, 170

Caslon, Captain (later Vice-Admiral) Clifford 155, 163, 336

Castelorizzo 158, 181, 336

Casten, Dr Virgil G. 290

'Castle', Operation 136

'Catapult', Operation 352; *see also* Oran

Caubergh, Colonel (later Lieut-General Baron) Alfred Van: career 319; in Belgian campaign 46, 48, 50

Ceylon 245, 246

Chamberlain, Rt Hon Arthur Neville: and aid to Poland 11, 12; and Fleet Air Arm 13, 22, 113; and Keyes's liaison with King Leopold 24; and Norwegian campaign 42, 43–4, 319; and Irish bases 162; and fall of Government 4, 6, 8, 72

Chamberlin, Lieut-General Stephen J. (USA): career 356; mentioned 280, 281, 291, 297

Channel Islands 186, 214

Charles, Prince of Belgium, Count of Flanders 48, 55

Chatfield, Admiral of the Fleet, 1st Baron (Alfred Ernle Montacute Chatfield): career 311; caution of 8, 10; and Fleet Air Arm 14, 21, 243; and Beatty 33; criticized by Keyes over Fleet Air Arm 112–14; criticized by Richmond 116, 162, 251; mentioned 226, 259, 261, 362

Cherbourg Peninsula 186, 214

Cherwell, 1st Viscount (Frederick Alexander Lindemann) 223

Chiefs of Staff Committee: and Operation 'Hammer' 5; and Keyes's proposal for Trondheim 38, 72; appoint Bourne commander of raiding operations 77, 86–8; relationship with Director of Combined Operations 78, 81; and proposal to capture Pantelleria 94, 95, 97, 100, 326; and Operation 'Workshop' 80, 104, 106–7, 109, 110, 132, 137–8, 139, 140, 141, 238, 333–4; and Operation 'Claymore' 154, 336; agree to amendments to DCO's directive 159–61, 209; approve formation of new amphibious striking force 164, 165, 204; and Operation 'Puma' 169; criticized by Keyes for delaying action 172, 186–7; and Operation 'Pilgrim' 191–2, 227, 341, 345; and combined operations

86–8, 93–4, 181, 190; suggest new inter-service organization for combined operations 84, 198–200, 201, 207, 209–11, 212, 227; mentioned 11, 179, 270
Churchill, Clementine, Lady 101, 105, 257, 327
Churchill, Diana 105, 328
Churchill, Lieut-Colonel J. M. T. F. 272–3, 275, 276, 354
Churchill, Mary 105, 328
Churchill, Randolph Frederick Edward Spencer: career 325; serves in Commandos 91, 135, 136, 146
Churchill, Brigadier Thomas B. L. 272, 273, 275, 276, 354
Churchill, Rt Hon Sir Winston Leonard Spencer: returns to Admiralty as First Lord 3, 8, 9, 10, 311, 312; and Fleet Air Arm 4, 19, 21, 112, 242–3, 261; and Norwegian campaign 4, 6, 22–5, 26, 44; and Keyes's proposals concerning Trondheim 5, 32, 34, 37, 39, 72, 104, 322–3; sends Keyes to Belgium 7, 90; and submarine service 21; and Belgian campaign 51, 53–6, 61, 62, 64, 65, 67, 69–70; attacks conduct of King Leopold 58, 59, 74, 322; and seizure of French Fleet 72, 322; appoints Keyes DCO 77, 88, 91, 115; personal relationship with Keyes causes difficulties 78, 83–4, 128–9, 216, 221, 231–3, 234–5, 236, 237, 331; and Pantelleria 79–80, 97, 100–1, 268, 324; and Operation 'Workshop' 102, 104–6, 109, 111–12, 119, 125–6, 130, 132–4, 211, 238, 332, 333–4, 346; rebukes Keyes for intemperate criticisms of naval staff 81, 142, 153; agrees to amendments to DCO's directive 159, 209; and Operation 'Menace' 128, 171, 223, 266, 268, 331, 352–3; broadcasts to Italian people 136, 333; and Operation 'Claymore' 156–7; and Dardanelles campaign 164–5, 172, 255; answers Lloyd George's criticism 169, 337–8; replies to critics in Parliament 172, 238, 338; orders Commandos in Middle East reconstituted 181; meets with Roosevelt in Newfoundland 186, 340; and Operation 'Pilgrim' 192, 193, 196, 197, 341; speech on war situation 206, 342; accepts Chiefs of Staff Committee proposals for new inter-service organisation for combined operations 84, 201–3, 207–8, 210, 227, 235; dismisses Keyes 84, 208, 211–12, 216, 228; rejects Keyes's proposal to go to the Middle East 85, 214; attempts to make Keyes Governor-General of Northern Ireland 85, 213, 214, 216, 343; avoids interview with Keyes 217–18, 233, 237, 268; and question of Keyes's age 207, 267, 268, 361; and motion of censure 222, 252, 254–5, 256, 267, 270; offers Keyes a peerage 222, 257, 258, 259, 269; approves Keyes's goodwill mission to Australia and New Zealand 223, 303; at unveiling of memorial plaque to Keyes in St Paul's 226; and Japanese threat in Indian Ocean 245–6; and death of Geoffrey Keyes 257, 269, 350; sends British Fleet to Pacific 277; mentioned 6, 34, 162, 248, 249, 266, 304, 361
'Chutney', Operation 165
Ciano, Count Galeazzo, 24, 316
Clarke, Captain (WAC) 280, 282
'Claymore', Operation 82, 154–7, 163–4
Coastal Command (RAF): and Fleet Air Arm 4, 17, 18; and proposals of Commander Bower 314; not supported by Bomber and Fighter Commands 19–20, 22, 113; Keyes and Richmond want naval control 113, 114, 116; and evacuation of Narvik 329–30; *see also* Royal Air Force, Fleet Air Arm
Cockburn, Major 55
Collins, Commodore (later Vice-Admiral Sir) John A. (RAN) 283, 290, 358
Colville, (later Sir) John Rupert: career 327; and Keyes 78, 101, 324, 327, 331
Colvin, Admiral Sir Ragnar Musgrave 253, 349
Combined Operations Organisation: and appointment of Keyes 77, 78; directive to General Bourne 86–8; changes in procedure proposed by Keyes 92; Keyes receives revised directive 159–61, 209; Chiefs of Staff Committee suggest new inter-service organisation 198–200, 201, 207, 209–11, 212, 277; *see also* Keyes, Commandos
Commandos: under C.-in-C. Home Forces to meet threat of invasion 78; and Atlantic Islands 79; and Operation 'Workshop' 125, 133, 137–8, 332, 333–4; and effects of delay in

operations 130, 138–9; sent to Mediterranean and Middle East 81, 99, 100, 165, 181; and Operation 'Brisk' 96, 97, 101, 327; and Crete 94, 96, 109; and training 110, 132; strength in December 1940 118–19; dispersal of 144, 146–8, 248, 254, 334; Castelorizzo 158, 336; Churchill orders reconstruction in Middle East 181, 182, 239, 248; operations in Syria 182, 218, 228, 339–40; and Operation 'Pilgrim' 194; Haydon recommends use in series of small raids 196–7; and Keyes 85, 204, 212, 215; Keyes favours use in Mediterranean theatre 215–16, 218; Keyes fears will not be properly employed 228–9, 230, 353; and landings in Sicily 269, 353; and South-East Asia 271; and Dalmatian Islands 272–3, 275–6; mentioned 98, 233, 293

Commandos (Units):
No. 2 275, 276, 354
No. 3 353
No. 7 181
No. 8 (Guards) 132
No. 11 (Scottish) 102, 182, 218, 228–9, 334, 335
No. 40 (Royal Marine) 275, 355
No. 50 (Middle East) 336

Conolly, Rear-Admiral (later Admiral) Richard L. (USN): career 355–6; meets Keyes in Hawaii 224, 228; at Manus 279, 282; at Hollandia 280, 281; Keyes's host during invasion of Leyte 282–7, 289, 290, 292, 294, 297; and landings in Sicily 293; and Keyes's proposal for night landings 298

Cooper, Alfred Duff; see Duff Cooper
Copenhagen 252, 253
Cork and Orrery, Admiral of the Fleet 12th Earl of (William Henry Dudley Boyle): career 315–16; and Norwegian campaign 23, 234; introduces Keyes in House of Lords 222, 351; conducts inquiry into Somerville's conduct after Cape Spartivento 231, 345–6; and debate in House of Lords over naval air 258, 259, 260; and Dudley North affair 266; report on Narvik suppressed in Admiralty 271–2; comments on destruction of *Scharnhorst* 272; mentioned 226, 362
'Corkscrew', Operation 330–1
Cornwallis, Admiral Sir William 162, 337
Corthouts, Major 48

Cowan, Admiral Sir Walter Henry: career 325; serves with Commandos in Adriatic 272–3, 275–6; mentioned 90, 158
Crete: and Commandos 94, 96; centre for raiding 98, 99, 109, 110; shortage of anti-aircraft guns 326; loss of 187, 206, 253, 338; mentioned 119, 127, 181
Cripps, Rt Hon Sir R. Stafford 262, 352
Cromwell, Oliver 161
Crutchley, Rear-Admiral (later Admiral Sir) Victor Alexander Charles 283, 358
Cunningham, Lieut-General (later General) Sir Alan Gordon 254, 350
Cunningham, Admiral (later Admiral of the Fleet, 1st Viscount) Andrew Browne: career 328; and Operation 'Workshop' 80, 111, 126–7, 158; success of 147; and Castelorizzo 158, 336; and Dudley North 223; and Normandy landings 223, 273; and inquiry into Somerville's conduct after Cape Spartivento 345–6; and reinforcements for south-east Asia 303–4; enters House of Lords 305, 362; mentioned 104, 142, 150, 164, 226
Cunningham, Vice-Admiral (later Admiral of the Fleet Sir) John Henry Dacres: career 329; and Operation 'Menace' 107, 266, 328; and Fleet Air Arm 113, 242
Curtin, Rt Hon John J. 302, 362

Daily Graphic 25
Daily Mirror 58, 321–2
Daily Telegraph: and Keyes 4, 8, 240–2; and Trenchard 253; mentioned 19, 304–5
Dakar: expedition to 78, 93, 136, 171; Keyes considers plan foolish 107; and General Irwin 331; Vichy reinforcements doom expedition 223, 266, 345, 352–3; mentioned 168, 170, 264; see also 'Menace'
Dalmatian Islands, see Adriatic
Dalton, Rt Hon Hugh (later Life Baron) 154, 157, 336
Daniel, Captain (later Admiral Sir) Charles Saumarez 105, 328
Dardanelles Campaign (1915): and Keyes 42, 72, 98, 225; and Churchill 128, 164–5; mentioned 6, 31, 33, 259; see also Gallipoli
Davies, Vice-Admiral Richard Bell 254, 350

Davis, Captain (later Admiral Sir) William W.: career 328; and Operation 'Workshop' 80, 104–6, 109, 133; and Operation 'Yorker' 143

Davy, Lieut-Colonel (later Brigadier) George Mark Oswald. career 320; and Belgian campaign 48–9, 50, 64, 65; mentioned 54, 55

Dechaineux, Captain E. F. V. (RAN) 290, 360

De Gaulle, Brigadier-General Charles Andre Joseph Marie 136–7, 266, 333

Denmark 4

De Pret-Roose, Captain Jacques 46

De Robeck, Admiral of the Fleet Sir John Michael 9, 312

De Valera, Eamon 14, 313

Diego Suarez 245

Dieppe 260, 298, 351

Dill, General (later Field Marshal) Sir John Greer: career 321; and Belgian campaign 54, 55, 62, 65, 68; relations with Keyes 205, 206, 207; mentioned 56, 59, 70, 71

Dinagat Island 285, 286

Divisions (Belgian):
15th (Infantry) 64

Divisions (British):
1st 330
10th 284
29th 284
46th 293
56th 293

Divisions (French):
60th 64
68th 62

Divisions (German):
1st Parachute 353
Hermann Goering 353

Divisions (United States):
1st Cavalry 285, 296
7th Infantry 284, 285, 288, 294, 296
9th Infantry 284, 285
24th Infantry 282, 285
96th Infantry 285

Dodecanese Islands: considered preferable to Pantelleria by JPS 99, 104, 326; attack considered inexpedient by Churchill, 103; and Keyes 109, 139, 233, 331; and Cunningham 158, 336; see also 'Mandible'

Dorling, Vice-Admiral James Wilfred Sussex 174, 338

Douglas-Pennant, Rear-Admiral (later Admiral Sir) Cyril Eustace 303, 362

D'Oyly-Hughes, Captain Guy 115, 265, 330

Drake, Sir Francis 161, 165, 252

Drax, Admiral Hon Sir Reginald A. R. Plunkett-Ernle-Erle 253, 349

Dreyer, Admiral Sir Frederic 305, 362

Du Cane, Peter 22, 23, 24, 315

Duff Cooper, Rt Hon Alfred (later 1st Viscount Norwich) 8, 311

Dunkirk 90, 140, 147, 321, 325

Eden, Rt Hon Robert Anthony (later 1st Earl of Avon): career 316; and Belgian campaign 24, 51, 52, 62; and Operation 'Puma' 82, 169, 170, 171, 338; and Operation 'Pilgrim' 198, 342

Egypt 164, 245, 246, 251, 253

Eichelberger, Lieut-General Robert Lawrence (USA) 282, 285, 357

Eisenhower, General (later General of the Army) Dwight David (USA) 259, 266, 351

Elisabeth, Queen of the Belgians 50, 53, 55, 64–5, 319, 320

Erben, Rear-Admiral Henry (USN) 284, 358–9

Esmonde, Lieut-Commander E. 247, 348

Evening Standard 243

'Excess', Operation 127, 129, 137–8, 331, 333, 336

Executive Planning Section (Joint Planning Staff): and proposal to capture Pantelleria 94, 97, 101; and Operation 'Workshop' 105, 106, 109, 110, 139, 336; criticized by Keyes for delaying action 172, 205, 228; and Operation 'Brisk' 327; and Operation 'Leapfrog' 189–90, 191, 206; and Norwegian campaign 206; and Maund 232; see also Joint Planning Staff

Eyre & Spottiswoode 164–5

Fell, Commander 135

Fergusson, Brigadier Sir Bernard Edward (later Baron Ballantrae) 85

Field, Admiral of the Fleet Sir Frederick L.: career 317–18, 362; and Keyes 34, 106, critized by Richmond 116, 162, 244; death of 304–5

Fighter Command (RAF) 19–20, 22, 113; see also Royal Air Force

Fisher, Admiral of the Fleet, 1st Baron (John Arbuthnot Fisher) 151, 172, 255, 335

Fisher, Admiral Sir William W. 116–17, 162, 330

Fleet Air Arm: and Coastal Command 4, 17, 18; and Norwegian campaign 6, 32; and difficulties en-

INDEX

countered on return to naval control 113, 242–4; success at Taranto 118, 243, 330, 347; debate in House of Lords 222, 260–1, 351; success against *Bismarck* 347; neglected by Admiralty 247–8, 260–1; and escape of *Scharnhorst* and *Gneisenau* 247, 348; Trenchard's criticism of answered by Portal 262, 263–4; and operations against *Tirpitz* 272, 354; mentioned 17, 21, 35

Fleets (United States):
3rd 285, 286, 289, 294, 295, 360
7th 292, 294

Fletcher, Vice-Admiral Frank Jack (USN) 282, 358

Foch, Marshal Ferdinand 184, 340

Forbes, Admiral Sir Charles 5, 226

Force 103, 331–2

Force H 127, 128, 322, 345

Force X 360–1

Force Y (French) 345

Forde, Rt Hon Francis Michael 301, 361

Forester, Cecil Scott 206, 342

Fortnightly 250, 254

Forward Operational Planning Section (Joint Planning Staff) 133, 143, 149; see also Joint Planning Staff

France: and Belgium 89; and African empire 175; Keyes recommends raids along coast (1941) 183–6, 211, 214, 215; see also Vichy

France (Army): defeated on Meuse 48, 58–60; and Belgian campaign 52, 56, 57, 61, 62, 64, 65, 90, 114; and attempts to block Zeebrugge (1940) 54, 73–4, 323

France (Navy): and Trondheim 32; and attempts to block Zeebrugge (1940) 54, 73–4; British action against at Oran 72, 74, 93, 322; Keyes wants to use in his plans 136–7; Keyes hopes to win over 152, 158, 171; Vichy Government sends reinforcements to Dakar 223, 231, 264, 345, 352–3

Franco y Bahamonde, Generalissimo Francisco 79

Fraser, Admiral (later Admiral of the Fleet, 1st Baron, of North Cape) Sir Bruce Austin 9, 151, 312, 354

Fraser, Rt Hon Peter 302, 362

Freeman, Lieutenant (USN) 282

Freetown 83, 191, 196, 341, 342

French, Admiral Sir Wilfred Frankland 174, 176, 177, 338

Gallabat 117, 330

Gallipoli: compared to Norwegian campaign 36, 39; and Churchill 128, 164, 172; lack of inter-service co-operation at 149; demonstrates costliness of daylight landings 298; mentioned 15, 31, 33, 189, 351; see also Dardanelles

Gambier, Admiral of the Fleet Sir James (1st Baron) 253, 349

Gando 189, 194, 341

Gaselee, Brigadier (later General) Sir Alfred 284, 358

Geddes, Rt Hon Sir Eric C. 150, 335

George V, King of England 51

George VI, King of England 54, 272

Germany: and threat to Belgium 3; attacks Norway 4, 239, 276; threat to Atlantic Islands 79, 166–7, 170, 185, 194, 195; attacks Russia 82, 176, 183, 186, 216; drive in Balkans anticipated 126; may reinforce Italians 127; danger British will be forestalled in Pantelleria 129–30, 132, 332; transport in English Channel 140; drive towards Egypt 164; and North Africa 175; and Sardinia 193

Germany (Air Force): and Norwegian campaign 6; dominates North Sea 19, 20; superiority in Belgium 45, 46, 55–7, 62–4, 69; arrives in Mediterranean theatre 81, 139, 140, 158, 336; resources strained by Russian campaign 183

Germany (Navy): and Trondheimfiord 5, 39, 41, 72, 89; and Narvik 23, 315, 317; and submarine war 251, 253

Gibraltar: and threat of Spanish intervention in war 78, 82; Operation 'Puma' may precipitate attack on 167; mentioned 186, 194, 195

Godfrey, General Sir William Wellington 91, 325

Goering, Reichsmarshal Hermann 91, 325

Golfini, Monsieur (ADC to Prince Charles) 48

Gort, General (later Field Marshal) 6th Viscount (John Standish Surtees Prendergast Vereker): career 320; meeting with Keyes 50, 55; misses meeting with Weygand 52; and conduct of King Leopold 57–9, 71–2, 266; and Belgian campaign 60–5, 67, 69, 71, 73, 114, 115; mentioned 54, 84, 147, 173, 206, 258

Graham, Lieutenant (USN) 282

Greece: assistance to 98, 99, 117; struggle against Italy 103, 109, 181, 238; and Operation 'Mandible' 125; and Operation 'Lustre' 158, 336; loss of 206
Grenfell, Captain Russell 301, 361
'Grind', Operation 129, 130, 331
Groves, Brigadier Percy Robert Clifford 252, 349
Grunne, Comte Guillaume de 53, 55, 321
Guest, Captain Rt Hon Frederick Edward 21, 113, 314

Hailey, Major (later Brigadier) John Malcolm 49, 65, 320
Haining, General Sir Robert Hadden 135–6, 204, 332–3
Halifax, Rt Hon 3rd Viscount (later 1st Earl) (Edward Frederick Lindley Wood): career 319; and Keyes 44, 129, 342; and King Leopold 68
Hall, Rt Hon George Henry (later 1st Viscount) 239, 346
Hall, Admiral Sir William Reginald: career 311; criticizes Admiralty conduct of the war 3, 9–10
Hallett, Vice-Admiral Theodore John 102, 327
Halsey, Admiral (later Fleet Admiral) William Frederick (USN): career 359; and invasion of Leyte 285, 286, 289, 295, 360; mentioned 293–4
Hamilton, General Sir Ian 299, 361
Hamilton, Rear-Admiral (later Admiral Sir) Louis Henry Keppel: career 338; and Operation 'Leapfrog' 83, 189, 190, 192, 193, 203; and Operation 'Puma' 169, 190; and Operation 'Pilgrim' 194, 204
'Hammer', Operation 5
Harcourt, Captain (later Admiral Sir) Cecil Halliday 24, 316
Harris, Air Marshal (later Marshal of the RAF Sir) Arthur Travers 177, 179, 339
Harrison, Jack 151
Harwood, Rear-Admiral (later Admiral) Sir Henry: career 327; and Operation 'Workshop' 102–4, 106, 110, 129
Hawke, Admiral of the Fleet Edward 33, 151, 317
Haydon, Brigadier (later Major-General) Joseph Charles: career 327; and Operation 'Workshop' 102, 105, 106, 110–11, 119–24, 330, 332; on effect of delay on Commandos 130, 333; prepares report on bringing Commandos up to full strength 147; and Operation 'Claymore' 154, 157, 163, 164; proposes series of raids (Sept 1941) 196–7; and Allied landings in North Africa 259, 351; mentioned 104, 135, 154, 215
Heffernan, Captain (later Rear-Admiral) John Baptist (USN) 289, 360
Heligoland Bight, action (1914) 12, 34
Hendaye 79
Henderson, Rt Hon Arthur 244, 347–8
Henderson, Admiral Sir Reginald Guy 264, 352
Herbert, Captain Godfrey 22, 315
Hitler, Adolf 79, 91, 169, 252
Hoare, Rt Hon Samuel John Gurney (later 1st Viscount Templewood) 21, 44, 113, 314, 319
Hodge, Lieut-General John R. (USA) 283, 358
Hollis, Colonel (later Lieut-General Sir) Leslie Chasemore: career 332; describes Admiralty suspicions of DCO 78; comments on dismissal of Keyes 84; and amendments to DCO's directive 208, 209, 210; mentioned 135, 212
Home Fleet 5, 238
Homonhon Island 285, 286
Hopkins, Harry L.: career 339; interview with Commander Woolley 82, 174–6, 177; interested in Azores 175; meets Keyes 175, 339; expects Keyes will command Operation 'Puma' 178; remarks on resentment of US Chiefs of Staff towards civilian interference 180
Hore-Belisha, Rt Hon Leslie (later 1st Baron) 52, 321
Hornby, Brigadier (later Major-General) Alan Hugh: career 328; and Operation 'Workshop' 104, 110; and preparations for offensive operations 134–6, 334; and Operation 'Claymore' 163
Horton, Admiral Sir Max Kennedy 41, 253, 318
Howe, Admiral of the Fleet Richard, 1st Earl 134, 151, 207, 268, 332

Indian Ocean 245–6, 255, 350
Information, Ministry of 155, 336
Inönü, General Ismet 137, 333
Inskip, Rt Hon Thomas Walker Hobart 1st Viscount Caldecote) 13–14, 21, 113, 313
Invergordon Mutiny 35, 74, 305, 362

INDEX

Ireland: bases denied British 14, 162, 244, 251, 313; Keyes suggests Dominion forces occupy 73
Ironside, Field Marshal (later 1st Baron) William Edmund: career 317; and Keyes's Trondheim scheme 31, 37-8; and Belgian campaign 50, 59
'Irrigate', Operation 203, 342
Irving, Major-General Frederick Augustus (USA) 282, 285, 357
Irwin, Major-General (later Lieut-General) Noel Mackintosh Stuart 107, 128, 328, 331
Ismay, Major-General (later General, 1st Baron) Hastings Lionel: career 325-6; Keyes tells of difficulties 94; and Operation 'Workshop' 100; mission to Russia 195, 196, 208, 342; and amendments to DCO's directive 209; conveys Keyes's messages to Churchill 217-18, 226; worried about Keyes's retention of secret papers 227, 230, 346; and Keyes's suspicion he was victim of intrigue 232, 234-7, 346; mentioned 77, 132, 211, 212
Italy: and Scandinavia 22-6, 239, 315; attitude causes anxiety 37, 40, 42, 89, 238; and Pantelleria 95, 126; expecting attack in Dodecanese 99; attacks Greece 109, 238; raids on mainland of 326; defeated in Libya 127; claims in Mediterranean 136; and Sardinia 183, 186; Keyes proposes amphibious operations against 215
Italy (Army): and desert war 80, 103, 187; garrison in Pantelleria 95-6, 125, 330; and Albania 117; in East Africa 330; and Castelorizzo 336
Italy (Navy): success at Alexandria 254, 349; and Cape Spartivento action 345; reverse at Taranto 347; mentioned 245, 261

Jacob, Lieut-Col (later Lieut-General Sir) Ian 101, 327
James, Wing-Commander (later Sir) Archibald W. H. 231-2, 234, 236, 345
James, Admiral Sir William Milbourne: career 317; as C-in-C Portsmouth 4, 31; and Keyes's Trondheim plan 309; on Pound 255; mentioned 89, 249
Japan: successes in Far East (1942) 221, 240, 244, 347; threat to Madagascar 245; mentioned 40, 225, 249
Japan (Navy): successes in Indian Ocean 245, 246, 249, 349, 350; and invasion of Leyte 285-7, 291-2, 295, 299, 360
Jellicoe, Admiral of the Fleet, 1st Earl (John Rushworth Jellicoe): career 318; and Beatty 34, 43; dismissed by Lloyd George 42, 151, 249; and Passchendaele offensive 108, 256; mentioned 72, 98, 240, 244
John, Captain (later Admiral of the Fleet Sir) Caspar 247, 348
Johnson, Captain (later Brigadier) James Robert 45, 48, 51, 52, 54, 319
Johnson, Robin E. A. 132, 332
Joint Intelligence Committee 172, 228
Joint Planning Staff: and Operation 'Workshop' 80, 105, 106, 109, 110, 139; relationship to DCO 159-60; and Norwegian campaign 206; and Operation 'Brisk' 96, 97; and Pantelleria 98, 101, 106, 326; criticized by Keyes for delaying action 172, 205, 228; see also Executive Planning Section, Forward Operational Planning Section
'Jubilee', Operation 351

Kassala 117, 330
Kemsley, Viscount (John Gomer Berry) 301, 361
Kenney, Lieut-General (later General) George Churchill (USAAF) 291, 360
Kenny, Commander (USN) 285-6, 290
Keppel, Admiral Augustus 151, 335
Kershaw, Captain Cecil A. 163, 337
Keyes, Diana Margaret 25, 132, 316
Keyes, Elizabeth Mary 25, 316
Keyes, Eva Mary Salvin Bowlby, Lady: illness of 4, 22, 89, 315; and Norwegian campaign 32, 309; cool towards offer of peerage 259; accompanies husband on goodwill mission to US, Australia and New Zealand 223-4, 277, 281, 283, 292-4 300; mentioned 74, 102, 132, 254, 323
Keyes, Lieut-Colonel Geoffrey Charles Tasker: career 316; serves in Commandos 81, 91; at Duchess of Montrose's Ball 131; and Litani River action 228, 339-40; and raid on Rommel's headquarters 221, 239, 241, 248, 300, 346-7; awarded posthumous Victoria Cross 221, 254, 347; honoured on plaque in St Paul's 226; mentioned 24, 48, 53, 102, 132, 174, 196, 225, 249, 281
Keyes, Katherine Elizabeth 24, 25, 74, 91, 132, 255, 316

Keyes, Lieutenant Roger George Bowlby (later 2nd Baron Keyes): career 321; serves in Royal Navy 53, 56, 131; in *Arethusa* 241, 250, 255, 347; in Adriatic 275; mentioned 48, 102, 132, 174, 196, 248

Keyes, Admiral of the Fleet, 1st Baron (Roger John Brownlow Keyes): unemployed at outbreak of war 3, 89; wants to be Chief of Naval Staff 3, 8–9; on loss of *Courageous* 8–9; sends *Sunday Chronicle* article to Churchill 10, 312; submits memorandum on conduct of war (Oct 1939) 11–14; seeks employment as Deputy First Sea Lord 15; comments on loss of *Royal Oak* 16; and Fleet Air Arm 4, 19–22, 112–14, 314–15; and Submarine Service 21, 151; secret mission to Belgian royal family 3–4, 24, 89, 114; and German attack on Norway 4, 167; gives interview to Italian journalist on meaning of Narvik 22, 23, 25, 315; interview with Churchill over Norwegian campaign 22–5; proposes attack on Trondheim 4–5, 6, 26, 27–8, 30–40, 72, 89, 309; speech in Parliament and fall of Chamberlain Government 7, 72; comments on Norwegian campaign 41–3, 44, 130, 233; and Dardanelles campaign (1915) 42, 107; comments on Dover Straits and Belgian coast operations during World War I 42; regrets advice to Beatty concerning Madden 34–5, 42; liaison officer with King Leopold during Belgian campaign 7, 44–6, 48–56, 66–9, 73–4, 89, 134; defends King Leopold's conduct 56–8, 59–66, 71–2, 74, 114–15, 226, 233, 321–2, 346; suggests occupation of southern Ireland 73; appointed Director of Combined Operations 77, 85, 88, 90, 91, 115; relationship with Pound 78; relations with naval staff, 78, 81; relationship with Churchill 78, 81, 85, 128–9, 216, 221, 331; comments on seizure of French Fleet 93; proposes capture of Pantelleria 79–81, 94–6, 97–9, 100; and Operation 'Brisk' 94, 96, 100, 103, 327; and Operation 'Workshop' 102–12, 118–19, 125, 129—34, 136–8, 211, 238–9, 268, 331–4; remarks on cancellation of 'Workshop' 138–142; and Operation 'Yorker' 81, 143–6, 149; proposes changes in planning procedure and organization 81–2, 92, 93–4, 159–61, 190, 208–9; and Operation 'Claymore' 82, 153–4, 156–7, 336; and Operation 'Puma' 82, 166—71, 190; and allegations about role of polo in pre-war Mediterranean Fleet 105–6; criticizes plan for Operation 'Menace' 107, 268, 334; describes preparations for Zeebrugge–Ostend operations (1918) 108–9, 110, 187; and French Navy 136–7, 152, 168, 171; submits memorandum on direction of combined operations 147–52, 153, 334–5; as DCNS under Beatty 151–2; forms new amphibious striking force 164–6, 204; criticizes interservice staffs for delaying action 172, 186–7; and President Roosevelt 173, 177, 224; opposes daylight assaults on defended beaches 181–2, 225, 297–8, 351; advocates capture of Sardinia 183–4, 186; and Operation 'Pilgrim' 83, 183–6, 190–2, 193–5, 197, 214–17, 340, 341, 343; and Operation 'Leapfrog' 83, 188–9, 190–1; opposes Chiefs of Staff Committee proposal to reduce his role to adviser 84, 190, 201–11; dismissed as DCO 84, 208, 212, 227, 235; proposes going to Middle East as adviser to newly planned combined operations organization 85, 213, 214; offered peerage by Churchill and proposed as Governor-General of Northern Ireland 213, 214, 216, 235, 238, 240, 343; unsuccessful in request for interview with Churchill 217–18, 233, 237, 268; fears Commandos will not be used properly after his dismissal 212, 215, 221, 228–30, 353; suspects his dismissal was due to intrigue 221, 231–7; speaks in Parliament on his dismissal 237–8, 346; loss of son Geoffrey 221, 239, 241, 257; criticizes slackness in dockyards 221, 248, 348, 361; seconds motion of censure against Churchill 221–2, 250, 252, 254–6, 267, 270, 349; meets Field Marshal Smuts 256–9; again offered peerage by Churchill 222, 228, 257–9, 269–70; and controversy over Fleet Air Arm 240, 241; replies to Trenchard in House of Lords 222–3, 260–1, 351; and Dudley North affair 223, 231, 264–7, 344; and Somerville 231; exchange with Churchill over his lack of employment (1943) 267–71, 299, 353, 361; suffers detached retina

223, 271, 272, 354; tours Normandy beaches 223; sent on goodwill mission to Australia and New Zealand 223-4, 277-9, 294, 301, 302-3, 361; visits Canada and the United States 224, 292-3; interview with Admiral King 224, 292; tours training establishments in California 224, 292, 293; observes exercises in Hawaii 224, 281, 293; visits New Guinea 224, 279-80, 281, 282; with Leyte invasion force 224-5, 281, 283-9, 294-6; suffers smoke poisoning 225, 289-90, 298-9; advocates Americans employ night landings 296-7, 298; strains heart flying without oxygen 225, 300; returns to England via Ceylon 225, 300-4, 361; reports on situation in south-east Asia 303-4; remarks on death of Admiral Field 304-5, 362; failing health 304, 305, 362; death 226
Kimmins, Major (later Lieut-General Sir) Brian 52
King, Admiral (later Fleet Admiral) Ernest J. (USN) 224, 292, 360
Kinkaid, Vice-Admiral (later Admiral) Thomas Cassin (USN): career 355; arranges for Keyes to observe Leyte landings 224; described by Royle 277; at Manus 279, 283; meets Keyes in New Guinea 279-80, 281; remarks on Fletcher Pratt's history 282; and invasion of Leyte 286, 290, 295; describes Surigao Straits and Samar Island battles 291-2; and Keyes's proposal about night landings 298; mentioned 284, 291, 294
Knox, Captain John 110, 328

Larken, Admiral Sir Frank 174, 339
Lausanne Conference 137
Laycock, Brigadier Sir Joseph 91
Laycock, Lieut-Colonel (later Major-General Sir) Robert 91, 136, 241, 254, 325
League of Nations Union 45
'Leapfrog', Operation 83, 189-93, 203, 204, 206
Leopold III, King of the Belgians: career 316; asks Keyes to come to Brussels 3, 24, 89, 114; and Belgian campaign 45-6, 48-57; and armistice 57-66, 66-71, 74, 84, 115, 321-2; refuses to leave country 64-5, 67-8, 70-1; encounters strong opposition towards return to throne 226; mentioned 7, 147, 266

Leros 99, 103
Le Touquet 214
Lewis, Commander 50
Leyte: invasion observed by Keyes 224, 225; mentioned 286-9, 295-7; see also Philippines, Surigao Straits, Samar Island
Libya: raiding operations on coast proposed 103, 104; land battles in 126, 127, 187, 206, 254; mentioned 143, 248, 346
Liners (British):
Aboukir 65
Aquitania 103
Bulolo 338
California 338
Queen Elizabeth 103, 279
Queen Mary 103
Litani River, action 241, 339-40
Little, Admiral Sir Charles James Colebrooke 9, 175-9, 312
Lloyd George, Rt Hon David (later 1st Earl): career 337; and Jellicoe 42, 249; and Churchill 169, 172, 337
Lloyd-Mostyn, 2nd Lieutenant Henry Pyers Ronald 54, 55
Lofoten Islands: first raid 82, 158, 191, 211, 336; second raid 241, 347; see also 'Claymore'
Logie, Colonel Marc J. (USA) 284, 359
London Naval Treaties 35, 43, 45, 116, 244, 248, 330
Londonderry, 7th Marquess of (Charles Stewart Henry Vane-Tempest-Stewart) 17, 314
Longmore, Air Chief Marshal Sir Henry Arthur Murray 253, 349
Lovat, Lieut-Colonel 17th Baron (Simon Christopher Joseph Fraser) 222, 271, 351, 354
Lucas, Colonel Burton K. (USA) 283
'Lustre', Operation 158, 336
Lynes, Commodore (later Rear-Admiral) Hubert 50, 320
Lyster, Rear-Admiral (later Admiral Sir) A. Lamley St George 244, 247, 347, 348
Lyttleton, Rt Hon Oliver (later 1st Viscount Chandos) 248, 348-9

MacArthur, General of the Army Douglas (USA): career 355; invites Keyes to visit headquarters 224; described by Royle 277; in *Nashville* 286, 287; meets Keyes 294; and Pacific Campaign 294-6; mentioned 225, 279, 280, 281, 284, 291, 298, 299, 303

MacDonald, Rt Hon James Ramsay 244, 347
Macfarlane, Major-General (later Lieut-General Sir) Frank Noel Mason 58, 322
Macmillan, Rt Hon Harold 7, 345
Madagascar 245, 246
Madden, Admiral of the Fleet Sir Charles E.: career 317; succeeds Beatty 34, 43; criticized by Richmond 116, 162, 244; mentioned 362
Mahan, Captain Alfred Thayer (USN) 251, 349
Mailliard, Lieutenant William Somers (USN) 281, 357
Malta: and Pantelleria 95, 103, 139; shortage of anti-aircraft guns 326; difficulty in supplying 158, 251; mentioned 98, 119, 140, 175
Manchester Guardian 253
'Mandible', Operation 125–7, 145, 146, 150; *see also* Dodecanese
Manners, Lieut-Colonel J. C., 275, 355
Manus: visited by Keyes, 279, 282–4, 290, 291, 294; mentioned 280, 281, 285, 289
Margesson, Captain Henry David Reginald (later 1st Viscount), 152, 335
Marshall, Captain (later Vice-Admiral) William J. (USN) 284, 359
Martin, Thomas B. 277, 355
Massawa 163
Matapan, Cape 246
Mathews, Admiral Thomas 267, 353
Maund, Captain (later Rear-Admiral) Loben E. H.: career, 332; writes paper seeking return of Combined Operations organization to Admiralty 135, 236, 332; and Keyes 232; and Cork and Orrery 234; mentioned 234, 254
Maxton, James 128, 331
Maxwell, Rear-Admiral Sir Wellwood George Courtenay, 254, 350
Mediterranean: Keyes wants to use amphibious force in 79, 94, 98, 119, 148, 149, 157, 181, 218; German air power arrives in 81; Keyes sees prospect of mortal blow to Italy 215; command of lost 250, 253, 254, 349–50; *see also* 'Workshop', 'Yorker', Cunningham, A. B.
Mediterranean Fleet 127
'Menace', Operation 107, 223, 331, 334, 345; *see also* Dakar
Menzies, Rt Hon Sir Robert G. 302, 361–2

Merchant Ships (German): *Hamburg* 164, 337
Merlimont 214
Michie, Allan A. 281, 357
Military Co-ordination Committee 5
Minorca 117
Mitscher, Vice-Admiral Marc Andrew (USN) 285, 359
Montgomery, General (later Field Marshal, 1st Viscount) Bernard Law 187, 269, 340
Montrose, Duchess of 131
Moore-Brabazon, Rt Hon John Theodore Cuthbert (later 1st Baron Brabizon of Tara) 113, 329
Morford, Brigadier Albert C. *see* St Clair-Morford
Morocco, Spanish 167
Morrison, Rt Hon Herbert Stanley (later 1st Baron) 248, 255, 259, 348
Morshead, Lieut-General Sir Leslie 282, 357–8
Mostyn, 2nd Lieutenant Henry Pyers, *see* Lloyd-Mostyn
Mountbatten, Captain (later Admiral of the Fleet, 1st Earl Mountbatten of Burma) Louis Francis Albert Victor Nicholas: career 343; succeeds Keyes 84, 212, 213, 217, 227–9, 255, 270, 271, 354; to retain Commandos 233; meets Keyes in Ceylon 225, 303–4; mentioned 140, 230, 301, 334
Munster, Captain the Earl of (Geoffrey William Hugh FitzClarence) 52, 55, 320–1
Muselier, Vice-Admiral d'Escadre Emile-Henry 136–7, 333
Mussolini, Benito 22, 25, 26

Namsos 4, 5, 36, 37, 39, 41
Napoleon I, Emperor 162
Narvik: seized by Germans 4, 5; Keyes's opinion on meaning of 22, 23, 315; naval action at 26, 265, 317; evacuation of, 114, 117 329–30; mentioned 33, 40, 234
National 251
Naval Staff: criticized by Keyes over Norway 6, 44, 78, 236, 238; and Keyes's Trondheim scheme 33, 35, 37; and Operation 'Pilgrim' 83; and Operation 'Workshop' 105, 106, 109, 111, 138–9, 140–1, 146, 147–8; and Operation 'Puma' 169; Keyes suspects they intrigue against him 207, 227, 232, 237; mentioned 34, 38, 41, 240; *see also* Admiralty, Pound

Needham, Major-General Henry 47, 48, 50, 52, 319
Nelson, Horatio, Viscount 74, 162, 226, 252
Newall, Marshal of the Royal Air Force (later 1st Baron) Sir Cyril Louis Norton 32, 302–3, 317, 362
New Guinea 279–82, 291, 304
News Chronicle 240, 241
New Zealand 223, 225, 300, 302
Nichols, Captain C. A. G. 283
Nimitz, Admiral (later Fleet Admiral) Chester William (USN): career 355; meets Keyes 224, 293; mentioned 277, 282, 292
Noble, Rear-Admiral Albert Gallatin (USN) 281, 357
Normandy, invasion of 223, 273, 274
Norrie, Major-General (later 1st Baron) Sir Charles Willoughby Moke 300, 361
North, Admiral Sir Dudley Burton Napier: career 345; Keyes becomes interested in case 223, 264–7, 344; treatment blamed on Keyes 231, 345; and action against French Fleet 266, 352
Norway: attacked by Germany 4; campaign in 4–6, 23–4, 27–8, 30–1, 39; raids on coast (1941) 155–7, 214–15, 241; mentioned 130, 206; *see also* Narvik, Trondheim, Namsos, 'Claymore'

Oldendorf, Rear-Admiral Jesse B. (USN) 286, 359–60
Oliphant, Sir Launcelot 48, 50, 319
Oliver, Admiral of the Fleet Sir Henry Francis 172, 338
Operations. *see under* respective code names, 'Workshop', 'Puma', etc
Oran 136, 168, 171, 266, 352
Osmeña, President Sergio 281, 282, 299, 357
Ostend: attempts to block (1918) 108–9, 150; plan to block in 1940 frustrated 73–4
O'Sullivan, Colonel (later Major-General) Curtis D. (USA) 284–5, 359
Overstraeten, Lieut-General Raoul F. C. Van: career 319–20; in Belgian campaign 48, 49, 52, 53, 56; on difficult position of Belgian Army 62, 63
Owen, Captain G. D. 174

Pacher, Lieut-Colonel (later Major-General) Francis T. (USA) 285, 359
Pacific, campaign in 224, 277, 279, 293–5, 297–9, 304; *see also* Philippines, Leyte, New Guinea, Admiralty Islands
Pantelleria: seizure proposed 79, 80, 94–9, 103, 109, 110, 268, 326; and COS and JPS 106, 187; capture in 1943 330–1; *see also* 'Workshop', 'Corkscrew'
Parker, Admiral Sir Hyde 74, 93, 323
Passchendaele 108, 256
Patton, Lieut-General (later General) George S. 269, 353–4
Peck, John (later Sir John) H. 211, 342
Peleliu 277, 355
Pell, Captain (later Lieut-Colonel) Beauchamp Tyndall 284, 358
Philippines 224, 293–6, 277, 304; *see also* Leyte
Phillips, Vice-Admiral (later Admiral Sir) Tom Spencer Vaughan: career 312; talks with Keyes 56; and proposal to capture Pantelleria 94; and loss of *Prince of Wales* 240, 337; and Fleet Air Arm 243; mentioned 9, 238, 323
'Pilgrim', Operation: evolved from 'Puma' 83, 190, 340; preparations tie up forces 183–4, 186, 218, 237, 341; criticized by Keyes as cumbersome 185, 191–2, 195–6; Keyes eliminated from planning 190, 191; small ships for operation sent to Freetown 192, 196, 202, 215–16, 341, 342, 345; Keyes proposes alternative plan 193–5, 197, 214, 217, 343; naval part of force untrained 204
Pitt, William, 1st Earl of Chatham 79, 147, 157, 176, 334
Poland 3, 11, 12
Portal, Air Marshal (later Marshal of the Royal Air Force, 1st Viscount): career 326; and Pantelleria 97; and Operation 'Workshop' 143, 144; and Keyes 205
Portal, Captain (later Admiral Sir) Reginald Henry 254, 261, 262–4, 350
Portugal 78, 167, 177; *see also* Azores
Pound, Admiral of the Fleet Sir A. Dudley P. R.: career 311; former Chief of Staff of Keyes 3, 8, 15; interview with Keyes concerning Norwegian campaign 5, 33, 34, 35, 38; Keyes suspects he is using his age against him 23, 89; advice to Keyes concerning Madden 34–5, 43; criticized by Keyes over Norway 44, 227, 238; difficult relationship with Keyes 78, 236; and Operation 'Work-

shop' 102, 104, 106; and Zeebrugge operation (1918) 108, 110, 111; nominates Hamilton for Operation 'Puma' 169; and Operation 'Pilgrim' 192; and abolition of Keyes's directorate 193, 203, 207, 258, 341; Keyes believes he sabotaged offensive plans 205, 239, 240; and Fleet Air Arm 242, 260; criticized by Keyes 248, 249, 255; criticized by Richmond 253, 254; and Dudley North affair 266, 267; mentioned 9, 14, 16, 232, 240, 266, 323

Power, Tyrone 283

Pownall, Lieut-General Sir Henry Royds: career 342; crit:cizes Keyes 83–4; at War Office 204; and Keyes 233, 258, 346; leaves War Office 237

Pratt, Fletcher 282, 358

'Puma', Operation: Keyes involved in planning 82, 190; advocated by Keyes 166–9; Keyes submits plan for 169; Keyes submits appreciation on 170, 171; described to Americans 174–8; expanded into Operation 'Pilgrim' 185, 190, 340; mentioned 189, 194, 197, 202, 237

Quebec 33, 37, 149
Quiberon Bay 33

Ramsay, Admiral Hon Sir Alexander Robert Maule: career 312; and Fleet Air Arm 9, 113, 242–4; describes Admiralty neglect of Fleet Air Arm 260–1

Ramsay, Admiral Sir Bertram Home: career 321, 354; and Normandy landings 223, 273, 274; mentioned 53, 223, 341

'Ransack', Operation 186

Red Sea 163, 250

Regiments (British):
3rd (King's Own) Hussars 48
12th (Prince of Wales's Royal) Lancers 46, 63, 101
Argyll and Sutherland Highlanders 149
Black Watch 284
Connaught Rangers 284
Queen's (Royal West Surrey Regiment) (2nd Foot) 149
Royal Scots (1st Foot) 102
Royal Scots Greys 254
Royal Welch Fusiliers 45

Regiments (United States):
9th Infantry 284
10th Infantry 284
11th Infantry 284

Reynaud, Paul 266, 353

Rhodes 99, 103, 336; see also Dodecanese, 'Mandible'

Richmond, Admiral Sir Herbert W.: career 329; praises Keyes's role in recovering control of naval aviation 112; criticizes former First Sea Lords 116–17, 162, 244; remarks on conduct of war 117–18, 221; plans for Syria during World War I 118; stresses importance of flotilla strength 162–3; letter of condolence on death of Geoffrey Keyes 241, 242; criticizes former First Lords for London Treaties 244; cites Japanese threat to Ceylon 245–6; remarks on necessity of air power and sea power 250–4; to host Keyes at Cambridge 258, 260

Ritchie, Captain Oliver (USN) 290

River Plate, Battle of 103, 314, 315

Roger II, King of Sicily 111–12, 329

Rommel, Field Marshal Erwin: career 349; headquarters raided 221, 239, 248, 346–7; mentioned 251, 253, 257, 263, 336

Romulo, Brigadier-General Carlos P. 281, 282, 357

Ronarc'h, Vice-Amiral Pierre 168, 337

Ronarc'h, Capitaine de vaisseau (later Vice-Admiral d'escadre) Pierre-Jean 168, 337

Roosevelt, President Franklin Delano: interview with Commander Woolley 82, 176–8; and Atlantic Islands 169, 177, 178, 214; and Keyes 173, 177, 193, 224, 292; interested in naval warfare 180; engages in defacto war against German submarines 193, 341; and public opinion 337; death of 303, 362

Roosevelt, Colonel James (USMC) 293, 360

Royal, Rear-Admiral Forrest B. (USN) 279, 280, 281, 285, 356

Royal Air Force: and Fleet Air Arm 4; attacks German naval bases 8, 12, 311; retains control of flying boats 13, 14; and Keyes's Trondheim scheme 31; and Belgian campaign 49, 56, 57, 62, 63, 69; in Red Sea area 330; and Ceylon 245, 246; mentioned 187, 251, 253; see also Air Ministry, Coastal Command, Fighter Command, Bomber Command

Royal Marines: Keyes plans use in

INDEX 395

Norwegian campaign 33, 37; Keyes proposes to employ in Mediterranean 149, 215, 229; mentioned 182, 226, 271
Royal Naval Air Service 20, 21; *see also* Fleet Air Arm
Royle, Vice-Admiral (later Admiral Sir) Guy Charles: career, 313–14; and Fleet Air Arm 16; and relations with Air Ministry 17, 18; on situation in Pacific 277, 355
Russia: attacked by Germany 82; situation discussed by Harry Hopkins 176; mentioned 40, 183, 186, 216

St Clair-Morford, Brigadier (later Major-General) Albert C.: career 326; and Operation 'Brisk' 96, 97, 101–3, 327
St Lawrence River 33
St Vincent, Admiral of the Fleet, 1st Earl (John Jervis) 134, 161, 207, 268, 332
Saipan, 277
Samar Island, Battle of 291–2, 295, 360
Sandford, Commander 49
Sardinia: capture suggested by Keyes 183–4, 186, 187; Germans occupy 144, 193; mentioned 81, 83, 143; *see also* 'Yorker', Cagliari
Saunders, Admiral Sir Charles 33, 37, 149, 317
Seal, Sir Eric: career 315; and Keyes's interview with Churchill 22, 23, 24; mentioned 53, 242
Sempill, 19th Baron (Commander William Francis Forbes-Sempill) 258, 351
Seversky, Major Alexander P. de 261, 292, 295, 299, 351–2
Shakespeare, Rt Hon Sir Geoffrey H. 8, 311–12
Sherwood, Lord 222
Shirer, William L. 239, 276, 346
'Shrapnel', Operation 107, 128, 129, 130
Sicily: German Air Force arrives in 139–40, 144, 145, 150, 336; Allied invasion of 269, 276, 293, 353
Sierra Leone 214, 215, 216; *see also* Freetown
Silverman, S. Sydney 255, 350
Simon, Rt Hon Sir John Allsebrook (later 1st Viscount) 42, 44, 318, 319
Sinclair, Rt Hon Sir Archibald Henry Macdonald (later 1st Viscount Thurso) 56, 321, 327
Singapore: creation of base 151; loss of 244, 245, 250, 347
Slayton, Lieut-Commander (USN) 284
Smuts, Field Marshal Jan Christian: career 350; and Keyes 256–7, 258, 259, 269
Somerville, Admiral of the Fleet Sir James Fownes: career 323; and action against French Fleet 73, 74, 322; and Dudley North affair, 223, 266, 345, 352; inquiry into conduct after Cape Spartivento action 231, 345–6; commands force sent to Indian Ocean 255, 350; mentioned 226
'Source', Operation 354
Spain: possible entry into war on side of Germany 78, 79, 82, 166–7, 331; action at Tangier 127, 167, 337; and defences of Atlantic Islands 170; mentioned 165, 216; *see also* Franco, Canary Islands, 'Puma', 'Pilgrim'
Special Service Troops, *see* Commandos
'Springboard', Operation 340
Stanhope, 1st Earl (James Stanhope) 244, 347
Stanhope, 7th Earl (James Richard Stanhope) 243, 347
Stanley, Rt Hon Oliver F. G. 44, 319
Stavanger 6
Steinkjer 38, 41–3; *see also* Trondheim, Trondheimfiord
Struble, Rear-Admiral (later Admiral) Arthur D. (USN) 286, 359
Sturges, Major-General (later Lieut-General Sir) Robert Grice 169, 215, 338
Submarine Service 21, 151
Suez Canal 158, 250
Sunday Chronicle 10, 32, 312
Sunday Graphic 25
Surigao Straits, Battle of 225, 291, 299
Sutherland, Lieut-General Richard K. (USA): career 356; meets Keyes 279–80, 291, 296–7; mentioned 281, 282, 298
Swift, Major-General Innis Palmer (USA) 282, 357
Syria: Richmond's plan for operations along coast 118; Commando operations in 182, 218, 339–40; *see also* Litani River

Talbot, Rear-Admiral (later Vice-Admiral) Arthur George 298, 360
Tangier 127, 167, 337
Tapp, Lieutenant (RAN) 277, 279, 281, 282

Taranto: Fleet Air Arm success 118, 243, 263, 330, 347; mentioned 117, 245–6
Tarawa 277
Thomas, Captain Edward Penry 277, 355
Thompson, Commander Charles Ralfe 105, 328
'Thruster', Operation 190, 194, 215, 340
Tientsin 284, 358
Times, The 8, 253, 305
Tito, Joseph Broz 275, 354–5
Tomkinson, Vice-Admiral Wilfred: career 323; and Admiral Field 304–5, 362; mentioned 239, 248, 249, 254
'Torch', Operation 351
Tovey, Vice-Admiral (later Admiral of the Fleet Sir) John Cronyn: career 335–6; and Operation 'Claymore' 153–6, 163–4
Trafalgar, Battle of 151
Tree, Ronald 331
Trenchard, Marshal of the Royal Air Force, 1st Viscount (Hugh Montague Trenchard): career 347; in House of Lords debates 222, 223, 259, 262, 351; influence over *Daily Telegraph* 240, 241, 253; criticized by Richmond 250–3; and Fleet Air Arm 260–1, 263–4; mentioned 244, 258
Trevelyan, Dr George Macaulay 258, 351
Trincomali 245, 246; *see also* Ceylon
Trondheim: seized by Germans 4; proposal to attack 4–5, 6, 89; Keyes plans attack 27–8, 30–40, 42, 309; Keyes believes Navy let the Army down 233; and Naval Staff 237; and Shirer 239, 276; mentioned 147, 206, 239, 265; *see also* Trondheimfiord, 'Hammer'
Trondheimfiord 5, 36–9, 41, 342; *see also* Trondheim, Steinkjer
'Truck', Operation 128, 138
'Tungsten', Operation 354
Tunisia 259, 265, 351
Turkey 99, 104, 125, 326
Tyrwhitt, Admiral of the Fleet Sir Reginald Yorke 226

United States: and Keyes's plans for Atlantic Islands 82, 83, 195, 197–8; and Spanish Atlantic Islands 168, 169; interest in Azores 175, 177, 178; opinions of British Joint Staff Mission on armed forces 179–80; possible assistance to British in Far East 244

United States (Army): and landings in Sicily 269, 353; and Normandy invasion 274; and Peleliu 277, 355; and Admiralty Islands 279; and New Guinea 280, 282; Ranger battalion in preliminaries to Leyte invasion 285, 286; and Pacific campaign 294
United States Marine Corps 293, 296
United States (Navy): at Manus and the Admiralties 279, 283–4, 294; work of engineers in New Guinea 280; and invasion of Leyte 285–9, 295–6, 359; and battles of Surigao Straits and Samar Island 291–2, 360; anticipated attempts to merge naval and army air services 292

Vandenheuvel, Major 46, 48, 51
Van Hook, Rear-Admiral Clifford E. (USN) 280, 291, 356
Varley, Commander C. H. 353
Vichy (France): and reinforcements for Dakar 223, 345, 352; and Madagascar 245, 246; mentioned 95
Vickers (firm) 21
Villeneuve, Vice-Amiral Pierre-Charles 162, 337

Warburton-Lee, Captain Bernard Armitage Warburton 265, 352
Wardlaw-Milne, Sir John S.: career 350; motion of censure against Churchill 221–2, 255, 270, 349
War Office: and Keyes 93; raises independent companies for raiding 87; discounts Richmond's suggestions about landing craft 117; and Commandos 118, 148, 212, 215, 229
Warren, Commodore (later Rear-Admiral) Guy 191, 341
Warships (Australian):
  Australia 283, 289, 290, 301, 361
  Shropshire 283, 287
  Sydney 283
Warships (British):
  Classes:
    'Dido' 102, 104, 106
    'Glen' (LSI) 94, 98, 101, 102, 104, 105, 107, 118–19, 129, 135, 138, 140, 144–6, 148, 151, 158, 175, 181, 334, 335
    'Maraciabo' (LST) 184, 340
    'R' (Battleships) 5, 23, 26, 37, 254, 350
    'U' (Submarines) 128
    'Ulster Monarch' (LSI) 103
    'X-craft' (Midget submarines) 272, 354

INDEX

Aboukir 13
Acasta 323
Ajax 17, 314
Ardent 323
Arethusa 250, 255, 347
Ark Royal 21, 166, 231, 232, 236, 254, 346, 347
Bachaquero 340
Baralong 22
Barham 127, 349
Britannia (Training ship) 305
Centurion 5, 27, 30, 37, 318
Colossus 8, 15
Cornwall 249, 349
Courageous 3, 8, 12, 13, 265, 312
Cressy 13
Dorsetshire 250, 349
Duke of York 272, 354
Exeter 17, 314
Formidable 143, 144, 350
Freesia 131
Glenearn 326, 334–5
Glengyle 326, 332, 334, 335
Glenroy 239, 326, 332, 334, 335, 347
Glorious 73, 114, 117, 231, 265, 323, 329
Hermes 350
Hogue 13
Howe 277
Hyperion 158
Indomitable 350
Illustrious 158, 336, 347
Karanja 106, 138, 140
Kingfisher 102
King George V 155
Malaya 127
Misoa 340
Nelson 155
Orangeleaf (RFA Oiler) 128
Oxley 313
Prince of Wales 255, 340, 347
Princess Beatrix 163, 330, 342
Queen Charlotte 149
Queen Elizabeth 48, 254, 349
Queen Emma 163, 330, 342
Ramilles 315, 350
Repulse 255, 347
Renown 26, 265, 315
Resolution 26, 315, 350
Revenge 315, 350
Royal Oak 16, 265, 313
Royal Scotsman 104, 106, 135, 327, 332
Royal Sovereign 26, 315, 350
Royal Ulsterman 327
Saumarez 354
Savage 354
Scorpion 354
Sheffield 128
Southampton 324, 336
Sturgeon 313
Suffolk 6
Swordfish 313
Talisman 347
Tartar 164
Tasajera 340
Torbay 347
Triad 318
Triton 313
Ulster Monarch 327
Ulster Prince 327
Ulster Queen 327
Valiant 174, 254, 349
Vernon (Training ship) 305
Victorious 348
Warspite 317, 350
Wyvern 53, 321
X.6 354
X.7 354
Warships (French):
  Dunkerque 73, 323
  Jean Bart 168, 337
  Strasbourg 323
Warships (German):
  Classes:
    'Blücher' 315
    'Deutschland' 21
    'Maass' 27
  Admiral Graf Spee 17, 21, 314
  Admiral Scheer 311
  Bismarck 21, 243, 263, 348
  Blücher 318
  Emden 311
  Gneisenau 246, 265, 311, 315, 323, 329, 348
  Lützow 318
  Prinz Eugen 348
  Scharnhorst 246, 265, 272, 311, 315, 323, 329, 348, 354
  Tirpitz 250, 354
  U.29 312
  U.47 313
  U.81 346
Warships (Italian):
  Conte di Cavour 347
  Duilio 347
  Littorio 347
Warships (New Zealand):
  Achilles 314
Warships (Norwegian):
  Stord 272, 354
Warships (United States):
  Appalachian 224, 225, 281, 283, 287, 288, 289, 290
  Augusta 340
  Canberra 359

Erben 284
Greer 341
Honolulu 289, 298
Houston 359
Hughes 286
J. Franklin Bell 290
Mount Olympus 283
Nashville 286, 287
Pennsylvania 279
Rocky Mount 285
Tennessee 225, 286, 289, 299
Wasatch 284, 286
Watson, Major-General Edwin Martin (USA) 177, 339
Wavell, General (later Field Marshal, 1st Earl) Sir Archibald Percival: career 328; offensive in desert war 80, 148, 187, 254; and East Africa 330; delivers Lee-Knowles lectures at Cambridge 157, 336; mentioned 104, 119, 129, 142, 150, 248
Wemyss, Lieut-General (later General Sir) Colville 177, 179, 339
Wemyss, Admiral Sir Rosslyn Erskine, see Wester-Wemyss
'Weserübung', Operation 4
Wester-Wemyss, Admiral of the Fleet, 1st Baron (Rosslyn Erskine Wemyss): career 313; as Deputy First Sea Lord 15; brings Keyes to Dover 90, 325; and Dardanelles campaign 128; mentioned 150, 335
Weygand, General Maxime: career 320; meets Keyes 51, 55, 60, 61; message to Lord Gort 62; Churchill has confidence in 67; Keyes hopes to win over 137, 152, 167, 171
Wilhelm II, Kaiser 51
Wilhelmshafen 8, 311
Wilkinson, Vice-Admiral Theodore Stark (USN): career 356; and invasion of Leyte 285-7; mentioned 280-3
William-Powlett, Major Peter de Barton Vernon 91, 255, 325
Williamson-Noble, Dr Frederick Arnold 286, 296, 359
Willis, Vice-Admiral (later Admiral of the Fleet Sir) Algernon Usborne 190, 215, 340-1
Willoughby, Brigadier-General Charles A. (USA) 280-2, 291, 297, 356
Wilson, Admiral of the Fleet Sir Arthur Kynvet 118, 330

Wilson, General (later Field Marshal) Sir Henry Maitland 182, 218, 339
Wilson, Sir Leslie Orme 279, 355
Winant, John Gilbert 174, 176, 339
Winster, 1st Baron (Commander Reginald Thomas Herbert Fletcher) 267, 353
Winterton, 6th Earl (Edward Turnour) 238, 346
Wolfe, Major-General James 33, 37, 149, 317
Wood, Rt Hon Sir H. Kingsley 19, 242-3, 314
Woolley, Paymaster Captain Herbert G. A.: sent to Washington 82, 173; and Operation 'Workshop' 100, 131, 132; meets Harry Hopkins 174-6; interview with President Roosevelt 177-8; opinion of American forces 178-80
'Workshop', Operation: proposed by Keyes 79-81, 100; under consideration by Chiefs of Staff Committee 102-7, 109-12; explained to Cunningham 119; General Haydon's brief for 119-24, 330; capture in 1943 330-1; supported by Churchill 124-6, 238, 346; opposed by Cunningham 126-7, 158; postponed 127-8, 130, 132-3, 135-8, 331, 332, 333-4; cancellation of 138, 139-41, 146, 334; Churchill wants Keyes to command 211; mentioned 143-5, 150, 169, 189, 190, 204, 233, 336; see also Pantelleria
Wrathall, Major W. P. 50, 320
Wright, Commander 290

'Yorker', Operation: proposals for 139; supported by Keyes 143-6, 150; mentioned 169; see also Sardinia
Yugoslavia: partisan operations in Dalmatian Islands 272-3, 275

Zeebrugge (1918): precedent cited for Operation 'Workshop' 80, 81; and Naval Staff 98; preparations for raid 108-9; operation described by Keyes 110; mentioned by Churchill 125; and delays 132; and inter-service co-operation 187; mentioned 33, 43, 51, 150, 238, 298; see also Ostend
Zeebrugge (1940) 54, 73-4, 323

Navy Records Society

(FOUNDED 1893)

THE Navy Records Society was established for the purpose of printing rare or unpublished works of naval interest. The Society is open to all who are interested in naval history and any person wishing to become a member should apply to the Hon. Secretary, c/o The Royal Naval College, Greenwich, London, SE10 9NN. The annual subscription for individuals is £5.50, the payment of which entitles the member to receive one copy of each work issued by the Society for that year. For Libraries and Institutions the annual subscription is seven pounds.

The prices to members and non-members respectively are given after each volume, and orders should be sent, enclosing no money, to the Hon. Secretary. Those volumes against which the letters 'A & U' are set after the price to non-members are available to them only through bookshops or, in case of difficulty, direct from George Allen & Unwin (Publishers) Ltd, PO Box 18, Park Lane, Hemel Hempstead, Herts HP2 4TE. Prices are correct at the time of going to press.

The Society has already issued:

Vols. 1 and 2. *State Papers relating to the Defeat of the Spanish Armada, Anno* 1588. Edited by Professor J. K. Laughton. (Vols. I and II). (*Reprinting.*)

Vol. 3. *Letters of Lord Hood,* 1781–82. Edited by Mr. David Hannay. (*Out of Print.*)

Vol. 4. *Index to James's Naval History,* by C. G. Toogood. Edited by the Hon. T. A. Brassey. (*Out of Print.*)

Vol. 5. *Life of Captain Stephen Martin,* 1666–1740. Edited by Sir Clements R. Markham. (*Out of Print.*)

Vol. 6. *Journal of Rear-Admiral Bartholomew James,* 1752–1828. Edited by Professor J. K. Laughton and Commander J. Y. F. Sulivan. (*Out of Print.*)

Vol. 7. *Hollond's Discourses of the Navy,* 1638 and 1658. Edited by J. R. Tanner. (*Out of Print.*)

Vol. 8. *Naval Accounts and Inventories in the Reign of Henry VII.* Edited by Mr. M. Oppenheim. (*Out of Print.*)

Vol. 9. *Journal of Sir George Rooke.* Edited by Mr. Oscar Browning. (*Out of Print.*)

Vol. 10. *Letters and Papers relating to the War with France,* 1512–13. Edited by M. Alfred Spont. (*Out of Print.*)

Vol. 11. *Papers relating to the Spanish War,* 1585–87. Edited by Mr. Julian S. Corbett. (*Out of Print.*)

Vol. 12. *Journals and Letters of Admiral of the Fleet Sir Thomas Byam Martin,* 1773–1854 (Vol. II.). Edited by Admiral Sir R. Vesey Hamilton. (*See* 24.) (*Out of Print.*)

Vol. 13. *Papers relating to the First Dutch War*, 1652–54 (Vol. I.). Edited by Dr. S. R. Gardiner. *(Out of Print)*

Vol. 14. *Papers relating to the Blockade of Brest*, 1803–5 (Vol. I.) Edited by Mr. J. Leyland. *(Out of Print.)*

Vol. 15. *History of the Russian Fleet during the Reign of Peter the Great. By a Contemporary Englishman.* Edited by Admiral Sir Cyprian Bridge. *(Out of Print.)*

Vol. 16. *Logs of the Great Sea Fights*, 1794–1805 (Vol. I.). Edited by Vice-Admiral Sir T. Sturges Jackson *(Reprinting.)*

Vol. 17. *Papers relating to the First Dutch War*, 1652–54 (Vol. II.). Edited by Dr. S. R. Gardiner. *(Out of Print.)*

Vol. 18. *Logs of the Great Sea Fights* (Vol. II.). Edited by Vice-Admiral Sir T. Sturges Jackson. *(Reprinting.)*

Vol. 19. *Journals and Letters of Sir T. Byam Martin* (Vol. III.). Edited by Admiral Sir R. Vesey-Hamilton. (*See* 24). *(£6.50/£12.00.)*

Vol. 20. *The Naval Miscellany* (Vol. I.). Edited by Professor J. K. Laughton. *(Out of Print.)*

Vol. 21. *Papers relating to the Blockade of Brest*, 1803–5 (Vol. II). Edited by Mr. John Leyland. *(Out of Print.)*

Vols. 22. and 23. *The Naval Tracts of Sir William Monson* (Vols. I. and II.). Edited by Mr. M. Oppenheim. *(Out of Print.)*

Vol. 24. *Journals and Letters of Sir T. Byam Martin* (Vol. I.). Edited by Admiral Sir R. Vesey Hamilton. *(£6.50/£12.00.)*

Vol. 25. *Nelson and the Neapolitan Jacobins.* Edited by Mr. H. C. Gutteridge. *(Out of Print.)*

Vol. 26. *A Descriptive Catalogue of the Naval MSS. in the Pepysian Library* (Vol. I.). Edited by Mr. J. R. Tanner *(Out of Print.)*

Vol. 27. *A Descriptive Catalogue of the Naval MSS. in the Pepysian Library* (Vol II.). Edited by Mr. J. R. Tanner. *(£6.50/£12.00.)*

Vol. 28. *The Correspondence of Admiral John Markham*, 1801–7. Edited by Sir Clements R. Markham. *(Out of Print.)*

Vol. 29. *Fighting Instructions*, 1530–1816. Edited by Mr. Julian S. Corbett. *(Out of Print.)*

Vol. 30. *Papers relating to the First Dutch War*, 1652–54 (Vol. III.). Edited by Dr. S. R. Gardiner and Mr. C. T. Atkinson. *(Out of Print.)*

Vol. 31. *The Recollections of Commander James Anthony Gardner*, 1775–1814. Edited by Admiral Sir R. Vesey Hamilton and Professor J. K. Laughton. *(Out of Print.)*

Vol. 32. *Letters and Papers of Charles, Lord Barham*, 1758–1813 (Vol. I.). Edited by Sir J. K. Laughton. *(Out of Print.)*

Vol. 33. *Naval Songs and Ballads.* Edited by Professor C. H. Firth. *(Out of Print.)*

Vol. 34. *Views of the Battles of the Third Dutch War.* Edited by Mr. Julian S. Corbett. *(Out of Print.)*

Vol. 35. *Signals and Instructions*, 1776–94. Edited by Mr. Julian S. Corbett. *(Out of Print.)*

Vol. 36. *A Descriptive Catalogue of the Naval MSS. in the Pepysian Library* (Vol. III.). Edited by Dr. J. R. Tanner. *(Out of Print.)*

Vol. 37. *Papers relating to the First Dutch War*, 1652–1654 (Vol. IV.). Edited by Mr. C. T. Atkinson. *(Out of Print.)*

Vol. 38. *Letters and Papers of Charles, Lord Barham*, 1758–1813 (Vol. II.). Edited by Sir J. K. Laughton. *(Out of Print.)*

Vol. 39. *Letters and Papers of Charles, Lord Barham*, 1758–1813 (Vol. III.). Edited by Sir J. K. Laughton. *(Out of Print.)*

Vol. 40. *The Naval Miscellany* (Vol. II.). Edited by Sir J. K. Laughton. (*Out of Print.*)

Vol. 41. *Papers relating to the First Dutch War, 1652–54* (Vol. V.). Edited by Mr. C. T. Atkinson. (*£6.50/£12.00*).

Vol. 42. *Papers relating to the Loss of Minorca in* 1756. Edited by Capt. H. W. Richmond, R.N. (*£6.50/£12.00.*)

Vol. 43. *The Naval Tracts of Sir William Monson* (Vol. III.). Edited by Mr. M. Oppenheim. (*£6.50/£12.00.*)

Vol. 44. *The Old Scots Navy, 1689–1710.* Edited by Mr. James Grant. (*Out of Print.*)

Vol. 45. *The Naval Tracts of Sir William Monson* (Vol. IV.). Edited by Mr. M. Oppenheim. (*£6.50/£12.00.*)

Vol. 46. *The Private Papers of George, second Earl Spencer* (Vol. I.). Edited by Mr. Julian S. Corbett. (*£6.50/£12.00.*)

Vol. 47. *The Naval Tracts of Sir William Monson* (Vol. V.). Edited by Mr. M. Oppenheim. (*£6.50/£12.00.*)

Vol. 48. *The Private Papers of George, second Earl Spencer* (Vol. II.). Edited by Mr. Julian S. Corbett. (*£6.50/£12.00.*)

Vol. 49. *Documents relating to Law and Custom of the Sea* (Vol. I.). Edited by Mr. R. G. Marsden (*£6.50/£12.00.*)

Vol. 50. *Documents relating to Law and Custom of the Sea* (Vol. II.). Edited by Mr. R. G. Marsden. (*£6.50/£12.00.*)

Vol. 51. *Autobiography of Phineas Pett.* Edited by Mr. W. G. Perrin. (*£6.50/£12.00.*)

Vol. 52. *The Life of Admiral Sir John Leake* (Vol. I.). Edited by Mr. G. A. R. Callender. (*£6.50/£12.00.*)

Vol. 53. *The Life of Admiral Sir John Leake* (Vol. II.). Edited by Mr. G. A. R. Callender. (*£6.50/£12.00.*)

Vol. 54. *The Life and Works of Sir Henry Mainwaring* (Vol. I.). Edited by Mr. G. E. Manwaring. (*£6.50/£12.00.*)

Vol. 55. *The Letters of Lord St. Vincent, 1801–1804* (Vol. I.). Edited by Mr. D. B. Smith. (*Out of Print.*)

Vol. 56. *The Life and Works of Sir Henry Mainwaring* (Vol. II.). Edited by Mr. G. E. Manwaring and Mr. W. G. Perrin. (*Out of Print.*)

Vol. 57. *A Descriptive Catalogue of the Naval MSS. in the Pepysian Library* (Vol. IV.). Edited by Dr. J. R. Tanner. (*Out of Print.*)

Vol. 58. *The Private Papers of George, second Earl Spencer* (Vol. III.). Edited by Rear-Admiral H. W. Richmond. (*Out of Print.*)

Vol. 59. *The Private Papers of George, second Earl Spencer* (Vol. IV.). Edited by Rear-Admiral H. W. Richmond. (*Out of Print.*)

Vol. 60. *Samuel Pepys's Naval Minutes.* Edited by Dr. J. R. Tanner. (*Out of Print.*)

Vol. 61. *The Letters of Lord St. Vincent, 1801–1804* (Vol. II). Edited by Mr. D. B. Smith. (*£6.50/£12.00.*)

Vol. 62. *Letters and Papers of Admiral Viscount Keith* (Vol. I.). Edited by Mr. W. G. Perrin. (*Out of Print.*)

Vol. 63. *The Naval Miscellany* (Vol. III.). Edited by Mr. W. G. Perrin. (*Out of Print.*)

Vol. 64. *The Journal of the First Earl of Sandwich.* Edited by Mr. R. C. Anderson. (*£6.50/£12.00.*)

Vol. 65. *Boteler's Dialogues.* Edited by Mr. W. G. Perrin. (*£6.50/£12.00.*)

Vol. 66. *Papers relating to the First Dutch War, 1652–54* (Vol. VI.; with index). Edited by Mr. C. T. Atkinson. (*£6.50/£12.00.*)

Vol. 67. *The Byng Papers* (Vol. I.). Edited by Mr. W. C. B. Tunstall. *(£6.50/£12.00.)*

Vol. 68. *The Byng Papers* (Vol. II.). Edited by Mr. W. C. B. Tunstall. *(£6.50/£12.00.)*

Vol. 69. *The Private Papers of John, Earl of Sandwich* (Vol. I.). Edited by Mr. G. R. Barnes and Lieut.-Commander J. H. Owen, RN. *(£6.50/£12.00.)*

Corregenda to *Papers relating to the First Dutch War,* 1652–54 (Vols. I. to VI.). Edited by Captain A. C. Dewar, R.N. *(£6.50/£12.00.)*

Vol. 70. *The Byng Papers* (Vol. III.). Edited by Mr. W. C. B. Tunstall. *(£6.50/£12.00.)*

Vol. 71. *The Private Papers of John, Earl of Sandwich* (Vol. II.). Edited by Mr. G. R. Barnes and Lieut.-Commander J. H. Owen, R.N. *(£6.50/£12.00.)*

Vol. 72. *Piracy in the Levant,* 1827–8. Edited by Lieut.-Commander C. G. Pitcairn Jones, R.N. *(£6.50/£12.00.)*

Vol. 73. *The Tangier Papers of Samuel Pepys.* Edited by Mr. Edwin Chappell. *(Out of Print.)*

Vol. 74. *The Tomlinson Papers.* Edited by Mr. J. G. Bullocke. *(£6.50/£12.00.)*

Vol. 75. *The Private Papers of John, Earl of Sandwich* (Vol. III.). Edited by Mr. G. R. Barnes and Commander J. H. Owen, R.N. *(£6.50/£12.00.)*

Vol. 76. *The Letters of Robert Blake.* Edited by the Rev. J. R. Powell. *(£6.50/£12.00.)*

Vol. 77. *Letters and Papers of Admiral the Hon. Samuel Barrington* (Vol. I.). Edited by Mr. D. Bonner-Smith. *(£6.50/£12.00.)*

Vol. 78. *The Private Papers of John, Earl of Sandwich* (Vol. IV.). Edited by Mr. G. R. Barnes and Commander J. H. Owen, R.N. *(£6.50/£12.00.)*

Vol. 79. *The Journals of Sir Thomas Allin,* 1660–1678 (Vol. I. 1660–66). Edited by Mr. R. C. Anderson. *(£6.50/£12.00.)*

Vol. 80. *The Journals of Sir Thomas Allin,* 1660–1678 (Vol. II. 1667–78). Edited by Mr. R. C. Anderson. *(£6.50/£12.00.)*

Vol. 81. *Letters and Papers of Admiral the Hon. Samuel Barrington* (Vol. II.). Edited by Mr. D. Bonner-Smith. *(Out of Print.)*

Vol. 82. *Captain Boteler's Recollections* (1808 to 1830). Edited by Mr. D. Bonner-Smith. *(Out of Print.)*

Vol. 83. *Russian War,* 1854. *Baltic and Black Sea: Official Correspondence.* Edited by Mr. D. Bonner-Smith and Captain A. C. Dewar, R.N. *(Out of Print.)*

Vol. 84. *Russian War,* 1855. *Baltic: Official Correspondence.* Edited by Mr. D. Bonner-Smith. *(Out of Print.)*

Vol. 85. *Russian War,* 1855. *Black Sea: Official Correspondence.* Edited by Captain A. C. Dewar, R.N. *(£6.50/£12.00.)*

Vol. 86. *Journals and Narratives of the Third Dutch War.* Edited by Mr. R. C. Anderson. *(Out of Print.)*

Vol. 87. *The Naval Brigades in the Indian Mutiny,* 1857–58. Edited by Commander W. B. Rowbotham, R.N. *(£6.50/£12.00.)*

Vol. 88. *Patee Byng's Journal.* Edited by Mr. J. L. Cranmer-Byng. *(Out of Print).*

Vol. 89. *The Sergison Papers* (1688–1702). Edited by Commander R. D. Merriman, R.I.N. *(£6.50/£12.00.)*

Vol. 90. *The Keith Papers* (Vol. II.). Edited by Mr. C. C. Lloyd. *(£6.50/£12.00.)*

Vol. 91. *Five Naval Journals,* 1789–1817. Edited by Rear-Admiral H. G. Thursfield. *(£6.50/£12.00.)*

Vol. 92. *The Naval Miscellany* (Vol. IV.). Edited by Mr. C. C. Lloyd. (*£6.50/£12.00.*)

Vol. 93. *Sir William Dillon's Narrative of Professional Adventures (1790–1839)* (Vol. I. 1790–1802). Edited by Professor Michael A. Lewis (*£6.50/£12.00.*)

Vol. 94. *The Walker Expedition to Quebec. 1711.* Edited by Professor Gerald S. Graham. (*Out of Print.*)

Vol. 95. *The Second China War,* 1856–60. Edited by Mr. D. Bonner-Smith and Mr. E. W. R. Lumby. (*Out of Print.*)

Vol. 96. *The Keith Papers,* 1803–1815 (Vol. III). Edited by Professor C. C. Lloyd. (*£6.50/£12.00.*)

Vol. 97. *Sir William Dillon's Narrative of Professional Adventures (1790–1839)* (Vol. II. 1802–1839). Edited by Professor Michael A. Lewis. (*£6.50/£12.00.*)

Vol. 98. *The Private Correspondence of Admiral Lord Collingwood.* Edited by Professor Edward Hughes. (*Out of Print.*)

Vol. 99. *The Vernon Papers* (1739–1745). Edited by Mr. B. McL. Ranft. (*£6.50/£12.00.*)

Vol. 100. *Nelson's Letters to his Wife and Other Documents.* Edited by Lieut.-Commander G. P. B. Naish, R.N.V.R. (*£6.50/£12.00.*)

Vol. 101. *A Memoir of James Trevenen* (1760–1790). Edited by Professor C. C. Lloyd and Dr. R. C. Anderson. (*£6.50/£12.00.*)

Vol. 102. *The Papers of Admiral Sir John Fisher* (Vol. I). Edited by Lieut.-Commander P. K. Kemp, R.N. (*Out of Print.*)

Vol. 103. *Queen Anne's Navy.* Edited by Commander R. D. Merriman, R.I.N. (*Out of Print.*)

Vol. 104. *The Navy and South America,* 1807–1823. Edited by Professor G. S. Graham and Professor R. A. Humphreys. (*£6.50/£12.00.*)

Vol. 105. *Documents relating to the Civil War,* 1642–1648. Edited by the Rev. J. R. Powell and Mr. E. K. Timings. (*Out of Print.*)

Vol. 106. *The Papers of Admiral Sir John Fisher* (Vol. II.). Edited by Lieut.-Commander P. K. Kemp, R.N. (*£6.50/£12.00.*)

Vol. 107. *The Health of Seamen.* Edited by Professor C. C. Lloyd. (*£6.50/£12.00.*)

Vol. 108. *The Jellicoe Papers* (Vol. I: 1893–1916). Edited by Mr. A. Temple Patterson. (*£6.50/£12.00.*)

Vol. 109. *Documents relating to Anson's Voyage round the World,* 1740–1744. Edited by Dr. Glyndwr Williams. (*£6.50/£12.00.*)

Vol. 110. *The Saumarez Papers: The Baltic,* 1808–1812. Edited by Mr. A. N. Ryan. (*£6.50/£12.00.*)

Vol. 111. *The Jellicoe Papers* (Vol. II: 1916–1935). Edited by Professor A. Temple Patterson. (*£6.50/£12.00.*)

Vol. 112. *The Rupert and Monck Letterbook,* 1666. Edited by the Rev. J. R. Powell and Mr. E. K. Timings. (*£6.50/£12.00.*)

Vol. 113. *Documents relating to the Royal Naval Air Service* (Vol. I: 1908–1918). Edited by Captain S. W. Roskill, R.N. (*£6.50/£12.00*).

Vol. 114. *The Siege and Capture of Havana: 1762.* Edited by Assistant-Professor David Syrett. (*£6.50/£12.00.*)

Vol. 115. *Policy and Operations in the Mediterranean*: 1912–14. Edited by Mr. E. W. R. Lumby. (*£6.50/£12.00.*)

Vol. 116. *The Jacobean Commissions of Enquiry: 1608 and 1618.* Edited by Dr. A. P. McGowan. (*£6.50/£12.00.*)

Vol. 117. *The Keyes Papers.* (Vol. I: 1914–1918). Edited by Dr. Paul G. Halpern. (*£7.50/£12.00—A & U.*)

Vol. 118. *The Royal Navy and North America: The Warren Papers,* 1736–1752. Edited by Dr. Julian Gwyn. (*£6.50/£12.00.*)

Vol. 119. *The Manning of the Royal Navy: Selected Public Pamphlets* 1693–1873. Edited by Professor J. S. Bromley. (*£6.50/£12.00.*)

Vol. 120. *Naval Administration,* 1715–1750. Edited by Professor D. A. Baugh. (*£6.50/£12.00.*)

Vol. 121. *The Keyes Papers* (Vol. II: 1919–1938). Edited by Dr. Paul G. Halpern. (*£6.50/£15.00*—A & U.)